REA

D0212105

Ireland and the Americas

Other Titles in ABC-CLIO's

Transatlantic Relations Series

Africa and the Americas, by Richard M. Juang and Noelle Morrissette
Britain and the Americas, by Will Kaufman and Heidi Slettedahl Macpherson
France and the Americas, by Bill Marshall
Germany and the Americas, by Thomas Adam
Iberia and the Americas, by J. Michael Francis

Ireland and the Americas

Culture, Politics, and History

A Multidisciplinary Encyclopedia

VOLUME II

EDITED BY

James P. Byrne

Philip Coleman

Jason King

Transatlantic Relations Series

Will Kaufman, Series Editor

Santa Barbara, California Denver, Colorado Oxford, England

Library of Congress Cataloging-in-Publication Data

Ireland and the Americas / edited by James P. Byrne, Philip Coleman, and Jason King.

p. cm. — (Transatlantic relations series)

Includes bibliographical references and index.

ISBN 978-1-85109-614-5 (hard copy : alk. paper) — ISBN 978-1-85109-619-0 (ebook : alk. paper) 1. America—Relations—Ireland—Encyclopedias. 2. Ireland—Relations—America—Encyclopedias. 3. America—History—Encyclopedias. 4. Ireland—History—Encyclopedias. 5. North America—History—Encyclopedias. 6. Latin America—History—Encyclopedias. 7. South America—History—Encyclopedias. 8. America—Politics and government—Encyclopedias. 9. Ireland—Politics and government—Encyclopedias. I. Byrne, James P., 1968– II. Coleman, Philip Michael Joseph, 1972– III. King, Jason Francis, 1970–

E18.75.I74 2008
327.730417—dc22

2007035381

12 11 10 09 08 1 2 3 4 5 6 7 8

Senior Production Editor: *Vicki Moran*
Editorial Assistant: *Sara Springer*
Production Manager: *Don Schmidt*
Media Editor: *Jason Kniser*
Media Resources Coordinator: *Ellen Brenna Dougherty*
Media Resources Manager: *Caroline Price*
File Management Coordinator: *Paula Gerard*

ABC-CLIO, Inc.
130 Cremona Drive, P.O. Box 1911
Santa Barbara, California 93116-1911

This book is also available on the World Wide Web as an ebook.
Visit www.abc-clio.com for details.

This book is printed on acid-free paper ♾
Manufactured in the United States of America

Contents

Faction Fighting

The *Oxford Companion to Irish History* (Connolly 1998, 184) defines faction fighting as follows: "fighting between rival groups who met at fairs, patterns and other venues to engage in pitched battles." Echoes of the Irish tradition of faction fighting continue to exist today. The small, shiny, black-painted sticks that are the staple purchases of the Irish diaspora—popularly referred to as "genuine Irish shillelaghs"—are resonant of another era. While the imagery of the "Fighting Irish" is universal in stereotype and cliché, the real social history and functions of faction fighting are an aspect of Irish culture that remains shrouded in mystery. Relatively little historical research has been undertaken into the phenomenon of faction fighting, and students of the subject are still heavily reliant on accounts of faction fights as described by travel writers and members of the Anglo-Irish ascendancy, for example, Le Fanu (1893), Inglis (1838), Hall (1843). Once-famous factions, such as the Carabhats and the Seanbheists, who fought bloody battles in Irish provinces such as Leinster and Munster, continue to be recalled in Irish song and story.

The heyday of faction fighting in Ireland occurred during the nineteenth century when it became a major social headache for the British colonial administration then in Ireland. The available evidence provided by historical and social records indicates, however, that faction fighting was a relatively short-lived phenomenon that peaked and died out as a practice within a span of about four decades. The term "faction" originated with the *factiones,* those fifth- and sixth-century groups of gladiators who fought and raced in the Roman Circus and in the Hippodrome of Constantinople. Two of the most famous of these factions were those referred to as the Greens and the Blues. There was a strong element of social-class delineation between each of these groups, the Blues supporters consisting of members of the wealthier upper classes while the Greens were primarily members of the poorer lower class. Each of these factions dressed differently and had thousands of supporters who fought one another on a regular basis. They were considered such a threat to the state that the Emperor Justinian felt obliged to crush them. The historian Procopius says that the phenomenon was wiped out when Justinian ordered the deaths of 30,000 Blues and Greens in the Hippodrome in the late sixth century.

In Ireland it is not clear when faction fighting began, although there are references to faction fights taking place in the early eighteenth century. Some surmise that it may have originally been an offshoot of the stick fighting or fencing that Continental armies practiced to hone their sword-fighting skills as long ago as the era of the ancien régime. Nineteenth-century colonial commentators frequently viewed Irish faction fighting as a remnant of a "barbarous" clan system or as evidence that Irish society was backward and less evolved than others. However, this underestimates the complex social dynamics that underlay this form of organized fighting. In Ireland factions appear to have generally comprised large groups of people who were related through their ties to a particular parish or region or to a particular extended family. Concepts such as family and regional honor were incorporated in the functioning of these groups so that factions frequently formed a separate society within a society in the era when Ireland was rebelling against its colonial masters. These groups had their own rules and regulations, and the fights frequently included a range of rituals, such as the use of particular war cries, insults, and challenges, or the practice whereby the faction leaders engaged in single combat before the fight proper.

Faction fighting was also a phenomenon that had a strong social and economic basis. The nineteenth century saw vast segments of the Irish population living a precarious and poverty-stricken existence on tiny landholdings that were commonly no more than 15 acres in size. The slightest deterioration in the economy brought severe hardship on an already oppressed Irish population, among whom were large numbers of rootless and semiliterate males. Crime was frequent and was a phenomenon that had a strong antiestablishment edge to it, and there are frequent references to riots between local civilians and the police and the army of the British colonists. A large social, cultural, and economic gap existed between the majority of the Irish populace and their colonial masters, a fact that meant the cogs of the state apparatus, whether in the form of the police or the courts, were little respected. A significant proportion of the Irish population was involved in antiauthoritarian activities, which included rebelling against the authorities, distilling whiskey, faction fighting, and joining agrarian secret societies such as the Whiteboys. In such an atmosphere, Irish people tended to leave their communities' resolution of public disputes or personal vendettas to the faction fight that took place at the fair, the country funeral, the pattern, the pilgrimage, or any similar public event where large numbers of people gathered.

Faction fighting crossed religious lines and particular fights, known as "party fights," and were especially common in the north of Ireland where groups of Catholics and Protestants such as the Ribbonmen and the Orangemen fought one another for sectarian and/or economic reasons. A wide range of factors could initiate faction fighting—a personal vendetta, economic jealousy between different groups of tradesmen, sectarian tension, and tensions or grievances between different townlands, parishes, or families. On occasion there was no ostensible reason as to why a fight would begin, a fact that is reinforced by the ritualized nature of these fights and the fact that people would prepare their weapons months in advance in the sure anticipation that a fight would take place. Fairs and markets were an important location for these fights, which were frequently conducted in an atmosphere of heavy drinking where illegal whiskey (poitín) was cheap and widely available. There is plenty of evidence that the local authorities actively encouraged these fights on occasion and some landlords even organized faction fighting, perhaps as a steam-valve process that might enable them to evade the anger and sense of grievance of the local peasantry.

Many factions were an offshoot of the secret and agrarian societies common in nineteenth-century Ireland, societies that were agitating for change in land reform and the rights of the Irish population to self-determination. These secret societies became particularly active at times of severe poverty and economic upheaval, and it is no surprise to find that the faction fighting tended to die down at these junctures. For instance, groups such as the Peep O' Day Boys and the Defenders in the north of Ireland evolved from two factions known as the Nappach Fleet and the Bawn Fleet. Faction fighting was not only a rural phenomenon but was also to be found in the cities with groups of tradesmen such as the Liberty Boys (tailors and weavers by trade) and the Ormond Boys (butchers) notorious as faction fighters in Dublin. The Irish also brought faction fighting with them upon emigration. In Scotland sectarian fights and fights between factions of Irish migratory workers and local Scottish factions were common. In the United States, where anti-Irish and anti-Catholic bigotry was common, the large immigrant populations of cities such as New York, Boston, and Philadelphia frequently formed themselves into communities within communities so as to agitate for labor reform and religious freedom, communities that had many similarities to the factions and secret societies they had left behind in their homeland.

Some Irish-American faction fights were fought on religious or economic grounds, with groups such as the Molly Maguires (named after a nineteenth century Irish secret society) faction fighting on the railroads. The practice of faction fighting also continued within Irish communities long after many Irish emigrants had resettled in the New World and were particularly associated with the followers of boxing where many aspiring Irish-Americans found an escape route from poverty. In Ireland faction fighting came to an abrupt end because of a number of factors that occurred almost contemporaneously. These included opposition from the Irish Catholic Church (including the threat of excommunication) and the advance of Father Mathew's temperance movement from the 1830s onwards. The influence of a new British under-secretary for Ireland named Thomas Drummond who was appointed in 1835 was not without significance also. He instituted increased controls on the sale of alcohol and imposed very severe prison sentences on those convicted of faction fighting in an effort to increase British administrative control in Ireland. The campaigns of Daniel O'Connell for Catholic Emancipation also had a strong effect on bringing an end to the phenomenon of faction fighting, and there are records of peace deals being brokered between different factions at the behest of O'Connell himself. A combination of increased governmental and clerical influence and a tightening of the state's grip on people's everyday lives and behavior seem to have brought an end to faction fighting in Ireland as some of the last references to large faction fights occurred in the late 1880s.

Michael O'hAodha

See also: MATHEW, Father Theobald; MOLLY MAGUIRES; O'CONNELL, Daniel

References

Bourke, E. "'The Irishman is no lazzarone': German Travel Writers in Ireland, 1828–1850." *History Ireland* 5, no. 3 (Autumn 1997): 21–25.

Connolly, S. J. *The Oxford Companion to Irish History.* Oxford: Oxford University Press, 1998.

Donnelly, James S. "Factions in Pre-Famine Ireland." In *The Uses of the Past: Essays on Irish Culture,* edited by Audrey S. Eyle and Robert F. Garrott. London and Newark: Associated University Presses/University of Delaware Press, 1988.

Donnelly, James S. "Pastorini and Captain Rock." In *Irish Peasants, Violence and Political Unrest, 1780–1914,* edited by S. Clark and James S. Donnelly. Manchester: Manchester University Press, 1983: 102–139.

Hall, Mr. S. C., and Mrs. S. C. Hall. *Ireland, its Scenery, Character &c.* London: How and Parsons, 1843.

Inglis, Henry. *A Journey Through Ireland.* London: Whittaker, 1838.

Le Fanu, William R. *Seventy Years of Irish Life.* London: Arnold, 1893.

O'Donnell, Patrick. *The Irish Faction Fighters of the Nineteenth Century.* Dublin: Anvil Press, 1975.

Owens, Gary. "A Moral Insurrection: Faction Fighters, Public Demonstrations and the O'Connellite Campaign, 1828." *Irish Historical Studies* 30, no. 120 (1997): 513–539.

FAHY (SOMETIMES FAHEY), ANTHONY DOMINIC (1805–1871)

Born in Loughrea, Co. Galway, son of Patrick Fahy (d. 1810) and Belinda Cloran (d. 1843), Fahy joined the order of Saint Dominic when he was about 20 years old, and received the habit on August 4, 1828. Immediately after profession he was sent to Rome to study for the priesthood in Saint Clement's College. Ordained a priest on March 19, 1831, he completed his studies in 1834. He left Rome for St. Joseph's convent (Somerset, Ohio), where he worked until 1836. Fahy returned to Ireland and in 1839 he was nominated prior of Black Abbey in Kilkenny.

In 1843 Fahy was appointed by archbishop of Dublin, Daniel Murray, to the Irish chaplaincy of Buenos Aires, replacing Father O'Gorman. From his arrival in Buenos Aires and up to his death twenty-eight years later, Father Fahy became the indisputable leader of the Irish Catholics in Argentina. He promoted a fund-raising campaign in 1847 for the victims of the Irish Famine. The following year, during the events leading to the execution of Camila O'Gorman, Fahy demanded an exemplary punishment. Perhaps to gain support from Buenos Aires governor Juan Manuel de Rosas, in 1849 Fahy made public his support of the government and acknowledged Rosas's favor toward the Irish of Buenos Aires.

Fahy organized his followers in chaplainries in Buenos Aires city and province, and appointed 12 Irish priests to these areas. He personally paid for their studies at All Hallows, Dublin. Sometimes there were conflicts between these chaplains and Fahy. Some of them recommended the use of the British Hospital instead of the Irish infirmary founded by Father Fahy. He also had to face accusations from the local clergy, in part under the influence of jealousy caused by his custom to isolate the Irish parishioners from the Spanish-speaking Catholic Church. Fahy had a reputation as a matchmaker. During five years ending in 1856 he blessed 185 marriages among Irish settlers. He introduced newly arrived girls from Ireland to their potential matches in Buenos

Aires, trying to respect their counties and towns of origin.

Father Fahy's chief mission was to create a Catholic English-speaking community in Argentina. He was also recognized by the Argentines for his role in public life. On May 19, 1864, President Bartolomé Mitre appointed Anthony Fahy as honorary canon of the Cathedral Church of Buenos Aires. On July 12, 1865, Fahy received a gift of about £600 as an evidence of the esteem of Irish, Anglo-Irish, and English settlers in Buenos Aires.

Fahy died of a heart attack on February 20, 1871, though chronicles report that he died a victim of the yellow fever owing to his attending to the sick. He suffered from heart problems long before his death.

Edmundo Murray

See also: O'GORMAN, Camila

References

Julianello, Maria Teresa. *The Scarlet Trinity: The Doomed Struggle of Camila O'Gorman against Family, Church and State in Nineteenth-Century Buenos Aires.* Cork: Irish Centre for Migration Studies, 2000.

Murray, Thomas. *The Story of the Irish in Argentina.* New York: P. J. Kenedy & Sons, 1919.

Ussher, James M. *Father Fahy: A Biography of Anthony Dominic Fahy, O.P., Irish Missionary in Argentina, 1805–1871.* Buenos Aires: Author's Edition, 1951.

FALKLAND/MALVINAS ISLANDS

The Falkland (the British name) or Malvinas Islands (the Argentinean name) are an archipelago in the south Atlantic, about 300 miles off the continental coast of South America. The islands were first occupied in 1764 by the French, who handed over their settlement to the Spanish naval flotilla on April 1, 1767. In 1820 Argentina claimed sovereignty as Spain's successor and has disputed Britain's claim to the islands since 1833, the year in which the British took possession of the archipelago. Irishmen may have been among the crew of John Davies's ship, the *Desire,* when he discovered the islands in 1592 or in the *Welfare* of John Strong, the first man to land on the Falklands/Malvinas in 1690. But if so, we have no record of their names.

The first recorded Irish visitor was Commander William Farmer, born in Youghal, Co. Cork, in 1732, who commanded the sloop *Swift* in West Falkland (Gran Malvina) waters in 1770 and was obliged to evacuate Port Egmont by a much larger Spanish force. The next Irish name in Falkland/Malvinas history is that of William Dickson of Dublin who was storekeeper for Louis Vernet's colonists and was entrusted with the care of the British flag by Captain Onslow after he landed at Port Louis in 1833. Dickson was among those murdered by the gauchos led by Antonio Rivera on August 26, 1833.

The first Falkland/Malvinas census, taken by Lt. Governor Richard Moody in 1842, noted five colonists who had been born in Ireland. But the Irish population was to increase sharply with the arrival of the military pensioners in 1849. A large proportion of the Victorian army came from Ireland, and the 1851 census counts 74 persons of the Irish nation: 15 were military pensioners and many of the rest their wives and children.

During the late 1840s, the second official in the islands was the magistrate, William Henry Moore, who had left his practice (and his wife) in Belturbet, Co. Cavan, and armed with a testimonial signed by many of the Dublin legal establishment, arrived in Port Louis in March 1845.

Moore was a caricature of a provincial lawyer: argumentative, self important, and a heavy drinker. He argued violently with the first two governors, Lt. Richard Clement Moody and Lt. George Rennie, and the former reported to London on June 25, 1846: "there are many Irishmen here, Mr. Moore is an Irishman, and the observation has been made that we have a 'Daniel O'Connell' among us." Moore eventually returned to London on leave in 1849 and was discovered offering legal advice to a company in dispute with the Colonial Office. He was sacked and disappears from view in a minor post in the Customs Office.

In the late 1830s some Irish began sheep farming in the Falkland/Malvinas Islands. Among others, Thomas Murray (aka "Thomas the Devil") owned a large flock, which he sold a few years later to purchase land on the continent. Most of the Irish were Catholics, but other Catholics in the islands were English, Chilean, French, and from other countries. A fundamental part of the life of Catholic islanders was the presence of priests among them. The islands were (and still are) under the jurisdiction of Propaganda Fide in Rome. In 1857 they wrote to Cardinal Wiseman, archbishop of Westminster, and to Cardinal Alessandro Barnabo, secretary of Propaganda Fide, to ask for a priest to attend their souls. The archbishop of Buenos Aires, Dr. Mariano J. Escalada, requested Anthony Fahy, O.P., to find a solution for the islanders, and he proposed that a priest from Buenos Aires visit them once every seven years. That same year, Father Lawrence Kirwan visited the islands and organized a committee to build a chapel and obtain land for a cemetery. Among the committee members were P. D. Lynch, Thomas Havers, Christopher Murray, and Patrick Maguire. In 1861, land was acquired to build a Catholic chapel. In 1865 Father Patrick J. Dillon visited the islands. At that time there were about 200 Catholics, and they had no priest. Father Dillon spent a few months among them and administered the sacraments. In 1872 Father William Walsh made a short visit to the islands, and before the end of the year he was gone on his way to his diocese of Brisbane in Australia.

Father James Foran was the first resident priest, and he was fundamental in establishing a Catholic position in the islands. He arrived in October 1875 and, after receiving permission from ecclesiastical authority, from 1880 to 1886 he spent half the year on the islands and the other half on the mainland. On June 15, 1873, Stella Maris chapel in Port Stanley was completed by the islanders, and later Father Foran moved it to a better location. Father Foran also started a school for Catholic children in the islands. When Father Foran finally left the islands in April 1886 he traveled to Buenos Aires and eventually returned to England. After 1888, the Catholics of the Falkland/Malvinas Islands were attended by the Salesian Fathers, beginning with Father Patrick J. Diamond, who arrived on April 19, 1888, in Port Stanley, together with Monsignor José Fagnano.

Father Diamond was able to continue the work that was carried out by Father Foran. Father Diamond built the parish priest house and directed the children's school. He also baptized *sub conditione* more than 25 Protestant adults. Father Diamond was followed in 1890 by Father Patrick O'Grady, who had been in Argentina since 1884. Father O'Grady replaced the old chapel with a new building, which opened in 1899. Other chaplains were Father Mignone, who remained in the islands until 1937, and Irish-born Fathers Drumm and Kelly. In addition, other priests assisted the resident clergy, including Monsignor Santiago M. Ussher in 1930, the Passionists Father Domingo Moore and Father Santiago Deane, and the Pallotine Father Celestino Butterly. The Salesian sisters *Hijas de María Auxiliadora,* among them Sister Mary Jane Ussher, established a mission in the islands and remained there for many years.

However, the Irishman who made the greatest impact on the history of the islands was certainly the Reverend Lowther Brandon, a Church of Ireland clergyman from Carlow who became colonial chaplain in 1877. A man of faith and drive, he was remarkable for tackling the social problems of Stanley, the capitol of the Falkand/Malvinas, in a series of practical steps. He founded the first savings bank, established abstinence societies to combat drunkenness, and launched the *Falklands Islands Magazine,* which he typeset and printed himself. He rode tirelessly around his broad parish, dragging after him a pack horse (*carguero*) laden with his magic lantern for shows to the camp settlements. Brandon also served as inspector of the government schools and was a constant advocate of better teaching for children in camp. He returned to Ireland in 1907 and died in Slaney, Co. Wicklow, in 1933.

Another Irishman in a senior post in government was Dr. Samuel Hamilton who arrived on the islands from Dublin in 1879 and served there for 25 years, returning to Ireland to retire. Prominent explorers who visited the islands included Captain Francis Crozier, from Banbridge, Co. Down, who commanded one of the ships (*Terror*) on the Antarctic expedition of 1841–1843 and Sir Ernest Shackleton, born in Athy, Co. Kildare, who visited Stanley on numerous occasions on his way to or from Antarctica. Another explorer, the Irish yachtsman Conor O'Brian, called at Stanley, and his boat remained in use in Falklands/Malvinas waters until she was returned to the Irish Maritime museum.

Two British governors came from Ireland, Thomas Fitzgerald Callaghan from 1877 to 1880 and Sir Cosmo Haskard, who served from 1964 to 1970 and then retired to Ireland. A third governor, Sir James O'Grady (1931–1935), was the son of an Irish family living in England. He started life as a jobbing carpenter, moved into trade union politics, was sent on a diplomatic mission to Bolshevik Russia, and was finally appointed colonial governor, first to one of the Australian states and then to the Falkland/Malvinas Islands.

During the opening decades of the twentieth century, the conflict between Argentina and England for the control of the Falkland/Malvinas Islands gained a wider awareness among the Irish in Buenos Aires and other provinces. The controversial and nationalistically opinionated *Fianna* newspaper never missed an opportunity to attack Britain's occupation of the islands. The integration process of Irish Argentines to a larger and wider society signified that most of them thought their loyalty was toward Argentina rather than Britain. Miguel Fitzgerald (b. 1926) perhaps best epitomized that general Irish-Argentine attitude, when twice flying from the mainland to the islands in 1964 and 1968. On both occasions he landed near Stanley, raised the Argentine flag, and with accompanying journalists tried (unsuccessfully) to interview British authorities. Nothing was achieved by these individual actions, but they do reveal the increasing nationalistic feelings of the Irish Argentines toward the adopted country of their forebears. In August 1966, another Irish Argentine, Eduardo F. McLoughlin (b. 1918), a former Air Force officer, was appointed Argentine ambassador to Britain; he would remain in London until 1970. Following Argentine policy, McLoughlin interfered with a British plan to hand sovereignty over to Falkland/Malvinas Islanders before 1982, which would have opened the way to a pacific settlement of the conflict.

The Falkland/Malvinas War (April 2–June 14, 1982) began when the Argentine military junta sent warships to land a party of scrap dealers on South Georgia with the intention of reclaiming the Falkland/Malvinas Islands. A full-scale military invasion followed. Attempts by the United Nations, the United States, and Peru to secure a peaceful resolution to the conflict failed. Britain dispatched a task force comprising some thirty warships, two aircraft carriers, assorted fleet auxiliaries, the *Canberra* (a requisitioned passenger liner), roll-on/roll-off ferries, and container ships to recover the islands. The 10-week conflict claimed the lives of nearly 1,000 British and Argentine military personel and civilians and ended with the surrender of the Argentine forces on June 14. The British victory contributed to the downfall of the Argentine military dictatorship and the reelection of Margaret Thatcher as prime minister. Argentina officially declared a cessation of hostilities in 1989.

Irish and Irish-Argentine soldiers were among those who fought on both sides of the war. Translation was one particularly skilled service rendered by many Irish Argentines during the Falkland/Malvinas War. For instance, Private Ronnie Quinn translated messages and Private Miguel Savage facilitated communications with the islanders and, after the surrender, onboard the *Canberra.* In the immediate aftermath of the Argentine invasion, Major Patricio Dowling acted as interpreter during the meeting with Governor Rex Hunt at his official residence. Dowling's hatred of all things British was remarkable, and he was later sent back to the continent in disgrace for overstepping his authority. The Falkland/Malvinas War was a turning point in the identity of most Irish Argentines. After decades of being *ingleses* and living voluntarily isolated in their own country, Irish Argentines finally began to feel truly Argentine.

Edmundo Murray

See also: DILLON, Patrick Joseph; FAHY, Anthony; SHACKLETON, Sir Ernest

References

Cawkell, Mary. *The History of the Falkland Islands.* Shropshire, England: Anthony Nelson, 2001.

Coghlan, Eduardo A., *Los Irlandeses en Argentina: Su Actuación y Descendencia.* Buenos Aires: Author's Edition, 1987.

Paul, James, and Martin Spirit. "Honour Regained: Naval Party 8901 and the Argentine Invasion." The Falklands War 1982 index. www.britains-smallwars.com/Falklands/NP8901.html (accessed August 23, 2007).

Tatham, David E. "A Coincidence of Incidents." *The Falklands Islands Journal* (1995): 117–135.

FARLEY, JAMES ALOYSIUS (1888–1976)

James Farley was born in 1888 in Grassy Point, New York, the son of Irish Catholic immigrants. His brickmaker father died when Farley was 10, and he and his four

A prosperous businessman, James Farley managed the key political campaigns that brought Franklin D. Roosevelt national attention. In appreciation of his political talent and efforts, President Roosevelt appointed Farley postmaster general in 1933. (Library of Congress)

brothers had to work to help support the family. Farley first became involved in politics in 1911, when he was elected town clerk of Grassy Point. In 1922–1923, he served on the state legislature. By 1928, he had risen to become secretary of the Democratic State Committee. He started in bookkeeping and went on to start his own building supply company. He became a close friend of Franklin D. Roosevelt, who at that time was in the New York State Assembly. Farley was instrumental in helping FDR win the governorship of New York State in 1928, even though it was widely expected FDR would lose if the Democrats lost the presidential election. Farley was again behind the scenes when FDR was reelected governor in 1930.

In 1932, Farley was instrumental in winning Roosevelt the Democratic nomination by convincing delegates for an opposing candidate, John Nance Garner, to throw their support to Roosevelt. Once Farley accomplished this, Garner gave his support to Roosevelt, ensuring his candidacy. Farley was again important in guiding Roosevelt to victory in the presidential election in November 1932, against the incumbent Herbert Hoover. Farley worked with Roosevelt's other confidant and strategist, Louis Howe. Farley was later named chairman of the Democratic National Committee. As a reward for his loyalty, Farley was named to the position of postmaster general. During his time as postmaster (1933–1940), Farley worked closely with President Roosevelt, who was an enthusiastic stamp collector. Among stamps issued under his tenure were a series of colorful National Parks stamps and a National Recovery Act stamp that Roosevelt hoped would help promote his New Deal.

Besides serving as postmaster general, Farley was a key adviser to Roosevelt, and helped end Prohibition. He wrote an autobiography in 1938. By 1940, there was friction between Farley and Roosevelt, stemming from a combination of Farley's belief that Roosevelt should not seek reelection and Farley's own desire to run for president. By this point, Farley had resigned as postmaster general. Farley was unsuccessful in his bid for higher office; the wildly popular Roosevelt was the Democratic nominee again in the summer of 1940. Farley did not mend fences with Roosevelt at that time, and he was not officially a supporter of FDR's 1940 reelection bid. Farley unsuccessfully attempted to win the nomination for governor of New York in 1958 and 1962.

Farley died in 1976 in New York City, at the age of 88. The main post office in New York City is named after him.

Richard Panchyk

References

Burns, James MacGregor. *Roosevelt: The Lion and the Fox, 1882–1940.* New York: Harcourt, Brace, & World, 1956.

Farley, James. *Behind the Ballots: The Personal History of a Politician.* New York: Harcourt, Brace, 1938.

Rollins, Alfred B., Jr. *Roosevelt and Howe.* New York: Alfred A. Knopf, 1962.

FARRELL, EDELMIRO JUAN (1887–1980)

Born on August 12, 1887, in Avellaneda, Buenos Aires, Edelmiro Juan Farrell was the grandson of Matthew Farrell (d. 1860) of Co. Longford and Mónica Ibañez. Farrell joined the army in 1905 and graduated as second lieutenant of the infantry regiment. He spent most of his career in Mendoza, where he specialized in mountaineering fighting units. In 1924 Farrell traveled to Italy to receive special instruction with the Alpine regiments of the Italian army. He was promoted to lieutenant colonel in 1927, colonel in 1931, and general in 1941, and was appointed director of the military mountaineering school.

Farrell was one of the main figures of the military coup d'état of June 4, 1943, led by Pedro Pablo Ramírez, which replaced the discredited administration headed by Ramón Castillo. Ramírez was appointed de facto president and Farrell his war minister. When the vice president, Rear Admiral Sabá Sueyro, died, Farrell was named in his stead. In February 1944, General Ramírez was deposed by the pro-German military group after announcing that Argentina would comply with U.S. requirements against the Axis governments. Farrell took over as president and was sworn in on March 12, 1944.

A leading figure of Farrell's administration was Col. Juan D. Perón. Perón became the most powerful man in Argentina by cornering such appointments as vice president, minister of war, head of the labor and welfare secretariat, and chairman of the council for postwar planning. Farrell and Perón were part of a secretive group of officers who came to be known as the Grupo de Oficiales Unidos. They were strong supporters of the Axis, sympathizing not only with the war efforts of Germany and Italy but also with the social model that Hitler and Mussolini had introduced in their countries (Franco's Spain was another source of inspiration). These officers conformed to a long tradition of nationalism, contempt for democracy, and pro-German sentiment in the Argentine army. Perón, as Farrell before him, had spent time in Italy training, and was deeply impressed above all with the personality and social policies of Mussolini. Both men found in European fascism a formula they believed could turn Argentina into a powerful nation capable of asserting its independence against the most powerful countries.

The end of the war and hopes for better times led to a dramatic rise in labor disputes. Civil war was in the air, and Farrell began to realize that the hour of defeat was near at hand. The pressure became too great, and the controversial vice president Juan Perón was forced to resign and was arrested on October 12, 1945. But Perón was no longer just an army officer, he was also

Argentina's foremost labor leader. Union leaders and young officers loyal to Perón began, with his wife Eva (known as Evita) Duarte's help, to mobilize resistance. Farrell's moment of truth came on October 17, 1945, when the working population of Buenos Aires took to the streets en masse, filled the Plaza de Mayo in front of the presidential palace, and demanded Perón's release. Farrell took the opportunity to resume control of the situation. Perón was instantly released, reinstated in all his appointments, and addressed a jubilant crowd of about 300,000 persons from the balcony of the presidential palace. This was the victory of the Argentine poor; *los descamisados* (the shirtless) and the despised *cabecitas negras* (small black heads) had now become a force to reckon with in Argentina's history.

Edelmiro Farrell was forced to announce that a presidential election would be held in February 1946. Perón was the obvious candidate and, with 54 percent of the votes cast, he defeated the candidate of the united opposition. Farrell gave way to Perón, who was sworn in as the new president on June 4, 1946. Edelmiro Farrell retired and died in 1980.

Edmundo Murray

References

Coghlan, Eduardo A. *Los Irlandeses en la Argentina: Su Actuación y Descendencia.* Buenos Aires: Author's Edition, 1987.

Rojas, Mauricio. *The Sorrows of Carmecita: Argentina's Crisis in a Historical Perspective.* Stockholm: AB Timbro, 2002.

FARRELL, EILEEN (1920–2002)

Eileen Farrell, who is of Irish ancestry, was born in Willimantic, Connecticut, in February 1920. Farrell's early musical studies were with her mother. She later studied singing with Merle Alcock and then with

Portrait of Eileen Farrell, American opera and concert singer. (Library of Congress)

Eleanor McClellan, initially concentrating on concert work before joining a CBS radio show in 1940. Her vocal talent was soon recognized, and she gained her own radio show. In the late 1940s she went back to concert tours and traveled throughout the United States and South America, always receiving acclaim for her style and performance. In 1951 she sang a concert version of Berg's *Wozzeck* with the New York Philharmonic at Carnegie Hall that created a sensation among the conservative patrons. However, her real breakthrough came when she was selected for the dubbed voice in the 1955 movie *Interrupted Melody,* which was the life story of the famous Australian Wagnerian soprano Marjorie Lawrence. Eleanor Parker played Lawrence. Operatic engagements quickly followed and Farrell made her debut in the role of Santuzza in the opera *Cavalleria Rusticana* in Tampa,

Florida. She then sang in Verdi's *Il Trovatore* at the San Francisco opera, where she was partnered with the great Swedish tenor Jussi Björling. She returned to San Francisco in 1958 where she sang in Cherubini's *Medea.* Throughout, the critics gave great praise to her vocal style and her vocal excellence.

In December 1960 the New York audience saw Farrell make her Metropolitan Opera debut in Gluck's *Alceste.* She was 40 years old. She only sang for five seasons at the Metropolitan Opera; however, her performances caused quite a sensation in New York and on tour where her large exciting voice placed her opposite some of the greatest Italian singers of the period. Her recording career blossomed. However, her relationship with the opera's management at the Metropolitan was not tranquil. Her vocal style and physical size were ideally suited for Wagner's operas, yet the Metropolitan's management continued to place her in the Italian repertory. Farrell was one of the early successful crossover artists. Her temperament and unique talent made her comfortable with various music styles in addition to opera. She frequently performed jazz and pop music and even worked with Louis Armstrong's musicians on one occasion. She made many records of popular song tunes. Her last recording was made in 1993, just before her seventy-third birthday.

In the 1970s she moved into teaching at the Indiana University Music School. Later she also taught at the University of Maine, where she had moved in 1980. In 1999 she coauthored her autobiography, *Can't Help Singing,* with writer Brian Kellow. It was published by Northeastern University Press. Farrell continued giving concerts until health problems slowed her down. She died in a nursing home in Park Ridge, New Jersey, in March 2002 at the age of eighty-two.

Basil Walsh

See also: HERBERT, Victor August; MUSIC IN AMERICA, IRISH

References

Davis, Peter G. *The American Opera Singer.* New York: Doubleday, 1997.

Steane, J. B. *The Grand Tradition: Seventy Years of Singing on Record.* New York: Scribner's, 1974.

Walsh, Basil. "Eileen Farrell." In *The New Grove Dictionary of Opera.* Vol. 1, edited by Stanley Sadie. London: Macmillan Press, 1992: 127–128.

FARROW, MIA (1946–)

Maria (Mia) de Lourdes Villiers Farrow was born in Los Angeles, California, on February 9, 1945, the daughter of Australian filmmaker and writer John Farrow and Irish actress Maureen O'Sullivan (who was born in Roscommon, Ireland on May 17, 1911). One of seven children, Mia was educated in Catholic schools in Spain, the United Kingdom, and California.

Farrow made her film debut in a small role in one of her father's films, *John Paul Jones,* in 1959, but began to establish herself with a well-received role in an off-Broadway production of *The Importance of Being Earnest* in 1963. Between 1964 and 1966 she starred in the hit TV show *Peyton Place,* and it was during this period that she met and married Frank Sinatra, who was almost 30 years her senior. Although the marriage ended in 1968 (reportedly over her refusal to turn down the role in Roman Polanski's *Rosemary's Baby*), they stayed on good terms until his death in 1998.

Farrow's breakthrough role was in Roman Polanski's *Rosemary's Baby* in 1968. Adapted from Ira Levin's best-selling novel, the film cast Farrow as the young wife who unsuspectingly becomes involved in a satanic plot when her husband (John Cassavetes) promises their unborn baby to a group of New York Satanists, in exchange for success in his career. Farrow's waif persona, and her apparent physical fragility (possibly the result of a bout with childhood polio), accentuated her character's vulnerability. The role in *Rosemary's Baby* was well received, and the film remains a seminal horror film. The film also brought her to the attention of a number of interesting directors, and in the 10 years that followed, she worked with veteran filmmakers such as Joseph Losey (*Secret Ceremony*), Claude Chabrol (*Docteur Popaul*), Jack Clayton (as Daisy in a poorly received film of F. Scott Fitzgerald's *The Great Gatsby*), and Robert Altman (*A Wedding*). Even though she took on roles that were often challenging and complex, she largely failed to win audience and critical acclaim in this period.

In 1982 she accepted a role in Woody Allen's *A Midsummer Night's Sex Comedy.* Although her performance received mixed critical reviews, it initiated a personal and professional relationship with Allen that lasted a decade. Their partnership was mutually productive: in the 10 years that followed, Allen produced films (*Broadway Danny Rose, Radio Days, The Purple Rose of Cairo, Crimes and Misdemeanors,* and *Husbands and Wives*) that are generally regarded by critics as his best work; Farrow's roles in these films revealed her to be an actress of depth, humor, and versatility. The partnership came to an abrupt and dramatic end in 1992, when it was revealed

Mia Farrow (right) and Woody Allen (left) on the set of Allen's film, A Midsummer Night's Sex Comedy, *in 1982. (Orion/The Kobal Collection)*

that Allen, with whom Farrow had three children (a birth son, Satchel, and two adopted children, Moses and Dylan), had begun a relationship with Farrow's adopted daughter (with second husband André Previn), Soon-Yi Previn. The breakdown of their relationship culminated in a protracted custody battle and well-publicized child molestation charges against Allen (subsequently dismissed by a U.S. court).

Although there has been some falling off in her career after the Allen controversy, Farrow has continued to take roles in films, often in Irish productions (e.g., *Widow's Peak* [1994] and *Angela Mooney* [1996]). Farrow is also well known for her charity work, and has served as a UNICEF (United Nations Children's Fund) special representative. She has been closely associated with the issue of adoption, having adopted (at last count) nine children from within the United States and abroad, as well as raising her birth children, Matthew, Sascha, and Fletcher (from her marriage with Previn), and Satchel (with Allen).

Gwenda Young

References

Groteke, Kristi (with Marjorie Rosen). *Woody and Mia.* London: Hodder and Stoughton, 1994.

Katz, Ephraim. *The Film Encyclopedia.* New York: Perigee Books, 1979.

Vinson, James. *International Dictionary of Films and Filmmakers: Actors and Actresses.* Chicago: St. James Press, 1986.

FAY, FRANCIS ANTHONY "FRANK" (1897–1961)

Frank Fay was born Francis Anthony Donner in San Francisco to parents of Irish ancestry who were both in the entertainment business. He attended school in New York until the fifth grade, when he left to work in a Shakespearean company. He appeared as a child actor in *Babes in Toyland* in 1903, and three years later he appeared on Broadway in a production of *Redemption of David Corson.* After a period spent working with Johnny Dyer, Fay became a solo performer in 1917. His solo act was one of the first that did not rely on costumes, and the focus of the show was entirely on Fay himself. Dressed in hat and tails, his interactions with the audience anticipated the comedy sketches of later stand-up comedians. In 1918 he appeared in *Girl o' Mine,* and four years later the show *Frank Fay's Fables,* which he both wrote and starred in, ran on Broadway for one month. He was responsible for discovering the actress Patsy Kelly when she performed a song-and-dance routine as a teen in his vaudeville act.

Fay married Barbara Stanwyck in 1928, and they both moved to Hollywood to pursue their acting careers. However, it was a turbulent marriage, and Fay's heavy drinking led to allegations of physical abuse being made against him by his wife. In 1932, in an attempt to rescue their marriage, they adopted a son named Dion. When Fay, in a drunken rage, threw their son into a swimming pool it eventually led to the end of their marriage, and they divorced in 1935. That same year Fay wrote his autobiography, entitled *How To Be Poor.* Later he married Frances White.

Fay starred in a total of 13 films throughout his career. His first, *The Show of Shows* (which he cowrote with J. Keirn Brennan), saw him playing the master of ceremonies, a role with which he felt at home and which drew on his earlier experience in vaudeville. He would repeat this role in the 1937 film *Nothing Sacred.* He played Irish Catholic priests in the films

They Knew What They Wanted and *Tom and Jerry.* As well as being an actor, he occasionally worked as a producer and writer. He both starred in and produced the film *A Fool's Advice,* which was later reissued under the title *Meet the Mayor.*

In 1936 Fay had a very successful radio program in which he recited the lyrics to popular songs and lampooned them. In the 1940s he revived his flagging career when he appeared as the alcoholic Elwood P. Dowd in Mary Chase's play *Harvey,* playing a man whose imaginary best friend was a six-foot-tall invisible white rabbit. The play won the 1945 Pulitzer Prize for Drama, and it ran for more than four years on Broadway. However it was to be his last appearance on Broadway. Five years later James Stewart was nominated for an Academy Award for his performance as the character in the film adaptation.

When Fay was once asked during a court appearance what his profession was, he replied, "I'm the greatest comedian in the world." He later turned to his lawyer and said, "I was under oath, wasn't I?" Although he was a vivacious character, his alcoholism not only contributed to the failure of his marriage but also led to increasingly unpredictable behavior and tensions with others, prompting Milton Berle to comment that "Fay's friends could be counted on the missing arm of a one-armed man." Toward the end of his life he worked in nightclubs and occasionally in television roles. He died in Santa Monica in 1961, having been declared legally incompetent and confined to a hospital a week before his death. He is buried in Calvary Cemetery, Los Angeles.

David Doyle

References

Fay, Frank. *How To Be Poor.* 1935. Reprint, New York: Prentice Hall, 1945.

Harrell, Joy. "Frank Fay." In *Encyclopedia of the Irish in America,* edited by Michael Glazier. Notre Dame, IN: University of Notre Dame Press, 1999.

Smith, Ronald L. *Who's Who in Comedy.* New York: Facts on File, 1992.

FEDERAL THEATRE PROJECT

The Federal Theatre Project (FTP) was part of President Franklin Roosevelt's Depression-era Works Progress Administration, and its goal was both to employ unemployed theater workers and establish an American national theater, one modeled partially after Ireland's national theater, The Abbey. Because of its nationalist agenda, the FTP strove to stage the American experience, a

Poster for The Living Newspaper *dramatic production* One-Third of a Nation, *produced by the Federal Theater Project. (Library of Congress)*

goal that was a result of FTP director Hallie Flanagan's research on the Abbey.

The FTP's goals made the Abbey and Irish playwrights a likely influence. Together with President Roosevelt and Harry Hopkins, the Federal Arts Project director, Hallie Flanagan outlined the goals of the FTP: to employ unemployed theater workers, to express American culture through theatrical performances, and to bring theater to every corner of America. The FTP easily met its employment goal by staging 924 separate productions that employed 12,700 theater workers in 40 states during its four-year run.

Irish playwrights helped the FTP meet its nationalistic and canvassing goals. In 1935, when Flanagan began to create the structure for the FTP, she looked to Europe for national theater models; she and her research staff reviewed most European national theaters. Yet, there was only one national theater she and her staff turned to first and continually researched during the FTP's four-year tenure: The Abbey. The Abbey's own cultural nationalist agenda of dramatizing Irish culture by staging plays written by native Irish playwrights provided Flanagan with a practical structure for capturing the American experience. Initially, Flanagan met with former and current Abbey Theatre directors to understand how they made their nationalist goals a dramatic reality. From these meetings, Flanagan conceived of the idea of producing plays written by Americans and that expressed American cultural moments. The most notable dramatic legacy was *The Living Newspaper.* These plays staged culturally significant events that the American people were currently experiencing. As a result of their subject matter, they came to be collectively and appropriately named *The Living Newspaper* because, like a newspaper, they reported the American peoples' 1930s narrative. And, much like how Sean O'Casey's *Dublin Trilogy* has left Ireland and the world with detailed narratives of the tragedy of Irish nationalism, *The Living Newspaper* has left America and all those who read them with moving portraits of depression-era life.

Additionally, Flanagan corresponded with George Bernard Shaw as she developed the FTP, and through this correspondence came the FTP's greatest gift: Shaw gave them unrestricted access to produce all of his plays. Shaw's support for the FTP is partially what gave the project its credibility and ultimate success. Through Flanagan's relationship with Shaw, the FTP attained its goal of bringing theater to every part of the American countryside. In a letter dated May 22, 1937, Shaw granted Flanagan and the FTP blanket permission to produce any of his plays as long as they kept the price of admission at 50 cents, thus allowing every American access to these federally sponsored dramas. Because of Shaw's artistic importance, each of the 158 federal theaters operating across America asked to produce a Shaw play. And when a Shaw play went up, audiences not only transformed federal theaters into standing-room-only experiences but also demanded that the performance runs be extended. Shaw's plays also instigated a new FTP phenomenon: play productions touring nationally. Of the nine Shaw plays the FTP produced, four of them toured nationally: *Arms and the Man, The Devil's Disciple, Pygmalion,* and *Androcles and the Lion.* In total, during the final two years of the FTP, American audiences enjoyed several thousand performances of Shaw's plays. By including Shaw's plays in the

FTP's canon, the American and worldwide opinion of the FTP changed from a second-rate theater project to one of an elite caliber and international acclaim. Today, the FTP is remembered for its *Living Newspaper* and Shaw productions, exemplifying the influence Irish theater had on the FTP.

Diane M. Hotten-Somers

See also: SHAW, George Bernard

References

Federal Theatre Project Papers. The Library of Congress. Washington, DC.

Flanagan, Hallie. *Arena: The History of the Federal Theatre.* Rahway: Quinn Boden, 1940.

Matthews, Jane De Hart. *The Federal Theatre, 1935–1939: Plays, Relief, and Politics.* Princeton, NJ: Princeton University Press, 1967.

O'Connor, John and Lorraine Brown, eds. *Free, Adult, Uncensored: The Living History of the Federal Theatre Project.* Washington, DC: New Republic Books, 1978.

FEENEY, CHARLES "CHUCK" (1931–)

Born into a working-class family in Elizabeth, New Jersey, Chuck Feeney was the son of an insurance underwriter and a nurse. His paternal grandmother originally came from near Kinawley in Co. Fermanagh. Feeney enlisted in the army after World War II and served in Japan and Korea. Upon his discharge he received a GI scholarship and studied hotel administration at Cornell University. After studying in Grenoble, France, and traveling in Europe, he ran a camp in southern France for children from the U.S. naval fleet. He met a fellow Cornell student, Robert Miller, in Barcelona and they agreed to go into business together to take advantage of the fleet's demand to purchase consumer goods. In 1960 they opened their first duty-free shops in Honolulu and Hong Kong. They called their company Duty Free Shoppers, and within the next few years they had opened dozens of shops around the world exploiting the rise in postwar tourism and tourists' demand for consumer goods.

In 1988 *Forbes* magazine placed Feeney in the top 20 in its list of the 400 richest people in America. They estimated his fortune at $1.3 billion, thereby making him the wealthiest Irish American of his generation. However, in 1982, after donating $700,000 to Cornell University, he set up Atlantic Philanthropies. This charitable foundation allowed him to fund projects while also preserving his anonymity. He then secretly arranged for his share of the company to be transferred to this charitable foundation, keeping less than $5 million for himself. He spent his time running the various businesses that constituted General Atlantic Group, Ltd. In 1997 when Duty Free Shoppers was purchased, and his relationship with his cofounder ended acrimoniously, he was forced to go public as the benefactor of the charity. The sale of his share of the company meant that Atlantic Philanthropies, the fourth largest charity in America, was worth $3.5 billion. Recently, it has moved away from its earlier project of funding universities and has focused on health and helping disadvantaged children in such countries as the United States, the Republic of Ireland, Northern Ireland, South Africa, Vietnam, and Bermuda.

His links with Ireland stretch back to the time when he grew up in an Irish-American neighborhood in New Jersey. He also traveled to Ireland during the 1970s to order whiskey for his duty-free shops. He holds both Irish and American citizenship. Following the Irish Republican Army (IRA) bombing in Enniskillen in 1987, he began to play an important role in the peace process, helping to bring about the first IRA ceasefire in 1994. Recently he has financed the establishment of a new Sinn Féin office in Washington, D.C. He also embarked on a program of funding Irish universities. He donated $10 million to Trinity College Dublin as well as $15 million to the University of Limerick. In total, he has donated more than $100 million to Irish universities while refusing all honorary degrees. In 1998 he organized a 50th reunion for the class of 1948 of St. Mary's High School in his hometown of Elizabeth, New Jersey, which took place in the Castletroy Hotel in Limerick.

In 2005 Feeney was embroiled in a political controversy in Ireland. He had announced that he would fund the Centre for Public Inquiry, an organization that was set up to investigate claims of corruption. The Centre included Justice Fergus Flood and broadcaster Damien Kiberd among its members. Its chief executive was the *Sunday Business Post* journalist Frank Connolly. However, Minister for Justice Michael McDowell, using parliamentary privilege, announced to Dáil Éireann that Connolly had travelled to Colombia on a false passport in April 2001 along with his brother Niall and Padraig Wilson, the former head of the IRA prisoners in the Maze Prison. McDowell said the purpose of their journey was to meet with Revolutionary Armed Forces of Colombia (FARC) guerrillas and share expertise in explosives. Connolly, whose brother Niall had been the Sinn Féin representative in Havana and had been arrested in Colombia on suspicion of training FARC guerrillas in 2001, denied the accusation. After meeting the minister for justice, Chuck Feeney decided to withdraw his funding for the Centre.

David Doyle

Reference

Molloy, Darina. "Charles Feeney." In *Encyclopedia of the Irish in America,* edited by Michael Glazier. Notre Dame, IN: University of Notre Dame Press, 1999.

FENIANS

The Fenians constituted a nineteenth-century revolutionary movement that was active in the United States and Ireland. Adapting their name from the Fianna, the legendary warrior army led by Finn MacCool, the Fenians rejected constitutional efforts to achieve Irish home rule. Although the Fenian designation originally served to distinguish the American cohort from the parallel Irish Revolutionary Brotherhood (IRB), the term became popular for militants on both sides of the Atlantic. Fenians sought a democratic and independent Irish republic.

From exile in Paris, James Stephens (1824–1901, born in Kilkenny), a participant in the Young Ireland 1848 Rebellion, began to plan—with John O'Mahony (1816–1877), Michael Doheny (1805–1863), and Joseph Denieffe—an insurrection that would be funded from abroad. With the promise of financial support from Irish Americans, Stephens, in Dublin on March 17, 1858, founded a group of oath-bound conspirators initially referred to only as the Organization, the Brotherhood, or the Society. In early 1859, Stephens took control of the group's parallel American faction, that under O'Mahony had taken the name of the Fenians. The tensions between the Fenians in America and Britain and those in Ireland would undermine their insurgent aims; while 1861–1866 would bring Fenian recruits from all three fronts, the attempts of Stephens at

Fenian banner, ca. 1866. The Fenians were Irish nationalists who harshly opposed British rule in Ireland. (Library of Congress)

dominating his comrades eventually weakened their plans for rebellion when, after the American Civil War, Irish and Irish-American veterans wished to continue fighting against the British for Irish independence. Stephens, lacking funds to battle, became shouldered aside by diehards eager to fight—no matter what their chances for nationwide success against the Crown.

American Fenians argued over how best to foment Irish revolution. A. M. Sullivan (1829–1884) published the newspaper *Nation* (1855–1874) to promote the Young Irelanders' advocacy of constitutional nationalism. Stephens opposed what he regarded as Sullivan's compromise, and countered with his own newspaper, not only as propaganda but as a personal investment. This action resulted in his demotion to European organizer. His publishing venture attracted unwelcome attention and penetration by the government. Stephens alienated support for the movement, however, when he started the *Irish People* newspaper; American Fenians believed this compromised the organization's secret, cellular hierarchy. This European-styled structure failed to prevent infiltration by spies, and the Fenians were never as secure as they believed from surveillance. In Ireland, Stephens joined with Thomas C. Luby (1821–1901) to build a nationwide network of support. Opposition from the Catholic Church, nationalist politicians, and law enforcement limited Fenian success. In 1863, a "Fenian Congress" in Chicago resolved that the Irish Republic desired by the Brotherhood be proclaimed as "virtually established." By 1865, the movement boasted 250,000 followers. In Philadelphia, a model Irish republican government had been proclaimed.

After the end of the American Civil War, 50,000 veterans from both sides supported the Fenians. British suppression of revolutionary activity led to imprisonment for Luby and Stephens and dissidents such as Jeremiah O'Donovan Rossa (1831–1915). The *Irish People* was suppressed in 1865. The British crackdown prevented a Fenian uprising. In Britain, there had been many rebel volunteers among Crown troops and the Irish emigrants, but Stephens, sprung from jail by his comrades in September 1865, would diminish hopes that a rising could succeed. Back in the United States, Stephens regained control over the Fenians, but without sufficient ammunition and funds, he lost the opportunity to spark an Irish insurrection. Later in 1866, hardline militants and Civil War veterans replaced Stephens. He failed to return for the 1867 rising they prepared. Their insurrection, with a minor February action and a larger, if still miniscule, attempt at a nationwide revolt on the night of March 4, met with defeat because of informers, a waiting array of British troops, and inclement weather. American Fenians had sent the ship the *Erin's Hope;* it arrived in Sligo Bay only after the rebellion had been crushed.

The year 1866 also marked the first of three abortive invasions of Canada by American-based Fenians. During the 1866 invasion the term "Irish Republican Army" was coined for the first time. Whether or not the British could be more easily defeated in Canada or Ireland divided the Fenians; a failed 1870 Canadian incursion ended the debate. Discredited, Stephens remained in exile again until his return to Dublin in 1891. After the Irish defeats of 1867, Fenian prisoners would revive agitation as their supporters rallied for their release. In September, 29 men were apprehended on charges of shooting an unarmed policeman who was transporting two prisoners. The November execution of three suspects (William Allen, Michael Larkin, Michael O'Brien), the "Manchester Martyrs," gained the insurgents not only popular sympathy but also a measure of condolence from the Catholic Church in Ireland. Home Rule efforts energized a counterrevolutionary campaign against such violence. The spread of Fenian sympathies would sway Gladstone to back this reform measure. Whether the Fenians were more accurately described as zealous revolutionaries or revelers seeking Irish camaraderie has been argued recently between revisionist and nationalist Irish historians. The Fenian legacy, nonetheless, endures in the popularity of their name and their mystique among their republican successors. Subsequently, the clandestine movement would reorganize, in America through Clan Na Gael and in Ireland as the IRB, both of which promoted physical-force separatism against the British Crown.

John L. Murphy

See also: IRISH REPUBLICAN ARMY; IRISH REPUBLICAN BROTHERHOOD

References

Comerford, R. V. *The Fenians in Context: Irish Politics and Society, 1848–92.* Dublin: Wolfhound Press, 1985.

Harmon, Maurice, ed. *Fenians and Fenianism.* Dublin: Scepter Publishers Ltd., 1968.

Kenny, Kevin. *The American Irish: A History.* New York: Pearson, 2000.

Miller, Kerby. *Emigrants and Exiles: Ireland and the Irish Exodus to America.* New York: Oxford University Press, 1985.

Moody, T. W., ed. *The Fenian Movement.* Cork: Mercier Press, 1968.

Newsinger, John. *Fenianism in Mid-Victorian Britain.* London: Pluto Press, 1994.

Ó Broin, Léon. *Fenian Fever: An Anglo-American Dilemma.* London: Chatto & Windus, 1971.

Rafferty, Oliver. *The Church, the State, and the Fenian Threat, 1861–75.* New York: St. Martin's Press, 1999.

FITZGERALD, BARRY (1888–1961)

William Joseph Shields, later known as Barry Fitzgerald, was born in Dublin on March 10, 1888. He attended the Civil Service College and obtained a position as a junior executive with the Unemployment Insurance Division in Dublin. He simultaneously worked as a supernumerary at the Abbey Theatre in Dublin.

Fitzgerald first acted in 1915 but flubbed his only line. He consequently turned to comedic acting as a vocation. In 1929 he left his executive job to become a full-time character actor. He shared lodgings with the Irish playwright Sean O'Casey, who wrote *The Silver Tassie* for his roommate. He also stared in O'Casey's play

The Juno and the Paycock. In 1930 Alfred Hitchcock offered Fitzgerald the same role for the movie version.

John Ford brought Fitzgerald to Hollywood in 1936 to act in the film version of *The Plough and the Stars,* a role he had played on stage. The diminutive (five-feet four-inches) Fitzgerald presented outstanding performances as Cocky in *The Long Voyage Home* with John Wayne in 1940 and as Henry Twite in *None but the Lonely Heart* with Cary Grant in 1944.

Fitzgerald, whose ethnicity was illustrated with his distinctive Irish brogue, was a lifelong Protestant nationalist. Ironically, his masterful acting as Roman Catholic priest Father Fitzgibbon in *Going My Way* garnered him an Academy Award. He made cinematic history when he was doubly nominated in 1944 for both Best Actor and Best Supporting Actor for *Going My Way.* He won for the Best Supporting Actor category. The Academy revised its classification system thereafter. He is also among the elite group of actors who have received Academy Award nominations for two films in one year.

He appeared in *And Then There Were None* in 1945 as Judge Francis J. Quinncannon with Walter Huston and as Dooley in *Two Years Before the Mast* in 1946. After 1944 Fitzgerald played variations of the earlier Father Fitzgibbon role. He appeared in *Duffy's Tavern* in 1945, *Two Years Before the Mast* in 1946, *Variety Girl* and *Welcome Stranger* in 1947, *Miss Tatlock's Millions* in 1948, and *Top o' the Morning* in 1949. His role in *The Naked City* in 1948 cast him against type.

Fitzgerald is mostly remembered for his memorable performance as Michaleen Oge Flynn in *The Quiet Man* with John Wayne and Maureen O'Hara in 1952. This was his last collaboration with Ford, who had also directed him in *How Green Was My Valley.*

Fitzgerald never became a famous movie star; rather, he always remained a character actor. His last role was in *Broth of a Boy* in 1959 in which he portrayed a 110-year-old man. Fitzgerald has a star on the Hollywood Walk of Fame for his work in films and another for his television performances. Fitzgerald died in Dublin on January 14, 1961.

Annette Richardson

FITZGERALD, F. SCOTT (1896–1940)

F. Scott Fitzgerald is ranked among the greatest American writers of the twentieth century. His parents, Edward and Mary (Mollie) Fitzgerald, were both of Irish descent. Edward Fitzgerald was a distant cousin of Francis Scott Key, composer of the American national anthem. The genteel Fitzgerald family left Maryland shortly after the Civil War to settle in St. Paul, Minnesota. Mollie Fitzgerald was of more recent Irish stock; her father, Philip Francis McQuillan, had emigrated from Ireland in 1843 and amassed considerable wealth as a wholesale grocer. The author, Francis Scott Key Fitzgerald, was born in St. Paul on September 24, 1896. When Edward Fitzgerald's wicker furniture business went bankrupt in 1898, he moved his family to New York State and went to work for Procter & Gamble. Young Scott Fitzgerald attended Catholic grammar schools in Buffalo, New York. The family returned to St. Paul in 1908, after Edward Fitzgerald once again lost his job. Mollie's family helped to support the Fitzgeralds, who

Writer F. Scott Fitzgerald and Zelda Sayre Fitzgerald on their honeymoon in 1920. Fitzgerald is best known for his novel The Great Gatsby. *(Library of Congress)*

struggled to maintain their social standing in highly stratified St. Paul. Scott Fitzgerald was always acutely aware of his father's professional failings and of the contrast in his parents' social backgrounds. The combination of factors, he later reported, gave him a "'two-cylinder inferiority complex."

A private-school education, followed by his acceptance at Princeton, did little to quell Fitzgerald's inferiority complex. He attended the nonsectarian St. Paul Academy from 1908 until 1911. As an Irish Catholic whose family lacked the social standing of many of his classmates' families, Fitzgerald felt like an outsider—a feeling that was to stay with him throughout much of his life and feature prominently in his fiction. A preoccupation with class and social standing is apparent in Fitzgerald's novels, particularly his masterpiece *The Great Gatsby,* and throughout many of his short stories. Fitzgerald's academic record at St. Paul Academy was mediocre at best. He apparently had little interest in schoolwork, devoting his time instead to writing stories for the school newspaper and plays for the drama club. His poor academic performance prompted his parents to send him to the Newman School, a Catholic boarding school in Hackensack, New Jersey. There, too, he felt isolated and unhappy; he later wrote about the experience in his semi-autobiographical novel, *This Side of Paradise.* While at the Newman School, Fitzgerald set his sights on attending Princeton. Above all, he was interested in the Princeton Triangle Club, an undergraduate club that wrote and performed a musical comedy each year.

Despite his poor academic track record, Fitzgerald was accepted at Princeton in 1913. His maternal grandmother, Louise McQuillan, died that summer, leaving enough money to cover her grandson's college expenses. Fitzgerald struggled academically at Princeton as well, and feelings of social inferiority continued to plague him. He wrote musical comedies for the Triangle Club, but academic probation kept him sidelined during performances. In December 1914, while home on Christmas break, Fitzgerald met and fell in love with the very beautiful and wealthy–and ultimately unattainable–Ginevra King. He would later create a number of fictional characters patterned on Ginevra King, including the title character in "The Debutante" (1917), Isabelle in *This Side of Paradise* (1920), and Daisy Buchanan in *The Great Gatsby* (1925).

While at Princeton, Fitzgerald formed close ties with two Irish Catholic intellectuals, Shane Leslie and Monsignor Sigourney Fay, both of whom encouraged Fitzgerald to embrace his Irish ethnicity. Under their influence, according to one Fitzgerald scholar, "from mid-May 1917 until early 1918, Fitzgerald was everywhere proclaiming himself Irish." When, in *This Side of Paradise,* the socially ambitious protagonist Amory Blaine expresses his concern that "being Irish was being somewhat common," Monsignor Darcy assures him that "Ireland was a romantic lost cause and Irish people quite charming, and that it should, by all means, be one of his principal biases."

In November 1915, a mild case of malaria provided Fitzgerald with an excuse to leave school rather than face his midyear exams. He returned a year later to repeat his junior year but never graduated from Princeton, choosing instead to enlist in the army. He received his commission as a second lieutenant in infantry in October 1917; a month later, he reported to Fort Leavenworth, Kansas, for training. Within three months Fitzgerald had completed a 120,000-word novel, *The Romantic Egoist.* The manuscript was rejected by Scribner's but later became the basis for *This Side of Paradise,* Fitzgerald's first successful novel. In June 1918 Fitzgerald reported to Camp Sheridan near Montgomery, Alabama, to prepare for overseas service. It was in Montgomery that he met his future wife, Zelda Sayre.

The war ended before Fitzgerald could be sent overseas, and he was discharged from the army in 1919. After working for a short time in an advertising agency in New York City, Fitzgerald returned to St. Paul to revise his manuscript. The novel was published as *This Side of Paradise* on March 26, 1920; Scott and Zelda Fitzgerald were married a week later. The novel was an overnight success, and the couple lived what appeared to be the charmed life of young celebrities, appearing on magazine covers and at high-profile social functions and dividing their time between the United States and Europe. In 1921 Zelda gave birth to a baby girl, Frances Scott (Scottie), and Fitzgerald began work on his second novel, *The Beautiful and the Damned* (1922). In 1925 he published his best known work, *The Great Gatsby.*

Beneath their glamorous image, the Fitzgeralds struggled with mounting financial pressures; Scott showed signs of alcoholism and Zelda of mental illness. Scott Fitzgerald turned his attention more and more to writing short stories, first to pay for their lavish lifestyle and later to cover his wife's medical expenses. By the time Fitzgerald published his fourth novel, *Tender is the Night* (1934), Zelda had already suffered several breakdowns and had been in and out of mental hospitals. The following year Fitzgerald began to write his three autobiographical "Crack-Up" essays in which he explores his own suffering and personal decay. After having Zelda transferred to Highland Hospital in Ashland, North Carolina (where she would eventually perish in a fire), Fitzgerald moved to Hollywood to begin work on a screenplay contract. While in Hollywood, Fitzgerald began an affair with gossip columnist Sheilah Graham. It was in her apartment that he suffered a fatal heart attack on December 21, 1940. Fitzgerald left his final novel, *The Last Tycoon,* unfinished at his death.

Kathleen Ruppert

See also: FARROW, Mia

References

Casey, Donald J., and Robert E. Rhodes, eds. *Modern Irish-American Fiction: A Reader.* Syracuse, NY: Syracuse University Press, 1989.

Myers, Jeffrey. *Scott Fitzgerald: A Biography.* New York: Harper Collins, 1994.

Prigozy, Ruth. *F. Scott Fitzgerald.* Woodstock, NY: Overlook Press, 2001.

FITZSIMONS, PATRICK (1802–1872)

Patrick Fitzsimons was a schoolmaster and educator born in Ennis, Co. Clare. In 1843, together with Cuthbert Collingwood Power, he founded the Springfield College for Catholic boys in Ennis and became its headmaster for about 20 years. Because of debts owed to their many creditors, Fitzsimons, his family, and Power left Ireland aboard the *Raymond,* and they arrived in Buenos Aires on October 1, 1862. They settled in Lobos, where Fitzsimons opened the Irish School. After this, he started schools in Flores and Paraná. In 1869 the Argentine President Domingo F. Sarmiento commissioned Fitzsimons to open the new Colegio Nacional in Corrientes, which became an educational achievement. A number of other institutions were annexed to it, including an elementary school, a model school for elementary teachers (which was based on the Irish national education system), and a normal school for teacher training. Fitzsimons also engaged in pioneering work in organizing night courses for workers and a special school for soldiers in the army. His two sons, Santiago and Guillermo (born James and William Fitzsimons in Ennis in 1849 and 1851, respectively), were appointed to positions of authority in these schools. *Los Tres Fitzsimons* are remembered in Corrientes as pioneering figures in the history of the city. Patrick Fitzsimons, his wife, Bidelia Kelly, and a son died during an outbreak of yellow fever in April 1872.

Edmundo Murray

See also: TRAVEL PATTERNS FROM IRELAND TO SOUTH AMERICA

References

Murray, Thomas. *The Story of the Irish in Argentina.* New York: P. J. Kenedy & Sons, 1919.

Ó Murchadha, Ciarán. "Springfield People: New Material on the History of Springfield College." *The Other Clare* 18 (April 1994).

Roger, María José. "The Children of the Diaspora: Irish Schools and Educators in Argentina, 1850–1950." *Irish Migration Studies in Latin America.* www.irishargentine.org (accessed October 21, 2004).

FLAHERTY, ROBERT J. (1884–1951)

Often called the father of the documentary film, Robert Joseph Flaherty was born on February 16, 1884, in Iron Mountain, Michigan. He was the oldest of seven children born to Robert Henry Flaherty (who was of Irish Protestant descent) and Susan Klöckner (who was of German descent).

Portrait of American filmmaker Robert Flaherty, who is most well known for his documentary Nanook of the North *in 1923. (Library of Congress)*

Robert Flaherty senior had mining interests in the United States and Canada, and he often traveled to remote mines accompanied by his eldest son. These early explorations and the nomadic nature of his childhood left Robert J. Flaherty with a taste for adventure.

Following sporadic attempts at education in Upper Canada College and Michigan College of Mines, Flaherty left his family to explore and prospect on the east coast of Hudson Bay. Many of the trips that he embarked upon between 1906 and 1913 were funded by large business interests, such as the engineering firm MacKenzie & Mann, and it was upon the request of William MacKenzie that Flaherty first used film to record his explorations. In 1913 he filmed his expedition to the Belcher Islands, an archipelago in Hudson Bay, but the footage was damaged through Flaherty's carelessness and lack of experience. In 1920 Flaherty was employed by a fur trading company, Revillion Frères, to film an expedition to a remote Inuit settlement on the northeast coast of Hudson Bay. Filming continued for nearly a year, during which time Flaherty's fascination with native cultures, lifestyles, and traditions deepened. Working with his editor, Charlie Gelb, Flaherty edited the vast amounts of footage, making a young Inuit, Nanook, the focus of the narrative. The resulting film, *Nanook of the North,* was released in 1923 and met with critical praise. Robert Sherwood, writing in *The Best Moving Pictures of 1922–3,* claimed that the film offered "drama rendered far more vital than any trumped-up drama could ever be by the fact that it was all *real.*" Although other critics echoed Sherwood's sentiments, *Nanook of the North* was never more than a romantic, poetic interpretation of the lives of the Inuits. During filming Flaherty had insisted that the Inuits wear traditional costumes—which they had ceased wearing many years before—to deepen the "authenticity" of the film's presentation of their lives. Despite the overt manipulation of reality that this entailed, *Nanook of the North* remains one of the cornerstones of the documentary film.

Following the success of *Nanook* Flaherty signed a contract with Paramount pictures to direct a South Seas film on location in Samoa. The result, *Moana,* was released in 1926, and its stunning cinematography was praised by critics. Flaherty returned to the South Seas in 1929 to shoot a film, *Tabu,* with German director F. W. Murnau, but the collaboration was fractious and ended before filming was completed.

In 1931 Flaherty traveled to Britain and was contracted by John Grierson, the creative organizer of the Empire Marketing Board and the father of the British documentary movement, to direct a documentary called *Industrial Britain,* which was released in November of that year. His next venture, financed by Michael Balcon of Gaumont pictures, was a film about the lives of the Aran Islanders living off the west coast of Ireland. Location filming took more than a year and the resulting film, *Man of Aran,* was a bleak but poetic film about the everyday hardships endured by the islanders.

In 1935 Flaherty worked with Zoltan Korda on *Elephant Boy,* an adventure film set in India and starring the Indian boy actor, Sabu. Flaherty shot much of the exterior footage in India, and Korda was responsible for interior scenes. Flaherty was disappointed that the finished film did not contain much of his footage and when it was released it met with mixed reviews.

As war broke out in Europe, Flaherty and his family returned to America and began work on one of his most important and controversial films, *The Land.* Produced for the U.S. Film Service and shot on location in the southern and eastern United States, *The Land* showed how the Depression affected rural communities. Flaherty spent two years working on the film (1939–1941), but when he presented his footage to his employers he was dismayed by the lukewarm reaction he received: Flaherty's film had become a victim of history and was considered out of date. *The Land* received a limited release in 1942, but it was withdrawn shortly after.

Flaherty's final film was *Louisiana Story,* produced for the Standard Oil Company and shot on location in Louisiana in 1946. Combining a fictional narrative with documentary-style footage, the film received warm reviews on its release in 1948. For the remaining three years of his life, Flaherty traveled around America and Europe promoting his films, being honored at universities and film festivals, and pitching ideas for new films. However, *Louisiana Story* was his last venture into filmmaking, and on July 23, 1951, he died of cerebral thrombosis at his home in Black Mountain, Vermont. He was survived by his wife and creative collaborator, Frances, and their three daughters.

Gwenda Young

References

Brownlow, Kevin. *The War, The West and the Wilderness.* London: Secker & Warburg, 1979.

Calder-Marshall, Arthur. *The Innocent Eye: The Life of Robert J. Flaherty.* London: W. H. Allen, 1963.

FLANAGAN, THOMAS (1923–2002)

Thomas (James Bonner) Flanagan was born in Greenwich, Connecticut, in November 1923, to Irish-American parents. He served in the U.S. Navy during World War II, and after the war studied at Amherst College. He taught at Columbia University from 1948 until 1960, and obtained his PhD from Columbia in 1958. His dissertation, *The Irish Novelists 1800–1850,* was published the following year. In 1960, he was appointed professor of English at the University of California at Berkeley; he was also awarded a Guggenheim fellowship, which enabled him to undertake the first of many visits to Ireland. Flanagan was an accomplished teacher and remained at Berkeley for 18 years before taking up the chair of English at State University of New York, Stony Brook. He was the author of numerous essays and reviews, and a posthumous selection of his criticism, *There You Are: Writings on Irish and American Literature and History,* was published by the New York Review of Books in 2004. In addition to these critical pieces, Flanagan was also the author of three historical novels set in Ireland: *The Year of the French* (1979), which deals with the failed Rebellion of 1798; *The Tenants of Time* (1988), which is set against the backdrop of the Land War; and *The End of the Hunt* (1994), which explores the troubled 1919–1923 period. Flanagan died in March 2002.

History is a central concern in all of Flanagan's work, and the narrative of history—and Irish history in particular—is always represented as something that is complex, profound, and uncertain. This point was registered early in Flanagan's career, in *The Irish Novelists,* when he described pre-Famine Ireland as "a fragmented culture, a dismaying and complicated tangle of classes, creeds, loyalties, and aspirations." To illustrate this point, *The Irish Novelists* comprises five extended essays on nineteenth-century authors who had different allegiances and who wrote in contrasting styles for specific audiences. Maria Edgeworth, Lady Morgan, Gerald Griffin, John Banim, and William Carleton receive detailed attention in this seminal piece of scholarship, and their manifold differences are used to underscore Flanagan's basic argument that his study should be considered "a study of five Irelands" rather than one. *The Irish Novelists* also argues against the idea of an established tradition of the novel in Ireland and suggests that literature and politics have always been intimately interrelated in Irish society. Questions of politics, audience, history, and style are also explored by Flanagan in his lengthy introduction to a 1982 edition of John Mitchel's classic *Jail Journal.*

Although Flanagan is well known for his academic work, he is perhaps more widely celebrated as the author of *The Year of the French.* This novel won the National Book Critics' Circle Award and was a commercial bestseller. It was subsequently adapted to the television screen by the Irish national broadcasting service, Radio Telefís Éireann, in association with the French station FR3 and Britain's Channel 4. *The Year of the French* takes as its theme the Rebellion of 1798—a much-mythologized episode in Irish history—when Catholics and Presbyterians joined forces and, with the assistance of a French expeditionary force, attempted to overthrow British rule in Ireland. Flanagan's treatment of this subject is subtle and sophisticated and gives the lie to any easy reading of this pivotal historical event. His novel is told by several conflicting narrators (a Protestant rector, a British army officer, a Gaelic schoolmaster, a Protestant United Irishman and his English patriot wife, and a conventional third-person storyteller), and it also includes a large cast of carefully delineated characters who have different aims and ambitions and who speak at cross-purposes, sometimes in different languages. By refusing to privilege any single perspective, Flanagan eloquently demonstrates that history is riddled with inconsistencies and contradictions and that any single narrative of the past, however valuable, is only ever partial.

Paul Delaney

See also: MITCHEL, John

References

Donoghue, Denis. "*The Year of the French.*" In *We Irish: The Selected Essays of Denis Donoghue.* Vol. 1. Brighton: Harvester Press, 1986: 258–266.

Kiely, Benedict. "Thomas Flanagan: The Lessons of History." In *A Raid into Dark Corners and Other Essays.* Cork: Cork University Press, 1999: 161–168.
Morrissey, Thomas J. "*The Year of the French* and the Language of Multiple Truths." *Éire-Ireland* 19, no. 3 (Fall 1984): 6–17.
Ward, Catherine. "Thomas Flanagan's *The Year of the French:* A Cautionary Tale." *Éire-Ireland* 22, no. 1 (Spring 1987): 59–71.

FLATLEY, MICHAEL (1958–)

Michael Flatley was born in Chicago in 1958. His parents had emigrated from Ireland in 1947 and had established a successful construction business in Chicago. Flatley's early interest was boxing, for which he won a Golden Gloves Championship at the age of seventeen. His parents were determined that their children would retain a sense of their Irish heritage, so from the age of eleven, he was enrolled in the Dennehy School of Irish Dance. At the age of 17, he became the first American to win the title of All-World Irish Dancing Champion. After graduating from high school, Flatley opened an Irish Dancing School. Although successful, Flatley's ambition was to perform rather than to teach. Eventually, he closed the school and began to forge a career for himself as a professional Irish dancer. In 1993, he was invited to dance at the Spirit of Mayo in Dublin, a unique festival of Irish dance and music. His performance caught the attention of the show's producers. He was subsequently commissioned to help create an interval act for the 1994 Eurovision Song Contest. *Riverdance* propelled Irish dance to worldwide attention and made Flatley a star overnight. He went on to star in the extended version of the show, which premiered in Dublin's Point Theatre in February 1995, before embarking on a number of international tours. Flatley left the show after a number of creative and financial difficulties arose and began choreographing, producing, and directing his own production, *Lord of the Dance.* This premiered in Dublin's Point Theatre in July 1996. It was an instant success, playing to sold-out venues, receiving standing ovations, and eventually setting records all over the world. Flatley followed *Lord of the Dance* with *Feet of Flames* in 2000. This was another astounding success, both in Europe and in the United States. Flatley has a number of entries in the Guinness Book of World Records for tap dancing speed, highest-paid dancer, and highest insurance premium placed on a dancer's legs. He retired from touring in 2001, and in 2004 he was awarded an honorary degree from University College Dublin for his contribution to Irish culture.

Aoileann Ní Eigeartaigh

See also: BUTLER, Jean

References

Lalor, Brian, ed. *The Encyclopaedia of Ireland.* Dublin: Gill and Macmillan Ltd., 2003.
Vallely, Fintan. *The Companion to Irish Traditional Music.* Cork: Cork University Press, 1999.

FLEMING, THOMAS J. (1927–)

Born on July 5, 1927 in Jersey City, New Jersey, Thomas J. Fleming was the son of Thomas James and Katherine (Dolan) Fleming, both of whom were of Irish ancestry. Fleming's father was a popular political ward leader in Jersey City who had a great influence on his son; Fleming recalled his father's impact on him in *Mysteries of My Father: An Irish-American Memoir* (2006). At an early age Fleming was exposed to politics, and this affected his later understanding of political and historical events. Fleming was educated in Catholic schools and later at Fordham University and the School of Social Work, after which he worked as a reporter for the *Herald Statesman.* Later he became executive editor of *Cosmopolitan* magazine from 1954 to 1961. He became a full-time writer in 1961 when he published his first novel, *All Good Men.* Since then he has written works ranging from biographies and historical works to novels and other pieces that have appeared in a variety of publications. His most recent book, *The Secret Trial of Robert E. Lee,* was published in 2006. He has received numerous literary awards for his work. Fleming is a fellow of the New Jersey Historical Society and the Society of American Historians and was the president of the American PEN from 1971 to 1973. He contributed to the PBS documentary *The Irish in America: The Long Journey Home,* which was broadcast in 1998. He is married, and his wife, Alice Mulcahey Fleming, also of Irish descent, is a writer. They have three sons and live in New York City.

Fleming's first published novel, *All Good Men,* deals with Irish-American city politics after World War II in a city that resembles Fleming's hometown of Jersey City. The same subject is explored in the later novels *King of the Hill* and *Rulers of the City.* Fleming has also explored his Catholic identity as an Irish American in some of his work. His 1970 novel *The Sandbox Tree*—which took him 17 years to write—aroused controversy on its publication because of its criticism of the pre-Vatican II Roman Catholic Church and the Church's repression of individual choice. His novel, *The Good Shepherd,* published four years later, depicts an archbishop's struggle between loyalty to the Catholic Church and his disagreement with some of the Church's teachings. In spite of Fleming's use of Irish and Catholic themes and concerns in his novels, he has stated that his Catholicism is incidental to his American identity. He has also said that growing up in an Irish-American community and with an Irish-Catholic identity has cut him off from the complete experience of being an American that others have enjoyed.

As well as exploring certain aspects of Irish-American life, Fleming has also written extensively about various periods in American history. His work, even when it is fiction, is intensely historical and relates the personal stories of individuals to the wider historical and political developments. He has focused on the American Revolution as a crucial moment in the country's history. His first published work, *Now We Are Enemies,* was a historical account of the battle of Bunker Hill. Three years later he published *Beat the Last Drum: The Siege of Yorktown.* Later, both *For Liberty Tavern* and *Dreams of Glory* dealt with the Revolutionary War. Recently, his work *Liberty! The American Revolution* accompanied the PBS series of the same name. His historical works not only deal with the public history of facts and events but also incorporate personal accounts written in diaries, letters, and journals.

His interest in the events of this time continued with his biography of Thomas Jefferson entitled *The Man from Monticello,* which won a Christopher Award. He has also written biographies of Benjamin Franklin, George Washington, and Harry Truman. He has written about twentieth-century American history, and World War II formed the subject of his novels *Time and Tide, Over There,* and *Loyalties.* In his best-selling novel *The Officers' Wives* he traces the history of postwar America by depicting the relationships among three women whose husbands graduate from West Point in 1950. He has also explored more recent American history in his novel *A Cry of Whiteness,* which is an account of the post-civil rights era busing of children for school integration.

David Doyle

See also: FLANAGAN, Thomas

Reference

Donnelly, Anna M. "Thomas J. Fleming." In *Encyclopedia of the Irish in America,* edited by Michael Glazier. Notre Dame, IN: University of Notre Dame Press, 1999.

FLYNN, ELIZABETH GURLEY (1890–1964)

Born in Concord, New Hampshire, in 1890, to an Irish-American working-class family whose identification with its Irish roots was strong, Elizabeth Flynn embraced socialism in her youth and by 1907 was an organizer for the Industrial Workers of the World (a radical group opposed to the perceived tameness of the American Federation of Labor and commonly known as the "Wobblies"). Among those with whom she developed personal bonds through labor activism was the Irish labor leader James Connolly. Flynn retained a lifelong affinity with the Irish nation, nurtured by parents with whom she remained close. Amongst her many associations as an activist were founding membership in the American Civil Liberties Union (ACLU) and, in 1937, the Communist Party. She faced criticism and even expulsion from the ACLU in 1940 as a result of her Communist sympathies. A renowned orator and energetic proponent of workers' organization, she was nonetheless, as a campaigner for women's rights, a frequent critic of male domination of formal trade unions. A Communist candidate for New York State representative in 1942, Flynn also held senior positions within the Communist Party. Caught up in the intense concern over communism in America after World War II, Flynn was arrested in 1951, tried, and convicted of violating the Alien Registration Act. After 28 months of incarceration, she resumed an active role in the Communist Party, becoming its chairman in 1961. Flynn died while on a trip to the Soviet Union in 1964. She was accorded a state funeral, with leading international Communist figures in attendance, including Nikita Khrushchev and Delores Ibarruri. She was an energetic figure who inspired both devotion and hatred, a tireless writer and speaker on behalf of various causes, and a figure whose prominence as a labor campaigner was coupled with a tumultuous private life. Flynn is remembered as a pioneer for labor and women's rights, an extraordinary orator, and one of the leading female labor leaders in twentieth-century America.

Kevin James

See also: BROPHY, John; CANALS AND THE IRISH INVOLVEMENT; DOMESTIC SERVANTS, IRISH; KNIGHTS OF LABOR; MITCHELL, John; MOLLY MAGUIRES; NO IRISH NEED APPLY; POWDERLY, Terence; QUILL, Michael Joseph

References

Baxandall, Rosalyn Fraad. *Words on Fire: The Life and Writings of Elizabeth Gurley Flynn.* New Brunswick, NJ: Rutgers University Press, 1987.

Camp, Helen C. *Iron in Her Soul: Elizabeth Gurley Flynn and the American Left.* Pullman: Washington State University Press, 1995.

Flynn, Elizabeth Gurley. *The Rebel Girl: An Autobiography, My First Life 1906–1926.* New York: International Publishers, 1973.

FOLEY (ALSO FOLI), ALLAN JAMES (1835–1899)

Born in Cahir, Co. Tipperary, in 1835, Allan Foley moved to America in 1853 at the age of 18 and settled in Hartford, Connecticut, at his uncle's home. Shortly afterwards he joined a local church choir and took vocal lessons. In 1861, on the recommendation of his New York vocal coach, Foley left for Naples, Italy, to commence vocal studies with Giovanni Bisaccia at the conservatory of San Pietro a Maiella. He made his operatic debut as Elmiro in Rossini's *Otello,* at Catania, Sicily, in December 1862. Engagements quickly followed at Modena, Turin, and Milan. During this period, Foley also became known as "Signor Foli," a title he retained to the end of his life. In 1864, he appeared at the Théâtre des Italiens in Paris, and in June 1865 he made his London debut as Saint-Bris, in *Les Huguenots.* Later that year he sang in *Norma* in Dublin. In London in July 1870, he created the role of Daland in the first English performance of *Der Fliegende Hollander.* In 1873, he appeared in Russia in *Mose, Der Freischutz* and Auber's *Masaniello* and in Italy in 1874. He participated in the first English performance of Berlioz's *L'enfance du Christ* in Manchester in December 1880. He also sang in oratorios and concerts. In 1878 Foley joined with the Mapleson Opera Company on an American tour as their principal bass vocalist. He was a great success in New York at the Academy of Music, where he performed leading roles in several operas. Foley later made an extended concert tour of Australia, New Zealand, and South Africa during 1892–1893. He had 60 roles in his repertoire, including Bertram in *Robert le Diable,* Caspar in *Der Freischutz,* Mephisto in *Faust,* Assur in *Semiramide,* and Rodolfo in *La Sonnambula.* Foley had a tall, imposing stage presence, and his large bass voice extended over two octaves in range. His career lasted 35 years. He died in Southport, England, in 1899.

Basil Walsh

See also: BALFE, Michael William

References

Brown J. D., and S. S. Stratton. *British Musical Biography.* Birmingham, UK: S. S. Stratton, 1897.

The Hartford Courant, March 18, 1859; October 21, 1899.

Mapleson, J. H. *The Mapleson Memoirs 1848–1888.* 2 vols. London: Remington & Co., 1888.

Reynolds, D. *A Neighbor's Child: The Life and Times of the Irishman Signor Foli.* Dublin: Millington Books Ltd., 1994.

FORD, HENRY (1863–1947)

In 1847 the Great Irish Famine drove William Ford from his farm in Clonakilty, Co. Cork, to Springfield Township, Michigan. There he built a log cabin and married Mary Litogot, who on July 30, 1863, gave birth to their second child, Henry Ford. Between 1871 and 1879 Ford attended school, absorbing from his teachers the values of diligence, self-reliance, and thrift. Despite his father's encouragement, Ford did not wish to be a farmer but instead became in 1879 an apprentice in a machine shop in Detroit. He worked nights for a jeweler and the next year began repairing steam engines for the Detroit Drydock Company. Ford credited his work on these engines with stoking his interest in the gasoline engine. In 1884 he returned to the family farm and in 1888 married Clara Bryant.

In September 1891, the couple moved to Detroit, where Ford became an engineer for Edison Illuminating Company. In 1893 he began designing a lightweight gasoline engine and on June 4, 1896, building on the work of Detroit engineer Charles B. King, tested his first automobile. Ford built a second automobile in 1899 and with capital from local investors founded the Detroit Automobile Company. Bankrupt the next year, Ford revived his fortunes by designing a 26-horsepower racing car and, in 1901, winning a race against Cleveland, Ohio, automaker Alexander Winton. Investors returned to Ford, helping him found the Henry Ford Company that year. Ford proposed to build another racer but investors wanted a commercial model. The rift led Ford to resign in 1902, and the remaining shareholders reorganized the firm as the Cadillac Motor Car Company. Ford built two racers and in 1902 set an American record of 5 minutes 28 seconds on the five-mile track at Grosse Pointe, Michigan.

Ford now turned, as investors had urged in 1901, to the manufacture of a commercial automobile. The decision marked a critical moment in the industry. Cadillac and the German automakers envisioned the automobile as a luxury and priced it beyond the means of most consumers. The American manufacturer Oldsmobile undercut these prices, and Ford proposed to price the automobile cheaper still. In pursuit of this aim Ford founded the Ford Motor Company in 1903. By manufacturing a standardized, inexpensive automobile Ford hoped to profit by the volume of sales. Implicit in this hope was the belief that a large market existed for the automobile. All an automaker needed to do was expand supply to meet demand. To stimulate sales he charged his office manager, James Couzens, with advertising, while Ford set himself the tasks of design, engineering, and production. In June 1903 Ford introduced the Model A at $850 and sold 1,708 cars by September 1904. To meet demand Ford enlarged his Mack Avenue plant in Detroit. Despite this success, Ford treasurer Alexander Malcolmson, clinging to the old vision of the automobile as a luxury, persuaded Henry Ford in 1905 to sell the Model B for $2,000. Profits the next year totaled $290,000 but Ford, ignoring Malcolmson, abandoned production of the high-end models B, C, and F. In July 1906 Ford bought Malcolmson's 255 shares and thereafter concentrated on the manufacture of inexpensive cars. That year Ford introduced the Model N at $600, although by year's end he had raised the price to $700. In 1906 Ford manufactured 10,000 Model Ns and grossed $1 million.

On October 1, 1908, Ford unveiled the Model T. The initial price of $850 made it more expensive than the Model N, but by August 1916 Ford had driven down the price to $325. By then he had revolutionized production. In 1913 he had introduced the assembly line. Rather than shuttle workers from place to place Ford moved automobiles in various stages of completion to them. Workers specialized in a small number of tasks that they repeated ad nauseam. Wherever possible Ford mechanized production, making the worker less a craftsman than a machine operator. As a result the assembly line and its machines set the pace of work. After touring a Ford plant Charlie Chaplin would distill the drudgery of the assembly line in *Modern Times* (1936). So high was turnover in 1913 that

Ford hired 52,000 workers just to maintain a workforce of 13,600. To attract and keep workers, in 1914 Ford reduced the workday from 9 to 8 hours and raised wages to $5 a day, double the rate in other industries. Yet not all workers were eligible for this pay. Ford established a sociology department to enforce his ideal of clean living at home and at work. Only workers who lived up to the values of diligence, self-reliance, and frugality that Ford had prized since childhood made $5 a day. By paying workers more than the prevailing rate Ford helped create a class of consumers able to afford the automobile. The durable Model T could travel poor rural roads, and farmers, prosperous during World War I as never before, made the Model T ubiquitous in the Midwest and Great Plains. Mass production had at last come to the masses. In 1921 the Model T accounted for 55 percent of U.S. auto sales, and by 1927 Ford had sold 15 million Model Ts.

By then General Motors (GM) rivaled Ford. In contrast to Ford, GM offered a range of styles and prices and unveiled new models each year to stoke demand. GM aimed to keep consumers dissatisfied with their current model. To fuel the purchase of expensive cars GM extended credit to consumers. Ford responded in May 1927 by halting production of the Model T and on December 1, 1927, unveiling his second Model A. Within two weeks Ford had 400,000 orders. Unable to meet demand, by the end of 1928 Ford held only 15 percent of the U.S. auto market and that year lost $74 million. In 1929 Ford rebounded, capturing 44 percent of U.S. auto sales. The Great Depression, however, cut sales and Ford shelved the Model A in August 1931. Between 1931 and 1933 Ford lost $125 million.

During the Depression Ford emerged as a spokesman for individualism as a counterweight to collectivism. Ford abhorred labor unions and the New Deal as antithetical to the value of self-reliance. To Ford the past was a saga of the pioneer and frontiersman. His upbringing on a farm, Ford believed, represented all that was good about the United States. To promote this idyllic vision of America, in 1933 Ford opened the Edison Institute and Greenfield Museum, an agrarian community. Ford turned against Congress in 1935 when it passed the Wagner Labor Relations Act, which allowed workers to bargain collectively. The formation that year of the United Auto Workers (UAW) exacerbated Ford's fear that government, labor, and communism were conspiring against him. Although GM and Chrysler signed contracts with the UAW in 1937, Ford refused and was criticized by the National Labor Relations Board for oppressing labor. Only in 1941 did Ford sign a contract with the UAW and then only because his wife threatened divorce.

World War II drew Ford into the production of armaments. The plant near Ypsilanti, Michigan, manufactured B-24 bombers for the U.S. Army Air Corps. Despite his role in wartime production Ford declared himself an isolationist. In 1938 he had accepted the Grand Cross of the German Eagle from Germany, leading critics to charge that Ford sympathized with Nazism. His anti-Semitism strengthened this charge as did Ford's refusal to manufacture engines for Great Britain.

Ford suffered strokes in 1938 and 1941. His only son Edsel died in 1943, and in September 1945 grandson Henry Ford II coaxed Henry Ford into retirement. He split his time between a mansion in

Michigan and a plantation in Georgia. Ford died of a cerebral hemorrhage at his Michigan estate. More than 100,000 mourners viewed his body at Greenfield Village. The family held a funeral service at Saint Paul's Cathedral in Detroit. Ford is buried at the farm his father had settled.

Christopher Cumo

See also: GREAT FAMINE, The; MICHIGAN

References

Brinkley, Douglas. *Wheels for the World: Henry Ford, His Company and a Century of Progress.* New York: Viking, 2003.

Ford, Carin T. *Henry Ford: The Car Man.* Berkeley Heights, NJ: Enslow, 2003.

Shores, Erika L. *Henry Ford: A Photo-Illustrated Biography.* Mankato, MN: Bridgestone Books, 2004.

Wood, John C., and Michael C. Wood, eds. *Henry Ford: Critical Evaluations in Business and Management.* New York: Routledge, 2003.

Zarzycki, Daryl. *Henry Ford: Cars for Everyone.* Hockessin, DE: Mitchell Lane, 2005.

FORD, JOHN (1895–1973)

An American film director with more than 100 productions, some of which are among the most influential films of the twentieth century, John Ford is one of Hollywood's best-known directors of westerns, but his career was complex and various. Whether his films are set in the majestic Monument Valley on the Arizona-Utah border or in the grimy streets of early twentieth-century Dublin, Ford's visions of rugged but disillusioned heroes (embodied in the actor John Wayne, who was made a star through Ford's films) are part of the American consciousness. He mastered a Hollywood narrative style, using sweeping images of a dangerous but profound moral landscape. Films such as *Stagecoach* (1939), *The Grapes of Wrath* (1940), *How Green Was My Valley* (1941), *The Quiet Man* (1952), *The Searchers* (1957), and *The Man Who Shot Liberty Valance* (1962) depict protagonists who are outsiders struggling to maintain bonds of family and community with courage, perseverance, duty, and honor. His work has influenced other directors, including Orson Welles, Stephen Spielberg, and Akira Kurosawa. Ford won the Academy Award for best direction four times (he was nominated six times) and was granted the first American Film Institute's Lifetime Achievement Award in 1973.

Born John Martin Feeney in Cape Elizabeth, Maine, in 1895, Ford alternately claimed his original name was Sean Aloysius O'Feeney, or O'Fearna, as a tribute to his Irish immigrant parents (his father came to the United States from Ireland in 1872). In 1914, Ford traveled to Hollywood to join his brother Francis (who had already taken the name "Ford"), who was then working with Universal Studios. John did some acting and had a few jobs as a prop man, but in 1917 he directed his first feature-length silent film, *Straight Shooting.* From that point on, John Ford and the Hollywood sound film matured in unison.

The year 1923, when "John Ford" became his official screen name, saw the production of *The Iron Horse* (1924), an epic American frontier drama detailing the building of the transcontinental railroad. This silent film established Ford in the top ranks of Hollywood directors and introduced the recognizable Ford elements of an idealized pioneer West and the rugged hero. The 1930s and early 1940s, however, were banner years for Ford. In 1935, *The Informer* (based on the novel by Irish writer Liam O'Flaherty) was released to critical acclaim and gave audiences a taste of Ford's more expressionistic style. Starring Victor

McLaglan as the dispossessed and hunted Gypo Nolan, *The Informer* and its Dublin location (shot on Hollywood sound stages) are presented in the texture and style of early film noir. *The Informer* won Academy Awards for best screenplay, best actor, and best picture. Ford's images of Dublin as a fogbound, dark, and despairing city of devastation echo the atmosphere of danger and destruction in many of his other films. In 1939 *Stagecoach* netted Ford another Oscar nomination and the film, with its open-air expansiveness of the West embodied in Monument Valley, revitalized the western genre for American audiences. *Stagecoach* also established John Wayne as a major Hollywood actor, and Wayne would continue to work on several films with Ford.

The permanence and power of nature, and resolute men fighting for justice, became trademark Ford elements with his next two major films, both of which won Academy Awards: *The Grapes of Wrath* (1940) and *How Green Was My Valley* (1941). These years saw Ford bring together a group of actors, writers, and film creators who would become known, unofficially, as Ford's stock company. The Hollywood careers of John Wayne, Henry Fonda, John Carradine, Ward Bond, and Dudley Nichols were interwoven with Ford's.

Ford was on active duty during World War II with the U.S. Navy as head of the Naval Field Photographic Unit. He was commissioned in the Naval Reserve with the rank of lieutenant commander and retired with the honorary rank of rear admiral (Ford's tombstone is inscribed "Admiral John Ford"). During the war, Ford made several documentaries, and two of them—*Battle of Midway* (1942) and *December 7th* (1943)—won Oscars. *Battle of Midway* won the Academy Award for feature-length documentary, a special award for the film's historical value in offering a camera record of one of World War II's most decisive battles. *December 7th* won for best documentary, short subject. The military ethos would find expression in several of Ford's fiction films. John Wayne's Lt. Col. Kirby Yorke in *Rio Grande* (1950) is but one such staunch army hero. Yorke, the leader of a military outpost in the years following the Civil War, faces his toughest battle against Apache warriors. Yorke's military training and discipline sustain his fight to redeem his honor and save his family's lives.

The postwar years saw an increasingly bleak vision in Ford's films, with the notable exception of *The Quiet Man* in 1952. Starring John Wayne (who always called Ford "Coach") as Sean Thornton, the film depicts Thornton's move from America back to Ireland to reclaim an ancestral homestead and find love with Mary Kate, played by Maureen O'Hara. *The Quiet Man* is well known for its use of stereotypical Irish icons from Celtic crosses and verdant glades to stormy weather and rollicking pub scenes. The film was popular in both the United States and the Republic of Ireland, although some Irish reviewers at the time were critical of what they saw as Ford's retreat into pastoral and sentimental images of Ireland. Nonetheless, *The Quiet Man* brought Ford an unprecedented fourth Academy Award.

Four years later, Ford made what many consider his best film, *The Searchers* (1956). Ethan Edwards (John Wayne) is a bitter, ruthless Civil War veteran on an epic quest for on orphaned niece kidnapped by Comanche natives. The hatred that propels his years-long search is made questionable and problematic as he realizes his niece has found family and community with the

Comanche. The power of family bonds and notions of military honor are more intricate in this late Ford classic. Ford's last film is *Seven Women* (1966), starring Anne Bancroft. The film holds true to signature Ford elements: an emphasis on action, colorful characters, a romanticized vision of the past, and a celebration of family or community ties.

Danine Farquharson

See also: FITZGERALD, Barry; O'HARA, Maureen; WAYNE, John

References

Bogdanovich, Peter. *John Ford.* Berkeley: University of California Press, 1968.

Eyman, Scott. *Print the Legend: The Life and Times of John Ford.* New York: Simon & Schuster, 1999.

Gallagher, Tag. *John Ford: the Man and His Films.* Berkeley: University of California Press, 1986.

McBride, Joseph. *Searching for John Ford.* New York: St. Martin's Press, 2001.

Rockett, Kevin, Luke Gibbons, and John Hill, eds. *Cinema and Ireland.* London: Routledge, 1987.

Sarris, Andrew. *The John Ford Movie Mystery.* Bloomington: Indiana University Press, 1975.

FORD, PATRICK (1837–1913)

Born in Galway on April 12, 1837, Patrick Ford immigrated with his parents to Boston in 1845. At the age of 15, Ford became a printer's devil at the abolitionist William Lloyd Garrison's newspaper *The Liberator* and remained there until he was 24. His experiences with Garrison had a lasting effect on his belief and advocacy for social reform. During the American Civil War, he fought on the side of the Union army in the Ninth Massachusetts Regiment. After the war, he spent a couple of years in Charleston, South Carolina, editing a Republican newspaper before moving to New York. In 1870, Ford settled in New York City and founded his own newspaper, the *Irish World.*

Portrait of Patrick Ford, Irish American nationalist and founder of the newspaper Irish World. *(Library of Congress)*

In the pages of the *Irish World,* Ford championed the need for radical social change. An advocate for various reform issues, Ford was a strong supporter of temperance, was against imperialism (both American and British), and argued for women's and African-American rights. After the outbreak of economic depression in America in 1873, he became a staunch defender of the rights of labor and industrial agitation. He backed labor union organization, the eight-hour work day, and the income tax, and he supported Greenback-Labor candidates and land nationalization. Ford argued that the root cause of the exploitation of the laboring poor was the monopolization of land and wealth by the privileged and nonproducing class of speculators and cartels. His adding the words *and American Industrial Liberator* to the title of the *Irish World* in 1878 is evidence of this new emphasis.

Unlike many of his contemporaries, Ford's belief in Irish independence went hand in hand with his struggle for social reform in America. He linked the cause of the industrial poor in America with that of the rural poor in Ireland, arguing that "the cause of the poor in Donegal is the cause of the factory slave in Fall River." His linkage of Irish nationalism and American radical social reform raised the ire of both moderate Irish-American nationalists like John Boyle O'Reilly and Patrick Collins, who argued for Irish-American middle-class respectability, and single-minded nationalists like John Devoy, who believed any focus away from Irish freedom was a dangerous diversion. Ford's troubled relations with other Irish-American leaders would prevent him from maintaining close and lasting relationships with contemporaries.

The outbreak of crop failure and agrarian unrest in Ireland in 1879 led to the formation of the Irish Land League by Michael Davitt and Charles Stewart Parnell, and the rise of this movement allowed Ford to be most influential during this period. The Land League was an attempt to use the rural unrest in Ireland to achieve political reform in Ireland by placing pressure on the British government. Both Davitt and Parnell undertook extensive fund-raising tours of the United States during 1880 and raised substantial funds for the Land League in Ireland. Another effect of the trip was the creation of an American branch of the Land League in May 1880. The Irish National Land League of America would provide for the most significant cooperation, albeit briefly, amongst Irish-American working-class, middle-class, and doctrinaire nationalists until the aftermath of the Easter Rising of 1916.

In January 1880, on his own volition, sensing the opportunity that the Land League and Parnell's visit presented, Ford placed a small ad in the *Irish World* telling readers that he would accept contributions to the Land League and would forward them to Ireland. Soon after, the *Irish World* began acknowledging donations and tabulating the amounts weekly under the heading "Land League Fund." In March, collections averaged more than $1,000 per week and were up to $2,500 per week the next month. By May, the *Irish World* had collected close to $25,000 for the Land League. Contributions came from a variety of sources, and local Land League branches began to sprout up across America. With the formation of the official American Land League in May, donations to the *Irish World* began to fall off. Ford countered this by drastically expanding coverage of local Land Leagues, detailing the formation of new branches, and following closely the activities of the League in Ireland. Regaining its earlier momentum, the *Irish World,* between January and September 1881, collected more than $100,000. Ford also established a "Spread the Light Fund," which allowed for the free distribution of thousands of copies of the *Irish World* in Ireland. The amount of funds collected and the transatlantic readership of the *Irish World* greatly increased Ford's influence. The British Prime Minister William Gladstone would later claim that without the *Irish World* and the money it collected, there would have been no agitation in Ireland.

In April 1882, Parnell and Gladstone reached an agreement to end Land League agitation, commonly known as the Kilmainham Treaty. Parnell, anxious to retain the momentum caused by the Land League, shifted his focus to achieving Irish Home Rule. This movement was dominated by middle-class Irish and Irish-American moderates, however, and more radical nationalists like Ford were pushed to the fringe. Because of this change, Ford concentrated more on achieving social reform in America than Ireland. In 1886, Ford supported social reformer Henry George's campaign for mayor of New York City. George had been a special correspondent for the *Irish World* in Ireland during the early 1880s, and George's book *Progress and Poverty*, which argued for land nationalization, was a major influence on Ford.

After 1886, however, in the aftermath of the Haymarket Riot and the increasingly militant labor movement, Ford retreated from his earlier radicalism, espousing more moderate, respectable reform until his death. Remaining editor of the *Irish World* until 1911, Ford became a supporter of John Redmond and Irish Home Rule, championed the Republican Party, and became a vehement opponent of socialism. He died at his home in Brooklyn in 1913.

Ely Janis

See also: DAVITT, Michael; PRESS, THE ETHNIC IRISH

References

Brown, Thomas N. *Irish-American Nationalism 1870–1890.* Philadelphia: J. B. Lippincott Company, 1966.

Foner, Eric. *Politics and Ideology in the Age of the Civil War.* Oxford: Oxford University Press, 1980.

Funchion, Michael. *Irish American Voluntary Organizations.* Westport, CT: Greenwood Press, 1983.

Joyce, William L. *Editors and Ethnicity: A History of the Irish-American Press, 1848–1883.* New York: Arno Press, 1976.

Rodechko, James. *Patrick Ford and His Search for America: A Case Study of Irish-American Journalism 1870–1913.* New York: Arno Press, 1976.

FOREIGN POLICY, IRISH

Article 29 of the Irish Constitution of 1937 directs that the Republic of Ireland's foreign policy follow a clear moral purpose in the pursuit of peaceful cooperation, international arbitration of disputes, and adherence to international law. In the early years of the twenty-first century, the Republic of Ireland continues to follow this mandate by focusing attention on international disarmament, human rights, and peace in Northern Ireland and by working through the United Nations (UN) and European Union (EU) to achieve these goals.

The most important objective of Irish foreign policy in the twenty-first century is to end the cycle of violence in Northern Ireland through a program of disarming the paramilitary groups and building democratic institutions for self-government. The Good Friday Accords of 1998, which were signed by the Irish and British governments as well as the representatives of the major sectarian parties, established the framework to meet these objectives. In May 1998 popular referenda in both Northern Ireland and the Republic of Ireland approved the Accords.

While the Accords have been successful in stopping the violence that had held the people of Northern Ireland in a state of terror since 1969, the agreement has stalled on the development of self-rule. In October 2002 Britain suspended the assembly of Northern Ireland. The Irish and British governments worked to get the process started again, but to no avail. Even though the assembly did not meet, elections were held in November 2003 and the voters moved away from the moderate parties on both sides toward the more hard-line positions. In April 2004 the Irish and British governments issued a joint report critical of the stance taken by the sectarian extremists. Ireland welcomed the announcement in July 2005 that the Irish Republican Army was giving up its armed struggle.

Proud of the progress made so far, the Irish government is still very concerned about the future of the Good Friday Accords and the long-term prospects of achieving a permanent peace in Northern Ireland. To build better relations between the citizens of the Irish Republic and Northern Ireland, in 1979 the Irish government established Cooperation Ireland, an aid program that promotes cross-border cultural ties. Between 1999 and 2004 the Irish government provided almost 14 million euros to 450 different groups as part of the program.

After issues in the north, Ireland has pursued several other important objectives with vigor. Primary among them is the cause of disarmament, including nuclear nonproliferation and the Ottawa Convention of 1997 to ban the use of antipersonnel landmines. The Irish government dedicates resources to the removal of land mines and education on the dangers of land mines in many parts of the world. A second objective is fostering human rights. Ireland stands firmly against the death penalty, torture, and terrorism. In 2002 Ireland ratified the UN convention against torture. In 2004 Ireland used its term of presidency of the EU to call for abolishing the death penalty. Later in the year the UN Committee on Human Rights adopted the resolution as well.

The primary method of Irish foreign policy is to act through international organizations. Representing a small country with a population of slightly less than 4 million persons, the Irish government feels it can only push its agenda by voicing its goals through larger organizations. In 1955 Ireland abandoned its neutrality and joined the UN. From 2002 to 2005 Ireland was a member of the UN Committee on Human Rights, which played an important part in Irish foreign policy goals. Ireland served on the UN Security Council in 2002 and worked to get resolution 1409 passed. Resolution 1409 sought to lessen the burden of sanctions against Iraq on its people, and focus the punishment instead on the regime of Saddam Hussein. Although Ireland is a peaceful nation, it is willing to allow, as a sign of its commitment to the UN, units of the Permanent Defense Force (PDF) to serve as peacekeepers. Between 2000 and 2006 more than 1,200 Irish UN peacekeepers were deployed to Cypress, East Timor, Eritrea, Ethiopia, and Liberia. In addition, individual members and smaller units of the PDF participate as observers in UN operations around the world. Ireland contributes forces to EU peacekeeping operations as well. Between 1999 and 2006 about 1,200 PDF peacekeepers served in Kosovo and the former Yugoslavia.

Membership in the EU has been a difficult balancing act for the Irish government. The government supports membership and full commitment to the EU. However, changes in the past decade have caused the Irish public to view the EU with considerably more suspicion. Throughout the 1990s Ireland moved toward meeting EU standards, including adopting the Euro with enthusiasm. The booming economy and double-digit economic growth bolstered the popularity of the EU. As the EU centralized, however, Ireland experienced some problems. It increasingly lost control of its agriculture policy, an important segment of its economy, and found itself in violation of many EU standards. Ireland also made clear that despite her commitment to the rapid deployment force, she did not consider the union a military alliance and reserved judgment on when her forces would be committed to action. In 2001 Irish voters rejected the Treaty of Nice, which called for the expansion of the EU into southern and central Europe. Ireland was only the European country to reject this treaty. The government resubmitted the treaty the following year and it was ratified. Ironically, it was during the Irish term of the EU presidency, in May 2004, that the 10 nations were added to the union. Since that time, the rift between the position of the government and the sentiment of the public continues to grow. In 2005, after the failure of France and the Netherlands to ratify the EU constitution, the Irish government suspended a referendum scheduled for the fall. It is conducting a public relations campaign to persuade a noncommittal Irish electorate that ratification would benefit the country. In a poll conducted in January 2006, 78 percent of Irish respondents stated that they wanted to see work permits reestablished as a way of preventing immigrants from southern and eastern Europe from taking jobs and driving down wages.

Under the Irish Aid Program (IAP) established in 1974, Ireland actively provides funds to underdeveloped countries around the world. In 2006 the total estimated amount of aid is about 750 million euros. IAP specifically targets education, medical care, and hunger in sub-Saharan Africa and East Timor. Aid is also distributed to other troubled places, such as recovery efforts from the devastating Indian Ocean tsunami of December 26, 2004. In 2006 the Irish government announced plans to place greater emphasis on environmental concerns in the distribution of IAP funds. IAP funds are distributed by approved Irish nongovernmental organizations, such as Trócaire, and international organizations, such as the Red Cross.

Like all governments, Ireland seeks to expand trade relations with other nations. In the last several years, Ireland has undertaken significant initiatives to establish trade and business agreements with a coordinated Asian strategy, focusing on China, a difficult task considering Ireland's support of human rights.

Gregory J. Dehler

References

Department of Foreign Affairs. *Annual Report 2003.* http://foreignaffairs.gov.ie (accessed May 1, 2006).

Department of Foreign Affairs. *Annual Report 2004.* http://foreignaffairs.gov.ie (accessed May 1, 2006).

Department of Foreign Affairs. *Challenges and Opportunities Abroad: White Paper on Foreign Policy.* http://foreignaffairs.gov.ie (accessed May 1, 2006).

Laffan, Brigid, and Ben Tonra. "Europe and the International Dimension." In *Politics in the Republic of Ireland,* edited by John Coakley and Michelle Gallagher. 4th ed. New York: Routledge, 2004.

Tonra, Ben, and Eilias Ward, eds. *Ireland in International Affairs: Interests, Institutions, and Identities, Essays in Honour of Professor N. P. Keatinge, FTCD and MRIA.* Dublin: Institute for Public Administration, 2002.

FOSTER, STEPHEN COLLINS (1826–1864)

The Fosters were of Ulster stock, the composer's great-grandfather having emigrated from Co. Derry to Pennsylvania in 1728. The family moved to Virginia and then back to Pennsylvania where Stephen Foster was born in Lawrenceville, near Pittsburgh, on July 4, 1826. His father tried a variety of ventures in business and politics with

Composer Stephen Collins Foster's songs speak of nineteenth-century dreams and nostalgia. Foster is famous for songs such as "Oh! Susanna" and "My Old Kentucky Home," the Kentucky state song. These familiar tunes, once popularized by blackface minstrel show performers are now prized Americana. (Library of Congress)

limited success, leaving the family with a somewhat tenuous hold on middle-class status. Yet there was a piano in the home, at least in the good times, and the young Foster learned to play guitar, flute, and the piano. He received formal musical training from a skilled German immigrant teacher in Pittsburgh.

Whatever Foster learned from studying the classics, however, it was popular music that claimed his talents. By the time he started writing songs, around 1844, the minstrel movement had begun, introducing two types of songs to the American public. The first was the fast-paced comic dance song that combined Scottish and Irish fiddle tunes with African-American banjo rhythms. It is not clear how much of this new American musical vernacular Foster picked up from the streets, so to speak, and how much was in imitation of the first minstrel performers. Nevertheless, his "Oh! Susanna" (1848) and "The Camptown Races" (1850) are among the few minstrel dance songs remembered today.

The minstrel stage also popularized the sentimental plantation songs, which projected onto African-American slaves white nostalgia for the lost childhood home, as in "My Old Kentucky Home, Good Night" (1853); for departed parents in the guise of "Massa's in the Cold Ground" (1852); for the separation of lovers, as in "Farewell My Lilly Dear" (1851); and for the death of the beloved, as in "Nelly Was a Lady" (1849). Improbable and embarrassing as these black-face conceits seem today, Foster's plantation songs were not as racist as many people assume. As Charles Hamm argues, the pieces bestow a level of human emotions and even nobility on the slaves depicted in the songs.

Although Foster had considerable success with his minstrel music, he wrote his best songs for another popular genus, the so-called parlor ballad, which at its best combined the strong flowing melodies of the Anglo-Celtic folk-song tradition with echoes of classical harmonies and decorations. Although requiring some formal training, most of these songs were within the vocal and pianistic range of a musically talented member (usually female) of the average middle-class family. From the beginning Foster's songs showed the influences of the British and Irish songwriters such as C. F. Horn, Thomas Linley, Samuel Lover, and, most important of all, Thomas Moore. Moore's poetry and songs, especially his *Irish Melodies,* were very popular in the United States. His music was the principal source in America for the traditional Gaelic airs upon which all of Moore's Irish songs were based. Charles Hamm finds Moore's influence in the structure of some of Foster's best melodies. In songs such as "Gentle Annie" (1856), "Old Folks at Home" (1851), and "Jeanie With the Light Brown Hair" (1854), Foster's melodic lines, like so many of the Irish airs Moore used, often contain an octave jump within the first phrase.

Foster, like many other American poets and songwriters, may also have been influenced by one of Moore's major themes—what William W. Austin has identified as "the dream of home." Many of Foster's parlor and plantation songs echo Moore's sense of nostalgia for the loss of the places and friends of childhood and youth. Although part of international popular culture, songs like Foster's "Old Dog Tray" (1853) had special meaning for restless Americans, who were ever on the move, always tearing down the physical reminders of the past to make way for the future. Although Moore's influence was significant, Foster assimilated many of the styles that shaped American popular music during his lifetime. He easily incorporated Scottish, German, and Italian elements into his songs, and this versatility helped make him one of America's best-loved and most respected songwriters during the nineteenth century.

William H. A. Williams

See also: MOORE, Thomas

References

Austin, William W. *"Susanna" "Jeanie," and "The Old Folks At Home": The Songs of Stephen C. Foster from His Time to Ours.* 2nd ed. Urbana: University of Illinois, 1989.

Hamm, Charles. *Yesterdays: Popular Song in America,* New York: W. W. Norton, 1983.

FOSTER, VERE HENRY LOUIS (1819–1900)

Born in Copenhagen on April 25, 1819, Vere Foster was a younger son of Sir Augustus John Foster, diplomat and plenipotentiary to the United States (1811–1812) and Denmark (1814–1824). After an education at Eton and Oxford, Vere Foster served as attaché at Rio de Janeiro (1842–1843) and Montevideo (1845–1847). During 1847, the worst of the Great Famine years, the 28-year-old bachelor visited Ireland for the first time and was deeply affected by the misery he witnessed. Leaving the diplomatic service to work for the poor on his brother's estate at Ardee, Co. Louth, he concluded that Ireland's problem derived from "excessive competition for employment." With this in mind, he sought immediately to remove from Ireland those who could profit from the greater opportunities available in America. His aim, as he said in the journal *Irish Female Emigration* in June 1855, was the "raising [of] the condition of the poorest families in the poorest districts of Ireland, by assisting the emigration to North America of one able-bodied member of each family (in most cases a woman), specially selected on account of her poverty, good character, and industrious habits, with the expectation that she will herself take the remaining members of her family out of poverty." Despite opposition—including at least one threatening letter from the notorious "Captain Rock"—Vere Foster persisted in his purpose to encourage female emigration, believing as he did that the demand for women in America exceeded that for men.

Before encouraging emigration, Foster set about collecting information on conditions, both on the emigrant ships and in North America. Following that, in 1850 he went to America, traveling more than 10,000 miles in an effort to ascertain the position of the working classes and the prospects for immigrants. He gave £25,000 to Irish women and men to assist their emigration. During the first phase of his emigration schemes he traveled steerage to New York on an emigrant boat. The conditions he and others experienced on the voyage led to public exposure in the newspapers and parliamentary inquiries, which resulted in transformative emigration laws. The publicity was very damaging to shipowners seeking to profit from short-changing emigrants. As a result of the incident Vere Foster found the cause that would occupy the rest of his life.

Once having found a goal for his life Foster expended all his abilities toward the best way to improve the lives of his countrypeople. A firm believer in education, he gave grants and helped in building several hundred new parish schoolhouses throughout Ireland. He also became the first president of the Irish National Teachers Organization and devised a series of copybooks, used widely by schools into the 1970s, which gave instruction in penmanship, drawing, and water coloring, skills he considered important for all children.

Foster's travels in Illinois in the 1850s were recounted in a fund-raising lecture that he gave years later. He described traveling at his own expense, accompanied by the ladies of an immigration society in "Incidents of Travel in America," a lecture delivered in the Rosemary Street Lecture Hall, Belfast, on January 27, 1879. In Springfield, Illinois, Foster placed one young woman with a distinguished Springfield lawyer, Abraham Lincoln.

Throughout his career Foster collected systematic information on conditions in North America by soliciting information through journals such as *The Freeman's Journal.* He gave away 250,000 copies of his *Penny Emigrant's Guide* before being forced to charge one penny apiece for it. Foster's papers in the Public Record Office of Northern Ireland attest to a single-minded, somewhat eccentric individual, who brooked no interference in his life mission. Despite the originality of his approach, however, Foster never became a controversialist and his papers show him always retaining a personal touch. His papers are full of correspondence with those he helped as well as those who solicited his help. Many distinguished people provided Foster with information about conditions in America, among them Horace Greeley, the well-known editor of the *New York Tribune.* Another was John Boyle O'Reilly, the distinguished editor of the Boston *Pilot* newspaper whose leadership of the Boston Irish-American community is still recalled in a statue of him in the Fenway area of the city.

Foster was entirely true to his principle of keeping any influence of religion or religious bias from influencing his efforts, and so he opposed proselytizing in any form. It was a view consistent with the concept of separation of church and state that influenced the Founding Fathers in the United States. Between 1880 and 1886 Foster estimated that he assisted almost 20,000 women between the ages of 18 and 30 to emigrate from the west of Ireland to the United States. In real terms this accounted for approximately 9.6 percent of the total female migration from Connaught from 1851 to 1856. Foster spent his last years in Belfast in charitable work. He died there, unmarried, on December 21, 1900, having spent his entire personal fortune on his life dream of helping Irish emigrants go to America. Foster's papers are on deposit in the Public Record Office of Northern Ireland.

Ruth-Ann M. Harris

See also: EMIGRATION; O'REILLY, John Boyle

References

Foster, Vere. *Origin and History of Vere Foster's Writing and Drawing Copy-books.* Privately printed, 1882.

Hall, Brendan. "Vere Foster and the City of Mobile." *Journal of the Genealogical Society of Ireland* 3, No. 1 (Spring 2002).

Harris, Ruth-Ann M. "'Where the Poor Man Is Not Crushed Down to Exalt the Aristocrat': Vere Foster's Programmes of Assisted Emigration in the Aftermath of the Irish Famine." In *The Meaning of the Famine,* edited by Patrick O'Sullivan, 172–194. London: Leicester University Press, 1997.

Harris, Ruth-Ann M. "Introduction." In *Search for Missing Friends: Irish Immigrant Advertisements Placed in the Boston Pilot,* edited by Ruth-Ann M. Harris and B. Emer O'Keeffe. Vol. IV, 1857–1860. Boston: New England Historic Genealogical Society, 1995: i-xxxiv.

Kohli, Marjorie. *The Golden Bridge: Young Immigrants to Canada 1833–1939.* Waterloo, Ontario: Natural Heritage Books, 2003.

McNeill, Mary. *Vere Foster 1819–1900: An Irish Benefactor.* Newton Abbot, UK: David and Charles, 1971.

Mullinger, Emma. "Cargoes of Virtue: The Work of Vere Foster and Charlotte Grace O'Brien for Nineteenth-Century Women Emigrants." Dissertation. University of Dublin, Trinity College, Dublin, 1996.

O'Connell, Anne. "Assisted Female Emigration: Vere Foster's Scheme 1880–1896." Dissertation. University of Limerick, 1998.

FURLONG, GUILLERMO (1889–1974)

Guillermo Furlong was born on June 21, 1889, in Arroyo Seco—a settlement of Irish and other sheep farmers in southern Santa Fe province in Argentina—to James Joseph Furlong and Anne Cardiff of Kilrane, Co. Wexford. He was educated in Rosario, in Mr. Woods's Protestant school and Mr. Robb's St. Bartholomew's School. Thanks to the Irish chaplain in Rosario, Father John Sheehy, Furlong entered the Colegio de la Inmaculada in the city of Santa Fe, where he began learning Spanish at the age of 13. In 1903, encouraged by Julián Hurley, S.J., he joined the Jesuit order as minor seminarian in Córdoba. In 1905 Furlong was sent to study in Spain, at the Monastery of Veruela (Aragón). He completed his studies in the United States, where he stayed from 1911 through 1913, studying in Woodstock College, Maryland, and obtaining a doctorate from the University of Georgetown, Washington, D.C.

Furlong returned to Argentina after his graduation, and in 1916 he was employed as a teacher of history at the Jesuit Colegio del Salvador in Buenos Aires and Colegio del Sagrado Corazón in Montevideo, Uruguay. He traveled to Spain and studied theology in Colegio Máximo of Sarriá, Barcelona, and was ordained in 1924. He returned to Argentina and taught literature, history, English, and other subjects in Colegio del Salvador. In 1939 Furlong was appointed a member of the national academy of history, and in 1942 he was one of the founders of the Society of Ecclesiastical History. In 1956 he founded the Society of Geography and became its first president. In 1970 he was appointed a member of the Instituto de Cultura Hispánica of Madrid.

As these details suggest, Furlong was interested in a wide range of subjects and disciplines. He was also involved in geographic explorations and conducted ethnological and linguistic studies of Indian peoples in Argentina, based on writings by missionaries of the colonial period. His publications included studies on music, libraries, architecture, mathematics, medicine, and natural history. He also did some work on the role of women in society at a time when women's history was just beginning to elicit some interest from the male-dominated history profession. In all his published work he relied heavily on the archival material available in Argentina, and this enabled him to resurrect some important individuals from the colonial time. He stoutly defended the Catholic religion and Argentina and wanted to revive faithfully the colonial period in the Rio de la Plata region. Father Furlong was against historical revisionism in Argentina, although he considered the Rosas regime as the first competent Argentine administration in the country. His quality research enabled him to produce numerous groundwork studies on colonial Argentina.

Furlong was awarded the National History Award (1952), the Spanish Order of Isabel la Católica, and *honoris causa* doctorates by Universidad del Salvador (1962) and Universidad de Buenos Aires (1971). He directed the history journals *Estudios* (1947–1952) and *Anales* (1957–1974). He was a remarkably productive writer, having published more than 2,000 studies—including more than 100 books—before his death. Frequently, he signed articles and reviews with pseudonyms or initials. Among his most notable books are *Glorias Santafecinas: Buenaventura Suárez S.J., Francisco Javier Iturri S.J., Cristóbal Altamirano S.J. Estudios Biobibliográficos* (1929), *El P. Pedro Lozano S.J.: Su Personalidad y Su Obra. Biobibliografía* (1930), *Los Jesuitas y la Cultura Rioplatense* (1933), *Nacimiento y Desarrollo de la Filosofía en el Río de la Plata, 1536–1810* (1952), *Historia y Bibliografía de las Primeras Imprentas Rioplatenses, 1700–1850* (1953), and *Historia Social y Cultural del Río de la Plata, 1536–1810* (1969). He died in Buenos Aires on May 20, 1974.

Edmundo Murray

See also: MURRAY, Luis Alberto; O'GORMAN, Edmundo and Juan; O'LEARY, Juan Emiliano; VICUÑA McKENNA, Benjamín

References

Auza, Néstor Tomás. "Guillermo Furlong: El Hombre, el Sacerdote y el Historiador." In *Homenaje de las Academias Nacionales al R. P. Guillermo Furlong S.J.*, 29–47. Buenos Aires: Academia Nacional de la Historia, 1992.

Geoghegan, Abel Rodolfo. "Apuntes para una biografía de Guillermo Furlong" *Archivum: Revista de la Junta de Historia Eclesiástica Argentina* 13 (1979): 31–41.

Larroca, Jorge. *El Padre Furlong: Proletario de la Cultura.* Buenos Aires: Editorial Retorno, 1969.

GAELIC ATHLETIC ASSOCIATION

The Gaelic Athletic Association for the Preservation and Cultivation of National Pastimes was founded in November 1884. Within weeks, the rather cumbersome name was shortened to the Gaelic Athletic Association, or GAA. The driving force behind the organization was Michael Cusack, an Irish-speaking civil servant and native of Co. Cork. Like other proponents of the Irish-Ireland movement, Cusack sought to preserve the native culture and halt the incursion of English habits and customs. In addition, he hoped that a revival of native Irish games would reverse what he perceived to be the moral and physical degeneration of the Irish countryside. In an anonymous letter printed in two prominent national weeklies, *United Ireland* and *Irishman,* on October 11, 1884, Cusack appealed to the Irish people to reject English sports and customs in favor of such distinctively Irish games as Gaelic football and hurling. Maurice Davin, a farmer near Carrick-on-Suir and a former athlete of international standing, responded with a letter supporting Cusack's ideas and offering to help establish a new sporting organization to promote national games. Near the end of October Cusack and Davin issued a circular announcing an organizational meeting for what would become the GAA; the meeting would be held at Hayes Hotel in Thurles on November 1, 1884.

The turnout at the first meeting was small—only 13 or 14 attended. Those present voted Davin president of the organization and agreed to invite Dr. Thomas William Croke, Charles Stewart Parnell, and Michael Davitt to become patrons. The subsequent acceptance by all three men—archbishop of Cashel, leader of the Irish Parliamentary Party, and head of the Land League, respectively—provided the GAA with nationalist credentials and contributed to the almost instant popularity and success of the GAA. Archbishop Croke's letter of acceptance was widely published in Irish newspapers supportive of the GAA. In the letter, Croke decries the fact that Ireland had begun importing from England not only manufactured goods but also fashions, literature, mannerisms, and "alien" games and pastimes. It is up to such organizations as the GAA, Croke maintained, to reverse the betrayal of Irish culture and nationality. Croke's letter continues to be reprinted in most GAA publications as a statement of the Association's founding principles.

Almost immediately upon its foundation, the GAA entered into controversy with a rival organization, the Irish Amateur Athletic Association (IAAA). At the third meeting of the GAA, held in January 1885, officers drew up rules for hurling and Gaelic football to codify and standardize those traditional games. When the GAA published the rules for those sports in the *United Ireland* newspaper on February 7, 1885 (and rules for weight-throwing and athletics in the two subsequent weeks), the IAAA, an Anglo-Irish body, roundly criticized the GAA for presuming to govern all athletic sports. As relations between the two groups deteriorated, the GAA banned members of any other sporting organization from joining its ranks. The following year, members of the GAA were banned from playing or attending English games, including football and rugby, on pain of expulsion from the Association. Despite the controversial bans, the GAA continued to expand quickly throughout Ireland. At the annual general meeting of 1886, 84 clubs were represented. The rapid expansion was due in large part to the decision to structure the GAA along parish lines, thus using an already familiar framework around which to organize clubs.

Recognizing the GAA as a potential recruiting ground for physical force nationalists, Dublin Castle took an immediate interest in the organization. The Royal Irish Constabulary (RIC) monitored GAA activities and kept detailed reports of information provided by local policemen, government agents, and informers from within the GAA. In response to such surveillance, the GAA banned members of the RIC from participating in Gaelic games. The link between the GAA and the extreme wing of the nationalist movement, while perhaps exaggerated by police at the time, was not without substance. As early as 1886, P. T. Hoctor, a well-known left-wing nationalist and a member of the Irish Republican Brotherhood (IRB), was elected vice president of the GAA. The following year tension between the constitutional and physical force nationalists within the organization ran high as the IRB gained substantial control of the central executive board. The increased politicization of the GAA prompted Davin to resign as president in May 1887, though he was reinstated the following January.

In addition to fostering local patriotism and national feeling in Ireland, the GAA also helped to promote and preserve a distinctively Irish ethnic identity among emigrants bound for North America and elsewhere. In the late nineteenth century especially, the GAA was one of a number of social, cultural, and political organizations that helped Irish immigrants adapt to life in urban America. In late September 1888, at the suggestion of Maurice Davin, a group of more than 50 athletes, hurlers, and officials embarked upon a six-week tour of American cities. Although the exhibition hurling games and athletic contests were less successful as fund-raisers than Davin had hoped, they did raise the profile of Gaelic games in America. Before long a number of clubs had been organized in areas with large Irish immigrant communities. Playing Gaelic sports eased the transition from Ireland to America (and elsewhere) by allowing participants to maintain a link to Ireland and thus preserve a sense of ethnic distinctiveness while adjusting to American life. The North American County Board of the GAA continues to promote hurling, Gaelic football, and camogie (hurling for women) throughout the United States.

Since the partition of Ireland, the GAA's political profile has remained high north of the border, as the organization has continued to espouse the goal of a united 32-county Ireland. So controversial has the GAA's presence in the north been that in October 1991 the Ulster Defence Association, a Protestant paramilitary group, added the GAA to its list of legitimate targets because of the Association's alleged sectarianism and support for the republican movement. Many criticized the retention of Rule 21, the controversial ban on members of the British security forces playing Gaelic games, as evidence that the GAA was unwilling to work toward a peaceful inclusive society. The ban was finally lifted, however, in November 2001.

Kathleen Ruppert

References

Darby, Paul. "Gaelic Sport and the Irish Diaspora in Boston, 1879–90." *Irish Historical Studies* 33, no. 132 (November 2003): 387–403.

Doherty, Gillian M., and Tomás O'Riordan. "History of the Gaelic Athletic Association (GAA)." http://multitext.ucc.ie/d/History_of_the_Gaelic_Athletic_Association_GAA (accessed July 30, 2007).

Lyons, F. S. L. *Ireland Since the Famine.* London: Fontana Press, 1985.

GALLAGHER, TESS (1943–)

Tess Gallagher was born Tess Bond to Leslie Bond, longshoreman and logger, and Georgia Morris, on July 21, 1943, in Port Angeles, Washington. Gallagher graduated from the University of Washington with a BA in 1963; she attended American poet Theodore Roethke's last writing workshop. That June she married Lawrence Gallagher, a Marine pilot; she worked as a hospital nurse, and they divorced in 1968. She received an MA from the University of Washington, studying under David Waggoner, in 1970. While at Iowa State, she married the poet Michael Burkard in 1973, but they divorced in 1977. In 1974 she received an MFA from Iowa State, where she worked with Mark Strand and Stanley Kunitz; that same year she began a series of teaching appointments at various colleges in New York State.

Gallagher's first full-length collection, *Instructions for the Double* (1976), probes the searing scars inherent in the process of love as it explores various dimensions of doubling. *Under Stars* (1978), which is dedicated to the poet and musician Ciaran Carson, contains anecdotes about her experiences in Ireland and the people she met there. The enlarged edition of *Portable Kisses* (1978; 1992) exhibits astonishing metaphysical conceits and the ebullient force of its psychology and style.

Gallagher had first met fellow Washingtonian Raymond Carver at a writer's conference in 1977, and she began living with him in 1979. They became inseparable, symbiotic writers who tirelessly collaborated with each other like tenor and soprano. *Willingly* (1984) paints longer narrative episodes in the lives of her mother, father, and lover—all set amid the forest landscape of the American Northwest. Carver encouraged her to write short stories, and her first collection, *The Lover of Horses and Other Stories,* appeared in 1986, followed by *The Owl-Woman Saloon* in 1999.

Just before Carver's death in 1988, they married. After Carver's death, Gallagher was afflicted with silence, but eventually began penning the startling elegies to Carver contained in *Moon Crossing Bridge* (1992); some of these poems are set in Japan and reveal the slight influence of an Eastern aesthetic. *Owl-Spirit Dwelling* (1994) further explores elegiac meditation, yet it contains a glimmer of fey humor. Gallagher worked with photographer Bob Adelman to produce *Carver Country* (1991) and collaborated with Robert Altman on the critically acclaimed movie *Short Cuts* (1993), based on Raymond Carver's stories. *Soul Barnacles* (2000) presents a miscellany of journal entries, mutual letters, and interviews with Gallagher and Carver.

Gallagher has a committed interest in the poetry of Eastern Europe, and she often gives readings there. She collaborated with Adam J. Sorkin on translating the selected poems of the Romanian poet Liliana Ursu, *The Sky Behind the Forest* (1996). In 2004 a selection of her poems appeared in Croatian. As an essayist, she published *A Concert of Tenses: Essays on Poetry* (1986). The largest collection of her poems remains *My Black Horse* (1995). Gallagher has received an honorary doctorate from both Whitman University and the University of Hartford.

Gallagher's poems recollect telling incidents in life when pathos, romance, and memory collide, breaking the planes of ordinary time. Her focus shadows the intuitive, emotional difficulties between the sexes, in this life and even in the afterlife, weaving together the ordinary and the ecstatic. During childhood she frequently rode horses on her uncle's Missouri farm, and she has written many poems with horse metaphors or themes. Her later meditative poems—lithely capable of nimble, sudden leaps or oblique introspection—employ a sinuous flowing syntax depicting a woman who has discovered strength of voice through vulnerability. Gallagher's autobiographical eloquence resides in a spontaneous exploration of the stream-of-consciousness interstices between events and the capricious journeys of the imagination. Her short stories display a warmly engaging investigation into the improvisatory qualities of life and conversation. Deep characterization, atmospheric detail, and witty dialogue remain the hallmarks of her stories. At her best, her work rises to lyric heights that transcend the phenomenological circumstances of this intimate and densely dramatic writer who can transform the ordinary into the hauntingly strange.

Kevin T. McEneaney

References

McFarland, Ron. *Tess Gallagher*. Boise, ID: Boise State University, 1995.

O'Neill, Charles. "Tess Gallagher and Irish Poetry." *Newsletter of the Poetry Society of America* 41 (Winter 1993): 8–12.

GARLAND, JUDY (1922–1969)

One of America's greatest performers, Judy Garland was born Frances Ethel Gumm on June 10, 1922, in Grand Rapids, Minnesota. She was the youngest daughter of former vaudevillians Frank Avent Gumm (b. 1886) and Ethel Marian Milne (b. 1893). Although in later interviews Judy would refer to her father as a "charming Irishman," he was, in fact, born in Murfreesboro, Tennessee, of mixed Scottish, French, and German ancestry. Judy's mother had direct, though distant, Irish lineage. She was born to John Milne and Eva Fitzpatrick in Michigamme, Michigan, in 1893. Although some of Garland's biographers have recorded that Eva Fitzpatrick was born in Dublin, Ireland, according to www.genealogy.com, she was actually born in Massena, New York, in 1865 and it was *her* grandfather, Peter Fitzpatrick (b. 1752) who could claim Irish birth. Despite this more remote Irish connection,

Garland remained proud of her Irish ancestry and would sometimes refer to it in interviews.

Soon after their marriage, Ethel and Frank became managers of a Grand Rapids cinema, and Ethel encouraged her two eldest daughters, Mary Jane and Virginia, to perform songs in the intervals of the film screenings. However, the arrival of Frances in 1922 changed the direction and focus of the Gumm Sisters act. From the age of two, Baby Gumm, as Judy was called, displayed a natural talent for performing, and very soon it was clear that she was the star of the show. Ethel was determined to pursue a theatrical career for her three daughters, and it was her ambition and drive that brought the family to California in 1927. Settling in Lancaster, California, Ethel built up connections within the entertainment industry, and the Gumm sisters made their professional debut on the bill of the "Meglin Kiddies Show" in Loew's State Theatre, Los Angeles, in December 1927. For the next five years, the Gumm sisters spent their childhood performing in vaudeville and auditioning for films. In later years Judy would recall her childhood as both exciting and unsettling: she loved the performing but the traveling and stress it brought took its toll on her already precarious health. Her parents' marital breakdown and unrelenting pressure from her ambitious mother would also contribute to the formation of a fragile and insecure young woman.

By 1933 Ethel had moved her daughters to Los Angeles and had enrolled Frances in the Lawlor School for Professional Children. Many of her classmates would go on to secure film contracts with varying degrees of success. It was at "Mom Lawlor's" that she first met Mickey Rooney, who would become a close friend and associate in Hollywood, and who signed a contract with Metro-Goldwyn-Mayer (MGM) studios in late 1933.

In 1934 Ethel brought her three daughters to perform at a restaurant/club on the outskirts of Chicago's World Fair. While there, they met George Jessel, a major vaudeville star, and performed on stage with him at Chicago's Oriental Theatre. He was impressed by the Gumm sisters, particularly by 12-year-old Frances, and he suggested that they should change their name to Garland. Almost a year later, Frances became Judy and her professional career began a steady ascent. In 1934, she was spotted by leading producer-director Joseph L. Mankiewicz, and he brought her to the attention of MGM's boss, Louis B. Mayer. Following an informal audition for Mayer, during which she sang a number of songs, including "Zing! Went the Strings of My Heart," she was signed to a long-term contract. Her cinematic debut was in a short film starring Deanna Durbin, *Every Sunday,* in 1936. More significant were her appearances in *Pigskin Parade* (1936) and *Broadway Melody of 1938* (1937), and her films with her former classmate Mickey Rooney, *Thoroughbreds Don't Cry* (1937) and *Love Finds Andy Hardy* (1938).

Her breakthrough came when a reluctant Mayer agreed to producer Arthur Freed's request that she be cast in a big-budget adaptation of L. Frank Baum's book *The Wizard of Oz* (1939). It turned out to be an inspired choice and the film, which won Garland rave reviews (and a special Academy Award) for both her acting and her singing, remains one of the most loved and most important films in Hollywood's history.

MGM teamed her with Rooney in three further films, *Babes in Arms, Andy Hardy Meets Debutante,* and *Strike up the*

Band (all 1940); the success of these films confirmed the popularity of the two performers, who were rapidly becoming MGM's most lucrative investments. In 1940, Garland branched out to star alongside George Murphy in the sentimental, Irish-themed film *Little Nellie Kelly* (1940); she followed it with a role opposite Lana Turner in *Ziegfield Girl* (1941). With audiences demanding a reteaming of Garland and Rooney, the two stars played together in *Life Begins for Andy Hardy* and *Babes on Broadway* (both 1942). During this time, she met and married the conductor/bandleader, David Rose. Although the marriage disintegrated within months, the couple did not divorce until 1945.

The 1940s saw Garland's physical and mental health constantly compromised by her gruelling work schedule and increasing reliance on prescription drugs. Yet this was the most fruitful time of her professional life, and she excelled in films that have remained much-loved classics. She acted with Gene Kelly in *For Me and My Gal* (1942), starred with Rooney again in *Girl Crazy* (1943), and entertained the troops for the USO. In 1944 she was cast, against her will, in *Meet Me in St. Louis,* a bittersweet musical drama about a family living in turn-of-the-century St. Louis. The film boasted strong performances from Mary Astor and Margaret O'Brien, but it was Garland who stole the show with her heartfelt portrayal of Esther Smith. The film featured some of her best known songs, such as "Meet Me in St. Louis," "The Trolley Song," and "Have Yourself a Merry Little Christmas." The production also inaugurated a romance with the film's director, Vincente Minnelli, resulting in a marriage in 1945 and the birth of a daughter, Liza, in 1946. Minnelli and Garland worked again the following year on a nonmusical film, *The Clock.*

Garland's hectic production schedule slowed down some after the birth of her daughter: she appeared in *The Harvey Girls* in 1946 and made a guest appearance as singer Marilyn Miller in *Till the Clouds Roll By* in 1947. She returned to a starring role in another Minnelli film, *The Pirate* (1948), in which she was cast opposite Gene Kelly, who was now a major star. The film was a troubled production, due mainly to Garland's mental problems and her increasingly fractious relationship with Minnelli. Although the film performed disappointingly at the box office, it remains a classic musical that features another Garland classic, "Be a Clown."

Garland and Minnelli's marriage was crumbling by the time they were teamed to make the Irving Berlin musical, *Easter Parade,* in 1948. The shoot was plagued with problems: Minnelli was replaced by Charles Walters, and the original male lead, Gene Kelly, was replaced by Fred Astaire. Garland's increasingly erratic behavior was becoming more difficult to hide, and her next two productions, *In the Good Old Summertime* (1949) and *Summer Stock* (1950), were difficult shoots. In between production of these two films, she was cast in *Annie get Your Gun* but was fired halfway through the shoot. Soon after, she was hospitalized with a mental breakdown but within weeks she had (inadvisably) returned to work on *Summer Stock.*

In 1950 she was cast in another film with Fred Astaire, *Royal Wedding,* but her unreliability resulted in her being replaced by Jane Powell during the shoot. In a devastating blow, MGM terminated her contract soon after. Garland was again hospitalized, and many commentators filed her among the ranks of washed-up stars.

In what must have been one of the bleakest periods of her life, Garland met and married a theatrical impresario, Sid Luft, and he was instrumental in encouraging her to revive her live career. She began doing radio appearances, and in 1951 audiences flocked to see her sell-out shows at London's Palladium Theatre and New York's Palace Theatre. In July 1951 she appeared for a number of sold-out shows at the Theatre Royal in Dublin. According to her biographer Gerold Frank, Garland sang to crowds outside the theater who had been unable to buy tickets. Her performances were greeted with rapture by Irish audiences and critics, and the press nicknamed her "America's Colleen."

The success of her live appearances reignited Hollywood's interest, and she was cast in the 1962 Warner Brothers production of *A Star is Born,* directed by George Cukor and costarring James Mason. The film was an apparently torturous shoot: the budget spiraled out of control, Garland was frequently absent or ill, and the film was extensively recut before its release. In spite of the problems of the shoot, the film was a complex, cynical, and deeply affecting portrait of Hollywood and the fragility of fame. With knowledge of Garland's subsequent tragic life, her performance becomes difficult to watch; its rawness and vulnerability seem to be more than mere acting.

Although Luft and Garland may have had high hopes for the renewal of her film career following the release of *A Star is Born,* Warner Brothers failed to fulfill the terms of her three-film contract and the remaining two films were not made. Garland returned to live performances for the next six years, with varying degrees of success. Her most triumphant runs were in London's Palladium Theatre in 1960 and, later that year, in New York's Carnegie Hall. Her performance at Carnegie Hall was later released as an album and won her five Grammy Awards.

By 1961, Hollywood was showing renewed interested in the enduring Garland, and she was cast in a small role in a prestigious Stanley Kramer film, *Judgment at Nuremberg.* Garland was featured in a cast of top actors that included Burt Lancaster, Spencer Tracy, Montgomery Clift, and Marlene Dietrich and her nine-minute appearance earned her an Academy Award nomination. She appeared again with Lancaster in a 1962 film, *A Child is Waiting,* and the following year signed with CBS television to make her own show. Unfortunately, the television show wasn't the popular success expected and, upon completion of *I Could Go on Singing* (her final film, made in Britain in 1963), she went back on the road.

By the mid-1960s Garland's life was beset by mental and financial problems, alcohol and drug abuse, and a turbulent private life. Following the breakdown of her marriage to Luft in 1963, she married an aspiring actor, Mark Herron, in 1964, but the marriage ended rapidly in divorce. She continued to tour in America and Europe throughout the 1960s and while appearing in London in 1969 she married her fifth husband, Mickey Deans.

On June 22, 1969, Judy Garland was found dead of an overdose, which was ruled accidental by the London coroner. She was survived by her three children, Liza

Minnelli (b. 1946), Lorna Luft (b. 1952), and Joey Luft (b. 1955).

Gwenda Young

References

Frank, Gerold. *Judy.* New York: Harper & Row. 1975.

Katz, Ephraim. *The Film Encyclopedia.* New York: Perigee Books, 1979.

"Liza Minnelli." www.genealogy.com (accessed May 15, 2006).

Morley, Sheridan. *Beyond the Rainbow.* London: Pavilion, 1999.

Shipman, David. *The Great Movie Stars: The Golden Years.* New York: Da Capo, 1986.

Vinson, James. *International Dictionary of Films and Filmmakers: Actors and Actresses.* Chicago: St. James Press, 1986.

GARSON, GREER (1904–1996)

Eileen Evelyn Greer Garson was born on September 29, 1904, in London, not Co. Down, Ireland, as is often believed. She was named after her mother Nina's ancestral name, MacGregor. Garson received an honors distinction in education at the University of London and began postgraduate studies at the University of Grenoble. At age 24 she left academia to pursue an advertising career and to experiment with drama as a hobby. Garson made her acting debut in 1932 with the Birmingham Repertory Theatre. She subsequently appeared in 13 plays on London's West End stages. She was noticed by Laurence Olivier, who offered her guidance to hone her talents.

Garson left London in 1934 for Hollywood after signing a contract with Louis B. Mayer of Metro-Goldwyn-Mayer (MGM). Garson's natural red hair, flawless complexion, and elegant manner allowed her an opportune entrance into Hollywood, because a number of leading actresses had resigned, leaving a void. Her first film for MGM, in 1939, was *Goodbye Mr. Chips* with Robert Donat. It earned enthusiastic reviews. Appearing at the beginning of World War II, it quickly became a classic.

Garson had married Edward Snelson on September 28, 1933, but she divorced him on May 8, 1940. Her role as Elizabeth Bennet in *Pride and Prejudice,* opposite her mentor Olivier in 1940, earned her increasing popularity. She appeared as the mother in the 1941 film *Blossoms in the Dust,* with Walter Pidgeon, and earned an Academy Award nomination. In 1942, Garson won her first Academy Award in *Mrs. Miniver,* starring again with Walter Pidgeon, for her role as British housewife Kay Miniver enduring the Blitz. It catapulted her to global fame. Garson's striking performance as Marie Curie in the 1943 film garnered her yet another Academy Award nomination.

On July 24, 1943, she married Richard Ney, who had played her son in *Mrs. Miniver.* Her role in *Mrs. Parkington* with Walter Pidgeon in 1944 earned her another Academy Award nomination. She repeated this feat for her performance as Irish housemaid Mary Rafferty in *The Valley of Decision* in 1945 opposite Gregory Peck. Her typecasting ensured great success during World War II.

The caliber of her projects waned post–World War II. In 1946, Garson played the love interest to Clark Gable in *Adventure,* but she was critically panned, although the advertising tag line "Gable's back and Garson's got him!" earned the film significant public interest. Her next role in *Desire Me* opposite Robert Mitchum in 1947 proved to be a humiliating disaster.

Meanwhile, conflicting career pressures doomed the Ney/Garson marriage; they could not weather their problems and divorced on September 25, 1947. The 1948 film *Julia Misbehaves* was well received. In 1949 Garson rebounded with *That Forsyte Woman* opposite Errol Flynn and Walter Pigeon, but the 1950 reprisal of *The Miniver Story* proved unpopular.

Garson's life took a major turn when she married wealthy Texan Colonel Elijah "Buddy" Fogelson, and she semiretired from acting. The happy couple spent their time on their ranch in New Mexico and a home in Dallas where she respectively devoted her energy to ranch life and community affairs. Garson's contract with MGM ended in 1954. She appeared on stage in *Auntie Mame* in 1957. Her last major role, as Eleanor Roosevelt in *Sunrise at Campobello,* earned her another Academy Award nomination in 1960. She also appeared in small roles in *The Singing Nun* in 1966 and in *The Happiest Millionaire* in 1967. Garson also accepted select television roles.

The philanthropic Fogelsons contributed to Santa Fe College by donating the E. E. Fogelson Library and the Greer Garson Theatre. Garson served as adjunct professor and received an honorary degree from Santa Fe College.

Fogelson died on December 1, 1987. Garson kept busy with administering their massive wealth by giving huge financial grants to various charities. She also gave considerable amounts of money to Southern Methodist University, her late husband's alma mater. Garson suffered a minor stroke in 1980 and endured several heart problems. She moved into a suite in the Dallas Presbyterian Hospital where she died on April 6, 1996. She was buried beside Fogelson in Sparkman-Hillcrest Memorial Park in Dallas.

Annette Richardson

References

Broderick, Marian. *Wild Irish Women: Extraordinary Lives from History.* Madison: University of Wisconsin Press, 2004.

Maltin, Leonard, and Spencer Green. *Leonard Maltin's Movie Encyclopedia: Career Profiles of More Than 2,000 Actors and Filmmakers, Past and Present.* New York: Plume Books, 1995.

Troyan, Michele. *A Rose for Mrs. Miniver: The Life of Greer Garson.* Lexington: University Press of Kentucky, 1998.

GAUGHREN, FATHER MATTHEW (1843–1914)

Main champion of and benefactor for the victims of the Dresden Affair, Matthew Gaughren was born in Dublin in 1843. He was one of three brothers who became Roman Catholic priests. Two of these, Matthew and Anthony, became bishops in the same vicariate. Their only sister was a Holy Faith Sister in Ireland. Gaughren joined the Oblates of Mary Immaculate and was ordained a priest in 1867. He had appointments successively in Holy Cross, Liverpool, St. Kevin's Reformatory in Glencree (Ireland), and Tower Hill, London, before becoming a provincial. After his term of office as provincial he became a superior in Leith.

During his ministry in London, Father Gaughren visited Argentina and collected funds in South America for lessening the debt on the church of Tower Hill. In February 1889, Gaughren met the Irish immigrants of the ship *City of Dresden* in Uruguay, when she called on Montevideo. He went onboard the steamer and shared the distresses experienced by settlers in Buenos Aires and later in the Irish Colony in Napostá, near Bahía Blanca. Father Matthew Gaughren was the only true friend of the immigrants. He discontinued his fund-raising, traveled to Napostá, and lived for some months with the poor unfortunates, attending to their spiritual needs.

Father Gaughren went back to Ireland and was appointed provincial, and in 1892 he established the Oblates in Australia. He remained as parish priest of Fremantle for a year. After serving as provincial he became a bishop in South Africa. On March 16, 1902, Father Gaughren was consecrated bishop in the parish church of Leith, Scotland, where he succeeded his brother. At the same time he was appointed administrator of the vicariate of Transvaal. He died on June 1, 1914, in Capetown, and was buried in Kimberly.

Edmundo Murray

See also: DRESDEN AFFAIR

Reference

Geraghty, Michael John. "Argentina: A Land of Broken Promises." *Buenos Aires Herald*, March 17, 1999.

GEORGIA

The best-known Irishman who settled in Georgia is a fictional character: Gerald O'Hara, the father of Scarlett, in Margaret Mitchell's *Gone With the Wind.* In spite of this and the fact that Georgia was not the destination for Irish immigrants to the same extent as other states were, those who did choose to emigrate there played a significant role in its development from a settlement to a state. Although Catholics were prohibited from settling in Georgia, in 1733 a ship carrying forty Irish convicts was allowed to dock at Savannah. However, as in many other states, particularly those in the South, the majority of early Irish immigrants to Georgia were Scots-Irish who came from an Ulster Presbyterian background. According to some reports, there were certain parts of Georgia where more than half the population were Ulster Presbyterians. In the 1820s a new wave of immigrants from Ireland was attracted by the various projects designed to develop the state's infrastructure. In 1834, after four years of construction, the state pulled out of the canal linking the port of Brunswick with the Altamaha River. To complete the project, a Boston firm brought in Irish Catholic workers whose roots lay not in Ulster like the previous immigrants, but in the south of Ireland. When the construction of the canal was completed, some of them returned to the north while others settled in Savannah. Soon, railways that were being built to link towns in Georgia were constructed by Irish immigrants in harsh working conditions. By the mid-1800s, Savannah was home to the greatest number of Irish immigrants in Georgia. Savannah and Co. Wexford in Ireland had a particularly strong connection, and a number of families originally from there later rose to prominence in the city. There was, however, a sharp division between the Scots-Irish who had settled there earlier and who were now established in society and the more recent, mainly Catholic, arrivals who were performing many of the menial tasks in the city.

The new immigrants, particularly in Savannah, set about establishing their own associations and societies to protect their interests and assert their identity. In 1812 the Hibernian Society had been founded in Savannah as an association for men of property. A sign of the changed nature of Irish immigration was seen when the Hibernian Society in Savannah elected its first Catholic president in 1856. Although it collected funds to provide help to poorer members the whole year round, one of its main focuses was Saint Patrick's Day, which provided an opportunity to bring together different parts of the community. In 1824 Bishop John England of Charleston, South Carolina, who had been born in Co. Cork, was the keynote speaker of the Society, and he was made an honorary member. There was also a chapter of Daniel O'Connell's Irish Repeal Association in both Savannah and Milledgeville during the 1840s. However, after O'Connell's condemnation of slavery in 1843, the chapters disintegrated. Later, the Civil War provided an opportunity for Irish immigrants to assert their loyalty to their new state, and many Irish volunteered to fight for the Confederacy and formed militias to do so. However, Irish immigration to Georgia never regained the numbers it had once held before the war.

As with Irish immigrants in other states, religious life provided one of the principal routes for Irish Catholics to occupy positions of authority. Georgia was no different; Bishop Francis X. Gartland, who was born in Dublin, became the first head of the diocese of Georgia in 1850. His successor, Bishop John Barry, was also born in Ireland. At the time, many of the parish priests ministering to Catholics in the state were either born in Ireland or were first-generation Irish Americans.

To this day, and partly because of the influence of the Hibernian Society and other Irish organizations, the legacy of the Irish has continued in Savannah. Each year, it holds the third largest Saint Patrick's Day parade in America after New York and Boston, and a statue of the Irish patriot Robert Emmet was erected in Savannah and a park was renamed Emmet Park in 1902.

David Doyle

See also: O'CONNELL, Daniel; SAINT PATRICK'S DAY PARADES

References

Gleeson, David T. *The Irish in the South, 1815–1877.* Chapel Hill: University of North Carolina Press, 2001.

Shoemaker, Edward M. "Georgia." In *The Encyclopedia of the Irish in America,* edited by Michael Glazier. Notre Dame, IN: University of Notre Dame Press, 1999.

GIBBONS, CEDRIC (1893–1960)

According to most sources, Austin Cedric Gibbons was born on March 23, 1893, in Dublin, Ireland, although in his 2005 biography of Louis B. Mayer, Scott Eyman records Gibbons's birthplace as Brooklyn and his birth year as 1890. The son of an architect, Gibbons studied painting at New York's Art Students League and became involved in the film industry when he took a job as an art director at the Edison studio in 1915. He was at the forefront of the movement toward greater realism in film set design, favoring the use of three-dimensional sets instead of theater-style painted backdrops. During the 1910s he worked for Edison and Goldwyn studios, but he rose to prominence after his 1924 appointment as head of the art department in the newly formed Metro-Goldwyn-Mayer (MGM) studios. For the next four decades he would shape the look of MGM films and, as stipulated in his contract, he received art direction credit for all MGM films released between 1924 and 1956, although he personally only designed a relatively small proportion of them. As head of the art department, Gibbons worked most closely with his team of skilled art directors, but ultimately 70 percent of all MGM staff was answerable to him (Balio 1995).

The look Gibbons pioneered was strongly influenced by the Moderne style (now more popularly known as Art Deco), a style that he had encountered when he attended the Exposition Internationale des Arts Décoratifs et Industriels in Paris in 1925. The impact of Art Deco's clean lines can be seen in some of the earliest films he designed for MGM, for example *Our Dancing Daughters* (1928) and *Grand Hotel* (1932), which feature lofty, streamlined sets and Art Deco furniture and props. Gibbons's importance in MGM is underlined by the fact that his sculptural sets often dictated the lighting styles used in MGM films—he favored high key lighting, which eliminated shadows and showcased the impressive set designs—and it was this glossy, sleek look that became the distinguishing feature of the MGM brand.

Nominated for 22 Academy Awards for art direction, Gibbons won Oscars for *The Bridge of San Luis Rey* (1929), *The Merry Widow* (1934), *Pride and Prejudice* (1940), *Blossoms in the Dust* (1941), *Gaslight* (1944), *The Yearling* (1946), *Little Women* (1949), *An American in Paris* (1951), *The Bad and the Beautiful* (1952), *Julius Caesar* (1953), and *Somebody Up There Likes Me* (1956). He retired shortly after winning his final Academy Award. In addition to the sets that he designed/ supervised for MGM films, Gibbons directed one feature for MGM, 1934's *Tarzan and His Mate,* perhaps a surprising choice for a man known for his sophisticated taste. Gibbons was also instrumental in establishing the Academy of Motion Picture Arts and Sciences, and he personally designed the Oscar statuette, which continues to be used by the Academy. Gibbons was married twice, to actress Dolores Del Rio and to actress Hazel Brooks. He died on July 26, 1960.

Gwenda Young

References

Balio, Tino. *Grand Design: Hollywood as a Modern Business Enterprise, 1930–1939.* Berkeley: University of California Press, 1995.

Eyman, Scott. *The Lion of Hollywood: The Life and Legend of Louis B. Mayer.* New York: Simon & Schuster, 2005.

Katz, Ephraim. *The Film Encyclopedia.* New York: Perigee Books, 1979.

Vinson, James. *International Dictionary of Films and Filmmakers: Writers and Production Assistants.* Chicago: St. James Press, 1987.

Gilmore, Patrick Sarsfield (1829–1892)

Born in Ballygar, Co. Galway, or Mullingar, Co. Westmeath, on December 25, 1829, Gilmore was a highly successful conductor of military bands, including his own

Portrait of Irish-born American composer Patrick Sarsfield Gilmore. (Library of Congress)

Gilmore's Band, and assembled thousands of performers that attracted enormous crowds at festivals in Boston in 1869 and 1872. Beginning in 1873 he was based in New York, and popular success never failed him throughout his distinguished career.

While his exact place of birth cannot be established, Gilmore grew up in Ballygar, Co. Galway. He began his musical career as a cornet player in an amateur band in Athlone, Co. Westmeath. In October 1849 he immigrated to Boston, initially working for the music dealer and publisher John P. Ordway. He began to lead a number of Massachusetts bands, including the Charlestown, Boston Brigade, and Salem Brass bands, the latter becoming famous under his direction (1855–1858) and performing at the inaugural parade for President James Buchanan in Washington in 1857. In 1858, he established his own Gilmore's Band, performing for the first time in the Boston Music Hall on April 9, 1859. His regular appearances were always favorably received. During the Civil War the band became attached to the 24th Massachusetts Infantry Regiment as part of the Union Army.

Gilmore's national reputation for mass events became established in 1864 at the inauguration of Governor Michael Hahn of Lousiana, when he assembled a band of 500 and a chorus of 6,000, plus 50 cannons and 40 soldiers to strike anvils. He also arranged for the simultaneous ringing of all the church bells in the city. For the National Peace Jubilee and Musical Festival at Boston in 1869, he organized a concert of 1,000 musicians (led by Ole Bull), including six military bands, and a chorus of 10,000. Of even larger dimensions was the World Peace Jubilee and International Music Festival in 1872, also at Boston, which featured 20,000 performers, including ensembles from England, France, and Prussia.

In 1873 Gilmore moved to New York to take up a position with the 22nd Regiment, which he turned into the foremost professional band of the United States for the next 19 years. Converting a popular hippodrome into Gilmore's Garden, he gave a series of more than 150 successful concerts there, also performing annually from 1879 at Manhattan Beach in the summer. The band toured to various locations all over the city and other states, including tours to the West Coast in 1876 and 1878. Gilmore also had an annual residency at the St. Louis Exposition, and it was during one such engagement that he died. Gilmore was buried in New York with many dignitaries and social leaders of the time attending the funeral.

As a composer, Gilmore is remembered for his many military arrangements of traditional music and for his own band marches and songs, which included the famous "When Johnny Comes Marching Home" as well as popular titles such as "Freedom on the Old Plantation," "The Spirit of the North," "God Save the Union," and the "Twenty-Second Regiment March." He also founded his own publishing company and engaged as a partner in brass instrument manufacturing businesses.

Axel Klein

See also: EMIGRATION; MUSIC IN AMERICA, IRISH

References

Damon, F. C. "P. S. Gilmore, Bandmaster." *Salem Evening News,* April 5, 1936 to July 2, 1937 (series of 23 articles).

Darlington, Marwood. *Irish Orpheus: The Life of Patrick Gilmore, Bandmaster Extraordinary.* Philadelphia: Olivier Maney Klein Co., 1950.

Gilmore, Patrick S. *History of the National Peace Jubilee and Great Musical Festival Held in the City of Boston, June, 1869.* Boston: Lee and Shepard, 1871.

GLEASON, JACKIE (1916–1987)

Born Herbert John Gleason, this comedian-actor was fondly nicknamed "The Great One," a reference both to his girth and his considerable comedic talents. In 1940, after spending a number of years performing on the vaudeville and cabaret circuits, Gleason was signed to a film contract by Warner Brothers. His screen debut was in *Navy Blues* (1941). His career was interrupted by World War II, but at the war's end Gleason returned to Hollywood, this time playing character roles in a number of films. He also performed in several Broadway shows. His major success was as the star of such television comedy series as *The Life of Riley, The Honeymooners* (which ran for only one season, 1955–1956, but achieved cult status as a result of reruns), and *The Jackie Gleason Show.* Gleason created a number of memorable comedic characters, such as Ralph Kramden (the loudmouth bus driver from *The Honeymooners*), Reggie Van Gleason, and Joe the Bartender. In 1959, Gleason returned to Broadway, winning a Tony Award for *Take Me Along.* He also continued to star in a number of films, including *The Hustler* (1961), for which he earned an Academy Award nomination for Best Supporting Actor; and the *Smokey and the Bandit* series of action comedies. His long career also included a period when he composed, arranged, and conducted recordings of mood music. Gleason died of cancer in 1987.

Aoileann Ní Eigeartaigh

References

Klein, Fred, and Ronald Dean Nolan, eds. *The Macmillan and International Film Encyclopaedia.* Basingstoke, UK: Macmillan, 2001.

Quinlan, David. *Quinlan's Illustrated Directory of Film Stars.* London: B. T. Batsford Ltd., 1996.

GLEESON, BRENDAN (1954–)

Brendan Gleeson was born in Dublin in 1954 and started performing as a child in local stage productions. After auditioning unsuccessfully for the National Theatre of Ireland, the Abbey Theatre, he became a secondary school teacher. During his 10-year teaching career, he continued to act and appeared in several productions, including *King of the Castle* at the Abbey Theatre and *Home* with the Passion Machine Company. In 1989, at the age of 34, Gleeson gave up his teaching job and began acting full time. In 1990, he made his film debut starring alongside Richard Harris in Jim Sheridan's *The Field.* Over the next five years, Gleeson played a number of supporting roles in movies such as *Far and Away* (1992), with Tom Cruise and Nicole Kidman, *Into the West* (1992) with Gabriel Byrne, and *The Snapper* (1993), based on the novel by Roddy Doyle. He also won critical acclaim for his portrayal of Michael Collins in the television production *The Treaty* (1991, shown in the United States in 1998). His role as Hamish, William Wallace's closest friend and ally, in Mel Gibson's epic *Braveheart* (1995) first brought Gleeson to international attention. He also starred in a supporting role to Liam Neeson in Neil Jordan's *Michael Collins* (1996). His status as an actor was enhanced by his first starring role in the black comedy *I Went Down* (1997), which was critically acclaimed on both sides of the Atlantic. It was his role as Martin Cahill, the real-life Irish criminal in John Boorman's *The General*, however, that garnered recognition and respect for the actor. Gleeson won several awards for his portrayal, including the Boston Society Film Critics Award for Best Actor, the Golden Satellite Award for Best Performance by an Actor in a Motion Picture, and the London Critics' Circle film award for British Actor of the Year. Gleeson balances his roles carefully between mainstream action and more low-key character driven roles. He has worked with many top directors, including John Woo, Stephen Spielberg, Martin Scorsese, and has played roles in major Hollywood films such as *Harry Potter and the Order of the Phoenix* (2007), *The Tiger's Tail* (2006), *Studs* (2006), *Black Irish* (2006), *Harry Potter and the Goblet of Fire* (2005), and many more.

Aoileann Ní Eigeartaigh

See also: HARRIS, Richard; JORDAN, Neil; NEESON, Liam; SHERIDAN, Jim

References

IMDB: Earth's Biggest Movie Database. www.imdb.com/name/nm0322407/ (accessed August 23, 2007).

Lalor, Brian, ed. *The Encyclopaedia of Ireland.* Dublin: Gill and Macmillan Ltd., 2003.

Pettit, Lance. *Screening Ireland: Film and Television Representation.* Manchester, UK: Manchester University Press, 2000.

GOGARTY, OLIVER ST. JOHN (1878–1957)

A native Dubliner, Oliver St. John Gogarty was educated at Oxford University and Trinity College Dublin. In 1907 Trinity conferred a medical degree upon him, and he subsequently enjoyed a successful career in Dublin as a surgeon. Distinguished by his enormous vitality, Gogarty became prominent more for the variety of his accomplishments than for any single achievement. He was, among other things, a champion bicyclist, a surgeon, a poet, a memoirist, a celebrated "wit," an aviator, an Irish senator, an enthusiast of archery, a hotel owner, and a skilled amateur classicist. His escape from Irish Republican Army kidnappers (he leapt into the Liffey and swam free of his assailants) added to his reputation for resourcefulness and good fortune. His greatest renown derived, however, from his social ubiquity; he enjoyed friendships with (to note only the most prominent) Æ (George Russell), Michael Collins, Arthur Griffith, Augustus John, James Joyce, George Moore, James Stephens, and W. B. Yeats. Despite maintaining generally good relations with these men, Gogarty's youthful friendship with Joyce famously soured into mutual suspicion, envy, and fascination. Joyce's depiction of Gogarty as the exuberant but frivolous Buck Mulligan in *Ulysses* is evocative, recognizable, and ungenerous. Joyce's skill in capturing elements of Gogarty's personality, and his accomplishment in translating them from reality to the fictional Buck Mulligan, saddled Gogarty with an unwanted, yet ineradicable, alter ego.

Gogarty spent almost the last two decades of his life in the United States. Having given lecture tours of North America in 1933 and 1937, he was engaged in a third lecture tour in 1939 when the eruption of World War II rendered a return voyage across the Atlantic impracticable. Gogarty's abiding detestation of Eamon de Valera further diminished the appeal of attempting a return to the British Isles, so in late 1939 Gogarty settled in Manhattan. He was to reside there for the rest of his life and, while living in New York City, he became an American citizen.

In the United States, Gogarty found a large and wealthy public interested in his reminiscences of the famous people he had known in Ireland and England. He accordingly wrote numerous memoirs, essays, and recollections about his friends and published them in popular American periodicals. He later gathered these pieces into book-length collections of inconsistent merit; they are impeccably entertaining and immoderately unreliable. Gogarty also gave occasional lectures to university audiences and literary societies throughout the United States and Canada. On at least four occasions he appeared on radio programs broadcast from New York City. From these lectures, essays, and reminiscences Gogarty derived a comfortable, if not lavish, retirement income. Although late in life he contemplated returning to Ireland, he died in Manhattan in 1957 of complications from a heart attack.

Gogarty's American period is often considered a dispiriting denouement to an otherwise distinguished and exciting life. Yet it was largely this period in which he wrote the memoirs that preserve some of the most intimate extant portraits of Ireland's twentieth-century cultural elite.

Andrew Goodspeed

See also: DE VALERA, Eamon; JOYCE, James Augustine Aloysius; YEATS, William Butler

References

Gogarty, Oliver St. John. *As I was Going Down Sackville Street.* London: Rich & Cowan, 1937.

Gogarty, Oliver St. John. *It Isn't This Time of Year At All!* New York: Doubleday, 1954.

Gogarty, Oliver St. John. *Rolling Down the Lea.* London: Constable. 1950.

Gogarty, Oliver St. John. *The Poems and Plays,* edited by A. Norman Jeffares. Gerrards Cross: Colin Smythe, 2001.

Gogarty, Oliver St. John. *Tumbling in the Hay.* London: Constable, 1939.

Lyons, J. B. *The Man of Many Talents.* Dublin: Blackwater, 1980.

O'Connor, Ulick. *The Times I've Seen.* New York: Ivan Obolensky, 1963.

GORDON, MARY (1948–)

With her 1978 debut novel, *Final Payments,* and its provocative emphasis on sexual politics and the Americanizing of Old World Catholic values, Mary Gordon established herself as a clear-eyed, unsentimental interpreter of the Irish-American experience. Since the popular and critical success of this first book, Gordon has published regularly and has honed her stylistic precision in a variety of genres. By turns lyrical and impassioned, cerebral and reflective, Gordon writes about such distinctly American themes as class and identity with an Irish-Catholic preoccupation with morality and faith.

Born in Queens, New York, and raised on Long Island's South Shore, Mary Catherine Gordon was a bookish child, keenly aware of being an outsider in her working-class family and parish. When she was seven, her father, David Gordon, died—a devastating event that left the precocious child bereft of a father and intellectual guide. A complex, literary, charismatic man whom Mary idolized, David Gordon was a Jew who had converted to Catholicism in 1937. In her 1996 memoir, *The Shadow Man: A Daughter's Search for Her Father,* Gordon's wrenching historical and emotional investigation uncovers her father's deep duplicity and grandiose self-invention. Remade as a devout Catholic, with an aristocratic pedigree and stints at Harvard and Oxford, David Gordon was actually a Lithuanian immigrant who dropped out of high school at 16. The truth revealed an overweening sense of her father's failure and diminishment, which was both "pathetic" and "tragic," but most horrific and unforgivable was the evidence of his raging anti-Semitism. "I had lost him as the figure in history I thought he was; I had lost my place in America," Gordon writes in the memoir with searching earnestness. She early found that language was the "place" to freely assert her powers, and she equates writing with consciousness itself. She read voraciously and describes Virginia Woolf's *Mrs. Dalloway* as inspiring her movement from poetry to lyrical, poetically charged prose.

Gordon was educated at Barnard and Syracuse University. She lives in Manhattan with second husband Arthur Cash—who is Laurence Sterne's biographer—and their two children and is the Millicent C. McIntosh Professor of Writing at Barnard.

The vexed "place" of religious life in a temptingly secular culture, the outmoded dictates of a church at odds with feminism and sexual liberty, and the need for self-determination and moral action are thematic mainstays in her work, although she is troubled by being labeled as a Catholic writer. "I guess when they start calling John Updike 'the Protestant writer,' then they can start calling me 'the Catholic writer,'" she says in a 1997 interview in the literary magazine *Ploughshares.* Yet the "formal beauty in Catholic liturgy" (*Ploughshares* 1997) informs her deepest sense of beauty and order in art. Her Catholic girlhood, her later disillusionment with Church teachings, and her subsequent, if conflicted, return to familiar religious ground all find their way into the internal and domestic dramas of her fictional characters. In the 1981 novel, *The Company of Women,* the central character, Felicitas, is cautioned by her mentor, Father Cyprian, to be wary of crass, unholy Americanism and its insipid, self-serving reduction of thorny spiritual truths. American mercantilism makes for shoddy spiritual goods, "an Elk's Club spirituality" that promotes false sentiment instead of deliverance from evil. Though Felicitas rebels against Cyprian's dour, hair-shirt diatribe against the way of the flesh, she ultimately can't escape her Irish Catholic past. The defining restraints of sin and servitude compete against the lush promise of expansive American worldliness, and though Gordon criticizes Church constriction, she is equally critical of American excess.

Her novel *Pearl* (2005), is set in Dublin. Twenty-year-old Pearl is dangerously close to dying after starving herself for six weeks in support of a barely discernable political, humanistic cause. Her mother, Maria, a take-charge New York liberal, journeys to Ireland to try to save her child and, in the process, is forced to cede control and confront her own ideals. Gordon's latest novel is *Circling My Mother* (2007). This book chronicles her mother's challenges with polio, alcoholism, and finally dementia, and describes her experience of caring for her mother in old age.

Kate Falvey

References

Bennett, Alma. *Mary Gordon.* New York: Twayne Publishers, 1996.

Gordon, Mary. *Seeing Through Places: Reflections on Geography and Identity.* New York: Scribner, 2000.

Lee, Don. "About Mary Gordon: A Profile." *Ploughshares,* Fall 1997, 218–226.

GORE, ROBERT (1810–1854)

British consul to Buenos Aires, member of Parliament, and officer of the British Royal Navy, Robert Gore was the fourth son of the 3rd Earl of Arran, William J. Gore (1767–1836), and Caroline Pym-Hale (d. 1853). He was born in Saunders Court in Co. Wexford, near the town of Crossabeg. On September 4, 1823, he entered the Royal Navy, and in 1832 he was promoted to the rank of lieutenant. From 1832 to 1834 Gore sailed in the *Melville* and the *Andromache* under Admiral Henry Ducie Chads, during which time he engaged in action with the Malay pirates. On July 15, 1837, grateful merchants and underwriters of Bombay presented him with a sword (which is now on exhibition in the National Maritime Museum, London). On May 9, 1839, Gore was promoted to commander, and he was put in charge of the *Serpent* on the West India Station. He was elected member of Parliament for New Ross, Co. Wexford, being a supporter of the Melbourne ministry and an advocate for free trade and abolition of monopolies. He returned to Ireland in 1841, and on October 23, 1846, was appointed as chargé d'affaires at Montevideo, Uruguay. His most important intervention in the River Plate was in March 1848, when he successfully put an end to the Buenos Aires blockade that the British had carried out since 1845 together with the French. On August 29, 1851, Gore was appointed as British consul in Buenos Aires.

Gore is remembered in Argentina for saving the life of the governor of Buenos Aires, Juan Manuel de Rosas, after the battle of Caseros, and for making possible his subsequent exile in Southampton. When he arrived home in the afternoon of February 4, 1852, Gore found Rosas sleeping in his bed. He spoke to Admiral Henderson, who allowed Rosas to board the *Locust.* With Rosas's daughter Manuelita disguised as a sailor, on the night of February 8 the family abandoned Buenos Aires. The British merchants, who had a poor relationship with the consul, accused Gore of receiving a sum of money to help Rosas. After the fall of Rosas, Gore met with General Justo José de Urquiza, who told him about his plans to develop the country, to open its rivers to all nations, and to attract "Saxon" (i.e., English-speaking) immigrants. In the fight between Buenos Aires and the Argentine Confederation that followed the battle of Caseros, Gore was perceived to be a friend of the provinces. However, in January 1853, when Gore complained that arms and ammunitions were being distributed among British subjects, he was expelled from Buenos Aires and returned to Montevideo. He died on August 4, 1854.

Edmundo Murray

See also: EMIGRATION

References

Escudé, Carlos, and Andrés Cisneros, eds. *Historia de las Relaciones Exteriores Argentinas.* www.argentina-rree.com/home_nueva.htm (accessed August 25, 2007).

Stenton, Michael. *Who's Who of British Members of Parliament, A Biographical Dictionary of the House of Commons.* Vol. 1, 1832–1885. Hassocks: The Harvestry Press, 1976.

GRACE, WILLIAM RUSSELL (1832–1904)

Born in Queenstown, Co. Laois, on May 10, 1832, to James Grace and Ellen Russell, William R. Grace had a boyhood ambition to gain a commission in the Royal Navy. His father would not allow him to join up, however, so he ran away to sea and spent two years sailing around the world. His father then bought him an interest in a firm

Portrait of William Russell Grace, philanthropist, entrepreneur, and New York mayor for two terms in the 1880s.

of ship chandlers in Liverpool and, becoming attracted by opportunities in South America, in the 1850s Grace went to Callao in Peru, where his father helped him to find a job. His brother Michael joined him, and in 1854 the firm Bryce & Co. became Bryce, Grace & Co., and finally Grace Bros. In 1860 the firm established a merchant steamship line to serve the Americas. Their fortunes increased but William Grace was forced to leave Peru on account of his health, leaving Michael in charge.

In 1865 Grace settled in New York and founded W. R. Grace & Co. to serve as a front for Grace Bros. of Callao, trading fabric, fertilizer, machinery, and other products. When Peru built its railway system, Grace secured practically all contracts for supplying iron, timber, food, and other elements to the builders of the railway. In 1875 he became adviser to the government of Peru, and handled the business of arming the Peruvian army. In 1879 he supplied munitions and battleships during the ill-fated war with Chile. Peru lost the war and Grace resigned as adviser. Peru was left owing $250 million to English bondholders.

With another Irishman, John Luke Heley-Hutchinson (Earl of Donaghmore), Grace bought up all the English and American bonds, and with the Grace Donaghmore contract of 1890 they secured a mortgage on the Republic of Peru, taking over the national debt and receiving many concessions in return. The Peruvian Corporation was formed to manage the concessions; it was directed by Heley-Hutchinson, but Grace was the power behind it. The company received outright the valuable silver mines of Cerro de Pasco, the entire output of the guano deposits, 5 million acres of land containing valuable oil and mineral deposits, the lease of two railways for 66 years, and the right to hold in perpetuity a road with generous grants for constructing it.

In 1895 the Grace companies united under an American charter and became William R. Grace & Co. The firm opened offices in all major Latin American countries and went into importing and exporting and establishing world contracts. Grace's exploits in Peru earned him the nickname of "The Pirate of Peru." On September 11, 1895, Grace married Lilly Gilchrist, the daughter of a shipbuilder. He returned home to Ireland with his bride and later went on a grand tour of Europe.

In Chile, William R. Grace & Co. developed the Nitrate Properties, built cotton and sugar mills, and set up traction, light, and power companies. In 1890, Grace acquired the New York and Pacific Steamship Co., which became the Grace Steamship Co., with regular services between New York and the west coast of South America. In 1900, Grace opened offices in Argentina.

Grace was elected mayor of New York in 1880, the first Roman Catholic appointed to this post. Opposing the famous Tammany Hall, Grace conducted a reform administration, attacking police scandals, patronage, and organized crime; reducing the tax rate; and breaking up the Louisiana Lottery. Defeated the following year, he was reelected in 1884 on an independent ticket, and lost again the following year. In 1897, he founded the Grace Institute to give young girls a practical education in stenography, dressmaking, and the domestic arts.

William R. Grace died on March 21, 1904. His company became a worldwide network with a particular focus on chemicals and packaging, but over time the company diversified into everything from sporting goods to tacos.

Edmundo Murray

See also: EMIGRATION; TAMMANY HALL

Reference

Marquis, James. *Merchant Adventurer: the Story of W. R. Grace.* Wilmington, DE: Scholarly Resources, 1993.

GRAY, DAVID (1870–1968)

David Gray was the American minister to Ireland from 1940 to 1947, one of the most tumultuous periods in American-Irish relations. Gray had no previous diplomatic experience before his appointment, and his Scottish Presbyterian background did not endear him to Eamon de Valera or the Irish political establishment. His ambition throughout his tenure was to cajole Ireland to aid Britain by any means possible. After 1943, Gary became increasingly concerned about Irish-American postwar efforts to end partition and the possible effects of those efforts on Anglo-American relations.

Gray was born on August 8, 1870, in Buffalo, New York. His early career included stints in the newspaper business and as a criminal lawyer. He eventually found some success as a writer, mostly of short stories, but also as a playwright. In 1914 he married Eleanor Roosevelt's aunt, Maude Waterbury. The Grays and the Roosevelts had a close relationship because Maude was only six years older than Eleanor and they were raised in the same house. Gray probably owed his appointment to Dublin to this relationship with the Roosevelts.

Gray's first efforts to engage Ireland in the war involved pressuring the Irish government to abandon its neutrality, an especially thorny proposition before December 1941, given American neutrality to that point. When it became clear to Gray that neutrality was so supported by the Irish people and the Irish government that there was no chance they would abandon it, his priority changed to finding ways to have the Irish government allow the British to use the treaty ports of Cobh, Berehaven, and Lough Swilly. These were ports that the British government maintained possession of after the 1921 Anglo-Irish Treaty until the Anglo-Irish Agreement of 1938. At that time, British Prime Minister Neville Chamberlain thought that because it would be almost impossible to use the ports effectively without Ireland being an active ally in a future war, returning the ports to Ireland might engender enough goodwill from the Irish government to allow that to happen. De Valera stressed that the return of the ports was the most important aspect of the agreement, one that finally allowed for Irish sovereignty over all the territory of the island that was not part of Northern Ireland. De Valera also reiterated a pledge he made years earlier that he would not allow Ireland to be used as a base by other states against Britain.

By 1943, realizing that his efforts to have Ireland join the Allies or relinquish the ports had failed, Gray hatched a plan that he hoped would discredit and isolate the Irish government, set up a scapegoat in case of failed Allied military plans, and short-circuit Irish-American postwar political efforts. This last point was especially important to Gray. He believed Irish-American influence after World War I had scuttled the League of Nations, and he feared that a similar lobbying effort by Irish Americans after World War II to end partition would drive a wedge in postwar Anglo-American relations. Having de Valera publicly deny a request from the Allies would serve all three of Gray's goals.

Gray delivered "The American Note," as it has come to be called, to de Valera in February 1944. Gray's first drafts included a demand for the ports, but State Department revisions simply made it a request that the Irish government expel the Axis representatives in Dublin because of the threat of espionage. Gray argued that allowing even the limited personnel from Germany and Japan to remain in Dublin, close to Allied bases, gave the Axis an advantage that the Allies did not have, thus constituting a breach in Irish neutrality. De Valera rejected the proposal and its assumptions about the level of Axis espionage, which Gray also knew to be overblown. Gray's hopes for the note came to fruition when news of it and the Irish refusal became public in March 1944. American and British newspapers and magazines widely condemned the Irish government, and Gallup Poll results showed that most Americans knew of the incident and believed Ireland should comply with the Allied request. De Valera, however, rode the wave of Irish support for his stand to an electoral victory later that year.

After the war, Gray worked actively to persuade Irish-American leaders that any efforts to lobby on behalf of ending partition would produce a Protestant backlash. He left his post as minister to Ireland in 1947, but continued to write on Irish issues. Gray died on April 12, 1968.

John Tully

See also: De VALERA, Eamon; WILSON, Woodrow

References

Cronin, Seán. *Washington's Irish Policy, 1916–1986: Independence, Partition, Neutrality.* Dublin: Anvil Books, 1987.

Davis, Troy D. *Dublin's American Policy: Irish-American Diplomatic Relations, 1945–1952.* Washington, DC: Catholic University Press of America, 1998.

Dwyer, T. Ryle. *Irish Neutrality and the USA, 1939–1947.* Dublin: Gill and Macmillan, 1977.

GREAT FAMINE, THE

The Irish Famine of 1845 to 1852 is central to understanding the development of modern Ireland. The deaths of more than 1 million people and the emigration of an even higher number within the space of five years made it one of the greatest catastrophes in Irish history. The tragic consequences of the crop failure were also unique within modern Europe, where famine had largely been eradicated by the mid-nineteenth century. The Famine's imprint, moreover, was also visible in the development of countries where famine refugees settled, particularly the United States, the main destination of the emigrants. Within the United States, the Irish Famine is commonly referred to as The Great Hunger, or its Irish name *An Gorta Mhór.*

No part of Ireland escaped the consequences of the Famine, although there were some marked regional variations; areas in the south and west, notably Skibbereen (Co. Cork) and Kilrush (Co. Clare), were indelibly linked with the Famine suffering. Even Ulster, the most industrially advanced part of the country, was affected, including Belfast, the flagship of Ireland's manufacturing and commercial progress. By 1847, there were daily accounts of dead bodies on the streets of Belfast, the local workhouse and hospitals were full, and the three major cemeteries (including the Protestant Shankill graveyard) were overflowing.

The tragedy was triggered by a mysterious blight that appeared on potatoes in the late summer of 1845, destroying approximately one-third of the crop. Potatoes were an important subsistence crop, and more than half of the population of 8.5 million people depended on this vegetable for their survival. The prime minister, Sir Robert Peel, responded swiftly by putting into place a series of measures that would become effective the following spring, when the shortages began to be felt. They included importing Indian corn (maize) from the United States and providing matching grants to local relief committees for the purchase of food or the establishment of public works. These measures, although short term and limited, were successful. In the year following the first appearance of blight, despite severe suffering, there was no excess mortality in Ireland. Many localities expressed their gratitude to Peel and his government for their intervention.

Peel used the Irish food shortages as an opportunity to repeal the Corn Laws, protective legislation that kept the price of imported corn artificially high. This action lost him support of many members of his Tory (Conservative) Party and ultimately led to the end of his premiership. The Tory government was also replaced in the summer of 1846 by a Whig (Liberal) administration led by Lord John Russell. The Whigs had been traditional allies of Daniel O'Connell, and within Ireland there was optimism that the Whigs would live up to their promise of "justice for Ireland." Political aspirations were pushed aside, however, as within a few weeks of coming into power, Russell's government was confronted by the reappearance of potato blight, even earlier than in the previous year. By September 1846, more than three-quarters of the crop had been destroyed, which meant the extent of distress would be far higher than in the previous year, and the impact of food shortages would be felt immediately. Russell was anxious not to alienate his British supporters by endorsing high expenditures on Ireland. Consequently, his relief measures placed a higher financial burden on Irish taxpayers than on the central government. Public works, based on hard, physical labor, were the main form of relief provision, and the cost of the works was repayable by the localities. This philosophy was in keeping with a widely held belief that "Irish property must support Irish poverty."

As a system of providing emergency relief, however, the public works system was flawed: the wages were kept deliberately low despite the steep rise in food prices; the hard physical labor and long hours of employment weakened the health of a people already debilitated by hunger;

the many layers of bureaucracy slowed down their effectiveness as a mechanism for relief and diverted money from the poor; and, moreover, the works undertaken served little purpose, resulting in their popular portrayal as "roads that led nowhere and walls that surrounded nothing." Despite the expense of the public works—by March 1847 outlay had reached more than £5 million, much of which was to be repaid by Irish taxpayers—they patently failed to save lives or maintain a basic level of health.

The new Whig government did not have a majority in parliament and, unlike the Tory Party, it derived a substantial part of its support from corn merchants and traders. One of the first things it did upon learning about the reappearance of blight was to assure the merchants that the government would keep its interventions in the Irish trade (both imports and exports) to a minimum. Nonetheless, a number of local corporations and prominent individuals asked for the Irish ports to be closed as a short-term expedient to keep food within the country. Although food imports did increase, most did not arrive until the following spring, by which time many people had already died or emigrated, or their health had been seriously jeopardized. The fact that Ireland was part of the United Kingdom, which was the richest and most industrialized empire in the world, did not protect the Irish poor at a time of deprivation and starvation.

In spring 1847, the government's policies again changed, indicating that the measures introduced only six months earlier had failed. The new procedures marked the most liberal phase of famine relief. Import duties were removed from corn, the restrictive Navigation Laws were temporarily relaxed, which meant that food could be carried on ships not registered in Britain, and sugar was allowed to be used in distillation in place of grain. All of these measures meant that more food was available and this, in turn, helped to bring prices down. The most important change in policy was that—for the first and only time during the Famine—for a limited period only, poor people could receive free food in specially opened soup kitchens. Although the portions given were meager, the soup kitchens meant that the poor had direct access to free food. The scale of demand provided a measure of the extent of need in Ireland. By July 1847 more than 3 million people were receiving free food rations daily while thousands of others, considered to be above destitution levels, were able to buy rations of food. Consequently, more than 40 percent of the Irish population was kept alive by the soup kitchens. Moreover, the soup kitchens demonstrated that the British government possessed both the administrative and logistical capability to feed the Irish poor. However, it lacked the political will or courage to do so for a prolonged period, despite unequivocal evidence of extensive need. Furthermore, the giving of gratuitous relief—especially to the Irish poor—was regarded with horror not only by orthodox supporters of political economy but also by British and Irish taxpayers who believed they were financing a flawed system of relief. Despite being cheap and effective, therefore, the soup kitchens were closed in the fall of 1847, and a more draconian phase of relief commenced.

Providentialist interpretations of the Famine were favored by leading Protestant British statesmen and administrators such as Charles Trevelyan of the Treasury and Charles Wood, the chancellor of the exchequer. This interpretation was enthusiastically supported by the London *Times.* Initially, some Catholic clergy viewed the food shortages as a judgment of God, requiring moral atonement by the population. However, this viewpoint was rejected by other Catholic clergy, including Archbishop Hughes of New York. At a fund-raising lecture given at the Broadway Tabernacle in March 1847, he averred that it was "blasphemy" to blame the tragedy on God, as the Famine was man's doing. He also pointed out that only one crop had failed in Ireland, while there was an abundance of other foodstuffs. Hughes, at a distance of 3,000 miles, was highlighting the central paradox of the Famine—how could people starve while vast amounts of foodstuffs were being grown and exported from Ireland?

There was little evidence of blight in the 1847 potato harvest, although the crop was very small. Nevertheless, the British government used the apparent disappearance of the blight to announce that the Famine was over and suggest that if further relief was necessary, it had to come totally from Irish sources. All relief, both permanent and emergency, was to be transferred to the Poor Law. The Poor Law had been introduced to Ireland in 1838 and was based on a system of workhouses, which were authoritarian, regimented institutions that provided a minimal amount of relief to families who were destitute. As the name implied, relief was given in return for work undertaken by the inmates, who were categorized as paupers. The 130 workhouses in Ireland could only hold a total of 110,000 inmates, but since 1846 they had been allowed to rent extra accommodation. After 1847, to deal with the additional demands placed on it, the Poor Law was also permitted to give a limited form of outside relief, thus allowing some paupers to remain in their own homes. For the British government, the key advantage of this form of relief was that each workhouse was supported by local taxation, which meant that the government could reduce its involvement in providing relief. The Famine, however, was far from over and, despite stringent regulations, in 1848 more than 1 million people were dependent on the Poor Law for survival. Moreover, the increase in local taxation and the inability of tenants to pay their rents on time had resulted in a policy of mass evictions. Consequently, the Irish poor now faced homelessness.

In 1848, the blight returned just as virulently as in 1846, yet the British government refused to deviate from its policies introduced in the previous year, determined that relief should be financed from Ireland, and not by British taxpayers. The result of this minimal intervention was disastrous, and in 1849 proportionally as many people died as in "Black '47." Again, the British government demonstrated its determination that the Irish poor would not be a financial drain on British resources. At the beginning of 1848 the British government gave a small grant of £50,000 for Irish relief, while insisting that no more money would come from the central government. Even this small contribution angered some British taxpayers whose sympathies toward Ireland had hardened as a result of the Young Ireland uprising in July 1848. To cope with the ongoing distress in Ireland a new tax was imposed on Irish ratepayers known as the "Rate-in-Aid." This taxation aroused the anger of some Protestant ratepayers in Ulster who argued—incorrectly—that they were being forced to subsidize the laziness and improvidence of paupers in the west of Ireland.

The impact of the Famine was not confined to Ireland. Newspapers throughout the world carried reports of the suffering, and by the end of 1846 an international fund-raising effort had commenced. Reports of the food shortages first reached the United States and Canada at the end of 1845, but the coverage about the seriousness of the scarcity was mixed. Within a few months, news from Ireland was dominated by the repeal movement and divisions between Young and Old Ireland. The second, more serious crop failure in 1846 appeared in the international press as early as October 1846. Even at this early stage it was clear that the situation was far more serious than in the previous year. It resulted in relief committees being organized in a number of cities. Their priority was to raise money to send to Ireland rather than alleviate the condition of famine refugees in America. In 1847 the usual Saint Patrick's Day dinners were canceled and the money sent to Ireland. Individual churches also raised money and sent it through the Society of Friends. In New York three ships were commissioned to take money and supplies to Ireland, the *New Haven*, the *Duncan* and the *Boston*. The *Macedonia*, donated by the secretary of the Navy, also included supplies for Scotland. It subsequently sailed from Boston, together with the *Jamestown*, which sailed directly to Queenstown (Cobh) in Cork. Paradoxically, as supplies left for Ireland, food was arriving in the United States from Irish ports, the British government having refused to close the Irish ports and keep food in the country. In the summer of 1847 conditions improved in Ireland, and mortality slowed down. This was partly attributable to the introduction of soup kitchens, but it was also because large donations and supplies of provisions were arriving from all over the world.

At the end of 1847, however, private donations to Ireland dried up. This was attributable to a combination of factors: the British government's declaration that the Famine was over; compassion fatigue; and frustration that despite large amounts of aid being sent to Ireland, paupers were emigrating and becoming an immediate burden on the taxpayers of their new country. These sentiments were evident in New York, which had raised money so generously for famine relief at the beginning of 1847. At the end of the year, the local authorities passed legislation making landing more difficult and introduced tighter housing legislation, which included restrictions on cellar dwellings. Nonetheless, the generosity of the American people following the second crop failure had been remarkable, not only in terms of the amount of aid raised, but also for the fact that donations had cut across national, religious, and ethnic boundaries, money being given by individuals and groups as diverse as the president of the United States, the Choctaw Indians, the Shakers of Albany, and Jewish synagogues in New York. In total, almost $2 million of relief was raised for Ireland, and its importance in saving lives was immeasurable.

Mass emigration extended the suffering of the Irish people beyond Ireland. Since the second crop failure in 1846, thousands of people had fled Ireland, selling what few possessions they owned to afford the fare. Their preferred destination was North America, often via the circuitous route of Liverpool and Canada, to obtain the cheapest fares. The journey across the Atlantic could vary between 17 and 90 days. Because the British-registered ships were subject to few regulations, many of the Irish immigrants arrived in a debilitated state. Ship fever had become commonplace, and so the immigrants inadvertently brought fever into the city. More than any other European immigrants, the Irish were undernourished, flea-ridden, and ill; they had little capital or the skills or robust health to ensure that they could find employment quickly. As early as November 1846 immigrants were arriving who were escaping from the destitution in Ireland. Because of their poverty many became applicants for relief, but the city authorities found it difficult to cope with the increased demands on their limited resources. In New York, for example, the city's almshouse could only hold 1,671 inmates, and it quickly became overcrowded. The ill health of many immigrants also meant that they filled up the hospitals and quarantine stations at the ports in which they landed.

Although Irish immigrants were evident in all walks of life, they predominated amongst the poorer classes. Despite being mostly from rural areas, many famine immigrants settled in East Coast cities. In New York, they congregated in the slums of the Lower East Side and Upper East and West sides. Ironically, they escaped the poverty of Ireland to live in overcrowded, polluted, unsanitary slums, where they were exploited by greedy landlords and corrupt city officials. Mortality was high, caused by ship fever or typhoid, and the Irish were also overrepresented in mortality resulting from the 1849 cholera epidemic. The Irish poor had exchanged one form of poverty for another. In 1850, approximately one-third of the Irish were living in cellar dwellings. The better-off Irish emigrants, who tended to be healthier and have some capital, generally escaped from the cities to move westward. Politically, however, Irish immigrants had more rights than they had had in their own country. The rise of anti-Irish nativism in the 1850s disguised the support and help given to the thousands of Irish arrivals who had fled from the Famine in the 1840s. The United States offered them a lifeline for survival and, without this safety valve, an even higher number of Irish people would have died.

Good potato harvests did not return to Ireland until after 1851. By then, more than 1 million people had died and an even higher number had emigrated. The return of good harvests, however, did not mark an end to hunger or social dislocation, and levels of disease, mortality, and emigration remained higher throughout the 1850s than they had been before 1845. The Great Hunger had not only changed Ireland dramatically; its repercussions also changed the development of other countries to which Irish people had fled.

Christine Kinealy

See also: AMERICAN CIVIL WAR; BOSTON; DOUGLASS, Frederick; EMIGRATION; FOSTER, Vere Henry Louis; GROSSE ILE; MITCHELL, John; NATIVISM AND ANTI-CATHOLICISM; NEW YORK CITY; O'CONNELL, Daniel

References

Hayden, Tom, ed. *Irish Hunger: Personal Reflections on the Legacy of the Famine.* Denver: Roberts Rinehart, 1997.

Hickey, Patrick. *Famine in West Cork: The Mizen Land and People 1800–1852.* Cork: Mercier Press, 2002.

Kinealy, Christine, and Gerard MacAtasney. *The Forgotten Famine: Hunger, Poverty and Sectarianism in Belfast 1840–1850.* London: Pluto Press, 2000.

Kinealy, Christine. *The Irish Famine: Impact, Ideology and Rebellion.* London: Palgrave, 2002.

Ó Gráda, Cormac. *Ireland: Before and After the Famine. Explorations in Economic History, 1800–1925.* Manchester: Manchester University Press, 1993.

Póirtéir, Cathal. *The Irish Famine.* Cork: Mercier Press, 1995.

GRENNAN, EAMON (1941–)

Born November 13, 1941, in Dublin to Thomas, an educational administrator, and Evelyn (Yourell) Grennan, Eamon was educated by the Cistercians at Roscrea and attended University College Dublin (BA, 1963; MA, 1964), where he studied English and Italian; he received a doctorate in English from Harvard University (1973). In 1972 he married Joan Perkins; they divorced in 1986, and he later married Rachel Kitzinger. Since 1974 Grennan has taught at Vassar College in Poughkeepsie, New York, and on occasion has been guest professor at Columbia, NYU, and Villanova.

His slim collection *Wildly for Days* (1983) announced a pastoral poet who etched in minimalist fashion an interior life open to appreciating the unexpected. *What Light There Is* (1987) attunes itself to poetry as visual painting with a broader syntactical brush that verges on the prose poem, displaying patrician approval of construction workers at their job or the way deer graze on a golf course. Grennan's breakthrough for a wider American audience occurred with the publication of *What Light There Is & Other Selected Poems* (1989). *As If It Matters* (1992) explores family outings, animals, insects, and an earnest attention to nature that recalls Cezanne's shifting planes or the affectionate detail of Bonnard's colorful interiors. The midlife poems in *So It Goes* (1995) mark a notable advance, both in the sensuality of their sinuous syntax and their porous exploration of memory, evoking Dantean inflections to meditate on childhood, daubing memorable portraits of his parents, especially his mother. *Still Life with Waterfall* (2001), which won the Lenore Marshall Award for Poetry in 2003 from the American Academy of Poets, returns to landscape sketches with more meditations on weather and landscape; here the poems are like a cornucopia bursting, more surreal and prolix in a profusion of lists that ramble with emotional predictability while the syntax engenders suspense. *Quick of It* (2004) delves into a more inward contemplation on landscape and reflection in densely textured, untitled, 10-line prose poems that push the boundaries of syntax, creating the frisson of collage, blurring the distinction between subject and object. Many of his landscape sketches are inspired by living on the west coast of Ireland near Tully Mountain.

Grennan's gently idiomatic and limpid translations of Leopardi's poetry earned him the 1997 PEN Award for Poetry in Translation. Grennan was also the recipient of a 1991 National Endowment for the Arts award and a Guggenheim Fellowship in 1995. His poems have won several Pushcart Prizes. With Rachael Kitzinger Grennan he has translated Sophocles' *Oedipus at Colonus* (2005).

Grennan's poetry exults in the casual: a cat listening to Mozart, his children's efforts at collecting mussels, cows in a field, the flight of a bird into a window; he often uses windows as framing devices. Occasionally, he experiments with second-person narration. The real virtue of his poetry resides in his affable voice: a charming immediacy, inquisitive about the small things in life, optimistic about the possibilities of dealing with difficulties, contemplatively shading nuances of mood in a landscape, as in a watercolor. Both tone and voice rejoice in intimate turns of phrase, couched in a genial appreciation of colloquial speech that effortlessly blends American and Anglo-Irish patterns with echoes of Dante and Leopardi. While devoid of Leopardi's pessimism and plangent self-pity, Grennan's approach shows the paramount influence of Leopardi's beguiling simplicity and impressionistic landscapes, especially in his gift for dramatizing tender empathy for the domestic ordinary, the delicate coloring of a pheasant, cobbled light off water, pale ambiance of a gentian sky.

In *Facing the Music* (1999), Grennan casts a poet's appreciative eye over the work of W. B. Yeats, James Joyce, Austin Clarke, Padraic Fallon, Patrick Kavanagh, Thomas Kinsella, John Montague, and Derek Mahon, emphasizing the effect of emotion and affection in their work within their historical context and the broader palette of Irish poetry; more recent poets garner brief reviews. Grennan remains a poet of insouciant buoyancy and visual delight in nature, cherishing familial events, the breathing of leaves, and birds.

Kevin T. McEneaney

See also: JOYCE, James Augustine Aloysius; KINSELLA, Thomas; MONTAGUE, John; YEATS, William Butler

References

Fitzgerald-Hoyt, Mary. "Vermeer in Verse: Eamon Grennan's Domestic Interior." *New Hibernia Review* 2, no. 1 (1998): 121–131.

Fleming, Deborah. "The 'Common Ground' of Eamon Grennan." *Eire-Ireland* 28, no. 4 (1993): 133–149.

Grennan, Eamon. *Leopardi: Selected Poems.* Princeton, NJ: Princeton University Press, 1997.

Grennan, Eamon. *Relations: New & Selected Poems.* St. Paul, MN: Graywolf Press, 1998.

GROSSE ILE

Formerly known as Ile de Grâce, Grosse Ile is a small island about two miles long by a half mile wide in the Saint Lawrence River approximately thirty miles downstream from Quebec City; from 1832 to 1937, the island served as a quarantine station for immigrants coming to Canada and was the scene of a major typhus epidemic in 1847 caused by the famine emigration from Ireland. Secret bacterial research was conducted there beginning in 1947; today the island is a Canadian historic site featuring the Irish Memorial and operated by the Canadian Parks Service.

Fearing contagion from Asiatic cholera, British colonial authorities established a quarantine station on the uninhabited island of Grosse Ile in 1832. Most of the 50,000 immigrants of that season were Irish. A hurried and generally inefficient system of quarantine that year resulted in the spread of cholera to the cities of Quebec and Montreal, where several thousand died of the disease. Cholera would again hit the colony in 1834, 1849, and 1854. However, Grosse Ile is infamously known as an Irish burial ground following the tragic events of the famine year of 1847, during which some 17,000 to 20,000 Irish immigrants lost their lives.

Two main reasons help explain the extremely high death toll at sea and on Grosse Ile during the 1847 season. First, being a British colony, Canada had little or no control over immigration to its shores, that being the responsibility of the imperial government. Unlike the independent United States, which saw the massive Irish exodus approaching on the horizon and took steps to curb the tide by refusing entry to the most overcrowded ships, Canada, via Grosse Ile, could do little but care for the sick and dying immigrants after they disembarked. Second, up to 1847, the average size of a season's immigration by the Saint Lawrence stood at 30,000 to 50,000. In 1847, no less than 100,000 immigrants came by way of the Grosse Ile quarantine station, many of them weak from starvation and diseased with typhus that they had contracted in ports of embarkation such as Liverpool or Cork. Their situation was further aggravated by cramped and unsanitary conditions on board ship and by the length of some passages; those vessels refused at American ports such as New York and Philadelphia made their way to Quebec. Some 5,000 were buried at sea that year and at least 5,424 found a grave on Grosse Ile. Another 6,000 Irish immigrants died and were buried at Pointe Saint-Charles in Montreal. Several doctors, priests, nurses, and employees of the quarantine station also became victims of the typhus epidemic that season.

With changes to ocean navigation, notably the development of faster transatlantic steamers, conditions on board and at the quarantine station generally improved. From 1869 to 1899, a bacteriologist, Dr. Frederick Montizambert, was medical superintendent of the quarantine station; he introduced the inspection and disinfection of vessels and luggage and saw to the examination and vaccination of passengers. Hospitals and hotels were erected on the island to treat and comfort passengers.

To commemorate the 50th anniversary of "Black '47," the Ancient Order of Hibernians of North America erected a Celtic cross on Grosse Ile. The cross, with inscriptions in French, English, and Irish, was displayed in 1909. Although immigration reached new highs in the early twentieth century (225,000 immigrants arrived at Quebec in 1914), the outbreak of World War I put a stop to the movement from Europe, and the quarantine station closed in 1937.

Shortly after World War II, secret bacterial research was conducted on Grosse Ile and the island was shut off from public scrutiny. The Canadian government declared the island a national historic site in 1984. An Irish Memorial was established in 1998 to mark the 150th anniversary of the catastrophic events of 1847. The site is today open to the public.

Robert J. Grace

See also: ANCIENT ORDER OF HIBERNIANS; EMIGRATION; GREAT FAMINE, The

References

Charbonneau, André, and André Sévigny. *1847, Grosse Île: A Record of Daily Events.* Quebec: Minister of Public Works, 1997.

O'Gallagher, Marianna, *Grosse Île: Gateway to Canada.* Quebec: Carraig Books, 1984.

GUEVARA, ERNESTO "CHE" (1928–1967)

One of the most famous revolutionary fighters of the twentieth century, Ernesto "Che" Guevara was the son of Ernesto Guevara Lynch and Celia de la Serna. A physician, better known for his role in the revolutionary forces in Cuba, Congo, and Bolivia, Che was born on June 14, 1928, in Rosario, Argentina. Owing to his poor health (he suffered from asthma), in 1932 the family moved to Altagracia, Córdoba province. In 1947, Guevara began studying medicine in the University of Buenos Aires and graduated in 1953. During this period he traveled throughout Latin America, including Argentina, Chile, Peru, Colombia, and Venezuela. The year of his graduation he went to Guatemala and got acquainted with the revolutionist Antonio Ñico López.

After the fall of Jacobo Arbenz, Guevara settled in Mexico. In July 1955 he enrolled in Fidel Castro's Granma expedition, which left Tuxpan on November 25, 1956, and landed a week later in Cuba. The rebels were defeated, but on January 17, 1957, they overpowered the regular army in Uvero (a battle that Guevara considered the maturity of the revolution). In June 1957, Guevara was appointed chief of the rebels' fourth regiment, which arrived the following year at Camagüey. By year end they occupied the city of Santa Clara, entering Havana on January 2, 1959. Guevara was awarded Cuban citizenship and on November 26 was appointed president of the national bank.

Between 1960 and 1965 Guevara traveled in commercial missions to countries in Europe, Asia, and Latin America to increase Cuban international trade, foster ideological dialogue, and support a military alliance against the threat of the United States. He also represented Cuba in international conferences and bodies. To resume military action, Guevara resigned his official appointments, left Cuba on October 3, 1965, and arrived in Bolivia with a Uruguayan passport and under the name of Adolfo Mena González. He joined the local guerrilla movement in November and after an encounter in Quebrada del Yuro he was seriously injured. On October 9, 1965, Che Guevara was executed in Higuera together with six other rebels. His body was discovered in 1997, and the remains were buried in Cuba.

On the belief that successful revolutions were only possible with the material support of well-organized armies, Guevara developed the primacy of military struggle and the guerilla foci, by which cumulative attacks over relatively small targets would develop the people's revolutionary awareness. Privately, he was critical of the Soviet Union and claimed that the world's northern hemisphere, including the United States and the Soviet Union, exploited the southern hemisphere. He supported the Vietnamese revolution and urged his comrades in South America to create "many Vietnams." Guevara's published works include *The Bolivian Diary, Guerrilla Warfare, The African Dream: the Diaries of the Revolutionary War in the Congo,* and *The Motorcycle Diaries.*

In Ireland and other places with Irish immigration, Guevara's life and thinking are sometimes linked with his ancestry. However, Guevara's family and cultural connections with Ireland were in fact far and remote. His paternal grandmother, Ana Isabel Lynch was the great-great-granddaughter of Patrick Lynch, born in 1715 in Lydican Castle, Co. Galway, and a member of a merchant family prominent in Jamaica and elsewhere in the West Indies. Patrick Lynch left Ireland in the 1740s and after traveling throughout the Americas settled in Buenos Aires in 1749. There is no evidence that Guevara identified with Irish culture. He was proud of his Argentine origin and Cuban nationality and regarded himself as Latin American. One of the possible sources of misinformation was an interview on March 13, 1965, by journalist Arthur Quinlan. Guevara was on his way back to Havana from Prague, and the Cuban Airlines aircraft developed mechanical trouble and landed in Shannon Airport. According to Quinlan, Guevara spoke in English and talked of his Irish connections through the name Lynch. He went with friends to Limerick and stayed in the

Hanratty's Hotel on Glentworth Street. Most likely, this was the closest connection that Che Guevara had with Ireland.

Edmundo Murray

See also: ARGENTINA; FARRELL, Edelmiro Juan

References

Anderson, John Lee. *Che Guevara: A Revolutionary Life.* New York: Grove Press, 1997.

Castañeda, Jorge G. *Compañero: Vida y Muerte de Che Guevara.* Mexico: Grijalbo, 1997.

Coghlan, Eduardo A. *Los Irlandeses en la Argentina: Su Actuación y Descendencia.* Buenos Aires: Author's Edition, 1987.

GUINEY, LOUISE IMOGENE (1861–1920)

A poet, essayist, and literary critic, Guiney was among the group of artists associated with the aesthetic revival in Boston during the 1890s. Her father, Patrick Robert Guiney, was born in Parkstown, Co. Tipperary, in 1835, and as a boy immigrated with his father to the United States. After briefly considering a career in the theater, Patrick Guiney decided to pursue a law career and was admitted to the bar in 1856. He later served with distinction as a Union soldier in the Civil War, winning a promotion to the rank of brigadier general from President Andrew Johnson. In 1859, he married Jeannette Margaret Doyle. Their daughter Louise Imogen Guiney was born in Roxbury, a prosperous Boston suburb, on January 7, 1861.

Portrait of poet, essayist, and literary critic Louise Imogene Guiney. (Library of Congress)

As an Irish-American Catholic, Guiney has been called "the ambassador between Boston's two cultures": the Boston Brahmin intelligentsia and the Irish. Her first published poem, "Charles Sumner," appeared in 1880 in the Boston newspaper the *Pilot,* edited by the prominent Irish-American journalist John Boyle O'Reilly, her father's close friend. Other poems, collected in *Songs at the Start* (1884) and *The White Sail and Other Poems* (1887), and her essays, collected in *Goose Quill Papers* (1885), soon attracted the attention of the Boston literary establishment, and by the mid-1890s she was firmly established in Boston artistic circles. Her well-known friends and patrons included Oliver Wendell Holmes, Thomas Bailey Aldrich, Thomas Wentworth Higginson, and Edmund Clarence Stedman. Her sentimental writing style, harking back to Romantic, seventeenth-century, and Civil War poets, reflects her Roman Catholicism and literary conservatism.

As the daughter of a well-off lawyer who held (unusually for an Irish immigrant at the time) politically liberal, antislavery views, Guiney's experience of growing up as an Irish Catholic in nineteenth-century

America was in some ways atypical. However, Guiney was proud of her Irish heritage, and many of her writings reflect her attempt to portray the Irish in a more positive light than was common at the time. In the late 1890s, Guiney turned to scholarship, focusing on the seventeenth-century Cavalier poets, but also writing on a variety of other subjects, including an entry on Chaucer for the *Catholic Encyclopedia* and a study of Robert Louis Stevenson on which she collaborated with her close friend, the writer Alice Brown.

Today, Guiney may be best remembered for her part in "discovering" the artist and writer Kahlil Gibran. Gibran had emigrated from Lebanon to the United States with his family at the age of 12, and in the 1890s his talent for drawing attracted the notice of local artists, including Guiney, who introduced him to the established artists of the aesthetic movement. Guiney was also generous in introducing other young writers, including the Canadian poet Wilfred Campbell, to American publishers. Although Guiney was a popular writer in her lifetime, by her own admission she did not take her own writing or fame very seriously. Her main ambition seems to have been to rescue the eclipsed reputations of other writers and notables, such as Robert Emmet, Hurrell Froude, Henry Vaughan, Lady Danvers, and Katherine Philips. After years of regular travel to and from England, Guiney settled there in 1901, dying in Gloucestershire in 1920.

Danielle Maze

See also: O'REILLY, John Boyle

Reference

Guiney, Louise Imogen, *Patrins: to Which Is Added an Inquirendo Into the Wit & Other Good Parts of His Late Majesty King Charles the Second.* Boston: Copeland and Day, 1897.

H

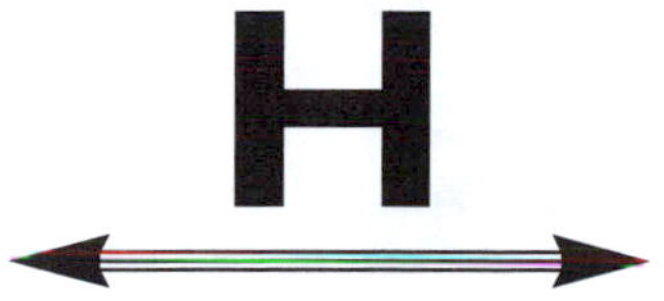

Hackett, Francis (1883–1962)

Francis Hackett was born in Kilkenny, Ireland, on January 21, 1883. At St. Kieran's College he met Thomas MacDonagh (1878–1916), the teacher and nationalist poet who was executed for his part in the Easter Rising in Dublin in 1916. MacDonagh and Hackett became regular correspondents after Hackett immigrated to the United States, aged eighteen. Hackett began his journalistic career at the *Chicago Evening Post,* eventually becoming editor of the literary review. In 1914, he became literary critic of the recently established *New Republic*: one memorable review, from March 1917, praises James Joyce's novel *A Portrait of the Artist as a Young Man.* In 1918, Hackett married Danish-born Signe Toksvig, also a promising writer, and completed his first full-length work, *Ireland: A Study in Nationalism* (1918). In it, Hackett blames British treatment of the Irish for the Easter Rising of 1916 and reasons that Home Rule, while not ideal, might herald "the beginnings of appropriate administration for Ireland." In a new preface for the third edition (1920), Hackett advocates complete separation from Britain. *The Story of the Irish Nation,* a romp through the history of Ireland, followed in 1922. Hackett also compiled two collections of criticism and reviews—*Horizons* (1918) and *The Invisible Censor* (1921). In one review Hackett affirms his "complete identification" with the United States.

Nevertheless, in 1922 Hackett and Toksvig left the United States for the South of France to start work on his first novel, *That Nice Young Couple* (1925). In 1926, the couple moved to Co. Wexford, Ireland, and then on to Co. Wicklow in 1929. Hackett worked as a freelance political writer to fund four years of research into his first historical biography. *Henry the Eighth* (1929) is a playful retelling of the Tudor monarch's life that simultaneously condemns his cruelty and praises his flair for leadership. Hackett produced another biography of a fallible but inspirational king, *Francis the First: Gentleman of France,* in 1934. In 1936 he finished his second novel, *The Green Lion.* The novel is semiautobiographical, describing the horrific childhood of a young boy in Kilkenny. However, it was banned by the Irish censors because the central character is the illegitimate offspring of a peasant girl and a church neophyte and because it condemns the Jesuit education system. Toksvig's second novel, *Eve's Doctor* (1937), was also banned in Ireland. In protest Hackett and

Portrait of author Francis Hackett, ca. 1935. (Library of Congress)

Toksvig left Wexford for Toksvig's native Denmark, settling in Copenhagen. Meanwhile, *The Green Lion* had been published in London.

In 1939, Hackett and Toksvig traveled to New York for a proposed dramatization of Hackett's fictional work, *Queen Anne Boleyn* (1939). However, the play was canceled, and the German occupation of Denmark had meant moving to Martha's Vineyard, Massachusetts, rather than back to Copenhagen. Hackett began contributing biweekly literary reviews to the *New York Times* and wrote his semiautobiographical political and social commentary, *I Choose Denmark* (1940), which extols the virtues of Denmark's constitution, suggesting a possible model for Ireland. Hackett's last novel, *The Senator's Last Night*—which details, with characteristic relish, the last moments of the life of a dissolute Washington senator—followed in 1943. Hackett returned to Copenhagen after the war, producing *Books in General and Particular,* a collection of essays and reviews, in 1947. He lived in Denmark until his death, on April 25 1962, aged seventy-nine.

In 1971, Toksvig published some of Hackett's early reminiscences, written in 1922–1923 about his life until 1913, under Hackett's self-penned title *American Rainbow.* Hackett's "rainbow" refracts his Irish past through the prism of his American present. *American Rainbow* commemorates Hackett's colorful life, counteracting his concern that "The rainbow does not vanish, but it recedes."

Tara Stubbs

See also: NATIONALISM, IRISH-AMERICAN

Reference

Toksvig, Signe, ed. *American Rainbow.* New York: Liveright, 1971.

HANLON, NED (1857–1937)

Although his Irish name was enshrined in the Baseball Hall of Fame roughly 90 years after his managerial career ended, Ned Hanlon's influence on the way baseball is played remains evident to this day. His 1,313 wins as a manager were notable in his day, but they pale in comparison to other Hall of Fame managers. Hanlon's influence, however, is best measured by the impression he left on his players who followed him as managers. Hanlon, best known for leading the Baltimore Orioles in the 1890s when it was a National League team, saw several of his players become successful managers in the major leagues, creating a legacy that remains vibrant. The managerial mentor of John McGraw,

Hanlon directly assisted in the managerial development of Hughie Jennings, Wilbert Robinson, Kid Gleason, and Miller Huggins. Although a mediocre hitter, Hanlon was among the many Irish-American ballplayers that spurred the burgeoning sport during the 1880s.

Hanlon joined the Orioles midseason in 1892 when they were among the worst teams in the league. He bought stock in the club and was elected president, which allowed him the freedom to acquire stars such as Dan Brouthers (with whom Hanlon earlier had formed a precursor to the baseball player's union), Jennings, Joe Kelley, and "Wee" Willie Keeler to join established players Robinson, McGraw, and Sadie McMahon. Hanlon's Orioles won their first pennant in 1894, and over the next six seasons his teams won four more pennants (two additional in Baltimore and Brooklyn during his first two seasons there).

If Hanlon was not considered the most combative manager, he likely placed among the top during an era renowned for rowdiness. Befitting the rules of the time, however, Hanlon was not allowed to leave the bench in his street clothes, which was the way nonplaying managers dressed. Hanlon's early legacy was in drilling his clubs in "baseball as she is played," which included players running into opposing fielders, holding or bumping base runners, interfering with catchers, and throwing equipment in front of opponents trying to score. Rules now preclude such tactics, yet the notion of aggressive baseball found its historic foothold in Hanlon's Orioles. Plays such as the hit-and-run and the sacrifice bunt, which he did not invent but his team implemented consistently well, did not always find favor with those players under his tutelage. McGraw detested the sacrifice. Hanlon's Orioles were among the first to have fielders back up each other on plays to reduce the opposition's advancement on errors. His development and innovation of "inside baseball" (the outguessing and outmaneuvering of the opposing team) found fertile soil in those managers who followed him, especially McGraw, who took inside baseball to a higher level and passed it further through the sport. When Hanlon's Baltimore club and attendance began to wane, Hanlon added a half interest in the Brooklyn franchise in 1899, trading himself several star players and establishing McGraw, who refused to leave, as his managerial successor and protégé in Baltimore. Managed by Hanlon, the Brooklyn Superbas won their first ever pennant and repeated the win in 1900. By 1910, most managers in both the American and National Leagues were men who had played for Hanlon during the 1890s. Among these was Connie Mack, an Irish American who began managing in the National League in 1894 and retired after 1950, following half a century at the helm of the Philadelphia Athletics.

Like McGraw, Mack was inducted into the Hall of Fame decades before Hanlon, who was selected in 1996. Despite Mack's unprecedented tenure, his legacy of successful managers has essentially died out. Among Hanlon's other protégés, Gleason (who pitched for Hanlon before becoming a second baseman), was the ill-fated manager of the 1919 White Sox, which lost the World Series when several players conspired with gamblers. Far more successful was Huggins, who led the New York Yankees to numerous American League pennants and World Championships during the 1920s. Like a family tree, successful managers trace through McGraw and Huggins particularly. For example, later Yankee dynasty leader Casey Stengel played for McGraw, but was also influenced by managers Bill Dahlen and Robinson, who both played for Hanlon. Huggins mentored Leo Durocher, whose influence upon Bill Rigney and Earl Weaver is still felt in the major leagues. Through Stengel, Hanlon's "great-grandsons" and "great-great-grandsons" include Billy Martin and Lou Piniella. Even successful managers of the 1990s such as Joe Torre and Tony LaRussa can trace their managerial influences back to Hanlon.

Matthew Sinclair

See also: BASEBALL; BASEBALL MANAGERS, IRISH-AMERICAN; MACK, Connie; McGRAW, John

References

Alexander, Charles C. *Our Game: An American Baseball History.* New York: Henry Holt and Co., 1991.

Solomon, Burt. *Where They Ain't: The Fabled Life and Untimely Death of the Original Baltimore Orioles.* New York: Free Press. 1999.

HARNETT, WILLIAM MICHAEL (1848–1892)

William Harnett was born in Clonakilty, Co. Cork, but his family moved to Philadelphia. He worked there as an engraver from 1865 until 1871 when he moved to New York, to study at the National Academy of Design and Cooper Union, returning to Philadelphia in 1876 where he continued his studies at the Pennsylvania Academy of Fine Arts. In 1880, he went to London, Frankfurt, and Munich, remaining in Munich until 1885. He returned to the United States via Paris, where he exhibited his paintings most successfully at the Salon. In 1886, he moved permanently to New York.

Initially, Harnett worked in the tradition of Raphaelle Peale, whose work, in turn, was rooted in seventeenth-century Dutch art. His early work brings together the significant elements of the artist's everyday life. His preferred still-life objects (fruit and vegetables, beer mugs and tobacco, books and musical instruments, writing materials and skulls) were additionally selected for their symbolic resonance.

In his work, conceptual realism explores tactile and intellectual considerations, as opposed to other such traditions in which the object is a vehicle for exploring formal, optical, and perceptual contemplation. Trompe l'oeil, at which Harnett excelled, is a further refinement of the former category of still-life painting in which the artist seeks illusionistically to re-create material reality. Harnett's mastery of trompe l'oeil challenged the new powers of the photographic age. His virtuosity was alternately acclaimed as the ultimate skill and derided as mere imitation. On the one hand, the content of still-life painting appealed to middle-class audiences, and the commodification of the art market facilitated the development of a middle-class consumer; thus, still-life painting can be credited with contributing to the democratization of art. On the other hand, the quotidian nature of the object, coupled with its mimetic execution, revealed the absence of those high moral qualities traditionally associated with great history painting. Such was Harnett's skill in hyperrealism that anecdotes abounded about the need to place guards beside his paintings to prevent anyone, for example, trying to take down the fiddle and bow, so illusionistically painted in *The Old Violin.* On another occasion, federal agents, disturbed by its remarkable illusionism, confiscated Harnett's painting of treasury bills in a New York saloon. Some indignantly went so far as to suggest that such imagery was actually intended to deceive the viewer

Harnett, however, described his work as one of "selective imitation," insisting that he did "not closely imitate nature." He believed the selection of objects was intended to convey states of mind. One such state was nostalgia, which in the late nineteenth century was understood as a way of either creating a sense of the past or holding on to values that were under threat. The objects he selected focused on a preindustrialized age; handmade objects were given added significance in the knowledge that they would soon be obsolete, amounting to what Robert Hughes called "a virtual fetishization of the mundane."

Harnett used predominantly male objects—drinking utensils, revolvers, pipes, and horseshoes—corresponding to his predominantly white, male, and middle-class audiences. Indeed, David Lubin argues that trompe l'oeil still lives were psychologically affirmative, and that these paintings "aesthetically demarcated gender and encouraged its stabilisation."

Stylistically, the visual effect is achieved by the use of a flat background pressing close to the picture plane, the shallowness of the depth heightening the illusion of three-dimensionality. The paint is applied in invisible strokes, worked to a hard-edged, highly polished finish. In contrast to the growing interest in sketchiness and spontaneity, which increased toward the end of the nineteenth century, the very perfection of the trompe l'oeil technique was almost enough to ensure its extinction.

Other Harnett paintings include *The Banker's Table, Golden Horseshoe, Old Refrain* and, most famously, *After the Hunt.*

Niamh O'Sullivan

References

Bolger, Doreen, et al., eds. *William M. Harnett.* New York: Amon Carter Museum, Metropolitan Museum of Art, and Harry N. Abrams, 1992.

Frankenstein, Alfred. *After the Hunt: William Harnett and Other American Still-life Painters, 1870–1900.* Rev. ed. Berkeley: University of California Press, 1969.

Lubin, David M. *Picturing a Nation: Art and Social Change in Nineteenth-Century America.* New Haven, CT: Yale University Press, 1994.

HARRIGAN, EDWARD (1844–1911) AND HART, TONY (1855–1891)

Harrigan and Hart were one of the most successful comic teams in the history of the American theater. Hart was a gifted actor, specializing in transvestite roles. Harrigan, one of the fathers of the American musical, wrote more than 80 sketches, 36 plays and musicals, and the lyrics to some 200 songs. Starting as a vaudeville duo, the two men developed a variety of comic ethnic types, including Germans, Italians, African Americans, and especially Irish characters. They placed the urban Irish immigrant on center stage of the late nineteenth-century popular American theater.

Born into an Irish family in Worcester, Massachusetts, Tony Hart (whose real name was Anthony Cannon) left home at an early age and found his way into show business. In 1871, at the age of 16, he teamed up with Edward Harrigan in Chicago. Hart's slight frame and light lyric tenor voice, combined with his acting talents, enabled him to play "wench" or "skirt" roles, as well as juvenile characters. His female impersonations were so successful that he is said to have once fooled the famous detective Allen Pinkerton.

Harrigan was third-generation Irish. His family migrated from Cork to Newfoundland and finally to New York City. He was born in the Corlear's Hook section on the Lower East Side. As a young man, he worked his way to San Francisco, following his father's trade as a ship's caulker. While there he began performing at the city's famous Bella Union variety theater in 1867. The satiric distance from which Harrigan would later view the New York Irish may have been influenced by his experience among the self-confident Irish of the Bay City, who had suffered none of the discrimination and hostility that characterized the Irish immigrant experience on the East Coast.

Working his way back East, Harrigan tried out several partners until he met Hart. The two had immediate successes with Harrigan's earlier material. However, they had a hit on their hands when they performed the sketch and song "The Mulligan Guards" at Pastor's Theater in New York City in 1873. The song became immensely popular. Unfortunately, Harrigan and British immigrant David Braham, who wrote the music, sold the rights to the publisher for only $50. It was a mistake they never made again. Braham, a skillful composer who set all of Harrigan's songs, soon became his musical director and eventually his father-in-law. Braham was in many ways the third partner in the Harrigan and Hart phenomenon.

Harrigan expanded the Mulligan Guard sketch, a satire of the Irish militia or "target companies" that proliferated around New York City. Finally, in 1879 he staged *The Mulligan Guard Ball,* the first of 11 musicals based on characters from the original Guard sketches. Set in the Five Points section of New York City, the series featured the comic and sometimes fractious rivalry among the district's Irish, German, and African-American residents. Following the lives of Irish immigrant Dan Mulligan, his wife Cordelia, and their friends and neighbors (played by Harrigan's repertory company), the musicals had many of the qualities of a modern situation comedy.

Harrigan's shows shared another characteristic with today's sitcoms: the placing of stereotypical characters within highly realistic settings. Contemporary critics commented on the striking realism of Harrigan's stage sets and the convincing behavior and appearance of the various urban types who peopled them. To ensure the authenticity of their wardrobe, Harrigan and his cast sometimes visited Castle Gardens, where they bought the clothes off the backs of arriving immigrants.

Other Harrigan musicals also featured the same ethnic mix that characterized the Mulligan Guard series. Harrigan was among the first playwrights to acknowledge the multiethnic character of America's rapidly growing cities, epitomized in the chorus of "McNally's Row of Flats'"(from *McSorley's Inflation,* 1883):

> It's Ireland and Italy, Jerusalem and Germany,
> O Chinamen and Nagers and a paradise for cats,
> All jumbled up together in snow and raging weather,
> They represent the tenants of McNally's Row of Flats.

Unfortunately, Harrigan's shows reflect the racism that was so characteristic of America in his day. With only a few exceptions, the African-American characters, played by white actors (including Harrigan and Hart) in blackface, were essentially products of the minstrel stage. However, this enabled Harrigan to allow his black characters to trade insults with the Irish on stage and to engage in dustups or melees, as Harrigan called them, a feature of most of the Mulligan Guard shows. Yet, Harrigan also depicted a remarkably free and easy relationship between the two races. In his plays they seem used to and familiar with each other, and if blacks were stereotyped, so too were the Germans and most of Harrigan's Irish characters.

At a time when many observers of urban America were becoming increasingly disturbed at the variety of races and nationalities pouring into the cities, Harrigan seemed to accept the emerging multiethnic America with uncommon optimism. When someone asked Harrigan if all the ethnic groups in New York really lived "sort of thick an' mixed like the innards of a mince pie," Harrigan assured the man that they were even thicker, and with "more spice in 'em" (Moody 109). When criticized for having so many immigrants and blacks in his plays, he responded: "Whoever votes the Republican or Democratic ticket in the United States must be an American, no matter what may be his mother tongue or color" (Kahn, Jr. 263–264).

However, it was the Irish who dominated most of Harrigan's plays and musicals. As one of his characters, an alderman says: "My district is the Tower of Babel, and the Irish flag floats from the top" (Kahn, Jr. 64). Although he satirized many aspects of Irish immigrant life, Harrigan also knew the New York Irish and had sympathy for their efforts to establish themselves amid the chaos and poverty of raw urban life. Many of his songs celebrated the more positive aspects of the Irish experience. Dan Mulligan's song "My Dad's Dinner Pail" (*Cordelia's Aspirations,* 1883) commemorated a working-class father who shared his lunch with his workmates. In "Babies on Our Block" (*The Mulligan Guard Ball,* 1879) the Irish fathers, in supporting their families, were not only "Quite easy with the shovel" but were also "handy with the pen." Although he made frequent use of the old Irish stereotypes, Harrigan could also depict, as he did in "Maggie Murphy's Home" (*Reilly and the 400,* 1890), the Sunday night dances in immigrant flats, without reference to either fighting or drinking.

Harrigan was also one of the first American writers to fully embrace urban life and to see the Irish as an integral part of the city. In "Going Home With Nelly After Five" from *The Mulligan Guard's Picnic* (1883), one of his Irish characters describes himself and his girlfriend as part of the great urban throng: "It's laboring men and working girls like bees out of a hive / Among the crowd I'm going home with Nelly after five."

Thanks to his company's annual tours, Harrigan's enormous popularity extended beyond New York City. Even the departure of Hart in 1886 did not impede his success. However, by the mid-1890s, New York had tired of Harrigan's multiethnic working-class comedies. By the time he died in 1911, Tin Pan Alley's Emerald Isles had replaced the crowded city as the preferred setting for "Irish" musicals and songs.

William H. A. Williams

See also: COHAN, George M.; McMANUS, George

References

Kahn, E. J., Jr. *The Merry Partners: The Age and Stage of Harrigan and Hart.* New York: Random House, 1955.

Moody, Richard. *Ned Harrigan: From Corlear's Hook to Herald Square.* Chicago: Nelson Hall, 1980.

Williams, William H. A. *'Twas Only an Irishman's Dream: The Image of the Irish and Ireland in American Popular Song Lyrics, 1800–1920.* Urbana: University of Illinois Press, 1996: 158–172.

HARRIS, RICHARD (1930–2002)

Richard Harris, along with Peter O'Toole, was part of a new generation of Irish actors to achieve international stardom in the 1960s. Of Welsh ancestry, he was born in Limerick on October 1, 1930, to Ivan Harris and Mildred Harris (née Harty) and was one of five children. Ivan Harris owned a well-known flour mill in Limerick, which he had inherited from his father. Although Richard mainly experienced a solidly middle class upbringing, the family mill was in constant financial difficulties in the 1920s and 1930s and would eventually close down in the 1950s.

Harris attended St. Philomena's junior school, which was run by the Jesuit order, and later enrolled in another Jesuit school, the Crescent Comprehensive. Although he did not excel in his academic studies (he was later diagnosed as dyslexic), he did stand out on the rugby pitch, and the sport would remain one of his great passions. He also became interested in acting and joined Limerick's Playhouse Theatre in 1947. Following a bout with tuberculosis in 1952, he resolved to pursue acting seriously and traveled to London to enroll in the London Academy of Music and Dramatic Arts; while there he met and married Elizabeth Rees Williams. During his time at the Academy he acted in plays and directed a 1956 production of Clifford Odets's *Winter Journey,* which received poor reviews.

Harris's big break was being spotted by Theatre Royal director Joan Littlewood, who cast him as Mickser in her 1956 production of Brendan Behan's *The Quare Fellow.* Signing him to her company, she cast him in a major role in *You Won't Always Be on Top,* an "angry young man" play written by Henry Chapman that received mixed reviews but gained publicity for both Littlewood and Harris when it was brought to court by the British censors. This performance was followed by a role in a Pirandello play, *Man, Beast and Virtue,* which won Harris more critical attention. In 1959 he made his screen debut in a television production of an Irish play called *The Irish Harp;* more significant was his appearance in an Associated British Picture, *Alive and Kicking,* which was made under contract to the film company.

In 1959 Harris returned to Ireland to take a role as an Irish Republican Army (IRA) gunrunner in a major American film, *Shake Hands with the Devil,* starring James Cagney. The film, while not a huge success, was important in the development of Harris's film career, and it attracted the attention of other American producers; soon after, he was cast in a supporting role in *The Wreck of the Mary Deare,* alongside two major Hollywood stars, Gary Cooper and Charlton Heston. The film received much publicity and was commercially successful.

Although Harris had certainly set his film career in motion, he also continued working in theater. He appeared in a number of Littlewood productions: a musical called *Fings Ain't Wot They Used T'Be;* a play, *The Dutch Courtesan;* and a minor role in Brendan Behan's *The Hostage,* staged by Littlewood in Paris. Returning to films in 1960, he took on another American-produced, IRA-themed film, *A Terrible Beauty,* shot in Dublin by Tay Garnett and starring Robert Mitchum.

Searching for challenging acting roles, Harris pursued the part of the Ginger Man in the play adapted from J. P. Donleavy's novel of the same name. Having scored a critical and commercial success during its

London run in 1960, it was transferred to Dublin's Gaiety Theatre, where it attracted a storm of criticism for its perceived sexual and religious profanity. The Dublin run was subsequently cut short, much to Harris's disappointment (and glee at having offended the moral majority). Returning to London, and still under contract to Associated British Pictures, he acted alongside Richard Burton and Laurence Harvey in *The Long and the Short and the Tall,* directed by Leslie Norman in 1960. Yet, despite having appeared in a range of American and British films, Harris was still not a widely recognized actor. This would change with his appearance in the troubled production of *Mutiny on the Bounty,* starring Marlon Brando and Trevor Howard and shot in Tahiti in 1961. Brando clashed with all his costars, including Harris, as well as his director, Carol Reed. Reed was replaced by Hollywood veteran Lewis Milestone, and the film was eventually released to a mixed critical reaction. Back in Britain, Harris was approached by film writer and documentary director Lindsay Anderson, who was preparing his first feature film, *This Sporting Life* (1963). The subject and the director appealed to Harris, and he accepted the lead role. The part of Frank Machin, the young rugby-playing protagonist, required weeks of intensive physical training, with the result that Harris delivered a performance that became the defining one of his career. Shortly after the film was released to critical acclaim he worked again with Anderson on a stage production of Gogol's *Diary of a Madman* at the Royal Court in London. This was to be his last stage role for 18 years.

Throughout the 1960s Harris divided his time among Ireland, Britain, and the United States, working with major Hollywood directors such as Sam Peckinpah (*Major Dundee* in 1965) and John Huston (*The Bible: In the Beginning* in 1965), as well as with emerging European auteurs such as Michelangelo Antonioni (*Deserto Rosso* in 1964). An important film was *Camelot,* in which he played King Arthur, a role that had already won Richard Burton considerable success on stage. *Camelot* was a musical, and Harris developed a lucrative side career as singer, releasing a number of successful albums between 1968 and 1974.

Soon after the release of *Camelot* in 1967, Harris accepted a role in *The Molly Maguires* (1968). Based on an Irish-themed script by the blacklisted Hollywood writer Walter Bernstein and directed by acclaimed director Martin Ritt, it was set in a mining community in nineteenth-century Pennsylvania and was notable for its sympathetic portrayal of the labor struggle. Harris was disappointed with the poor performance of the film at the box office, although he remained proud of the film and of his part.

Harris's next choice surprised many who regarded him as a republican sympathizer. He took on the title role in Ken Hughes's *Cromwell* (1970), the story of the seventeenth-century soldier and brutal oppressor of Catholic Ireland. Harris explained that he was drawn to the role because of his interest in Ireland's history and because he felt paradoxically drawn to the character of Cromwell, whom he regarded as a complex, tormented man.

In 1970 he traveled to Israel to shoot *Bloomfield.* The shoot was a difficult one, and the original director, Uri Zohar, was fired and replaced by Harris himself. This would prove to be Harris's first and only venture into directing and when the film was released it was dismissed by many critics as an ego trip for its director and star. His output was prolific in the 1960s and 1970s and, although his choices were not always governed by artistic ambition, he did star in a number of hit films such as *Caprice* (1967), *The Cassandra Crossing* (1976), and *A Man Called Horse* (released in 1969, it spawned two sequels: *Return of a Man Called Horse* in 1976 and *Triumphs of a Man Called Horse* in 1982).

By the mid-1970s, Harris was an international star with a reputation for hard drinking and a volatile temper, if not for outstanding films. He battled personal problems that included tax debts, drug and alcohol abuse, and the breakdown of his marriages to Elizabeth and his second wife, Ann Turkel. After a decade of starring in mostly forgettable films, Harris returned to Camelot, this time in a stage production that traveled throughout the United States, Australia, and London in 1981–1982. As with the 1967 film, Harris took over the King Arthur role from Richard Burton, who had been forced to bow out because of ill health. Harris's return to the stage after an absence of nearly two decades was almost his last performance: after years of alcohol and drug abuse his health was deteriorating rapidly, and he was warned by doctors that his body could not withstand much more ill treatment. Soon after, he resolved to stop drinking, and for the last two decades of his life he remained a moderate drinker.

The 1980s saw Harris taking on fewer roles: there were some appearances on television and in moderately budgeted films, but to many it appeared that Harris was washed up as an actor. This perception changed, and Harris's career emerged from the doldrums, when he met Irish producer Noel Pearson in 1989. Pearson had just achieved a major hit with *My Left Foot,* his film of the life of Irish writer Christy Brown, which was directed by Jim Sheridan. Having scored five Academy Award nominations for *My Left Foot,* the winning team of Pearson and Sheridan was set for their next project: a film version of John B. Keane's complex play of Irish identity and the land, *The Field.* Pearson had already cast veteran Irish stage and screen actor Ray McAnally in the central role of Bull McCabe, and he offered Harris a supporting role as a priest. However, as the film was going into production McAnally died suddenly and Harris sought to take over his part. Despite the initial reluctance of the film's financiers, Granada television, Harris succeeded in winning the role, resulting in a performance that was rated as a career high point. For Harris, winning the role of Bull McCabe was his last chance to prove that he was a great actor, that he had fulfilled the promise so evident in *This Sporting Life.* It proved to be a role that reconnected him to his country, to its troubled and complex history, and it caused him to reassess his own attitudes to work, roots, and family. In an interview during the making of the film, he observed that "*This Sporting Life* was my *Hamlet. The Field* will be my *Lear.*" And indeed the role of Bull McCabe had many parallels with the story of Shakespeare's doomed king: both were abrasive and ruthless characters whose own flaws led to their pathetic downfall. Tellingly, many of Harris's friends and colleagues believed it was a self-revelatory performance, a view tacitly endorsed by Harris himself. Harris's Bull McCabe was heralded as a return to form and garnered him Academy Award and BAFTA (British Academy of Film and Television Arts) nominations. (Much to his disappointment, he won neither.)

Harris's performance also rekindled the interest of leading producers and directors and in the 10 years that followed, he acted in 22 films and made a triumphant return to the stage in a production of Luigi Pirandello's *Henry IV* in 1990. Many of the films he made in the last decade of his life were high-profile and traded on the public's perception of him as an aging hell-raiser and raconteur. He appeared as a flamboyant rogue, English Bob, in Clint Eastwood's acclaimed western, *Unforgiven* (1992), and as a Sinn Féin leader in Philip Noyce's film of a Tom Clancy novel, *Patriot Games* (1992). He also appeared in several Irish films, including *Trojan Eddie* (1996) and *This Is the Sea* (1998).

In 2001 Harris had the opportunity to play another Lear-like role, in Dan Boyd's independent film, *My Kingdom,* which recast Shakespeare's king as a dying criminal boss in Liverpool. Although the film did not receive a wide release, it won critical praise, particularly for Harris's performance.

The last two years of Harris's life brought him to an even wider, younger audience. He appeared in a major role in Ridley Scott's 2000 blockbuster, *Gladiator,* and as Professor Dumbledore in two Harry Potter films, *Harry Potter and the Sorcerer's Stone* (2001) and *Harry Potter and the Chamber of Secrets* (2002). Soon after he completed the shoot on *Harry Potter and the Chamber of Secrets,* he was diagnosed with Hodgkin's disease. Although he went through a course of chemotherapy, the prognosis was terminal. He died in London on October 25, 2002. He was survived by his two ex-wives, Elizabeth and Ann, and his three children with Elizabeth, Damian (b. 1958), Jared (b. 1961), and Jamie (b. 1963).

Gwenda Young

References

Callan, Michael Feeney. *Richard Harris: Sex, Death & the Movies.* London: Robson Books, 2003.

Caughie, John, and Kevin Rockett. *The Companion to British and Irish Cinema.* London: British Film Institute, 1996.

Katz, Ephraim. *The Film Encyclopedia.* New York: Perigee Books, 1979.

HARRISON, FRANK LLEWELLYN (1905–1987)

Born in Dublin on September 29, 1905, Frank Harrison was one of the most important Irish musicologists of the twentieth century. He taught at Kingston (Canada); Yale, Stanford, and Princeton (the United States), Oxford (United Kingdom), and Amsterdam and Utrecht (the Netherlands). Harrison's career began as a musician, singing in the choir of Saint Patrick's Cathedral, Dublin, studying at the Royal Irish Academy of Music and at Trinity College Dublin (Bachelor of Music, 1926; Doctor of Music, 1929). He won prizes for his organ playing at the Feis Ceoil (festival of music) and became the organist at Kilkenny before emigrating to Nova Scotia in 1930. He also contemplated a career as a composer, and studied with Marcel Dupré (1933) and later with Paul Hindemith at Yale (1945–1946).

Harrison was the first professor of music at Queen's University, Kingston, Ontario (1935–1945). With an interruption to study with Hindemith at Yale, he continued to teach at Colgate University at Hamilton, New York (1946–1947), and at Washington University, St. Louis (1947–1952), a position he left early for political differences of opinion in 1950. Following this, he took another doctorate in musicology at Oxford (1951), where he became senior lecturer in

1956. It was here that he developed his specialization in medieval music, which he continued while teaching at Amsterdam (1970–1980) and Utrecht (1976–1980).

Harrison's main research interests lay in the medieval music of the British Isles and continental Europe as well as in ethnomusicology. His *Music in Medieval Britain* (1958) has been a standard reference work for many years, while his anthology *Time, Place and Music* (1973) represents a culmination of his ethnomusicological achievements. In all his published books and essays he achieves a remarkable combination of positivistic research and anthropological and sociological interpretations. Later in life he increasingly worked on Irish music, contributing important research on music in the age of Swift (published in *Eighteenth-Century Ireland,* 1 [1986]) and on traditional music in *Irish Traditional Music—Fossil or Resource?* (1988). In 2004, the Society for Musicology in Ireland began to award an annual Harrison Medal in the memory of this first internationally renowned Irish musicologist.

Axel Klein

References

Chadd, David F. L. "Francis Llewellyn Harrison, 1905–1987." *Proceedings of the British Academy* 75 (1989): 361–380.

Klein, Axel. *Die Musik Irlands im 20. Jahrhundert.* Hildesheim, Germany: Georg Olms, 1996.

White, Harry. "Frank Llewellyn Harrison and the Development of Postwar Musicological Thought." *Hermathena* 146 (1989): 39–47.

HAYES, CATHERINE (1818–1861)

Ireland's first internationally renowned soprano, Catherine Hayes was born on October 25, 1818, in Limerick. Her musical talents were recognized at an early age by the bishop of Limerick, who sponsored her. She initially studied singing in Dublin, then in 1842 she went to Paris to study with famed teacher Manuel Garcia, who had trained the soprano Jenny Lind. After two years with Garcia and at his direction she moved to Milan for further study and coaching with Felice Ronconi. She made a successful debut at the Italian Opera in Marseille in May 1845 in Bellini's *I Puritani.* In November that year she appeared at La Scala in Milan, in the title role in Donizetti's *Linda di Chamounix.* Her career immediately blossomed. She was invited to La Fenice opera in Venice and later to the opera in Vienna where she sang opposite leading singers of the day. By now she had the most famous *Lucia di Lammermoor* of the period. In 1846, Giuseppe Verdi (1813–1901) became interested in Hayes for one of his new operas.

Hayes was awarded a diploma from the Academy of St. Cecilia in Rome in 1848. Toward the end of that year, she accepted a contract offered by the Italian representative of the Royal Italian Opera at Covent Garden in London. Her London debut took place in April 1849. The critics praised her performances highly. Hayes returned to Ireland in November 1849 to great acclaim as she was the first Irish woman to achieve such international fame. She gave performances in Dublin, Limerick, Cork, and Waterford before returning to London for more operatic activity and concerts tours in the provinces over the next twelve months. Her mother traveled with her everywhere throughout her career.

In September 1851, Hayes arrived in New York, where Jenny Lind had been creating sensational headlines under the sponsorship of showman P. T. Barnum. Hayes initially gave a series of concerts at Tripler Hall, on Broadway and Mercer Street. She went on tour to more than 40 cities, to places such as Hartford, Connecticut; Albany and Syracuse, New York; Toronto; Philadelphia; and Boston, (where Daniel Webster attended her concerts). President Millard Fillmore attended her Washington, D.C., concert with his family. Wherever she went she was acclaimed. She traveled on to Richmond, Virginia; Savannah, Georgia; Augusta, Georgia; and Mobile, Alabama, eventually arriving in New Orleans where she gave an extended series of concerts. Two of the sold-out concerts were performed at the urging of Father James Mullon, an Irish priest who had the responsibility for raising funds to complete the construction of Saint Patrick's Church. The church, which still stands today, is now a U.S. historic landmark and is known as Saint Patrick's Cathedral. Hayes went up the Mississippi River giving concerts on river boats and in river towns. She eventually arrived in St. Louis, where she gave more concerts before traveling on to Chicago, Detroit, and the Great Lakes towns, eventually returning to New York. In New York she gave a benefit concert for Father Theobald Mathew (1790–1856), who was on a fund-raising trip in America. P. T. Barnum invited Hayes's mother to his home and to his daughter's wedding. Through Barnum Hayes met her future husband, William Avery Bushnell, a former Jenny Lind manager. Her plans, sponsored by Barnum, next took her to San Francisco via Panama. In San Francisco she performed in costumed concert versions of various Donizetti and Rossini operas, sometimes traveling to the goldfields to sing for the miners and leading politicians of the day. She amassed a great fortune, and in July 1854, along with her mother and Bushnell, she left for Australia. In Sydney her arrival was greeted by an enormous turnout of leading politicians, businessmen, and others. She performed in Sydney, Melbourne, Hobart, and the Bendigo goldfields to sold-out houses.

After two years in Australia and side trips to Calcutta, Java, and Singapore Hayes returned to London in August 1856. Two years later her husband Bushnell died of consumption. In August 1861, Hayes suffered a stroke in a friend's home in Sydenham, just outside London, where she died on August 11. Her signature song throughout her career was "Kathleen Mavourneen." In pursuit of her career she traveled around the globe, perhaps being the first prima donna to do so.

Basil Walsh

See also: EMIGRATION; MATHEW, Fr. Theobald

References

Sadie, Stanley, ed. *The New Grove Dictionary of Opera.* London, Macmillan Press: 1992.

Walsh, Basil. *Catherine Hayes: The Hibernian Prima Donna.* Dublin: Irish Academic Press, 2000.

HAYES, HELEN (BROWN) (1900–1993)

The "First Lady of American Theater" was born on October 10, 1900, in Washington, D.C. Her mother was Catherine Estelle Hayes, whose father, Patrick Hayes, was the nephew of the Irish singer Catherine Hayes, "The Swan of Erin." Helen Hayes's father, Francis Brown, worked as a salesman for a meat producer. Failing in her own attempts to succeed as an actress, Hayes's mother encouraged her daughter to try out for child roles in regional theater. At the age of nine Helen made her professional debut in a New York production of *Old Dutch* produced by Lew Fields. More stage roles followed, and in 1910 she made her film debut in a two-reeler for Vitagraph called *Jean and the Calico Doll.*

Despite her early foray into cinema, Hayes stayed mainly in theater for the next two decades, initially building up a reputation as a child actress, before maturing into ingenue and flapper roles in the 1920s. Her theater successes in the 1920s included *Pollyanna* (1917–1918), *Clarence* (1919) with Alfred Lunt, *Babs* (1920), and a 1928 production of George Bernard Shaw's *Caesar and Cleopatra.* In 1928 she met and married Charles MacArthur, a journalist, wit, and noted playwright (*The Front Page,* with Ben Hecht). In 1930 both Hayes and MacArthur signed contracts with major Hollywood studios and moved to California; MacArthur wrote the script for Hayes's debut in sound films, *The Sin of Madelon Claudet,* a maternal melodrama that won her a Best Actress Oscar in 1932. She followed it with roles in a number of prestigious productions, such as John Ford's film of Sinclair Lewis's *Arrowsmith,* Clarence Brown's adaptation of Antoine de Saint-Exupéry's *Night Flight,* and Frank Borzage's film of Hemingway's *A Farewell to Arms* (1932). These films, while worthy, failed to show off her talents as an actress and, more importantly, failed to appeal to movie audiences. Hayes herself admitted that films were not her best medium, and in 1934 she announced that she was "leaving the screen because I don't think I am very good in the pictures and I have a beautiful dream that I am elegant on the stage."

Hayes's elegance on stage was confirmed with her highly acclaimed performance as Queen Victoria in the long-running Broadway show *Victoria Regina* (1935–1939). At the peak of her career in the 1930s and 1940s she tackled a diversity of roles, from Shakespeare to Tennessee Williams. In 1949 Hayes and MacArthur suffered the loss of their only daughter, Mary, to polio; henceforth, Hayes would be actively involved in fund-raising for a number of charities. In 1952 she returned to films with an appearance in the anticommunist film *My Son John.* After the death of MacArthur in 1956, she occasionally appeared in films and television, earning a second Academy Award for her role in *Airport* in 1971. However, her first love remained theater, and the respect and admiration she inspired in theater circles was underscored in 1955 when a New York playhouse was renamed in her honor.

Hayes's last great theater triumph was in a 1972 production of Eugene O'Neill's *Long Day's Journey into Night.* She published several volumes of autobiography, including *On Reflection* (1968) and *My Life in Three Acts* (1990). She died on March 17, 1993, at her home in Nyack, New York, and is survived by her adopted son, James MacArthur.

Gwenda Young

See also: FORD, John; O'NEILL, Eugene

References

Hayes, Helen. *On Reflection: An Autobiography.* New York: Evans Press, 1968.

Moore, Stephen, and Donn Murphy. *Helen Hayes: A Bio-Bibliography.* Westport, CT: Greenwood Press, 1995

HAYES, ARCHBISHOP PATRICK JOSEPH (1867–1938)

Patrick Hayes was born in New York City on the site of Saint Andrew's Church rectory in Manhattan. His parents, Daniel and

Portrait of Patrick Joseph Hayes, Archbishop of New York, 1931. (Library of Congress)

Mary (Gleason) Hayes, were both Irish immigrants from Killarney, Co. Kerry. When he was five years old his mother died, and his mother's sister and her husband raised him. He attended Transfiguration School, the De La Salle Institute, and Manhattan College in New York City. In 1888 he entered St. Joseph's Provincial Seminary in Troy, New York. He was ordained on September 8, 1892, by Archbishop Michael A. Corrigan. He then attended the Catholic University of America in Washington, D.C. Hayes was appointed curate to St. Gabriel's parish on East 37th Street in New York City, where he became the secretary to the pastor, John Murphy Farley. When Farley was named archbishop of New York in 1902, he appointed Hayes as chancellor of the archdiocese and president of Cathedral College in 1903. Hayes remained in these positions until October 28, 1914, when Cardinal Farley consecrated him titular bishop of Tagaste. He served as pastor of St. Stephen's parish on East 29th Street in New York City from 1915 until America's entry into World War I in 1917. The war required a rapid growth in the number of army chaplains ministering to American troops. Because of this situation, Pope Benedict XV created a new American military ordinariate and appointed Hayes as its first head on November 24, 1917. Within a year the number of chaplains in the U.S. Army had increased from 25 to nearly 900. Although Hayes did not visit the Western Front in Europe, he toured military camps in America during this time. He was one of the four signatories of the Program of Social Reconstruction in 1919 that was issued by the National Catholic War Council. Later, he strongly supported its successor, the National Catholic Welfare Conference.

On March 10, 1919, Hayes succeeded Cardinal Farley as the fifth archbishop of New York. Five years later, on March 24, 1924, he was made a cardinal. The most significant legacy of his administration was the founding in 1920 of Catholic Charities, an organization set up to unify and strengthen Catholic charitable works. Because of this he was often referred to as the "Cardinal of Charities." Although he supported the temperance movement he opposed the child labor amendment on the grounds that it infringed states' rights. Apart from these issues, his administration was marked by a shunning of controversial issues and a limited involvement in public affairs. An exception was in 1935 when he preached against Margaret Sanger's proposal that poor people be urged to use birth control. One of his principal legacies was the expansion of the archdiocese; it had grown by sixty new parishes by the end of 1929.

Although Hayes was friendly with the Irish-American politician Alfred E. Smith, he avoided commenting directly on politics. He celebrated a Memorial Mass for the Lord Mayor of Cork, Terence MacSwiney who died on hunger strike in Brixton Prison in London in 1920. He donated $5,000 to the Catholic Charities fund, but he maintained that political violence in Ireland would only weaken the cause in America. He attended the International Eucharistic Congress, which was held in Dublin in 1932. However, the day after the congress closed, at the home of his host, Frederick A. Sterling, he suffered a heart attack. Over the next six years until his death on September 4, 1938, he was to be stricken by his weakened health and lingering illness. In spite of his illness, he retained his position as military ordinary until his death and he attended the National Eucharistic Congress at Cleveland, Ohio, in 1935 as the personal representative of Pope Pius XI. He also served as president of the Catholic Near East Welfare Association. He was succeeded as archbishop of New York and military ordinary by Cardinal Spellman. Since the time of Cardinal Hayes, the archbishop of New York has always held the position of military ordinary. He is buried in the crypt under the altar at Saint Patrick's Cathedral in New York City.

David Doyle

References

Brown, Mary Joseph. "Cardinal Hayes." In *The Encyclopedia of the Irish in America,* edited by Michael Glazier. Notre Dame, IN: University of Notre Dame Press, 1999.

Kelly, J. B. *Cardinal Hayes: One of Ourselves.* New York: Farrar and Rinehart, 1940.

Walsh, James J. *Our American Cardinals.* New York: D. Appleton and Company, 1926.

HEALY, MICHAEL MORRIS (1796–1850)

Born in Ireland, Michael Healy emigrated from Co. Roscommon, arriving in New York in 1815. He settled in Jones County, Georgia, near the city of Macon. In 1818 he took the oath of allegiance to his adopted country at the courthouse in Jones County.

Healy participated in the lotteries that were redistributing land that had been seized from the Cherokees, the Creeks, and other Native American tribes. In the lotteries of 1823 and 1832 he won land just across the Ocmulgee River from the town of Macon. He prospered as a cotton farmer and a landowner, eventually owning 1,500 acres of land. At a time when the average number of slaves was only 14, Healy owned 49 slaves. The value of these was $34,000, roughly equivalent to half a million dollars today. In 1829 he took Mary Eliza Smith, a 16-year-old mulatto slave girl from Georgia, as his common-law wife. She had been a domestic slave on the plantation of cotton magnate Sam Griswold until Healy purchased her. Although it was common for slave owners to have sexual relations with their female slaves, neither Healy nor Smith ever married anyone else, and they lived together until their deaths within a few months of each other in 1850. Although they did not formally marry, as such a union would have been impossible in Georgia at that time, they considered each other man and wife in all but name. Consequently, the relationship went directly against the strong attitudes held by the antebellum South regarding the idea of interracial marriage.

Together they had 10 children, nine of whom survived until adulthood. Because the children were of mixed race and were considered slaves, they were denied the opportunity to be educated in the South. Consequently, Healy sent each of the boys to the North to receive their education. At first they were educated by the Quakers in Long Island, New York, and then in Burlington, New Jersey. Later, in 1844, Healy had a chance meeting on a steamboat with the Roman Catholic bishop of Boston, John Bernard Fitzpatrick. Fitzpatrick encouraged Healy to send his sons to the College of the Holy Cross in Worcester, Massachusetts, where the younger boys could receive their primary education and the older ones could finish their secondary education and then proceed to college. While attending the school, the boys were baptized as Catholics. In spite of the restrictions placed on children of interracial marriages, many of Healy's nine children found success in their chosen fields, and a number opted to become Catholic priests or nuns. Healy's eldest son, James Augustine Healy (1830–1900), was perhaps the best known. He became a priest in Boston and eventually rose to become the second bishop of the diocese of Portland from 1875 to 1900. Hugh Clark Healy (1832–1853) became involved in the hardware business in New York City and was later killed in a boating accident. Patrick Francis Healy (1834–1910) became a Jesuit and was the first African American to hold a doctorate. He became the president of Georgetown University in Washington, D.C., revitalizing and restructuring the campus and the student curriculum to such an extent that he is called the second founder of the university. Alexander Sherwood Healy (1836–1875) became the rector of the Catholic Cathedral of the Holy Cross in Boston. Martha Ann Healy (1838–1920) became a housewife in Boston, and Michael Augustine Healy (1839–1904) was a captain in the U.S. Revenue Cutter Service. Two sisters became nuns in Montreal, Amanda Josephine Healy (1845–1879) in the Religious Hospitallers of Saint Joseph and Eliza Dunamore Healy (1846–1919) in the Congregation de Notre Dame. The youngest surviving child, Eugene (1849–1914) became a salesman.

David Doyle

References

Foley, Albert S. *Bishop Healy: Beloved Outcaste.* New York: Arno Press, 1969.

O'Toole, James M. "Michael Morris Healy." In *The Encyclopedia of the Irish in America,* edited by Michael Glazier. Notre Dame, IN: University of Notre Dame, 1999.

O'Toole, James M. *Passing for White: Race, Religion and the Healy Family, 1820–1920.* Amherst: University of Massachusetts Press, 2002.

HEANEY, SEAMUS (1939–)

The eldest of nine children, Seamus Heaney was born on April 13, 1939, to Patrick and Margaret Kathleen (née McCann) Heaney. The 50-acre family farm, Mossbawn—located near Castledawson, County Derry—provides the backdrop for several of Heaney's early poems. From 1945 until 1951, Heaney attended the local Anahorish School, a "mixed" elementary school that enrolled both Catholic and Protestant students. At the age of 12, Heaney won a scholarship to St. Columb's College, a Catholic boarding school in Derry. After attending St. Columb's from 1951 to 1957, Heaney went on to study at Queen's University, Belfast. His first poems were published in the university's literary magazine in 1959. Heaney graduated from Queen's in 1961 with a first-class degree in

English Language and Literature, and he earned a Teacher's Training Diploma the following year from St. Joseph's College of Education in Belfast.

During his first year of teaching Heaney was introduced to the poetry of Patrick Kavanagh, an encounter that would significantly influence the direction of Heaney's early writing. Following Kavanagh's example, Heaney chose as his subject matter his own quotidian experiences growing up in the rural north of Ireland. In 1963, while teaching English at St. Joseph's College, Heaney joined the "Belfast Group," a poetry workshop established that year by Philip Hobsbaum. The group was part of a larger effort among Northern Irish intellectuals to preserve and rehabilitate Ulster's cultural traditions. In the summer of 1965 Heaney married Marie Devlin, a native of Co. Tyrone and a graduate of St. Mary's College of Education in Belfast. The following year Heaney joined the faculty at Queen's University, published his first collection of poems, *Death of a Naturalist,* and took over Hobsbaum's role as leader of the Belfast Group. His wife also gave birth to the first of their three children.

Heaney's first two volumes of poetry, *Death of a Naturalist* (1966) and *Door into the Dark* (1969), are largely autobiographical and reveal a great deal about the importance of place and cultural traditions with which the poet at once identifies and feels estranged. With the renewal of the conflict in Northern Ireland, and especially after the escalation of violence surrounding Bloody Sunday (January 30, 1972), Heaney felt called upon to confront the contemporary political situation both in his poetry and in several collections of prose writing. The essays in *The Government of the Tongue* (1988) and *The Redress of Poetry* (1995), in particular, address the question of the poet's responsibility to respond to immediate political and social concerns. It was a question that exercised Heaney for much of his career, as he found himself thrust into the role of a public commentator on affairs in Northern Ireland. Having grown up a Catholic in the Protestant-dominated North, Heaney was well positioned to observe his society's divisions along religious and political lines. The intensification of the crisis in Northern Ireland is reflected in much of Heaney's poetry from the 1970s and early 1980s, most notably among the poems in *Wintering Out* (1972), *North* (1975), *Field Work* (1979), and *Station Island* (1984).

During the academic year 1970–1971 Heaney taught as a guest lecturer at the University of California at Berkeley. In July 1972, he resigned his lectureship at Queen's University and moved with his family to a cottage in Glanmore, Co. Wicklow, where he worked full time as a freelance writer. Heaney accepted a faculty position at Carysfort Teaching Training College in Dublin in 1975 and moved his family to Sandymount shortly thereafter. It was at this point in his career, while hosting a program called *Imprint* for Radio Eireann, that Heaney struck up a friendship with American poet Robert Lowell.

In 1979 Heaney spent a semester at Harvard, beginning what would become a long-term relationship with the American institution. After publishing *Field Work* in 1979 and *Preoccupations,* his first collection of essays, in 1980, Heaney left Carysfort in 1981 to accept a post as a visiting professor at Harvard. He divided his time between the United States and Ireland for the next five years, teaching workshops in creative writing and courses in British and Irish modern poetry at Harvard for one semester of each year. In the meantime Heaney coedited *The Rattle Bag: An Anthology of Poetry* (1982) with Ted Hughes and cofounded Field Day Publishing—an outgrowth of Field Day Theatre—in 1983 with playwright Brian Friel and others. During his tenure at Harvard Heaney also continued to publish his own prose and poetry, including *An Open Letter* (1983) and *The Haw Lantern* (1987). He also gained recognition as a translator with *Sweeney Astray* (1984), his version of a medieval Irish text.

After five years at Harvard, Heaney became a professor of poetry at Oxford University. He published his second collection of essays, *The Government of the Tongue,* in 1988 and *Seeing Things* in 1991. The position at Oxford, also a five-year post, required Heaney to deliver three public lectures each year. The Oxford lectures were published in 1995 under the title *The Redress of Poetry.* In that same year Heaney was awarded the Nobel Prize for Literature.

Heaney has remained prolific in the years since; recent publications include *The Spirit Level* (1996), *Opened Ground* (1998), *Beowulf* (2000, translation), *Electric Light* (2001), and *District and Circle* (2006). He has also maintained ties with Harvard as the Ralph Waldo Emerson poet-in-residence. Heaney has been the recipient of honorary degrees from numerous American universities and is a foreign member of the American Academy of Arts and Letters.

Kathleen Ruppert

References

Collins, Floyd. *Seamus Heaney: The Crisis of Identity.* Newark, DE: University of Delaware Press, 2003.

Foster, Thomas C. *Seamus Heaney.* Boston: Twayne Publishers, 1989.

Murphy, Andrew. *Seamus Heaney.* Plymouth, UK: Northcote House Publishers, 1996.

Vendler, Helen. *Seamus Heaney.* Cambridge, MA: Harvard University Press, 1998.

HEFFERNAN, MICHAEL (1942–)

Born and raised in a working-class area of Detroit, Michael Heffernan is the son of parents of Irish descent. As a child he attended Catholic schools in Detroit. He attended the University of Detroit for his undergraduate degree before proceeding to graduate school at the University of Massachusetts, where he received his MA and his doctorate. Heffernan has combined his work as a poet with teaching at various universities. He has taught at Oakland University in Rochester, Michigan, as well as Pittsburgh State University. He is currently professor of English at the University of Arkansas at Fayatteville, and he teaches creative writing there. He codirects the International Writers' Course at the National University of Ireland, Galway. He helped to establish this course in 1990 and since then has taught there on three occasions. Heffernan has received three fellowships from the National Endowment for the Arts. His verse has appeared in such publications as the *American Poetry Review, Boulevard, Crazyhorse, Gettysburg Review, Iowa Review, Poetry, Kenyon Review, Southern Review,* and *Shenandoah.* He has also published some short stories. Heffernan currently lives in Elkin, Arkansas.

Heffernan's first poetry collection, *The Cry of Oliver Hardy,* was published in 1979. Five years later *To The Wreakers of Havoc* was published. This was followed in 1989 by *The Man at Home. Love's Answer,* which was published in 1993, was the winner of that year's Iowa Poetry Prize. The following year, Heffernan published *The Back Road to Arcadia.* This was his first collection of poetry to be published by Salmon Press, an independent Irish publishing house based in Co. Clare and founded by an American, Jessie Lendennie. His most recent collection of poetry, *The Night Breeze off the Ocean,* was also published by Salmon Press in 2005.

Heffernan traces his decision to become a poet to the time when, aged 13, he discovered his mother's copy of Walt Whitman's *Leaves of Grass.* He also credits his parents and the love of language that existed in their household as being a major influence on his decision to become a poet and on all of his subsequent work.

Citing W. B. Yeats and Wallace Stevens as the major influences on his work, he has drawn upon both poets in his own work. As if to illustrate this, one of his poems "Land of Heart's Desire" is named after Yeats's play of the same name. In his more recent work, with his decision to publish his poetry with an Irish publisher and his involvement with the National University of Ireland, Galway, Ireland as a place has become much more evident in his work. This presence has primarily taken the form of an examination of Irish rural life and the people who populate it.

David Doyle

References

Heffernan, Michael. *Another Part of the Island.* Cliffs of Moher, Clare, Ireland: Salmon Publications, 1999.

Wall, Eamonn. *The Encyclopedia of the Irish in America,* edited by Michael Glazier. Notre Dame, IN: University of Notre Dame, 1999.

HENRY, JOHN (1746–1794)

John Henry's early years are not well documented. He was born in Dublin Ireland, but little is known about his parents, upbringing, or earliest professional acting. He performed in Dublin and London, at Drury Lane, and possibly at Belfast. In 1762 Henry departed Ireland, accompanying the performer Charles Storer and his family to Jamaica, where some time before 1767 Henry married Storer's daughter, Helen. In 1767 Henry set out for the mainland colonies intending to join the American Company of Comedians of David Douglass. Disaster struck when their ship, the *Dolphin,* caught fire, killing Henry's wife and their two children. In October 1767 Henry performed for Douglass's American Company in Philadelphia at the recently constructed Southwark Theatre (also known as the South Street Theatre) and then at the new John Street Theatre in New York, the first permanent theater in that city. He also appears to have become intimate with another of Storer's daughters, Ann, who bore Henry's third child. Henry later married the youngest Storer sister, Maria.

Henry's career blossmed in America, in part because his acting talents were complemented by his good looks, acrobatic abilities, and musical talents. His most important acting performances included a number of lead roles from Shakespeare (he played both Othello and Shylock), but also others from plays by Richard Brinsley, George Farquhar, and Thomas Otway. Richard Brinsley Sheridan's *The School of Scandal* (1777) provided Henry with the role of Sir Peter Teazle. The disruptions of the War for American Independence (1776–1783) saw Henry return to Jamaica and then sail to London, in 1777, where he performed at Drury Lane. He returned to

America in 1782, and by 1785 he and Lewis Hallam, Jr. (Douglass's stepson) were comanaging the Old American Company. The company did well, mostly performing tried-and-true classics and expanding its geographical base beyond the centers of New York and Philadelphia. For instance, a theater was opened in Baltimore, Maryland, and the company performed as far south as Richmond, Virginia. Henry's ostentatious lifestyle (his private coach, with driver and coat of arms, was noted by contemporaries) was frequently the source of gossip during these years, as was his unconventional relationship with the Storer sisters.

Henry's activities and interests progressed naturally from performing to managing, promoting, and writing. He wrote *School for Soldiers; or, the Deserters,* which had been performed in Jamaica before it was printed in 1783, and which was also performed in New York, until at least 1788. Other plays written by Henry include *The American Soldier, a Comedy, The Convention; or, the Columbian Father,* and *True Blue; or, the Sailor's Festival: A Farce.* Henry was involved with reprintings of Sheridan's *School of Scandal,* by Hugh Gaine (New York, 1786) and Prichard & Hall (Philadelphia, 1789). He also helped promote American playwrights, such as Royall Tyler whose *The Contrast,* which was modeled on Sheridan's *School of Scandal,* the Old American Company produced in 1787, celebrating Tyler as "A citizen of the United States." In 1790 Henry aimed to have Boston repeal its anti-theatrical legislation. In the early 1790s Henry also traveled to England with the aim of encouraging talented actors to return with him to America. That task was not always an easy one, and Henry's relationships with some of the rising stars he promoted were not always congenial. His conflicts over roles with the British-born actor John Hodgkinson, whom Henry had encouraged to come to America, for instance, were well known. Those tensions played a part in Henry's decision to quit the company in 1794, selling out to Hallam for about $10,000. He died in 1794, on board a ship sailing for Rhode Island.

Mark G. Spencer

References

Brown, Jared. "John Henry." In *American National Biography,* edited by John A. Garraty and Mark C. Carnes. New York: Oxford University Press, 1999.

Dunlap, William. *A History of the American Theatre.* 2 vols. New York, 1832.

Hornblow, Arthur. *A History of the Theatre in America from its Beginnings to the Present Time,* 1919.

Hughes, Glenn. *A History of the American Theatre, 1700–1950.* New York: S. French, 1951.

Nathans, Heather S. *Early American Theatre from the Revoution to Thomas Jefferson: Into the Hands of the People.* Cambridge, UK: Cambridge University Press, 2003.

Rankin, Hugh F. *The Theater in Colonial America.* Chapel Hill: University of North Carolina Press, 1964.

Taubman, Howard. *The Making of the American Theatre.* New York: Coward McCann, 1965.

Wilmeth, Don B., and Christopher Bigsby, eds. *The Cambridge History of American Theatre, Volume One: Beginnings to 1870.* Cambridge, UK: Cambridge University Press, 1998.

HERBERT, VICTOR AUGUST (1859–1924)

Victor Herbert was one of America's best composers of light opera. Although born in Dublin, Herbert was raised in Germany, where he received his musical training. When his wife, the singer Terese Förster, was recruited for New York City's Metropolitan Opera in 1886, Herbert was given

Portrait of Victor August Herbert, composer and conductor of light opera. (Library of Congress)

the first chair as cellist in the company's orchestra. He quickly established himself as a soloist and conductor, leading a number of ensembles. In addition to the Victor Herbert Orchestra, he also directed Patrick S. Gilmore's 22nd Regimental Band and the Pittsburgh Symphony Orchestra. He continued to compose works for the cello, frequently performing his successful *Second Cello Concerto, op. 30* (1894).

Herbert also began composing operettas, starting with *Prince Ananias* in 1894. However, he did not really concentrate on that genre until 1903, when he brought out his successful *Babes in Toyland.* His most popular operettas, such as the *Red Mill, Naughty Marietta* (1910), and *Sweethearts* (1913), were made into films and continued to appear in revivals, especially in summer stock, well into the middle of the century. Hit songs from his operettas and later comic Broadway musicals became standard repertory items for singers.

Although Herbert's family left Ireland shortly after he was born, he maintained a strong, public attachment to the land of his birth. This was due in large part to childhood visits with his grandfather, the Irish writer Samuel Lover. There are interesting parallels between grandfather and grandson. Both lived outside Ireland, Lover spending much of his adult life in England. Both wrote songs and performed, Lover being famous in England and America for his "Irish Evenings." Finally, both were romantic nationalists.

Herbert's sense of himself as an Irishman was probably encouraged after he arrived in the United States. Given his training in the great tradition of German musical culture, he could have easily associated himself with German America. Yet it was the New York Irish who benefited from his attention and talents. Of course, Herbert did not frequent the Five Points in Manhattan. He moved in the upper echelons of the city's Irish society. He conducted the glee club for the Friendly Sons of St. Patrick, and in 1914 became the society's president. By that time the Home Rule crisis had become a major concern among Irish Americans, and Herbert was outspoken in his support for Irish nationalism and in his criticism of the British government. In May 1916 he opened the Irish Race Convention where he was elected president of the Friends of Irish Freedom. The following year when Peadar Kearney's "The Soldier's Song" (destined to become Ireland's national anthem) was published in New York, Victor Herbert was listed as the arranger. Although Herbert wrote fiery newspaper articles condemning

Britain and, at lest by implication, supporting Germany, once the United States entered World War I, the composer loyally supported his adopted country. He continued, however, to publicly support the cause of Irish nationalism into the early 1920s.

Given his dedication to Ireland, it is not surprising that Herbert was interested in writing an operetta with an Irish theme. In 1915 he had staged *Princess Pat,* a romantic fantasy that featured the song "Two Laughing Irish Eyes." His major effort to present a musical vision of Ireland, however, was *Heart of Erin* (later renamed *Eileen*), which debuted on New Year's Day in Cleveland in 1917. A romance set amid the Rising of 1798, the show was as musically strong as anything Herbert had written. Instead of drawing upon traditional Irish tunes, he followed his grandfather in composing his own material. Although his power as a popular composer rested in large part on his mastery of the Viennese tradition, Herbert tried to write in the "characteristic spirit of the music of my native country—Ireland." Although successful at the time, the show did not become established on the American stage. This was partly because tastes were changing in the postwar years and operettas were falling out of fashion. Herbert shifted to writing musical comedies for Broadway, including songs for the Ziegfeld Follies, but he produced little that had the charm and musicality of his earlier operetta pieces. He died suddenly in New York City on May 26, 1924.

William H. A. Williams

See also: FARRELL, Eileen

References

Kaye, Joseph. *Victor Herbert: The Biography of America's Greatest Composer of Romantic Music.* New York: G. Howard Watt, 1931.

Waters, Edward N. *Victor Herbert: A Life in Music.* New York: Macmillan, 1955.

HINDS, CIARÁN (1953–)

Ciarán Hinds was born in Belfast in 1953 and has played starring roles on screen and stage. He studied law in Queen's University Belfast, before leaving to study acting at London's Royal Academy of Dramatic Art. His first professional job was with the Glasgow Citizen's Theatre. Hinds stayed with the company for several years and starred in a number of productions, including *Arms and the Man* (1983), *Arsenic and Old Lace* (1985), and *Faust* (1985). He also worked and toured with the Field Day Company, starring in *Antigone* (1984) and *High Time* (1984). In 1987, Hinds had one of his big breaks when he was spotted by acclaimed English director Peter Brook, who cast him in *The Mahabharata,* a production that toured the world. Hinds also starred in the film version of *The Mahabharata* (1989). He played lead roles in *The Cuchulaine Cycle* in the Abbey Theatre in Dublin, *Assassins* (1992) at the Donmar Warehouse in London, and *Machinal* (1993) and *Closer* (1997) at the Royal National Theatre in London. Roles at London's Greenwich Theatre included *The Way of the World* (1984) and leads in *Richard III* and *The Lady From the Sea.* He has starred in several productions with the Royal Shakespeare Company, including *Edward II* (1990–1991), *Troilus and Cressida* (1990–1991), *Two Shakespearian Actors* (1990–1991), *The Last Days of Don Juan* (1990–1991), and the title role of *Richard III* (1993), which also went on a world tour. Hinds made his film debut in 1981, in John Boorman's *Excalibur,* but he did not make another film until 1989, when he played a supporting role in Peter Greenaway's *The Cook, the Thief, His Wife, and Her Lover.* This was followed by roles in Thaddeus O'Sullivan's *December Bride*

(1990) and Pat O'Connor's *Circle of Friends* (1995), which finally brought him to the attention of an international audience. More substantial roles followed in Roger Mitchell's adaptation of Jane Austen's *Persuasion* (1995), Terry George's *Some Mother's Son* (1996), a drama based on the 1981 hunger strike in a Belfast prison, and Gillian Armstrong's *Oscar and Lucinda* (1997). Recent films have included *The Tale of Despereaux* (2008), *Hallam Foe* (2007), *Rome*—13 episodes (2005–2007), *The Nativity Story* (2006), *Munich* (2005), and *The Phantom of the Opera* (2004). In addition to his film work, Hinds has also continued to star in both television and stage productions, including the popular English series *Prime Suspect* (1994 season) and the BBC television serialization of *Ivanhoe* (1997).

Aoileann Ní Eigeartaigh

See also: O'CONNOR, Pat

Reference

Pettit, Lance. *Screening Ireland: Film and Television Representation.* Manchester, UK: Manchester University Press, 2000.

HOBAN, JAMES (1762–1831)

James Hoban's most lasting effect on the United States is found in his design of the president's residence, the White House, in Washington, D.C. Three centuries after he submitted his original plans, the core of the structure still functions as a home and a place of business and statecraft for America's first families, a place where they welcome leaders from all over the world as well as live out their private and public family lives.

Hoban was born in Desart, near Callan, Co. Kilkenny. He studied at the Dublin Society of Architecture School, where he learned the neoclassical style of Robert Adam, a style that emphasized clean lines and spare proportions along with classical detail, and which came to be known as Georgian after the reigning British monarch of the period. Crossing the ocean in the minds and pattern books of craftsmen, builders, and architects such as Hoban, in the United States it would become the Federal style.

Hoban came to the United States in the 1780s, first settling in Philadelphia and then moving to South Carolina. In South Carolina he designed the state capitol building, which was built in 1792 and burned during the American Civil War in 1865. This design was based in part on Pierre L'Enfant's proposed design for Federal Hall in New York City. In incorporating ideas from a published design or pattern book, Hoban was following common architectural practice of his day, and it was a practice he turned to again when in 1792 he decided to enter a competition to design a house for the president of the new republic of the United States of America. Leinster House in Dublin was one building to which he turned, and he is also believed to have referred to drawings in James Gibbs's *Book of Architecture* (London, 1728).

George Washington had encouraged the Irishman to enter the competition, and his design beat out a number of entries, including one believed to be from Thomas Jefferson, who entered under an assumed name. Hoban won the commission to build the presidential home, which would come to be called the White House because of its white painted front walls, as well as a $500 prize and a lot for himself in the District of Columbia.

Work on the White House lasted from 1793 to 1801, and President John Adams and his family were the first to live in the newly completed building. They found a design that reflected an interest in proportion and balance as was common in Georgian architecture, and use of fanlights and window details that combined both Georgian ideas and republican and federal motifs. From 1793 to 1802, Hoban also worked as one of the superintendents of the building of the United States Capitol building designed by William Thornton. Hoban also designed several hotels in Washingon, D.C. When the White House was burned by the British during the War of 1812, James Hoban was called on to supervise its reconstruction, and in 1818, his last federal commission was the design of the State and War Department offices.

Kerry Dexter

See also: WASHINGTON, D.C.

References

Grace, Catherine. *The White House: An Illustrated History.* New York: Scholastic, 2003.

McDermott, Matthew. *Ireland's Architectural Heritage.* Dublin: Folens, 1975.

Truman, Margaret. *The President's House.* New York: Ballantine, 2003.

HODGINS, JACK (1938–)

Jack Hodgins is an award-winning Canadian novelist and short story writer of Irish ancestry. He was born in 1938 in the town of Merville, in the Comoz Valley of Vancouver Island. He studied English literature at the University of British Columbia, where he took a course in creative writing. He graduated from the University of British Columbia with a Bachelor of Education degree, and taught English in a Vancouver High School until 1979. His first publication was in 1968. Thereafter, he began to regularly publish short stories in a number of publications, including *Descant, The Capilano Review,* and *Canadian Forum.* His first volume of short stories, entitled *Spit Delaney's Island,* was published in 1976. It was nominated for the 1976 Governor General's Award. His first novel, *The Invention of the World,* was published a year later to critical and commercial success. It won the Gibson's First Novel Award.

The publication of *The Resurrection of Joseph Bourne* in 1979 marked a turning point in Hodgins's career. The novel won the 1979 Governor General's Literary Award for English Language Fiction. Hodgins resigned from his teaching post and began to write full-time. He published another collection of short stories, *The Barclay Family Theatre,* in 1981, and a collection of excerpts from unpublished and unfinished works, *Beginnings: Samplings from a Long Apprenticeship,* in 1983. Later that year, he accepted a full-time position as a professor of creative writing at the University of Victoria, a decision that allowed him and his family to return to Vancouver Island. Since then, he has continued to publish regularly. He has written a guide to writing fiction entitled *A Passion for Narrative: A Guide for Writing Fiction* (1994, revised and reprinted 2001), a children's book entitled *Left Behind in Squabble Bay* (1988), and a book about his own travels in Australia entitled *Over Forty in Broken Hill* (1992). He also published a number of novels: *The Honorary Patron* (1987), *Innocent Cities* (1990), *The Macken Charm* (1995), *Broken Ground* (1998), and *Distance* (2003), and a collection of short stories entitled *Damage Done by the Storm* (2004). Many of his stories have also been televised or adapted for radio and the stage. His work has been translated into a number of languages, including Dutch, Hungarian,

Japanese, German, Russian, Italian, Polish, and Norwegian.

In June 1995, the University of British Columbia awarded Hodgins an honorary DLitt for—according to the *UBC Chronicle*—bringing "renown to the university and the province as one of Canada's finest fiction writers and as an innovative stylist and distinguished academic." In the spring of 1998 he was given an honorary DLitt by Malaspina University-College, and in 2004 he received an honorary DLitt from the University of Victoria. He was elected a Fellow of the Royal Society of Canada in 1999.

Aoileann Ní Eigeartaigh

HOLKERI, HARRI (1937–)

In 1995, Harri Holkeri, the former prime minister of Finland in the late 1980s and member of the board of Bank of Finland, was invited to participate in an international body headed by former U.S. Senator George Mitchell, to find a way to conduct negotiations that might provide the basis for a peace agreement in Northern Ireland. The Mitchell Commission was given the task of holding the multiparty talks in which the Unionist and Nationalist parties of Northern Ireland discussed the peace plan themselves without the national (British and Irish) governments. Under Holkeri's chairmanship, multiparty negotiations started in June 1996. Holkeri's most important task in the beginning, as he recalls, was to build up an environment of trust so that the negotiations could go ahead. After two difficult years, Holkeri and rest of the commission managed to bring the negotiations to a successful conclusion with the Belfast or Good Friday Agreement, which was signed in April 1998. After his mission in Northern Ireland, Mr. Holkeri has acted as president of the 55th United Nations General Congress, and in the summer of 2003 he assumed the position of head of the United Nations Interim Administration in Kosovo. For his efforts in the Northern Ireland peace process, Holkeri was made a knight of the Order of the British Empire (OBE) in 1998.

Aki Kalliomäki

See also: MITCHELL, George

References

Holkeri, Harri. "The Ten Commandments of Peace Talks." Public Lecture at University of Helsinki, April 28, 2000.

Iloniemi, Jaakko. *Harri Holkeri: Former Prime Minister of Finland, Peacemaker.* Virtual Finland, 2000. www.finland.fi/netcomm/news/showarticle.asp?intNWSAID=26160 (accessed August 25, 2007).

HOLLAND, JOHN PHILLIP (1841–1914)

Born February 24, 1841, in Liscanore, Co. Clare, the son of Mary (Scanlon) and John Holland, John Phillip Holland was an officer in the British Coastguard Service. Educated at St. Macreehy's National School and the Christian Brothers' school at Ennistymon, he showed an aptitude for science. He joined the teaching order of the Irish Christian Brothers in 1858 and taught music and science at various institutions across Ireland until 1872.

Holland immigrated to America in 1873, where he took a job teaching in Patterson, New Jersey, while continuing his work on underwater propulsion. Holland had read the scanty literature on submarines, including the works of Robert

Portrait of inventor John Phillip Holland climbing up the hatch of the USS Holland. *(Library of Congress)*

Fulton and David Bushnell: their failures did not deter his plans. In 1875 he introduced his design to the U.S. Navy, which rejected his scheme as the fanciful dreamings of a shore-bound civilian.

Searching for a backer, Holland was introduced to the Fenian Brotherhood in 1876 by his younger brother, Michael; unlike the U.S. Navy, the Irish nationalist group was intrigued with his plans and agreed to finance construction of a prototype. The Fenians supplied Holland with some $23,000 from their Skirmishing Fund; it was hoped Holland could construct a fleet of submarines to harass British shipping and lead to the creation of an independent Ireland. The first experimental craft, a 14-foot-long, steam-powered, single-person craft, was tested on the Passaic River in 1878. A more sophisticated version of this vessel, *The Fenian Ram,* was launched from New York City's Delameter Iron Works into the Hudson River in May 1881. In effect, *The Fenian Ram* embodied the chief principles of the modern submarine in terms of balance and control, and it was able to dive by inclining its axis and plunging to the desired depth. At 31 feet long, *The Fenian Ram* was a three-person vessel that displaced 19 tons and was powered by an internal combustion engine. The vessel made several practice runs in New York harbor, once diving to the depth of 60 feet and remaining submerged for an hour. Disagreements over the disbursement of the Skirmishing Fund led the Fenians to steal Holland's prototype, and he severed all relationships with the nationalist group.

In 1888, Holland won a U.S. Navy–sponsored competition for his design of a submarine torpedo boat, a feat he repeated in 1889 and 1893. Unfortunately, no appropriations were attached to these honors. Undeterred, Holland founded the Holland Torpedo Boat Company in 1893; in 1895 he was awarded a government contract to build a submarine, *The Plunger,* to Navy specifications. Naval engineers largely controlled the design of the vessel, and Holland, although made manager, was excluded from many design decisions. Not surprisingly, the design floundered and was never adopted.

Returning to a design he had envisioned years before, Holland launched a self-named submarine, the *Holland VI,* in 1897. At over 53 feet long, and with a displacement of some 75 tons, the *Holland VI* was fitted with torpedoes, dynamite guns, and a hybrid motor, using gasoline for surface propulsion and electric storage batteries for underwater propulsion. The *Holland* was the first boat to be designed in such a manner and, in fact, was the first submarine that could be run to any significant distance when submerged. Furthermore, the *Holland* was capable of remaining underwater for some 40 hours. While this was by far Holland's most impressive submarine, its success was due largely to elements in his earlier designs, namely its fixed center of gravity, rapid diving capability, and positive reserve buoyancy.

After several rigorous tests, the U.S. Navy purchased the *Holland* and six additional submarines from the inventor. Holland later designed submarines for Japan and was awarded the Order of the Rising Sun in 1910. Holland's company became a subsidiary of Electric Boat in 1899; forced out by shrewd lawyers, Holland retired from active life in 1907.

Holland died of pneumonia August 12, 1914, so he never saw the disastrous effect his vessels would have on shipping during World War I. Holland had always hoped his invention would be used for peaceful exploration of the ocean depths for the good of humankind. He was survived by his wife of 20 years, Margaret (Foley), and their four children.

Tim Lynch

See also: FENIANS

Reference

Morris, Richard K. *John P. Holland, 1841–1914: Inventor of the Modern Submarine.* Annapolis, MD: United States Naval Institute Press, 1966.

HONDURAS

The region of Central America that became Honduras was discovered by Christopher Columbus on his last voyage to the Americas in 1502. It became a Spanish colony in 1526 and within 50 years was under attack by pirates from the British Isles. English and Irish seafarers continued to attack Spanish ships and settlements for more than a century and occupied the Bay Islands off the north coast of Honduras. One of the ship captains, Sir Nathaniel Butler (1557–ca. 1643), who was based in Ireland during the 1620s, seized the town of Trujillo close to the Bay Islands, in 1639.

In 1779, when Spain, to support the American declaration of independence, declared war on Britain, the Royal Navy was sent to attack Spanish interests, and in October the Irishman Sir Peter Parker (1721–1811) was involved in an attack on the Spanish at Omoa, Honduras.

During the nineteenth century, Irish involvement with Honduras was intermittent. Honduras gained its independence in 1821, and in the 1830s Juan Galindo, an Irish-born Roman Catholic of Spanish descent, went to Central America to try to get the republics to stop encroachment from the British. He served with the Liberals in Honduras and was killed at the battle of El Petrero on January 30, 1840—Juan Galindo is still regarded as a national hero in Honduras. Seventeen years later, Honduran forces were involved in crushing the forces of American adventurer William Walker, who included some Irishmen in his band of adventurers.

During the early twentieth century, two doctors of Irish descent made major advances in the study of tropical medicine in Central America. Rupert (later Sir Rupert) Boyce (1863–1911), son of an engineer from Carlow, made some discoveries in the spread of yellow fever in 1905, and Dr. Daniel Murrah Molloy (1882–1944) continued this work in 1918. Molloy worked on providing supplies of clean water for Tegucigalpa, the Honduran capital, and by teaching basic hygiene to local doctors, he helped reduce infection from hookworm and lowered the infant mortality rate in the country.

In late 1900s, an American of Irish descent, Guy Ross Molony (1883–1972), arrived in Honduras fresh from his exploits in South Africa during the Anglo-Boer War. In 1910 Molony joined with another adventurer, Lee Christmas, and the two supported a banana exporter, Samuel Zemurray, in his bid to take over the country and reinstate a former president, Manuel Bonilla, who was in exile in New Orleans. This was successful, and U.S. banana interests in Honduras were protected—Molony served in the U.S. forces in World War I, and then he returned to New Orleans where he was elected mayor. Molony later became chief of police in New Orleans but in 1925 quarrelled with the new city administration and left for Honduras where he established a brewery.

In 1932, when rebels supporting the Liberal faction tried to take over the country, Molony flew an aircraft with New Zealander Lowell Yerex (1895–1968) as observer and bomber. Together they took part in the first ground-air battle in Honduran history. However, the fight was unnerving and Molony was only just able to land the plane before losing consciousness. Molony then involved himself in the rice industry in Honduras before retiring to New Orleans in 1961.

In the mid-1930s, while Molony was still a household name to many in Honduras, Walter Edward Guiness, Lord Moyne (1880–1944) visited the Bay Islands. He described his visit there in his 1938 book *Atlantic Circle*. Since then, there has been limited Irish contact with Honduras. Irish diplomatic representation in Honduras is handled by the Irish Embassy to the United Nations in New York.

Justin Corfield

See also: BELIZE

Reference

Griffith, William J. "Juan Galindo: Central American Chauvinist." *Hispanic American Historical Review* 40, no. 1 (1960): 25–52.

HORGAN, PAUL GEORGE VINCENT O'SHAUGHNESSY (1903–1995)

On August 1, 1903, Paul Horgan was born into a Buffalo, New York, family with strong interests in music, art, theater, and language. Horgan later recalled that he was writing for and acting in family theatricals by the time he was six. His father, a business executive of Irish descent, was employed by the Erie Railroad, and then by insurance and printing companies. His mother came from a large family of German immigrants, which included his maternal grandfather, an established journalist, poet, and businessman, who, along with his mother and a German nurse, taught him German at an early age.

Members of his extended family, and their experiences, were to be reflected in many of Horgan's subsequent writings. So was his fascination with the catafalque on display in the Buffalo and Erie County Historical Society Museum. This catafalque had been used to transport Abraham Lincoln's coffin to and from Buffalo's St. James Hall so his body could be viewed by an estimated 100,000 mourners, during a 15-hour stop of the funeral train taking him home to Springfield after his assassination.

Horgan was a precocious young student in Buffalo's private French-Catholic

Miss Nardin's Academy before his family moved in 1915 to Albuquerque, then a town of 10,000 in the new state of New Mexico, because of his father's tuberculosis. There he attended public schools for the first time, in a strikingly different environment, although his freshman English teacher at Albuquerque High was to be Willa Cather's sister Elsie. The culture was mixed Hispanic-Anglo-Native American. The setting was the broad, dry, sand-and-soil colored Rio Grande Valley, situated between two visible mountain ranges.

Horgan spent his two middle years of high school at New Mexico Military Institute (NMMI) in Roswell, from 1919 to 1921, before returning home upon his father's death. He became a junior reporter for the *Albuquerque Journal,* where he worked under city editor and later U.S. Senator Clinton Anderson. After a year at the *Journal,* where he had also become a book reviewer and the music, art, literary, and drama critic and had managed to offend some of the local gentry with occasional lampoons, he returned to NMMI for a combined senior year of high school and first year of college. By this time Horgan's friends included fellow NMMI student Peter Hurd, later a Southwestern artist and the husband of artist Henriette Wyeth of the Pennsylvania art family, and J. Robert Oppenheimer.

Horgan returned to the East in 1923, to study voice at the Eastman School of Music in Rochester, New York. He stayed there until 1926, designing scenery for the opera department; becoming production assistant to Rouben Mamoulian, director of the Eastman School of Dance and Dramatic Action; and acting and singing in productions of the Eastman Theatre. He then returned to the NMMI as its librarian, taking his mornings off to write. This time Horgan stayed until he joined the army's Information and Education Division in 1942. His NMMI activities during this period included teaching, advising student publications, designing sets for student balls, coaching the tennis team, and starting his own magazine of book reviews, poems, and translations. His army duties included working on films with director Frank Capra.

After his army service, which also included time in the Pentagon with the army's General Staff Corps, Horgan briefly taught at the University of Iowa, then returned to NMMI as a faculty member from 1947 to 1962. He went East again in 1960, for semesters as a fellow of the Center for Advanced Studies at Wesleyan University in Middletown, Connecticut, before leaving NMMI for the final time to become the Center's director from 1962 to 1967. Horgan also lectured as a Hoyt Fellow of Yale's Saybrook College in 1965. He remained at Wesleyan for the remainder of his life, as an adjunct and then a professor of English from 1967 to 1971, and thereafter—while making frequent trips back to the West—as Wesleyan's permanent author in residence. He died on March 8, 1995, in Middletown. He never married.

Horgan was highly prolific, the author of more than forty books and numerous short stories, articles, poems, and librettos. Many of his works concerned the Southwest, from Texas to California. Lawrence Clerk Powell called him the "Dean of Southwestern Writers." His *Great River: The Rio Grande in American History* won a Pulitzer Prize for history, and his *Lamy of Santa Fe,* about the archbishop who had been the subject of an earlier Willa Cather novel, won a Pulitzer Prize for Biography.

But Horgan also wrote of Lincoln (including *Citizen of New Salem*); of the loses of childhood innocence in a novel set in upstate New York (*Things as They Are*); of artists, architects, and musicians; and of the writing process itself. Although he had many prominent friends, he remained ready to skewer attitudes and acts he found pretentious, notably those of Buffalo heiress and Southwestern art patron Mabel Dodge. *The Clerihews of Paul Horgan,* first published when he was eighty, is a set of drawings and short poems lampooning historical figures from Achilles and the Emperor Tiberius to Maria Montessori and Howard Hughes.

Steven B. Jacobson

References

Gish, Robert Franklin, *Paul Horgan.* Boston: Twayne, 1983.

Horgan, Paul. *Nueva Granada: Paul Horgan and the Southwest.* College Station: Texas A&M University Press, 1995.

Horgan, Paul. *Approaches to Writing.* 2nd ed. Middletown, CT: Wesleyan University Press, 1988.

Horgan, Paul. *A Certain Climate: Essays in History, Arts, and Letters.* Middletown, CT: Wesleyan University Press, 1990.

Horgan, Paul. *Of America East and West: Selections from the Writings of Paul Horgan.* New York: Farrar, Straus and Giroux, 1884.

Horgan, Paul. *The Richard Trilogy: Things as They Are, Everything to Live For, The Thin Mountain Air.* Middletown: Wesleyan University Press, 1990.

Horgan, Paul. *Tracings: A Book of Partial Portraits.* New York: Farrar, Straus and Giroux, 1993.

Horgan, Paul. *Whitewater.* Austin: University of Texas Press, 1987.

Horgan, Paul. *Writer's Eye: Field Notes and Watercolors.* New York: Harry N. Abrams, 1988.

McCullough, David C. "Historian, Novelist, and Much, Much More." *New York Times Book Review,* April 4, 1984.

HORSE RACING

Racehorses and racecourses have frequently brought Ireland and America into competition and collaboration. The most famous of British (and Irish) traditional sporting ballads, "Skewball" (sometimes "Stewball"), which celebrates the victory of Mr. Marvin's Skewball over Sir Ralph Gore's gray mare (usually identified, almost certainly incorrectly, as Griselda) in a match at the Curragh in March 1752, crossed the Atlantic early on. It exists in a number of American versions, and in some of these the race is presented as an affair of transatlantic rivalry. In the eighteenth and nineteenth centuries, Irish emigrants took their skills in horsemanship in all its aspects to America. One of the most influential of early American breeders, James Jackson of Alabama, was born in 1782 in Co. Monaghan. The traffic has not, however, all been one way—wealthy American patrons have always been welcome in Irish racing and noteworthy successes have been recorded.

The controversial Democratic politician Boss Croker relocated to Ireland and funded a racing empire at Glencairn, winning the English and Irish derbies of 1907 with Orby. After some decades of inactivity, Glencairn would be revived as a racing stable by Joe McGrath, an Irishman who made his fortune selling the Irish Sweepstakes lottery to the U.S. market. An American of a very different type, Republican grandee J. H. "Jock" Whitney, won the Cheltenham Gold Cup in 1929 and 1930 with the Irish-bred Easter Hero (and might well have made it three in a row had the race not been canceled in 1931). Later came Bing Crosby's notable triumph in the 1965 Irish Sweeps Derby (a race that attracted more financial interest in the United States than it did in Ireland) as co-owner of

Meadow Court. In the late twentieth century, other Americans to have enjoyed success with horses trained in Ireland include Bertram R. Firestone, Allen Paulson, Bob Fluor, Franklin Groves, Henry de Kwiatowski, and Virginia Kraft Payson.

Occasionally, American trainers have enjoyed success in Ireland as well, most notably when Michael O'Brien sent out the New York–based Fourstar's Allstar to win the 1991 Irish 2000 Guineas at the Curragh. Although his horses were bred in the United States and trained in England, Paul Mellon demands a mention as an Irish American who has enjoyed considerable success in Irish racing, notably with Forest Flower in the 1987 Irish 1000 Guineas. American owners and Irish trainers have also combined to win big in Britain, as with Betty Moran's Papillon in the 2000 Aintree Grand National. Irish-bred horses have also enjoyed considerable success in the United States, both at stud and on the track, such as Round Table, the 1958 Horse of the Year in the United States, and the endlessly influential (and famously temperamental) stallion Nasrullah.

However, from the 1970s onward the story of Irish-American exchange in horse racing is essentially the story of two Irishmen, trainer Dr. Vincent O'Brien and stallion master John Magnier, and their systematic acquisition of American-bred racehorses, with a view to racing them in Europe and making them into globally attractive stallions. By doing this, O'Brien and Magnier revolutionized the world bloodstock industry and made Ireland into Europe's foremost producer of thoroughbreds, capable of competing with the previously all-powerful American industry.

O'Brien had been Ireland's most successful trainer from the late 1940s, at first in National Hunt racing and then on the Flat, winning a succession of big races for American owners across Europe and beyond. For John McShain, O'Brien trained Ballymoss (winner of the Irish Derby and King George and Queen Elizabeth Stakes at Ascot in 1957, followed by the 1958 Prix de l'Arc de Triomphe) and Gladness (winner of the 1958 Ascot Gold Cup). In 1962 he sent out Larkspur to win the 1962 Epsom Derby for the then U.S. ambassador to Ireland, Raymond Guest, before recording a series of triumphs with the brilliant Sir Ivor (the English 2000 Guineas and Derby, the Eclipse Stakes, and the first Irish-trained winner of the Washington International) for the same owner in 1968. Guest is also notable as the owner of L'Escargot—the only horse to win the Cheltenham Gold Cup (1970 and 1971) and the Grand National (1975). In 1970, O'Brien won the English Triple Crown for Charles Engelhard with the peerless Nijinsky (bred in Canada). For John Galbreath, he won the 1972 English Derby with Roberto, who went on to inflict an unprecedented defeat at York on the undisputed English Champion, Brigadier Gerard. In the York race the positive U.S. riding tactics of Roberto's Panamanian jockey, Braulio Baeza, caused a sensation.

In 1973, O'Brien and his future son-in-law Magnier bought a substantial share of a relatively modest stud farm, Coolmore. The two men had determined that the future of Irish racing and breeding lay in buying the choice lots at the yearling sales in Kentucky, bringing them back to Ireland for racing, and then standing them at stud in Ireland or selling shares in them back to the American market at a substantial profit. This high-risk policy was founded on a total faith in O'Brien's ability to identify potential champions in their infancy and Magnier's instinct for what would make a marketable stallion pedigree. In the late 1970s and early 1980s, they enjoyed remarkable success on the racecourses of Europe. Running in the colors of their most substantial backer, Robert Sangster, and usually ridden by top jockey of the day Lester Piggott, horses trained by O'Brien won all of the major European races: the English Derby with The Minstrel (1977) and Golden Fleece (1983), the King George at Ascot with The Minstrel (1977), consecutive Prix de l'Arc de Triomphes with Alleged (1977 and 1978), and the English 2000 Guineas with Lomond (1983) and El Gran Señor (1984).

Many of these expensively bought horses went on to be successful at stud, but the policy's success attracted imitators, and by the mid-1980s the yearling market had become ludicrously inflated, notably by the emergence of oil-wealthy owners such as Khalid Abdullah and Sheikh Mohammed bin Maktoum of Dubai. Mistakes of judgment became even more expensive, and the Coolmore operation consolidated. O'Brien's last great triumph came in improbably romantic circumstances in the United States, when Royal Academy won the 1990 Breeder's Cup Mile, ridden by the veteran jockey Lester Piggott, who was lured out of retirement by O'Brien to win yet another big prize for the Coolmore connections.

With O'Brien in semiretirement, Magnier set about expanding Coolmore's stud operation into the United States and Australia. Shrewd and adroit financial management, aligned with good luck, ensured his success. In Australia, the relatively modest and inexpensive racehorse Danehill turned out champion after champion, while in Europe, Sadler's Wells began in short order to sire one top-class racehorse after another. More significantly, Sadler's Wells was a homebred, a sire of sires who had cost Coolmore nothing. A winner of the Irish 2000 Guineas, Eclipse Stakes, and Irish Champion Stakes in 1984, he had nevertheless been rated second in O'Brien's stable to the brilliant El Gran Senor (famously defeated in the English Derby by Secreto, trained by Vincent O'Brien's son, David), but Sadler's Wells provided Coolmore with a stallion of global renown. With the acquisition of the Ashford Stud in Kentucky, Coolmore also established a stronghold in the United States that set the scene for greater expansion.

In the mid-1990s, a young Irish trainer, Aidan O'Brien, exploded into racing consciousness, producing record numbers of winners in Ireland over jumps and on the flat. Magnier and his coinvestors quickly decided that Aidan O'Brien was a worthy successor to Vincent (although no relation), and installed him in the latter's training headquarters, Ballydoyle. Coolmore also went back to the now-deflated yearling sales and reinvested in another generation of American yearlings by new stallions, notably Storm Cat. Instantly, O'Brien produced a multiple Group One winner for Coolmore, Desert King (Irish 2000 Guineas and Derby in 1997), and since then a succession of top-class racehorses and potential stallions has been produced.

Coolmore's global scale of ambition can be measured in its range of successes on the international stage, and particularly in that many of O'Brien's horses' finest performances have come at the Breeder's Cup, the meeting that crowns and culminates the U.S. season. Johannesburg won the Breeder's Cup Juvenile in 2001 and High

Chaparral the Breeder's Cup Turf in 2002 and 2003. In addition, Rock of Gibraltar narrowly lost the 2002 Breeder's Cup Mile (ending a run of seven consecutive wins in Group One races) and Giant's Causeway just lost out to Tiznow in the finish of the 2000 Breeder's Cup Classic, the richest horse race in the world.

Ballydoyle and Coolmore look set to continue their dominance, but it is also important to recognize that other Irish trainers have done equally well in U.S. racing in recent years. John Oxx won the Breeder's Cup Mile with Ridgewood Pearl in 1995 and other big American prizes with Timarida in 1996. Most notably, however, Dermot Weld remains the only trainer from outside the United States to have won an American Triple Crown race; Go and Go's victory in the Belmont Stakes of 1990 confirmed Weld's unrivaled gift for producing horses to win anywhere in the world. Weld has since produced many other winners in America from his base on the Curragh, including Pine Dance (2002) and Dimitrova (2003).

Michael Hinds and Stephen Wilson

See also: CROKER, Richard; CROSBY, Bing

References

O'Brien, Jacqueline, and Ivor Herbert. *Vincent O'Brien: The Official Biography.* London: Bantam, 2005.

Robinson, Nick. *Horsetrader: Robert Sangster and the Rise and the Fall of the Sport of Kings.* London: Harper Collins, 1994.

Thoroughbred Times. www.thoroughbredtimes.com (accessed February 12, 2005).

HOVENDEN, THOMAS (1840–1895)

Thomas Hovenden was born in Dunmanway, Co. Cork, to parents who died during the Great Famine. He was brought up in an orphanage until he was apprenticed to George Tolerton, a carver and gilder, who recommended him to the Cork School of Design in 1858. Hovenden emigrated to New York in 1863, where he worked as a photographic colorist. Here he entered the school of the National Academy of Design. He moved to Baltimore in 1868.

The Last Moments of John Brown *by Thomas Hovenden.* (©*The Metropolitan Museum of Art*)

Hovenden worked across a range of genres: history painting, genre painting, paintings of literary themes, landscapes, and portraits. In 1874, he went to France for six years. In Paris, he studied at the premier school, the École des Beaux-Arts, under Alexandre Cabanel, bringing his work to the level of sophistication associated with the European experience. He also painted in Pont-Aven, Brittany, where he joined other Irish and American artists. Here he met the painter Helen Corson (1846–1935), whom he married in 1881. In Pont-Aven, he painted *The Hunter's Tale, The Poacher's Story* (1880), *The One Who Can Read* (1877), and *In Hoc Signo Vinces*

(1880). The latter, based on the Wars of the Vendée (1793–1795), treated the peasant uprisings against the revolutionary government in western France. The reemergence of the historical antagonism between clericalism and republicanism in Brittany in the 1870s revived the War of the Vendée as a theme, allowing artists to comment politically on contemporary events without appearing to do so. The painting was exhibited at the Paris Salon in 1880 and made his name. Hovenden returned to New York and showed the picture at the National Academy of Design to great acclaim. He was elected academician of the National Academy of Design and member of the Society of American Artists, the New York Water Color Society, the New York Etching Club, and the Philadelphia Society of Artists. In 1881, he and Helen Corson moved to Plymouth Meeting, where the Corsons were established as Quakers.

Robbins Battell commissioned Hovenden to paint John Brown, the renowned abolitionist, in *The Last Moments of John Brown* (1882–1884), now in New York's Metropolitan Museum of Art. Although the incident, showing Brown kissing a black child on his way to the scaffold, transpired to be apocryphal, Hovenden imbued it with high moral purpose. His wife's family was involved in the abolitionist movement, and Hovenden's own studio was used as a stop along the Underground Railroad. He painted several African-American subjects that, to our eyes, may be somewhat patronizing, but he had significant links with the black artist, Henry Ossawa Tanner, and both produced visually defining images that challenged racial stereotypes

In the Hands of the Enemy (1889) depicts an imaginary Union family caring for a wounded Confederate soldier after the Battle of Gettysburg. The theme of Christian, fraternal reconciliation transcending political or racial difference earned Hovenden a record $5,500. His largest and last painting, *The Founders of a State* (1895), remained unfinished at his death. It shows the opening of the Southwest in response to the pressure from frontiersmen and the resulting occupation of Cherokee land by homesteaders.

Although renowned in his own time, Hovenden was undeservedly overshadowed by painters such as Thomas Eakins and Thomas Anshutz, who also taught at the Pennsylvania Academy of Fine Arts where Hovenden taught from 1886 to 1888. Hovenden's blend of history/narrative/genre painting went out of critical favor. His reputation, however, was revived with a major exhibition at the Woodmere Art Museum in Philadelphia in 1995.

Hovenden sought to uphold the traditional American values that appealed to the morality of his age. *Breaking Home Ties* (1890) enshrined his ideas about the home hearth—where the virtues of loyalty in a traditional God-fearing rural family are promoted—but the stylistic characteristics of his work were now less rapturously received as the influence of Impressionism increasingly modernized American painting. But if the critics were less than enthusiastic, the public was ecstatic. Exhibited at the World's Columbian Exposition in Chicago in 1893, it was considered the most popular of all 1,000 paintings on show.

Niamh O'Sullivan

References

Gregory, Anne, Sylvia Young, and Naurice Frank Woods, Jr. *Thomas Hovenden (1840–1895): American Painter of Hearth and Homeland.* Philadelphia: Woodmere Art Museum, 1995.

Wunderlich, R. "Thomas Hovenden and the American Genre Painters." *Kennedy Quarterly* 3, no. 1 (April 1962): 2–11.

HOWARD, MAUREEN (1930–)

Born on June 30, 1930, Maureen Howard was raised in an Irish neighborhood in the industrial town of Bridgeport, Connecticut. Her father was an Irish immigrant to America who later became the detective for Fairfield County. Like her mother, Howard was educated at Smith College and received her bachelor's degree in 1952. After graduating, she worked for advertising and publishing firms before becoming a full-time writer. She published her first novel, *Not a Word About Nightingales,* in 1960. Five years later her second novel, *Bridgeport Bus,* was published. Her third, *Before My Time,* appeared in 1975. Two years later, she edited *Seven American Women Writers of the Twentieth Century* before publishing *Facts of Life,* a memoir of her childhood and early adulthood, in 1978. For this work, she was awarded the National Book Critics Circle Award for general nonfiction in 1980. She also edited *The Penguin Book of Contemporary American Essays* in 1984. Her novels *Grace Abounding, Expensive Habits,* and *Natural History* were all nominated for the PEN/Faulkner Award in 1983, 1987, and 1993, respectively. *A Lover's Almanac* appeared in 1998, and three years later she published *Big as Life: Three Tales for Spring,* a collection of short stories and memories. Howard has contributed to Irish-American fiction by writing the foreword for *Cabbage and Bones: An Anthology of Irish American Women's Fiction.* She has combined her writing with teaching, and from 1967 to 1968 she taught English and creative writing at the New York School for Social Research. She has also held positions at Amherst College, Brooklyn College, Yale, Princeton, and the University of California at Santa Barbara. Howard is currently on the faculty of the writing program at Columbia University. She was awarded a Guggenheim fellowship in 1967. She has contributed articles to the *New Yorker,* the *New York Times,* and the *Yale Review.* She is married and has one daughter. Currently, she lives in New York City.

Much of Howard's work involves women characters who are at odds with society and who are searching for their own sense of identity and place in a hostile world. This has led some critics to accuse her of being a woman's writer, confining her work to issues that only concern women. Her upbringing in an Irish-Catholic community in Bridgeport has formed the basis for much of her work. In many ways, Bridgeport is a character in all her work, and Howard has drawn upon experiences from her own childhood and incorporated them into her novels. In *Bridgeport Bus,* she tells the story of 35-year old Mary Agnes Keely, an Irish-Catholic girl who leaves her widowed mother in Bridgeport and travels to Manhattan to begin a life of her own. The novel ends with the protagonist, pregnant and unmarried, returning home to her mother and forced to deal with the change in the circumstances of her life. The consequences of Howard's own upbringing in an Irish Catholic community are examined in her memoir *Fact of Life.* This work also explores her parents' relationship with each other, their attitude toward their children, and what Howard has termed their "diseased attitude towards money." Bridgeport also forms the setting of *Natural History,* a work that combines a fictional narrative with a collection of facts about Bridgeport. It mixes different literary genres, combining a screenplay, the encyclopedia, diary entries, and historical narratives to tell the story. The plot deals with a county detective who bears a resemblance to Howard's own father and his life in Bridgeport. This mixing of different literary genres continued with *Big as Life: Three Tales for Spring,* which was published in 2001. This work combines short stories with memoirs and, as the second part of a proposed quartet of novels dealing with the seasons, focuses on themes of renewal and regeneration. *The Silver Screen,* her most recent novel and the third in the quartet, continues this concern with Irish-American themes by dealing with Isabel Maher, a star of silent movies and her relationship with her children.

David Doyle

Reference

Kearns, Caledonia. "Maureen Howard." In *The Encyclopedia of the Irish in America,* edited by Michael Glazier. Notre Dame, IN: University of Notre Dame Press, 1999.

HOWE, FANNY QUINCY (1940–)

Born in Buffalo, New York, on October 15, 1940, Fanny Howe was reared in an intellectual household in Cambridge, Massachusetts. She was the daughter of a distinguished Harvard Law School professor, Mark DeWolfe Howe, and an Irish immigrant from Dublin, Mary Manning Howe, later known as Molly Howe, who was an actress, novelist, playwright, and cofounder of the Poets Theater. Fanny was the middle child, and her elder sister Susan Howe also became known as a poet and a playwright. Starting at age 14, Fanny Howe would meet and become a part of the poetic community through the Poets Theater. There, also, Howe fell in love with Irish singer and actor Liam Clancy. Through the Poets Theater she was exposed to performances of Irish poetry and drama but also developed an appreciation for American poets of the time. Fanny Howe was dismissed from Buckingham School in Cambridge in 1957; she subsequently studied at Stanford from 1958–1961, but did not obtain a degree. Howe returned to the East to write and became involved in the civil rights movement. She assisted in the birth of a literary magazine called *Fire Exit.* There she met Carl Senna, a writer of mixed Chicano and black ancestry, who was also an activist. On October 27, 1968, Howe and Senna married. They had three children: Annlucien, Danzy, and Maceo. This interracial marriage, the process of bearing and rearing children of African-American-Chicano-Irish descent, and the racial turmoil of Boston during the 1960s and 1970s influenced her experience and writing deeply. Howe began writing novels and poetry that dealt with issues of race relations, class, and social justice in Boston during those decades. However, even before her marriage, Howe believed she was from mixed ancestry, referring to her powerful, charismatic, artistic Irish mother and her retiring, unexpressive, academic father. Howe was reared in an unreligious Protestant household, but she began attending Mass with her mother-in-law. She eventually converted to Roman Catholicism, though she never became an orthodox Catholic. Howe describes herself as an atheist Catholic and says she is attracted to Catholicism because of its many contradictions, and her spiritual beliefs are often explored through her poetry in which she probes matters of the material and spiritual world.

Howe worked at Tufts University as a lecturer in creative writing from 1968 through 1971. Then in 1973 Howe worked with the Massachusetts Poetry-in-the-Schools program. In 1974 she lectured in creative writing at Emerson College in Boston. That same year, Senna and Howe divorced. Then from 1975 through 1978 Howe lectured, again in creative writing, for the Columbia University Extension and School of the Arts in New York City. In 1976 Howe was a lecturer in poetry at Yale University, and then in 1977 she lectured in fiction at the Harvard Extension. From 1978 though 1987 Howe was a visiting writer and lecturer in fiction and poetry at MIT. In 1987 she became a professor at the University of California in San Diego. In 1991 Howe was a professor of language and literature and codirector of the MFA program in writing at Bard College. From 1993 through 1995 Howe was the associate director of the University of California Study Center in London, England. In 1996 and 1997 she was the distinguished visiting writer-in-residence at Mills College. In 1998 Howe was writer-in-residence at Small Press Traffic in San Francisco.

Howe is known as an experimental poet with an extraordinary sense of the sound of language and an exacting use of words. Her work is considered strong, yet quiet and passionate, often with no identifiable voice or persona. Howe's work has been called unclassifiable and avant-garde. She frequently deals with issues of race, religion, social justice, politics, and metaphysics in her writings, often leaving questions unanswered. In her novels, Howe writes of troubled, lonely, ethical women of poverty, most often in the setting of Boston, the environment where she experienced the day-to-day challenges of racism. Howe has published more than 20 books of fiction and poetry. Her work has been most frequently compared with that of Emily Dickinson. Howe feels a closeness to early Celtic poetry with its four-line stanzas and first-person observer viewpoint.

"O'Clock," a series of poems published first as a work in 1995, then in an almost complete form as part of *Selected Poems* in 2000, is set in Ireland, the birthplace of Howe's mother. However, most of Howe's work is set in America, most commonly New England and particularly in Boston where Howe was reared. The influence of Howe's Irish heritage seems to manifest itself most often in her interest in mixed heritage and race relations in America in general. Race, poverty, and class relationships became a primary concern for Howe after her marriage.

The recurrent themes of homelessness and loneliness revealed through Howe's characters originated when Howe and Senna's Irish-African-American family were ostracized during the explosive times they lived in the Boston area. After her divorce, Howe began moving with her children, and she has been moving ever since, working at numerous institutions and changing apartments often. She says she is most comfortable when she is traveling from place to place. Even her style of working reflects this. Rather than write in an office setting, she prefers to carry her work in her pocket, writing and revising as she moves throughout the day. Howe considers herself a modern-day nomad, a wanderer, as are many of her characters.

Robeson Street is a book of poetry set on Robeson Street in Jamaica Plain, Massachusetts, where she and Senna purchased a dilapidated Victorian home after living in the racially troubled West Roxbury. In West Roxbury, Howe and her family were continually assaulted by racial prejudice and confronted with violence. In the house on Robeson Street, Howe and Senna would entertain people from their diverse ethnic backgrounds. In *Robeson Street,* Howe expresses a multitude of feelings and perspectives: of isolation and fear, "with white boys banging the lids of garbage cans, calling racial zingers into our artificial lights." "On Robeson Street anonymous was best. . . ." Sometimes the feeling is ambiguity: "This America is a wonderful place, one immigrant said. If it's a cage, then it's safe."

Many of her works deal with characters facing loneliness or homelessness as Howe, herself the mother of three ethnically mixed children, felt alienated and alone—outside white middle-class society, but not accepted in black neighborhoods. *One Crossed Out,* published in 1997, tells the story of May, a homeless madwoman. Even the jumbled ramblings of May contain passages referring to the metaphysical, a constant in Howe's writing. Many consider Howe to be a religious author. May, like some of Howe's other characters is a wanderer—homeless, nomadic, and lonely. These themes are recurrent in Howe's writings.

Howe's 1980 novel *The White Slave* is based on a true manuscript. A white baby is taken from his mother and given to a black slave to rear as her own. The child experiences the life of a slave firsthand, as well as the love and compassion of his adopted mother. Again, through this book, Howe deals with the racial dichotomy of American society.

In "The Right Thing" Howe tells the story of a white liberal couple in Boston who adopt a black boy as a social obligation and three years later return him, believing it is the right thing to do, but condemning him to a future of foster homes and life on the streets. One of Howe's common themes is that of white, middle-class hypocrisy.

In Howe's poem "Jasmine and the Gypsies," she addresses being lost, alone, destitute, abandoned, and nomadic. In the following line she expresses nomadism in the global terms of her family ethnic makeup: "I'm walking the globe from Africa to Ireland. . . ." Howe is known to write the story of the outsider, one not fully accepted into American society.

Howe has been the recipient of numerous awards, including fellowships with the McDowell Colony in 1965 and 1990 and the Bunting Institute in 1974. She received the St. Botolph Award for fiction in 1976 and the Writers Choice Award for Fiction in 1984. Howe was the recipient of the Village Voice Award for Fiction in 1988 and the California Council on the Arts Award for poetry in 1993. She received the National Poetry Foundation Award and the Chancellor's Associates Faculty Award for Excellence in the Arts from the University of California in San Diego in 1998. Also in 1998, Howe received the Best of the Small Presses Award for *Standards.* In 1999 Howe received the America Award for *Nod,* and in 2001 she won the Lenore Marshall Poetry Prize for *Selected Poems.* That same year she was a finalist for the Griffin Poetry Prize.

Howe's writing offers extreme and poignant portraits of the American urban landscape and the real cultural and class battles encountered by the poor and forgotten in American. But Howe is often most concerned with what occurs inside, emotionally and spiritually, and the loneliness of the outsider, the one who has not fit in or been accepted by main stream society. She is known as one of the most important experimental American poets today. Howe has spent more than 30 years exploring her cultural background in relationship to American society and against the backdrop of American inner-city settings. Her Irish heritage has been crucial to her unique perspective on American social class, race relations, and her view on homelessness and loneliness.

Melanie Zimmer

References

Clancy, Liam. *The Mountain of the Women: Memoirs of an Irish Troubadour.* New York: Doubleday, 2002.

Kane, Daniel. *What Is Poetry?* New York: Teachers and Writers Collaborative, 2003.

HUGHES, ARCHBISHOP JOHN (1797–1864)

John Joseph Hughes was born in Co. Tyrone in Ireland, but he is indelibly linked with Catholicism in the United States. For 26 years, from 1838 until his death in 1864, Hughes led the Catholic Church in New York. In some respects, he was the embodiment of the Irish-American dream. His father was a poor farmer in Co. Tyrone. Hughes, who had little formal education or money, immigrated to the United States in 1817. After his arrival he worked as a builder and a gardener, but when he died he was archbishop of New York.

Portrait of Archbishop John Hughes, Catholic archbishop of New York from 1838 to 1864 and founder of Freeman's Journal. *(National Archives)*

Through the intervention of Mother Elizabeth Seton the uneducated Hughes was admitted to Mount Saint Mary's seminary in 1820. Hughes's success and rise to prominence was rapid. He was ordained in Philadelphia in 1826, and by 1838 he had been consecrated a bishop. Unlike that of his predecessors, Hughes's style of leadership was energetic and forceful rather than contemplative. In 1840 he helped to found the *Freeman's Journal* in New York, which provided a vehicle for expressing his views to a wide audience. His forceful personality was particularly evident in his handling of anti-Catholic bigotry and Protestant attempts at proselytism, both of which were widespread. The movement by fundamental Protestants to promote their religion and maintain Anglo-Saxon supremacy in the States was referred to as "nativism." It was a powerful movement and appeared unassailable as Protestantism permeated many institutions in the United States. Moreover, schools were Protestant controlled, and reading the Protestant bible was prevalent in the curriculum. In 1843, the American Protestant Society had been formed for the purpose of converting Catholic immigrants. In 1847 Hughes issued a pastoral letter condemning the Protestant clergy's attempts to convert Catholics in institutions. He believed

Catholics had the right to defend themselves against Protestant attacks. In the 1840s also, Catholic churches and convents were burnt in Philadelphia and Boston. In 1842, the year Hughes became bishop of New York, his house was stoned and ransacked by nativists, and the windows of the Catholic cathedral were smashed. Hughes responded with characteristic vigor. He issued a robust admonition to Protestant extremists, warning them that "if a single Catholic church were burned in New York, the city would become a Moscow." Significantly, no churches were burnt in New York. In 1844 he again called on Catholics to physically defend themselves and church property against nativist rioters. Three thousand Irishmen answered his call, armed with a variety of weapons ranging from shillelaghs to guns, and he formed them into cadres.

In addition to using physical force, Hughes realized the political potential of Irish Catholics. A number of politicians were aware of the power of the Irish vote and made attempts to woo them at election time. By 1839, there were about 60,000 Catholics in New York, many of whom were Irish. This number increased substantially in the wake of the Famine exodus. Hughes believed education was the key to unlocking the opportunities available in the United States to Irish immigrants, and one of his enduring aspirations was for Catholics to have their own parochial schools, financed by the government. Hughes therefore challenged the New York Public School Society, which was responsible for providing an exclusively Protestant education system. He was supported by Governor William Seward but opposed by powerful nativists, including John Quincy Adams and John Calhoun.

After the 1841 New York City election, Hughes was successful in getting the authorities to introduce legislation allowing wards to run their own Catholic schools. This legislation angered nativists, and their vehement opposition meant the bill was not passed and no money was made available for Catholic schools. After 1842, however, religious education was barred from public schools. Hughes's victory at winning public funds for Catholic parochial education was short lived, but defeat made him more determined. Following this disappointment, Hughes threw his energies into creating a separate Catholic school system in New York. One of his greatest achievements was the creation of a parochial school system paid for by Catholic parishioners, which ran parallel with the official system. At the time of his death, there were 100 such Catholic schools within his diocese. Moreover, he was instrumental in founding Fordham University and Mount St. Vincent College.

In 1850, largely because of Hughes's reputation, New York became an archdiocese and he became archbishop. This was not only an achievement for Hughes personally, but it was also a tribute to the success of the Catholic Church in America. As archbishop, Hughes continued to fight for separate Catholic education. Hughes remained concerned with the fact that many public and private establishments were Protestant, and sometimes priests were denied access to patients in hospitals and other institutions. In some cases, Protestant authorities even took advantage of their monopoly by seeking to convert the inmates. Hughes therefore wanted distinctive Catholic institutes, such as orphanages, hospitals, banks, and social societies. In 1846 Hughes invited the Sisters of Mercy from Ireland to New York—to increase the number of clergy and create a female workforce for hospitals and schools. Hughes's sister, Sister Mary Angela Hughes, was also in religious orders, and she and her fellow Sisters of Charity ran St. Vincent's Hospital, which opened in 1849 in Lower Manhattan. As the Famine Irish arrived in New York, however, it was hard for such institutions to keep pace with the demands made on them. By the 1850s, various religious bodies, including the St. Vincent de Paul Society and the Sisters of Mercy, were operating a network of welfare provision for the poorest members of society, providing alms, medical support, shelter, clothing, and advice about education, employment, and saving. The nuns within the New York diocese also organized employment agencies, finding work for female immigrants from Ireland, who outnumbered male immigrants. Hughes encouraged the foundation of the Society for the Protection of Destitute Catholic Children, which was known as the Catholic Protectory.

Hughes's growing power coincided with the massive Irish Catholic immigration triggered by the Great Famine. More than any earlier generation of immigrants, the latest influx viewed themselves as exiles, and their religion and their ethnicity fused to give them a new social identity. As Hughes realized, the Church allowed the immigrants to bridge the gap between Ireland and America, while providing them with an outlet for expressing their Irish identity. To ensure that the Church played a central role in their new homes, Catholic institutions were established to look after their social as well as their spiritual needs. The establishment of parochial schools gave the Catholic Church more visibility in everyday life, as did the increased number of parish churches, all of which made the Catholic Church more accessible to ordinary people. The Catholic clergy undertook missions to the worst slum districts in New York, where they attempted to bring the poorest immigrants back to the Church. Chastity, temperance, avoidance of sin, and piety were at the core of the Church's teachings. Significantly, many Irish Americans defined themselves by their parishes, which became a centers of their lives. Overall, Irish Catholics were more devout in the United States than they had been in Ireland. Devotion to the Catholic Church was also helped by nativist opposition, which was histrionically anti-Catholic. However, Hughes was an integrationalist, and he wanted the immigrants to combine their Irishness with American patriotism. He described himself as being "an American by choice, not by chance." Despite his love of Ireland, he supported a program of Americanizing Irish immigrants, although he rejected the idea that this process should involve a move to Protestantism. The creation of a Catholic Irish-American identity, however, excluded Irish immigrants who were Protestants, and it was contrary to the secular, nonsectarian view of the radicals of both 1798 and 1848.

For Irish people throughout the world, the late 1840s were dominated by the unfolding of a prolonged famine in Ireland. Within the United States, massive amounts of money were raised by individuals and specially formed committees for the distressed poor in Ireland. On March 20, 1847, Hughes spoke at a fund-raising event on behalf of the New York Famine Relief Committee. His impassioned speech indicated that he was more critical of the British government than many of his fellow bishops in Ireland. His lecture was entitled

"Antecedent Causes of the Irish Famine" and made it clear that the Famine was not attributable merely to the potato blight, but that it was necessary to ask why the lives of so many had been "left dependent on the capricious growth of a single root?" He attributed the Famine to a number of causes that he classified as the incompleteness of conquest, bad government, and a defective or vicious system of social economy.

Although Hughes laid many of the ills of Ireland at the door of the British government, he did not support rebellion, even in the midst of a famine. Essentially, Hughes was a social conservative, although he had been an admirer of the constitutional methods of Daniel O'Connell, the leader of the Irish Repeal Movement. After O'Connell's death in 1847, the political vacuum was filled by a group of radical intellectuals, known as "Young Ireland." In 1848, believing Ireland could never get justice from a British government, the Young Ireland leadership prepared for a rebellion. Yet, despite his advocacy of physical force in New York, Hughes opposed it in Ireland, continuing to support constitutional methods. He believed the 1798 uprising had been an unmitigated catastrophe for Ireland and that a fresh one would be similarly disastrous. Nonetheless, in August 1848 Hughes attended a meeting in New York on behalf of the Irish republican movement, and he even made a donation, which he insisted should be used to purchase shields and not weapons should there be an uprising in Ireland.

At this stage, supporters in the United States were unaware that a small uprising had already taken place in Ballingarry in Co. Tipperary and that it had been easily defeated by the Irish Constabulary, with only two casualties. Following the failure of the 1848 uprising Hughes once again became an implacable enemy of the Young Ireland movement. His antagonism was most apparent in his attacks on Thomas D'Arcy McGee, who had escaped from Ireland in 1848 and founded the *New York Nation.* McGee opposed Hughes's attempts to involve the Catholic Church in education, as he believed education should be secular. As more Young Irelanders sought exile in the United States, including the renowned leaders, Thomas Francis Meagher and John Mitchel, Hughes remained a firm opponent of Irish republicanism, secret societies, and radical movements.

The success of the Catholic Church in the United States was apparent in August 1858 when, in front of more than 100,000 people, the cornerstone of Saint Patrick's Cathedral was laid. It was to replace the smaller, original Saint Patrick's Cathedral. This project was completed in 1879, by which time Hughes was dead. Nonetheless, it remained a tribute to his imagination and vision. The building of the cathedral was suspended during the Civil War. Hughes supported the Union in this conflict, and he believed the involvement of Irish soldiers in the war would link the Irish with American patriotism. He gave his blessing to the formation of Irish brigades, seeing it as a way of protecting Catholics in an overwhelmingly Protestant army. Hughes supported the war in a less obvious way. In the early months of 1862 he undertook a covert visit to Europe on behalf of the American government to raise support for the Union. However, Hughes opposed the Conscription Act of 1863, which was an attempt to bring more men into the Union Army. It required 200,000 men to be drafted, but permitted people to buy exclusion for $300. Hughes opposed the act on the grounds that it discriminated against the poor. In the violent riots that followed the introduction of the act, Catholic priests mediated between police and rioters, both sides being predominantly Irish. Although ill, Hughes attempted to mediate between the different sides in the riot, but he was saddened by what he viewed as the reemergence of nativism in the midst of a war.

Archbishop Hughes died January 3, 1864, unaware that the riots marked an end rather than a continuation of nativism, which he had so vigorously opposed during his lifetime.

Christine Kinealy

See also: CATHOLIC CHURCH, the; GREAT FAMINE, The; McGEE, Thomas D'Arcy; NATIVISM AND ANTI-CATHOLICISM

References

Bayor, Ronald H., and Timothy J. Meagher. *The New York Irish.* Baltimore, MD: Johns Hopkins University Press, 1996.

Billington, Ray Allen. *The Protestant Crusade: A Study of the Origins of American Nativism.* New York: Macmillan, 1938.

Carthy, Margaret. *A Cathedral of Suitable Magnificence. St Patrick's Cathedral, New York.* New York: Health Policy Advisory Center, 1983.

Hassard, John R. G.. *Life of the Most Reverend John Hughes D.D. First Archbishop of New York with Extracts from His Private Correspondence.* 1866. Reprint, New York: Arno Press, 1969.

Shaw, Richard. *Dagger John. The Unquiet Life and Times of Archbishop John Hughes of New York.* New York: Paulist Press, 1977.

HURLING IN ARGENTINA

In 1887, just three years after the founding of the Gaelic Athletic Association (GAA) in Ireland, hurling was being widely played in Argentina, particularly in Mercedes and Capitán Sarmiento. However, the game was not played on any competitive basis. The first organized game was played on May 1900 in a field belonging to the Irish Catholic Association in Caballito, a district of Buenos Aires, which is today a public square known as Plaza Irlanda. Another game was played on July 15, 1900, between Palermo and Almagro. Each team had only nine players because of the shortage of hurleys.

The Buenos Aires Hurling Club—the local branch of the GAA—was founded on August 5, 1900; James P. Harte (d. 1932) of Co. Cork was its first president and William Bulfin was a committee member. Bulfin was a key sponsor of hurling in Argentina through his articles in the *Southern Cross* newspaper, which published hurling rules, a plan of the hurling field, and indications on how teams were to be placed. Initially, teams were to be formed by 17 players a side. However, in practice games played in Caballito there were as many as 30 players a side. Enthusiasm for the game spread rapidly, and soon clubs were founded in departments with significant Irish populations. The most noteworthy were in towns such as San Andrés de Giles, Rojas, and Chacabuco. Hurling was introduced in the 1930s to the Fahy Institute, a boarding school for Irish Argentines in Capilla del Señor, and its ex-pupils were to form two of the outstanding teams of the countryside, the Capilla Boys and the Fahy Boys.

Up to 1914, games were organized every weekend on a regular basis. These games received good coverage from the local press, including *La Nación* newspaper. The playing of hurling declined when it became difficult to import hurleys from

Ireland during World War I, but resumed after the end of the war. In 1919 the hurling field in Buenos Aires was located in the corner of Neuquén and Bellavista.

One of the persons who did most to further the game in Argentina was Miguel E. Ballesty (1876–1950) of Salto, son of Patrick Ballesty and Ann Kelly of Co. Westmeath. On August 16 and 27, 1920, Miguel Ballesty organized meetings with representatives of three clubs, St. Patrick's College, Capilla Boys, and Bearna Baoghail, and founded the Argentine Hurling Federation. On October 21, 1921, a special game was played in Mercedes in honor of Laurence Guinell, diplomatic envoy of the Irish Republic, who was on special mission in Argentina. Another game was played at the same place on October 31, 1921, when a team of Irish Argentines defeated a team of Irish-born players. On October 15, 1922, the first hurling championship was won by the Wanderers, followed by Capilla Boys.

From October 1922 the playing field was rented from Club Banco Nación in Vélez Sarsfield, a suburb of Buenos Aires, where a fine wooden clubhouse was erected and painted green, white, and orange. Because of the construction of a new street, the club was moved to Villa Devoto. These grounds were to witness the golden age of hurling in Argentina during the next 22 years. Most of the great games between the leading teams were played there, and it also held many of the great Irish-Argentine gatherings. The club made one further move in 1948 and settled in Hurlingham, where it still continues to flourish through rugby and field hockey.

On October 18, 1923, the Hurling Club celebrated its Silver Jubilee with hurling games, speeches, and a barbecue. Gerald Foley (1868–1927) of Co. Offaly, Bulfin's successor as editor of the *Southern Cross* and supporter of the GAA in Argentina, paid tribute to all those who had worked hard to keep hurling alive, especially James P. Harte, Miguel Ballesty, and Patricio F. Byrne.

Numerous clubs were formed during the 40 years the game prospered in Argentina: Buenos Aires, Almirante Brown, Fahy Boys, Capilla Boys (Capilla del Señor), St. Patrick's College (Mercedes), St. Paul's College (Capitán Sarmiento), Juniors Hurling Club, and National Hurling Club. Frequently, the idea to establish these and other clubs came from Roman Catholic priests. The Irish chaplain Father Edmund Flannery promoted the first games played in 1900 in the grounds of the Argentine Catholic Association in Caballito. Father Santiago Ussher was an ardent supporter of hurling, as were many of the Passionist and Pallotine fathers established in Argentina. Passionist Brother Clement Roche coached St. Paul's College pupils and they soon became proficient in the game. Father Stanislaus Gill, C.P., director of the same school in 1938, was an outstanding hurler in his youth and even in ripe old age was not slow to challenge the skill of men of a younger generation. Some of these priests used their contacts in Ireland to promote hurling in Argentina. In the 1930s Father Vincent O'Sullivan, S.C.A., was given 100 hurleys and six sliothars (hurling balls) by the Cork County Board for the boys of the Fahy Institute. Thurles Sarsfield Club sent hurleys to Father Tony Kelly, S.C.A., an ex-member of the club who labored many years in Buenos Aires. Father Pat O'Brien, born in Argentina, became a skilful hurler while studying in Ireland.

It is commonly accepted that World War II put an end to hurling in Argentina, when it became very difficult or impossible to import hurleys from Ireland. However, there were other reasons. Some members of the Irish-Argentine community thought that hurling, instead of being a uniting factor, was causing quite an amount of discord and division in the community. Some old players still remember the scandal of some fights among hurlers after the game. Hurling was almost entirely confined to people of Irish origin, the number of people playing hurling was relatively small, and clubs were few in number. Clubs were playing each other too often, which was not a happy state of affairs, and it often led to tension and even bitterness among members of a community that was small in relation to the population of the country. From the 1930s onward there was a steady transference of players, resources, and enthusiasm from hurling to field hockey, a sport popular in England and that some historians claim had its origins in hurling. The Hurling Club won the national hockey championship for five years. Half of the players on the Argentine hockey team that played in the 1948 Olympic Games in London were from the Hurling Club.

In Argentina, hurling and teaching the Irish language did not follow the same patterns of success. The Argentine branch of the Gaelic League was founded on May 1889 in the Passionist monastery of Capitán Sarmiento; J. E. O'Curry was its first president. Initially, the Gaelic movement took strong hold among many Irish and Irish-Argentine residents in the countryside of Buenos Aires and Santa Fe. However, on October 28, 1902, the *Southern Cross* editor Gerald Foley wrote to William Bulfin and remarked that although hurling was very successful the Gaelic League was advancing very slowly. As they came from English-speaking areas in Ireland, most of the Irish settlers in Argentina were not native speakers of Irish. Additionally, their interest in Irish nationalism was socially driven and motivated by the opportunities to make connections in their circles. Furthermore, in the first decades of the twentieth century the majority of the upper segment in the Irish-Argentine community was already incorporated into the Argentine landed bourgeoisie, which was markedly Anglophile, and thus had little interest in supporting Irish nationalists and their efforts to teach the Irish language.

In Argentina the nationalist discourse behind the practice of hurling and learning the Irish language was more popular among young members of the Irish landless proletariat, particularly the sons of waged rural laborers and railway company employees, who felt a need to be recognized as different from other immigrants' children, and belonging to a culture perceived by many as superior to that of the Italian or Spanish settlers. Hurling was an important element in building the identity of this segment, a process in which members of the Roman Catholic clergy saw an opportunity to differentiate their flock from the upper social segments influenced by Protestant cultures. Hurling represented a factor of identity against that characterized by cricket, soccer, and polo, which were predominantly played by English, Anglo Argentines, and wealthy Irish Argentines. Hurling was also viewed as a masculine entertainment, in contrast to lawn tennis, which in the beginning was practiced primarily by women. Perceptions changed in the second half of the twentieth century, when rugby football began to be regarded as the ultimate masculine sport, and field hockey was adopted as a popular entertainment among Irish and other private schools for girls.

Edmundo Murray

See also: BULFIN, William; EMIGRATION

References

Hayes, Seán S. "Hurling in Argentina." *Gaelic Athletic Association: A Century of Service, 1884–1984.* Dublin: Cumann Luthcleas Gael, 1984

King, Seamus J. *The Clash of the Ash in Foreign Fields: Hurling Abroad.* Cashel: Author's Edition, 1998.

Passionist Fathers of Argentina. *Golden Jubilee of the Monastery Saint Paul's Retreat of the Passionist Fathers.* Capitán Sarmiento: Passionist Fathers, 1938.

Raffo, Víctor. *El Origen Británico del Deporte Argentino: Atletismo, Cricket, Fútbol, Polo, Remo y Rugby Durante las Presidencias de Mitre, Sarmiento y Avellaneda.* Buenos Aires: Author's Edition, 2004.

HUSTON, ANJELICA (1951–)

Anjelica Huston was born in Santa Monica, California, on July 8, 1951, the first daughter of film director John Huston (1906–1987) and ballet dancer Enrica (Ricki) Soma (1929–1969). She spent most of her childhood at St. Cleran's, Huston's country house outside Galway, and attended Kylemore Abbey School. From an early age she had aspirations of becoming an actress and, at the age of 18, was cast in the lead role in her father's production of *A Walk with Love and Death* (1969), which was adapted from a short story by Hans Koningsberger. The film was neither a critical nor a commerical success, and Anjelica's performance was particularly panned. The devastating reviews that she received led to the curtailment of her acting career and for a number of years she focused her attention on her modeling career. Although unconventional in the context of ideals of beauty within 1970s fashion, her statuesque looks attracted the attention of top photographers, including Richard Avedon.

During the 1970s Huston took a variety of minor roles and cameos in films (e.g., *The Last Tycoon* [1976], *The Postman Always Rings Twice* [1981], *Frances* [1982], and *This Is Spinal Tap* [1984]), but it was her major role in *Prizzi's Honor* (1985), directed by John Huston and starring her partner, Jack Nicholson, that propelled her back into the limelight. Her superb performance as the scheming Maerose Prizzi won her a Best Supporting Actress Oscar. Two years later she took the lead role in her father's final film, *The Dead* (1987), based on James Joyce's short story. The film was one of the high points of John Huston's career, and Anjelica's performance as Gretta Conroy won her much critical acclaim. Her subsequent career has seen her taking on mainstream projects such as *The Witches* (1990), *The Addams Family* (1991), *The Addams Family Values* (1995), and gritty film noirs and dramas like *The Grifters* (1990), which earned her a Best Actress Oscar nomination. She also appeared in *The Crossing Guard* (1995), and in a number of nonmainstream and independent films such as *Buffalo 66* (1998).

In recent years Huston has started to direct and produce her own films. Her directorial debut, a searing and courageous drama about child abuse called *Bastard Out of Carolina* (1996), though critically praised, was shelved by its original production company following concerns about its uncompromising, controversial material. She returned to directing—and to Ireland—with her 1999 adaptation of Brendan O'Carroll's comic play, *The Mammy* (retitled *Agnes Browne*), in which she also took the lead role. The film received mixed reviews. Throughout her career as an actress she has worked with many of the top established directors, including John Huston, Woody Allen, and Francis Ford Coppola, as well as working with actor-directors such as Sean Penn and Vincent Gallo. Her acting range has also developed, and she has proved herself equally adept at comic and dramatic roles.

After her long-term relationship with Jack Nicholson ended, she married the distinguished Mexican-born American sculptor, Robert Graham, in 1992. Her latest directorial effort was *Riding the Bus with My Sister* in 2005.

Gwenda Young

See also: HUSTON, John

References

Huston, John. *An Open Book.* London: Columbus Books, 1988.

Grobel, Lawrence. *The Hustons.* Revised ed. New York: Cooper Square Press, 2000.

HUSTON, JOHN (1906–1987)

John Marcellus Huston was born on August 5, 1906, in Nevada, Missouri, the son of actor Walter Huston and journalist Rhea. Brought up by his mother after his parents' divorce, John only established a closer relationship with his father during his teenage years. At the age of 10 Huston was diagnosed with Bright's disease, a diagnosis that limited his physical activities for two years. However, in 1920 he entered the San Diego Army and Military Academy and soon developed an interest in boxing (as a teenager John even toyed with the idea of training to be a professional boxer).

Huston made his stage debut in a minor role in a New York production of *The Easy Mark,* starring his father, Walter. He continued to take small roles in productions for the Provincetown Playhouse Theater, during which time his father established himself as one of the American theater's most important actors.

By 1929 John Huston was dabbling in writing: he published his first short story, "Fool," in the prestigious *The American Mercury* magazine; worked as a journalist for *The New York Graphic;* and wrote a short play for marionettes, *Frankie and Johnny.*

In 1931, John followed his father to Hollywood, where he secured a screenwriting job at Universal studios. His first credit was for work on one of his father's films, *A House Divided,* work that caught the attention of the film's director, William Wyler, and Universal's boss, Carl Laemmle Jr. More films followed, including *Law and Order* (starring Walter Huston) and an uncredited contribution to the screenplay of the influential horror film *Murders in the Rue Morgue.*

Despite some initial success at Universal, Huston found the life of a Hollywood screenwriter frustrating: many of his ideas and treatments remained unproduced, and in the early 1930s he also battled with personal problems (including involvement in a car accident that resulted in the death of a female pedestrian). Huston left Hollywood in 1934 and moved to Britain, where he signed a contract with British-Gaumont. However, his experiences with British studios—he also worked, very briefly, for Ealing studios—were largely unproductive, and in 1935 he returned to the United States.

In 1935 Huston starred in a Works Progress Administration (WPA) theater production of Howard Koch's *The Lonely*

Man in Chicago, but by 1937 he had returned to Hollywood, where he secured a screenwriting contract with Warner Brothers. The period 1937–1941 was immensely productive for him: he contributed to or cowrote eight A-budget films, including William Wyler's production of *Jezebel,* starring Bette Davis; *The Amazing Dr. Clitterhouse* and *Dr. Ehrlich's Magic Bullet,* both starring Edward G. Robinson; *Wuthering Heights,* with Laurence Olivier and Merle Oberon; *High Sierra,* with Humphrey Bogart; and *Sergeant York,* starring Gary Cooper. Huston's work on *Dr. Ehrlich's Magic Bullet* garnered him an Academy Award nomination for best screenwriter (with Norman Burnstine and Heinz Herald).

In 1941 Huston made his directorial debut with an adaptation of Dashiell Hammett's *The Maltese Falcon.* This was the third film adaptation of Hammett's 1931 novel, and it proved to be the most effective at depicting the noir world of Sam Spade. The film's star, Humphrey Bogart, had already worked with Huston on *High Sierra* and *The Amazing Dr. Clitterhouse,* and despite not being the studio's first choice for the role of Sam Spade (Warner Brothers favored George Raft), his performance firmly established him in the first rank of American screen stars. The film also featured a cameo from Walter Huston (as the dying sea captain, Jacobi), and supporting performances from Mary Astor, Sydney Greenstreet, and Peter Lorre. Huston also took a screenwriting credit for the adaptation (which followed Hammett's novel very faithfully), and his work earned him a second Academy Award nomination.

Huston's next directing effort, an adaptation of Ellen Glasgow's crime melodrama, *In This Our Life,* was generally considered to be less successful than *The Maltese Falcon,* but its sympathetic depiction of African Americans was evidence of Huston's liberal politics. Huston's third film, *Across the Pacific,* reunited him with Bogart and Greenstreet and successfully injected the action genre with wartime ideology. Soon after completing production on *Across the Pacific,* Huston left Hollywood to join the U.S. Signal Corps and was stationed in the remote Aleutian Islands. Huston spent the war years directing documentaries, beginning with *Report from the Aleutians* in 1943 and followed by *San Pietro* (aka *The Battle of San Pietro*), which was filmed in Italy in 1943–1944. He completed his wartime trilogy with the controversial and moving *Let There Be Light,* which depicted the troubles of soldiers suffering from mental illnesses as a result of war service. The U.S. Army deemed the film too disturbing and controversial, and it was not theatrically released until 1980.

In 1947 Huston returned to Warner Brothers and began production on one of his most acclaimed films, *The Treasure of the Sierra Madre.* Shot on locations in Mexico and California, the film showed how gold fever affects three prospectors; the grueling production tested the endurance of its cast and crew (including Bogart and Walter Huston). The film also made Academy Award history in 1949 when both Walter and John won awards for acting, directing, and screenwriting. Huston worked with Bogart again the following year on his production of *Key Largo,* which also reunited him with Edward G. Robinson.

Huston's liberal politics were increasingly challenged in the growing conservatism of postwar America, and in 1947 he was instrumental in establishing the Committee for the First Amendment, a group comprising leading Hollywood writers, actors, and directors, protesting the House Un-American Activities Committee's (HUAC) treatment of the Hollywood Ten. Although the Committee for the First Amendmet traveled to Washington as HUAC was questioning the Hollywood Ten, they were not successful in preventing the jail sentences imposed on them. Despite this setback, Huston remained supportive of the Hollywood Ten and would continue to lend his name to a variety of liberal causes.

Huston's next film, an adaptation of W. R Burnett's crime novel *The Asphalt Jungle,* featured a strong cast, including Sterling Hayden, Sam Jaffe, and Marilyn Monroe in a small role. The film remains one of the seminal examples of the heist genre. Soon after the film was released, Huston was dealt a personal blow with the sudden death of his father, Walter. While *The Asphalt Jungle* had been a relatively modest production, his next film, an ambitious production of Stephen Crane's *The Red Badge of Courage,* was anything but: the film's troubled shoot and edit were the subject of a series of articles by Lillian Ross that were later collected and published as a book, *Picture,* in 1952. The film, which starred real-life war hero Audie Murphy in a lead role, was drastically cut down and released to lukewarm reviews.

The rise of McCarthyism and greater opportunities for filming in Europe spurred Huston to base himself outside the United States for most of the 1950s. In 1951 he traveled to the Belgian Congo (now Zaire) to shoot a film of C. S. Forester's novel *The African Queen.* Featuring a script by acclaimed writer (and Huston fan) James Agee, the film costarred Humphrey Bogart as Charlie Allnutt, a rogue riverboat captain, and Katharine Hepburn as Rose Sayer, a straitlaced missionary. The film's shoot, which was later fictionalized by Peter Viertel in his novel *White Hunter, Black Heart,* was a taxing experience for the cast and crew, many of whom were struck down with malaria and dysentery. The production was also marked by personal happiness for Huston: during the shoot he received news that his wife, Ricki Soma, had given birth to his first child, Anjelica.

The next few years saw Huston work mainly in Europe. In 1952 he shot a film about fin de siècle Paris and the life of Toulouse Lautrec (*Moulin Rouge*), and the following year *Beat the Devil,* a crime caper comedy based on a script by Truman Capote and featuring an all-star cast that included Bogart, Jennifer Jones, Peter Lorre, and Gina Lollobrigida. The reviews for both films were mixed: *Beat the Devil* divided critics, who either loved or loathed its freewheeling style. Huston's European sojourn became more permanent when he purchased a rundown mansion called St. Cleran's in Co. Galway in 1957. The next few years were spent restoring the house, and the Huston family—which now included a son, Tony (b. 1952)—relocated to St. Cleran's in 1959.

Ireland was the main location for Huston's next project, an ambitious film of Herman Melville's *Moby Dick,* adapted by Ray Bradbury and starring Gregory Peck in the role of Captain Ahab. Filmed mainly in Youghal, Co. Cork, the film performed disappointingly at the box office, despite some positive reviews. Huston's next location was the Caribbean island of Tobago, where he shot *Heaven Knows, Mr. Allison,* the story of a nun (Deborah Kerr) and a marine (Robert Mitchum) stranded on a remote island during World War II. The film made effective use of Mitchum and Kerr—both favorite actors of Huston's—and remains one of Huston's most underrated films. Huston's experience of working in Japan with John Wayne on his next film, *The Barbarian and the Geisha,* was less happy: director and actor clashed, and the resulting film was poorly received by critics and the public. In addition, 1958 saw the release of another Huston film, *The Roots of Heaven,* another production that fared badly at the box office.

Huston's last film of the decade was *The Unforgiven,* starring Burt Lancaster, Audrey Hepburn, and veteran actress Lillian Gish. The film's western theme anticipated his next production, *The Misfits,* which was shot in Nevada the following year. Based on Arthur Miller's screenplay and featuring a heavyweight cast that included Miller's then wife, Marilyn Monroe, screen icon Clark Gable, and Montgomery Clift, the film was a complex and perceptive treatment of broken dreams and troubled lives. The film shoot was difficult for all involved, and Gable died shortly after the film was completed. Upon its release in 1961, the film garnered positive reviews, and the performances by all three leads were highly praised. Huston worked again with Montgomery Clift the following year on *Freud,* another troubled production that resulted in a film that received mixed reviews.

Huston returned to Europe in 1963 to shoot *The List of Adrian Messenger,* which featured cameos by Frank Sinatra, Burt Lancaster, and Robert Mitchum, cameos that were not enough to win the film critical praise or box office success. Despite Huston's busy directing schedule throughout the 1960s, he continued to pursue other interests: he took several acting jobs in large productions (e.g., appearing in Otto Preminger's *The Cardinal* in 1963, in a performance that won him an Academy Award); he took out Irish citizenship in 1964 and began making representations to the Irish government in an effort to establish an Irish Film Board. Huston's collaborations with leading American writers continued through the 1960s: he directed an adaptation of Tennessee Williams's *The Night of the Iguana* in 1964 and a film version of Carson McCullers's *Reflections in a Golden Eye,* featuring Marlon Brando and Elizabeth Taylor, in 1967. Huston's next collaboration was with his daughter, Anjelica, on the 1969 film, *A Walk with Love and Death,* but the experience was difficult for the young and inexperienced Anjelica, and her performance was poorly received.

After the release of his next film, a thriller called *The Kremlin Letter,* Huston began production on *Fat City,* the story of a down-and-out boxer (played by Stacy Keach). The film's assured representation of the boxing world reflected Huston's familiarity with that milieu, and its gritty urban noir look and strong performances won it acclaim upon its release in 1972. During the 1970s Huston continued to be prolific: he released seven films in all, including a Paul Newman western, *The Life and Times of Judge Roy Bean* in 1972, a big-budget version of Rudyard Kipling's *The Man Who Would Be King,* partly shot in Morocco and starring Sean Connery and Michael Caine, and a well-received adaptation of Flannery O'Connor's Southern Gothic novel *Wise Blood.*

Huston's output slowed down in the 1980s, becaue of increasing health problems (he was diagnosed with emphysema), and some of the film choices he made were surprising (e.g., his production of the musical *Annie* in 1982), but he was back on form with his comic gangster film, *Prizzi's Honor,* in 1985. The film featured strong performances by the leads, Jack Nicholson and Kathleen Turner, but the film's revelation was the superb performance by Anjelica Huston, a performance that won her an Academy Award for Best Actress.

Anjelica Huston took the lead in Huston's final film, a subtle, moving adaptation of James Joyce's short story *The Dead.* Huston had been a long-time admirer of Joyce, and the production of the film was the fulfillment of a long-cherished ambition to successfully adapt Joyce to the screen. He was helped in this task by his son Tony, who took the screenwriting credit. The film was released soon after Huston's death and received positive reviews.

John Huston died of emphysema on August 28, 1987, in Rhode Island. He was survived by his children, Pablo (whom he adopted in the 1940s), Anjelica, Tony, Danny, and Allegra (Ricki Soma's daughter, whom he adopted after Soma's death in 1969).

Gwenda Young

See also: HUSTON, Angelica; HUSTON, Walter; JOYCE, James Augustine Aloysius; O'CONNOR, Flannery; PECK, Gregory; WAYNE, John

References

Desser, David, and Gaylyn Studlar. *Reflections in a Male Eye: John Huston and the American Experience.* Washington, DC: Smithsonian Books, 1993.

Grobel, Lawrence. *The Hustons.* New York: Scribners, 1989.

Huston, John. *An Open Book.* London: Columbus Books, 1988.

HUSTON, WALTER (1884–1950)

Walter Huston (born Walter Houghston) was born in Toronto, Canada, on April 6, 1884, the fourth child of Elizabeth McGibbon (b. 1848) and Robert Houghston (b. 1848, of Irish descent). From an early age Walter showed an interest in performing, and at the age of 16 he took his first role in a traveling production of *The White Heather,* a popular nineteenth-century melodrama. Over the next four years he appeared in minor roles in a number of theater productions in Canada and America, the most notable of which were *In Convict Stripes,* with Lillian Gish, and *The Sign of the Cross.* In 1904 he met and married Rhea Gore (b. 1881); they had one son, John Huston (b. 1906). Soon after, Walter was appointed an operating engineer for the Union Electric Power Company, and by 1909 he was running a power plant in Weatherford, Texas. The lure of acting remained strong, however, and having separated from his wife at the end of 1909, he returned to popular theater and vaudeville shows.

For the next 14 years Huston built up a vaudeville act alongside his second wife, Bayonne Whipple. In 1923 he gave up his Canadian citizenship to become an American citizen; in the same year he moved into legitimate theater, starring in a play called *Mr. Pitt* that won him good reviews. However, his big break came when he accepted the role of 75-year-old patriarch Ephraim Cabot in a New York production of Eugene O'Neill's *Desire Under the Elms.* Critics praised Huston's ability to transform himself into O'Neill's character; this chameleon-like quality would become a trademark of Huston's acting persona in theater and in films.

During the 1920s Huston found further success in the theater, starring in plays such as *The Barker* (1926), *Elmer the Great* (1928), and *The Commodore Marries* (1929). In 1928 he also appeared in his first film, Paramount's production of Ward Morehouse's *Gentleman of the Press.* In the spring of 1929 he received $20,000 for four weeks' work as a villain in Victor Fleming's film of Owen Wister's novel *The Virginian,* starring Gary Cooper; this was followed by his lead role in D. W. Griffith's *Abraham Lincoln* (1930). Throughout the 1930s Huston divided his time between New York theater and Hollywood films, winning critical acclaim on stage with *Dodsworth* (1933) and *Knickerbocker Holiday* (1938), as well as in films such as *The Criminal Code* (1931), *American Madness* (1932), *Beast of the City* (1932), *The Wet Parade* (1932), *Rain* (1932), and *Of Human Hearts* (1938).

Huston's on-screen persona was often that of a man of integrity, holding simple values and adhering to a (sometimes inflexible) moral code. Huston's commitment to his craft and his unfailing professionalism won him the respect and affection of leading directors, actors, and producers in Hollywood. In 1941 he took an uncredited cameo role as the dying sea captain Jacobi in *The Maltese Falcon,* the directorial debut of his son, John; he would also take another unbilled role in John Huston's second film, *In This Our Life.* This was followed by one of his most humorous roles, that of the puckish Mr. Scratch in William Diertele's 1942 adaptation of Stephen Vincent Benet's *The Devil and Daniel Webster.* Although not eligible for active war service during World War II, he nonetheless played an important role in promoting the efforts of America and its allies by appearing in a number of patriotic films, including *Edge of Darkness, Mission to Moscow,* and *The North Star* (all 1943) and *Dragon Seed* (1944).

Following the end of the war, Huston's film output slowed somewhat, though he found time to appear in Joseph Mankiewicz's *Dragonwyck* (1946), as well as King Vidor's epic western melodrama, *Duel in the Sun* (1946). His most memorable role came in a fourth collaboration with his son, this time in an Oscar-winning lead role as the greedy, amoral prospector Howard in *The Treasure of the Sierra Madre.* His final film, a western called *The Furies,* was released in 1950. Though primarily a stage and screen actor, Huston also acted on radio and recorded a popular song, "September Song," which became a major hit in the 1940s.

After a party to mark his sixty-sixth birthday, Huston suffered an abdominal aneurysm and died in California on April 7, 1950.

Gwenda Young

See also: HUSTON, Angelica; HUSTON, John; O'NEILL, Eugene

References

Huston, John. *An Open Book.* London: Columbus Books, 1988.

Grobel, Lawrence. *The Hustons.* Revised ed. New York: Cooper Square Press, 2000.

Illinois

The state of Illinois, named after the native Illiniwek or Illini, became part of the French empire in the late seventeenth century before passing to the British in 1763 as a result of the Seven Years' War. In the aftermath of the American Revolution the area became part of the Northwest Territory (1783), Illinois Territory (1809), and finally the 21st U.S. state in 1818. A significant proportion of the early settlement in southern Illinois comprised Irish republicans who made a deep impression on the emerging political and cultural landscape. Eight of the first 16 governors were of Irish descent, and other notable descendants included Stephen A. Douglas. The population then spread north, displacing tribes in the process (e.g., the Black Hawk War, 1832). Chicago was organized in 1833 and soon became a popular destination for immigrants moving out west.

An Irish population of a few hundred was already established in Chicago by the time a significant growth in the number of Irish immigrants occurred in the 1830s. Chicago was incorporated as a city in 1837 and consolidated itself rapidly, destination for many thousands escaping the Potato Famine. By 1850, Irish immigrants made up approximately one-fifth of the city's population (54 percent of the city's population was foreign born), and by 1860 Chicago had the fourth largest Irish population in the United States. Chicago soon became one of the most important transport hubs in the country, with canals and particularly railroads, and from the late nineteenth century it grew into a powerful city industrially and politically. Its population grew rapidly, making it, by the turn of the century, the nation's second largest city after New York. Chicago's population growth was attributable to large-scale immigration to the United States and the migration of thousands of African Americans from the southern states from the 1910s onwards. The Irish population in Illinois was 27,786 in 1850 and 87,000 in 1860, but a large proportion lived in the city.

Thousands of Irish laborers worked in railroad construction, and many settled along the new routes that were established, especially in Illinois. Many also came by river, and while the prospect of cheap midwestern land attracted some, the vast majority gravitated to urban centers. Irish laborers worked on the Illinois and Michigan Canal (1836–1848) and were strongly represented in the police and fire services and in the public school system. Margaret

Haley's Chicago Teachers' Federation became the first teachers' union in the country. From the 1830s onwards, the majority of Irish in the city were working class, many of whom lived in depressed neighborhoods, often on the South Side of the city. (The Great Chicago Fire of 1871 started at a property owned by Irish immigrants Patrick and Catherine O'Leary.) Slums led to a variety of organizations forming to alleviate conditions. In 1839, Chicago's Mayor Buckner Stith Morris donated his salary to relief for Irish workers. While the number of Irish immigrants did not dramatically decline in the second half of the nineteenth century, their proportion within the state, and particularly Chicago, did decrease, because of the large influx of immigrants from southern and eastern Europe.

The Irish community in Chicago remained fairly cohesive, owing first to a strong involvement in local politics, which would result in one of the most famous city mayoral dynasties in Richard J. Daley (1955–1976) and his son, Richard M. Daley (1989–present) Overwhelmingly Democratic, the Irish became the most significant and influential ethnic group in the city's political machine. In addition to the Daleys, Irish-American mayors were John Hopkins (1893–1895), Edward F. Dunne (1905–1907), William Dever (1923–1927), Edward Kelly (1933–1947), Martin Kennelly (1947–1955), and Jane Byrne (1979–1983). Second, Irish and German Catholics established the foundations of the city's Catholic churches in the 1830s and 1840s, including Saint Patrick's for the Irish in 1846. Until 1916 all of Chicago's Catholic bishops except one were either of Irish birth or first-generation Irish. The smaller number of Irish Protestants tended to distance themselves from the Catholics. Third, among many Irish immigrants there was a strong sense of Irish nationalism, which manifested itself in providing financial support and sometimes volunteering for various nationalist campaigns, notably the Fenians in the 1860s.

The fusion of Irish and Catholic identities at a real or perceived level meant the Irish suffered from the national wave of anti-immigration and anti-Catholic sentiment spearheaded by the Know-Nothing Party in the 1850s. This resulted in Chicago electing a Know-Nothing mayor in 1855 and a Know-Nothing–controlled city council, and waves of anti-Catholicism would hit the city again in the 1890s and again with the second phase of Ku Klux Klan activity in the 1910s.

Illinois would receive much of its popular recognition through its association with Abraham Lincoln, who lived and worked in Springfield (which became state capital in 1837) before becoming the 16th president. During the Civil War Illinois often provided troops by ethnicity or occupation, including Irish, German, Scottish, and Jewish units. James Mulligan, an Irish-American lawyer in Chicago, capitalizing on the famed Fighting Irish regiment from New York, was instrumental in forming the Illinois Irish Brigade, which became the first Irish regiment, followed by a second, the Irish Legion. Interracial and interethnic conflict, often over job competition, spilled over on several occasions (as well as general labor unrest as seen in the Haymarket Riot in 1886), such as the Springfield race riot of 1908, the East St. Louis race riots of 1917, and the Chicago race riot of 1919 in which much of the violence was Irish against blacks, although there was also friction with Italian immigrants over the same period.

Irish immigration slowed in the first half of the twentieth century because of quota systems generally applied to immigration in 1921 and again in 1924 (although aimed primarily at reducing new immigration) and also because of the Depression. The numbers of Irish immigrants resumed in the 1950s and rose significantly again in the 1980s. In the 2000 census people of Irish ancestry represented 12.2% of the state's 12,419,293 inhabitants, and Chicago had the fourth largest concentration of Irish in the United States. The city is famous today, among other things, for its Saint Patrick's Day parades, which involve dyeing the river green, and the city's Irish culture has been highlighted by the success of Michael Flatley, the Chicago-born dancer who featured in *Riverdance.*

Sam Hitchmough

INDIANA

Modern-day Indiana was for hundreds of years a part of the Mississippian culture that stretched across large tracts of America. The area was claimed as part of the French empire in the seventeenth century before passing to the British as part of the post-Seven Years' War settlement in 1763. In turn, the area became part of the new American Republic after the Revolution, within the Northwest Territory. With such turbulence, many Native American tribes throughout this period, especially the Shawnee and the Miami, faced dilemmas regarding issues of loyalty and neutrality, and these often resulted in internal disagreement. Organized as Indiana Territory in 1800, Indiana became the nineteenth state on December 11, 1816.

The first Irish settlers before statehood were predominantly Scotch-Irish, often from other states, such as Kentucky. These settlers established a number of Presbyterian churches. The town of Ireland would later be the natural consolidation of some of the land informally known as the "Irish Settlement." Emigration over the first few years of statehood saw the population mushroom to more than 145,000. Early Irish settlements were in the southern portion of the state along the Ohio River as workers began moving into the state in pursuit of canal and road construction work beginning in the 1830s. These settlers resied in rural worker camps, before a process of urbanization and increased immigration led to more permanent settlement patterns and movement into the central areas of the state. Indiana was not a state that saw particularly large numbers of immigrants as a result of the Famine in the 1840s, although the state population grew significantly during the decade as people relocated from the East Coast, including many Germans (who form the largest ancestry group in modern-day Indiana). From the late 1840s onward, railroad construction would also attract Irish workers (the first large railroad project was completed in 1847). Irish immigration doubled in the 1850s before peaking between 1860 and 1920; the year 1870 witnessed the largest number of Irish when around 29,000 Irish-born immigrants lived in the state. Compared with other states, this population was relatively small, as the state's total population was nearly 1.7 million, but the number nevertheless made up around 14 percent of the foreign-born immigrant population. When, in 1860, 8.8 percent of the population was foreign born, the Irish, perceived as being overwhelmingly

Catholic, were a noticeable element of society, and one that was often subject to a significant level of discrimination. It was, however, a population large enough to shape the community around it, and a range of organizations and societies were formed in the 1870s onward. The Catholic population from different countries had also been influential, and had established, for example, Notre Dame, a Catholic university founded in 1842. The sporting teams from the university famously bear the name the Fighting Irish, but the genuine origin of the name is vague and open to competing stories.

Although most Irish regiments in the Civil War were mustered in the East, Indiana was asked to produce an Irish and a German regiment in addition to regular recruitment (more than 180 regiments). Efforts focused around cities such as Terre Haute and Indianapolis but also the smaller Ohio River communities and, interestingly, tried to allay fears about discrimination by suggesting that proven loyalty would have long-term social benefits. The 35th Indiana Infantry, or the 1st Irish, prominently involved at the Battle of Stones River, were notable for the fact that they were issued emerald-green wool kepis (caps) with a shamrock wreath on the front, adopted for the entire service of the unit from December 11, 1861, to October 23, 1865, as well as a green regimental flag that was presented at a gathering of Irish women and leading Democrats.

While many other states witnessed a further rise in Irish immigration in the 1920s, Indiana once again did not share the same experience; the Irish population proportionally fell across the state, with the exception of a few areas, such as the Lake County mill industry. Indiana's modern economy relies heavily on corn, soybeans, dairy products, melons, tomatoes, and tobacco, as well as manufacturing, including a large steel industry. Indiana's population in the 2000 census was 6,080,485; those of Irish heritage numbered 656,369 and represented 10.8 percent of the state population, the third largest ancestry group in the state.

Sam Hitchmough

References

Doyle, David Noel, and Owen Dudley Edwards, eds. *America and Ireland, 1776–1976: The American Identity and the Irish Connection.* Westport, CT: Greenwood Press, 1980.

Giffin, William W. *The Irish. Peopling Indiana, Volume 1.* Indianapolis: Indiana Historical Society Press, 2006.

Kenny, Kevin. *The American Irish.* London and New York: Pearson Education Ltd., 2000.

Miller, Kerby A. *Emigrants and Exiles: Ireland and the Irish Exodus to North America.* 1985. Reprint, New York: Oxford University Press, 1988.

Peckham, Howard Henry. *Indiana: A History.* Champaign: University of Illinois Press, 2003.

INGRAM, REX (1893–1950)

Born on January 15, 1893 in Rathmines, Dublin, Reginald Ingram Hitchcock would become famous as one of the great film directors of the 1920s. Reginald, or "Rex" as he was more commonly known, was the first of two children born to Francis Hitchcock, an Anglican minister, and his wife, Kathleen Ingram. Francis Hitchcock's ministering duties meant that the family moved several times during Rex's childhood, and by the time Rex was 12 years old he had lived in Offaly, Tipperary, and Dublin. Educated at St. Columba's College in Dublin, Rex's skills as an artist and sportsman attracted more attention than his academic record. His mother's sudden death in 1908 had a profound effect on him, and he would later adopt her maiden name as his surname. In 1911 Rex abandoned plans to study at Trinity College Dublin and boarded the American-bound White Star liner *Celtic* at Queenstown (Cobh) in Cork. Ingram would never return to Ireland, though he remained fiercely proud of his Irish identity. After some initial employment in New Haven, Connecticut, Ingram enrolled in a fine arts program at Yale University in 1912. During his time at Yale he met Charles Edison, son of Thomas Edison, and this encounter seems to have sparked a new, more serious interest in films. By 1913 Ingram had decided that his future lay in filmmaking, and he joined the Edison Company as a general helper. His work there included scriptwriting, set design, acting, and even painting portraits of the actors. After serving his apprenticeship at Edison, Ingram moved on to stints at Vitagraph and Fox before signing with Carl Laemmle, head of Universal studios, in 1916. Laemmle was a veteran of the film industry. He had entered films in 1906 and was known as a risk taker. Laemmle offered Ingram what the other studios would not: a chance to direct his first feature. Ingram's debut as a director was a melodrama, *The Great Problem,* starring Violet Mersereau. He followed this with a number of dramas, most of which were set in foreign locales and boasted exotic themes. These films attracted the attention of film critics who particularly praised Ingram's sophisticated pictorialism and attention to detail. Some months after America's entrance into World War I, Ingram suspended his promising film career and joined the Canadian Flying Corps, but he returned to the film industry at the end of 1918. Although he directed two more films for Universal, he had grown dissatisfied with the studio, and in 1920 he signed with Metro-Goldwyn-Mayer (MGM). In the eight years that followed, he established himself as one of the top directors in the American film industry, balancing critical acclaim with box office success.

Foremost amongst his films of the 1920s was *The Four Horsemen of the Apocalypse* (1921), based on a novel by Vincente Blasco Ibanez and adapted for the screen by June Mathis. This film propelled a minor actor, Rudolph Valentino, to stardom. Though debate continues to rage about who precisely discovered Valentino, there can be no doubt that Ingram was the first director to recognize the charisma and star quality of the Italian actor. The female lead in *The Four Horsemen of the Apocalypse* was given to Alice Terry, an actress who had been in films since 1916 and who would become Ingram's second wife in 1921, after his divorce from Doris Pawn. Terry was herself from an Irish-American background: her father was born in Kildare but immigrated to America as a young man.

The success of *The Four Horsemen of the Apocalypse* was due, in part, to its superior production values and the charisma of Valentino, but the careful attention paid to the presentation of the film in theaters also helped to draw audiences in. Critics lavished praise on the film, and Robert Sherwood claimed that the film "lifts the silent drama to an artistic plane that it has never touched before." Following the critical and commercial success of *Four Horsemen,* Ingram brought a number of classics to the screen, including a version of Balzac's *Eugenie Grandet,* which was filmed as *The Conquering Power* in 1921, and *The Prisoner of Zenda* with Alice Terry and Lewis Stone in 1922.

Ingram's prolific output and commercial success meant that he initially flourished in the film industry. However, as the 1920s wore on and Hollywood became an industry dominated by producers, not directors, he increasingly resented what he perceived to be the intrusions of the so-called "money men" in the making of his films. His resentment toward the studio system was exacerbated by MGM's failure to award him the contract to direct *Ben Hur,* a prestigious project that would have a turbulent production history. In 1924 he traveled to Europe to shoot *The Arab* at the Victorine studios in Nice, France, and on location in North Africa. The positive experience of shooting away from Hollywood convinced Ingram that his future now lay in Europe, and he continued to shoot in Europe and North Africa throughout the 1920s. His last project, a sound film called *Baroud,* was released in 1932. Although Ingram never returned to directing, he remained interested in cinema and the fine arts and was an accomplished painter and sculptor. He died in Hollywood on July 21, 1950.

Gwenda Young

References

Brownlow, Kevin. *The Parade's Gone By.* London: Columbus Books, 1989.

O'Leary, Liam. *Rex Ingram: Master of the Silent Cinema.* 1980. Reprint, London: British Film Institute, 1993.

IOWA

Iowa was first explored in 1673 by French explorers (Joliet and Marquette). From this point forward the numerous local Indian tribes lost land through a blend of forced land sales, encroachment, and removal, some in the fallout of the Black Hawk War (1832). The first official American settlement was established in 1833 on some of the land gained in the latter conflict. Many families settled in the area from a number of states, including Pennsylvania, Kentucky, and Ohio. Less official settlements before this date included a small community of fifty miners, approximately 35 of them Irish, in Dubuque in 1830. This group was notable for writing the Miner's Compact, which was one of the state's first written laws. Numbers of settlers increased in the early to mid-1830s, as did trade using the Mississippi River. With consolidated communities many Irish settlers were able to establish positions of some prominence. Patrick Quigley became the first justice of the peace. F. K. O'Farrell was mayor from 1844 to 1846.

Iowa became the twenty-ninth state on December 28, 1846, and significant increases in the new state's population occurred in the ensuing decades. The Irish population grew from 4,885 in 1850 to 28,072 in 1860. Many Irish were encouraged to settle in the area by those already established in the state both before and after the Civil War, having been urged to avoid the heavily overcrowded cities in the East. This included many letters sent to Ireland, often by religious leaders, urging emigration and discussing the possibilities of settling predominantly Irish towns. Consequently, a number of prominently Irish settlements emerged, such as Keokuk and Temple Hill, and the southern part of Dubuque quickly became known as Little Dublin. Many, including Irish migrants from Pennsylvania and St. Louis, were attracted by the prospect of canal and railroad jobs, as well as cheap land at $1.25 per acre.

In 1853, the Reverend Timothy Mullen brought a number of Irish families to an area south of Des Moines that would become known as the Irish Settlement, which soon embraced several townships. In 1874, a handful of Irish families settled in northern Iowa and established what would become Emmetsburg. Named after the Irish patriot Robert Emmet, the town became the Irish capital of Iowa, and the small town today commemorates its past with a bronze statue of Emmet. However, such numbers attracted a level of resistance reflecting the Know-Nothing knee-jerk popularity of the 1850s, and many Irish experienced discrimination from the anti-Catholic and anti-immigrant group. In 1856, for example, a group of Irish in Des Moines built a new church out of the town center in order to avoid confrontation with Know-Nothings.

By 1860, only a portion of the state could be considered frontier any longer, as the population swelled from 674,913 in 1860 to a postwar 1,194,020 in 1870 (Iowa did not experience any Civil War battles but provided approximately 75,000 men for the Union Army). Indeed, the post–Civil War immigration boom was encouraged by the state itself, which dubbed itself "The Home of Immigrants," and the call was answered by large numbers of Germans and notable numbers of Scandinavians among many others. After a brief surge in the popularity of the Fenian movement in the years immediately after the Civil War, mostly centered around Baltimore, Iowa continued to attract a steady stream of immigrants. However, immigration reflected the nationwide trend of attracting new immigrants in the latter half of the century onward; many Italians and Croats, for example, came to work in the state's small number of coal mines.

Agriculture continued, and still does, to form the economic foundation of the state, with companies such as Quaker Oats originating in the area. Despite being supplemented by a manufacturing base, the state has been involved in the phenomenon of rural flight that has affected several Great Plains states, witnessing population losses. Of the 2000 population, those of Irish ancestry accounted for 13.5 percent of the total, the second largest group behind those of German descent (35.7 percent)

Sam Hitchmough

References

Doyle, David Noel, and Owen Dudley Edwards, eds. *America and Ireland, 1776–1976: American Identity and the Irish Connection.* Westport, CT: Greenwood Press, 1980.

Miller, Kerby A. *Emigrants and Exiles: Ireland and the Irish Exodus to North America.* 1985. Reprint, New York: Oxford University Press, 1988.

Kenny, Kevin. *The American Irish.* London and New York: Pearson Education Ltd, 2000.

Schweider, Dorothy. *Iowa.* Iowa City, IA: University of Iowa Press, 1996.

IRELAND, JOHN (1838–1918)

Born in Co. Kilkenny, John Ireland was raised in Minnesota. He received his early education at local cathedral schools and completed theological studies at Meximieux and Toulon. In 1867 Father Ireland was appointed rector of St. Paul's Cathedral, where he organized the first total alcohol abstinence society in the state. He represented Bishop Grace of St. Paul at Vatican Council I (1869–1870). Pope Pius IX appointed him coadjutor with the right of succession for Bishop Grace. After his consecration in 1875, Ireland initiated a Minnesota settlement scheme for Catholic immigrants in eastern cities, the most successful rural colonization program ever sponsored by the Catholic Church in the United States.

Portrait of John Ireland, archbishop of St. Paul, Minnesota, and founder of the University of Saint Thomas. (Library of Congress)

Bishop Ireland went on to represent his diocese at a number of high-profile church councils. His address on "The Catholic Church and Civil Society," given at the Third Plenary Council of Baltimore (1884), has since been cited as a fundamental tenet of the progressive position in church-state discussions. In 1886, at the Provincial Council of Milwaukee, Ireland successfully petitioned the Holy See to create a new archdiocese west of Milwaukee to accommodate the growth of his diocese. Shortly thereafter, Archbishop Ireland instituted a plan where parochial schools could be rented to local public school boards for use during the school day but be retained for religious instruction outside public school hours. Critics within the Church argued that his plan weakened the position of Catholic education recommended by the Plenary Council, and opponents outside the Church charged him with violating the principle of separation of church and state. Yet he clearly supported the decisions of the Council in other ways, for example, in his assistance in establishing what would become the Catholic University of America. Within his own archdiocese he also founded the College of St. Thomas (1885) and St. Paul Seminary (1894).

Archbishop Ireland's forthright opinions often drew him into controversy. A tireless patriot, he urged the laity to accept the ways and language of their new country and stifled activities, such as those of Peter Paul Cahensly, a zealous lay leader who lobbied for the establishment of dioceses staffed with German-speaking clergy. Ireland's interest in politics, and his allegiance with the Republican party drew some criticism but also the opportunity to perform additional diplomatic duties. In 1887, Ireland was entrusted with a delicate mission to negotiate with the Holy See on behalf of American archbishops who were concerned that the Vatican's censure of the Knights of Labor would alienate a significant portion of their laity. In 1898 the Holy See asked Ireland to use his influence to intercede and possibly avert the impending Spanish-American War. His attempts were in vain, but upon the conclusion of the war he served on the commission that negotiated a settlement between the United States and the Vatican for the friars' lands in the Philippine Islands. As an official guest of the French government, Ireland preached a sermon in Orléans honoring the anniversary of the raising of the siege of that city by St. Joan of Arc. A year later he returned to France at the request of President McKinley to present a statue on behalf of the American people. In return he was invested with the Cross of the Legion of Honor.

In spite of his considerable administrative duties, Ireland produced a significant body of essays, which provide a thoughtful, coherent statement on the challenges the Church faces in a pluralistic and democratic society. His final great project was the construction of a cathedral in St. Paul that was commensurate with the growth and dignity of his archdiocese.

Mike Cottrell

See also: KNIGHTS OF LABOR

References

Barry, Colman James. *The Catholic Church and German Americans.* Milwaukee, WI: Bruce, 1953.

Browne, Henry. "The Catholic Church and the Knights of Labor." *Studies in American Church History* 38 (1949).

Ireland, John. *The Church and Modern Society: Lecture and Addresses.* Chicago: D. H. McBride & Co., 1896.

Moyhnihan, James. *The Life of Archbishop John Ireland.* New York: Harper, 1953.

O'Gorman, Thomas. "The Educational Policy of Archbishop Ireland." *Educational Review* 3 (1892): 462–471.

Reardon, James Michael. *The Catholic Church in the Diocese of St. Paul.* St. Paul, MN: North Central Publishing Co., 1952.

IRISH DANCING IN AMERICA

Records of Irish dancing among the diaspora start with the emigrant ships, which transported hundreds of thousands of people to the United States and Australia during the mid-nineteenth century. Musicians and dancing masters are listed among the ships' crews on long crossings. Dancing was a common feature of the departure parties in Ireland, often called "American wakes." Evidence suggests that as well as constituting a form of entertainment, dancing on board

Dancer Michael Flatley leaps in the air against the Chicago skyline. Flatley, a former Golden Glove boxer, became an international star through the production of Riverdance *and* Lord of the Dance. *(Time & Life Pictures/ Getty Images)*

the emigrant ships was used to express homesickness and fear of what lay ahead. Dancing continued to be an important part of cultural expression among communities where newly arrived immigrant lived. Some of the oldest forms of Irish dancing are still found in the areas first settled by these immigrants, for example the Appalachian Mountains.

Historians suggest that Irish dancing was more readily accepted in the United States than in other countries like Canada, Australia, or New Zealand, where the powerful British influence suppressed Irish culture. The lack of British influence, combined with the contribution Irish immigrants had made to American independence, meant that Irish music and dance were readily accepted and quickly became popular.

As the dances were handed down as part of an oral tradition, their origins can be difficult to trace. There are few written references to the specifics of Irish dancing in North America in the nineteenth century, and even in the twentieth century little has been published. Many of the traditional elements of Irish dance have persisted, but it also evolved and absorbed elements of the existing American culture. This integration of old and new can be found in certain forms of folk dance, such as the Kerry Four-Hand in Florida, American tap dance, and popular minstrel dances. The interest in Irish dance was helpful to many early nineteenth-century immigrants. With discrimination against the Irish common at this time (signs reading "No Irish Need Apply" were common in some eastern cities), many turned to careers in show business. On Broadway, Irish step dancers were commonly included in vaudeville shows. In the early 1900s, Irish show bands traveled around the country and entertained their audiences with Irish music and dance. Festivals of Irish dance (*céilí*) became common in Appalachia during the 1930s, when the first of the great Irish dance masters came to America to teach. In the 1950s, Irish dancing continued to flourish as a performance medium and was featured on such popular television shows as *The Ed Sullivan Show.*

The rapid growth of Irish dancing in the late 1950s and early 1960s meant that there was an urgent need to organize and standardize its teaching. Almost every major North American city with a significant Irish population was hosting annual competitions (known as *feiseanna*). The need to standardize syllabus content and other fundamental elements of the dances became obvious. In March 1964, the first meeting of what became the Irish Dancing Teachers Association of North America (IDTANA) was held in the Irish Institute in New York City. The charter members of the association were Cyril McNiff, Peter Smith, Mae Butler, Anna O'Sullivan, Fidelma Davis, and Kevin McKenna. Their aim was to preserve and promote the best in Irish dancing. Lower air fares made it possible for them to work closely with dancing teachers in Ireland, who were organized through the Irish Dancing Commission (or *An Coimisiún* as it was commonly known). The first commission exams for dancing teachers were held in New York in 1967. Around 50 candidates sat the exams. These teachers formed the backbone of the development of Irish dancing in North America. In 1968, the North American Feis Commission was founded to regulate competitions in North America. Discussions began about the possibility of running a national championship every autumn, in which the winners of the regional summer *Feiseanna* could compete for National Honors. The syllabus was approved by the commission in Dublin, and there was agreement that the nationals would serve as a qualifying event for the Irish Dance World Championships that had been inaugurated in Dublin in 1969. On Thanksgiving weekend 1969, the first National Oireachtas was held in New York. The following spring, the committee brought the qualifers to Dublin for the first all-world championship. Donny Golden was the first North American dancer to place in the world competition. In 1975, Michael Flatley of Chicago became the first North American to win the World Championships. In 1976, steadily increasing participation in Irish dancing competitions necessitated the division of IDTANA into five regional branches: Eastern, New England, Canadian, Mid-Western, and Western. The nationals are rotated among the regions in turn.

Irish dancing has continued to provide the diaspora with a sense of community and heritage. Irish dancing continues to be supported and developed through dancing classes, competitions, and festivals. Research indicates that these events constitute important social gatherings for Irish communities outside Ireland and that they continue to attract participation from those of Irish descent. Irish dance also provides participants with the opportunity to compete in national dancing championships and, through participation in international events, to forge closer links with Ireland.

Aoileann Ní Eigeartaigh

See also: BUTLER, Jean; FLATLEY, Michael; MUSIC, COUNTRY AND IRISH; MUSIC IN AMERICA, IRISH

References

Cullinane, John P. *Aspects of the History of Irish Dancing in the New York Area. Produced as Part of a St. Patrick's Day Lecture Series Delivered In New York, 1991.* Cork: Ballineaspaig Publications, 1991.

Cullinane, John P. *Aspects of the History of Irish Dancing. Produced as a Souvenir of the World Irish Dancing Championships, Galway City, Ireland, 1987.* Cork: Ballineaspaig Publications, 1987.

Cullinane, John P. *Further Aspects of the History of Irish Dancing (Ireland, Scotland, Canada, America, New Zealand and Australia).* Cork: Ballineaspaig Publications, 1990.

Lalor, Brian, ed. *The Encyclopedia of Ireland.* Dublin: Gill and Macmillan Ltd., 2003.

Morrison, J'aime. "Dancing Between Decks: Choreographies of Transition During Irish Migrations to America." *Éire-Ireland: Journal of Irish Studies* 36, no. 1–2 (Spring-Summer 2001): 83–97.

IRISH FESTIVAL SINGERS

Alternatively named Feis Éireann, the Irish Festival Singers are a group of Irish professional singers of varying members that gathered under this name for successful U.S. concert tours and long-playing records in the 1950s and 1960s. Most members of the group were well-known professional singers of their time in Ireland. Mainly recruited from the RTÉ Singers, the first group included the well-known Dublin soprano Veronica Dunne as soloist, Sylvia O'Brien, Claire Kelleher, Celestine Kelly, and Ethna McGrath. The male section was headed by the tenor Dermot Troy, the baritones Austin Gaffney and Tomás Ó Súilleabháin, plus James Cuthbert, Arthur Agnew, and Liam Devally. Further members were Sheila Larchet (harp) and Terry O'Connor (violin), the former director of the Irish String Orchestra. The ensemble was directed by Kitty O'Callaghan, who also accompanied at the piano.

The group was formed in 1955 to undertake a concert tour through the United States—culminating in a recital at New York's Carnegie Hall—and to sell the purpose-made LP record on the New York-based Angel Records label. The record is remarkable for its combination of traditional music in both English and Irish and for its selection of skillful arrangements by acknowledged Irish composers such as Herbert Hughes, John F. Larchet, Carl Hardebeck, and Seóirse Bodley. After the success of the first such venture, it was repeated in the following year, again accompanied by an LP, with some personnel changes for the concert tour. In 1966, the group was re-formed under the name of Feis Éireann Group of Singers. This time the group comprised 10 male singers (among them the young Frank Patterson) and nine female singers and was conducted by Eileen (Eily) O'Grady. By this time, however, audiences had changed, and both the American tour and the LP record were less ambitious.

Axel Klein

IRISH FESTIVALS IN THE UNITED STATES

Festivals have been celebrated through the ages to mark births, weddings, anniversaries, battles, good harvests, and religious events. Festivals also celebrate the visual and performing arts, flowers, folklore customs, and seasons, and just anything that people want to celebrate.

Irish festivals promote Irish culture. Some of the festivals and events are well established and internationally renowned, provide a showcase for the best of Irish and international talent, and draw large audiences that create a festive atmosphere in the towns and cities in which they are held. Others are small, local events, full of character and charm, which usually include lots of music and dancing, sporting events, lectures and singsongs, beer and food tents, carnival attractions, and vendors hawking shamrock-green merchandise. Most have the celebration of the Mass sometime during the festival.

These Irish festivals are regional; many are more tolerated than officially accepted and are often categorized as carnival events. They stand apart from the usually accepted definition of festive events and celebrations but many have been a part of the American landscape since the Puritans. They now wind their way through Fairfield, Glastonbury, and New Haven, Connecticut; Billerica, Boston, Easton, and Malden, Massachusetts; Newport and Providence, Rhode Island; Milwaukee, Wisconsin; Philadelphia; Phoenix; Brooklyn, New York; and Sioux Falls, South Dakota.

Saint Patrick's Day

The best known is Saint Patrick's Day. This major event, held on March 17, has been observed by the Irish as both an ethnic festival and a national celebration for thousands of years on St. Patrick's religious feast day and the anniversary of his death in the fifth century. It is not a national holiday in the United States, but it is nationally observed. Today, St. Patrick's Day is a boisterous festival of parading and revelry, dancing and drinking, emblazoned with shamrocks and harps, all in emerald green. The parades are perhaps America's most public display of ethnic pride, often with political overtones disguising the strong Irish nationalism.

Non-Holiday Events

Other festivals, usually less boisterous than the Saint Patrick's Day parades, exist on a more local or regional level, and most are held in the summer. They have gained in popularity since the 1980s and many have begun to replace parades as better representations of Irish folk life. With its large Irish population, many of these festivals are especially prominent in the Northeast.

Beginning in New England, there is the Burlington Irish Heritage Festival, usually held in March; it offers a week packed with activities, both fun-filled and informative, which celebrate Irish-American culture and community. The combination of music, lectures, movies, drama, and dance provides a little something for everyone. Most of the festival events are presented with free admission, making the fund-raising raffle a great draw, with wonderful prizes to win.

In Canton, Massachusetts, there is an annual Irish Connections Festival, sponsored by the Irish Culture Centre of New England at its headquarters outside Boston; it is usually held in June. First started in 1991, this event is considered an open house for the region's large Irish community. The main stage is sponsored by Compass Records, which supports many new Celtic artists. Other stages throughout the festival grounds include The Point, which celebrates contemporary Celtic music with Celtic rock bands and an "Urban Ceili." A new addition is the Abbey Theatre, which highlights dramatic performances, poetry readings, and other literary presentations. Sports activities include Gaelic football and hurling matches, along with the traditional aspects of the festival, such as an Irish tea house, children's entertainment, pipe bands, Irish cottage exhibition, and music sessions. (Web site: http://irishculture.org/festival.)

Also in Massachusetts, the Lowell National Historical Park, Lowell Festival Foundation, National Council for the Traditional Arts, and the City of Lowell sponsor the Lowell Folk Festival, considered the largest free folk festival in the nation. It is three days of traditional music, dance, craft demonstrations, street parades, dance parties, and ethnic foods, presented on six outdoor stages throughout the city of Lowell, usually in late July. (Web site: http://lowellfolkfestival.org.)

A festival held at summer's end, over the Labor Day weekend, is the Newport Waterfront Irish Festival, a popular three-day event in Rhode Island, at the historic Newport Yachting Center. The festival, which started in 1998, celebrates both the Irish culture of arts, music, dance, and food and the beautiful, historic town of Newport, with its famous waterfront. Entertainers have included Tommy Makem, Screaming Orphans, and the Barley Boys.

The Midwest hosts a well-known, very popular Irish festival in Sioux Falls, South Dakota, the Irish Fest, sponsored by the Sioux Falls Irish Club. This festival, which only began in 1999, celebrates the traditions of Irish music, song, and dance and provides continual food feasts and Irish dancing. (Web site: www.irish.org/SFICmenu.htm.)

Further west, the Colorado Irish Festival is operated by the Colorado United Irish Societies, a qualified nonprofit organization incorporated in 1995 as a 501(c)(3). Currently it comprises 12 individual organizations, many of which are also nonprofit organizations. The festival is usually held in July. (Web site: www.coloradoirishfestival.org.)

Another major festival has been the Milwaukee Irish Fest, held in August. It is renowned as the world's largest Irish culture festival and was established in 1980 by members of Milwaukee's Irish community to showcase its rich Irish heritage and to establish an Irish cultural center in that city. Under the direction of Ed Ward, curator of the Irish Music Archives, Irish Fest premiered in Milwaukee, the city of festivals, in 1981. Irish Fest showcases Irish music, history, dance, drama, sports, and culture. The festival features Irish and Irish-American talent and serves as a stage for up-and-coming local performers. Located on Milwaukee's Lake Michigan shoreline, Irish Fest is held annually during the third weekend of August. During its four-day run, the event annually hosts more than 100,000 guests from around the globe. (Web site: www.irishfest.org.)

Further Developments

Mostly, these Irish festivals are traditional annual events that are named for their locations and designated as Irish festivals or simply Irish fests. At most of these festivals, music and dance are a main element, featuring top Irish and Irish American entertainers from around the world, along with numerous regional groups that perform on the festival's stages. In addition, roaming performers dressed in traditional costumes entertain guests as they stroll the grounds. With the recent surge of interest in Irish dance, stages featuring step dancing have become a popular attraction, and guests can also learn ceilidh and set dancing at daily workshops.

Cultural exhibits, displays, theater, poetry readings, and demonstrations bring alive the spirit of Old Ireland's folklore and charm while contests, raffles, sporting events, and comedy shows add to the levity. To promote traditional Irish culture, many groups and organizations get assistance from local government, businesses, and media, as well as from organizations in Ireland, such as the National Gallery of Ireland, the National Museum of Ireland, Arts Council, and the Irish Tourist Boards, including Galway, Sligo and Lisburn, the Shannon Development Corporation, RTE, and Aer Lingus.

With the increase of interest in family lineage and heraldry, genealogical resources and organizations have become an increasingly popular attraction, with many Irish genealogical societies. For those with a competitive nature, Irish fests offer plenty of sports contests, such as rugby, hurling, currach racing, Gaelic football, and games, which can range from children's red hair and freckle contests to bingo, treasure hunts, and a baking contest.

Many festivals were established as small community events to promote Irish culture. The Phoenix Irish Festival started in 1984 with the support of the valley Irish organizations. Its sole purpose was to promote and encourage all forms of Irish culture. Grand National Irish Fair and Music Festival, sponsored by the Irish Fair Foundation, Pasadena, California, began in 1974 at Notre Dame High School as a small ethnic fair that grew to a large festival held in the Rose Bowl.

The Irish Heritage Weekend was created by the Heritage Foundation as a bicentennial committee that was formed to promote the ethnic heritage of Louisville, Kentucky. It began having ethnic weekends in 1979.

The Fitchburg Irish Festival, set up by the Irish American Association of Fitchburg in 1982, claims to be the first Irish festival in New England. Two years later, the New England Irish Festival celebrated its first event in Sullivan Stadium, in Foxboro, Massachusetts; it was started by the Irish-American family who owned the stadium, home of the New England Patriots. The family wanted to create a family event.

The Great Irish Fair, sponsored by the Ancient Order of Hibernians, began in 1981 in Brooklyn, New York, as a fund-raiser for Brooklyn Catholic Charities. Further upstate, the Buffalo Irish Festival was created in 1982 as an offshoot of Irish music programs held at the Shannon Pub to benefit Buffalo Irish organizations. The Irish Cultural Festival of Cleveland, Ohio, was established in 1983 to raise money for Project Children to bring children from Northern Ireland to the United States. Proceeds also went to students of Irish music.

In Pennsylvania, the Irish Center of Pittsburgh Feis was set up in 1968 to bring together participants from the Northeast, Midwest, and Canada for a dancing competition, while in Wilkes-Barre the Donegal Society started Irish Days in 1980 to support local ceilidh dancers who wanted to go to a competition. Profits from the festival benefited most groups from Wilkes-Barre but also others from the Philadelphia area, upstate New York, and Ireland.

The North Texas Irish Fest was begun in 1983 by the Southwest Celtic Music Association in Dallas, Texas, as a ceilidh, and it was held on the state fairgrounds. In San Antonio, the Texas Irish Festival began as a multiethnic event in 1985 to benefit St. Mary's Catholic Church.

Rose of Tralee

Probably the best-known Irish festival is the Rose of Tralee International Festival, held annually at the end of August in Tralee, Co. Kerry, Ireland. This international Irish festival, the premiere festival of the Emerald Isle, now includes representation from the United States. It hosts approximately 150,000 visitors annually. Started in 1959 to promote Co. Kerry, the now 10-day festival boasts nonstop street entertainment, concerts, parades, and horse racing leading up to the final televised two-night competition, the crowning of the Rose. In 2005, it was considered the number one television attraction in Ireland and drew 1.6 million viewers. The festival queens, the Roses of Tralee, are always Irish but not necessarily Ireland-born. In 2007, some Roses were Katie Crean (London), Grainnie Fox (Longford), Jackie Maher (Luxembourg), and Rosie Dempre (New Orleans). (Web site: http://www.roseoftralee.ie.) American centers for the festival are located in Boston/New England, New York, Philadelphia, San Francisco, Southern California, Texas, and Washington, D.C.

Martin J. Manning

See also: NATIONALISM, IRISH-AMERICAN; SAINT PATRICK'S DAY PARADES

References

Eleuterio-Comer, Susan K. *Irish American Material Culture: A Directory of Collections, Sites, and Festivals in the United States and Canada.* New York: Greenwood, 1988.

Feintuch, Burt, and David H. Watters, eds. *Encyclopedia of New England Culture: The Culture and History of an American Region.* New Haven, CT: Yale University Press, 2005.

Glazier, Michael, ed. *Encyclopedia of the Irish in America.* Notre Dame, IN: University of Notre Dame, 1999.

Heideking, Jurgen, Genevieve Fabre, and Kai Dreisbach, eds. *Celebrating Ethnicity and Nation: American Festive Culture from the Revolution to the Early Twentieth Century.* New York: Berghahn Books, 2001.

Henderson, Helene, and Sue Ellen Thompson, eds. *Holidays, Festivals, and Celebrations of the World Dictionary.* 2nd ed. Detroit, MI: Omnigraphics, 1997.

Roy, Christian. *Traditional Festivals: A Multicultural Encyclopedia.* Santa Barbara, CA: ABC-CLIO, 2005.
Shemanski, Frances. *A Guide to Fairs and Festivals in the United States.* Westport, CT: Greenwood, 1984.

IRISH LINEN IN NORTH AMERICA

Irish linen was a fine cloth made, with some reputation in Ulster, from flax fibers; but more than that, it was an object that deepened the story of Irish-American connections. The migration of Irish people to North America in the eighteenth and nineteenth centuries was accompanied by a translocation of culture, in both the anthropological and agricultural senses of the word. Before linen production was even a critical industry in Ireland, Irish immigrants brought flax to the New World. They grew it for making linen and for exporting seed to Ireland. In the nineteenth century, demand for North American seed declined, even though the Irish linen industry required vast new quantities of flax. Irish linen, however, grew increasingly popular among consumers in North America.

The Scots-Irish in New England and Pennsylvania were the first Irish Americans to grow flax and produce linen in significant quantities in the eighteenth century. Many were skilled linen weavers when they migrated from Ulster. Because of English protective tariffs on the wool trade, linen had become a popular alternative for weavers in Ireland. The linen industry in Ulster has a long history of its own, but its influence on Irish-American relations is not well-known. The Ulster Scots who migrated to North America in the eighteenth century carried with them knowledge of flax production and a use for home-manufactured linen. Probate records show that Irish immigrants on the Pennsylvanian frontier in the 1720s and 1730s had linen cloth in abundance, and people of almost all specializations raised some flax and owned spinning wheels and other tools of linen making. Linen production did exist in the colony before Irish immigration, especially in areas like Germantown, but the Scots-Irish stimulated the trade.

In New England, one center of linen production and Irish immigration was Londonderry, New Hampshire. By the mid-eighteenth century, the town was known for its linen. Scots-Irish immigrants played important roles in the cultivation and production of flax fibers and linen fabrics, although it is incorrect to think they introduced the trade to this region. Domestic linen found wider markets in New England than it did in Pennsylvania, but still, consumers relied heavily on imported linen. In fact, families sold home-produced linen so they could afford fancier materials manufactured in the British Isles. Women were the active producers in this exchange, and flax production often involved deeply gendered divisions of labor.

Cloth was extremely valuable in the colonies, and both the processing equipment and the skills of the trade were assets to these early migrants. In the 1760s, when Irish migrants from New England resettled in the Truro area of Nova Scotia, they grew flax, built flax mills, and produced enough linen to sell in neighboring towns. British officials, however, encouraged the export of North American flax and flaxseed to the mother country. In 1770, one of the first settlement projects to what would become Prince Edward Island attempted to establish a flax colony based on the mercantilist model. The project failed, but the export of flaxseed from North America did form an important connection to the Irish linen industry. Ireland imported seed because its flax crop was harvested before maturity to produce finer linen fibers. Colonials met part of this need by tolerating a coarser fiber and exporting surplus seed to Ireland.

In the nineteenth century, flax cultivation declined, and cotton produced a more efficient textile. Much of the massive immigration movement to British North America came out of Ulster's declining linen industry, but at this point the skills of the trade were less useful in the New World. Immigrants who claimed to be farmers and weavers usually turned their full attention to farming. Yet, when the home production of linen began to be regularly recorded in censuses, we see a more complicated pattern of Irish North American linen makers. As the history of Scots-Irish settlers in Canada suggests, in 1871 large concentrations of linen producers and Scots-Irish settlers were coincidental but not co-related. The earlier 1842 census shows townships in Johnstown District, later part of Ontario, where both Irish immigration and home production of linen were high. Linen production amounted to 1.52 yards per person in Bastard Township, in a district where the average person produced only 0.59 yards. Bastard had among the highest Irish immigrant per capita in the district, but further research is necessary to determine if those immigrants were responsible for the linen production and if the connections were based on skills and farm strategies developed in Ireland.

Industrial linen production grew slowly in North America, and the influences of the Irish linen industry were sometimes abstruse. Three brothers from New York started the first linen mills in Canada in the 1850s, and their longtime mill foreman was Robert Printer, an Irish Presbyterian immigrant. A few years later, the American Civil War raised the price of cotton in the United States, and the linen industry began to grow faster. The large linen thread manufacturer, William Barbour and Sons of Lisburn, upgraded its American agency in Patterson, New Jersey, to a full thread factory. The expansion was profitable because of import tariffs implemented in the United States during the Civil War, and the infrastructure was possible because of large injections of machinery and labor from Lisburn to New Jersey.

Josh MacFadyen

See also: AMERICAN CIVIL WAR; PENNSYLVANIA; SCOTS-IRISH; SCOTS-IRISH PATTERNS OF SETTLEMENT, CANADA; SCOTS-IRISH PATTERNS OF SETTLEMENT, UNITED STATES

References

Collins, Brenda, and Philip Ollerenshaw, eds. *The European Linen Industry in Historical Perspective.* Oxford: Oxford University Press, 2004.

Coons, Martha. *All Sorts of Good Sufficient Cloth: Linen-Making in New England, 1640–1860.* North Andover, MA: Merrimack Valley Textile Museum, 1980.

Griffin, Patrick. *The People with No Name: Ireland's Ulster Scots, America's Scots Irish, and the Creation of a British Atlantic World, 1689–1784.* Princeton, NJ: Princeton University Press, 2001.

Ulrich, Laurel Thatcher. *The Age of Homespun: Objects and Stories in the Creation of an American Myth.* New York: Alfred A. Knopf, 2001.

IRISH REPUBLICAN ARMY

The Irish Republican Army (IRA) is seen as a militant separatist group of the physical force tradition for establishing a fully

Irish Republican Army takes over Dublin barracks in 1922. (Corbis)

independent, 32-county Irish republic. With the old IRA emerging from the separatist Irish Volunteers in the aftermath of the 1916 Easter Rising, the continuity of the armed struggle granted, for those who fought for complete freedom from British rule, the IRA legitimacy to again take up a guerrilla campaign against the Crown forces. In 1917 and 1918 the Irish Volunteers began active maneuvers that sparked suppressive measures by British authorities. Resentful at Sinn Féin politicians who increasingly took credit for the Easter Rising and the subsequent republican movement, the Volunteers determined to return to physical force. After all-Ireland elections obtained a mandate for Sinn Féin in December 1918, which led to the inauguration of the first Dáil Éireann in January 1919, the Irish Volunteers assumed an unsanctioned role as the Irish Republican Army, whose members took an oath of allegiance to the Dáil and who claimed to act as the Republic's military wing. In fact, the Dáil and the Army headquarters never gained complete control over the Volunteers. This ambiguous relationship between political governance and militant operations would characterize the IRA throughout its evolution during the twentieth and twenty-first centuries.

After the end of the Anglo-Irish War, the Treaty divided the IRA. The subsequent civil war pitted "irregulars" against the Free State army, and IRA veterans were found on both sides of the battle. Those loyal to the opposition lost the effort to achieve complete Irish freedom from British control. The anti-Treaty forces refused recognition not only of the six Ulster counties under the Crown, but also of the Dáil at Leinster House as a "partitionist assembly." Denouncing any collaboration with what republican purists saw as an illegitimate Free State within the British Commonwealth, the defeated IRA asserted itself as the army of the 1918 First and the 1921 Second Dáil, the last governing bodies elected throughout all of Ireland which had voted in Sinn Féin as the majority party. Although the Treaty had led to a Third Dáil Éireann, the IRA and Sinn Féin abstained from entering this assembly if elected—unless they had enough members to engineer its overthrow for a return to a 32-county republic faithful to the broadly socialist policy asserted in the 1916 Proclamation and the 1919 Democratic Programme.

This emphasis on abstaining from entering into the government's convening in Dublin, Stormont, or Westminster became not only Sinn Féin's policy but a justification for the IRA to assert itself as the legitimate army of the pre-Treaty, 1916–1922 Irish Republic. The IRA believed this republic could not be disestablished by the Free State. Opposed to constitutional compromise with what the IRA perceived as pro-British sympathizers, the IRA split from Sinn Féin. In 1925, Eamon de Valera decided to seek entry into the Dáil for his Sinn Féin faction, who would in 1926 become Fianna Fáil. This party, once it gained power in 1932, suppressed or co-opted the activities of many former comrades-in-arms. De Valera banned the IRA in 1936.

Throughout the 1930s, republicans became divided as Fianna Fáil's success grew. Leftist and right-wing divisions weakened the remaining IRA and Sinn Féin activists. Saor Éire and the Republican Congress attempted to mobilize a socialist popular front. The Spanish Civil War attracted IRA veterans to both factions. Physical force proponents revived a bombing campaign in Britain. By 1938, the surviving Second Dáil members delegated to a dwindling cadre within the IRA the powers of government until the All-Ireland Republic could be restored. Although this transfer of authority attracted few adherents, this mantle of succession ensured that the revival of the IRA and Sinn Féin in future decades would gain moral and political approval among a significant number of Irish at home and abroad, as IRA emigrants sustained republican loyalists throughout America.

In 1939, Seán Russell led the hardline IRA to revive a Fenian-style bombing war in England, but this inept operation resulted in a crackdown by both the British and the Free State, which led to the imprisonment of many IRA members at the Curragh in Kildare during what was called "the Emergency." By 1944, its leaders betrayed, incarcerated, or retired, the IRA had ceased to function. After World War II, the dormant IRA reestablished links with Sinn Féin; an armed campaign in the North of Ireland from 1956 to 1962 again failed.

By 1964, a remnant of the IRA, recently released from jail, began to rethink strategy. Guided by British Marxists, and expanding ideological and community effort through the Wolfe Tone Society, the IRA and Sinn Féin revised their methods. They now determined to spark political, economic, and military agitation to rouse popular solidarity. They also built networks with third world anticolonial liberation movements. Under the Stalinist-influenced stages theory, organizers among 1960s republicans endorsed an end to abstentionism so they could be voted into government assemblies to promote socialism.

This new departure from republican doctrine split the IRA and Sinn Féin in 1969–1970 into an official Marxist group claiming to be the true inheritors of doctrinal legitimacy to the Republic of Pearse and especially Connolly, against what would soon be the dominant Provisional traditionalist wing, which was bent on continuing the armed struggle. Along with this formal disagreement over republican policy, the renewal of violence in the north had contributed to this latest fracture within the IRA. The Provisionals emphasized the physical force tradition and proclaimed that they alone continued as legitimate heirs of 1916, the Second Dáil, and as an all-Ireland army and governing body. The Officials distrusted Catholic-directed militancy and asserted that support could be drawn from the Unionist community, as their party would eventually attain a nonsectarian worker's republic. After infighting between the Officials and the Provisionals damaged both their military and political aims, the Officials retreated from the armed struggle in 1972; a militant faction founded the Irish National Liberation Army in 1974.

By now, the few hundred active volunteers attracted international attention to their fight for freedom from British rule of the north. The all-Ireland base of the IRA predecessors—who ironically had lacked an effective force in Ulster during the 1919–1921 war—now shifted to Belfast, Derry, and rural areas along the border. The leadership in Dublin supported a full-scale military campaign as the Troubles mounted; their counterparts in Belfast, now acting as defenders of Catholic enclaves there and in Derry, faced stalemate. Failing to quickly oust the British or to hasten a united Ireland, the IRA fought an attenuated guerrilla war against not only an occupying army but also provincial police, informants, spies, undercover units, and Loyalist brigades. Their attacks against high-profile targets such as Lord Mountbatten in 1979 and Margaret Thatcher in 1984 gained notoriety for the IRA. Army, police, and sectarian retaliation for thousands of less publicized victims of the armed struggle ensured that the IRA itself declined on a military front and in media sympathy. Counting all casualties of the Troubles, the Provisional IRA killed the most—about 1,770 of more than 3,660 civilians, state representatives, and military personnel—during the 1969–1998 armed campaign.

Under the policies of Gerry Adams and Martin McGuinness, the IRA's northern command eased out Dublin's faction. After the H-Block and hunger strikers' protests galvanized widespread popular support for republicans, a move emerged pairing, in Danny Morrison's phrase, "the armalite and the ballot box." Although the 1969 Provisionals had rejected entering constitutional politics, by the 1980s IRA commanders prepared for negotiations to transform the guerrilla war into a broader effort. Through a revived Sinn Féin, republican tacticians argued that they could achieve justice for the nationalist minority in the north by agreeing to a settlement with the governments that they had earlier derided as "partitionist assemblies."

This shift again alienated physical-force adherents. Republican Sinn Féin had split from the main movement in 1986 over abstentionism; the Continuity IRA allied with this purist faction. Many IRA members in rural areas, such as Louth, South Armagh, and Fermanagh, resisted such a compromise as leading to the decommissioning of arms and the practical—as well as symbolic—end to their armed struggle. This led to another break in the late 1990s, of a group calling itself the "Real IRA," which became allied with the 32-County Sovereignty Movement, and rejected the end of the physical-force tradition. For the majority in the IRA, the appeals of the leadership to enter into the peace process convinced volunteers that the military campaign was at a standstill and that the British occupiers could not be removed by force. The 1994 ceasefire preceded a brief return to the bombing war, but with the 1997 truce, the Adams-McGuinness policy has ensured the publicized dominance of Sinn Féin's ballot boxes over the IRA's hidden armalites. The future of the IRA, in the wake of its suspension since 1998's Good Friday Agreement, remains uncertain. Some within its ranks continue to delay full and irrevocable decommissioning of their weaponry, and political uncertainty continues as various entities attempt to integrate Sinn Féin into Stormont, the Dáil, and Westminster while excluding their IRA comrades. Allegations that IRA volunteers since the peace process have remained armed—to intimidate community activists, smugglers, pushers, and those labeled as criminal elements—persist.

Throughout the history of the IRA, North American support has provided clout for its republican aims. Fund-raising appeals have continued from the rise of the Fenians in the 1860s to the founding of Irish Northern Aid in 1970. After the defeats of the old IRA in the 1920s, many volunteers, rejecting the Free State and on the run (or prevented from seeking employment), left for the United States. Their loyalty to physical-force strategies ensured that at times more support for the cause would come from America rather than Ireland. Arms and finances both flowed east. In the 1980s, a Federal Bureau of Investigation crackdown on gunrunning from U.S. ports effectively put an end to large-scale smuggling to Irish republicans. Media stereotypes also flourished: the image of the bomb-throwing, rosary-clutching "Paddy" would become as common on screens as it was in Fenian caricatures for earlier American audiences. By the mid-1990s, Gerry Adams would bring a more diplomatic approach to the White House of the Clinton administration. The *Irish Voice* newspaper, its sister magazine *Irish America,* and Irish-American philanthropists have crafted a respectable role for the mainstream Irish republican that has supplanted the terrorist thug cartoons of previous decades. Today, Friends of Sinn Féin, based in Washington D.C., lobbies for the party; critics have alleged that, as with Noraid (Irish Northern Aid Committee) and earlier organizations, many of its donations have directly funded the IRA.

John L. Murphy

See also: CLINTON, William Jefferson; De VALERA, Eamon; IRISH REPUBLICAN BROTHERHOOD; MITCHELL, George J.; MITCHELL PRINCIPLES, The; NATIONALISM, IRISH-AMERICAN; NATIONALISM IN THE TWENTIETH CENTURY, IRISH-AMERICAN; NORAID

References

Bell, J. Bowyer. *The Secret Army: The IRA.* 3rd ed. New Brunswick, NJ: Transaction Publishers, 1996.

English, Richard. *Armed Struggle: The History of the IRA.* New York: Oxford University Press, 2003.
Feeney, Brian. *Sinn Féin: A Hundred Turbulent Years.* Dublin: O'Brien Press, 2002.
Holland, Jack. *The American Connection: U.S. Guns, Money, and Influence in Northern Ireland.* Niwot, CO: Roberts Rinehart, 1999.
Moloney, Ed. *The Secret History of the IRA.* New York: W. W. Norton, 2002.
Patterson, Henry. *The Politics of Illusion: A Political History of the IRA.* London: Serif, 1997.
Smith, M. L. R. *Fighting for Ireland? The Military Strategy of the Irish Republican Movement.* London: Routledge, 1997.

IRISH REPUBLICAN BROTHERHOOD

A revolutionary movement of the late nineteenth and early twentieth centuries, emerging from the Fenians, the Irish Republican Brotherhood (IRB) continued the oath-bound, clandestine, and physical-force separatist agitation that had characterized the earlier factions that had coalesced after the Young Ireland defeat in 1848. The Fenians had established networks not only in Ireland but also in the United States, Britain, and Australia—from which funds, personnel, and ammunition supplied the international organization, which was hierarchically structured but designed around small cells of activists to discourage infiltration. As with the Fenians, however, the IRB was compromised—most infamously by the "Prince of Spies," Henri Le Caron (the Englishman Thomas Beach, 1841–1894). But the IRB persisted longer than the Fenians, as Brotherhood members supported the Land War of 1879–1882, led bombing campaigns in England in the 1880s, revived to assist Sinn Féin, directed the 1916 Easter Rising, and endured under their leader, Michael Collins, through the Anglo-Irish war until the founding of the Free State.

Its origins intertwined with the Fenians, the IRB gradually superseded the earlier organization after the defeat of the Irish uprising of 1867. After the arrests later that year of Fenian insurgents, the death of the "Manchester Martyrs" (William Allen, Michael Larkin, and Michael O'Brien), and the spread of support for the rebels from not only the Irish people but also from some within the Catholic establishment, the IRB began to regroup. In 1871, it emerged under Jeremiah O'Donovan Rossa (1831–1915) and John Devoy (1842–1928). Two years later, a constitution for the IRB determined its function as a secret society democratically governed by a partially elected supreme council. Agrarian activism attracted many of its members during the 1870s populist struggle against large landholders; however, it was not until the 1880s that the IRB leadership directed a bombing campaign in Liverpool, Glasgow, and especially London, where for five years attacks were carried out against prominent targets.

Operating from America, Devoy organized the secret Clan Na Gael while O'Donovan Rossa gathered the "skirmishers" to sustain the dynamite war in Britain. Devoy backed the New Departure negotiated by Michael Davitt and Charles Stewart Parnell in which they agreed on a unified front to bring parliamentary nationalists together with revolutionary agents to further the causes of Home Rule and land reform. Devoy supported moderation; O'Donovan Rossa asserted physical-force strategies. The division between the two leaders weakened the American movement as Parnellism and Home Rule appealed more to many in the 1880s than the perpetuation of Fenian aggression. With the demise of Parnell in the 1890s, the constitutional nationalists weakened too, but the prospect of revolution remained distant until the appearance of Sinn Féin in the new century inspired Clan Na Gael veteran and convicted skirmisher Tom Clarke (1857–1916) to return to Ireland in 1907, after 15 years in a British prison and a long American residence. Under Clarke and *Irish Freedom,* a paper appearing in 1910, separatism invigorated both old Fenians and young militants. Home Rule failed to satisfy a generation inspired by the Celtic Revival and radicalized against John Redmond's commitment of the Irish Volunteers to aid the British military in 1914. With Home Rule postponed when World War I began, the IRB planned for action.

The next year, Patrick Pearse gave his famous Glasnevin oration evoking Fenian continuity over O'Donovan Rossa's grave, the body having been returned from New York. The connection between American support and Irish responsibility endured as the IRB calculated its opportunity. Under Pearse, with the cooperation of James Connolly's Citizen Army, the IRB resolved to rebel while World War I divided the attention of the Crown. Despite the failure of the Easter Rising, the aftermath echoed that of the 1867 defeat. The deaths of Fenians then had provoked widespread support; the executions of Pearse, Connolly, and their comrades angered many Irish people who felt little sympathy for the Easter Rising but now acclaimed them martyrs for a new cause, that of yet another guerrilla assault against the British.

The IRB, however, now found itself part of a larger revolution. The Irish Republican Army, under the leadership of IRB president Michael Collins, edged out the IRB during the War of Independence from 1919 to 1921. After the Anglo-Irish Treaty, and the ensuing civil war between treaty proponents and opponents, the IRB found itself increasingly relegated to a nominal role after the death of Collins in 1921. Three years later, military members of the IRB demanded an end to post–Civil War demobilization and renewed progress toward a full republic. This March 1924 aborted mutiny of Irish Republican Army veterans within the Irish army resulted in the Free State's disbandment of the Brotherhood.

John L. Murphy

See also: DAVITT, Michael; DEVOY, John; FENIANS, The; IRISH REPUBLICAN ARMY; NATIONALISM, IRISH-AMERICAN

References

Brennan, Michael. *The War in Clare, 1911–1921: Personal Memoirs of the Irish War of Independence.* Dublin: Four Courts Press, Irish Academic Press, 1980.

Cole, J. A. *Prince of Spies: Henri Le Caron.* London: Faber and Faber, 1984.

Denieffe, Joseph. *A Personal Narrative of the Irish Revolutionary Brotherhood.* New York: The Gael Publishing Co., 1904.

Devoy, John. *Recollections of an Irish Rebel.* 1929. Reprint, Shannon, Ireland: Irish University Press, 1969.

Golway, Terry. *Irish Rebel: John Devoy and America's Fight for Irish Freedom.* New York: St. Martin's Press, 1998.

O'Donovan Rossa, Jeremiah. *Irish Rebels in English Prisons.* Dingle, Ireland: Brandon, 1991.

Ó Broin, Léon. *Revolutionary Underground: The Story of the Irish Republican Brotherhood, 1858–1924.* Dublin: Gill and Macmillan, 1976.

O'Leary, John. *Recollections of Fenians and Fenianism.* 2 vols. London: Downey & Co., 1896.

Smart, K. R. M. *The Dynamite War: Irish-American Bombers in Victorian Britain.* Dublin: Gill and Macmillan, 1979.

IRISH TRAVELERS IN THE UNITED STATES

Irish Travelers constitute a small population of scattered groups that have resided predominantly in the southern United States since emigrating from Ireland in the 1800s. Members of the community divide themselves based on historical residence in Mississippi, Georgia, Texas, and Ohio. Those identified as Northern Travelers include all Travelers who work along the eastern seaboard. Contemporary Traveler men earn their living traveling in all-male family groups for most of the year, asphalting, laying linoleum, and spray painting. Travelers are descendants of a historically nomadic Irish community known as "tinkers" or, more recently, "Travellers," which were defined as an ethnic minority in British and Irish law in 1998 and 2000, respectively, and with whom they share many cultural traits. The term "tinker"—currently derogatory—and its English and Irish-language cognates were used in Ireland for perhaps centuries to refer to indigenous itinerant people who provided tinsmithing, peddling, horse-trading, and craft services to the majority culture. Certain oral accounts suggest that eight Traveler families, led by a pioneer named Tom Carroll (1830–1910), who is buried in Westview Cemetery, Atlanta, emigrated from either Ireland or England sometime soon after the mid-nineteenth century, and spread throughout the urban Northeast, where they practiced their ancestral occupations. Oral tradition also enshrines the memories of other nineteenth-century Traveler founding fathers such as Peter Sherlock and Pat O'Hara. Numbers increased through ongoing Traveler emigration from Ireland, and intermarriage within the community. Before the Civil War, Travelers had begun to winter in the southern states, where they very successfully traded mules and horses. Travelers appear to have been one of the more successful segments of Irish emigrants to America at this point. When the demand for these animals decreased in the North in the late 1800s, Travelers ceased summering there and took up permanent bases in Nashville, Tennessee, Fort Worth, Texas, and Atlanta, Georgia, migrating thence to Mississippi and other parts of the South. The less documented Ohio Travelers migrated to the Midwest as other Travelers went south. Contact between the southern communities continues, but has lessened somewhat in recent decades.

Although Travelers provided mules for the government during World War II, a 1927 Georgia law that heavily taxed traveling horse traders and the increasing mechanization of American agriculture after the Depression era caused the trade to dwindle among members of the group. Strikingly, the twentieth-century economic and occupational patterns of Travelers in Ireland followed the model of American Travelers somewhat, although there was no formal contact between the groups until the 1990s. Since the 1960s, Travelers have abandoned the tents, brightly colored covered wagons, and trucks of previous generations for camps or villages of luxury mobile homes and, increasingly, houses. Despite these adaptations to sedentary norms, business transactions continue to be cash based, and trading and bartering are still used in dealings. Contemporary Travelers appear to have remained more seasonally nomadic than their Irish counterparts. Overall, Traveler culture remains as independent, self-reliant, and enclosed as when it first emerged in the United States, a tendency that sometimes leads to mutual suspicion between Travelers and members of the wider society.

Culture and Ethnicity

Although allusions to tinkers abound in Ireland and Britain before the nineteenth century, Sharon Gmelch's discovery of references to the tinker lifestyle in an 1835 report on Irish indigence is understood to be the earliest description of tinkers as what would currently be recognized as an ethnic, as opposed to an occupational minority. American anthropologists generally describe Travelers in the United States as an ethnic minority, although this has yet to be acknowledged in U.S. law. Irish Travelers are occasionally identified as Irish Gypsies by non-Travelers and the U.S. media because of their semi-itinerant lifestyle, but they reject this ascription. A minority of contemporary Travelers is aware of their Irish roots and keeps abreast of Traveler issues in "the old country." Like their Irish counterparts, Travelers in the United States share common descent and have discrete cultural practices: boundary rules against most non-Travelers, early marriage, an aspiration to be mobile, a tradition of self-employment and involvement in trades or services not generally pursued by members of the settled community, a unique material culture, customs surrounding cleansing, and an oral culture. They also use a cryptolect called "Cant" or "Gammon," which is traditionally used instead of or alongside English in certain trading situations and has been variously theorized as deriving from a lost pre-Celtic language, Irish, Romani, English, or various combinations of these languages. Most importantly, in both Traveler cultures, the extended family was and remains the key unit of social and cultural reproduction. Traveler men alone are involved in business dealings and traditional trades requiring seasonal traveling in groups. In the past, peddling and bartering were the only occupations allowed to women, although young women have begun to enter the unskilled mainstream labor force for short periods before marriage. Additionally, in recent years a small proportion of young Traveler women have taken up administrative and nursing posts. Upon marriage, women take responsibility for the home, family, finances, all aspects of religious observance, and dealings with outside agencies such as schools and hospitals.

Although Traveler settlements are effectively matriarchal when the men take to the road for months on end, Traveler gender roles are rigid. Girls are thrust into caretaking roles from an early age, and boys are encouraged to assist their fathers. Marriages are endogamous; they are initially arranged by the mothers and occur at a very young age. Substantial dowry payments are involved when the families are affluent. Marriage between second cousins is allowed by Traveler culture and is within the law of most southern states. Divorce is rare among Travelers, and the birthrate is lower than that of their Irish counterparts, with an average of two to three children per family. Elderly women help rear grandchildren. Travelers appear to have always practiced Catholicism, and the culture remains predisposed to public displays of religiosity. In line with Catholic teaching, all Travelers are baptized and receive the sacraments of first communion and confirmation. In the past, having arranged for the storage of bodies with funeral homes, southern Travelers buried their dead once a year in spectacular and large funeral ceremonies in Atlanta and Nashville so that kin from various states could reaffirm Traveler ties. This practice has been discontinued, but Catholic Church funerals with a Mass remain the norm. In contemporary Traveler culture, large get-togethers continue to be organized around Christmas, weddings and other family occasions.

Status in American Society

Travelers are generally markedly wealthier and better educated than their Irish counterparts, and this appears to make them less visible and liable to public scrutiny. No formal Traveler organizations exist, and unlike their Irish counterparts, Travelers have not founded any Traveler-specific organizations, or allied themselves with broader national or international Roma political and cultural networks, despite the fact that they have been victims of prejudice since their early itinerant days. Travelers have little inclination toward integration, and for this reason the community appears to be unknown in mainstream American society, bar a handful of recent popular culture representations centering on alleged Traveler sharp business practices in which the minority has been presented as a kind of mysterious grifter subculture. In 1889, Frederick Arnold first drew attention to members of a culturally and linguistically distinct Gypsy-like Irish tinker "caste" he encountered in New York State who were, he stressed, *not* Gypsies. However, despite the fact that it was American author Charles Godfrey Leland who first revealed the existence of the "Irish tinkers' tongue" in 1880 (prompting a flood of material on the subject of the Irish tinker in the Victorian period), and although Irish-American Travelers sporadically came to attention as a peculiar and picturesque Irish Gypsy culture throughout the twentieth century in popular folklore, ephemeral animal trade and trailer lifestyle publications, Catholic periodicals, and tourist guides, they were largely undocumented by serious commentators in the United States until the 1970s. Academic studies of the community remain scant, due in part to Traveler itinerancy and the community's suspicion regarding researchers from majority culture. For these reasons, and also because the U.S. Census does not recognize Travelers as a unique ethnic group, population figures are unavailable. Relatively recent estimates suggest that the Georgia Traveler community consists of approximately 500 families, the Mississippi Traveler camp consists of approximately 200 families, and the Texas Traveler community, which emerged of late, has fewer families. Ian Hancock, an expert in Romany culture based at the University of Texas at Austin, has suggested that there are upwards of 30,000 Irish Travelers in the United States, although estimates of 5,000–10,000 are more usual.

Transatlantic Travel(l)er ties

The Traveller community in Ireland has been and continues to be discriminated against by mainstream society to a huge extent, but a growing awareness of marginalization led to the politicization of the minority during the 1960s and 1970s, and the increasing assertion of Traveller ethnicity. The awareness of a worldwide fraternity of nomadic peoples engendered by the involvement of Irish Traveller leaders with the founding of the international Romani rights lobby in the 1960s laid the groundwork for formal contacts between the Travel(l)er communities in Ireland and America. In 1994, and with the assistance of the pioneering scholar of southern Traveller culture, Jared Vincent Harper, Irish Traveller activist Michael McDonagh accompanied Belfast anthropologist Robbie McVeigh to Murphy Village, a noted and prosperous Georgia Traveler settlement of about 2,000 people established in the 1960s near North Augusta, South Carolina, with the assistance of Father Joseph Murphy. This was the first of a number of cross-Atlantic fact-finding missions between the Traveller communities. Irish Traveller leaders are anxious to disseminate knowledge of their American counterparts in mainstream culture in Ireland as they believe the survival and development of Traveler culture in America counters arguments (particularly prominent in Ireland during the 1970s) that rather than being a distinct ethnic group, Travellers were merely post-Great Famine dropouts from sedentary society who require reintegration. This belief is, of course, contradicted by the fact that Irish Travellers first immigrated to America as a distinct group just after the Famine period and have maintained their ethnic identity there since. (Numerous nineteenth-century Catholic Church registries in the South record the baptism and marriages of "Irish Tinkers.") Significantly, the largest body of research on Traveller culture in Ireland to emerge in the late twentieth century was generated by the American anthropologists, George and Sharon Gmelch, who produced valuable scholarship on the community in the 1970s and 1980s, a period when it was largely ignored in Irish academic circles. The Republic of Ireland government's first official report on the minority in 1963, which claimed to be a comprehensive investigation of Traveller culture and lifestyle, made no mention of the related community in the United States. Despite a handful of scholarly and popular articles and television documentaries on the subject in recent decades, awareness of or interest in this Irish minority abroad among the non-Traveller population in Ireland remains scant. Likewise, the Traveler tradition has yet to be generally recognized or claimed by Irish America.

Mary Burke

See also: AMERICAN CIVIL WAR; CATHOLIC CHURCH, the; GREAT FAMINE, The

References

Andereck, Mary E. *Ethnic Awareness and the School: An Ethnographic Study.* Sage Series on Race and Ethnic Relations, Vol. 5. Newbury Park, CA: Sage, 1992.

Arnold, Frederick S. "Our Old Poets and the Tinkers." *The Journal of American Folklore* 11, no. 42 (1898): 210–220.

Bond, Pat. "The Irish Travellers in the United States." *Sinsear: The Folklore Journal* 5 (1988): 45–58.

Gmelch, Sharon. *Tinkers and Travellers.* Dublin, Ireland: O'Brien, 1975.

Harper, Jared Vincent, and Charles Hudson. "Irish Traveller Cant in its Social Setting." *Southern Folklore Quarterly* 37, no. 2 (1973): 101–114.

Leland, Charles Godfrey. "Shelta, the Tinkers' Talk." *New Quarterly Magazine* 3 (1880): 136–141.

McDonagh, Michael, and Robbie McVeigh. *Minceir Neeja in the Thome Munkra: Irish Travellers in the USA.* Belfast, Ireland: Belfast Travellers' Education and Development Group, 1996.

Radharc: Stories from Irish America. "Travellers of Murphy Village." Directed by Joe Dunn. Transmitted on RTE (Ireland), April 23, 1995.

IRISH YANKEES

In the 1820s, particularly in Argentina and imperial Brazil, there was a current of Irish from North America emigrating to Latin America, who were collectively styled as the "Irish Yankees." Some were born in Ireland, emigrated to Canada or the United States, and after a period of settlement there traveled to the Atlantic coast of South America. Although the numbers of immigrants were not significant (in 1827 there were only 150 Irish residents in Buenos Aires), they often pioneered new trades in Buenos Aires and Rio de Janeiro as tailors, cobblers, or coach builders, and they shaped the first prosperous urban middle classes in South American cities.

Some of the Irish Yankees became well known in Buenos Aires. Bernard Kiernan was a renowned astronomer who arrived from the United States in 1824. Kiernan was born in 1780 in Ballybougham, Moneymore (Co. Derry). In 1810 he settled in St. John, New Brunswick, with his family, and then went to Argentina with his own ship. He worked in the countryside as a surveyor, mathematician, and astronomer, and died in 1863 in Morón. His son James Kiernan (1806–1850) was a well-known journalist and owner and director of the *Gaceta Mercantil* newspaper together with Stephen Hallett. John Hayes arrived in Argentina from New York and settled in Esquina in the Corrientes province as a cattle rancher and sheep farmer. During the Triple Alliance War with Paraguay, Hayes was correspondent for *The Standard,* with the pseudonym Simbad. Patrick Fleming, brother of Dr. Michael A. Fleming, bishop of Newfoundland (1829–1850), established a naval store and a coffee shop that was the meeting point for the Irish residents up to the 1850s. On his way to Cuyo Patrick Fleming was kidnapped by Ranqueles Indians and rescued by the Rosas expedition of 1833. The merchant Patrick Lynch emigrated from the United States to Buenos Aires and had good commercial connections with North America. Mrs. Hanlon, who came in 1822, as well as Bartholomew Foley, James McGuire, Richard Sutton, Patrick Donohue, and physicians Conyngham and Brown of the republican army were other immigrants of this group in Argentina. John Devereux was under the influence of this group when he visited Buenos Aires in 1816, but returned to North America when he could not convince the Argentine authorities to obtain a loan in London. In Bolivia Edmond Temple was involved in the mining industry, and the Garrett family in the import of textiles.

The Irish Yankees also had some rural settlers. The first three Irishmen to tend flocks of sheep in the province of Navarro were from North America. Also, some of the first sheep farmers in Mercedes, near the city of Luján, were North Americans with Irish names.

Edmundo Murray

See also: DEVEREUX, John

References

MacLoughlin, Guillermo. "The Forgotten People: The Irish in Argentina and other South American countries." Paper read at the conference The Scattering of Ireland and the Irish Diaspora: A Comparative Perspective. University College Cork, September 24–27, 1997.

Murray, Thomas. *The Story of the Irish in Argentina.* New York: P. J. Kenedy & Sons, 1919.

JACKSON, ANDREW (1767–1845)

In 1765, Andrew Jackson, Sr., Elizabeth (Hutchinson) Jackson, and their two eldest sons emigrated from Carrickfergus, Ireland, to Waxhaw, South Carolina, where Mrs. Jackson gave birth to her third son, Andrew Jackson, in March 1767, a month after his father died. Elizabeth inculcated a hatred of the British in her son, an emotion natural given centuries of British oppression of Ireland. In 1779, the eldest son Hugh died in battle against the British, and the two surviving sons, Andrew and Robert, joined the local militia, fought at the battle of Hanging Rock, and were taken prisoner in 1781. While captive Andrew Jackson enraged a British officer by refusing to shine his boots, and the latter slashed Jackson across the face with a sword. The brothers contracted smallpox and both Robert and Mrs. Jackson died in 1781, leaving Andrew Jackson an orphan. In 1784, he settled in Salisbury, North Carolina, to study law in the office of local attorney Spruce McCay and later with Col. John Stokes. In September 1787 Jackson was admitted to the bar, and in October 1788 he settled in Nashville, which was then part of North Carolina. In 1791 Jackson married Rachel (Donelson) Robards, who was separated from, but had not divorced, her husband Lewis Robards. Only later did Jackson learn this fact, and upon her divorce Jackson and Rachel Robards held a second wedding in 1794. The circumstances of their courtship and marriage led opponents to defame them throughout their lives.

The taint of scandal never alienated Jackson from his friends, and they created opportunities for Jackson at critical junctures in his life. In 1788 Superior Court Judge John McNairy, who had studied law with Jackson, appointed him prosecuting attorney, and in 1791 William Blount, governor of the western counties of North Carolina (what would become the state of Tennessee in 1796), named him attorney general of the Mero District. In 1796 Jackson won election as Tennessee's first congressman. That year he was the only congressman to vote against a tribute to President George Washington; he did so because Washington had supported the 1794 Jay Treaty. Critics condemned Jackson's vote as unpatriotic. In 1797 the Tennessee legislature appointed Jackson to the U.S. Senate but he resigned in April 1798 to become a superior court judge. In 1802 he ran against former Tennessee governor John Sevier in the election for major general of the state militia. The contest was even until Tennessee governor Archibald Roane, a supporter of Jackson, broke the deadlock by voting for his friend. In 1804 Jackson resigned as judge, keeping only his commission in the militia. That year he bought the Hermitage, a 640-acre plantation, and adopted the lifestyle of a cotton planter. A penchant for settling scores by violence led him to kill slave trader Charles Dickinson in a duel in 1806. Jackson himself nearly bled to death from the gunshot wound Dickinson inflicted near Jackson's heart. In 1813 Jackson took a bullet in his left shoulder after having been a second in another duel.

The War of 1812 elevated Jackson to fame. In command of the Tennessee militia he defeated the Creek Indians at the battle of Horseshoe Bend in 1814. The victory won him the rank of major general in the U.S. Army. In 1814 he defended New Orleans against a British assault. The battle coincided with news that the United States and Great Britain had signed a peace treaty, leading Americans to mistakenly believe Jackson had won the war. Commander of the Seventh Military District, in 1817 he pursued the Seminole Indians into Spanish Florida and captured St. Marks; then in 1818 he captured Pensacola, declared Florida a U.S. possession, and executed two British citizens for inciting the Seminoles against the United States. These actions brought the United States to the brink of war with Spain and Britain. President Monroe countermanded Jackson and returned Florida to Spain, though Secretary of State John Quincy Adams persuaded Monroe not to rebuke Jackson. In 1819 Spain sold Florida to the United States, and in 1821 Monroe appointed Jackson the first governor.

That November Jackson resigned, as he had his seats in the House and Senate, and returned to the Hermitage, but his friends would not countenance his retirement. In October 1823 the Tennessee legislature returned him to the U.S. Senate, and in the 1824 presidential election he won the popular vote and carried the Electoral College. His total, however, was not decisive, throwing the election into the House of Representatives, where Speaker of the House Henry Clay tilted the vote to Adams. In return Adams named Clay secretary of state, infuriating Jackson and his supporters. The 1828 election again pitted the populist Jackson against the aristocrat Adams. As he had in 1824, Jackson styled himself the champion of the common people. This time his electoral tally of 178 won him the presidency. Jackson appointed his friends, among them Martin Van Buren, to the cabinet, though Jackson and Vice President John C. Calhoun drifted apart over the tariff. Calhoun sided with South Carolina against the tariff of 1828 and even suggested that states had the right to nullify unpopular laws. This position emboldened some South Carolinians to speak of secession, but Jackson threatened to hold the state by force. In 1832 Congress followed Jackson's recommendation to lower the tariff, but it was not enough to satisfy South Carolina. In 1830 he disappointed the proponents of economic growth by vetoing a bill to fund construction of a road between Maysville and Lexington, Kentucky. The Second Bank of the United States suffered the same fate. With the charter due to expire in 1836 bank president Nicholas Biddle, calculating that Jackson would not risk a veto in an election year, asked Congress to recharter the bank in 1832. Congress obliged but Jackson vetoed the bill, charging that the bank benefited the wealthy and foreign investors but hurt ordinary farmers and debtors. The veto cast the 1832 election, in the mold of the previous election, as a contest between Jackson the champion of democracy and Clay the defender of privilege. Jackson totaled 124,000 more votes than Clay and the third party, the Anti-Mason Party, combined. The victory left Jackson free to erode the rights of Native Americans. In 1835 he permitted Georgia to defy the U.S. Supreme Court by taking land from the Cherokee and settling them in Arkansas. In 1836 Jackson secured the nomination of Van Buren, then his vice president, as the Democratic presidential candidate. In 1837 he returned to the Hermitage, where he died in 1845. He is buried in its garden beside his wife.

Christopher Cumo

See also: SCOTS-IRISH AND MILITARY CONFLICT; SCOTS-IRISH POLITICS; TAMMANY HALL

References

Behrman, Carol H. *Andrew Jackson.* Minneapolis: Lerner Publications, 2003.
Brands, H. W. *Andrew Jackson, His Life and Times.* New York: Doubleday, 2005.
Burstein, Andrew. *The Passions of Andrew Jackson.* New York: Alfred A. Knopf, 2003.
Ellis, Richard E. *Andrew Jackson.* Washington, DC: CQ Press, 2003.

JAMES, JESSE WOODSOM (1847–1882)

Arguably the most infamous outlaw in American history, save perhaps Billy the Kid, Jesse Woodsom James was born in 1847 in Centraville (now Kearny), Missouri. His father was Robert Sallee James, a Baptist minister, who is sometimes described as an immigrant from Ireland, but who in fact was born in Missouri. His mother was Zerelda Cole, who had been educated in a Catholic convent and so may have been Roman Catholic. Cole's family's presence in the United States dated back to the Revolutionary War, according to her grandson Jesse James, Jr. These and other facts make it unclear whether James's ancestry was Irish or Scots-Irish. Some confusion undoubtedly has arisen because of a false claim in recent years that Robert Sallee James was an immigrant from Co. Kerry, a fabrication that attracted some international publicity.

Portrait of Jesse James, one of the most infamous outlaws in American history. (Library of Congress)

At the age of 15, during the Civil War, Jesse James joined a band of pro-Confederate guerrillas led by William C. Quantrill. The guerrillas raided farms and communities sympathetic to the Union. In 1862 Quantrill was commissioned a captain in the Confederate Army; that same year Union authorities declared him an outlaw. On August 21, 1863, Quantrill and his guerrillas, including James, burned and pillaged the town of Lawrence, Kansas, slaughtering more than

150 unarmed men, women, and children. In October, they killed about 100 Union soldiers at Baxter Springs, Kansas. Two years later the guerrillas were looting in Kentucky when a small force of Union soldiers surprised them and fatally wounded Quantrill, which led to the dissolution of his gang. After the Civil War, James formed his own gang with his brother Frank James and several other men. They held up banks, stagecoaches, and trains until 1876, when the gang was decimated while attempting to rob a bank in Northfield, Minnesota. The James brothers escaped and formed a new gang. In 1875, James married his cousin Zerelda after a nine-year courtship. They had two children, Mary and Jesse. On April 3, 1882, in St. Joseph, Missouri, James was shot and killed by Robert Ford, a fellow gang member motivated by the substantial reward money that had been offered for James's death. James was buried at his childhood home in Missouri. Rumors persist that James faked his death and lived until the 1940s under an assumed name, usually that of Frank Dalton. These were definitively proven false in 1995 when DNA tests of James's exhumed body determined that it was indeed his corpse that had been buried in 1882.

The facts and myths of Jesse James's life are an enduring part of American legend and have been treated in numerous books, films, and popular songs. Some recent historical assessments of James have cast a more critical eye upon his character and exploits, but there are still many for whom he remains a hero of the Confederacy. A longstanding, popular myth contends that James was an Old West Robin Hood who bestowed part of the proceeds of his robberies to needy family members and former neighbors, but there is no historical evidence for this.

Danielle Maze

See also: BONNEY, William "Billy the Kid"; SCOTS-IRISH

References

James, Jesse Edwards. *Jesse James My Father, written by Jesse James, Jr.: The First and Only True Story of His Adventures Ever Written.* New York, 1899.

Walker, Dale L. *Legends and Lies: Great Mysteries of the American West.* New York: Tom Doherty Associates, Inc., 1997.

JEANIE JOHNSTON, THE

The *Jeanie Johnston* is a full-size replica of a sailing vessel of three masts used to transport Irish immigrants from Tralee, Co. Kerry, to Baltimore, New York, and Quebec during the Irish Famine. The original vessel was built in Québec in 1847 by the Scottish-born shipbuilder John Munn and made a total of 16 voyages to North America between 1848 and 1855 carrying over 2,500 Irish people across the Atlantic; the ship has the enviable reputation of having never lost a passenger or crew member to death or disease; in 1858 en route from Québec to Hull, the ship became waterlogged and sank, but the crew was saved. Today, the recreated *Jeanie Johnston* is a floating museum that recalls the momentous Irish migration that saw some 1.8 million people leave their homes between 1845 and 1855 because of the ravages of famine.

More than 100 sailing vessels were built at John Munn's shipyard in Québec City between 1821 and 1857. The *Jeanie Johnston,* launched in 1847, was purchased one year later by Nicholas Donovan, a Tralee hardware merchant. The ship made her maiden voyage in April 1848 transporting a total of 193 passengers from Tralee to Québec. During the panic-driven migration caused by the Great Irish Famine of the late 1840s, it is remarkable that the *Jeanie Johnston* never lost a life as many "coffin ships" out of Liverpool and Cork were noted for their extremely high death tolls, which at times reached 50 percent. The *Jeanie Johnston*'s happy record is no doubt attributable to the sturdiness of the ship; the experience of Captain James Attridge, who had been at sea 28 years when he joined the ship in 1848; and to the presence on board of Dr. Richard Blennerhassett, who had been educated in Edinburgh. While on average the voyage from Tralee to Québec aboard the *Jeanie Johnston* took 47 days, in October 1853 the passengers had already been at sea nearly two months when the ship was blown out of the Gulf of Saint Lawrence twice by gale force winds, and the captain put in at Saint Andrews, New Brunswick.

The modern full-size replica was designed by Fred M. Walker, chief naval architect with the National Maritime Museum in Greenwich, who had supervised the re-creation of the eighteenth-century Captain Cook *Endeavour II* ship. The re-creation of the *Jeanie Johnston* followed closely the restoration of the seventeenth-century Dutch East India ship, the *Batavia*, in Lelystad, Holland.

Born in the early 1990s as a project to recall the great migrations of the Famine years in Ireland, the $6.6 million (U.S.) undertaking involved the employment of a group of 300 young people from the United States and Canada and from the nationalist and unionist traditions in Belfast as well as some from Dublin and Kerry. Completed in 2002, the *Jeanie Johnston* undertook a series of visits to ports in the United Sates and Canada in the summer and fall of 2003. In September 2003, a commemorative plaque was unveiled in John-Munn Park in Québec City, which recalls the city's shipbuilding past and the contributions of its Scottish and Irish inhabitants. The modern *Jeanie Johnston* is 123 feet long by 26 feet of beam and 14 feet of draft. She is 510 tonnes and her rigging consists of three masts with four square sails each and single topsails.

Robert J. Grace

See also: EMIGRATION; GREAT FAMINE, The

Reference

Marcil, Eileen. *The Charley-Man: A History of Wooden Shipbuilding at Quebec, 1763–1893.* Kingston, ON: Quarry Press, 1993.

JEFFERS, ROBINSON (1887–1962)

Born in Pittsburgh, Pennsylvania, Robinson Jeffers was the son of a Presbyterian minister who was of Irish ancestry. Jeffers's paternal grandfather had immigrated to America from Co. Monaghan in 1810. Jeffers was educated at the University of Western Pennsylvania and Occidental College, where he received his bachelor's degree in 1905. After graduation he studied medicine at the University of Southern California, where he met Una Call Kuster, who was also of Irish lineage. In 1913 they married and had four children together. At the height of his popularity, Jeffers was the first American poet to appear on the cover of *Time* magazine, on April 4, 1932. However, after World War II there was a change in the critical reception to Jeffers's work.

Although his staunch opposition to American involvement in the war can account for part of this, his postwar work was also received negatively by several influential literary critics such as Yvor Winters and Kenneth Rexroth. Jeffers died in Carmel on January 20, 1962. A posthumous collection of his poems, *The Beginning and the End* appeared the following year.

Along with the Carmel coastline and Big Sur Mountain, Ireland had a considerable influence upon Jeffers's work. He visited Ireland with his wife on a number of occasions. In 1929 they spent six months traveling around Ireland, England, and Scotland. He returned to Ireland in 1937, traveling around the country from June to October. His final journey there was in 1956. The principal work in which Ireland is visible is *Descent to the Dead: Poems Written in Ireland and Great Britain* (1931), which contains poems that were inspired by his travels there and his stay on the northeastern coast. The poems in this collection were included in the later collections *Give Your Heart to the Hawks* (1933) and *Selected Poetry* (1938). Ireland is also present in *Visit to Ireland* (1954), a prose work that includes excerpts from Una's diaries recounting her travels in Ireland. This volume was edited by Jeffers, and it includes some entries by him.

Evidence of their trips to Ireland and the influence the country exerted over Jeffers and his wife can be seen in the granite house where they lived in Carmel, California, and which formed the setting for many of his poems. Overlooking the Pacific Ocean, Tor House was partly built by Jeffers himself and he continued to add to the structure throughout his life. (*Tor* is a Celtic term for a large outcropping of rock.) Jeffers built a large four-story, 40-foot stone tower called Hawk Tower on the same site. The tower was named after a hawk that appeared while Jeffers was working on the structure and disappeared the day it was completed. The structure was based on similar structures Jeffers and his wife had seen while traveling through Ireland and reflected his wife's interest in stone towers and Irish literature. In addition, a Celtic cross without an inscription was taken from a gravestone in Co. Donegal during one of their visits there and was embedded in the walkway to the gardens of their house in Carmel.

David Doyle

Reference

McLean, Andrew M. "Robinson Jeffers." In *The Encyclopedia of the Irish in America,* edited by Michael Glazier. Notre Dame: University of Notre Dame Press, 1999.

JOHNSON, SIR WILLIAM (1715–1774)

William Johnson was a pivotal figure in British colonial and early Native American fortunes. Born in 1715, in Smithstown, Co. Meath, Johnson was the eldest son of Christopher and Anne Johnson. His father was a Catholic middleman and tenant farmer, while his mother was the descendant of Catholic Irish gentry, the Warrens. Johnson's uncle, Sir Peter Warren, had been raised as a Protestant and had gained fame and fortune with the Royal Navy. As Peter Warren began to accumulate vast properties in New York, he encouraged William to emigrate and help him in managing these properties.

In 1738, at the age of 23, Johnson emigrated to America with 12 Protestant families to settle and manage his uncle's estate in New York's Mohawk River Valley. He quickly established a trading post for white settlers and native Indians, and it was through these dealings that he was to develop the relationship of trust and goodwill with the Indians that would become the focal point of his later life in America. As he became a major landowner in his own right, he began to learn the Indians' language, dress in their clothes, and welcome them into his own home. This intimacy led to his being appointed superintendent of Indian Affairs for the Six Nations by the governor of New York in 1744. As tensions with the French escalated, Johnson's role became instrumental to the success of British affairs in America. In 1746 he was made "Colonel of the Forces to be raised out of the Six Nations" and, as a diplomat for British colonial interests, managed to keep the tribes of the Six Nations from aligning with the French in King George's War (1744–1748).

Johnson's position and abilities were crucial to British success in the French and Indian War (1754–1763). In 1754 he led the negotiations with the Indians at the Albany Congress. In 1755, commissioned as a major general, he led the British forces in the expedition against Crown Point. Though he failed to capture Crown Point, his defeat of the French at Lake George and subsequent capture of the French commander, Baron de Dieskau, was the only success in a campaign that had been disastrous thus far. Feted in London as a British hero, he received the thanks of Parliament and a baronetcy. In 1756 Johnson was appointed as sole agent and superintendent of Indians and their affairs; now only subordinate, he recruited 700 Iroquois for the Niagara campaign and, when the commander of the British forces was killed, took command and seized Fort Niagara, the key to the West. The following year he raised a force of 600 Indians and served under Jeffrey Amherst in the campaign to take Montreal. The success of this campaign helped end French power in Canada, and Johnson was rewarded with a king's grant of 100,000 acres of land north of the Mohawk Valley.

This addition to his already substantial land holdings made him one of the largest landholders in the English colonies. After the war, Johnson retired to his large estate to live in the style of an English baron, with many servants and slaves. In 1762, he founded the community that would become Johnstown, by building Johnson Hall and a village three miles north of Fort Johnson (which he had fortified in 1743). In 1763 and 1764, he again won approbation for persuading the Iroquois to stay out of Pontiac's Rebellion. In 1768, Johnson was the lead negotiator in the first Treaty of Fort Stanwix, in which the Iroquois ceded lands in western Pennsylvania and New York (as well as dubious claims to territory in Ohio) for a payment of £10,000.

Johnson displayed genuine respect and love for the Indians of the Six Nations, particularly the Mohawks. In turn, they adopted him into the tribe, making him a sachem and naming him Warraghiaghy, meaning "he who has charge of affairs." After the death of Catharine Weisenberg, a German servant girl who may or may not have been his wife, Johnson first took Caroline and then Molly Brant, two Mohawk women, into his home and fathered several children by them. Though he had been ill for several years, Johnson's actual death resulted, fittingly, from overexertion in addressing an Indian council on a very warm day. His paper on "The Language, Customs, and Manners of the Six Nations," published by the Philosophical society of Philadelphia in 1772, remains an invaluable insight into the Indian nations of the North American territories.

James P. Byrne

References

Deedy, John. "Johnson, Sir William." In *The Encyclopedia of the Irish in America,* edited by Michael Glazier. Notre Dame, IN: University of Notre Dame Press, 1999: 482–483.

Drew, Paul Redmond. "Sir William Johnson—Indian Superintendent." *The Early America Review.* Fall 1996. www.earlyamerica.com/review/fall96/johnson.html (accessed July 31, 2007).

O'Toole, Fintan. *White Savage: William Johnston and the Invention of America.* London: Faber and Faber, 2005.

JORDAN, KATE (1862–1926)

Born on December 23, 1862, in Dublin, Kate Jordan was the daughter of Michael James and Katherine Jordan. Her father was a professor who traced his ancestry back to an artist in the court of King Henry VIII of England. His family had a rich tradition of the arts, and nearly all his relations were either writers, professors, singers, or artists of one type or another. As a one-year-old child, Kate left Dublin and immigrated with her family to America, eventually settling in New York. She was educated in public and private schools as well as at home by private tutors. When she was only 12 years old her first short story was published, and this motivated her to become a full-time writer. In 1897 Jordan married Frederic M. Vermilye, a broker from New York. They had no children. Although she took his name as her surname, because of her fame as a writer she continued to publish her works under her maiden name. Throughout her life Jordan contributed many stories to different magazines. One of her most popular stories was "The Kiss of Gold," which was published in *Lippincott's Monthly Magazine* in October 1892. She published seven novels in total, including *The Other House* (1892), *A Circle in the Sand* (1898), *Time the Comedian* (1905), *The Creeping Tides* (1913), *Against the Winds* (1919), and *The Next Corner* (1921). Her final book, *Trouble-the-House* (1921), consisted of true stories remembered from the author's own childhood. As well as writing novels, Jordan also wrote plays. Her plays include *A Luncheon at Nick's* and *The Pompadour's Protégé,* both of which were written in 1903; *Mrs. Dakon,* which was written in 1909; and two years later, *The Right Road.* Her final play, *Secret Strings,* was published in 1914. Jordan traveled all over the world and spent extended periods living in England and France. When she lived in London she was a member of the Lyceum, the Pen and Brush Club, and the Writers' Club. In America she was a member of the Society of American Dramatists and the Authors' League of America.

Jordan's work, both in drama and fiction, exhibited a wide breadth, which showed her to be at ease in her depiction of diverse characters inhabiting different worlds. For several years toward the end of her life she suffered failing health. Because of anxiety partly caused by her inability to complete a novel, she suffered from insomnia in her final years. In the spring of 1926 she left her home in New York and traveled with her niece to Mountain Lakes, New Jersey, where she spent a couple of months. There, on the morning of Sunday, June 20, 1926, in the woods near her niece's home, she committed suicide by poisoning herself. After her death her body was cremated, and her ashes were buried in Sleepy Hollow Cemetery.

David Doyle

Reference

Harrell, Joy. "Kate Jordan." In *The Encyclopedia of the Irish in America,* edited by Michael Glazier. Notre Dame, IN: University of Notre Dame Press, 1999.

JORDAN, NEIL (1950–)

One of Ireland's most well-known and leading contemporary filmmakers, Neil Jordan began his artistic career as a writer, but he has established himself as a filmmaker with an original and affecting style. His stories have mythic underpinnings, folkloric sensibilities, and characters capable of abiding passions; the tales will often have a gothic or horrific twist. Recurring themes in his films deal with alienation and freedom, the violence at the heart of humankind, and the potential hope in emotional connections between people. His most celebrated film, and one that embodies so many of his signature elements, is *The Crying Game* (1992). Issues of race, sexuality, national tensions, and political violence are all woven into this unconventional romantic tale that surprised international audiences.

Born in Sligo, Jordan grew up in Dublin and studied Irish history and literature at University College Dublin. He began writing at an early age and became involved in fringe theater while at university. Jordan's writing career was established with the publication of *Night in Tunisia* (1976), a collection of short stories that won the prestigious Guardian Fiction Prize. He then went on to publish two novels, *The Past* in 1980 and *The Dream of a Beast* in 1983, both of which are erotic and lyrical depictions of different states of desire.

It would be film, however, that brought Neil Jordan's name to international audiences. Jordan's first involvement in film came when he worked as a creative assistant on John Boorman's 1981 *Excalibur,* and Jordan went on to make a documentary on the making of the film. His first full-length feature was *Angel* (1982), which was released in the United States under the title *Danny Boy.* Starring Irish actor Stephen Rea, who would have a career-long association with Jordan's films, *Angel* is a bleak and violent revenge story about a musician who inadvertently becomes embroiled in sectarian killings in Northern Ireland. The stark surrealism of *Angel* was followed by *The Company of Wolves* (1984), a cinematic adaptation of the fairytale-inspired story by Angela Carter. Full of symbolic imagery and expressionistic cinematography, this reworking of the Little Red Riding Hood story brought Jordan the Best Film and Best Director awards from the London Critics Circle. His next film was even more successful at the box office and pulled Jordan into the international spotlight, winning the Best Picture at Cannes: *Mona Lisa* (1986) stars Bob Hoskins as an ex-con who falls in love with a chic prostitute, played by Cathy Tyson.

The late 1980s saw Jordan direct two unremarkable Hollywood-financed films. Despite the involvement of major Hollywood stars such as Sean Penn and Robert De Niro, *High Spirits* (1988) and *We're No Angels* (1989) were not commercial successes. However, the 1990s proved to be Jordan's most successful decade so far. *The Miracle* (1991) is a darkly sensuous coming-of-age story set in Ireland. The film is modestly produced compared with his earlier films and returns to the world of psychosexual dynamics. His most critically acclaimed and popular film came out the following year. *The Crying Game* reunited Stephen Rea and Neil Jordan and became the most talked about film of that year, due in no small part to the surprising plot twist near the end. Jordan's direction is convincing as he worked with his own script. The film returns Jordan to the struggle of complex characters who find love in a politically and racially complicated world. *The Crying Game* was nominated for six Academy Awards, and Jordan won the award for best original screenplay.

The success of *The Crying Game* led Jordan to adapt Anne Rice's cult classic, *Interview With a Vampire,* in 1994, but Jordan soon returned to Irish content with *Michael Collins* (1997) and *The Butcher Boy* (1998), based on the novel by fellow Irishman Patrick McCabe. Both *Michael Collins* and *The Butcher Boy* showcase Jordan's skill at adaptation: either of historical events (the 1916 Easter Rising and later War of Independence) or of literary works. After *The Butcher Boy,* a disturbing portrait of mental disintegration, Jordan adapted Graham Greene's novel of London during the blitz, *The End of the Affair* (1999). One of Jordan's most ambitious projects was the 2002 remake of the 1955 film noir by Jean-Pierre Melville, *Bob le Flambeur.* Casting Nick Nolte in the lead as an American drug addict and art thief, Jordan's version (titled *The Good Thief*) is considered his best adaptation. Neil Jordan's career continues in both film and fiction. In 2004 he published his third novel, *Shade,* and 2006 saw the release of *Breakfast on Pluto.* He has two films in production at the time of writing.

Danine Farquharson

See also: BYRNE, Gabriel; GLEESON, Brendan; NEESON, Liam; O'CONNOR, Pat; PATTERSON, Frank

References

Jordan, Neil. *A Neil Jordan Reader.* New York: Vintage, 1992.

Rockett, Emer, and Kevin Rockett, *Neil Jordan: Exploring Boundaries.* Dublin: Liffey, 2003.

Rockett, Kevin, Luke Gibbons, and John Hill, eds. *Cinema and Ireland.* London: Routledge, 1987.

Rogers, Lori. *Feminine Nation: Performance, Gender, and Resistance in the Works of John McGahern and Neil Jordan.* Lanham, MD: University Press of America, 1998.

JOYCE, JAMES AUGUSTINE ALOYSIUS (1882–1941)

James Joyce was born on February 2, 1882, in Rathgar, a suburb of Dublin. His youth was spent in numerous homes throughout the city, as declining family circumstances

Portrait of Irish author James Joyce, whose work includes Dubliners, A Portrait of the Artist as a Young Man, *and* Ulysses. *(Library of Congress)*

brought ever greater privations. He nonetheless developed a formidable intellect, attending Clongowes Wood College, Belvedere College, and University College Dublin. In 1904 he met the woman who would be his lifelong companion, Nora Barnacle (1884–1951); they married in 1931 and had two children, Giorgio (1905–1976) and Lucia (1907–1982). Joyce and Nora left Ireland in 1904. After brief periods in Zurich and Pola, they settled for a decade in Trieste. There Joyce taught languages by day and wrote at night. The family spent much of World War I in Zurich, then in 1920 made their most significant move, to Paris. While in Paris Joyce became world famous upon the 1922 publication of his novel *Ulysses.* Joyce spent most of the rest of his life writing the experimental novel *Finnegans Wake.* Critical incomprehension, worsening eye disease, chronic poverty, and his beloved daughter's degenerative mental condition tormented his last years. After the Nazi invasion of France the Joyces fled to Zurich, where Joyce died of a duodenal ulcer on January 13, 1941. He is buried in the Flunturn Cemetery there.

Joyce is one of the most important prose writers of the twentieth century. His 1914 collection of short stories, *Dubliners,* exposes the spiritual paralysis he saw at the center of Dublin life, using tightly written episodes that suggest the influence of George Moore. His next work, *A Portrait of the Artist as a Young Man* (1916), depicts the Joyce-like Stephen Dedalus in an experimental bildungsroman, as he grows from Dublin youth to the first stirrings of artistic endeavor. Dedalus reappears in Joyce's masterpiece, *Ulysses* (1922), which is widely considered the greatest novel of the twentieth century. With relentless stylistic invention, *Ulysses* tells the story of Leopold Bloom, a Dublin Jew whose wanderings on June 16, 1904—Bloomsday—echo the wanderings of Odysseus in the *Odyssey.* Despite its complexities, *Ulysses* remains one of the most admired and accomplished novels in modern literature. Joyce's last work, *Finnegans Wake* (1939), is often considered alienatingly indecipherable. In it Joyce mutates words into multilingual puns, attempting to recreate (or at least to suggest) the flood of images and cross-references encountered in dreams. The resultant novel is a technical accomplishment of merit, yet one in which the plot is, for many readers, incomprehensible.

Joyce never visited North America, nor is that continent a significant element in his writings. Yet Joyce has several important connections to the United States, as he received irreplaceable support from several Americans. His most prominent benefactor was the poet Ezra Pound, who promoted Joyce to publishers with his characteristic volcanic generosity. His most important American acquaintance, however, was the bookseller Sylvia Beach. She not only befriended Joyce, but also published *Ulysses* from her Paris bookshop, Shakespeare and Company, and then advanced him funds from the proceeds in his frequent periods of insolvency. Finally, Joyce made legal history in the United States, as *Ulysses* was at the center of an important legal case, *The United States v. One Book Entitled* Ulysses. This 1933 decision, which held that *Ulysses* was not obscene and was therefore not legally excludable from the United States, has continued to influence American legal discrimination between artistry and obscenity.

Andrew Goodspeed

See also: BEACH, Sylvia; COLUM, Mary; COLUM, Padraic; ELLMANN, Richard David; GOGARTY, Oliver St. John; HUSTON, John; RESEARCH COLLECTIONS, IRISH, IN CANADA; RESEARCH COLLECTIONS, IRISH, IN THE UNITED STATES

References

Ellmann, Richard. *James Joyce.* Rev. ed. Oxford: Oxford University Press, 1982.

Joyce, Stanislaus. *My Brother's Keeper.* London: Faber and Faber, 1958.

McCourt, John. *The Years of Bloom: James Joyce in Trieste.* Dublin: Lilliput, 2001.

K

Kearns, Thomas (1862–1918)

Born in Oxford County, Ontario, the fourth child of recently arrived Irish Catholic immigrant parents, Thomas Kearns moved with his family to the Irish-American agricultural colony of O'Neill, Nebraska, when he was seven or eight. His education was limited to grammar school. He left the family farm at 17 to work as a prospector and teamster in the Black Hills, Tombstone (Arizona), and Tintic (Utah) mining areas, before settling in the silver mining town of Park City, Utah, in 1883.

Upon arriving in Park City, Kearns went to work in its Ontario Mine as a shaft man and mucker, while self-studying geology and mineralogy in the evenings and prospecting on his own. In late 1888 he became a tunneling contractor for a new mine, where he soon observed that its vein of silver ore came from the direction of an adjacent abandoned property. He quickly leased the abandoned property with partners, and by early 1889 they had struck silver. Noticing that the silver vein in the newly leased property similarly came from the direction of other properties, Kearns acquired them, too, and with his partners organized the Silver King Mining Company in 1892. The Silver King soon became one of the West's most profitable silver mines, making Kearns and his remaining partner multimillionaires.

Kearns himself managed the Silver King mine, which featured state-of-the-art equipment, including a 7,300-foot aerial tramway taking buckets of silver-lead concentrate from the mine to railway cars near Park City's rail station. Another feature was excellent employer-employee relations. Kearns and his partner refused to cooperate with other mine owners who sought to lower wage rates when silver prices fell in 1897. They recognized their employees' comparative seniority and how many dependents they had when making necessary layoffs, and they created their own form of in-house workers' compensation. During the tempestuous 1890s, there were no strikes at the Silver King. Kearns's mining interests further expanded in 1907 when the Silver King was combined with other mines as part of the newly formed Silver King Coalition Mining Co.

Kearns used some of his millions to build a French Renaissance mansion for himself, his wife (the former Jennie Judge), and his three children, on Salt Lake City's South Temple Street. Their home, which now houses Utah's governor, included nine turrets, nine fireplaces, and a bowling alley. Kearns also became involved in other businesses, organizing a railway between Salt Lake City and Southern California with other western business and political figures in 1900, acquiring Salt Lake City's largest newspaper—the *Tribune*—in 1901, and financing an 11-story office building—still called the Kearns Building—to house Utah's leading corporations.

Kearns's political career began with his election as a Park City alderman in 1893. He was chair of the committee on mines and mining at Utah's 1895 constitutional convention, held in anticipation of Utah's 1896 statehood, where he successfully sponsored a constitutional provision establishing an eight-hour day for persons working on public works, together with an instruction to Utah's first legislature to pass occupational health and safety laws protecting factory, mine, and smelter workers.

Kearns joined other western delegates in leaving the 1896 Republican National Convention after it endorsed the gold standard and refused a proposed plank calling for the free coinage of silver. He then joined other independent or "silver" Republicans in campaigning for Democratic presidential candidate William Jennings Bryan, who easily carried Utah in 1896. Kearns was a delegate to the Republican National Convention again in 1900. That year he supported the Republican's national ticket of William McKinley and Theodore Roosevelt.

Kearns was elected by Utah's legislature to a vacant U.S. Senate seat in 1901, after 22 ballots, with the support of the Latter-day Saints (LDS or Mormon) church's president. His senate candidacy was controversial because of concerns over his rough manner and knowledge level (he had described Alaska as an island and Utah's rivers as flowing into the Gulf of Mexico) and an 1897 lawsuit by a woman who claimed he had fathered her child. He was elected, in large part, because of LDS influence.

Kearns served in the Senate for four years, during which he advocated reclaiming agricultural lands, expanding Utah's Fort Douglas, and making part of northwestern Arizona Territory a part of Utah. He was, however, defeated when he sought reelection in 1905. He had angered LDS leaders by opposing LDS businessman and apostle Reed Smoot, a fellow organizer of the Salt Lake and Los Angeles Railroad, in Utah's 1903 U.S. Senate election—although Smoot had stepped aside at the urging of LDS leaders to allow Kearns's election in 1901. He had also upset Utah's sugar industry by supporting a sugar reciprocity agreement for Cuban sugar. His successor in the Senate was George Sutherland, another non-Mormon, who later became a U.S. Supreme Court Justice.

Kearns remained active in politics until 1912. Bitter over his reelection defeat, and despite his LDS support in 1901, he lashed out at LDS leaders as having too much statewide political and economic influence and in speeches and on the pages of his *Salt Lake Tribune* accused some of them of continuing polygamous relationships. He became a supporter of the anti-LDS American Party, which held municipal offices in Salt Lake City from 1905 through 1911, but then disbanded. Kearns returned to the Republican Party, supporting President Taft for reelection in 1912, and cutting back the *Tribune*'s anti-LDS rhetoric.

Kearns spent his last years tending to his business interests. He died in 1918 after being hit by a car while crossing through downtown Salt Lake City's main intersection.

Steven B. Jacobson

References

Alexander, Thomas G. *Mormonism in Transition: A History of the Latter-Day Saints, 1890–1930.* Urbana: University of Illinois Press, 1986.

Alexander, Thomas G., and James B. Allen. *Mormons and Gentiles: A History of Salt Lake City.* Boulder, CO: Pruett Publishing Company, 1984.

Bringhurst, Newell G. "Thomas Kearns: Irish-American Builder of Modern Utah." *Journal of the West* 31 (April 1992): 24–32.

Malmquist, O. N. *The First Hundred Years: A History of the Salt Lake Tribune, 1871–1971.* Salt Lake City: Utah State Historical Society, 1971.

Peterson, Richard H., *The Bonanza Kings: The Social Origins and Business Behavior of Western Mining Entrepreneurs, 1870–1900.* Lincoln: University of Nebraska Press, 1977.

Poll, Richard D., ed. *Utah's History.* Provo, UT: Brigham Young University Press, 1978.

Thompson, George A., and Fraser Buck. *Treasure Mountain Home: A Centennial History of Park City, Utah.* Salt Lake City: Deseret Book Company, 1968.

Entertainer Gene Kelly in mid-air dance step. Best known for his role in Singin' in the Rain, *Kelly was an extremely talented and versatile entertainer in the twentieth century. (Library of Congress)*

KELLY, GENE (1912–1996)

Born in Pittsburgh, Pennsylvania, in 1912 to parents of Irish descent, Eugene Curran Kelly started early in show business, appearing with his siblings as the Five Kellys. They sang and tap-danced while their mother Harriet served as their manager and booked their appearances. Young Gene soon became an expert dancer. By the age of 16, Harriet Kelly had opened two locations of the Gene Kelly Studio of Dance, where Gene taught pupils for 50 cents a lesson. Gene was now appearing with his brother Fred, billed as the Kelly Brothers. After graduating high school, he was educated at Penn State College and the University of Pittsburgh. He left for New York City in 1938. His first big break came that year when he appeared in the chorus of a Broadway show called *Leave it to Me.* In 1940 he choreographed Billy Rose's *Diamond Horseshow* and had a starring role in a show called *Pal Joey.* In 1941, he choreographed a Broadway musical, *Best Foot Forward.* His first film appearance was in 1942, when he costarred with Judy Garland in *For Me and My Gal.* He rose in popularity during the 1940s after signing a contract with Metro-Goldwyn-Mayer (MGM). After a stint in the military during World War II, he returned to Hollywood, more popular than ever. Along with Fred Astaire, Gene Kelly was considered among the top American dancers of the era. His dance routines were the highlights of his films, imaginatively choreographed and visually interesting.

In 1945, Kelly was nominated for a Best Actor Academy Award for his role in the musical *Anchors Aweigh* (opposite Frank Sinatra). In 1946 he appeared in *Ziegfeld*

Follies. In 1949, Kelly was the star, choreographer, and codirector of *On the Town.* In 1951, he appeared in *An American in Paris,* which showcased a 17-minute dance sequence. He was awarded a special Oscar for his work in that film. Perhaps his most famous film role was in the 1952 musical *Singin' in the Rain,* which he codirected and co-choreographed. That film contained a lavish 14-minute dance sequence called "Broadway Ballet." That sequence alone cost about $6 million to make, but the film was still a great moneymaker for MGM and is today considered one of the best musicals ever made. Kelly continued to appear in films after that, but by the end of the 1950s the decline of the musical led to fewer roles. His last MGM film was in 1957. In 1962, he appeared in *Going My Way,* a short-lived television situation comedy based on a 1944 film starring Bing Crosby. He was nominated for a Best Supporting Actor Oscar in 1973's drama *Forty Carats.* He remained in the spotlight for 1974's *That's Entertainment* and 1976's *That's Entertainment, Part II,* compilation films that he co-narrated.

Richard Panchyk

References

Hay, Peter. *MGM: When the Lion Roars.* Atlanta: Turner Publishing, 1991.

Karney, Robin, ed. *The Movie Stars Story.* New York: Crescent Books, 1984.

Yudkoff, Alvin. *Gene Kelly: A Life of Dance and Dreams.* New York: Back Stage Books, 1999.

KELLY, GEORGE "MACHINE GUN" (CA. 1897–1954)

George Kelly Barnes, who later became one of the most notorious gangsters in American history, is variously reported as having been born in 1895, 1897, and 1900. It is agreed that he was born in Memphis, Tennessee, to a prosperous middle-class family. Although he began criminal activities early in his life, particularly running liquor, he was nonetheless able to enroll in the predecessor institution of what is now Mississippi State University. He studied agriculture.

Kelly continued a minor criminal career, including bank robbery and illegal liquor distribution, throughout the 1920s. He was apprehended several times and served sentences for punishment at both Leavenworth Penitentiary and the State Penitentiary in New Mexico. At some point in the late 1920s he met Kathryn Thorne who, although she was romantically involved with another small-time criminal, spotted George's potential and began dating him regularly. They subsequently married. It is thought that it was she who bought him a machine gun, urged him to master it, and to promote himself as "Machine Gun" Kelly. This self-promotion scheme worked, and the public became fascinated and alarmed by the notion of a master machine gunner. He enjoyed the peculiar allure of a notorious criminal and eventually became Public Enemy Number One in the United States.

On July 22, 1933, Kelly and Thorne perpetrated their most daring criminal action when they kidnapped one of the wealthiest citizens of Oklahoma City, Charles Urschel. They held him for ransom for more than a week and, when paid, released him near Norman, Oklahoma. Unfortunately for them, Urschel proved to be a cunning and attentive hostage; he was able to provide the authorities with good information about where Kelly and Thorne had taken him and where they might be heading. That information, combined with a trace run on the numbers of the money they were given, resulted in their apprehension by Federal Bureau of Investigation (FBI)

George "Machine Gun" Kelly, handcuffed and shackled, is led under heavy guard in 1933 from Shelby County Jail to Oklahoma City to be tried for the kidnapping of Charles F. Urschel. (Library of Congress)

agents in cooperation with the Tennessee State Police. According to FBI lore, Kelly cried out to the arresting officers some variation of the phrase "Don't shoot, G-men" (for government men), an appellation for FBI agents that the bureau happily appropriated. The story is likely untrue, but Kelly is still widely attributed with coining—or at least popularizing—the term.

Kelly was sentenced to Leavenworth penitentiary in 1933, but was soon transferred to the famous prison island of Alcatraz, near the city of San Francisco. There he led an incongruously decorous life, earning the reputation of a model prisoner. He even served, for a time, as an altar boy in the prison chapel. He was retransferred back to Leavenworth in 1951, where he died of a heart attack on July 17, 1954.

Kelly was not notable for his interest in, or contribution to, Irish-American relations. Only by heredity can he be considered a significant figure in Irish life in America. Yet he is perhaps the most notorious criminal figure in the life of Irish America, and was, for a time, the most wanted man in the nation.

Andrew Goodspeed

References

Breuer, William. *J. Edgar Hoover and His G-Men.* Westport, CT: Praeger, 1995.

Burrough, Bryan. *Public Enemies.* New York: Penguin, 2004.

Hamilton, Stanley. *Machine Gun Kelly's Last Stand.* Lawrence: University of Kansas Press, 2003.

Hoover, J. Edgar. *Persons in Hiding.* Boston: Little, Brown, 1938.
Johnston, James A. *Alcatraz Prison and the Men Who Live There.* New York: Scribners, 1949.

KELLY, GRACE (1929–1982)

Grace Patricia Kelly was born on November 12, 1929, in Philadelphia, Pennsylvania, to Irish Catholic John Brandon Kelly, Sr., who made his fortune in bricklaying, and his athletic wife, Margaret Majer Kelly. Kelly had one brother, John, and two sisters, Lizanne and Peggy. She was educated at the Academy of the Assumption at Ravenhill, Philadelphia, from 1934 to 1943. She graduated from the Stevens School in Germantown in May 1947. Thereafter she enrolled at the American Academy of Dramatic Arts in New York. She refused her father's financial support and accepted modeling and television assignments.

Kelly's beauty and innate regal bearing worked to her advantage. She made her stage debut in a 1949 Broadway production, *The Father,* and her first film role was in *Fourteen Hours.* She gained considerable recognition in 1952 for her role as the wife of Gary Cooper's character in *High Noon.* She signed a contract with Metro-Goldwyn-Mayer and appeared as Linda Nordley in *Mogambo,* with Clark Gable and Ava Gardner, for which she received an Academy Award nomination for Best Supporting Actress.

Alfred Hitchcock selected Kelly for roles in *Dial M for Murder* and *Rear Window* in 1954. She won the Best Actress Academy Award for her role as Georgie Elgin in *The Country Girl,* also in 1954. That same year she also played in *Green Fire,* and she appeared in *The Bridges at Toki Ri* and another Hitchcock film, *To Catch a Thief,* in 1955.

Kelly met His Serene Highness Prince Rainier III (1928–2005) of Monaco on a publicity stunt during the Cannes Film Festival in 1955. The couple began a secret long-distance relationship. In 1956 she completed *The Swan* and *High Society.* Her duet with Bing Crosby, "True Love," reached platinum status. Kelly is listed as 13th on the American Film Institute's list of the greatest actresses of the classic era.

On April 25, 1956, Kelly married Prince Rainier at the St. Nicholas Cathedral in Monaco. She gave up her film career to concentrate on being Monaco's princess and raising a family. The couple had three children: Caroline Louise Marguerite was born on January 23, 1957; the heir to the throne, Albert Alexandre Louis Pierre, was born on March 14, 1958; and Stephanie Marie Elisabeth was born on February 1, 1965. As Princess Grace, she focused her energies on enhancing the principality. She established foundations, charities, and public buildings and supported the arts. Her constant media presence put Monaco on the world stage. She never acted again. Instead she gave poetry readings in aid of charitable causes. Her 1977 narration of the documentary *Children of Theatre Street* was well received.

On September 12, 1982, Princess Grace and Princess Stephanie were returning to the palace after leaving the family farm Roc Agel, in the French mountains above Monaco. As Kelly was negotiating the last tricky hairpin curve of the Moyenne Corniche, she suffered a stroke, causing her vehicle to veer off the road. She was gravely injured, and Stephanie suffered minor back injuries. Princess Grace died after two days on life support. Her funeral was attended by luminaries from across the world and was televised globally. The sympathy for the grief-stricken Prince Rainier was astounding, but he never recovered from the shock. Princess Grace helped her husband revolutionize Monaco's image; it is now an inviting country in which to conduct business and a delight to visit. Princess Grace is buried in St. Nicholas Cathedral in Monaco, the site of her wedding.

Annette Richardson

References

Bradford, Sarah. *Princess Grace.* London: Weidenfeld & Nicolson, 1984.

Edwards, Anne. *The Grimaldis of Monaco: The Centuries of Scandal, the Years of Grace.* New York: William Morrow and Co., 1992.

Eglund, Steven. *Grace of Monaco: An Interpretive Biography.* New York: Doubleday & Co., 1984.

Robinson, Jeffrey. *Rainier and Grace: An Intimate Portrait.* New York: Atlantic Monthly Press, 1989.

Taraborelli, J. Randy. *Once Upon a Time: Behind the Fairy Tale of Princess Grace and Prince Rainier.* New York: Rose Books, 2003.

KELLY, "HONEST" JOHN (1822–1886)

Born on April 21, 1822, in New York City to poor Irish immigrant parents, John Kelly received little formal education. He worked from an early age, eventually prospering as a stone cutter. The religious Kelly was also an amateur boxer and actor. Drawn to politics, he joined Tammany Hall, the New York City Democratic Party machine. After a stint as an alderman, Kelly served two terms in the U.S. House of Representatives, during which time he was the only Roman Catholic in Congress. In 1858 he left Congress to become the county sheriff, a position rich in patronage and financial rewards.

Although Kelly was part of the leadership of Tammany Hall, he did not support Boss William Tweed. Kelly disapproved of Tweed's extravagant corruption. After the deaths of his wife and son and a bitter quarrel with Tweed, Kelly resigned as sheriff in 1868 and took a tour of Europe.

The exposure of the corruption of the Tweed ring led to the boss's loss of political control of Tammany Hall. Kelly quickly emerged as the new leader because he was one of the few city Democrats who had no involvement in Tweed's corruption. Kelly systematically removed known Tweed supporters from important positions and courted reformers. Kelly rationalized the political system he inherited and firmly established centralized control in his own hands. To hold the system together, Kelly replaced the Tweed method of corrupt business contracts with a greater reliance on political patronage. To pay for campaigns Kelly instituted a system of assessments from candidates and civil servants who owed their jobs to political connections. For the day, it was a standard, although controversial, practice used by both parties. Controlling two newspapers, Kelly ensured that he had direct communications with the grassroots voters. He was the first Catholic and Irish leader of Tammany Hall and permanently oriented its focus to the growing immigrant population.

The strength and weakness of Kelly's leadership was his attempt to win over the reformist elements inside the Democratic Party with some modest changes. He invited leading reformers to become members of Tammany. This policy aided him in making Tammany Hall stronger in the wake of the Tweed scandals than it had been before. A testament to Kelly's leadership was his avoidance of scandal during his reign as boss. At the same time, however, he never did enough to satisfy the reformers and angered many of his own supporters who viewed him as giving away too much in search of approval that never came. This tension was no more evident than during the depression of 1877, when Kelly sided with the reformers and their policy of fiscal retrenchment while the Tammany faithful called for government-financed public works projects to put the unemployed to work. To the chagrin of many of his supporters, when Kelly received the appointment of comptroller of New York City he refused to open the treasury.

If he disappointed his supporters, he still failed to win over the Protestant reformers, many of whom harbored xenophobic contempt for the Irish Catholics of Tammany Hall. Governor Tilden proposed an amendment to the state constitution that would have established a board to oversee all the city's financial transactions. Although Kelly successfully defeated the measure, he did so at a great cost. Kelly showed his anger in 1878 when he stormed out of the Democratic state convention with the entire Tammany Hall delegation in tow. Kelly was able to broker a deal with the reformers in 1880, but it was only a temporary rapprochement. Kelly convinced the reformers to support his choice of mayor, William Grace, the first Roman Catholic to hold that office. However, Grace turned out to govern completely independently of Tammany Hall, which infuriated Kelly. In 1884, Kelly did what he could to defeat both Grace and the Democratic presidential candidate, Grover Cleveland, another anti-Tammany reformer. When both candidates won their respective elections, Kelly became a bitter and broken man. He effectively retired from politics and passed the torch to Richard Croker, a protégé he had groomed for the position. Kelly died on June 1, 1886.

Gregory J. Dehler

References

Allen, Oliver. *The Tiger: The Rise and Fall of Tammany Hall.* Reading, MA: Addison Wesley, 1993.

Genen, Arthur. "John Kelly: New York's First Irish Boss." PhD dissertation, New York University, 1971.

Mandlebaum, Seymour J. *Boss Tweed's New York.* New York: John Wiley and Sons, 1965.

Werner, M. R. *Tammany Hall.* Garden City, NY: Doubleday, Doran, and Co., 1928.

KENNEDY FAMILY

The Kennedy family dominated Irish-American politics for most of the twentieth century and continued to be influential into the twenty-first. The first prominent representative was John Francis "Honey Fitz" Fitzgerald (1863–1950). A well-educated banker, Fitzgerald could not resist the lure of Boston ward politics. He served two terms as mayor of Boston but failed in comeback races for Congress, the Senate, and the governorship. Nevertheless, his high visibility in the Irish community guaranteed fast political tracks for his grandsons. In 1914 his daughter Rose (1890–1995) married Joseph P. Kennedy (1888–1969), the Harvard-educated son of a wealthy liquor dealer. Joe built the family fortune with brilliant forays into banking, shipbuilding, motion pictures, real estate, and (just before prohibition ended) a heavy investment in upscale imported liquor. He moved the family base from Boston to New York in 1927, where it remained until his son John Fitzgerald Kennedy (1917–1963) returned to Boston in 1946. Joe was noted for his fierce devotion to promoting his children, his notorious love affairs, his ruthless business dealings, and his major roles in the New Deal. He built the new Securities and Exchange Commission into a powerful watchdog of Wall Street. Joe reached the pinnacle of esteem as ambassador to the Court of St. James (1938–1940), cruising elegantly in the highest circles of London society, in contrast to his maligned reputation in American high society. His daughter Kathleen (1920–1948), became Marchioness of Hartington when she married the heir to a dukedom; she later died in a plane crash. Recalled as ambassador because of his isolationism and support for Chamberlain's appeasement of Germany, Joe nevertheless endorsed Franklin Roosevelt in the critical 1940 election. Unlike Al Smith and other prominent Irishmen, he refused to attack Roosevelt and thereby preserved presidential options for his sons. Joe was increasingly isolated after 1941, keeping his distance from the clubhouse politicians who clustered around Honey Fitz, as well as the Yankee businessmen he thought had denied him entry into the most elite Harvard circles. His business enterprises flourished, and he established daughter Eunice (1921–) in Chicago, where her husband Sargent Shriver (1915–) operated the family's giant office building, the Merchandise Mart. Although Shriver led the antipoverty programs in President Johnson's Great Society and was the Democratic nominee for vice president in 1972, as an in-law he never broke into the inner circle. The Chicago ties paid off handsomely when Mayor Richard J. Daley, boss of the city's powerful Democratic machine, enthusiastically supported the Kennedys' national political campaigns. Realizing his leadership status as one of the half dozen most powerful Irishmen in America, Joe played up his ties with Francis Cardinal Spellman of New York and with the nation's most prominent Irish Republican, Senator Joseph McCarthy, even encouraging the bachelor senator to date his daughters.

Joe and Rose instilled remarkably high levels of solidarity and competitiveness in their four sons and five daughters. Rosemary (1918–2005) was mentally retarded and institutionalized, which led to family involvement in numerous charities, such as the Special Olympics for athletes with disabilities. Of the sons, only Robert (1925–1968) followed his mother in becoming a devout Catholic with high moral standards regarding sexual behavior; he fathered 11 children. Joe never ran for office himself but devoted his political ambitions to putting Joseph Jr. (1915–1944) in the White House. But Joseph Jr. died before his father achieved his ambition; his Navy bomber exploded on a combat mission in Europe in 1944, and he became the first of many Kennedys to die violently. John (1917–1963) then became heir apparent, returning to Boston to take a seat in Congress in 1946 and defeating the prototypical Yankee, Senator Henry Cabot Lodge, Jr., in 1952. Robert entered politics as an aide to Senator Joseph McCarthy, but he built his reputation as an aide to Senator Kennedy in highly publicized investigations into racketeering in the Teamsters Union, the largest labor union and one that had broken with the Democratic phalanx of the AFL-CIO unions. John Kennedy's presidential campaign in 1960 was a family affair, funded by the father and orchestrated by Robert. John preferred Ivy League policy advisers, but unlike his father he enjoyed the give and take of Massachusetts politics and built a largely Irish team of campaigners, headed by Larry

O'Brien and Kenneth O'Donnell. The new president shook off nepotism charges and appointed his brother Robert attorney general in 1961.

Meanwhile, First Lady Jacqueline Bouvier Kennedy (1929–1994) added fresh glamour to the family, even as she disdained the roughhousing of her in-laws. John Kennedy's 1963 assassination turned him into a martyr and, indeed, a saint in the Catholic community. It also shifted the glare of publicity away from Joe (who had suffered an incapacitating stroke) and John's surviving children, and onto widow Jacqueline. She remarried in 1968 to Greek shipping magnate Aristotle Onassis, and became in her own right a celebrity who overshadowed her in-laws. Robert, increasingly at odds with President Lyndon Johnson, resigned his cabinet post in 1964 to run for the Senate from New York. In 1968 he broke decisively with Johnson on the issue of the Vietnam War. Liberals who had long distrusted this former McCarthyite rallied to his side, fighting not just the forces of Johnson and Hubert Humphrey, but also those of Eugene McCarthy, an Irish senator who claimed primacy in the antiwar movement. Multiple chasms opened in the Democratic Party: the intellectual and radical student wings supported McCarthy, the conservative southern whites rallied to George Wallace, and Kennedy and Humphrey battled for control of the blue-collar white ethnics and the African-American voters. At the climax of a bruising, nasty, and often violent primary season Robert won the decisive California primary, but he was assassinated immediately after leaving the podium where he claimed victory.

In the presidential election, the Irish Catholic vote splintered for the first time, showing that at long last the iron grip of the Democratic Party had been permanently broken. Edward (Ted) Kennedy (b. 1932) became the head of the Kennedy family and, to the surprise of critics who saw him as shallow and indecisive, emerged as the most successful politician in the family's history. Entering the Senate in 1962, Ted succeeded because of his ability to build coalitions inside the Democratic Party and, on occasion, with Republicans. As a tireless campaigner and powerful orator, he used the family reputation to solidify his position as the strongest figure on the left of the Democratic Party. His own presidential aspirations collapsed in 1969 when he drove an automobile off a bridge, watching helplessly as his lady companion Mary Jo Kopechne drowned. When he finally did seek the nomination in 1980, he was badly outmaneuvered by incumbent president Jimmy Carter. The old city machines were long gone, the Irish were divided politically, and they no longer acknowledged a Kennedy as automatically entitled to a presidential nomination.

Scandals and tragedy tarnished the third generation of Kennedys, Joe's grandchildren. Two died in violent accidents, another of a drug overdose; one was acquitted in a highly publicized rape trial; an in-law was convicted of murder. Worst of all the younger generation did poorly at politics; none could move higher than the federal House of Representatives. The first woman in the family to run for high office, Kathleen Kennedy Townsend (b. 1951) lost the traditional Democratic stronghold of Maryland when she ran for governor in 2002. Fresh blood was needed, and although the family had never promoted its in-laws, they were astonished to watch Arnold Schwarzenegger, the Republican husband of Maria Shriver Schwarzenegger (b. 1951), seize the governorship of California in 2003 and emerge as the dominant politician on the West Coast.

Richard Jensen

See also: BOSTON; KENNEDY, John Fitzgerald; MASSACHUSETTS; McCARTHY, Joseph

References

Kearns Goodwin, Doris. *The Fitzgeralds and the Kennedys: An American Saga.* New York: St. Martin's Press, 1987.

O'Brien, Michael. *John F. Kennedy: A Biography.* New York: Thomas Dunne Books, 2005.

Smith, Amanda, ed. *Hostage of Fortune: The Letters of Joseph P. Kennedy.* New York: Viking, 2001.

KENNEDY, JOHN FITZGERALD (1917–1963)

John Fitzgerald Kennedy (often referred to as JFK) is widely regarded as the most important Irish-American figure in recent history. Educated at private schools and (following in the footsteps of numerous relatives) Harvard University, he was an indifferent student until the war in Europe focused his attention. Extensive interviews with major British politicians and observers led to an unusually precocious senior thesis that became an influential book: *Why England Slept* (1940). As second son in the Kennedy family, John was marked for an intellectual career as a writer or journalist, and his older brother Joseph was slated for politics by their hypermanipulative father, Joseph P. Kennedy. Yet the elder brother's death in combat, combined with JFK's heroic war record, set the stage for his political debut as a congressional candidate in 1946. Although the father had abandoned Boston, JFK's return to the city restored the family's traditional power base among the large and powerful Irish-American community in Massachusetts. Strong family connections with the Chicago Irish political community (led by Mayor Richard J. Daley) augmented his national Catholic base. JFK always had two sets of advisers, an inner circle of Irish politicians who planned his campaigns, and a Protestant-Jewish coterie of intellectuals (mostly from Harvard) who promoted his stature as the intellectual in politics. That image was solidified by the Pulitzer Prize awarded his book *Profiles in Courage* (1956).

JFK possessed powerful assets: his ability as an excellent speaker and glib commentator on major issues, a middle-of-the-road political record that offended no one, strong expertise in foreign policy, articulate anti-communism, unfailing charm and stage presence, a national network of Irish allies, a Catholic base that comprised a fourth of the electorate, and an immense purse that was ready to fund his ambitions, not to mention innumerable relatives who campaigned endlessly on his behalf. JFK fought his way into the Senate in 1952 by defeating incumbent Henry Cabot Lodge, Jr., the archetypical Yankee. With the national Democratic Party leaderless, JFK largely ignored the old-boy Senate (controlled by his rival Lyndon Johnson) to display his talents through newspaper and television interviews, magazine articles, and highly publicized speeches to Democratic Party gatherings in every part of the country. Aided by his closest adviser, his brother Robert, JFK appealed to conservatives by tolerating Joe McCarthy and instead launching relentless attacks on corrupt labor leaders, especially Jimmy Hoffa of the Teamsters. Many liberal Democrats, led by Eleanor Roosevelt, distrusted JFK, primarily because they could never forget his father's break with Franklin Roosevelt or the family's support for

McCarthy. Yet with the fading away of Adlai Stevenson, liberals lacked a viable candidate of their own. By 1960 JFK was the front-runner for the Democratic presidential nomination, and the biggest question remaining was whether his Catholic base of support would be outweighed by anti-Catholicism of the sort that hurt Al Smith so badly in 1928. Of course prohibition was no longer an issue, and fear of Tammany-like bossism had faded away with the demise of most big city machines. The Kennedy juggernaut defeated rival Hubert Humphrey in the West Virginia primary, a state with so much poverty and so few Catholics that party leaders were convinced they had a winner. Kennedy won over the party's intellectuals by his effective academic connections, while shaming doubters by a brilliant performance before the Protestant ministers of Houston. There he enunciated the position that he did not speak for the Catholic Church on matters of religion, and it did not speak for him on public affairs. He was able to take that position because there were no high-intensity moral issues such as abortion before the public. Although JFK's religiosity consisted of nominal attendance at Sunday Mass, he excited tens of millions of Catholics who saw his election as president as confirmation of their full recognition as true Americans. With eight of 10 Catholics voting for Kennedy, he ran up majorities in ethnic strongholds like Chicago that barely provided the margin of victory against Richard Nixon. Apart from a few pockets of antipopery among some Midwestern Lutherans and Southern Baptists, fears of Catholicism had largely disappeared from the voting booth.

President Kennedy was primarily interested in foreign policy. Weeks after his memorable inaugural address sounded the bell for vigorous anticommunism, he encountered disaster when his invasion of Cuba failed, and he was forced to ransom thousands of soldiers who were captured by Fidel Castro. Soviet leader Nikita Khrushchev, sensing weakness, pushed hard on the Berlin issue, and was able to build the Berlin Wall despite Kennedy's anguished rhetoric, "Ich bin ein Berliner!" Khrushchev and Castro went too far in 1962, secretly setting up medium-range missiles in Cuba equipped with nuclear warheads that threatened the southeast United States as far inland as Atlanta. In his greatest moment, Kennedy rejected invasion plans but imposed a blockade and demanded that the missiles be removed immediately. Khrushchev publicly backed down, but privately got Kennedy to remove American missiles from Turkey, while Castro secured the promise that the United States would never invade his island. The Cuban Missile Crisis reversed JFK's image of ineptness in foreign policy, but his quiet, continuous escalation of military involvement in Vietnam set the stage for the whirlwind reaped by his successor.

As a senator, JFK had shown limited interest in domestic affairs apart from labor union corruption. As president he ignored that issue. Working with his high-powered economic advisers he proposed a Keynesian program to stimulate the economy, not by higher spending but by tax cuts, but none of his domestic policy initiatives went anywhere. Congress was effectively controlled by a conservative coalition of Republicans and southern Democrats; the alignment remained unchanged after the status-quo midterm elections of 1962. A new issue that Kennedy had not anticipated blazed into view as the civil rights movement in the South, led by Martin Luther King, produced dramatic confrontations with segregationist Democrats, especially Governor George Wallace of Alabama and Governor Ross

Barnett of Mississippi. A month before the 1962 election, Kennedy sent federal marshals and army military police to enforce a federal court order that African-American student James Meredith be admitted to the University of Mississippi. Violent resistance by townspeople left two civilians dead, hundreds injured, and 166 federal agents injured. The confrontation in Alabama in 1963 was nonviolent and boosted Wallace's visibility as a leader of southern Democrats. JFK ignored the risks to his southern base and spoke out in favor of civil rights legislation, but as in so many instances, no legislation was passed.

Kennedy's assassination in November 1963 was a stunning shock to all Americans. The Irish Catholic community took it hard, and immediately elevated JFK to a sort of sainthood status, celebrating the miracle that he had liberated them from second-class citizenship. Lyndon Johnson claimed Kennedy's mantle, and pushed through most of the legislation that had languished for three years, together with new initiatives of his own. He successfully retained the Catholic base JFK had fostered, but that was the last hurrah. By 1966 Catholics started showing their disillusionment with Johnson, who never recovered from the wave after wave of urban riots that followed his civil rights bills, nor from the disillusionment of the intellectuals with his Vietnam policy. With the assassination of Robert Kennedy in 1968, and the failure of Ted Kennedy to recover his brothers' national base, the Kennedy legacy increasingly became the romantic memory of Camelot. Disclosures of JFK's astonishing sexual involvements and detailed reports of his multiple grave medical problems fascinated the public in recent years but failed to break the myth that if only JFK had lived his second term would have been a story of political triumphs that would restore the people's faith in their government.

Richard Jensen

See also: AMERICAN IRELAND FUND; BOSTON; CATHOLIC CHURCH, The; CLINTON, William Jefferson; DE VALERA, Eamon; EIRE SOCIETY OF BOSTON, The; ETHNIC AND RACE RELATIONS (IRISH AND AFRICAN AMERICANS); KENNEDY FAMILY; MASSACHUSETTS; McCARTHY, Joseph; O'NEILL, Thomas "Tip," Jr.

References

Dallek, Robert. *An Unfinished Life: John F. Kennedy, 1917–1963.* Boston: Little, Brown and Co., 2003.

Maier, Thomas. *The Kennedys: America's Emerald Kings.* New York: Basic Books, 2003.

O'Brien, Michael. *John F. Kennedy: A Biography.* New York: Thomas Dunne Books, 2005.

Parmet, Herbert S. *JFK: The Presidency of John F. Kennedy.* New York: Dial Press, 1983.

KENTUCKY

Although the Irish are recorded as being present in Kentucky from the earliest days, it was in the years around the American Revolution that they first rose to prominence in the state's history. When the explorer Daniel Boone established Fort Boonesboro on the banks of the Kentucky River, some Irish were documented as being appointed trustees of the settlement. In the years before the Declaration of Independence the Scots-Irish in Kentucky began to play an increasingly important role in the leadership of the independence movement in the state. However, their influence in Kentucky was quite limited because of the isolated and fragmented nature of their settlements. When Harrod's Fort was founded by Captain James Harrod in 1774, a number of Irish Catholic families were there. In 1792, the first Catholic church in Kentucky was built by Irish settlers at Pottinger's Creek. By 1811, a Frenchman, Benedict Joseph Flaget, had been appointed the first bishop of Kentucky. With the establishment of Catholic settlements in the state, which were frequently populated by people with Irish surnames, there was an increase in the number of Catholic churches being built.

In 1821 St. Mary's College was founded and managed by Father William Byrne, who had been born in Co. Wicklow, Ireland. He ran the school for 12 years, during which time the school educated more than 1,000 children, including John Spalding, who later became the second bishop of Louisville and archbishop of Baltimore. Following Father Byrne's death from cholera in 1833, the school was taken over by the Jesuits. In 1848, the Trappist monastery, the Abbey of Gethsemani, was founded in Nelson County, Kentucky. The land the monastery was built on had originally been donated to the monastery by the Sisters of Loretto. The monastery had a strong Irish presence: of the 176 monks who entered between 1848 and 1948, 32 monks were born in Ireland and 18 were of Irish descent.

After the Great Famine in Ireland some Irish Catholics settled in Kentucky. Although their numbers were not on the scale of other states, they performed manual labor, mostly working in construction as stonemasons building fences but also as farm laborers and railroad workers. The Scots-Irish and Irish have also played an important role in horse breeding, for which Kentucky has become famous. Samuel Riddle was the Scots-Irish owner of Man O'War, who was regarded by many as the best racehorse ever. He also owned War Admiral, a horse who won the Triple Crown in 1937. An Irishman, Price McGrath, was the winner of the first Kentucky Derby, which was held in 1875. The home of the famed Kentucky Derby, Churchill Downs, was built by Matt J. Winn, who was the son of Patrick and Julia Flaherty, both of whom were of Irish ancestry. There has also been much speculation as to the links between Kentucky mountain music and Irish and Scottish traditional music.

In spite of the relatively thin history of the Irish in Kentucky compared with other states—even other states in the South—in recent times there has been a growing awareness of Irish ancestry on the part of people living in Kentucky. In the 1990 census conducted in the state, 696,000 people, out of a total state population of 3.6 million, claimed to be of Irish ancestry.

Kentucky's newspapers have made an important contribution to the state's documentation of its Irish demographic and ethnic activities. Chief among these is the *Kentucky Irish American* newspaper, established in 1898 by William M. Higgins. The paper was originally a four-page weekly, and its chief readership was the Irish community in Louisville, Kentucky. The paper flourished until 1968; its last issue is dated November 30, 1968. Issues of the *Kentucky Irish American* are preserved in microfilm at the University of Louisville Archives, Louisville, Kentucky.

David Doyle

References

Clark, Thomas D. *The Rampaging Frontier: Manners and Humors of Pioneer Days in the South and Middle West.* Indianapolis, IN: Bobbs-Merrill, 1939.

Mattingly, Sister Mary Ramona. *The Catholic Church on the Kentucky Frontier 1785–1812.* Washington, DC: University of America, 1936.

McLaughlin, Raymond F. "Kentucky." *The Encyclopedia of the Irish in America,* edited by Michael Glazier. Notre Dame, IN: University of Notre Dame, 1999.

special.library.louisville.edu/display-collections.asp?ID=601 (accessed Sept. 26, 2007).

KEOUGH, DONALD R. (1926–)

Horatio Alger could not have spun a better story than that of Donald R. Keough. The business legend grew up in the golden cornfields of northwest Iowa; within 30 years he was comfortable in corporate boardrooms in New York City. He helped mastermind what *Forbes* calls "one of the greatest growth stocks ever, the world's best known brand—Coca Cola." An inspiration to the Irish and Irish Americans, Keough's long career is a dual model of ethical business practice and Irish studies patronage. In a December 15, 2005 interview, musing over his principles as a business leader, Keough said, "Maintaining a competitive, nervous edge is not only very Irish, it's good for business. My associates and I at The Coca Cola Company had a huge challenge, absolutely daunting: we had to maintain sales around the world in one product over several decades of changing consumer tastes and demographics . . . and we did it. We had to change and adapt, just like Ireland now. And that whole process in Ireland is just starting up. It's a fascinating situation, a whole new paradigm for that special island."

Keough is president emeritus of one of the world's largest and most iconic multinational companies. His management record has drawn respectful attention from business leaders throughout the globe. When he accepted the 1993 Gold Medal of honor from the American Irish Historical Society in New York City, Keough observed, "It's often been said that Ireland's national emblem, the shamrock, is a good teaching tool because it's all about unity in diversity. How true! Why, a few decades ago, Ireland was but a spit of land in the Atlantic, a tiny exclamation mark. Who went there? A few ardent Irish Americans seeking their

Donald Keough is president emeritus of The Coca Cola Company, Atlanta, Georgia, and also chairman of the board of Allen & Company, Inc., New York City. His patronage of Irish Studies resulted in the founding of educational institutes in Dublin and at Notre Dame University, Indiana. (Foster & Associates, Atlanta, 1994. With kind permission.)

roots, I suppose, but it was mostly tourists who visited, tourists curious about 'the Ol' Sod' or needing to play a little golf at Smurfit's luxury digs in Kildare. Now, with Ireland's new Financial Centre and the economy's strong corporate backing, the unique isle of saints and scholars has joined the modern world—Ireland is happening, it's earned a seat at the party. The thrill of my life is being a celebrant at that table.

"Ireland's challenges in 2006 are different: they're facing ethnic identity issues, they're negotiating the current influx of foreign cultures, and they're smart enough to educate their youth to the new bio-tech markets. These are serious undertakings."

Complementing his broad credits in corporate management, Keough has used his formidable resources and corporate savvy to distinguish himself as a valued patron of Irish studies. The Keough-Naughton Institute for Irish Studies at Notre Dame University in Indiana and the Keough-Naughton Notre Dame Centre in Dublin have swiftly become busy hubs of serious scholarship, teaching, and learning; they also serve as a visible working model of Irish-American relations. Martin Naughton of Ireland has been a co-builder of the Institute. At the Institute, scholars from Ireland, the United States, and points well beyond find archival resources for their projects, as well as a nurturing, cosmopolitan climate for collegial dialogue. Reflecting strong international interest in the Keough-Naughton Institute, Paris was the host city for the Keough Irish Seminar in the summer of 2006, under the directorship of Seamus Deane, Luke Gibbons, and Kevin Whelan.

Donald R. Keough was born on September 4, 1926, in Maurice, Iowa, the third child of Leo Keough and Veronica (Henkels) Keough. His father was a farmer and a cattleman whose ancestral roots went back to Co. Wexford, Ireland. After graduating high school at the age of 16, Keough enlisted in the Navy in 1944. After World War II he attended Creighton University, in Omaha, Nebraska, on the G.I. Bill. Keough set his cap for a career in big business, but he began modestly, with small steps. After graduating from college in 1949, Keough worked as a talk show host in Omaha. Then he moved on to advertising for the Butter-Nut Coffee Company of Omaha, which was eventually sold to the Duncan Coffee Company of Houston, and acquired by The Coca-Cola Company in 1964. Keough rose to executive marketing and administrative positions at The Coca-Cola Company within a few years. By 1981, he was president of the world's soft drink giant and chairman of the largest bottling system. Not overlooking his Irish roots, Keough and his managers established a Coca-Cola plant in Drogheda, Co. Louth, and later opened a larger, and more efficient plant in Ballyna in Connemara, the major supplier of the drink's concentrate to Europe and elsewhere. Few were surprised when Keough was selected for the 1988 Horatio Alger Award in Washington, D.C. After a tenure of nearly 30 years at Coca-Cola, Keough stepped down in 1993, although he continues to serve as a member of the Board.

In 1993, Keough was elected chairman of Allen & Company Inc., an investment banking firm in New York City. Keough names as his career models and mentors his father, Leo Keough, as well as Robert Woodruff, Clarke A. Swanson, and Warren Buffett; he also has great admiration for Tony O'Reilly, Martin Naughton, Herbert Allen, Michael Smurfit, and Fr. Theodore Hesburgh.

Keough's impressive business career notwithstanding, his most memorable legacy may well be his great contribution to Irish Studies, both in the United States and in Ireland. Not only did he serve as founder and patron of new Irish Studies institutes on two continents, but he was also personally instrumental in building the Institutes' important scholarly resources through an ongoing commitment to rare book acquisition. At present, Hesburgh Library at Notre Dame University is a premier site for Irish Studies researchers.

Determined to wear out, not rust out, Keough maintains a whirlwind schedule even into his eighth decade. In addition to frequent visits to the Keough-Naughton

Irish Studies institutes in Flanner Hall at Notre Dame and at O'Connell House in Dublin, Keough serves on the boards of IAC/InterActive Corp, Global Yankee Holdings, Convera Corporation, Berkshire Hathaway Inc., and The Coca-Cola Company. He has also served for many years as a member of the boards of McDonald's Corporation, the Washington Post Company, H. J. Heinz Company, and Home Depot. Maintaining strong ties to the scholarly community, Keough is chairman emeritus of the board of trustees, a life trustee of the University of Notre Dame, and co-chair of its Ireland Council with Martin Naughton of Ireland. He is also a trustee of several other educational, charitable, and civic organizations.

Keough's career achievements, as well as his broad philanthropic and patronal activities, have garnered many distinctions and awards over the years, including honorary doctorates from the University of Notre Dame, Creighton University, Emory University, Clark University, Trinity College Dublin, and University College Dublin. In 1993, Keough was given two prestigious awards: the Laetare Medal, the University of Notre Dame's highest distinction; and the Gold Medal from the American Irish Historical Society in New York City. In 2002, he became an elected fellow of the American Academy of Arts & Sciences. In 2003, Keough was inducted into the Junior Achievement National Business Hall of Fame. In 2006, he was inducted into the American Advertising Hall of Fame. In 2007, Mr. and Mrs. Keough were awarded full Irish citizenship by the minister for justice at a ceremony at the University of Notre Dame; this award was celebrated at Slane Castle, Ireland, at an event hosted by Dr. Martin Naughton.

Keough divides his time between his family office in Atlanta, Georgia, and Allen & Company Incorporated in New York City. He presently resides in suburban Atlanta with his wife of over 50 years, Marilyn or "Mickie" (Mulhall) Keough. "And don't forget," he enjoys reminding interviewers, "I've also been a busy father. I guess I did a few things right! Of my six children—Kathleen, Mary, Michael, Patrick, Eileen, Clarke—five graduated from Notre Dame University. Kathleen graduated from my alma mater, Creighton University, Nebraska. That's a happy record of credits, sure to make any parent proud."

Donald R. Keough's media image is that of a hard-working, no-nonsense professional, a sturdy Midwesterner who cherishes traditional ethical values of fair play and equal treatment. Those who know Keough best hasten to emphasize his affectionate spirit, capacity for humor, unstinting love of family and friends, inspirational advice, and need to launch a pipedream now and again.

Maureen E. Mulvihill

References

Bergin, John. "Donald R. Keough: Irish American of the Year." *Irish American Magazine,* March/April, 1993, 42–49.

Forbes.com. Selected media coverage on Donald R. Keough and The Coca Cola Company. http://www.forbes.com/finance/mktguideapps/personinfo/FromMktGuideIdPersonTearsheet.jhtml?passedMktGuideId=74489 (accessed August 30, 2007).

Horatio Alger Association of Distinguished Americans website. Donald R. Keough. http://www.horatioalger.com/members/member_info.cfm?memberid=keo88 (accessed August 1, 2007).

Keough, Donald R. Acceptance speech. Gold Medal Awards, American Irish Historical Society, New York City, 1993.

Keough, Donald R. Acceptance speech. Advertising Hall of Fame Awardee, New York City, 2006. http://www.advertisinghalloffame.org/members/member_bio.php?memid=2420 (accessed August 1, 2007).

Mulvihill, Maureen E. On site interviews with Donald R. Keough, Allen & Co., New York City. March 1997, December 2005.

Mulvihill, Maureen E. "Wall Street Irish: The Making o' the Green." *World of Hibernia,* April 1995, 140–159. With photos.

New York Times. "57th Annual Advertising Hall of Fame." February 27, 2006, C5. Full-page ad, placed by American Advertising Federation for induction of Keough, March 17, 2006, Waldorf Astoria, New York City.

KILMER, (ALFRED) JOYCE (1886–1917)

Joyce Kilmer was born in New Brunswick, New Jersey, on December 6, 1886, to Frederick Barnett Kilmer and an Irish mother, Annie (Kilburn). Educated at Rutgers University (1904–1906) and Columbia University, he graduated in 1908, and in the same year he married Aline Murray. Soon thereafter he took a job teaching in Morristown, New Jersey. Kilmer moved to New York City, where he found sporadic employment; from 1909 to 1912 he worked as an editor on the Funk and Wagnall's dictionary. He served as literary editor of *The Churchman,* an Anglican newspaper (Kilmer converted to Catholicism toward the end of 1913), and in 1913 became a member of the staff of *The New York Times.*

Kilmer supplemented his work on *The New York Times* with other activities. An avowed socialist, Kilmer often dined with emerging writers like Bliss Carman and Richard La Gallienne to discuss political radicalism. Poetry, though, was his passion. In 1914 he published *Trees and Other Poems*; two years later came *The Circus,* which was followed by *Dreams and Images* (1917), *Main Street and Other Poems* (1917), and *Literature in the Making* (1917), a series of interviews with literary personages. When the United States declared war on Germany in 1917, Kilmer was a family man with a wife and five children. Nevertheless, he enlisted as a private in the Seventh Regiment, New York National Guard. At his request, he was transferred into the 165th Infantry, the old Fighting 69th. Once in France he quickly attained the rank of sergeant and was attached to the newly organized Regimental Intelligence staff. His responsibilities included gathering information that would be of tactical importance to the Allied Forces.

In his position on the Regiment's Intelligence staff, Kilmer had no front-line responsibilities during combat operations, but on July 30, 1918, during the battle of the Ourcq, he attached himself as adjutant to Major William Donovan, who was commanding the First Battalion. It was a fateful decision; a sniper's bullet ended the soldier-poet's life at age 31. Posthumously, Kilmer was awarded the French Croix de Guerre for bravery, and for many Americans, he became the symbol of soldierly courage and poetic idealism.

As a poet and author, Kilmer is remembered today mostly for the poem "Trees," published in 1914. (The poem begins: "I think that I shall never see / A poem lovely as a tree," and ends "Poems are made by fools like me, / but only God can make a tree.") At the time of his entry into military service Kilmer was considered the premier American Catholic poet alive, and much of his work expressed his deep religious beliefs. Examples of this include "Rouge Bouquet,"

"Memorial Day" (which was written in 1917 shortly before his departure overseas), and "Prayer of a Soldier in France." One can only wonder how Kilmer's poetry would have developed, and what his position in the pantheon of American literature would be, had his talent not been cut down at so early an age.

Tim Lynch

Reference

Covell, John E. *Joyce Kilmer: A Literary Biography.* Brunswick, GA: Write-Fit Communications, 2000.

KING, JOHN (1800–1857)

A member of the Argentine naval forces that fought against Brazil under the command of William Brown, John King was born on October 26, 1800, in Newport, Co. Mayo, son of Miles and Mary King. He served in the British navy, and in 1820 was a midshipman in the frigate *Heroine,* under Captain David Jewett. King joined the Argentine forces in January 1826 as a second lieutenant during the war against Brazil. Given his experience, he was appointed master in the barque *Congreso,* under Captain William R. Mason. His first battle in the River Plate was on February 9, 1826, at Punta Colares, in which *Congreso* was hit by 13 shots from the Brazilian ships. During the attack on Colonia del Sacramento in February and March, King acted as the barque's second commander and later captain. He was promoted to lieutenant on May 12, 1826. In this same year he married the Irish teacher Sarah McGaw (d. 1874), niece of the Buenos Aires shipwright James McGaw.

On June 11, 1826, in the battle at Los Pozos, the powerful Brazilian fleet attacked, and was repulsed by, the Argentines. The subsequent action was in Quilmes, when Brown's squadron was attacked by the Brazilian ships on July 29. King acted as second commander of *Congreso,* under the orders of Captain José Fisher. He then accompanied William Brown in his attacks at Brazilian coastal cities, and was transferred to the brig *República,* the Argentine flagship, as its second commander. In this facility King fought in the battle at Monte Santiago in April 1827. When surrounded by the enemy, he was ordered by Brown to evacuate and set fire to his ship to avoid its capture by the Brazilians.

King retired from active service in May 1827. During the following months he successfully acted as privateer with the schooner *Sin Par* against Brazilian ships. On April 22, 1828, King reentered the naval service with the rank of captain and fought until the end of the war against Brazil in August of that year. He was discharged from service and during the next 10 years became a pilot in the River Plate and captain of the merchant ship *Esperanza,* sailing frequently to Carmen de Patagones and Rio de Janeiro. He also worked in a ranch in Corrientes. Reincorporated as sergeant-major in 1840, King was appointed by Brown as commander-in-chief of the Argentine squadron, in charge of the frigate *25 de Mayo,* in which he fought in Montevideo and Punta Indio against the naval force of John H. Coe. Between 1842 and 1844 King participated in the blockade of Montevideo as captain of the brig *General Belgrano.* The following year he played a key role in the attack of Montevideo in combination with the land forces of general Oribe.

Two scandals dishonored King's public image. The first occurred in 1841, when he was accused of receiving 3,000 patacones (silver pesos) from Captain Coe to cross over to the Uruguayan side. This was rapidly denied by witnesses, and on October 3 of that year William Brown celebrated King's reincorporation into service. The second was his lifetime addiction to alcohol. During the remainder of the Rosas régime, King worked in administrative positions in the maritime department of Buenos Aires. Considered partial to Rosas, King was discharged of service after the governor's fall in 1852. He died penniless in Buenos Aires on August 22, 1857. A street in the district of Almagro has borne his name since 1904.

Edmundo Murray

See also: BROWN, William; CAMPBELL, Peter.

References

Cutolo, Vicente Osvaldo. *Buenos Aires: Historia de las Calles y Sus Nombres.* Buenos Aires: Elche, 1994.

Rodríguez, Horacio, and Pablo E. Arguindeguy. *King 1995,* Buenos Aires: Instituto Browniano, 1995.

KINSELLA, THOMAS (1928–)

Thomas Kinsella was born in 1928 in Inchicore to John Kinsella, a worker at the Guinness Brewery, and Agnes (Casserly). John Kinsella's life and work are commemorated in a number of his son's poems, most notably "The Messenger" (1976). Kinsella's school education took place at the Inchicore Model School and with the Christian Brothers. He attended University College Dublin, initially as a science student, but he left shortly afterwards to join the Civil Service. From 1950 he worked in the finance department, a period of his life recorded and satirized in "Nightwalker" (1967/1968). During this time he also attended evening lectures in Arts at University College Dublin and wrote his first poems. Encouraged by Liam Miller of the Dolmen Press, he began to translate from the Irish, and some of these translations were published in the mid-1950s. He married Eleanor Walsh in 1955. A number of his early poems, culminating in "Phoenix Park" (1966), refer to her serious illness early in their relationship. His first book of original poetry, *Poems,* was published in 1956, followed by *Another September* (1958) and *Moralities* and *Downstream* (1962). By 1963 he had begun his translation of the Old Irish epic the *Táin Bó Cuailnge,* which was published six years later.

In 1965 Kinsella left the civil service to pursue a full-time writing career, and he became writer-in-residence and, subsequently, professor of English at Southern Illinois University. In 1970 he moved to Temple University, Pennsylvania, where he remained as a professor of English until his retirement in 1990, dividing his time between Ireland and the United States. In 1973 he established Temple University's program in Irish studies.

Kinsella's early poems are typically written in strict closed forms. A number of critics have seen the influence of W. H. Auden in the early work—other influences include W. B. Yeats, James Joyce, and the Irish-language poetry Kinsella translated. During the 1960s, and particularly after his exposure to American poetry, Kinsella began to experiment with more open forms. Some critics have seen the influence of William Carlos Williams in these works. Even before Kinsella's move to the United States, as early as 1962's *Downstream,* Ezra Pound functioned as an influence and antagonist in his work. Nonetheless, Irish cultural geography is vital to works as different as *Butcher's Dozen* (1972), a bitter satire on the Widgery Report, and *New Poems* (1973), a self-analysis that draws on Jungian psychology and Old Irish mythic texts.

Kinsella established the Peppercanister Press in 1972 to facilitate the quick printing and distribution of *Butcher's Dozen.* He subsequently used the press to issue limited-edition chapbooks of poetry, which were later collected in trade editions. Peppercanister pamphlets function as a kind of draft publication, showing the poet's interest in matters of revision and renewal. The third Peppercanister chapbook, *The Good Fight* (1973), is of particular interest to students of Irish-American relations, as it commemorates the 10th anniversary of John F. Kennedy's assassination. As well as exploring the psychology of the president's assassin, the poem examines Kennedy as a cultural icon particularly important to Irish Americans. Kinsella continued to publish Peppercanister pamphlets, mostly of poems, although the publications also included literary criticism in the form of *The Dual Tradition* (1995), throughout the next three decades. He was involved in two important anthologies in the 1980s: *An Duanaire: Poems of the Dispossessed 1600–1900,* a collection of Irish-language poems edited by Seán Ó Tuama, for which Kinsella provided the translations, and in 1986 the *Oxford Book of Irish Verse,* controversial for Kinsella's editorial dismissal of Northern Irish poetry and omission of women poets. Trade editions of his *Collected Poems* appeared in 1996 and 2001. In 2001 the poet left his Wicklow home and took up residence in Pennsylvania.

With his exact contemporary John Montague, Kinsella is often credited with introducing the techniques of American modernism to Irish poetry. Exactly how influential he has been remains a matter for critical debate. Although he has spent long periods of his life in the United States and has engaged substantially with American culture, his main interests and sensibility remain Irish, and his particular contributions to the translation of Irish-language texts cannot be underestimated. In the words of Derval Tubridy, "Kinsella's is a complex and dense poetry that, in its later years, eschews lyricism for a narrative development that relies on the poetic sequence and an engagement with sources as divergent as Irish mythology, European Enlightenment and contemporary US history."

Kit Fryatt

References

Abbate, Donatella. *Thomas Kinsella.* New York: Twayne, 1996.

John, Brian. *Reading the Ground: The Poetry of Thomas Kinsella.* Washington, DC: Catholic University Press, 1997.

Tubridy, Derval. *Thomas Kinsella: The Peppercanister Poems.* Dublin: University College Dublin Press, 2001.

KNIGHTS OF LABOR

The Noble and Holy Order of the Knights of Labor reached its apex of influence under the leadership of the son of Irish immigrants. By far the most significant of the early labor groups, in 1879 the Knights organized as a national industrial union under the leadership of Terrence V. Powderly, who led the organization from 1878 to 1893. The order was founded in 1869, as a secret society that was suspicious of modern industrial capitalism, by garment cutter and Freemason Uriah S. Stephens (1821–1882) and eight to 10 others at a tailors' meeting in Philadelphia. Drawing freely from the Freemasons, the Knights used a complex set of rituals ranging from secret oaths and handshakes to signs and passwords to further their ends of reforming labor conditions from within specific industries. Emphasizing brotherhood that extolled virtues like family duty, personal integrity and responsibility, honesty, and activism, the Knights stressed organization, education, and political agitation as the best ways to build a new society. Organized into mixed local and district assemblies, the group aimed to forge the entire labor movement into a single disciplined army. Although its mottos "equal pay for equal work" and "an injury to one was a concern to all" were inclusive, the secrecies prevented the organization from becoming very large.

At first the Knights of Labor was a kind of idealistic labor lodge and fraternal organization designed to organize individual workers, rather than uniting existing trade unions into one big union to which all gainfully employed skilled and unskilled persons, except bankers, lawyers, professional gamblers, stockbrokers, saloon keepers, and physicians, were eligible to join. However, skilled craftsmen remained aloof, and for a decade the Knights' growth was only moderate. After 1878, when Terrence Powderly of Scranton, Pennsylvania, became its grand master, the Knights of Labor took on new life. Powderly, born in 1849, began working as a switch tender at the age of 13. As a machinist he took so prominent a part in the work of the Machinists' and Blacksmiths' Union that he not only lost his job but was also blacklisted by the employers, after which he was elected mayor of Scranton in 1878 on the Greenback-Labor ticket. When a meeting was held to reorganize the Knights, Powderly dominated the proceedings and for the next 15 years his name and the Knights of Labor were almost synonymous.

Powderly took a small salary, traveling at his own expense wherever he felt he could gain more recruits. From a membership of only 28,000 in 1880 the organization increased to more than 700,000 in 1886. Its rapid growth was a result of dropping many of the secrecies that dominated the early organization and keeping membership open to all trades and skill levels. Favoring an eight-hour day, the use of arbitration as a substitute for strikes, and improvements in the legal status of labor had national appeal. Such women as Susan B. Anthony, Elizabeth Cady Stanton, and Mary Harris "Mother" Jones, as well as more than 90,000 African Americans, joined its ranks, enhancing its national appeal, which led to its being the first labor organization strong enough to challenge industry on its own ground. This occurred when New York financier Jay Gould conferred with the Knights' executive board in 1884 and acceded to their demands during the great railroad strike in the Southwest. Moreover, the Knights won several minor victories in the mid-1880s, such as in 1885 when the Missouri-Pacific was forced to restore cut wages.

However, the central organization's control over the behavior of the local organizations disintegrated, and strikes were increasingly undertaken against the advice of the general executive board. In spite of trying to avoid strikes, the Knights were involved in a series of violent strikes like the 1886 Texas-Pacific strike led by Martin Irons. Events culminating in the Haymarket Riot (1886) resulted in loss of prestige, and internal disputes slowed its political and social agenda. As a result the skilled workers, alienated by the way unskilled workers precipitated conflicts, began to withdraw from the Knights to build up their own unions. Specifically, the 1881 formation of the Organized Trades and Labor Unions (called the American Federation of Labor after

1886), along with factional disputes, overcentralization, mismanagement, and squandering of financial resources through unsuccessful strikes led to the rapid demise of the Knights. By 1900 the Knights of Labor was virtually extinct.

Mark Connolly

See also: POWDERLY, Terence Vincent

References

Fink, Leon. *Workingmen's Democracy: The Knights of Labor and American Politics.* Urbana: University of Illinois Press, 1985.

Powderly, Terence. *The Path I Trod: The Autobiography of Terrence V. Powderly,* edited by Harry Carman, Henry David, and Paul Guthrie. 1940. Reprint, New York: AMS Press, 1968.

Voss, Kim. *The Making of American Exceptionalism: The Knights of Labor and Class Formation in the Nineteenth Century.* Ithaca, NY: Cornell University Press, 1993.

Weir, Robert. *Beyond the Veil: The Culture of the Knights of Labor.* College Station: Pennsylvania State University Press, 1996.

Ladies' Land League (1880–1882)

The Ladies' Land League in Ireland and America allowed women to participate publicly in the Irish nationalist struggle for the first time. The Ladies' League movement began in America after a request by Fanny Parnell (sister of Charles Stewart Parnell) for Irish-American women to revitalize the Land League's fund raising. From this beginning, several Ladies' Land League branches were founded across the United States. Buoyed by its success in America, Michael Davitt convinced Anna Parnell to head a Ladies' Land League in Ireland. Parnell and her fellow Ladies' Land Leaguers would play a prominent role in the land struggle after the arrest of the male leaders of the movement. The women attempted to implement the radical rhetoric emanating from the imprisoned male leaders and were successful in providing relief to evicted tenants and urging nonpayment of rent. Upon his release from prison and his agreement with the Prime Minister William Gladstone to end the land agitation, however, Charles Stewart Parnell attempted to rein in the Ladies' Land League. Rather than be placed into a subservient and background position, the Ladies' Land League voted to disband. With the end of the Ladies' Land League, women were effectively pushed out of the nationalist movement. The memory of the Ladies' League, however, would provide an important inspiration to the next generation of Irish women nationalists and their participation in the struggle for Irish independence.

Fanny and Anna Parnell were the guiding lights behind the formation of the Ladies' Leagues of America and Ireland. Fanny was discouraged with the slow start of the Land League in America, and after consulting with Michael Davitt, decided to form a Ladies' Land League of America (LLLA) in the hopes that competition from the women would spur both Leagues' fund-raising efforts. On August 12, 1880, she sent a letter entitled "The Coming Struggle" to the *Irish World* and several other newspapers calling on Irish-American women to organize. Responses to this letter began to trickle in and on October 15, 1880, a meeting was held to establish the New York Branch of the Ladies' Irish National Land League. Branches were quickly established across the country, from Boston to Denver, and as far west as San Francisco; a branch was even formed in Montreal, Canada.

Certain areas became strongholds of LLLA activity. Philadelphia was the home of eight ladies' branches with a total membership of more than 600. New York City was another area of activity, where, because of their size, Ladies' Land League branches were organized by wards. A mass meeting in Hartford, Connecticut, attracted 2,000 women, and it was unanimously voted that the turnout was too large for one league, so three branches were formed. The LLLA was not only a phenomenon in the eastern states but also in the Midwest and on the West Coast, especially in St. Louis and San Francisco. The Irish-American women involved in the LLLA took advantage of the opportunity offered to them by the land war in Ireland and took an active role in shaping local Irish-American nationalist politics.

Inspired by the success of the Ladies' Land League in America, a Ladies' Land League in Ireland (LLLI) was formed on January 31, 1881. Most Irish leaders, with the exception of Davitt, were resistant to incorporating women into the Land League struggle but were persuaded by the argument that the women could carry on the struggle if the male leaders were arrested. Shortly after the establishment of the LLLI, almost all of the male national leaders, including Davitt and Parnell, were arrested under a new Coercion Bill. This left the Land League movement in Ireland primarily under the control of the LLLI. The women of the LLLI kept a strict record of finances, expenditures, and evictions and were fairly successful in continuing the land agitation.

After his agreement with Gladstone to stop the land agitation, Parnell moved to undermine the LLLI. Disillusioned by the animosity toward them by the male leadership, the Ladies' Land League disbanded. With the end of the LLLI, the American branches slowly died out. Unfortunately, the rise and fall of the LLLI would effectively push Irish women out of the political sphere until the twentieth century and would leave intact, though challenged, the male-dominated structure of Irish nationalist politics.

Ely Janis

See also: DAVITT, Michael; PENNSYLVANIA

References

Cote, Jane. *Fanny and Anna Parnell: Ireland's Patriot Sisters.* London: Macmillan, 1990.

Ward, Margaret. *Unmanageable Revolutionaries: Women and Irish Nationalism.* London: Pluto Press, 1995.

Parnell, Anna. *Tale of a Great Sham,* edited by Dana Hearne. Dublin: Arlen House, 1986.

Funchion, Michael, ed. *Irish American Voluntary Organizations.* Westport, CT: Greenwood Press, 1983.

LAND LEAGUE (1879–1882)

The Land League movement in Ireland and America in the early 1880s had an enormous impact on the history and character of contemporary Ireland and Irish America. The Land Leagues of Ireland and America, as well as their sister Ladies' Land Leagues, provided a stimulus and mobilization of Irish and Irish-American men and women in the cause of Irish nationalism that was unmatched until the period after the Easter Rebellion of 1916.

In 1879–1880 several events in Ireland provided an impetus for the rise of a united front between Irish and Irish-American nationalists. In 1879 Ireland experienced its worst season since the Famine because of a combination of bad weather, poor harvests, and low prices. The value of the potato crop, valued at £12 million in 1876, dropped to £3.5 million. A slump in the U.S. economy from 1873 to 1879 curtailed

Portrait of Michael Davitt, founder of the Land League. (Library of Congress)

immigration, while a poor harvest in Great Britain depressed the income of migratory laborers. Sensing an opportunity, John Devoy; the Irish-American Clan na Gael leader, Michael Davitt; and the leader of the Irish Parliamentary Party, Charles Stewart Parnell, arrived at the New Departure, an agreement that linked the land and national questions, providing for a united front between physical force and constitutional nationalists.

On August 16, 1879, Michael Davitt and a convention of tenant farmers in Mayo founded the Land League of Mayo. Following this success, the Irish National Land League was formed in Dublin on October 21, 1879, with Parnell as president. From this beginning, Land League branches were quickly established across Ireland. The aim of the Land League was to exploit rural unrest in Ireland to gain what became known as the "three Fs": fair rents, fixity of tenure, and free sale. The Land League committed itself to pursuing only nonviolent means to accomplish its goals. This distinction, however, was often blurred as Irish leaders spoke with increasingly forceful rhetoric and agrarian unrest spread in the rural districts.

In 1880, both Davitt and Parnell undertook extensive fund-raising tours of the United States, and Parnell himself traveled more than 16,000 miles, spoke in 62 cities, addressed a joint session of Congress, and raised more than $300,000 for rural relief and the Land League. The movement quickly spread across the country, and thousands of Irish Americans participated in branches in their local communities. Patrick Ford, editor of the *Irish World and American Industrial Liberator,* devoted considerable space in his columns to the movement in America and raised more than $340,000 for the Land League.

The Land League movement was the first transatlantic movement to unite all strands of Irish nationalist politics, bringing together agrarian radicals, physical force advocates, and parliamentary constitutionalists. In Ireland, small farmers and radical leaders like Davitt sought to overthrow the agrarian order through the use of boycotts and nonpayment of rent, while more prosperous farmers and Parnell sought Parliamentary land reform. Across the Atlantic, Irish Americans used Irish-American nationalism and the apparatus of the Land League to participate in a variety of American social movements. Working-class Irish Americans were often members of both the Land League and the Knights of Labor. Henry George, the San Francisco author and land reformer, traveled to

Ireland as a special correspondent for the *Irish World* and published a pamphlet on the Irish land question, linking Irish land reform to American struggles for land nationalization. Middle-class Irish Americans such as John Boyle O'Reilly and Patrick Collins, both of Boston, attempted to use Irish-American nationalism to raise the status of Irish Americans and to assert their fitness to participate in the American middle-class social and political world by freeing Ireland from England's yoke and proving the Irish not to be a feckless and colonized people.

Fanny Parnell, the sister of Charles Stewart Parnell, after consulting with Michael Davitt, decided to form a Ladies' Land League of America (LLLA) in the hopes that competition from the women would spur the both Leagues' fund-raising efforts. On October 15, 1880, a meeting was held to establish the New York Branch of the Ladies' Land League. Inspired by the success of the LLLA, Michael Davitt asked Anna Parnell to form a Ladies' Land League in Ireland, and it was founded in Dublin on January 31, 1881.

The Land League was able to exert tremendous pressure on the British government to enact changes in the landholding system in Ireland. In August 1881, the government enacted a Land Act that established the three Fs the Land League had called for: fixity of tenure, fair rent, and free sale. However, leaseholders and those in arrears were left out of the bill, and the land courts set up to implement the bill heavily favored the landlords. The bill began to break down the class alliance within the Land League as tenant farmers, who had effectively reached their goals through the Land Act, began to accept the terms of the bill. Alongside this new legislation, the British Government introduced a new Coercion Bill and arrested Charles Stewart Parnell and most of the other Irish leadership.

After the arrest of the male leaders in late 1881, Anna Parnell and the Ladies' Land Leagure were left effectively leading the Land League and kept the movement going. The imprisoned leaders issued the "No Rent Manifesto," which called on tenants to hold their rents until the British government released the prisoners. The manifesto put a major strain on the movement by putting an immense strain on the League's finances, and it alienated the Catholic hierarchy and conservative elements of the Land League, both in Ireland and America.

The Land League agitation was effectively ended when Parnell, increasingly anxious to leave prison, reached an informal agreement with Prime Minister William Gladstone known as the Kilmainham Treaty. Under the terms of the agreement, the government would amend the Land Bill to extend the fair rent provision to leaseholders, deal with rent arrears, and release the prisoners. For his part, Parnell agreed to rein in the agrarian discontent in the countryside. Though his actions were resisted by radical elements in the Land League, any further attempts to keep the agitation going were fatally undermined by the murder in Phoenix Park in Dublin of the new chief secretary Lord Frederick Davendish and undersecretary of Ireland Thomas Henry Burke, on May 6, 1882. In October 1882, a new organization, entitled the Irish National League, was formed to replace the Land League. Although it continued to receive support from many Irish nationalists, the Irish National League lacked the widespread appeal of the Land

League, and its effectiveness never reached the same level as that of the Land League.

Ely Janis

References

Brown, Thomas N. *Irish-American Nationalism 1870–1890.* Philadelphia: J. B. Lippincott Company, 1966.

Clark, Samuel. *Social Origins of the Irish Land War.* Princeton, NJ: Princeton University Press, 1979.

Davitt, Michael. *The Fall of Feudalism in Ireland; or, The Story of the Land League Revolution.* Shannon: Irish University Press, 1970.

Foner, Eric. "Class, Ethnicity, and Radicalism in the Gilded Age: The Land League and Irish-America." In *Politics and Ideology in the Age of the Civil War.* Oxford: Oxford University Press, 1980.

Jordan, Donald. *Land and Popular Politics in Ireland.* Cambridge: Cambridge University Press, 1994.

Palmer, Norman. *The Irish Land League Crisis.* New Haven, CT: Yale University Press, 1940.

LANGUAGE, THE IRISH

Many early Irish immigrants to the United States spoke Irish, either as their only tongue or along with English. With the advantage of widespread familiarity with English, most immigrants abandoned the use of Irish, or conversed in Irish only with other first-generation arrivals. Unlike many ethnic groups, the Irish rarely passed on their language to their children. Today, use of Irish in America continues at an attenuated level. A mixture of Irish-born speakers and American learners challenge stereotypes of a method of communication long belittled as poor, isolated, and backward, working to refashion it into a relevant medium, allowing new generations to enter into the cyber-*Gaeltacht,* along with native and second-language users worldwide.

To find out how many Irish came to America knowing Irish, estimates of how many departed from the Irish-speaking areas—*Gaeltachtaí*—must be examined. Up to and during the Famine, many who came to America would have spoken Irish. Kerby Miller estimates that one-fourth to one-third of all Famine-era emigrants spoke Irish; half of these left Connacht and Munster, where at least half the people used Irish as late as 1851. At this time Irish speakers, concentrated most heavily near the western seaboard, would be less likely to find the funds to emigrate. Education in Ireland enforced English. Irish became scorned. By the end of the 1870s, the collapse of subsistence farming and the traditional lifestyle spurred emigration from destitute *Gaeltachtaí.* More than half of later American arrivals from Ireland came from these areas, and half of them would have spoken Irish. By 1900, the peasant culture had eroded, and later emigrants to the United States likely knew English before they left Ireland.

Reginald Byron, analyzing the Irish history of Albany, New York, questions Miller's interpretation. He counters that the 1861 Irish census recorded 98 percent bilinguals or English monoglots. He criticizes Thomas Ihde's pioneering work as overlooking bilingualism as the emigrant norm. Yet Miller notes that a quarter of the Irish emigrants after the Famine may not have been active speakers, but their children were passive listeners. In Albany, Byron found that the new Irish advanced more quickly than other Europeans because of their abilities in English. By contrast, Kevin Kenny observes how native Irish speakers formed the core of the Molly Maguires. Many of the immigrants, in whichever language, arrived as illiterate.

Their efforts to read and write in their new county would necessarily emerge through English. Little pride in Irish could be found when so many of its people suffered discrimination and ridicule for their accents, dress, religion, and culture. Assimilation usually jettisoned Irish in favor of the practical reliance on English, however broken its mastery seems to have been by some who learned it only in America. Following the pattern of many immigrants, Irish newcomers depended on sponsors—often from the home county or community—for assistance before employment could be obtained. Therefore, patterns of settlement for nineteenth-century (or even later) Irish speakers tended to place emigrants into specific American locales. Kenneth Nilsen's study of Portland, Maine, links Irish language use to arrivals from Corr na Móna and Cois Fharraige in Galway. Connemara and the Aran Islands supplied Boston; Dingle sent speakers to Hartford, Connecticut, and Springfield, Massachusetts. Donegal supplied emigrants to Brooklyn and Staten Island, New York, as well as Bayonne, New Jersey. Achill Island and Cleveland were linked, as were Connemara and Pittsburgh. Around 1910, the language in Philadelphia's Schuylkill district and in the mining towns near Scranton and Wilkes-Barre, Pennsylvania, survived. Chicago, Minneapolis-St. Paul, and Butte, Montana, also gained speakers who left the traditional ports of arrival for Irish America to travel further west.

For instance, Archbishop John Ireland arranged for 390 emigrants from the Mayo and Galway *Gaeltachtaí* to settle in Graceland, Minnesota. Here, an Irish-speaking community was attempted in 1880. Such efforts were few, however, as the practicality of using English rather than loyalty to Irish undermined long-term survival of the language in a sustained form. New immigrants ensured that some form of native language exposure to Irish marginally survived, in Boston and New York notably, but this failed to slow the pattern of language loss by the second generation.

Often, the Catholic Church, dominated after 1795 by Maynooth-trained clergy, suspected the use of Irish at home and abroad. Unlike Hebrew, Greek, or Russian in liturgical functions by other emigrants, Irish played no necessary role for the survival of its communal religious tradition. Few followed the example of the German priest and linguist, St. John Neumann, who learned Irish to hear the confessions of his Pennsylvania congregation. Fenianism and agitation tainted the reaction to Irish by many other clerics. Ethnic pride in the post-Famine period contributed to cultural nurturing of the language. The *Irish-American* paper in 1857 began columns in Irish. The Ossianic and the Philo-Celtic learned societies and a New York preservation group formed over the next two decades. From 1881 to 1898, *An Gaodhal/The Gael* appeared monthly. As the Celtic Revival flourished, periodicals included learner's lessons, and luminaries from Ireland began touring America, raising consciousness and gaining funds that would support both the nationalist and the linguistic campaigns for an Irish Ireland.

Douglas Hyde's deanglicization efforts and his founding of the Gaelic League in 1893 aided American retention of Irish. Branches grew all over America, and contributors came not only from the East Coast but also from San Francisco, Butte, and Denver. Hyde toured in 1905–1906 to fund his Gaelic League; missions followed in 1910–1912 and 1914–1915. Anticolonialism joined pro-Celtic promotion. As with the parent organization, Irish-American political and cultural divisions over how best to regain control of the homeland weakened the cohesion of the League. By the time of Ireland's partial independence, Irish-language efforts reverted to the Free State. Government bureaucrats rather than bands of enthusiasts were entrusted with the revival of Irish, and its survival overseas came to be regarded as irrelevant.

Miller maintains that the emphasis in Irish language expressions upon patience rather than action tainted the mentalities of those who spoke it. A conservative, dependent, and collective worldview limited personal responsibility and implied that fate trumped choice. This Whorfian analysis remains controversial, yet it represents one academic theory that explains the willing and rapid loss of Irish among so many of its speakers in the post-Famine period of emigration and demoralization. American immigrants, Miller suggests, sought attainment of a refined English to replace their humble accents and unfamiliar native tongue. The Irish language earned no status in the New World. This situation intensified as students in the Free State and the Republic often resented the regimen of compulsory Irish taught in the postindependence decades. Those emigrating brought fewer native speaker experiences and more memories of a language on life support, too often unimaginatively taught and frequently caricatured as a symbol of peasant poverty, clerical punishment, and fanatical jingoism. For Irish choosing to move into the cities, at home and abroad, English accompanied their global diaspora.

By the 1980s, improved media, increased immigration, Irish cultural fairs and centers, republican activism, and a rebirth of ethnic pride among Irish Americans emphasized attainment of Irish. Dictionaries, tapes, and now software and Internet materials enable fluency within an international network. Distance from Ireland no longer prevents immersion. Organizations such as *Daltaí na Gaeilge* and *An Teanga Mhartanach* join the Gaelic League and classes, academic or less formal, that encourage learners from all backgrounds to learn the language. The National Association of Celtic Language Teachers ensures sophisticated instruction applying linguistic and sociological methods. Hartford, Connecticut, families have piloted an urban *Gaeltacht* program modeled on those in Belfast in their efforts to keep Irish as a chosen and maintained language today.

John L. Murphy

See also: CATHOLIC CHURCH, the; EMIGRATION; GREAT FAMINE, The; IRELAND, Archbishop John.

References

Connolly, Bridget. *Forgetting Ireland: Uncovering a Family's Secret History.* St. Paul, MN: Borealis Press, 2003.

Ihde, Thomas W., ed. *The Irish Language in the United States: A Historical, Sociolinguistic, and Applied Linguistic Survey.* Westport, CT: Bergin & Garvey, 1994.

Kenny, Kevin. *Making Sense of the Molly Maguires.* New York: Oxford University Press, 1998.

Miller, Kerby A. *Emigrants and Exiles: Ireland and the Irish Exodus to North America.* New York: Oxford University Press, 1985.

Moran, Gerard. "'In Search of the Promised Land': The Connemara Colonization Scheme to Minnesota, 1880." *Éire-Ireland* 31, no. 3–4 (Fall-Winter 1996): 130–149.

Ní Bhroiméil, Úna. *Building Irish Identity in America, 1870–1915: The Gaelic Revival.* Dublin: Four Courts Press, 2003.

Nilsen, Kenneth E. "Thinking of Monday: The Irish speakers of Portland, Maine." *Éire-Ireland* 25, no. 1 (Spring 1990): 6–19.

Ó Annracháin, Stiofáin, ed. *Go Meireceá Siar.* Dublin: An Clóchomar, 1979.

Uí Fhlannagáin, Fionnuala. *Micheál Ó Lócháin agus "An Gaodhal."* Dublin: An Clóchomar, 1990.

LAVIN, MARY (1912–1996)

Mary Lavin was born in East Walpole, Massachusetts, in 1912, and was the only child of Irish parents. Her mother was unhappy with life in America, and the young Lavin accompanied her on her return to Ireland in 1921. They moved initially to Athenry, Co. Galway, and subsequently (after her father's return from the United States), to Dublin and then Bective, Co. Meath. Each of these Irish locations is important to the stories that Lavin wrote from the time she was a student in the 1930s. Her first collection of short stories, *Tales from Bective Bridge,* was published to popular and critical acclaim in America in 1942. It was reissued the following year in England, and included a prefatory note by Lord Dunsany in which the elder writer generously remarked that Lavin was one of the finest young writers to have ever come to his attention. *Tales from Bective Bridge* won the James Tait Black Memorial Prize for the year's best work of fiction in 1943 and was selected as a Readers' Union choice. It marked the beginning of an auspicious career, and over the next four decades Lavin published many volumes of stories, including *The Becker Wives* (1946), *A Single Lady* (1951), *A Likely Story* (1957), *The Great Wave* (1961), *In the Middle of the Fields* (1967), *A Memory* (1972), and *A Family Likeness* (1985).

Although Lavin also wrote two successful novels, *The House in Clewe Street* (1945) and *Mary O'Grady* (1950), she is principally remembered for her work as a short story writer. In the preface to her 1959 volume, *Selected Stories,* she defined her understanding of that craft in the following terms: "Short story writing—for me—is only looking closer than normal into the human heart. The vagaries and contrarieties there to be found have their own integral design."

Questions of love and the heart are central to Lavin's writing, and her stories often engage with intimate relationships and domestic concerns. Often, though, these relationships are not as close as they initially appear, and characters who seem to be intimate or familiar (such as lovers, spouses, friends, or family members) are in danger of loneliness, betrayal, or misunderstanding. Many of Lavin's stories are set in small-town provincial Ireland, and her work often dramatizes the conflict between the values of these communities and the convictions of an individual morality. This conflict is frequently underscored by questions of money, respectability, and class. The theme of loneliness and broken relationships is given an added significance in her work in her celebrated sequence of stories that explore the experiences of widowhood. Lavin herself was a young widow and a mother to three girls—her first husband died in 1954, and she didn't remarry until the late 1960s. Relationships between women are particularly significant in her stories, and these relationships are variously arranged and often complex.

Lavin's work is predominantly realist in mode, and her best stories are subtle, restrained, or spare in style. Many of her stories are open-ended or ambivalent, and it has sometimes been suggested that this ambivalence is evidence of a "double vision" in Lavin's eye, which enables her to move between tragedy and comedy and to fuse local issues with universal concerns. According to the critic Janet Egleson Dunleavy, this is a consequence of her twinned inheritance as an Irishwoman and an American. Whatever the truth of this claim, it is certainly the case that abstract or insular issues like nationalism and the nation occupy little place in her work.

Lavin was the recipient of numerous awards and prizes in recognition of her work as a story writer. These included two Guggenheim Fellowships, the Ella Lynam Cabot Award, the Katherine Mansfield Prize, the Gregory Award, the Éire Society Gold Medal (Boston), and the Irish American Foundation Literature Prize. She was granted an honorary DLitt from her Alma Mater, University College Dublin, and she was a member of Aosdána, the affiliation of creative artists in Ireland. In 1992, the members of Aosdána elected her Saoi—that organization's highest honor. Lavin died in Dublin in 1996.

Paul Delaney

References

Bowen, Zack. *Mary Lavin.* Lewisburg, PA: Bucknell University Press, 1975.

Deane, Seamus. "Mary Lavin." In *The Irish Short Story,* edited by Patrick Rafroidi and Terence Brown. Gerrards Cross, UK: Colin Smythe, 1979: 237–247.

Egleson Dunleavy, Janet, "Mary Lavin, Elizabeth Bowen, and a New Generation." In *The Irish Short Story: A Critical History,* edited by James F. Kilroy. Boston: Twayne, 1984.

Harmon, Maurice, ed. "Mary Lavin Special Issue." *Irish University Review* 9, no. 2 (Autumn 1979): 207–312.

Kelly, A. A. *Mary Lavin: A Quiet Rebel.* Dublin: Wolfhound Press, 1980.

LAW, ANDREW BONAR (1858–1923)

Often referred to as the "Unknown Prime Minister," Andrew Bonar Law is perhaps more endearingly known as "Britain's Canadian Prime Minister," although Canada had yet to become a country at the time of his birth. The Ulster Presbyterian heritage of his father undoubtedly played a strong role in the political outlook Law had as an adult. Taken ill in 1877, James Law left New Brunswick to resettle in his native Ulster, where he died five years later; living in Glasgow, the young Law traveled nearly every weekend to visit his ailing father during this period, another aspect that might have further strengthened his political resolve on the "Irish Question" in later years. Law repeatedly defended the will of Ulster Unionists and regularly, in the pre–World War I days, campaigned with Edward Carson in Britain and Ulster, addressing crowds on the necessity of the Union. He viewed Home Rule as inevitably leading toward civil war and defended his support of Ulster Unionists in their position because of this threat. He was influential in ensuring that the six counties now composing Northern Ireland were left out of the Irish Free State Bill that enacted the arrangements of the 1921 Anglo-Irish Treaty. While detractors, and especially Irish nationalists, argue that Law was racist in his stance and rhetoric against Irish Catholics, his defenders argue that he was only against the politicians who claimed to be acting in the interests of the Irish while they ignored the desires of the majority of those in the northeast.

Born on September 16, 1858, in Kingston (now Rexton), Kent County, New Brunswick, Law was the fourth of five children born to the Reverend James Law and his wife Eliza Anne (Kidston). James Law had immigrated from Co. Antrim to New Brunswick in 1845 after graduating from the University of Glasgow and spending a brief period as a minister in Coleraine. He administered the Free Church of Scotland's St. Andrew's Church in Kingston, where he had a formidable reputation for his sermons. His family had in turn emigrated from the Scottish Lowlands to Ulster in the late seventeenth-century wave of the northeast's plantation. Bonar Law (his first name was rarely used by family, friends, or others) left New Brunswick to live with his mother's wealthy Kidston relations in Glasgow at the age of 12 following her death and his father's remarriage. He would never return to the land of his birth.

The Kidston branch of his family, who were Presbyterians and conservatives, took Law in as one of their own, sending him to Gilbertfield House in Hamilton and later the prestigious Glasgow High School. At 16 years old he left school to become a clerk in the Kidston's family business, which would later merge with Clydesdale Bank. In 1885, with a loan from his relatives, he bought a partnership in an iron wholesale company that would in future provide him with the financial independence one needed to pursue public office. In 1891 he married Anne Pitcairn Robley, the daughter of a prosperous Glasgow merchant, with whom he would have six children before her premature death in 1909.

Law was first elected as a member of Parliament for the Unionist Party during the "Khaki Election" (a national election where the outcome is strongly influenced by wartime or postwar sentiment) of 1900 for the working-class constituency of Glasgow Blackfriars. Over the years he would represent the ridings of Dulwich, Bootle, and Glasgow Central, the first two after election defeats and subsequent by-election victories. Law himself claimed that his two great concerns as a politician were tariff reform and Ireland, although his time and role in the wartime coalition government that helped to bring about Allied victory and British political stability has also had a significant impact on his legacy. He became leader of the Unionist Party in 1911 and prime minister in late 1922, achieving the former as a compromise candidate and the latter after the downfall of Prime Minister Lloyd George. He remained prime minister only until May 1923 because of failing health, finally succumbing to cancer on October 30, 1923. His 211 days spent in office represent the shortest British government of the twentieth century.

Brad Kent

See also: NEW BRUNSWICK

References

Adams, R. J. Q. *Bonar Law.* Stanford, CA: Stanford University Press, 1999.

Blake, Robert. *The Unknown Prime Minister: The Life and Times of Andrew Bonar Law, 1858–1923.* London: Eyre & Spottiswoode, 1955.

LIDDY, JAMES (1934–)

Born July 1, 1934, to a dispensary doctor in Dublin, James Liddy was raised in counties Clare and Wexford. Educated by the Benedictine monks of Glenstall Abbey in Co. Limerick, he graduated from King's Inn (Dublin) and practiced as a barrister for some time before becoming disenchanted with law and acquiring an MA from University College Dublin. He considered his education capped by the company of Patrick Kavanagh, the bohemian poet-sage of McDaid's pub.

In the early 1960s he coedited *Arena* magazine with the poet Michael Hartnett; *Arena,* with its lively contents and attractive typography, became the leading venue for both established Irish writers like Austin Clarke and Patrick Kavanagh and emerging writers like John Montague and Derek Mahon. Liddy was also instrumental in founding the more long-lived periodical *Poetry Ireland.*

Dolmen Press published Liddy's *Esau, My Kingdom for a Drink* (1962), *In a Blue Smoke* (1964), and *Blue Mountain* (1968). These slender books promised a writer alive to unusual but graceful syntactical rhythms that avoided the awkward self-consciousness of projective verse, but *Baudelaire's Bar Flowers* (1975) displayed an energy and vitality that melded the street with the library, as Liddy ran modern riffs on the French poet; he developed a humorous vision of the demimonde as the landscape of the saved rather than damned. *Corca Bascinn* (1977) turns to a more intimate, chatty style that investigates minimalism, culminating in Blakean parody and transformation. *A White Thought in a White Shade* (1987) professes an inward meditative style, combining the discursively confessional with an inscape of the numinous.

Collected Poems (1994) gathers an immense body of work from fugitive chapbooks and selections from his principal books; as well as lyrics, the collection features letter poems, narratives, religious poems, epigrams, and prose poems. Many of Liddy's preoccupations—Roman Catholicism, same-sex orientation, the telling family anecdote—shine at their brightest in *Gold Set Dancing* (2000), where the influences of his San Francisco and Milwaukee experiences bloom. Portraits of friends, living and dead, appear in *I Only Know That I Love Strength in My Friends and Greatness* (2003). *Yeats: New Ways of Falling in Love* (2003) contemplates the erotic. Liddy published an autobiographical novella set mostly in Spain, *Young Men Go Walking,* in the volume *Triad* (1986) and a short autobiography, *The Doctor's House* (2004). His literary essays are found in numerous periodicals.

Since 1976 Liddy has taught at University of Wisconsin at Milwaukee, spending summers either writing at his family home in Wexford or teaching in Dublin. The landscape of his poems paints the countryside of Ireland and the streets of San Francisco and Milwaukee, as well as glancing glimpses of Cuba and New Orleans. He has written many vivid portraits of his mother. Like many Irish writers he has been haunted by the ghosts of W. B. Yeats, James Joyce, and Patrick Kavanagh, finding affinities with Yeats (folkloric appreciation), Joyce (musicality of phrasing), and Kavanagh (transformation of the ordinary). A literary outsider, he wittily peppers his memory-monologues with amusing asides and startling observations, while his exuberant and puckish personality floats an energetic spontaneity that avoids the trivial or hieratic, remaining richly layered with surreal juxtapositions and the raw emotion of heartfelt romance. A comic realist who unearths joy in extreme subjectivity, he provides a critique of the banal in culture both high and low, plundering memory like a picaresque pirate, raising casual or impulsive anecdote to near-liturgical significance.

Kevin T. McEneaney

See also: JOYCE, James Augustine Aloysius; YEATS, William Butler

References

Arkins, Brian. *James Liddy: A Critical Study.* Galway: Arlen House, 2001.

Stanley, George. "Beyond the Sublime: Reading James Liddy." *Irish University Review* 28, no. 1 (Spring-Summer 1998): 92–109.

LITERATURE, AMERICAN CHILDREN'S

The range of Irish-related literature for children in America has gradually broadened since the nineteenth century. In children's stories earlier than 1900, Irish male characters are generally superstitious and good humored, and they usually work with horses or pigs. Less visible are Irish women, often domestic servants in the background, referred to as "Bridget" with no other explanation. Irish children, such as the street urchins who are the "sworn enemies" of the March girls in Louisa May Alcott's *Little Women* (1869), are seldom portrayed in a favorable light.

Irish fantasy, folk tales, and legends have had a greater impact in America than realist fiction. *Granny's Wonderful Chair*, by Donegal-born Frances Browne (1816–1879), published in 1856, went through numerous editions and reprints, especially between 1890 and 1940.

With Pádraic Colum's emergence as a prominent writer of children's books, the American view of Ireland changed. Colum (1881–1972) left Ireland in 1914 and spent most of his life in the United States. He was one of the most respected writers of children's editions of Greek, Norse, Hawaiian, and Irish myths and legends. His work helped raise the image of Ireland from a land of poverty to one rich in oral tradition.

Colum is one of only two Irish authors to have achieved Newbery Honor status, the other being Ella Young (1867–1956). *The Golden Fleece and the Heroes who Lived before Achilles* was a Newbery Honor book in 1922, *The Voyagers: Being Legends and Romances of Atlantic Discovery* in 1926, and *The Big Tree of Bunlahy: Stories of My Own Countryside* in 1934. Colum's work was featured on the Federal Bureau of Education List (1925) of 40 books "all children should read before they are 16 years of age."

Following the popularity of Colum's stories, James Stephens (1882–1950) and Eileen O'Faolain (1900–1988) wrote stories of magic, leprechauns, and animals that helped to establish American expectations regarding Irish fiction. Fairies, leprechauns, and "wee folk" remain popular in American expectations of Irish literature.

In fiction, by the mid-twentieth century, Irish surnames are no longer limited to characters in rural or domestic spheres, but they do stay with occupations that are more typically associated with Irish Americans. Clancy is a Boston policeman in Robert McCloskey's classic, *Make Way for Ducklings* (1941), and the hero of Virginia Lee Burton's *Mike Mulligan and His Steam Shovel* (1939) also has an Irish surname.

In recent years, collections of legends and folktales by Irish authors have been available in American editions, but editions of single stories based on tradition are usually American-written. Thus, Sheila McGill-Callahan's *The Children of Lir* (1993), in which two pairs of twins are turned into swans by their stepmother and reunited with their father after seven years, is one of the most visible American versions of that story. Tomie dePaola has produced some of the picture books of Irish stories most readily available in America, including *Fin M'Coul: The Giant of Knockmany Hill* (1981) and *Jamie O'Rourke and the Pooka* (2000). Older collections of folktales are often used as source material for contemporary American retellings, such as *Brave Margaret* by Robert San Souci (1999) and *Billy Beg and his Bull* by Ellen Greene (1994).

From the 1980s on, there has been an increasing interest in Irish historical fiction, both in Ireland and America. Most of the American historical fiction centers on the Famine and the ensuing immigration to

America. One exception, *A Family Apart* (1987) by Joan Lowery Nixon, tells of an Irish immigrant family sent west on an Orphan Train in the mid-nineteenth century. In another exception, Gary Schmidt invents a young English soldier stationed in Dublin in the seventeenth century. In *Anson's Way* (1999), Anson witnesses colonialism and the Penal Laws and chooses his own path.

Nory Ryan's Song (2000) by Patricia Reilly Giff, *Beyond the Western Sea* by Avi (1996), and *The Grave* by James Heneghan (2000) are all set in Famine times. Siobhán Parkinson critiques American famine novels with a rough guide to the "famine myth," which concludes with "some lucky/plucky Irish people" who "escaped and were welcomed into America." Heneghan's *The Grave* does not conform to this pattern; this novel is one of time travel centering on a mass grave that was found in Liverpool in 1974.

One of the most successful Irish-born authors of children's books in the United States is Eve Bunting (b. 1928), who grew up in Maghera, Northern Ireland. She and her family settled in the United States in 1960. Of the wide range of books she has written, a few are set in Ireland. *Dreaming of America* (1999) is a story of Annie Moore, the first person to pass through the Ellis Island Station. *Market Day* (1996) is interesting as it does not conform to the image of rural isolation often associated with Ireland. It features a town rather than a village, and the market includes a cosmopolitan, even exotic cast of characters. A novel for older children, *Spying on Miss Muller* (1995) is a story of students in a Belfast girls' boarding school during World War II who think their teacher is a German spy.

The current large increase in the publishing of children's books by Irish authors and their success in America (e.g., Martin Waddell, Sam McBratney, Eoin Colfer, Roddy Doyle) may influence the future range of representation of Irish in American children's literature.

Aedín Clements

LITERATURE, IRISH-ARGENTINE

Irish-Argentine literature is the artistic representation of a unique array of cultural values expressed in English and Spanish, as they are portrayed by the Irish settlers in Argentina and their descendants. Recognizing a strong association with *Southamericana* literature of the English-speaking communities in Latin America, Irish-Argentine writers historically demonstrated a distinct set of characteristics, including a preference for simple, yarn-type stories occurring in the rural milieu and presenting explicit divisions between the Irish and characters with other origins.

One of the most frequent motifs in Irish-Argentine literature is the experience of the emigrants. The dominant subjects are the oppressive conditions in Ireland and British imperialism as the reason for their emigration as well as the transatlantic journey and the encounters with the otherness of Argentines and other immigrants. These recurrent subjects were present in spontaneous literary contributions sent to the editors of Irish and other newspapers that usually published short stories and poems contributed by readers. William Bulfin (1864–1910), who began publishing stories in Father Feeney's *Irish Argentine* and then in the *Southern Cross,* appealed to his readers' homesickness and their relations with gauchos, the cowboys of the pampas. In *Tales of the Pampas,* a collection of short stories published by Bulfin in London (1900), characters include gauchos, shepherds, scoundrels, Spanish immigrants, match-makers, and other persons typical of late nineteenth-century rural Argentina. These characters use a comic mixture of English, Irish, and Spanish, which reflects less a historical linguistic reality than the author's nationalistic strategy to bring the Irish nearer to the Argentines and therefore to veer them away from the British.

Kathleen Nevin's novel *You'll Never Go Back,* completed by her sister Winnie and published in Boston in 1946, is a fictionalized autobiography based on the oral memoirs of the author's mother, Catherine Smyth of Ballymahon, Co. Longford (a traditional area of immigration to South America). The novel covers the time before emigration, the transatlantic journey, the initial settlement in the city of Buenos Aires and in the Irish sheep farms, and the narrator's decision to stay in her new country after her engagement to another Irish immigrant. The text is full of reflections on the different culture that Kate, the principal character, is confronted with in the new country, and the gradually changing effect this contrast has on her feelings toward home.

Another common theme in Irish-Argentine literature is the scientific or pseudoscientific observation of nature and people, that is, the "traveler's style" popular in the British Isles. John Brabazon (1828–1914) of Mullingar, Co. Westmeath, left his memoir *The Customs and Habits of the Country of Buenos Ayres from the Year 1845,* which was translated into Spanish, edited, and published in 1982 by the genealogist Eduardo Coghlan (*Andanzas de un irlandés por el campo porteño*). The different meaning of the title in English and Spanish is an indication of the translator's intention to add a Quixotic type of adventure to the original Brabazon's purpose of describing the society and places he visited. Other examples of published travel accounts are William MacCann's *Two Thousand Miles' Ride through the Argentine Provinces* (1853), Thomas J. Hutchinson's *Buenos Ayres and Argentine Gleanings* (1865), J. Macnie's *Work and Play in the Argentine* (1925), and Barbara Peart's *Tia Barbarita: Memories of Barbara Peart* (1933).

Twentieth-century Irish-Argentine authors revealed diverse identities in their texts, with the increasing use of Spanish and of *gauchesca* themes indicating their connection with the newly created Argentine identity. Benito Lynch (1882–1951), descendant of a Galway family resident in Buenos Aires since the eighteenth century, published *El Inglés de los Güesos* (1922), a novel within the themes and styles of Argentine rural literature that adds the foreign (*inglés,* i.e., English-speaking) character to emphasize the *Argentineness* of the local culture. Maria Elena Walsh (b. 1930) enjoyed immediate success with her first collection of poems, *Otoño Imperdonable* (1947). But she is better-known for her children's songs and stories, in which she recognizes the crossbred influence of her English, Irish, and Andalusian ancestors. In *Novios de Antaño* (1990), Maria Elena Walsh included a chapter with family letters describing the life of Anglo-Irish railway workers in 1880s Argentina. Rodolfo Walsh (1927–1977), unrelated to the previous writer, was a journalist who published nonfiction novels (*Operación Masacre,* 1957) and short stories (including *Irlandeses*

Detrás de un Gato, 1964). Rodolfo Walsh's most popular texts occur in a political milieu and expose a political intention. As an intelligence officer of the Montoneros group, Walsh was involved in violent action against the military dictators. He was killed by a military death squad after publishing an *Open Letter to the Military Junta,* which, according to Nobel Prize winner Gabriel García Márquez, is "one of the jewels of universal literature." Enrique Anderson Imbert (1910–2000) published *Mi Prima May,* dealing with a mysterious leprechaun, *Patricio O'Hara, el Libertador,* comparing Celtic and Argentine mythologies, and *Mi Hermana Rita,* in which he used Irish folklore. Miguel Rice Treacy (1903–1971), known by tango musicians as "El irlandesito," wrote tango lyrics under the pen name Carlos Viván. He published the famous Argentine tangos "Cómo se pianta la vida!" and "Moneda de cobre" and played jazz in the United States. Luis Alberto Murray (1923–2002), a poet and historian who was well-known for his radical positions within Argentine nationalism, published *América Clavada en Mi Costado* (1968) and *De Pie Entre los Relámpagos* (1980), among other works. He also translated poetry and tango lyrics into English. One of his poems, "A los Poetas Irlandeses" was published by the *Southern Cross* in the centenary edition (1975). John Walter Maguire (1906–1981), an antiquary and writer of rural stories, published special editions of *Loncagüé* (1967) and *La Pezuña de Oro* (1980). Juan José Delaney is one of the latest authors to publish short stories; *Tréboles del Sur* (1994), and the novel *Moira Sullivan* (1999) reflect the influence of Bulfin's *Tales of the Pampas* and of Nevin's *You'll Never Go Back,* respectively.

Other Irish-Argentine writers include Guillermo Sullivan (1888–1927), a playwright and author of literary essays; Bernardo Carey, a short-story writer and a well-known playwright; Eduardo Carroll, a poet and novelist; Alfredo Casey, a poet, playwright, and translator of Pádraic Pearse's texts; Patricio Gannon (1901–1977), an essayist in English literature; Luis Francisco Houlin, a poet; Esteban Moore, a poet and translator of Irish poetry; and Pacho O'Donnell, a playwright and historian.

Edmundo Murray

See also: BULFIN, William; COGHLAN, Eduardo Aquilio; WALSH, Rodolfo

References

Delaney, Juan José. *The Language and Literature of the Irish in Argentina,* 1999.

Graham-Yooll, Andrew. *The Forgotten Colony.* Buenos Aires: Literature of Latin America, 1999.

Izarra, Laura. "The Irish Diaspora in Argentina." *British Association for Irish Studies Newsletter* No. 32, October 2002.

Murray, Edmundo. "How the Irish became 'Gauchos Ingleses': Diasporic Models in Irish-Argentine Literature." *The Representation of Ireland/s: Images from Outside and from Within,* edited by Rosa González, 369–380. Barcelona, Spain: Promociones y Publicaciones Universitarias, 2003.

LYNCH, BENITO EDUARDO (1882–1951)

Benito Eduardo Lynch was born on July 25, 1880, in Buenos Aires, the second child of Benito Lynch (1852–1902) and Juana Beaulieu (d. 1937). Lynch's fourth grandfather, Patrick Lynch, was born in Lydican Castle, Co. Galway, in 1715 and settled in Buenos Aires in 1749, where he founded a large and well-known family in Argentina, Chile, and Uruguay. Benito Lynch, Jr., grew up in El Deseado, a ranch in Bolívar

(Buenos Aires province). His father was Bolívar's major, provincial member of Parliament, and mayor of the city of La Plata. The family belonged to the wealthy group of ranchers who owned lands in Buenos Aires province.

Growing up on the family *estancia* (ranch), Benito Lynch learned the linguistic idiosyncrasy of the gaucho, the cowboy of the pampas, and acquired a firsthand knowledge of the life and work in the countryside, particularly in the use of horses. In the early 1890s the family moved to La Plata, and Lynch was educated by a private tutor. He stood out as a good sportsman (rowing, box, and fencing), and learned the *lunfardo,* the urban jargon of Buenos Aires. Lynch completed his studies in the Colegio Nacional of La Plata. In 1902, using the pen name Thyon Lebic, Lynch began writing as a journalist for *El Día,* a paper in which his father was a shareholder. In 1910 Lynch joined the Conservative Party in Buenos Aires province, and worked for the communications committee. Some of his first published works were "*El Potrillo Roano,*" a short story, and the novel *Los Caranchos de la Florida* (which was translated and published in Italy in 1916). The celebrated *El Inglés de los Güesos* appeared in 1924. On August 11, 1939, Lynch was sworn in as doctor *honoris causa* of the University of La Plata. In 1941 he published *La Nación de Medallas de Oro, Nuestra Novela,* and *Cartas y Cartas,* and retired from fictional writing. In 1949, blind and deaf, he was run over by a tramway in La Plata. He was hospitalized with concussion and died two years later on December 23, 1951.

Between 1903 and 1941 Lynch published 34 short story volumes, six novels, and more than 100 articles and short fictional pieces. In addition to those mentioned, some of the published works are *Plata Dorada* (1909), *Raquela* (1918), and *El Romance de un Gaucho* (1933). In *El Inglés de los Güesos,* with a recognized influence of Charles Darwin's *Diary,* the principal character Mr. James represents the contrast between the European culture and the native values of the pampas. In many of his books there are detailed descriptions of the life in Argentine ranches, and accurate depictions of the main attitudes of the ruling elites in the first decades of the twentieth century.

Edmundo Murray

See also: LITERATURE, IRISH-ARGENTINE

References

Coghlan, Eduardo A. *Los Irlandeses en la Argentina: Su Actuación y Descendencia.* Buenos Aires: Author's Edition, 1987.

Petit de Murat, U. *Genio y Figura de Benito Lynch.* Buenos Aires: Eudeba, 1968.

LYNCH, ELISA (ELIZA) (1835–1886)

First lady of Paraguay and concubine of dictator Francisco Solano López until his death in 1870, Elisa Lynch was born in Co. Cork to a middle-class family that left Ireland and settled in France in 1845. In 1850, at the age of 15, she married Jean Louis Armand de Quatrefages, a French military surgeon. The unhappy marriage dissolved after three years. Lynch was living in Paris with her mother, and perhaps a Russian nobleman, when she met López in 1853. It was love at first sight: López was overwhelmed by Lynch's beauty and Lynch was attracted by the security López offered with his position as heir to Paraguayan first post. Despite arguments with his younger brother Benigno, who did not want the affair carried across the ocean, López left Lynch with funds and instructions on how to get to Paraguay, and he departed to South America.

Lynch arrived at Buenos Aires in October 1855 and gave birth to a son, who was baptized in a private ceremony as Juan Francisco ("Panchito") López after her arrival in Asunción in December. After an initial depression on encountering Paraguay and its people, Lynch learned to take political and financial advantage of her status, despite her unofficial position and the López family's dislike of her. By 1858 she was the social leader of the community, even though she was almost always pregnant and perceived by the bigoted local elite—particularly by the patrician ladies—to be "living in sin."

"Madame Lynch"—as she styled herself, though she was popularly known as "La Lynch"—was something of a snob and delighted in displaying her new ways to the Paraguayans, refusing to ride sidesaddle and serving elegant French cuisine to guests. She became a lady to emulate if not like, and her social example almost placed her in the ranks of the foreign diplomats, for she did her part to modernize Paraguay and its fashion, and began a cultural transfer of French (not English or Irish) customs to replace the native ones. She set the style with her home and her lover's house, as well as clothing, cuisine, champagne, cosmetics, sewing machines, certain music, formal dances, and lithographs and other objets d'art.

Photographs taken around 1860 show Elisa Lynch looking less like a young lady and more like a matron. Between 1855 and 1861 she gave birth to five sons, all of whom openly carried the López name. She rose high in the world in a material sense, and received gift after gift from her admiring general. She became the world's largest female landowner. By 1865 she owned several large ranches and at least 26 urban properties. During the Triple Alliance War against Argentina, Brazil, and Uruguay, perhaps to place in her name huge properties in order to protect some wealth in case he lost the conflict or had to abdicate, López ordered the sale to Lynch of more than 800,000 acres of land and forests of the state located in the Chaco. Furthermore, she acquired 12 million acres in eastern Paraguay and another 9 million acres of *yerbales* and forests in the contested area north of Rio Apa. All her properties were confiscated in 1869.

In 1870, López was killed in Cerro Corá. Lynch buried her lover and their son Panchito and fled to Paris with more than $500,000 in jewels, gold, and cash. In 1875 she returned to Paraguay, invited by President Juan B. Gill, who supported her claims to lost properties. But she was deported again to France and finally settled in Paris, where she died in 1886, penniless and largely forgotten.

Lynch's life fascinated modern writers of fiction and biography in English and Spanish, and several books about her life were published. In the 1970s Lynch was proclaimed Paraguayan national heroine, and her remains were removed from a grave in Montmartre to her adopted country. A central street in Asunción was named "Madame Lynch."

Edmundo Murray

See also: O'LEARY, Juan Emiliano

References

Baptista, Francisco. *Elysa Lynch, Mujer de Mundo y de Guerra.* Buenos Aires: Emecé, 1987.

Barrett, William. *Una Amazona.* Asunción: Servilibro, 2003.

Cawthorne, Nigel. *The Empress of South America.* London: Heinemann, 2003.
Hoyt Williams, John. *The Rise and Fall of the Paraguayan Republic, 1800–1870.* Austin: University of Texas at Austin, 1979.
O'Leary, Juan E. *El Mariscal Solano López.* Asunción: Ediciones de la Casa América,1920.
Rees, Siân. *The Shadows of Elisa Lynch: How a Nineteenth-Century Irish Courtesan Became the Most Powerful Woman in Paraguay.* London: Review, 2003.

LYNCH, ARCHBISHOP JOHN JOSEPH (1816–1888)

Born in Co. Monaghan, John Joseph Lynch was the son of a schoolteacher. After training at the College of St. Lazare in Paris, Lynch was ordained and served as a professor with the College of Castleknock. In 1846 he accepted a placement to conduct missionary work in the United States. Father Lynch's health suffered during his labors in Texas, and he retreated to a Lazarist college in Missouri, where he was appointed president and first demonstrated his considerable abilities as an administrator.

In 1857, Father Lynch founded the Seminary of Our Lady of Angels at Suspension Bridge. Accounts of his generosity and dedication reached the Vincentian Superior in Paris who recounted them to Bishop of Toronto Comte Armand de Charbonnel. Charbonnel thought Lynch would make an appropriate successor for the Toronto diocese and thus permit his own retirement. In 1859, Father Lynch was elected coadjutor to the bishop of Toronto with right of succession. He was consecrated in Toronto and became the third bishop of the diocese the following year.

Bishop Lynch more than doubled the Catholic infrastructure in Ontario in order to combat the challenges of an industrializing society. He obtained the services of the Sisters of Charity of St. Vincent de Paul and the Sisters of the Good Shepherd to found the Notre Dame Institute, an industrial school for girls, and the Magdalen Asylum, a refuge for indigent and troubled women in the city. The Saint Nicholas Home, an Agricultural and Industrial School, was established for wayward boys. Lynch also provided the services of devout priests and teachers in penitentiaries and institutes for the insane. He vociferously fought for the economic and political interests of the urban Irish Catholics of Toronto. Lynch's success in this regard is remarkable because Toronto was the strongest center of the Orange Order outside the British Isles.

Lynch promoted the doctrine of the Immaculate Conception and encouraged expressions of Marian devotion in the diocese. In doing so, he embodied and reflected a religious revival in Ireland that was being intensified through continuing emigration to North America. Lynch believed he had a duty as leader of a minority to promulgate the views of his faith and his people. In his role as spokesman for Irish Catholicism in Toronto, he often became embroiled in disputes with Protestant spokesmen.

Lynch expected obedience within his diocese. He sought to reduce clerical problems with financial misconduct and excessive drinking by educating his own priests. He also hoped to improve the behavior of Catholic laypeople and thereby mitigate the prejudice of the Protestant majority. However, he did not fully appreciate the desire of the laity for greater freedom and ultimately proved powerless to halt an ongoing process of secularization. Particularly problematic were a series of attacks emanating from the city's Separate School Board concerning his staunch opposition to the use of the ballot in Separate School Board elections.

Lynch visited Rome and Ireland in 1862, using the opportunity to support Home Rule for Ireland. He was formally received by the Canadian high commissioner and became the first Roman Catholic bishop since the reign of James II to attend a royal levee. In 1869 he participated in the Vatican Council, where he delivered forcible arguments in favor of the dogma of papal infallibility. During the council, his diocese was raised to an archbishopric by Pope Pius IX.

Mike Cottrell

See also: ONTARIO; ORANGE ORDER

References

"Archbishop John Joseph Lynch, C.M." Archives of the Roman Catholic Archdiocese of Toronto website. www.archtoronto.org/archives/bishops/lynch.htm (accessed August 5, 2007).

Cottrell, Michael. "St. Patrick's Day Parades in Nineteenth-Century Toronto: A Study of Immigrant Adjustment and Elite Control." In *A Nation of Immigrants: Women, Workers, and Communities in Canadian History, 1840s–1960s,* edited by Franca Iacovetta, Paula Draper, and Robert Ventrescan. Toronto: University of Toronto Press, 1998.

Kelly, Edward. "Archdiocese of Toronto." In *The Catholic Encyclopaedia,* Volume 14, Robert Appleton Company, 1912. Online Edition K. Knight, 2003. www.newadvent.org/cathen/14781d.htm (accessed August 5, 2007).

Nicolson, Murray W. "The Other Toronto: Irish Catholics in a Victorian City, 1850–1900." *Polyphony* (Summer 1984: 19–23.

Stortz, Gerald J. "Archbishop John Joseph Lynch of Toronto: Twenty-eight Years of Commitment." *CCHA Study Sessions* 49 (1982), 5–23.

LYNCH, P. J. (1962–)

P. J. Lynch was born in Belfast on March 2, 1962, the son of Anna (McKillen) and Liam Lynch. Lynch attended Jordanstown Polytechnic and Brighton Art College, where he received his BA degree in 1984. Although he spent some years in England, he now lives in Dublin. His career as an illustrator began when he illustrated Alan Garner's *A Bag of Moonshine* (1986), which won the Mother Goose Award in 1987. He later illustrated fairy tales and gave new life to stories by E. Nesbit, Oscar Wilde, Hans Andersen, and W. B. Yeats. His *Oscar Wilde: Stories for Children* (2000) was translated into many languages. Lynch's witty style, fantastic settings, and expressive characters recall the illustrations of Arthur Rackham, whose influence Lynch acknowledges.

Lynch received recognition in the United States with *The Christmas Miracle of Jonathan Toomey,* written by Susan Wojciechowski and published in 1995. It was the Bisto Book of the Year in Ireland, and in Britain it received the Kate Greenaway Medal, among other awards. Jonathan Toomey is a woodcarver, embittered by personal tragedy, whose love of humanity reemerges at Christmas when he carves a set of nativity figures for a widow and her son. Lynch traveled to the Shelburne Museum in Vermont to ensure the accuracy of his setting. His watercolor paintings combine realistic details with lighting effects that enhance the mood of the story. Among the strengths of the illustrations are the use of light and shade to mirror Jonathan Toomey's psychological state, the evocative detail of the New England setting and the woodcarver's home, and the facial expressions that depict the developing relationship between the adult and the child. Since this book, his style in realist painting has developed in tandem with his dramatic works of fantasy.

Lynch's next major award-winning work, *When Jessie Came Across the Sea,* by Amy Hest, won the Greenaway Medal in 1997. In Ireland it won a Bisto Merit

Award, and in the United States it was an International Reading Association Notable Book for a Global Society. The book, with paintings in watercolor and gouache, contains a number of striking two-page spreads. The cover shows immigrating passengers, viewed from a lower point, standing on deck as their ship passes the Statue of Liberty. A review in *The New Statesman* comments that "Lynch clearly relishes the contrast between old faces and young ones."

Lynch has continued to bring new interpretations to old stories, with witty and fantastic illustrations for Marie Heaney's *The Names Upon the Harp,* (2000), Brendan Behan's *The King of Ireland's Son* (1997), and Frank Stockton's *The Bee-Man of Orn* (2004). His realist-style book, *Grandad's Prayers of the Earth* (2000), by Douglas Wood, has received awards and critical recognition in the United States. The story of a boy's experience of nature and prayer is illustrated in two-page spreads throughout. The close-up and lower points of view employed enhance the effect of the magnitude of nature, and again, Lynch has visited the setting, this time Minnesota, to ensure the accuracy of his art. His latest book is *East o' the Sun and West o' the Moon* (2006) by Naomi Lewis.

Lynch's cover illustration in *For Every Child,* a book on the United Nations Charter for the Rights of the Child, with illustrations by top illustrators from a number of countries, was a finalist in the Illustrator's Ireland awards in 2002. This illustration shows a child in the embrace of an old woman. Illustrators Ireland selected Lynch's *Ignis,* the story of a dragon, for the award for the best "series of illustrations" in a book for publication. This juxtaposition nicely demonstrates the two kinds of illustration Lynch has become well known for—sensitive portraits of people and exuberant works of fantasy. That he has been three times a recipient of the Christopher Medal, for works that "affirm the highest dignity of the human spirit" is a comment on the works he elects to illustrate as well as on the quality of his artistic interpretation.

Aedín Clements

See also: BEHAN, Brendan; WILDE, Oscar; YEATS, William Butler

References

Craig, Amanda. "Children's Books." *New Statesman,* December 5, 1997: 62.
Lynch, P. J. "Digging for Story Gold." *Chalk Talk* (Autumn 2002): 4–5.

LYNCH, THOMAS (1948–)

A well-respected poet and award-winning essayist, Thomas Lynch has also been a funeral director in Milford, Michigan, for several decades. Lynch was born in Detroit in 1948. He was educated in Catholic schools before attending Oakland University in Rochester, Michigan, during the late 1960s. He left the university without a degree but was later awarded an honorary doctorate of humanities. Lynch, whose father was also a funeral director, graduated from mortuary school in 1973 and took over the family's funeral home in Milford. All four of Lynch's children have attended mortuary school as well. In much of his writing, both poetry and prose, Lynch reflects on lessons learned in his life as an undertaker.

Lynch published his first collection of poetry, *Skating with Heather Grace,* in 1987. He has since published two other collections of poetry—*Grimalkin & Other Poems* (1994) and *Still Life in Milford* (1998)—as well as three collections of essays. The first of these, *The Undertaking: Life Studies from the Dismal Trade* (1997), won an American Book Award and has been translated into seven languages. In his second collection of essays, *Bodies in Motion and at Rest* (2000), Lynch writes about American attitudes toward death and addresses a wide range of other topics from alcoholism to Catholicism to the breakup of his first marriage.

In his most recent publication, *Booking Passage: We Irish and Americans* (2005), Lynch explores the ties that he and many Irish Americans feel to their ancestral homeland. Lynch first visited Ireland in 1970, when—having drawn a high enough lottery number to avoid the Vietnam draft—he decided to pursue an interest in reading Irish poetry and fiction. While in Ireland, he met and established close ties with his cousins Tommy and Nora Lynch in the small town of Moveen, Co. Clare. Lynch's great-grandfather had left Moveen in 1890 and immigrated to America. *Booking Passage* documents Lynch's search for family and his evolving relationship to his great-grandfather's home country. Lynch now owns the ancestral cottage in Moveen; while pursuing his dual vocation as writer and mortician, he divides his time between West Clare and Milford.

Lynch is a regular op-ed contributor to the *New York Times,* the *Boston Globe* and the *Times of London.* He also writes for Beliefnet, a website unaffiliated with any particular religious organization or movement but dedicated to issues concerning spirituality. In addition, his work has appeared in *The New Yorker, Poetry, The Paris Review, Harper's, Esquire, Newsweek, The Washington Post, The Los Angeles Times,* and *The Irish Times.* Lynch has been a guest speaker at universities throughout the United States and Ireland, as well as elsewhere in Europe, Australia, and New Zealand. He regards his two seemingly disparate vocations—poetry writing and funeral directing—as quite similar in that both represent attempts to articulate what is often difficult to put into words.

Kathleen Ruppert

Reference

Wake Me When I'm Dead: A Documentary about Poet and Undertaker Thomas Lynch. Compiled by Seamus Kelly. First broadcast December 31, 2002.

MacDonald, Michael Patrick (1966–)

Michael Patrick MacDonald is both an award-winning author (his memoir, *All Souls: A Family Story from Southie,* won an American Book Award and a New England Literary Lights Award) and an activist against crime and violence. MacDonald was born in Boston in 1966 and grew up in the Old Colony Housing Project of South Boston, an area with the highest concentration of impoverished whites in the United States. In *All Souls* (1999) MacDonald writes about growing up in the predominantly Irish Catholic neighborhood, which was plagued by drugs, organized crime, and extreme poverty. The ninth of 11 children, MacDonald lost one of his brothers to suicide and two others to crime-related violence. Another brother died of pneumonia as an infant, after he was denied emergency room treatment for lack of insurance, and MacDonald's sister sustained permanent brain damage when she was thrown off a roof during an argument over drugs. Despite the heartbreak of his youth, MacDonald refers to Southie as "the best place in the world," and his memoir encapsulates the fierce loyalty of its residents to their community.

MacDonald spent the first year of his life in the Columbia Point Project, a predominantly black housing development on the South Boston/Dorchester waterfront, an area characterized by heavy pollution and a large rodent population. In the mid-1960s, when the MacDonald family lived in Columbia Point, the neighborhood was a high crime area—drug dealings and shootings were common—and racial tensions ran extremely high. MacDonald's mother struggled to raise her large family without the help of Dave MacDonald, her abusive and typically absent husband. In 1967 she moved with her children into her parents' home in Jamaica Plain, where they lived for the next six years in a neighborhood of working-class Irish-American families. MacDonald's mother, Helen MacDonald (later King), supplemented her welfare income by playing the Irish accordion at local barrooms. Although the family was not living in a housing project at the time, MacDonald recalls spending a great deal of time visiting the project nearby and playing with other children whose families were on welfare.

When, in the summer of 1973, MacDonald's grandfather decided to sell the house in Jamaica Plain, MacDonald and his siblings moved with their mother to the Old Colony Housing Project in Southie. MacDonald attended St. Augustine's grammar school, where his mother struggled to make tuition payments so that her children would not be bused to primarily black neighborhoods. In his memoir, MacDonald chronicles the antibusing riots in Southie that made national news in the mid-1970s. He also writes about organized crime and specifically about James "Whitey" Bulger, a politically connected mobster and drug lord who ruled the streets of Southie and enforced a strict code of loyalty and silence among its residents.

After all his family members either died or moved away, MacDonald relocated to downtown Boston in 1990 and began working as an antiviolence activist with Citizens for Safety. He helped to start Boston's gun buyback program and worked with other activists and victims to give voice to survivors of violence and the drug trade. His early work connected him with families in Boston's largely black and Latino neighborhoods of Roxbury, Dorchester, and Mattapan. Those families, MacDonald discovered, had experienced many of the same tragedies and hardships as their counterparts in the predominantly Irish community of Southie. The difference was residents of Southie were typically unwilling to talk about the problems that plagued their neighborhood. In 1994 MacDonald broke the code of silence when he agreed to an interview with *U.S. News & World Report* about the "white underclass" in Southie. In the summer of 1994, MacDonald moved back to Southie and founded the South Boston Vigil Group for families who, like MacDonald, have lost loved ones to drugs, violence, or suicide.

Kathleen Ruppert

See also: Boston; Bulger, James "Whitey;" Ethnic and Race Relations (Irish and African American)

Reference

McNaught, Sarah. "No Place Like Home: Michael Patrick MacDonald Talks about His New Book, *All Souls,* and Changing Times in South Boston." www.bostonphoenix.com/archive/features/99/10/14/MACDONALD.html (accessed August 8, 2007).

MacGowan, Michael (1865–1948)

Michael MacGowan was a Donegal-born Irish speaker whose memoir offers an outstanding insight into the life of an immigrant laborer in late nineteenth-century North America. Published posthumously in 1959, *Rotha Mór an tSaoil* (*The Great Wheel of Life*) is a compilation of autobiographical stories collected from MacGowan by his son-in-law, Seán Ó hEochaidh, a folklorist with the Irish Folklore Commission. It was subsequently translated into English by Valentin Iremonger and published in 1962 as *The Hard Road to Klondike.*

Born the eldest of twelve children in 1865 in Cloghaneely, Co. Donegal, MacGowan first left home at the age of eight via the hiring fairs in Letterkenny. At the age of 15 he departed for Scotland, and spent five years as a migrant worker before leaving for Bethlehem, Pennsylvania, to join a relation who worked in the iron mills. He earned a dollar a day at his first job in Bethlehem: hauling sand for the construction of the then-expanding city, which was attracting Irish and other immigrants. While he soon moved to a job in the iron works, he found the long hours and low pay no more appealing than they had been in Scotland, so he ventured by rail to the rich silver and copper mines near Butte, Montana. He spent nearly a decade mining at Granite Mountain, alongside fellow Cloghaneely men. Economic forces moved him on, however: the price of silver collapsed in the mid-1890s, making work difficult to find. In 1897 MacGowan heard that gold had been discovered in the Klondike region in Canada's Yukon Territory.

The next year, he made the arduous, six-month journey to join friends who had already ventured north to Canada for the early days of the gold rush. He journeyed much of the way west to Seattle as a hobo, stealing train rides in freight cars. From Seattle, he traveled north, mostly by boat but sometimes on foot: first up the coast, then through the Bering Sea and finally up the Yukon, fighting the ice that became more of a menace as winter set in. After a series of life-threatening episodes, MacGowan reached the large miners' settlement at Dawson City in December 1898. He spent the next three years in nearby All Gold Creek, working the tedious, difficult task of mining a claim. While the work was gruelling, MacGowan and his fellow Irish miners developed a strong sense of community and retained a sense of Irish identity. In his memoir, he describes an impromptu Saint Patrick's Day parade: a crowd of miners marched behind a lone piper from their cabins to the town, where they celebrated the day in the hotel bars.

MacGowan's emigrant story was ultimately one of triumph: in 1901, he returned home to Cloghaneely for a visit, having earned enough money in the Klondike to travel first class. While at home, he fell in love with a local woman, Maire Bawn Dickson, and decided not to return to America. Instead, he married in 1902 and bought the house of a local landlord, where the couple raised a family of 11 children, and where he lived until his death in 1848.

The strength of MacGowan's legacy is in the vividness of the account he provides of his migrant experience; he articulately explores such experiences as his homesickness, the camaraderie he felt with his fellow migrants, the excitement of the gold rush, and the difficulties of his work. In addition, his memoir provides insightful observations into the effects of larger historical forces on MacGowan and those he encounters. His depiction of Native Americans, for example, whom he portrays sympathetically, reveals his sensitivity to their suffering and his sense of commonality with them as colonized people.

A video documentary entitled *Rotha Mór an tSaoil,* based on the work, was produced for RTÉ in 1998 and directed by Desmond Bell.

Noreen Bowden

See also: EMIGRATION; SAINT PATRICK'S DAY

MACGOWAN, SHANE (1957–)

Shane MacGowan was lead vocalist and songwriter for 1980s London-Irish punk-folk band The Pogues. He subsequently fronted the Popes and worked as a solo singer and guest musician. MacGowan combines the content and craft of traditional Irish tunes with the style and delivery of punk and rock music. Born in Tonbridge, Kent, and raised in Puckaun, Co. Tipperary, MacGowan returned to England with his family in 1964. Accepted in 1971 to London's Westminster public school on scholarship, he was ejected a year later for narcotics possession. Hospitalization for drug abuse preceded a combination of odd jobs, street living, and appearances as an early punk fan, "Shane O'Hooligan." Press attention in *The New Musical Express* after a concert where his ear was bitten led to his singing for the Nipple Erectors, later called the Nips, from 1978 to 1981.

By 1983, MacGowan cofounded Pogue Mahone, later the Pogues. This North London band pioneered a fusion of traditional ballads, chants, and anthems with MacGowan's own original tunes, drawing on folk and contemporary influences. The band's shambolic performances and MacGowan's drug and alcohol abuses led to notoriety and success among British and American audiences. Their first album, *Red Roses for Me* (1984), revealed raw talent, while the Elvis Costello–produced *Rum, Sodomy & the Lash* (1985) introduced the band to the United States. On the four-track extended-play *Poguetry in Motion* (1986), "The Body of an American" chronicles the prejudices and stereotypes within the Irish-American community. American and worldwide tours and their next two albums heightened the band's reputation as gritty chroniclers and celebrators of urban "Paddies." *If I Should Fall from Grace with God* (1988) displays MacGowan's ability to croon as well as bluster; "Fairytale of New York" is a duet with Kirsty MacColl, daughter of Ewan MacColl, himself a folksinger from the previous generation. By collaborating with the Dubliners, too, MacGowan sought to prove to younger listeners that the Irish musical tradition could survive in a contemporary milieu, even if it proved offensive to some purists.

Touring and conflicts over musical direction weakened the band. *Peace and Love* (1989) and *Hell's Ditch* (1990) diversified into Mediterranean, Latin, and American styles, which were at odds with MacGowan's commitment to concentrate on Celtic themes. Increasingly under physical and mental strain, MacGowan failed to show up for dates on a 1989 U.S. tour supporting Bob Dylan. While "Five Green Queens and Jean" on the 1990 album produced by Joe Strummer (of the Clash) attests to MacGowan's ability to assimilate Dylan's attitude, the globalized itinerary and increasing interest in world music of his fellow musicians proved too diverse for MacGowan. He and the band parted in 1991.

Duets with Nick Cave ("What a Wonderful World," the Pogues' "Rainy Night in Soho," and Cave's "Lucy") appeared in 1992, but a solo album from MacGowan emerged only in 1994. He assembled some long-time friends into a sextet christened the Popes. *The Snake* mixed a more rock-oriented singer-songwriter approach with ballads like "Nancy Whiskey" and "The Rising of the Moon." With guests ranging from Johnny Depp and Sinead O'Connor to members of the Pogues and the Dubliners, the range of this album boded well for MacGowan's solo ambitions. A long-delayed successor, *The Crock of Gold* (2000), failed to sustain this energy, however. Live albums have followed; the Popes recorded *Across the Broad Atlantic* live from both Dublin and New York on Saint Patrick's Day in 2001.

Throughout his career, MacGowan has strived to express the plight of the emigrant Irish, as his English counterparts John Lydon (Johnny Rotten of the Sex Pistols), Morrissey (of the Smiths), and Kevin Rowland (of Dexy's Midnight Runners) had done as punk crested and then subsided for their displaced generation. MacGowan's recent work with diverse artists attests to his determination to express the Irish experience across the diaspora in both lyrics and music. Death-metal Irish band Cruachan, songwriter-activist Christy Moore, traditional singer Colm O'Donnell, noise-pop band the Jesus and Mary Chain, Boston punk-folk hardcore band Dropkick Murphys, Breton harpist Alan Stivell, and American country artist Steve Earle all have performed with MacGowan after his departure from the Pogues.

John L. Murphy

See also: MOORE, Christy

References

Clarke, Victoria Mary. *A Drink With Shane MacGowan.* New York: Macmillan, 2002.

MacGowan, Shane. *Poguetry: The Lyrics of Shane MacGowan.* London: Faber & Faber, 1990.

Merrick, Joe. *Shane MacGowan: London Irish Punk Life and Music.* London: Omnibus Press, 2001.

Prendergast, Mark. *Isle of Noises: Rock and Roll's Roots in Ireland.* New York: St. Martin's Press, 1987.

Stanage, Niall. *Down All the Days: The Life and Times of Shane MacGowan.* London: Omnibus Press, 1991.

MacGowran, Jack (1918–1973)

John Joseph McGowran (he later changed the spelling of his surname) was born on October 13, 1918, in Ranelagh, a southern suburb of Dublin. Growing up, he attended the Christian Brothers School where, despite his somewhat unstudious nature, he developed a love of literature that he maintained throughout his life. His first love, from early adolescence, was acting. In 1940 he debuted in the Gaiety Theatre, one of Dublin's major theatrical venues. During the war years he worked at the Gaiety and, for several years after the war, at the Abbey Theatre, then the foremost Dublin venue. He began to develop reputations as both an astounding acting talent and an unreliable frequent drinker. He also began to appear in film roles, some undistinguished, but several that attained fame (his most famous film was *The Quiet Man,* opposite John Wayne and Maureen O'Hara, although he later also appeared in several of Roman Polanski's lesser films). But in the early 1950s theatrical work remained, as often in Dublin, scarce and uncertain, so MacGowran resolved to try his luck in London.

In 1954 he debuted in London as The Young Covey in Sean O'Casey's *The Plough and the Stars.* He had become friendly with O'Casey, and MacGowran's performances were notable for his extraordinary ability to replicate the simultaneous desperation and humanity of O'Casey's Dubliners. Yet it was in 1957 that MacGowran made his most fruitful friendship with an Irish playwright—Samuel Beckett. MacGowran originally encountered the author through a vocal appearance on the radio play *All That Fall,* and he became intrigued by Beckett's gloomy humor and lyrical genius. The men met, became friends, and for the rest of his life MacGowran remained the definitive male performer of Beckett's works. His rumpled face and prominent nose—which had long worked against him in the theater—perfectly captured the ravaged looks the dramatist described. MacGowran performed in many of Beckett's plays, including *Waiting for Godot, Endgame,* and the teleplay that was written expressly for him, *Eh Joe.* His greatest success, however, was a one-man show of excerpts from Beckett's plays, novels, and short stories entitled *Jack MacGowran in the Works of Samuel Beckett.* This play was wildly popular on Broadway, making MacGowran a respected name in American theater and further encouraging Beckett's fervent following in the United States.

Although MacGowran was able to conquer his alcoholism, he still suffered from depressions and self-doubt. Compounding his health problems, MacGowran routinely overcommitted and overworked himself. He died on January 30, 1973, in New York City. His biographer ascribes his death to angina.

MacGowran's major contribution to Irish-American relations was his extraordinary embodiment of Beckett's characters on the American stage. Although he had several failures in his American theater career—most notably, a disastrously misconceived version of O'Casey's *Juno and the Paycock* as a musical comedy—MacGowran did more to impress North American audiences with the theatrical value and moral humanity of Beckett's work than any other actor. His complete faith in Beckett's writings, combined with his nearly inhuman submersion of himself in the writer's outcasts and tramps, made for performances that are still regarded as among the most accomplished ever given on an American stage.

Andrew Goodspeed

See also: BECKETT, Samuel

References

MacGowran, Jack. *MacGowran Speaking Beckett.* Dublin: Claddagh Records, 1966.

MacGowran, Jack. "Working with Beckett." In *Beckett at 60: A Festschrift,* edited by John Calder. London: Calder & Boyars, 1967.

Toscan, Richard. "MacGowran on Beckett." In *On Beckett: Essays and Criticism,* edited by S. E. Gontarski. New York: Grove Press, 1986.

Young, Jordan R. *The Beckett Actor: Jack MacGowran, Beginning to End.* Beverly Hills, CA: Moonstone Press, 1987.

MACK, CONNIE (1862–1956)

Connie Mack was born Cornelius McGillicuddy on December 22, 1862, in East Brookfield, Massachusetts, to Michael McGillicuddy, a wheelwright, and Mary (McKillop) McGillicuddy, both Irish immigrants. Mack was a catcher who was signed to a professional baseball contract in 1884, earning $90 per month to play for Meriden of the Connecticut State League. Two years later he made his major league debut with Washington of the National League. In 1887 he married his childhood sweetheart, Margaret Hogan; when she died five years later, she left him three children. After three years with Washington, Mack led a player's revolt against the arbitrary salary limits used by National League clubs. He invested his savings in the new Players League, and spent two years with the Buffalo club. When the Players League folded, Mack was assigned to Pittsburgh of the National League, playing with them for six years (1891–1896).

Mack's style has been described as combative and crafty; he used such tactics as chatting with batters to distract them, conversing with umpires to influence them, and tipping bats so as to make swings ineffective. These attributes earned him managerial responsibilities in 1894, a position he held for three years. In 1897 he became manager and part owner of the Milwaukee franchise, learning the business side of the game, and reassessing his earlier stance on player-owner grievances.

Portrait of professional baseball player and manager Cornelius "Connie Mack" McGillicuddy. (Library of Congress)

In 1901 Mack was named manager—and made 25 percent owner—of the expansion Philadelphia Athletics, of the new American League. He recruited star National League players to the fledgling club, and with the backing of investors such as Ben Shibe, he built one of the flagship franchises in all the game. Under Mack's tutelage the Athletics won six of the first 14 American League pennants and four pennants in five years from 1910 to 1914.

Known as "the grand old gentleman of the game," Mack eschewed the uniform of his day and managed in a business suit, high starched collar, tie, and straw hat. He was a keen judge of talent who scouted colleges and high schools for players. He sought young, intelligent players who could pressure opponents with their athleticism and talents. His players were expected to be well behaved, and Mack treated them with deference and respect, attributes not seen in many managers. As he had promised his pious mother, who believed all ballplayers were profane gamblers, Mack exuded professionalism and tact. He banned smoking, card playing, and drinking from the clubhouse and rigidly enforced curfews during road trips. On the field, Mack introduced such innovations as pregame and postgame strategy sessions and defensive substitutions. He often coordinated his pitchers with his defense; knowing how his pitchers would fare against certain batters, he positioned his fielders accordingly, using his manager's scorecard to wave players into position.

For all his knowledge of the game, Mack was seen as a penurious, ruthless competitor. He was rumored to have employed special coaches whose job it was to steal signs from opposing players from a seat in the centerfield bleachers, and he routinely slashed salaries if the team lost money. During one such spree, Mack sold the contracts of many of his stars, and the Athletics finished last in every season from 1915 to 1922. The onset of the Great Depression forced Mack to liquidate even his most notable players, ending a run of three pennants from 1929 to 1931.

Mack managed the Athletics until 1950 and remained principal owner until 1954. During his time at the helm, the Athletics won nine pennants and five world championships. In 1955, over Mack's objections, the Athletics were sold and relocated to Kansas City. It was the end of a half-century association between Connie Mack and the Athletics. During his 53-year managerial career, Mack accumulated many records, including most games managed (7,755), won (3,776), and lost (3,948). Elected to the Baseball Hall of Fame in 1937, Mack was survived by his second wife, Katherine Hallahan (whom he had wed in 1910), and his eight children when he died on February 8, 1956, in Germantown, Pennsylvania.

Tim Lynch

See also: BASEBALL; BASEBALL MANAGERS, IRISH-AMERICAN

References

Davis, Ted. *Connie Mack: A Life in Baseball.* Philadelphia: Writers Club Press, 2001.

Jordan, David M. *The Athletics of Philadelphia: Connie Mack's White Elephants.* New York: MacFarland and Company, 1999.

Mack, Connie. *My Sixty-Six Years in the Big Leagues.* Philadelphia: Amereon Press, 1950.

MACKENNA, JOHN (1771–1814)

Governor of Osorno and a general in the Chilean War of Independence, John Mackenna was born on October 26, 1771, in Clogher, Co. Tyrone, the son of William McKenna and Eleanor O'Reilly. He went to Spain with his uncle, the Count O'Reilly, and studied in the Royal School of Mathematics in Barcelona. In 1787 he was accepted in the Irish Brigade of the Spanish army and joined the army fighting in Ceuta in northern Africa. While there, Lt. Col. Luis Urbina promoted him to second lieutenant. In 1791 Mackenna resumed his studies in Barcelona and acted as liaison with mercenaries recruited in Europe. The following year he was promoted to lieutenant in the Royal Regiment of Engineers. In the war against the French, John Mackenna fought in Rosellón under General Ricardos and met the future liberator of Argentina, José de San Martín. For his merits in the defense of Plaza de Rozas, he was promoted to captain in 1795.

Following a new assignment in October 1796, Mackenna left Spain for South America. He arrived in Buenos Aires and then traveled to Mendoza and to Chile across the Andes. Once in Lima, Viceroy Ambrose O'Higgins appointed Mackenna the governor of Osorno. In this capacity, John Mackenna convinced families of Castro, in the isle of Chiloé, to move to Osorno to found a colony there. He built a storehouse, two mills, and the road between Osorno and present-day Puerto Montt. His successful administration provoked jealously from Chile's Captain-General Gabriel de Avilés, who feared that John Mackenna and Ambrose O'Higgins would create an Irish colony in Osorno. Both Irishmen were loyal to the Spanish crown, however; John Mackenna had good relations with O'Higgins's son Bernardo, the future emancipator of Chile, and was also connected with the Venezuelan Francisco de Miranda and his group of supporters of South American independence. When Ambrose O'Higgins died in 1801, Avilés was appointed viceroy of Peru. It took him eight years to remove O'Higgins's protégé John Mackenna from Osorno.

In 1809 John Mackenna married Josefina Vicuña y Larraín, an 18-year-old Chilean woman from a family with revolutionary connections. The following year he was called to the defense committee of the new republic of Chile, and in 1811 he was appointed governor of Valparaíso. Owing to political feuds with José Miguel Carreras and his brothers, John Mackenna was dismissed from the post and imprisoned. He supported the faction of Bernardo O'Higgins, who appointed him one of the key officers to fight the Spanish army of General Antonio Pareja. Mackenna's major military honor was achieved in 1814 in the battle of Membrillar, in which the general ensured a temporary breakdown of the royal forces. He was appointed commandant-general by Bernardo O'Higgins, but after a coup d'état led by José Luis Carreras both were banished to the Argentine province of Mendoza. John Mackenna died on November 21, 1814, in a duel with José Luis Carreras in Buenos Aires.

Edmundo Murray

See also: O'HIGGINS, Ambrose

References

Tellez Yañez, Raúl. *El General Juan Mackenna: Héroe del Membrillar (Ensayo Histórico).* Santiago, Chile: Alonso de Ovalle, 1952.

Vicuña Mackenna, Benjamín. *La Guerra a Muerte: Memoria Sobre las Últimas Campañasde la Independencia de Chile, 1819–1824.* Santiago, Chile: Imprenta Nacional, 1868.

MADDEN, RICHARD ROBERT (1798–1886)

Richard Madden was born in Dublin in August 1798, on the same day the French arrived off the Co. Mayo coast. On the night of his birth his father's house was searched for arms by the notorious Major Sirr, attended by a company of yeomanry. The 1798 Rising became throughout his life what Madden called "a sort of ruling passion." His seminal seven-volume *The Lives and Times of the United Irishmen,* the first of which was published in 1842, revived the memory of United Irish leaders such as Theobald Wolfe Tone and Lord Edward Fitzgerald, names that had lain in near oblivion if not disgrace for some 40 years. Madden is also associated with Anne Devlin, Robert Emmet's housekeeper. Devlin had been imprisoned and tortured in 1803 and was alone and poor by the time Madden befriended her in the 1840s.

Madden's father, Edward Madden, was a descendent of an important Gaelic family that had held large tracts of land in the southern part of Co. Roscommon and the contiguous northern area of Galway. Edward Madden was a fairly prosperous silk and woolen manufacturer and merchant in Dublin. He had 21 children by two wives. Richard was the last of the 21; his mother was a woman by the name of Forde from Co. Leitrim.

After attending various schools in Dublin as a boy, Madden's contact with medicine began when he was apprenticed to a surgeon in Athy. While still a teenager he went to France in a bid to fight incipient tuberculosis. He worked and studied for a while in Paris and Bordeaux, before finding himself practicing for a while as doctor in Naples, Italy. In Naples he formed part of the British emigré set who lived in that city, developing contacts among elements of the

British liberal intelligentsia and aristocracy that were to survive throughout his life. From Naples he went on to live for some years in the Middle East before returning to practise as a doctor in England.

In 1833 the British government named Madden as one of a group of magistrates to go to Jamaica "to carry out the liberation of the Jamaica slaves from their bondage." Of the six special magistrates appointed, four were dead from disease within a year. Madden survived, but he left Jamaica in rather cloudy circumstances. He had made many enemies among the slave owners on the island and appears to have been the victim of death threats. On one occasion "a mere accident averted from him the assassin's dagger."

From Jamaica Madden was posted to Cuba, where in 1836 he was appointed "Superintendent of Liberated Africans," to serve in Cuba under the terms of the Anglo-Spanish Treaty of 1820, an agreement that had, on paper, put an end to the Spanish slave trade. In 1839 he received an additional duty, when he was named acting judge-advocate on the International Commission Court sitting at Cuba. During Madden's three years in Cuba he traveled all over the island and became familiar with the slave system. He visited the barracoons (barracks-like structures) in Havana, where slaves were lodged when they arrived in Cuba, before they were dispersed throughout the island. He became acquainted with the Cuban slave-poet Juan Francisco Manzano and translated his poetry and autobiography to English. The knowledge of slavery Madden acquired in Cuba became the subject for his book *The Island of Cuba,* published after he left the island.

In 1839 53 Africans were purchased by two Spanish sugar planters at Havana and put aboard the schooner *Amistad* for shipment as slaves to a plantation on the east of Cuba. Once at sea the Africans seized the ship and ordered the planters to sail to Africa. However, the vessel drifted for weeks and eventually was sighted off the coast of Long Island, New York. The Africans were detained and lodged in U.S. federal custody in Connecticut. Spain had abolished slavery in her possessions in 1820, but Africans in bondage before that date had to remain in slavery. The petition of the Spanish "owner" of the slaves for the return of his "property" prompted a landmark case in the United States courts. Essentially, the matter hinged on whether or not the African mutineers had been slaves before 1820, or whether they were recently kidnapped from Africa.

Of his own initiative Richard Madden sailed from Cuba to Connecticut to take part in the U.S. Circuit Court proceedings. He gave his testimony before the U.S. District Court in Hartford, Connecticut, on November 20, 1839. His evidence focused on the question of whether these were Bozales—Africans recently and therefore illegally kidnapped from Africa—or Ladinos—slaves who had been brought to Cuba before 1820. Using linguistic and other evidence, supported by his intimate knowledge of the operation of Spanish slave markets in Cuba, Madden showed that the captives were recently kidnapped from Africa. He exposed the extent to which slave traffic was still occurring, even though it was supposedly outlawed. In January 1840, the presiding judge ruled that the Amistad captives were "born free" and kidnapped in violation of international law. The U.S. administration appealed the decision to the Supreme Court, but the high court agreed that the Amistad captives were "kidnapped Africans, who by the laws of Spain itself were entitled to their freedom."

Madden's human rights work continued in the years after the Amistad case. In 1840 he went with others on a fact-finding mission to Egypt to investigate alleged persecution of Jews in that country. He then found himself sent to the British possessions in West Africa, enquiring into the treatment of blacks at the hands of the colonists. There are some indications that the publication of his *Lives* in the 1840s lost him favor with the British government, because after his stint in Africa he had to accept a job as Spain and Portugal correspondent of the *Morning Chronicle*. He spent three years in the Iberian Peninsula, mostly in Lisbon. Back in favor, he undertook one further brief colonial posting in Australia, before returning around 1850 to settle in his native Dublin for the remainder of his life. He had published dozens of books on a wide range of topics before his death in 1886.

Madden always maintained that his support for justice and freedom abroad was another manifestation of his support for the same values in his native country. He saw his human rights advocacy as fully coherent with his Irish nationalism, a position that was restated a generation or two later by Roger Casement.

David Barnwell

See also: CASEMENT, Roger

References

Burton, Gera. *Ambivalence in the Colonized Subject : The Counter-discourse of Richard Robert Madden and Juan Francisco Manzano*. New York: Peter Lang, 2004.

Madden, Richard. *The island of Cuba: its resources, progress, and prospects, considered in relation especially to the influence of its prosperity on the interests of the British West India colonies*. London: Partridge and Oakey, 1853.

Madden, Richard. *The memoirs (chiefly autobiographical) from 1798 to 1886 of Richard Robert Madden. Edited by his son Thomas More Madden*. London: Ward & Downey, 1891.

Madden, Richard. *Poems by a slave in the island of Cuba, recently liberated; translated from the Spanish, by R. R. Madden M.D. With the history of the early life of the Negro poet, written by himself; to which are prefixed two pieces descriptive of Cuban slavery and the slave-traffic*. London: Thomas Ward, 1840.

Madden, Richard. *The United Irishmen: Their Lives and Times*. Dublin: Duffy, 1846.

O Broin, Leon. *An Maidíneach: starái na nÉireannach Aontaithe*. Baile Átha Cliath (Dublin): Sairseal agus Dill, 1971.

MAGUIRE, JOHN WALTER (1906–1981)

Writer, rancher, and notable collector of old books, coins, silver artifacts, and Argentine traditional artwork, John Walter Maguire was born in 1906, son of Eduardo Pedro Maguire (1865–1929), a large landowner in Buenos Aires province, and Catalina Murray (1866–1940). He was the grandson of John Maguire (1825–1905). He later became the president of the Buenos Aires Institute of Numismatics and Antiques. Maguire's unique collection of horse-driven carriages was stored in his ranch, Tres Bonetes, of Lincoln department, Buenos Aires province. He was also the author of *Loncagüé* (1967) and *La Pezuña de Oro* (1980). *Loncagüé* includes stories of the frontier and the Indians, folklore tradition of the pampas, and an essay about Argentine silverwork by E. Greslebin. In *La Pezuña de Oro* (the golden hoof) Maguire describes the pampas of Buenos Aires province and the life in old *vaquerías* (ranches), including information about livestock brands of Buenos Aires and Santa Fe; relations among gauchos, politicians, bandits, Indians, and landowners; work with cattle; and the cattle business. The volume contains a glossary and color illustrations.

Maguire's books are full of anecdotes and stories that reflect everyday life of pioneer Irish settlers in the west of Buenos Aires province. In the early 1860s John Walter's grandfather, John Maguire, James Gaynor, and Patrick MacDonnell visited the area of Loncagüé and La Unión lagoons, in today's department of Nueve de Julio. They began sheep farming with a flock of 3,400 sheep in 1865, facing frequent attacks by Indians. In 1876 they obtained a lease contract from the provincial government (by the system of emphytheusis) and in 1882 Maguire and Gaynor owned approximately 18,000 hectares each in the area. In a language typical of Argentine traditionalist narrative, Maguire recounts in his book *Loncagüé* the encounters with the Indians, and how the first Irish *estancieros* (ranchers) regarded Indian and gaucho culture and life.

Maguire's writing was influenced by the nationalist ideology that developed in the last decades of the nineteenth century. He conceived gauchos and their life as a central part of Argentine identity. Maguire's writings also reflect the era of massive immigration, by which the contribution of the immigrants to the development of their new country was given literary expression.

Edmundo Murray

See also: ARGENTINA

Reference

Coghlan, Eduardo A. *Los Irlandeses en la Argentina: Su Actuación y Descendencia.* Buenos Aires: Author's Edition, 1987.

MAHAN, ALFRED THAYER (1840–1914)

Alfred Thayer Mahan was born September 27, 1840, in West Point, New York, to noted military theorist and tactician Dennis Hart Mahan and Mary (Okill). After attending Columbia College for two years, he graduated second in his class from the U.S. Naval Academy at Annapolis in 1859. Mahan was made a lieutenant in August 1861 and served aboard the *Pocahantas, Macedonian,* and *Seminole,* where he was primarily engaged in blockade duty throughout the American Civil War. Promoted to lieutenant-commander in 1865, he undertook a long cruise in the *Iroquois* to Japan via Rio de Janeiro, Brazil; Capetown, South Africa; Aden (now part

Portrait of Alfred Thayer Mahan, author and naval strategist during the American Civil War. (Library of Congress)

of Yemen); and Bombay, India. Returning to the United States in 1869, he served on shore patrol for the next 20 years, a not unwelcome relief from the seasickness that constantly ailed him. In 1872, the same year in which he was promoted to the rank of commander, he married Ellen Evans; the union produced three children. In 1885 he was promoted to captain.

In 1883, while serving in the Brooklyn Navy Yard, Mahan composed *The Gulf and Inland Waters* for Charles Scribner's series *The Navy in the Civil War*. The book caught the eye of Stephen Luce, founder and president of the new U.S. Naval War College in Newport, Rhode Island. Mahan was invited to join the faculty, where he lectured extensively on naval history and tactics, linking international relations with naval operations and the broad issues of military thought. From 1886 to 1889 he served as president of the college; the following year, he published his lecture notes as *The Influence of Sea Power upon History, 1660–1783,* a tome that revolutionized the study of international affairs and the role of the armed forces in shaping them. A second volume, *The Influence of Sea Power upon the French Revolution and Empire, 1793–1812,* was published in 1892. Together, the volumes served as perfect propaganda for the international naval expansion then taking shape. The volumes were translated into many languages and were required readings for all naval officers.

Mahan's work emphasized the role that merchant and naval fleets played in establishing overseas empires; he effectively expanded naval thinking beyond battle tactics and technical issues, linking naval affairs to wider national and international themes. According to his interpretation, a nation that had a vibrant merchant fleet and a strong navy to protect it would be prosperous in times of peace and invulnerable in times of war. By necessity this meant modernizing and expanding America's naval capabilities and acquiring overseas territories to support a two-ocean, coal-dependent fleet. In addition to his espousal of a modern navy and the related coaling stations to support it, Mahan believed in the importance of major fleet battles to win command of the sea, drawing attention to the sea lanes of communication. Many found in Mahan and his theory a prophet who could show them the way to international respectability via economic, military, and diplomatic power. Appearing at a time of expansionist fervor, Mahan's work exercised tremendous influence over United States and international foreign policy and is widely regarded as the motivating force behind the growth of the battleship navy in the late nineteenth century.

Feted around the world, Mahan received honorary degrees from Oxford and Cambridge. Mahan again served as president of the Naval War College in 1892, and he was given command of the cruiser *Chicago* the following year. Mahan retired with the rank of rear admiral in 1896, although he was recalled to service two years later to serve on the strategy board directing naval operations during the Spanish-American War. In 1902 he was elected president of the American Historical Association, where he continually expounded the need for historical study as the foundation for all knowledge. Few other historians so widely influenced the political thought and policies of their own time as did Mahan, and his theories still hold currency today. Alfred Thayer Mahan died from heart failure in Washington,

D.C., on December 1, 1914. He is interred at Quogue, New York.

Tim Lynch

See also: AMERICAN CIVIL WAR

References

Livesay, William E. *Mahan on Sea Power.* Norman: University of Oklahoma Press, 1981.

Mahan, Alfred Thayer. *The Influence of Sea Power Upon History, 1660–1783.* New York: Dover Publications, 1987.

MAINE

Maine is a frontier state. The present boundary of the northern part of the state was not formally settled until the Webster-Ashburton Treaty of 1842. Maine's isolation and peripheral location within the United States as a whole is similar to Ireland's historical geographical isolation relative to the rest of Europe. In each case there are conflicting notions of inclusion and exclusion, of commonality and distinctiveness.

The first Irish to visit Maine, long before it became a separate state in 1820, were Scots-Irish emigrants from Ulster. They were largely Presbyterian and were fleeing from what they perceived to be discriminatory treatment by the Anglican establishment, both British and Irish, in their native Ulster. As early as 1718 there is a record of the arrival in Casco Bay (Falmouth, later known as Portland) of the ship *McCallum* bearing 20 families, largely from (London)Derry. Subsequently, other Scots-Irish immigrants would settle the mid-coast region east of Brunswick and Topsham.

The first prominent Irish Catholic community in Maine was in Newcastle (Damariscotta Mills), centered on two successful merchant families, the Kavanaghs and the Cottrills. Saint Patrick's Church, erected in 1808 by these families, is the oldest standing continuously used Catholic church in New England. These families dominated the local lumber and merchant trade, and in 1843 Edward Kavanagh, son of James, became the first Catholic governor in New England.

One intriguing variation from the norm in Irish immigration to America occurred in the southern part of Aroostook County in far northern Maine. Here, after 1833, Bishop Benedict Fenwick of Boston financed and initiated an Irish rural enclave in the heart of this potato-growing region. Fenwick's idea was to recreate an American environment for these immigrants similar in nature to the region they were leaving in Ireland, as opposed to their more traditional arrival in the overcrowded urban landscapes of America, such as Boston and New York. He also hoped to create a seminary that would educate future generations of Catholic priests to serve the spiritual needs of the Irish, French, and Native American inhabitants of this part of Maine. The settlement was named Benedicta in Fenwick's honor, and to this day a strong Irish presence is in evidence there, with dominant family names such as Qualey and McAvoy.

The greater numbers of these Irish immigrants, however, were lured to Maine's major cities, such as Portland, Lewiston, and Bangor. These urban centers offered the magnet of promised employment for men along the various waterfronts, railroads, mills, and canals, and in forest-related industries, and for the Irish women work in hotels and as domestics in the homes of the wealthy. This mid-nineteenth-century period was marked by economic opportunity for these newcomers. Many Yankees (Maine-born

Protestants, usually of English heritage) had recently left or were leaving Maine for the more fertile farmlands of the Midwest. Often their farming daughters were drawn further south in New England by the lure of jobs in the mills of Lawrence or Lowell, or other mills and factories in Connecticut or Rhode Island. This same period marked a time of economic and demographic catastrophe in Ireland known as the Great Hunger or the Potato Famine of 1845–1850. Negative factors pushed emigrants out of Ireland just as positive factors pulled these immigrants to Maine and elsewhere in America. The Irish in Maine seized these economic opportunities.

The Irish were not universally welcomed in nineteenth-century Maine. Their Catholic religion set them apart from the majority in this nearly universally Protestant state and region. In terms of social class the Irish were largely unskilled laborers, both male and female, and some of these families needed assistance upon arrival. Opposition to immigration in Maine and elsewhere in America took the form of the American Party (better known as the Know-Nothings). These so-called "native Americans" feared the loss of control and the degree of change being fostered by these new arrivals. An anti-Catholic nativist movement locally resulted in the tarring and feathering of Father John Bapst in Ellsworth (1854) and the burning of the Old South Church in Bath, which was then being used for Catholic services (1854). Perhaps the Irish in Maine got off lightly when one considers what was happening just to the south of Maine. These nativist episodes included the burning of the Ursuline Convent in Charlestown, near Boston, in 1834, and the Irish-nativist riots in the Five Points area of New York City, recently made famous by Martin Scorsese's film, *The Gangs of New York* (2001).

By the early twentieth century the Irish in Maine were better established. They had proven their willingness to fight and die for their adopted country in the Civil War and World War I. Now, however, another nativist threat appeared in the form of the Ku Klux Klan, whose targets in Maine included Catholics, Jews, and immigrants in general. Another difference from the Yankee majority had since evolved. Most Irish in Maine were loyal Democrats in a state that had been dominated by the Republican Party since the time of Hannibal Hamlin, Lincoln's first vice president (1861–1865).

By the late twentieth century, this Irish adherence to the Democratic Party would result in the election of Joseph Brennan, whose parents came from Co. Galway, as two-term governor of Maine (served 1979–1987). A nationally known figure from Maine emerged in the form of Senator George Mitchell who served as the Senate majority leader (1989–1995) and was subsequently asked by President Bill Clinton to help shepherd the search for peace in Northern Ireland; his actions resulted in the Belfast or Good Friday Agreement of 1998. Another Maine-born celebrity was the movie director John Ford. He won Academy Awards for several films: *The Informer* (1935); *The Grapes of Wrath* (1940); *How Green Was My Valley* (1941); two documentaries, *The Battle of Midway* (1942) and *December 7th* (1943); and finally the quintessential Irish nostalgia film, *The Quiet Man* (1952). Ford was born John Feeney and grew up in Irish neighborhoods of Portland, such as Gorham's Corner and Munjoy Hill. He was known as "Bull" Feeney when he played football at Portland High School (1910–1914). The

Americanization of his surname is an indication of ethnic and religious tensions that still existed in this period, and certainly there is no indication that the name Ford hindered in his search for fame.

By the late twentieth century the Irish in Maine had become largely assimilated. However, the state would continue to reflect clear lines of demarcation between a predominantly rural, conservative, Republican, Protestant constituency versus an urban, liberal, Democratic, Catholic constituency. Perhaps these lines are blurring at the start of the twenty-first century with the spread of suburbia and an ever-increasing mobility, both physical and social, even in a frontier state like Maine. The Irish in Maine have faced some particular challenges, but, like their counterparts in the rest of America, they have largely succeeded in living the American dream.

Michael Connolly

See also: EMIGRATION; FORD, John; NATIVISM AND ANTI-CATHOLICISM; MITCHELL, George J.

References

Connolly, Michael C., ed. *They Change Their Sky: The Irish in Maine.* Orono: University of Maine Press, 2004.

Lapomarda, Vincent A. *The Catholic Church in the Land of the Holy Cross: A History of the Diocese of Portland, Maine.* Strasbourg, France: Les Editions du Signe, 2003.

Lucey, William L. *The Catholic Church in Maine.* Francestown, NH: Marshall Jones, 1957.

Mundy, James H. *Hard Times, Hard Men: Maine and the Irish 1830–1860.* Scarborough, ME: Harp Publications, 1990.

Syrett, John. "Principle and Expediency: The Ku Klux Klan and Ralph Owen Brewster in 1924." *Maine History* 39, no. 4 (Winter 2000–2001): 215–239.

Whitmore, Allan R. "'A Guard of Faithful Sentinels': The Know-Nothing Appeal in Maine, 1854–1855." *Maine Historical Society Quarterly* 20, no. 3 (Winter 1981): 151–197.

MALONE, DOROTHY (1925–)

Dorothy Malone was born Eloise Maloney on January 30, 1925, in Chicago. She was a child model, and at age 18 she was noticed by an RKO talent scout when she appeared in a play at Southern Methodist University in Dallas. She signed on as an actress and moved to California with her mother, deeming the experience to be a paid vacation because she did not expect a strong career, and indeed, her earliest parts were nonverbal. However, in 1945 she signed a contract with Warner Brothers and subsequently changed her name.

Malone had a speaking part in *The Big Sleep* and *Night and Day* in 1946. She appeared in *One Sunday Afternoon* and *Two Guys from Texas* in 1948 and *South of St. Louis,* filmed in 1949. No longer contracted to Warner Brothers, she appeared in *The Nevadan, Saddle Legion,* and *The Bushwackers* from 1950 to 1952. *Private Hell 36* was filmed in 1954. In 1955 she appeared in *Five Guns West, Artists and Models,* and *Battle Cry,* which brought her fame. Her most famous role was in *Written on the Wind* in 1957, for which she won a Best Supporting Actress Academy Award and a Golden Globe. She also appeared in *The Tarnished Angels* and *Tip on a Dead Jockey* in 1957. That year she also had roles in *Man of a Thousand Faces, Tarnished Angel,* and *The Last Voyage.*

Malone married French actor Jacques Bergerac in 1959. The couple had two daughters, Mimi and Diane. They divorced in highly publicized proceedings in 1963. Thereafter Malone married Robert Tomarkin, but she divorced him and then married Charles Huston Bell whom she also divorced.

Malone's career fell into a downward spiral because of a lack of parts for mature actresses. Malone appeared in *Beach Party* in 1963. In 1964 her career was revived when she starred for four years as Constance Mackenzie Carson in *Peyton Place,* a popular nighttime soap opera. When she was removed from the cast, she sued the production company for breach of contract and won a $1.6 million settlement. Malone next played the role of Patty Hearst's mother in *Abducted* in 1975 and appeared in one scene in *The Man Who Could Not Die,* also in 1975. She filmed *Winter Kills* in 1979. Meanwhile, she appeared in numerous television movies.

Malone continued to act in a variety of television shows and appeared in the series *High Hopes* (1978). She made numerous appearances in B movies in the 1980s and ended her acting career with her last noteworthy role in *Basic Instinct* in 1991.

Annette Richardson

Reference

Maltin, Leonard. *Leonard Maltin's Movie Encyclopedia.* New York: Plume, 1994.

MARITIME PROVINCES (CANADA)

Located on the eastern coast of Canada, the Maritime Provinces consist of New Brunswick, Nova Scotia, and Prince Edward Island. The Irish experience in this region dates back to the latter part of the eighteenth century, shortly after the British conquest of the territory was complete. Although their proportion of the population within the growing colonies was rather small, Irish Protestants played a prominent role within their administrations. The unsuccessful attempts to apply the name "New Ireland" to Prince Edward Island (known as St. John's Island until 1799) in 1779, and New Brunswick in 1780, reflect the influence of Irish-born Walter Patterson and Thomas Carleton, the first governors of these colonies.

Large-scale emigration by the Irish to the Maritime Provinces commenced in the early 1800s. Lured by the promise of opportunity, tens of thousands would pour into the region during the first half of the century. While immigration to North America is often viewed as a response to famine in the motherland, it should be noted that immigration to Nova Scotia and Prince Edward Island during the famine years was minimal; only a single "coffin ship," the *Lady Constable,* docked in the latter colony. The status of Saint John as a major port of entry, on the other hand, led to a substantial increase in Irish immigration to New Brunswick in this period, peaking at 15,279 in 1847.

The Irish influx during the first half of the 1800s had a significant impact on the ethnic composition of the Maritime Provinces. Formerly dominated by the Scots, English, and French, by the 1870s approximately 35 percent of New Brunswick, 25 percent of Prince Edward Island, and 15 percent of Nova Scotia were of Irish origin. While Protestants dominated the eighteenth-century Irish population within the region, the nineteenth-century immigrants shifted the dynamic: Roman Catholics formed approximately 53, 66, and 90 percent of the total Irish population within New Brunswick, Nova Scotia, and Prince Edward Island, respectively.

The arrival of the Irish led to the emergence of a variety of socio-fraternal organizations. The Charitable Irish Society in Halifax (1786), the Saint Patrick's Society in Saint John (1819), and Prince Edward Island's Benevolent Irish Society (1825) were established to provide immigrant aid and cultural support within their respective communities. All three continue to play the latter role. Irish immigration also gave rise to nativist tensions, directed toward the Roman Catholic component and articulated through the rapid expansion of the Orange Order throughout the region. Not to be discouraged, Irish Roman Catholics flourished in the region and became noted for their prodigious output of clergy. Likewise, the Irish, both Protestant and Roman Catholic, would go on to play an important role in the fields of business, politics, and education.

Irish culture has played an important role in the social fabric of the Maritime Provinces. Although the language and sporting traditions of Ireland failed to take root, the same cannot be said for the musical tradition. Celebrated annually in a series of festivals, most notably the Irish Festival on the Miramichi (founded in 1973), it is also an important component of the region's popular Celtic amalgam, known widely as "East Coast" music.

Ryan O'Connor

See also: EMIGRATION

References

Houston, Cecil J., and William J. Smyth. *Irish Emigration and Canadian Settlement: Patterns, Links, and Letters.* Toronto: University of Toronto Press, 1990.

O'Driscoll, Robert, and Lorna Reynolds. *The Untold Story: The Irish in Canada.* Toronto: Celtic Arts of Canada, 1988.

O'Grady, Brendan. *Exiles and Islanders: The Irish Settlers of Prince Edward Island.* Montreal: McGill-Queen's University Press, 2004.

Power, Thomas P. *The Irish in Atlantic Canada, 1780–1900.* Fredericton, New Brunswick: New Ireland Press, 1991.

Toner, P. M., ed. *New Ireland Remembered.* Fredericton, New Brunswick: New Ireland Press, 1988.

MARYLAND

John Cabot explored some of the area that would become Maryland as early as 1498, but it was not until 1632 that Cecilius Calvert inherited the charter for the area of Maryland given to his father by King Charles I and named it after the king's wife, Henrietta Maria. His brother, Leonard Calvert, led the first group of settlers on the *Ark* and the *Dove* in 1633, and his Roman Catholicism led him to envisage Maryland as a progressive place of religious toleration, an escape from the popular anti-Catholicism in England. Indeed, in 1649 a religious Act of Toleration was passed and while it became one of the few predominantly Catholic areas in the colonies, the Catholicism of the area would be subject to fairly frequent opposition, including a Puritan revolt.

Early Irish immigrants settled continuously, one of the earliest being Daniel Carroll, who arrived in 1659 from Littemourna. His family would become one of the most influential families in U.S. political history as his grandson, Charles Carroll (1737–1832), was a delegate to the Continental Congress, signed the Declaration of Independence, and became a Maryland senator. Maryland would also be represented at the Continental Congress by a recent Scots-Irish immigrant from Ulster, James McHenry. He was a Revolutionary War army medic before being elected to the Maryland legislature and, like Carroll, attended the Continental Congress before representing Maryland at the Constitutional Convention.

For a short period, November 26, 1783, to June 3, 1784, Annapolis was the country's capital. It was the last state to ratify the Articles of Confederation, and the seventh state to ratify the Constitution.

The state had a significant strategic involvement in the War of 1812. Two major encounters occurred, the second of which, the defence of Fort McHenry, inspired a local Baltimore resident, Francis Scott Key, to write the "Star Spangled Banner."

Discrimination flared up intermittently, early signs manifesting themselves in 1704 when a tax of 20 shillings was levied on Irish immigrants arriving in Maryland as servants. In the same year Catholic masses were outlawed. The main brunt was borne during the 1840s–1850s as the Know-Nothings gained popular currency with a campaign resting on a crude blend of anti-Catholicism, anti-immigration, and a fear of being overwhelmed by waves of people. In 1856 there was street fighting between Know-Nothing supporters and Irish democrats. "No Irish need apply" signs were reported, and the state gave its electoral votes to the Know-Nothing presidential candidate, Millard Fillmore.

In the aftermath of the American Revolution, the restrictions on Catholic worship were significantly relaxed in a number of states, Maryland included, and in 1784, John Carroll, of Irish descent and cousin to Charles Carroll, became the superior of missions in the United States of North America. He subsequently became America's first bishop (bishop of Baltimore) in 1789, helped establish the first Catholic cathedral in America (Baltimore, 1806), and became archbishop in 1808 of the new Baltimore archdiocese. (John Carroll also established the Catholic Georgetown University in Washington, D.C.)

The church, as well as a host of social organizations, helped new immigrants settle into the community, particularly important in the periods of heightened discrimination. The Hibernian Sons of Baltimore was, for example, established in 1803 and provided limited financial assistance. The group established the Hibernian Free School and met annually on Saint Patrick's Day.

In time, the majority of Irish immigrants, who were mostly unskilled, would either seek out work in the western half of the state in the coal mines, start laying track for the B&O Railroad (the first commercial long-distance railroad in the country), dig the Chesapeake and Ohio Canals, and establish mining and railroad towns such as Frostburg and Cumberland or they would settle, as most did, around Baltimore in the emerging shipbuilding and ironwork industries.

Baltimore, planned in 1730, became the second-largest port of entry for Irish immigration in the nineteenth century. Large numbers arrived during the Famine years, and of a state population of 418,000 in 1850, 20,000 were Irish born. The B&O railroad constructed "immigrant pier" to help move numbers further into the state and beyond. Immigrants on the infamous coffin ships that transported people to the United States could suffer anything up to a 40 percent loss of life in the crossing, but a replica of the *Jeanie Johnston,* which included Baltimore on its route, was recently rebuilt in 2000 to celebrate the fact that it made 16 transatlantic voyages without the loss of a single life.

Baltimore offered a myriad of jobs from sweatshops to the large sugar-refining trade in the city, and Irish workers became involved in union activity such as the Knights of Labor, organized in Baltimore in 1878. Many thousands lived close to their places of work, such as Locust Point near the port and Fells Point (Fells Point had a Catholic church as early as 1796), often enduring severe overcrowding. Thousands of terraced houses were built throughout the 1880s to accommodate growing numbers. A number of companies, such as B&O, whose owners were of Irish descent, provided a limited number of benefits for employees, such as savings plans.

Maryland was a slave state and had strong Confederate support, but it did not secede. As a result, significant numbers of men volunteered to fight with the Confederacy, but the majority fought for the Union. The state witnessed the bloodiest single day in U.S. military history—the dual-named Battle of Sharpsburg (as known in the South) or the Battle of Antietam (as known in the North) on September 17, 1862. Meagher's New York Irish Brigade suffered particularly heavy losses at "Bloody Lane." The battle proved influential on two counts: first, it marked the end of General Lee's attempt at taking the offensive into the north, and second, the victory allowed Lincoln the position of strength he required from which to issue the Emancipation Proclamation.

Today the proportion of Maryland's population with Irish ancestry stands at 11.8 percent (2000), and the Irish are the second largest group after Germans. Catholicism remains the largest single denomination in the state. The majority of the population is relatively in the Washington-Baltimore metropolitan area, and the eastern and southern areas have a much more scattered populace. There has been a general trend of out-migration of whites in the 1990s, and more have left the state than moved into it throughout the decade. Its politics have been historically Democratic, and it is widely regarded as one of the most liberal states in the Union.

Sam Hitchmough

References

Brugger, Robert J. *Maryland, A Middle Temperament.* Baltimore, MD: Johns Hopkins University Press, 1996.

Doyle, David Noel, and Owen Dudley Edwards, eds. *America and Ireland, 1776–1976: The American Identity and the Irish Connection.* Westport, CT: Greenwood Press, 1980.

Kenny, Kevin. *The American Irish.* London: Longman, 2000.

Miller, Kerby A. *Emigrants and Exiles: Ireland and the Irish Exodus to North America.* Oxford: Oxford University Press, 1988.

MASSACHUSETTS

Contrary to the myth of a wholly English colonial Massachusetts, people from Ireland were among the earliest settlers in New England. The Irish have a long and distinguished history in the Bay State despite the inveterate hostility of the Puritans and Yankees. Colonial Massachusetts militia muster rolls and town, church, and court records include many Irish names. Indentured servants from Ireland were common, and uncounted numbers of children kidnapped from Irish ports were bound out as servants in Massachusetts. By 1660, more than 10,000 Irish immigrants lived in the American colonies, and so many arrived in Massachusetts that the colonial legislature banned them in 1654. Anne Glover, an elderly Irish servant, was the last woman hanged in Boston as a witch (1688), probably for speaking Gaelic and mumbling Catholic prayers in her senility.

Although Catholics were the first Europeans in America, anti-Catholic prejudice was deeply rooted in New England Protestants. It reflects the bitter conflict between England and its Catholic rivals, France and Spain. French and Indian raids from Quebec on Massachusetts towns like Deerfield in 1704 aroused bitter resentment. Massachusetts at times disarmed or barred Catholics from the militia, public office, voting, and jury service, and it expelled all priests. Even the 250,000 Protestants from Ireland who immigrated to America by 1750 were unwelcome in Massachusetts. In 1720 the legislature passed an ordinance directing that "certain families recently arrived from Ireland be warned to move off," and later ordered Ulster immigrants to register with the town selectmen in 1723. Hostile Yankees in Worcester burned a Scots-Irish Presbyterian church in 1734. The Irish settled in more remote communities; some had moved to Maine by 1718, then part of Massachusetts, and introduced flax and potatoes to Yankee farmers. However, the need for labor and the profits from selling indentured servants' contracts overcame Yankee prejudice. The *Boston News-Letter* announced the auction of Irish boys in 1730. Women transported from Belfast as convicts were sold in Boston in 1749.

Twenty-six Protestant Irish gentlemen in Boston established the Charitable Irish Society in 1737 to assist 1,000 Irish immigrants who arrived on more than 50 ships from 1714 to 1738. By 1750, Irish Catholic men joined this oldest Irish organization in the nation. These Irish pioneers founded many New England towns and counties named for their homeland: Antrim, Bangor, Belfast, Colerain, Derry, Dublin, Keegan, Kilkenny, Limerick, Orange, and Sullivan. Famine in Ireland in 1740 prompted more Irish Catholics and Protestants to immigrate to Boston, but most settled in western Massachusetts or other parts of New England.

Patrick Carr, another Boston Irishman, was one of the five colonists killed by British troops in the Boston Massacre in 1770. At least one of the Sons of Liberty involved in the Boston Tea Party (1773) was Irish, William Molineux from Dublin. Boston's first Saint Patrick's Day celebration by Irish soldiers in the British army outraged patriots in 1775. However, the hero of the siege of Boston on March 17, 1776, General Henry Knox, was the son of Irish immigrants to Massachusetts, and this event is celebrated in Boston as Evacuation Day on Saint Patrick's Day. Massachusetts elected Governor James Sullivan in 1808, the son of Irish immigrants to Maine. His brother, General John Sullivan, was governor of New Hampshire in 1786. A memorial (1949) on Boston Common honors Commodore John Barry, the father of the U.S. Navy, who was born in Ireland in 1745 and served in Boston during the Revolution, when as many as 450,000 Irish lived in America.

General George Washington condemned the nativist and anti-Catholic Pope's Day riots in 1776 at Boston, Salem, Marblehead, and Newburyport, but prejudice subsided only slightly after the Revolution despite loyal service in the army and navy by countless Irishmen. The failed Revolution of 1798 sent more Irish refugees to Massachusetts, and many contributed to the state's economic development by building canals and roads in the 1820s. Irish workers built the Pawtucket Canal in Lowell in 1822, and walked 50 miles from Boston to Worcester to build the Blackstone Canal in 1826, and the new railroads in the 1840s. Many subscribed to the *Catholic Sentinel,* the first Catholic newspaper in the United States in 1829, and later to the *Boston Pilot* published by Patrick Donahoe in 1835. They worshipped at the first Catholic church in Boston, the Cathedral of the Holy Cross built in 1800. The Celtic cross in Lowell (1979) and Worcester (1976) and the Irish Round Tower in Milford (1857) honors these Irish settlers.

After the Napoleonic Wars, the Irish were the first impoverished group to leave Europe in large numbers, prompted by the enclosure movement favored by British landlords, discriminatory penal laws, and rising poverty. By 1825, about 125,000 people left Ireland for the United States, and Boston had 8,000 Irish residents in 1830. The Potato Famine (1845–1850) forced a million Irish refugees to flee to America, often on disease-ridden and unsafe Irish "coffin ships." Rest Haven Cemetery at Deer Island contains the graves of 850 Irish immigrants who died at the quarantine station in Boston Harbor in 1847. A memorial in Cohasset recalls the wreck of the brig *St. John* in 1849, when 104 immigrants from Galway drowned. Memorials to the contributions of the Famine Irish are located in Cambridge (1997) and Boston (1998).

Because of the 4 million Irish immigrants who had entered the United States by the end of the nineteenth century, Boston's population increased rapidly from 136,881 in 1850 to 250,000 in 1870, of whom 56,900 were Irish. By 1850, the Irish were the largest ethnic group in Boston, Cambridge, Fall River, Lawrence, Lowell, Lynn, and Worcester, which made Roman Catholics the state's largest denomination. Young Irish women found work in domestic service, and by 1860 two-thirds of the servants in Boston were Irish. Irish men worked in construction jobs, building railroads, streets, sewers, and water lines, or in quarries and on the docks. Their labor modernized the state in the Industrial Revolution.

Irish immigration stimulated religious intolerance, however, when the dynamic Congregational preacher Lyman Beecher aroused a Charlestown mob that burned the Ursuline convent in 1834. A Yankee fire company rioted for days after an Irish Catholic funeral procession on Boston's Broad Street in 1837, and John Bapst, a Jesuit missionary to Native Americans, was tarred and feathered by a Protestant mob in Ellsworth, Maine, in 1854. Father Bapst survived to become the first president of Boston College in 1863. Even the Civil War Draft Riots revealed nativism and anti-Catholicism, when Irish men and boys clashed with the police and Union Army troops in Boston's North End on July 14, 1863.

Col. Thomas Cass and Col. Patrick R. Guiney inspired loyal service in the Civil War by Irish soldiers of the Ninth Regiment. They and other Irish regiments formed in Massachusetts, including the 15th, 19th, and 20th Massachusetts Volunteer Infantry Regiments, did much to reduce ethnic and religious intolerance. However, after the war newspaper want ads still read "Americans only" or "No Irish Need Apply." Discrimination in employment persisted, and most Irish remained in low-paid jobs as laborers, but many worked as teachers or in public utilities and municipal fire and police departments and as priests. However, their descendants would prosper to make Massachusetts the most Irish state in the nation: 26 percent of the residents claimed Irish origins in 2004.

The Boston Catholic diocese offered effective Irish leadership with bishops John B. Fitzpatrick, John J. Williams, and William H. O'Connell. A new leader appeared in 1869 with John Boyle O'Reilly, an Irish rebel who escaped from the penal colony in Australia. As a popular poet, orator and editor of the *Boston Pilot,* he bridged the gap between Boston Brahmins and Hibernian Boston until his sudden death in 1890. This most influential Irishman of the era, an eloquent spokesman for the downtrodden, was honored by Daniel Chester French's memorial sculpture on the Fenway in 1896.

Irish contributions were varied, and many Bay State Irish men and women were prominent in art (John Singleton Copley), music (Patrick Sarsfield Gilmore), sculpture (Augustus Saint Gaudens), sports (John L. Sullivan and James B. Connolly), poetry (Louise Imogen Guiney), architecture (Charles D. Maginnis and Louis Sullivan), vaudeville (Jeremiah Cohan), comedy (Fred Allen), education (Annie Sullivan), and women's rights (Mary Kenny O'Sullivan and Margaret L. Foley).

Other leaders arose from the Irish immigrants and their offspring, and they transformed the Democratic Party after the Civil War. The Irish penchant for politics was evident when Lawrence (1881), Lowell (1882), and Boston (1884) elected the first Irish Catholic mayors. The 1880s saw an increasing number of Irish candidates elected to public office. Patrick Collins (1844–1905), a Democrat in the state legislature and in Congress (1883–89) was the mayor of Boston (1902–1905) and played roles in presidential campaigns by 1876. Joseph H. O'Neil (1853–1935) served Boston in the House of Representatives (1889–1895) until he was succeeded by John F. Fitzgerald (1895–1901), the grandfather of President John F. Kennedy. David I. Walsh (1872–1947) was the first Irish Catholic to serve as governor (1914–1916) and as U.S. Senator (1919–1925, 1926–1947) in Republican-dominated Massachusetts. The son of immigrants from Co. Cork who settled in Leominster, Walsh was the first Democrat elected governor in 1914. A statue on the Charles River Esplanade (1954) honors Walsh.

The state's most memorable Irish politician may be James M. Curley (1874–1958), who served as mayor of Boston four times and as congressman and governor in a colorful half-century career. The man Senator Walsh dubbed the mayor of the poor is remembered in Edwin O'Connor's novel (1956) and John Ford's movie *The Last Hurrah* (1958), and by two statues at Boston City Hall (1980). Curley was a fierce critic of the anti-Catholic Ku Klux Klan that revived in Worcester and other New England communities in the 1920s.

In national politics, Massachusetts has been a unique breeding ground for political leaders and party operatives at all levels, and among these Irish names stand out. John W. McCormack was Speaker of the House (1962–1970), and mentor to Speaker Thomas P. "Tip" O'Neill, Jr. (1977–1987). Senator John F. Kennedy was the first Catholic elected president (1961–1963), and his brother, Edward M. Kennedy, succeeded him as Democratic U.S. senator from Massachusetts. Their brother Robert F. Kennedy served as attorney general and as senator from New York. Lawrence F. O'Brien, a Springfield Democrat, served as a key Kennedy White House adviser, was postmaster general, and was twice chairman of the Democratic National

Committee. The rise of Irish Americans to positions of power in Massachusetts and in national government was a hallmark of the twentieth century. The election of Boston's Jack Kennedy, a turning point in Irish-American history, marked the end of a long, hard road to acceptance and integration in mainstream American society.

Peter C. Holloran

See also: CURLEY, James Michael; EMIGRATION; FORD, John; KENNEDY FAMILY; KENNEDY, John Fitzgerald; O'CONNOR, Edwin

References

Kenny, Kevin. *The American Irish: A History.* New York: Longman, 2000.

O'Connor, Thomas H. *The Boston Irish: A Political History.* Boston: Northeastern University Press, 1995.

O'Connor, Thomas H., Marie E. Daly, and Edward L. Galvin. *The Irish in New England.* Boston: New England Historic Genealogical Society, 1985.

Quinlin, Michael P. *Irish in Boston: A Lively Look at Boston's Colorful Irish Past.* Guilford, CT: Globe Pequot Press, 2004.

Savage, Neil J. *Extraordinary Tenure: Massachusetts and the Making of the Nation.* Worcester, MA: Ambassador Books, 2004.

MASSACRE AT SAINT PATRICK CHURCH, THE

In the early hours of Sunday, July 4, 1976, a few months after the military ousted the democratic government of Argentina, a navy death squad gunned down five members of the Pallotine community in Saint Patrick's Church of Buenos Aires. The killing was a major tragedy, one of the worst in the 400-year history of the Roman Catholic Church in Argentina. It was the product of an ideological division between Irish Argentines in favor of the armed forces and their illegal methods to fight terrorism, and those who were against it. The bodies of three priests, Alfie Kelly (parish priest), Alfredo Leaden, and Eduardo Dufau, and two seminarians, Emilio Barletti and Salvador Barbeito, were found later that day lying in a pool of blood in the living room of the parish house. Slogans were written on the walls and on the carpet: "For our colleagues of Federal Police headquarters," and "This is what happens if you poison the minds of the young." The victims were tortured between 1 a.m. and 3 a.m. and ultimately gunned down with more then 65 bullets. Their killers were members of a death squad composed of six members of the armed forces. According to the declaration of a witness before the International Human Rights Commission in Geneva, Navy Lieutenant Antonio Pernias was their commander. The local police had knowledge of the killers' plans but did nothing to prevent the crime. No one was charged with responsibility, although the journalist Eduardo Kimel, author of a book denouncing the judge Guillermo Rivarola's complicity with the killers, was condemned for libel.

Edmundo Murray

See also: WALSH, Rodolfo

References

Kimel, Eduardo. *La Masacre de San Patricio.* Buenos Aires: Lohle-Lumen Editores, 1986.

O'Neill, Kevin. *Apuntes Históricos Pallotinos.* Buenos Aires: Editora Palloti, 1995.

Seisdedos, Gabriel. *El Honor de Dios.* Buenos Aires: Ediciones Paulinas, 1986.

MATHEW, FATHER THEOBALD (1790–1856)

Father Theobald Mathew (1790–1856) spearheaded the national temperance movement that swept Ireland in the late

1830s to the mid-1840s. He also took his temperance message to the emigrant Irish in Scotland, the United Kingdom, and the United States. Mathew is a much-neglected figure in Irish history, but in the past 20 years, his life and work have received more considered study.

Several biographies have been written about him; however, some were motivated to remember Mathew in the most glowing terms. They ignored his character flaws, his poor organizational skills, his financial difficulties, and his strained relationships with some of the Irish Catholic hierarchy. More recently, Colm Kerrigan and John F. Quinn have examined the roles of Father Mathew and the temperance movement in Irish history. Kerrigan has focused on the Irish context, while Quinn has expanded this to discuss Mathew's trip to America in 1849–1851.

Theobald Mathew was born at Thomastown, Co. Tipperary, on October 10, 1790, to James Mathew and Anne Whyte. Elizabeth Malcolm (1986) gives a detailed account of the family in her chapter on Mathew. James Mathew worked as an agent for his relation, the first Earl of Llandaff. During his childhood, Theobald spent much time at Thomastown Castle, the original family seat, and developed a close relationship with the earl's family. Mathew studied briefly at the seminary in Maynooth in 1807. He joined the Capuchin Order in Dublin. In 1814 he was ordained a priest and was sent to Cork. The Quaker, William Martin, with a group of like-minded reformers was attempting to promote temperance in Cork, and he guessed the young friar would attract the Catholic masses to the cause.

With Mathew's dedication, temperance fever spread around Ireland and millions took the pledge. Handsome and mannerly, Mathew was generous and a very hard worker, renowned for his dedication to his parishioners' spiritual and material needs. Likewise, the wealth and interdenominational nature of his family allowed him the confidence to move within wealthier circles and gave him an ecumenical outlook on the work of the temperance movement. Mathew was interested in the social and economic welfare of the members, and reading rooms and temperance bands were established. Mathew avoided political associations, yet the temperance movement allowed Daniel O'Connell to have peaceful monster meetings and to spread the idea of repeal among the network of temperance groups.

Mathew took his temperance work to Scotland in 1842, England in 1843, and, despite very poor health, America from 1849 to 1851. In America, he wished to travel both in the northern and southern states and did not want a political issue to impede his independence. However, Mathew became embroiled in the slavery controversy. He declined William Lloyd Garrison's offer to speak at an antislavery commemoration. This led to an outcry in the northern states. The southern states were also concerned when they learned that Mathew had signed the "Anti-Slavery Address to Irish Americans in 1841," but Mathew explained that he would not become involved in any discussions of American institutions and was accepted there. In Washington, D.C., he was honored by the House of Representatives and admitted to a seat in the House. After some objections and a subsequent vote, the honor was repeated in the Senate. Following this exhausting tour his health continued to decline, and when he died on December 8,

1856, the temperance organization was in a weak and disorganized state.

Ann Coughlan

See also: DOUGLASS, Frederick; O'CONNELL, Daniel

References

Kerrigan, Colm. *Father Mathew and the Irish Temperance Movement 1838–1849.* Cork: Cork University Press, 1992.

Maguire, John Francis. *Father Mathew: A Biography.* London: Longman, Green, Longman, Roberts, & Green, 1865.

Malcolm, Elizabeth. "Mathew the Martyr." In *Ireland Sober, Ireland Free: Drink and Temperance in Nineteenth-Century Ireland,* 101–150. Dublin: Gill and Macmillan, 1986.

Quinn, John F. *Father Mathew's Crusade: Temperance in Nineteenth-Century Ireland and Irish America.* Amherst: University of Massachusetts Press, 2002.

Portrait of Matthew Fontaine Maury, oceanographer and author of Physical Geography of the Sea, *which is considered the first comprehensive book on oceanography to be published. (Library of Congress)*

MAURY, MATTHEW FONTAINE (1806–1873)

Matthew Fontaine Maury, who became known as the "Father of Oceanography," was born in Virginia on January 14, 1806, to Richard and Diana Maury. Maury joined the navy in 1824, and between 1825 and 1834 he sailed on three expeditions, visiting the South Pacific and Europe as well as traveling around the world aboard the *Vincennes.* It was likely during these voyages that he realized the importance of understanding global patterns of winds and ocean currents for commerce and warfare. In 1834, upon his return to Virginia, he married Ann Herndon and began work on *A New Theoretical and Practical Treatise on Navigation,* a tome that received positive reviews when it was published in 1836. The following year, he was promoted to lieutenant and assigned as surveyor on the famous Charles Wilkes expedition to the Pacific. Upset at his appointment, Maury begged off the exploring expedition to the South Seas and instead was assigned to surveying duties along the Gulf Coast. During this time he penned a series of anonymous attacks on the secretary of the Navy, regarding inefficiency and suggesting reforms, including the establishment of a naval academy. It was also during this time that Maury was seriously injured in a stagecoach accident and made permanently lame. Ineligible for sea duty, in 1842 Maury was appointed superintendent of the Depot of Charts and Instruments of the Navy Department at Washington. It was here that Maury began to study the huge assemblage of ship's reports in the Depot's archives. From this information, be began to put together a global database on currents, winds, and weather patterns, devoting nearly all his time to assembling information on the physical properties of the ocean across the globe. His charts revealed for the first time the worldwide patterns of oceanic currents and winds.

In 1847, Maury issued his famous *Wind and Current Charts of the North Atlantic,* which he added to by using data sent to him by ship captains all over the world. His compendium of ocean currents, surface temperatures, and wind patterns sliced transportation times and costs appreciably: as a result of his work, sailing times between New York and San Francisco were reduced from 180 to 133 days. In the fall of 1853, he was appointed the U.S. Representative to the International Congress in Brussels, where he urged the recording of oceanographic data aboard naval and merchant marine vessels; soon his system of recording currents and winds was adopted worldwide.

In 1855, Maury published what is considered to be his greatest contribution to oceanography, *The Physical Geography of the Seas.* The book contained detailed information on the Gulf Stream, bathymetric maps with contours at depths exceeding 4.5 miles, and a wealth of information on currents and meteorology. The tome, which some call the first textbook of modern physical oceanography, was translated into many languages and brought the author international fame.

At the outbreak of the American Civil War, Maury resigned his commission and proceeded to Richmond, where he was sworn in as commander in the Confederate States Navy. Assigned to harbor defense, Maury devised riverine fortifications for the Confederacy and developed underwater mines to disable Union ships. Recognizing his international reputation, the Confederacy sent Maury as an emissary to England and France, where he worked to gain recognition for the rebels. At the conclusion of the war, Maury espoused the settlement of former Confederates in Mexico, a plan that met with little support. He subsequently lived in England for two years, publishing a series of geography textbooks and earning an honorary degree from Oxford. Returning to the United States in 1868, Maury taught meteorology at the Virginia Military Institute until his death in 1872. He was survived by his wife and eight children and is interred at Hollywood Cemetery in Richmond, Virginia.

Tim Lynch

See also: AMERICAN CIVIL WAR

Reference

Williams, Frances Leigh. *Matthew Fontaine Maury: Scientist of the Sea.* New Brunswick, NJ: Rutgers University Press, 1963.

McCANN, COLUM (1965–)

Irish-born short story writer and novelist Colum McCann has achieved critical and popular success in Ireland and America with his vivid, symbolic prose style. McCann elucidates the stories of those who live at the margins of society—often exiles, immigrants, the homeless, homosexuals, or the incarcerated.

McCann is one of five children born to journalist, author, and editor Sean McCann and Sally (McGonigle) McCann, a housewife. He grew up in south Co. Dublin and frequently summered with family in rural

Co. Derry. McCann was an excellent student, studying communications at Rathmines and later pursuing graduate studies at the University of Texas at Austin. He worked as a freelance journalist for several newspapers in Dublin and then in New York City, where he first moved in the early 1980s. As he made the transition from journalist to author, he took various jobs, such as taxi driver in Cape Cod, bartender, and volunteer for a troubled youth program in Texas. He spent two years on a bicycle tour of the United States and taught English in Japan to broaden his range of life experience.

McCann's early success followed upon the heels of the short story "Tresses," which garnered two Hennessy Awards in 1991. His first collection of short stories, *Fishing the Sloe-Black River,* earned him the Rooney Prize for Irish Literature in 1994. His first novel, *Songdogs,* was published the following year. *Songdogs* features a son who recreates his father's life via a series of flashbacks evoked by the father's photographs. McCann's next novel, *This Side of Brightness* (1998), is set in New York City in the twentieth century, and features a cast of characters that ranges from the "sandhogs" who built the subway tunnels below the Hudson River, up to the construction workers who bolted the steel girders of the city's skyscrapers together, and back down to the "mole people" who inhabit New York's underground network of abandoned tunnels. In 1999, McCann won a Pushcart Prize for the short story "As Kingfishers Catch Fire." In *Everything in This Country Must: A Novella and Two Stories* (2000), McCann turns to an Irish landscape as he writes about the Troubles through teenage eyes. His acclaimed novel, *Dancer* (2003), traces the life of renowned ballet dancer Rudolf Nureyev from World War II Russia up to his AIDS-related death in the early 1990s by way of Leningrad, France, Italy, and New York's discos of the 1970s and 1980s. His latest novel, *Zoli* (2007), is the story of a Gypsy girl in Slovakia who flees Nazi persecution during World War II. She teaches herself to read and write and becomes a poet. McCann has also been involved in adapting his writing to screen and stage, and served as the Sidney Harman writer-in-residence at Baruch College, City University of New York, in the spring of 2004. He lives in New York with his wife, Allison Hawke, and their two children.

Kelly J. S. McGovern

References

Lennon, Joseph. "McCann, Colum." In *Dictionary of Literary Biography, Volume 267: Twenty-First-Century British and Irish Novelists.* Detroit: Gale, 2002.

"McCann, Colum." In *Contemporary Authors: New Revision Series.* Vol. 99. Detroit: Gale, 2002.

McCann, Donal (1943–1999)

Born in Dublin, Donal McCann was the son of John J. McCann, who was a playwright and the lord mayor of Dublin on two occasions. He was educated at Terenure College, and while he was there he acted in a production of his father's play *Give Me a Bed of Roses.* He studied architecture before taking a position as a subeditor in the *Evening Press.* He also began to take classes at the Abbey School of Actors before joining the Abbey Players. His first major performances were in W. B. Yeats plays—*On Baile's Strand* and *Cathleen Ni Houlihan* in the Abbey Theatre. He soon became identified with roles in plays by Irish writers, especially the theatrical adaptation of Patrick Kavanagh's *Tarry Flynn,* Dion Bouccicault's *The Shaughran,* J. M. Synge's *Riders to the Sea,* and Oliver Goldsmith's *She Stoops to Conquer.* In 1969 he appeared in Samuel Beckett's *Waiting for Godot,* in which he played Estragon opposite Peter O'Toole as Vladimir. In 1981 he embarked on an American tour in Sean O'Casey's *The Shadow of a Gunman,* and in 1986 he played the part of Captain Boyle alongside Geraldine Plunkett as Juno and John Kavanagh as Joxer in the Gate Theatre's landmark production of Sean O'Casey's *Juno and the Paycock.*

Later he became associated with Brian Friel's work, particularly with the 1974 film version of *Philadelphia, Here I Come,* in which he played the public self of Gar, who is preparing to leave Ireland and emigrate to America. He also appeared in other Friel plays, such as *Translations* and *Wonderful Tennessee,* as well as giving a much praised performance in *Faith Healer* in the Abbey Theatre in 1980. His most celebrated role in the theater was in Sebastian Barry's play *The Steward of Christendom.* For his performance in the Royal Court in London he was awarded the London Critics' Circle Theatre Award (Drama Theatre) in 1995. The play later had a 12-week run at the Brooklyn Academy of Music. There, his performance was praised by the *New York Times,* which called him "an astonishing Irish actor . . . widely regarded as the finest of them all" and he was hailed by *Newsweek* as a "world-class star."

As well as working in the theatre, he played numerous roles in films, beginning with Disney's *The Fighting Prince of Donegal* (1966). He also starred in John Huston's *Sinful Davey* (1969), Neil Jordan's *Angel* (1982), and played the father of the title character in Pat O'Connor's *Cal* (1984). The film for which he is best remembered is the adaptation of James Joyce's short story *The Dead* (1987), which was directed by John Huston and in which he played the part of Gabriel Conroy with Anjelica Huston as his wife. He appeared in a television adaptation of Sean O'Casey's *The Silver Tassie,* as well as in Granada Television's *Who Bombed Birmingham?* One of his most celebrated performances was as Barney Mulhall in RTÉ's adaptation of James Plunkett's *Strumpet City* (1980). He appeared in Bob Quinn's Irish language film *Poitin* (1979) and later in his experimental drama *The Bishop's Story* (1995). In 1999 he was the subject of a documentary made by Quinn entitled *It Must Be Done Right,* which was broadcast on RTÉ. In 1997 he was awarded an honorary doctorate by Trinity College Dublin for his contribution to acting in Ireland. After battling both alcoholism and depression, he died of pancreatic cancer in 1999.

David Doyle

Reference

Laffan, Pat, and Faith O'Grady, eds. *Donal McCann Remembered.* Dublin: New Island, 2000.

McCarey, Leo (1898–1969)

Leo McCarey was one of American cinema's most distinguished film directors, a recipient of multiple Academy Awards for writing and directing, and the man credited with teaming Stan Laurel with Oliver Hardy. He was born in Los Angeles on October 3, 1898, the son of Thomas McCarey, a boxing promoter of Irish lineage, and Edna Mistral. He attended St Joseph's Catholic School and Los Angeles High School, before entering the University of Southern California to study law. Although he did practice briefly he was, on his own admission, a poor lawyer, telling Peter Bogdanovich in 1969 that "a discouraging factor in my legal career is that I lost every case."

In 1919 McCarey abandoned the legal profession to take up work in Universal studios, where he became third assistant to film director Tod Browning on *The Virgin of Stamboul.* In 1921 he made his debut as a film director with a film called *Society Secrets,* which was not well received. McCarey left Universal to work for Hal Roach who, along with Mack Sennett, was the leading producer of comedies in American cinema of the 1920s. McCarey initially worked as a gagman on the *Our Gang* comedies, before graduating to directing Charley Chase films beginning in 1924. It was during this time that he first worked with Oliver Hardy; three years later he made the highly successful decision to team Hardy with Stan Laurel and, by his own estimate, he directed or supervised at least 100 films featuring the pair.

In 1930, he left the Hal Roach studios and, after some work with Fox studios and the independent producer Samuel Goldwyn, he signed with Paramount. Here his experience as a comedy director proved essential: his initial assignments saw him direct the Marx Brothers (*Duck Soup,* 1933), Mae West (*Belle of the Nineties,* 1934), W. C. Fields (*Six of a Kind,* 1934), and Harold Lloyd (*The Milky Way,* 1937).

By the end of the 1930s, McCarey had established himself as one of American cinema's most distinguished writer-directors. Although he is traditionally associated with comedies, including the classic screwball comedy, *The Awful Truth* (1937), his versatility can be seen in his bittersweet 1937 drama about aging, *Make Way for Tomorrow,* and in the classic melodrama, *Love Affair* (which he remade in 1957 as *An Affair to Remember*). McCarey always excelled at directing actors, and his work with stars such as Cary Grant and Irene Dunne proved seminal in the development of their careers.

McCarey's Catholic faith found expression in a duo of films that he made in the 1940s: *Going My Way* (1944) and *The Bells of St. Mary's* (1945) cast Bing Crosby as a Catholic priest, and the successful fusion of humor and sentiment ensured the films' success at the box office.

McCarey, always a political conservative, became increasingly right wing in the later 1940s, and in 1952 he directed the red-baiting *My Son John,* which featured the last performance of Robert Walker (who died before the film's completion). McCarey's later career seems to have been beset by a number of personal and professional problems, and he directed his last film, *Satan Never Sleeps,* in 1962.

McCarey died of emphysema in Los Angeles on July 5, 1969. He was survived by his wife, Stella, whom he married in 1920, and their daughter, Mary Virginia.

Gwenda Young

See also: CROSBY, Bing

References

Bogdanovich, Peter. "Interview with Leo McCarey." In *Who the Devil Made It: Conversations with Legendary Film Directors.* New York: Ballantine, 1997.

Poague, Leland. "Leo McCarey." In *Hollywood Professionals.* Vol. 7. New York: A. S. Barnes, 1980.

Wood, Robin. "Leo McCarey." In *Cinema: A Critical Dictionary,* edited by Richard Roud. Vol 2. New York: Secker and Warburg, 1978.

McCARTHY, JOSEPH (1908–1957)

Born to a poor Irish farm family in Appleton, Wisconsin, Joseph McCarthy was a hyperactive, extroverted youth who dropped out of school after eighth grade to start his own poultry business. After the chickens all died, he enrolled in the local public high school. Thanks to enormous energy and a retentive mind, he finished his coursework in less than a year at age 20. After two undergraduate years at Marquette University, a leading Jesuit school in Milwaukee, McCarthy entered Marquette Law School, acquiring the rudiments of the profession as he knit together a statewide network among Irish and German Catholics. McCarthy was a practicing Catholic his entire life but rarely referred to religion or ethnicity in his speeches. He actively supported President Franklin Roosevelt in the Young Democrats, but he did not join Irish organizations. Although he was defeated in his 1936 race for district attorney, McCarthy displayed remarkable campaign abilities and an astonishing memory for faces. He had the energy and determination to meet every voter in person, exuding charm and a concern for each voter as an individual. The same tactics paid off in 1939, when he was successful in a nonpartisan contest for a regional judgeship.

In 1942, McCarthy volunteered for the Marine Corps (as a judge he was draft exempt), becoming an intelligence officer in an aviation unit heavily engaged in combat in the South Pacific. Although assigned a desk job, McCarthy flew numerous combat missions as a tail gunner—he exaggerated the number to qualify for a Distinguished Flying Cross. McCarthy had his name entered in the Republican primary for U.S. Senate in 1944, opposing a well-entrenched incumbent. The absentee war hero ran a strong second, making a name for himself statewide. Why McCarthy suddenly changed parties was never explained, but prospects for ambitious Wisconsin politicians were dim inside the poorly organized Democratic party, for most New Dealers supported the state's Progressive Party. During the war, however, the Progressive Party collapsed, torn apart between its New Deal domestic liberalism and its intensely isolationist opposition to Roosevelt's foreign policy. Increasingly out of touch with Wisconsin, its leader, Robert LaFollette, Jr., looked to his family's past glories and made the blunder of trying for reelection to the Senate in 1946 as a Republican. "Tail Gunner Joe," who endlessly crisscrossed the state while his opponent stayed in Washington, offered an alternative in the Republican primary to old-guard Republicans who had opposed the Lafollettes for a half century. McCarthy brilliantly captured the frustrations citizens felt about massive strikes, unstable economy, price controls, severe shortages of housing and meat, and the growing threat from the far left. He narrowly defeated LaFollette in the primary. The slogan "Had Enough?—Vote Republican" gave the Republicans a landslide victory all across the state, electing a new junior senator from Wisconsin.

In Washington, McCarthy was a mainstream conservative in domestic policy, and, like many veterans, was an internationalist in foreign affairs, supporting the Marshall Plan and the North Atlantic Treaty Organization. His speeches rarely mentioned domestic communism or flaming issues like the Alger Hiss espionage case, but that suddenly changed in early 1950 when his vivid anticommunist rhetoric drew national attention. Alleging there were many card-carrying communists in Truman's State Department, McCarthy forced a Senate investigation led by Millard Tydings, Democrat of Maryland. McCarthy named numerous suspect diplomats but failed to convince the three Democrats on the panel; they concluded his allegations were "a fraud and a hoax," while the two Republicans dissented. McCarthy retaliated by campaigning against Tydings, who was defeated for reelection in November 1950. What the senator himself called McCarthyism was a factor in key races across the country; all of the McCarthy-supported candidates won, and his stock soared. A few weeks later American forces were crushed by the Chinese in Korea, and in the spring of 1951 Truman tried to shift the blame by firing General Douglas MacArthur. McCarthy now became the dominant figure in American politics, with strong support among both Republicans and Catholic Democrats, as he alleged that Truman's top people had betrayed America. He singled out Secretary of State Dean Acheson and Secretary of Defense George Marshall. Liberals were aghast; Truman had picked General Marshall to head the defense department precisely because he thought the elderly statesman would always be above criticism, no matter that China turned from a staunch ally to a bitter enemy on his watch. McCarthy's blistering attacks on Marshall as "part of a conspiracy so immense, an infamy so black, as to dwarf any in the history of man" fueled the belief McCarthy was a wild man, a pathological liar who overstepped the bounds of political discourse.

With Eisenhower crusading against "Korea, Communism and Corruption" in the 1952 presidential campaign, Republican victory was ensured. As a senior member of the majority party McCarthy for the first time became a committee chairman, with control of staffing and agenda. He used his Government Operations Committee to open highly publicized hearings in 1953–1954 alleging disloyalty in the State Department, the Central Intelligence Agency, the U.S. Information Agency, and finally the Army. His furious attacks on the Army led to the televised "Army-McCarthy" hearings in spring 1954, which exposed his bullying tactics to a national audience. As McCarthy's poll rating plunged, his enemies finally pulled together to introduce a censure resolution focused on McCarthy's contempt for the federal government and especially for his fellow senators.

McCarthy's charges that overeducated liberals tolerated Communism at home and abroad had baffled the liberals. He alleged that they had corruptly sold out the national interest to protect their upper-class privileges and were so idealistic about world affairs that they radically underestimated the threat posed by Stalin, his spies, and the worldwide Communist movement. Instead of refuting the allegations, liberals tried one of two approaches. Some became intensely anticommunist and claimed they were more effective than McCarthy and the Republicans in eliminating communism in the unions and Democratic Party and containing the Stalinist menace in Europe. The other approach was to counterattack, to charge that "McCarthyism" had never found a single spy but had only hurt innocent people in hunting for nonexistent witches; thus, it represented an evil betrayal of American values. In an appeal to upscale conservatives and liberal intellectuals, critics ignored the Communist infiltration of labor unions and liberal causes and focused on stereotyping anticommunists as ill-mannered ignorant troglodytes, oblivious to American traditions of free speech and free association. McCarthy's exaggerations and false charges encouraged opponents to stress the second approach, but it escalated the controversy to a pitch of hatreds and fears unprecedented since the days of reconstruction. McCarthy's superb sense of timing and his media instincts kept his partisan attacks on the front page every day; his willingness to do battle in the election campaigns with Democratic opponents across the country strengthened his base in the Republican Party. His religion and ethnicity, refreshed with highly visible friendships with leading Irish Catholics, especially the Kennedy family, bolstered his standing among Democrats.

According to Gallup polls, McCarthy's popularity crested in January 1954. His core support came from Republicans and Catholics who had not attended college. McCarthy, however, failed to create any sort of grassroots organization. He had no organizational skills; he did not effectively use his talented staffers (such as Robert Kennedy). He was a loner who lurched from issue to issue, misled by the enormous media publicity into believing a one-man crusade was possible in a complex society honeycombed with local, regional, and national organizations. By operating within the Republican Party apparatus he lost the opportunity to create an independent grassroots political crusade in the style of Teddy Roosevelt, Huey Long, or Ross Perot. He never launched his own magazine or radio show, nor did he form alliances with publishers who agreed with him. McCarthy's strained relations with Senate colleagues created a trapdoor. It was sprung after many Republicans realized that he had shifted the attack away from the Democrats. What use was his slogan "20 Years of Treason" once Eisenhower was in office? McCarthy's answer was "21 Years of Treason!" Eisenhower's supporters could no longer tolerate such a loose cannon, and as McCarthy unwisely shifted his attacks to Eisenhower's beloved army, his cause was doomed. Although many Americans distrusted Ivy League, "striped pants" diplomats, soldiers were held in high regard; McCarthy's charges of subversion were flimsy (one communist dentist had been automatically promoted); he sabotaged his own reputation by finagling favors for an aide who had been drafted. The televised hearings proved fatal to an ill-prepared bully. After the Democrats regained control of Congress in 1954 the censure motion carried, 67–22. McCarthy's appeal, so widespread yet superficial, evaporated overnight and the senator faded into the shadows.

Richard Jensen

See also: KENNEDY FAMILY

References

Crosby, Donald F. *God, Church and Flag: Senator Joseph R. McCarthy and the Catholic Church, 1950–1957.* Chapel Hill: University of North Carolina Press, 1978.

Herman, Arthur. *Joseph McCarthy: Reexamining the Life and Legacy of America's Most Hated Senator.* New York: Free Press, 2000.

Reeves, Thomas C. *The Life and Times of Joe McCarthy: A Biography.* New York: Stein and Day, 1982.

McCARTHY, JOSEPH VINCENT "JOE" (1887–1978)

Joe McCarthy, the son of Benjamin McCarthy and Susan Connolly Bradley, was born in Germantown, Pennsylvania.

McCarthy played college baseball at Niagara University in 1905 and 1906, before beginning his professional career. He played for Wilmington of the Class B Tri-State League in 1907, moving up to Toledo of the American Association in 1908. He played various infield and outfield positions, but spent most of his time at second base. By his own admission, he was a mediocre player, wielding a more powerful glove than bat. McCarthy joined his last team, Louisville of the American Association, in 1916. He became the player-manager in 1919 and ended his playing career in 1921, after an on-field collision. The closest he came to playing in the majors was in 1916, when he signed with Brooklyn of the Federal League. The league collapsed before the season began.

As manager, McCarthy led Louisville to the pennant in 1921 and again in 1925. The second pennant brought him to the attention of Cubs owner William Wrigley, who hired McCarthy for the 1926 season. The Cubs finished fourth in 1926 and 1927, rising to third in 1928. McCarthy promised a pennant if the Cubs obtained second baseman Rogers Hornsby from the Boston Braves. The Cubs made the trade and won their first pennant since 1918, but lost the World Series in five games to the Philadelphia Athletics. The Cubs faltered slightly the next year, and McCarthy was fired toward the end of the season with the club in second place.

In 1931, Yankees owner Jacob Ruppert hired McCarthy. McCarthy led them to the World Series in 1932, culminating in a four-game sweep of the Cubs. It was their last championship of the Babe Ruth era. The Yankees released Ruth in February 1935, leaving McCarthy as the undisputed leader of the team. Beginning in 1936, McCarthy's Yankees dominated the baseball world in a way not seen again until the 1950s. Between 1936 and 1943 the Yankees won the pennant every year but 1940, finishing behind Detroit and Cleveland. Of those eight World Series, the Yankees won seven, only losing to the Cardinals in 1942, in five games. The Yankees needed six games to dispatch the Dodgers in 1941, but needed no more than five games in the other six. The Yankees, like every other team, lost stars to military service during World War II and finished third in 1944 and fourth in 1945, McCarthy's worst year as Yankees' manager. Illness aggravated by drinking and interference from the front office led McCarthy to resign at the start of the 1946 season.

In 1948, McCarthy replaced Joe Cronin as manager of the Red Sox. He came within one game of first place in each of his two full seasons. The Red Sox and the Indians tied in 1948, but Cleveland won a one-game playoff to win the pennant. McCarthy started journeyman Denny Galehouse in the game, defending the move on the grounds that no other pitcher was available. In 1949 the Yankees defeated the Red Sox in the last two games of the season to win the pennant. After a mediocre start in 1950, McCarthy retired for good.

A Chicago sportswriter gave McCarthy the nickname "Marse Joe," noting McCarthy's reputation as a taskmaster. McCarthy did not hesitate to crack the whip or get rid of players. In 1926 he had the Cubs trade future Hall of Famer Grover Cleveland Alexander because McCarthy concluded the pitcher was a troublemaker. McCarthy's first action in the Yankee clubhouse in 1931 was to have a card table chopped up and hauled away in full view of the players. He may be considered the father of the idea of "Yankee pride." He got along with anyone who played hard. As Cubs manager, McCarthy got the most out of the talented but heavy-drinking outfielder Hack Wilson. McCarthy's tensions with Babe Ruth came not from Ruth's off-field antics, which McCarthy ignored, but from Ruth's unfulfilled desire to manage the Yankees. McCarthy was famous for requiring players to wear neckties in public. Ted Williams was equally famous for refusing to wear neckties. To defuse a potential conflict, McCarthy came to spring training in 1948 wearing an open-collared shirt with no necktie.

McCarthy ended his career with a winning percentage of .615, the highest of all time. In 1957 he was elected to the Hall of Fame, the first manager to be elected without any major league playing experience.

Robert Smith

See also: BASEBALL; BASEBALL MANAGERS, IRISH-AMERICAN

References

Graham, Frank. *The New York Yankees: An Informal History*. New York: G. P. Putnam's Sons, 1943.

Honig, Donald. *The Man in the Dugout*. Chicago: Follett Publishing Co., 1977.

McCarthy, Mary (1912–1989)

Mary McCarthy was born in Seattle, Washington, into a privileged family of Irish Catholic, New England Protestant, and Jewish descent. When she was six years old her parents died of Spanish influenza. For the next five years Mary and her three younger brothers were raised in Minneapolis by her aunt and her husband, where they were treated harshly and subject to frequent

Portrait of Mary McCarthy, author of Memories of a Catholic Girlhood *and* The Group. *(Library of Congress)*

physical abuse. When Mary was still in school she won a state essay contest, including $25 in prize money, for her essay "The Irish in America." When her treatment at the hands of her aunt and uncle became intolerable, she was taken in by her maternal grandparents, who sent her to Annie Wright Seminary in Tacoma. McCarthy credited her grandfather, a lawyer from Seattle, with the liberal views she later espoused in her writings. The events of her childhood were explored in her best-selling memoir, *Memories of a Catholic Girlhood* (1957). She attended Vassar College where she majored in English before graduating as a Phi Beta Kappa in 1933. Vassar was the setting for her hugely successful novel, *The Group* (1963), which dealt with eight female graduates and their subsequent lives in 1930s America. The book remained on the *New York Times* best-seller list for almost two years and was later adapted as a movie of the same name.

In the same year McCarthy graduated from Vassar she married Harold Johnsrud. She also began to review novels for *The Nation* and *The New Republic.* By 1936 she had divorced Johnsrud and moved to Greenwich Village in New York City, where she became active on the American left, mingling with Dwight McDonald, Fred Dupee, William Phillips, and other anti-Stalinist writers associated with *Partisan Review.* She became the drama critic for *Partisan Review,* a position she held from 1938 until 1962, and she lived with the periodical's editor Philip Rahv. McCarthy. She married the writer Edmund Wilson in 1938, and he encouraged her to write fiction. Later that same year she gave birth to her only child, a son named Ruel. Her first stories appeared in publications such as *Harper's Bazaar* and *Partisan Review.* Her debut novel, *The Company She Keeps* (1942), was a collection of loosely connected stories that depicted a group of New York intellectuals in the late 1930s. In 1946, while teaching at Bard College, she divorced Wilson and married Bowden Broadwater. They were married until 1960, during which time they traveled to Europe together. This period was one of McCarthy's most productive, during which she published some of her most important work. She also taught at Sarah Lawrence College and won two Guggenheim Awards in 1949 and 1959.

After World War II, McCarthy opposed both the Stalinism of Russian communism and the anticommunism of McCarthyism, and she became known as one of the most prominent liberal intellectual voices in postwar America. She married her fourth husband, James Raymond, in 1962, and they spent most of their time living in Paris. In 1968 she went to Hanoi to write about the Vietnam War for the *New York Review of Books.* Her writings on the war were published as *Report from Vietnam* (1967) and *Hanoi* (1968). She also wrote about Watergate, publishing *The Mask of State: Watergate Portraits* (1974). She enjoyed a particularly warm relationship with Hannah Arendt, and their correspondence was later published. Her final novel, *Cannibals and Christians* (1979), explored the psychology of terrorism.

Late in life McCarthy was touched by scandal when, as a guest on the *Dick Cavett Show* on television, she accused the writer Lillian Hellman of lying, saying "every word she writes is a lie, including 'and' and 'the.'" Hellmann filed a $2.5 million lawsuit against McCarthy but died before the case came to trial.

McCarthy was a member of the National Institute of Arts and Letters, and she won the National Medal for Literature, the Edward MacDowell Medal, and the first Rochester Literary Award. McCarthy died of lung cancer in New York City on October 25, 1989, and she is buried in Castine, Maine, where she and her fourth husband had a summer vacation home.

David Doyle

References

Brightman, Carol. *Writing Dangerously: Mary McCarthy and Her World.* San Diego: Harcourt Brace, 1994.

Gelderman, Carol, ed. *Conversations with Mary McCarthy.* Jackson: University Press of Mississippi, 1991.

Gelderman, Carol. *Mary McCarthy: A Life.* New York: St. Martin's Press, 1988.

Kiernan, Frances. *Seeing Mary Plain: A Life of Mary McCarthy.* New York: W. W. Norton & Co., 2000.

McCarthy, Patrick "Paddy" (1871–1963)

A professional boxer, soccer player, and pioneer athletics coach in Argentina, Patrick McCarthy, kown as "Paddy," was born on March 17, 1871, in Cashel, Co. Tipperary, where he studied with the Christian Brothers and obtained sound marks in swimming and other sports. He arrived in Buenos Aires in 1900 to teach English and athletic activities in the Escuela Superior de Comercio, directed by Co. Clare–born James FitzSimons (1849–1944).

McCarthy coached professional and amateur boxers at the Boxing Club of Buenos Aires in Florida. The activity was still unlawful, but he managed to train and hire several professionals. Sparring amateur boxers were recruited among sailors on call in Buenos Aires, who were invited to boxing festivals by the Reverend Henry Brady, assistant chaplain in Saint John the Baptist Anglican church, who was responsible for the Missions to Seamen in the port of Buenos Aires.

The first professional boxing match in Argentina was fought on October 9, 1903, by Paddy McCarthy and the Italian Abelardo Robassio. The match to finish—with no preset number of rounds—was organized by *El Gladiador* magazine in their rooms. Carlos Delcasse was the referee, and the chief of police, Francisco Beazley, acted as timekeeper (though boxing was still banned). Paddy won the match by knockout in the fourth round, collecting the gate money, a record $500. McCarthy abandoned boxing because of family reasons, but he was appointed member of the sports municipal committee in Buenos Aires together with James FitzSimons's son Juan and others.

McCarthy began playing soccer in Argentina with several Irish Argentines in Lobos Athletic Club. When some players joined those of Lanús Athletic Club to form the team of the English High School, McCarthy left and joined Club Atlético Estudiantes. He also played in Central Athletic Club, a small institution in the port of Buenos Aires. In 1904 McCarthy was hired by Club Atlético Gimnasia y Esgrima of Buenos Aires to train its players. He was also coach of Boca Juniors, and referee of the Argentine Association Football League for 18 years.

Soccer and boxing were some of the athletic activities of the upper classes of Buenos Aires and other Argentine cities. They were considered restricted to men and perceived as manly activities. Although in the beginning these activities were limited to the English-speaking community, by the time McCarthy and other professional players and trainers were active in Argentina, members of the local elite were actively involved in these sports. McCarthy not only taught hundreds of Argentines the techniques and rules of these and other athletic activities, but he also helped to popularize these sports among humbler children in the first decades of the twentieth century through his job in the Dirección de Deportes of Buenos Aires municipality. McCarthy retired in 1943 and died on August 10, 1963, at the British Hospital of Buenos Aires; he is buried in Chacarita cemetery.

Edmundo Murray

See also: SOCCER, EARLY ARGENTINE

Reference

Raffo, Víctor. *El Origen Británico del Deporte Argentino: Atletismo, Cricket, Fútbol, Polo, Remo y Rugby Durante las Presidencias de Mitre, Sarmiento y Avellaneda.* Buenos Aires: Author's Edition, 2004.

McCormack, John (1884–1945)

John Francis McCormack was born in Athlone, Ireland, in 1884. His interest in singing was evident from a very young age. In 1903, he was offered a salaried position in the Palestrina Choir of the Pro-Cathedral in Dublin. The choir was directed by Vincent O'Brien, who recognized McCormack's potential immediately. O'Brien encouraged him to enter the Irish National Music Festival, the Feis Ceoil, in 1903. With very little formal training, McCormack won the gold medal in the tenor competition. This commendation was a turning point for McCormack, and he began to give recitals in different parts of Ireland. In 1904, McCormack also began to make some recordings. Realizing that he would benefit from further training, he began to save up until he could go to Milan, Italy, to study under Vincenzo Sabatini. With Sabatini's encouragement, McCormack made his operatic debut in 1906, singing under the pseudonym Giovanni Foli (the pseudonym being a marketing ploy). In 1906, he went to live in London, seeking opportunities to sing professionally. He signed a recording contract with Odeon and played a number of minor operatic roles. His breakthrough came in 1907, when he met Albert Vesetti, a professor of singing at the Royal College of Music. In 1907, he made his debut at Covent Garden. At age 23, he was the youngest principal tenor ever to sing there. By 1910, he was singing opera in the United States. He also began a career on the recital stage that would make him one of the most successful singers of all time. Between 1914 and 1919, McCormack gave more than 400 concerts in the United States. During World War I, he toured widely on behalf of the Red Cross. He also performed for servicemen at military bases and hospitals. In 1919, he became a citizen of the United States.

Portrait of world-famous Irish tenor John McCormack. (Library of Congress)

At the end of the war, McCormack began to tour Europe again. After a series of concerts and operatic appearances in the early 1920s, McCormack achieved celebrity status. He continued to tour widely but returned to New York regularly. He also continued to record. In addition, he began to broadcast regularly on the radio in the United States. He continued to perform for a number of charitable organizations, paying particular attention to Catholic charities, and he made a point of including religious music in his recitals whenever he could. The Church bestowed a number of honors on McCarthy in recognition of his contributions. In 1928, the pope made him a count of the Holy Roman Empire, a title of which McCormack was very proud. In 1930, he starred in a musical film, *Song o' My Heart.* He became a Hollywood celebrity after the film was released. Tired of the onerous touring, by 1936 McCormack was ready for a change. He gave his last concerts in the United States during 1937, although he continued to make radio broadcasts throughout 1938. He moved to London in 1938 to be nearer to his family. His farewell tour of Ireland and the United Kingdom took place at the end of that year, culminating with an appearance in London's Albert Hall. With the outbreak of World War II, McCormack resumed his charitable work. From 1939 to early 1942, he toured on behalf of the Red Cross. He also made regular broadcasts for the BBC. His activities on behalf of the war effort greatly endeared him to the British public. Ill health forced him to retire in 1943, and he died in 1945.

Aoileann Ní Eigeartaigh

References

Boylan, Henry. *A Dictionary of Irish Biography.* Dublin: Gill and Macmillan, 1998.
Lalor, Brian, ed. *The Encyclopaedia of Ireland.* Dublin: Gill and Macmillan Ltd., 2003.
McRedmond, Louis, ed. *Modern Irish Lives.* Dublin: Gill and Macmillan Ltd., 1996.
Randel, Don Michael, ed. *The Harvard Biographical Dictionary of Music.* Cambridge, MA: The Belknap Press of Harvard University Press, 1996.

McCourt, Frank (1930–)

Frank McCourt was born in 1930, in Brooklyn, New York. He was the first of seven children of immigrant parents. In 1934, unable to find work in the depths of the Depression, the family decided to leave New York and return to their native Ireland. They settled in Limerick in southwest Ireland. McCourt's father, an alcoholic, was unable to hold down a job. He eventually abandoned the family, leaving them penniless. Three of the seven children died of poverty-related diseases. Frank McCourt himself contracted tuberculosis at the age of 10 and spent a number of months in a sanatorium. He left school at the age of 13 and worked at various menial jobs until he had saved enough money to return to New York when he was 19. McCourt was drafted into the U.S. Army at the start of the Korean War and spent the war stationed in Germany. At the end of his tour of duty, he took advantage of the GI Bill to go to New York University—in spite of failing to complete his secondary education. After graduation, he went to work for the New York City public school system, and spent almost 30 years teaching creative writing in a number of schools. After his retirement, McCourt worked on his own memoirs. *Angela's Ashes* was published in 1996 and spent 117 weeks on the *New York Times* best-seller list. It was awarded the National Book Critics Circle Award in Biography/Autobiography (1996), the Los Angeles Times Book Award (1996), the ABBY Award (1997), and the Pulitzer Prize for Biography (1997). *Time Magazine* and *Newsweek* chose *Angela's Ashes* as the best nonfiction book of 1996. The second volume of McCourt's memoir's, *'Tis,* was published in 2000. It was also a best seller. The film of *Angela's Ashes,* directed by Alan Parker, was released in 1999. McCourt provided a voiceover for much of the film. McCourt's 2005 book *Teacher Man,* describes his experiences as a teacher in New York schools.

Aoileann Ní Eigeartaigh

Reference

Lalor, Brian, ed. *The Encyclopaedia of Ireland.* Dublin: Gill and Macmillan Ltd., 2003.

McDermott, Alice (1953–)

Alice McDermott was born on June 27, 1953, in Brooklyn, New York. Inspired by her childhood on New York's Long Island, most of McDermott's works explore the complex lives of characters within tight-knit Irish-American communities. Of her frequent choice of subject matter, McDermott has said, "Being Irish-American myself, Irish-American material is readily at hand to me. I know Irish-American people."

McDermott's writing has garnered both popular success and critical acclaim. Critics have especially praised her rich prose style and keenly observed characters. In 1978, McDermott's first published stories appeared in *Ms.* and *Seventeen* magazines. Her first novel, *A Bigamist's Daughter* (1982), was widely acclaimed. *That Night* (1987), her second book, was a finalist for the Pulitzer Prize, the National Book Award, and the *Los Angeles Times* Book Prize. *At Weddings and Wakes* (1992), her third novel, was a *New York Times* best-seller. McDermott won the National Book Award for her fourth novel, *Charming Billy* (1998), with its tragic tale of the alcoholic Billy Lynch. Her most recent novel (2006) is *After This.*

McDermott received her BA in 1975 from the State University of New York at Oswego, and her MA in 1978 from the University of New Hampshire. She has taught at the University of California at San Diego, American University, and the University of New Hampshire. She also has been a writer-in-residence at Lynchburg and Hollins colleges in Virginia. McDermott currently resides in Bethesda, Maryland, and is a writer-in-residence at Johns Hopkins University.

Danielle Maze

Reference

Fanning, Charles. *The Irish Voice in America: 250 Years of Irish-American Fiction.* 2nd ed. Lexington: University Press of Kentucky, 2000.

McDonald, Richard "Dick" (1909–1998)

Born in New Hampshire to Patrick and Margaret McDonald, both of whom were Irish immigrants, Dick McDonald attended Manchester High School West before moving to California. There, he and his brother Maurice "Mac," opened a hot dog stand near the Santa Anita racetrack in Arcadia in 1937. The business prospered, and the brothers decided to open a drive-in barbecue restaurant in San Bernardino in 1940. Realizing that the majority of their sales were hamburgers, they decided to focus on this aspect of the restaurant's business. In December 1948 they opened a hamburger restaurant that they named McDonald's; it was one of the first of the new breed of fast-food restaurants that began to appear in the United States after World War II. In many ways, the success story that later became McDonald's represents the postwar economic boom in America. The restaurant offered cheap food in an environment that was easily accessible and family friendly. The brothers also developed the concept of a self-service, high-volume, drive-in restaurant. The menu was fixed and consisted of 15¢ hamburgers, 19¢ cheeseburgers, 20¢ malts, and 10¢ French fries.

Dick designed the Golden Arches logo and the red and white tiles for which McDonald's later became famous. He also devised the "Millions Served" signs outside the restaurant. While he focused on the marketing of the restaurant, his brother was in charge of the day-to-day running of the restaurant. In 1952 the success of the brothers' restaurant led to their being featured on the cover of *American Restaurant* magazine. Soon after, they proceeded to franchise eight of the restaurants. In 1955, Ray Kroc, a salesman who owned the rights to the mixers the brothers used to make the milkshakes, was granted the exclusive rights to develop the McDonald's franchise in the United States. He formed McDonald's System Inc., and in the same year he opened his first franchise and the ninth restaurant altogether, in Des Plaines, Illinois. In 1961, Dick and Mac sold their rights in the business to Ray Kroc for $2.7 million. Dick retired to live in New Bedford, New Hampshire, and his brother Mac died in 1971.

In Kroc's biography, *Grinding It Out: The Making of McDonald's,* he traced the origins of the fast-food giant to his takeover of the company. Later, however, he would come to an agreement with Dick McDonald in which he acknowledged the contribution Dick and his brother had made to the global franchise.

Today McDonald's has more than 23,000 restaurants and 4,500 franchisees in more than 111 countries. The first branch of the McDonald's franchise opened in Dick and Mac McDonald's ancestral home of Ireland in May 1977. In 1984, Dick, who had grilled the first hamburger in the restaurant in San Bernardino, was served the 50 billionth hamburger by Ed Rensi, the president of McDonald's USA, in a public ceremony in New York City. In 1992 he attended a ceremony where a plaque was unveiled at the site of the original McDonald's restaurant at 14th and E Street in San Bernardino. Dick McDonald died in Manchester, New Hampshire, on July 14, 1998.

David Doyle

References

Halberstam, David. *The Fifties.* New York: Villard Books, 1993.

Harrell, Joy. "Richard McDonald." In *The Encyclopedia of the Irish in America,* edited by Michael Glazier. Notre Dame, IN: University of Notre Dame Press, 1999.

Kroc, Ray. *Grinding it Out: The Making of McDonald's.* Chicago: H. Regnery, 1977.

McEnroe, John (1959–)

John Patrick McEnroe, Jr., was born in Wiesbaden, Hessen, Germany, on February 16, 1959, where his father was stationed while serving with the Air Force. Before McEnroe's first birthday the family returned to the United States, eventually settling in Douglaston, New York. In 1977, McEnroe shot to worldwide prominence when at the age of 18 he became the youngest player and the first qualifier to reach a Wimbledon semifinal, where he was beaten by Jimmy Connors. In 1978, McEnroe attended Stanford University, where he led the team to an NCAA (National Collegiate Athletic Association) title and won the men's singles.

Although he was born in Germany, McEnroe is of Irish Catholic descent, and his fiery antics on the court were sometimes attributed—especially in the British press—to his Irish ancestry. In 1979, McEnroe won his first of four U.S. Open Titles, beating Vitas Gerulaitis in straight sets. However McEnroe's talent was quickly ignored, in particular by the British tabloid press, which labeled him "Superbrat" and concentrated on his on-court antics rather than his talent as a player. His temper, emotional outbursts, and the constant comparisons and competition between him and the calmer, crowd-pleasing Björn Borg meant that when McEnroe did beat Borg and win Wimbledon for the first time in 1981, he was the first player in history not granted honorary membership to the All-England Club. During this tournament he was fined by the All-England Club, and it was here that he used the phrase "you cannot be serious" for the first time when he disagreed with an umpire's decision. McEnroe's response was his refusal to attend the champion's dinner the same night. McEnroe won Wimbledon twice more for a total of three times, and he appeared in two other singles finals: in 1979 he was beaten by Borg and in 1982 he was beaten by Jimmy Connors. He was eventually granted membership.

McEnroe's combination of shots and volleying skills continued to be masked by his volatile makeup, which resulted in outbursts and temper tantrums on court. McEnroe's temper also meant that he failed to get many of the lucrative endorsement contracts that other players of his generation obtained. Yet he was one of the first sports professionals to sign a deal with Nike. By the time McEnroe retired in 1992 he had won 77 singles titles, including 17 Grand slams—nine in men's doubles and one in mixed doubles. He also helped the United States to five Davis Cup wins, and became the then-youngest player to be ranked number one. McEnroe has been married twice, the first time to actress Tatum O'Neal in 1986 (daughter of actor Ryan O'Neal). They had three children before they divorced in 1994. In 1997 he married the singer Patty Smyth, and they have two children. McEnroe is also stepfather to Patty's daughter.

Since retiring, McEnroe has been recognized for his unique blend of talents: in 1996 he was named Father of the Year by the National Father's Day committee, and in 1999 his name was enshrined in the Tennis Hall of Fame in Rhode Island. McEnroe has continued to work in the world of sports. He managed the U.S. Davis Cup team for 14 months in 1999–2000, he works as a television commentator for major tennis events, and in 2003 he published his autobiography, *You Cannot Be Serious.*

Brid Nicholson

Reference

Harbridge, John. *Please Play On: A Biography of John McEnroe.* London: Central Publishing, 2001.

McGEE, THOMAS D'ARCY (1825–1868)

Thomas D'Arcy McGee was known as an ardent supporter of Irish republicanism in his youth, an agitator for better treatment of Irish immigrants to North America, and a founding figure and visionary of Canadian Confederation. His changed views regarding Irish republicanism in later life resulted in his assassination in 1868.

McGee was born in Carlingford, Co. Louth, on April 13, 1825 to James McGee and Dorcas Catherine Morgan. His family moved to Wexford when he was a child. In 1842, at the age of 17, McGee went to the United States. A speech he made soon after at Providence, Rhode Island, on the repeal of the Union between England and Ireland, brought him an offer to join the staff of the *Boston Pilot,* a Catholic newspaper. His editorial and other contributions to the paper and his public addresses gained the attention of the famed Irish revolutionary leader Daniel O'Connell, who called them "the inspired utterances of a young exiled Irish boy in America." When he was only 19 years old, McGee became the *Pilot's* editor, using his position to lobby for Irish independence from Great Britain and the rights of Irish Catholic immigrants in the United States. He also supported the American annexation of Canada.

The young McGee was also a prolific poet and historian. Most of his poems, such as "Home Sonnets Addressed to Ireland," treat subjects such as Irish independence, Irish patriotism, and emigration. His historical works include *Irish Writers of the Seventeenth Century* (1846), *History of the Irish Settlers in North America* (1854), *History of the Attempt to Establish the Protestant Reformation in Ireland* (1853), *Catholic History of North America* (1854), and *History of Ireland* (1862).

In 1845 McGee returned to Ireland, where he worked at the *Freeman's Journal.* In 1847 he married Mary Teresa Caffrey in Dublin. He became involved in the Young Ireland movement, serving as secretary of the Irish Confederation, and was arrested and imprisoned for a short time for one of his political speeches. When the British government began to suppress the movement and to arrest its leaders, McGee escaped to the United States disguised as a priest. In New York he started a paper called *The Nation* but soon had a run-in with the local bishop over his violent revolutionary ideas and diatribes against the Catholic priesthood in their relation to Irish politics. Changing the name of the paper to *The American Celt,* he moved to Boston, then to Buffalo, and finally back to New York City. In 1857, McGee moved to Montreal, Canada, at the invitation of the local Irish community.

McGee's attitudes toward Canada had changed by the time he came to Montreal. He no longer supported American annexation, and in fact he urged new Irish immigrants to choose Canada over the United States. In Montreal, McGee became editor of the *New Era,* which he used to discuss Irish politics and the future of Canada. McGee's editorship of the *New Era* was a springboard for his start in Canadian politics. In December 1857, he was elected to the Legislative Assembly of the Province of Canada, in which his ability as a speaker put him at once in the front rank. His political views changed radically during this time; as he advanced in official prominence, he advocated British supremacy as loyally as he had formerly promoted the revolutionary doctrines of his youth. The Confederation of the British colonies of North America as the Dominion of Canada in 1867 was due largely to McGee's initiative. He also supported issues such as constructing a railroad and creating a province for Canada's Indian tribes.

As he grew older, McGee's views on Irish republicanism also altered, and he became vehemently opposed to it. His outspoken criticism of the Irish independence movement and Irish republicanism alienated many in the Irish community, in Canada and elsewhere. McGee's religious views changed, too, and he became a devout Catholic.

By 1866, McGee was planning to leave politics for a job in the civil service. On April 7, 1868, he attended a late-night session in the Canadian House of Commons in Ottawa, where he gave a passionate speech in favor of national unity. Returning home, he was shot and killed as he entered his rooming house. It is generally believed McGee was killed for his anti-Republican views. However, although Patrick James Whelan was convicted and hanged for

McGee's murder, the prosecutor never accused Whelan of being an Irish Republican. McGee was given a state funeral.

See also: O'CONNELL, Daniel

Danielle Maze

References

Burns, Robin G. "McGee, Thomas D'Arcy." In *Dictionary of Canadian Biography,* edited by Frances G. Halpenny. Vol. 9. Toronto: University of Toronto Press, 1976: 489–494.

McGee, Thomas D'Arcy. *The Poems of Thomas D'Arcy McGee,* edited by James Sadlier. London: D. & J. Sadlier, 1869.

McGINLEY, PHYLLIS LOUISE (1905–1978)

A prolific, Pulitzer Prize–winning author of light verse, essays, and children's stories, Phyllis McGinley celebrates the seemingly mundane lives of ordinary women and finds plenitude and worth in the challenges and moral complexities of the domestic sphere. As a woman's lot was being redefined during the first wave of postwar feminism, McGinley remained a steadfast advocate of the domestic arts and traditional gender roles. She dignifies the choices of housewife and mother, cherishes homes and homemaking, and recognizes the creative and spiritual purpose in the quiet little dramas of day-to-day living. Beneath her glib and glittering poetic surfaces—her attention to form, her verbal dexterity, her incisive intelligence, her artful and playful precision—is an abiding belief that our deepest humanity lies within and responds to right behavior. To McGinley, manners, as well as a mother's responsibility to translate and teach ethical rules to her children, are the pathways to joy and the foundations of an honest and honorable life.

McGinley was born in Ontario, Oregon, and lived in various far western towns until, after her father's death in 1917, her family settled in Ogden, Utah. The stability she prized in her own married life certainly owes something to this unsettling early loss. Her deep affection for her "charming" and imperfect suburban homes in Larchmont, New York, and, after her two daughters were grown, Weston, Connecticut, is made poignantly comprehensible when contrasted with the rootlessness of her earliest years. "But we were happy as meadowlarks," she writes in the 1964 paean to the American housewife, *Sixpence in Her Shoe.* "We married our house for love."

Her father's business as a land speculator may have forced a peripatetic life, but Julia and Daniel McGinley also provided roots in Catholicism and an Irish inclination toward the life of the mind. McGinley graduated from the University of Utah in 1927, taught school, and then moved to New York in 1929, where she began her writing career in earnest. Here she taught English in a suburban junior high, joined the staff of *Town and Country,* wrote advertising copy, and devoted herself to honing her craft. She published widely and regularly in a host of popular magazines, such as *The New Yorker, Vogue, Ladies' Home Journal,* and *Reader's Digest,* establishing herself as a canny humorist and social commentator. Throughout her five-decade-long career, she was a familiar and reliable fixture of the American literary scene, and she had a large and loyal readership. She married Charles L. Hayden in 1936, two years after her first collection of poetry, *On the Contrary,* was published. Ten more volumes of poetry would follow, including the 1960 collection *Times Three: Selected Verse from*

Three Decades with Seventy New Poems, for which she was awarded the 1961 Pulitzer Prize. She also published 17 children's books and four essay collections and wrote the lyrics for a Broadway musical revue. Though after her marriage she maintained that housekeeping was her "native vocation," her steadily determined devotion to the "occupation" of writing produced a remarkable body of work—a veritable chronicle of twentieth-century life.

Light verse has often been relegated to a kind of poetic substatus; the term itself is often used dismissively to denote insubstantial, if clever and amusing, verbal parlor tricks. More recently, especially with the Library of America's 2003 publication of *American Wits: An Anthology of Light Verse,* the term has been applied with a generic distinction and broader inclusiveness. McGinley shares space in this volume not only with well-known wits Dorothy Parker and Ogden Nash but also with the serious likes of Edna St. Vincent Millay, Ezra Pound, and James Merrill. In *The Writer Observed,* McGinley distinguishes between poetic types and intents: "the appeal of light verse is to the intellect and the appeal of serious verse is to the emotions." In a 1965 essay in *The American Scholar,* she describes herself as "a technician" whose "virtue is to beguile." Her work's mass appeal, she goes on to say, in wistful deference to poetry more "serious" than her own, may urge unsuspecting readers along the road to true poetic perception. Yet despite her somewhat arch protestations to the contrary, her work yields more than wry surprises. In much the same way that "manners are morals," as she says in *Sixpence in Her Shoe,* McGinley's "lightness" contains glimmers of what Marianne Moore calls "the genuine." W. H. Auden wrote an appreciative introduction to "Times Three" in which he compares McGinley to Moore, Jane Austen, and Virginia Woolf.

Though her work has fallen out of favor in the wake of the feminist revolution of the sixties (she wrote *Sixpence in Her Shoe* in direct response to Betty Friedan's 1963 classic, *The Feminist Mystique*), the time is ripe for a reevaluation of her work, especially in light of more expansive, post-feminist attitudes toward women's roles and choices.

Kate Falvey

References

Auden, W. H. *The Dyer's Hand.* New York: Random House, 1962.

Breit, Harvey. *The Writer Observed.* New York: Collier Books, 1961.

Hollander, John, ed. *The American Wits: An Anthology of Light Verse.* New York: Library of America, 2003.

McGinley, Phyllis. "The Light Side of the Moon." *The American Scholar* 34, no. 4 (Autumn 1965): 555–568.

McGinley, Phyllis. *Saint-Watching.* New York: Viking, 1969.

Wagner, Linda W. *Phyllis McGinley.* New York: Twayne Publishers, 1971.

McGonigle, Thomas (1944–)

Born on October 25, 1944, to Hugh and Marion (Whitney) McGonigle in Patchogue, Long Island, New York, McGonigle attended Hollins College, but transferred to Beloit College for his BA. He then received an MA from University College Dublin. McGonigle frequently writes about the theme of the writer as an exile. All three of his novels treat this theme: *St. Patrick's Day, Dublin, 1974* (only fragments have appeared in journals) paints one day in the life of an Irish-American exile in a bohemian Dublin setting; *Going to*

Patchogue (1992) depicts a New York writer's ironic pilgrimage to the hometown he grew up in and left in the mundane suburban setting of Patchogue, which would seem uncongenial to literary treatment; *The Corpse Dream of N. Petkov* (1997) presents a surreal journey into the mentality of fascism, dramatizing the absurd rationalizations of tyranny within a hallucinatory framework. This novel mixes fantasy and fact about an exile returning home to Sofia to challenge the communist leadership who tried, tortured, and hung Petkov in 1947. The novel was made possible by a traveling fellowship to Bulgaria from the International Research and Exchange Board.

As a personality, McGonigle remains uniquely himself: a dry absurdist humor permeates his portrayal of conversations, memories, observations, newspaper clippings, and even narcissistic self-meditations. His work abounds in temporal discontinuities, as in the work of Alain Robbe-Grillet, whom he has interviewed for the *Village Voice.* His fascination with the rootless wanderings of the Dutch novelist Nees Cootebaum led to a *BookForum* interview with the Dutch master. McGonigle has written introductions to books by Julian Green and E. M. Cioran. For the *Review of Contemporary Fiction* he has written articles on Charles Bukowski, Aidan Higgins, B. S. Johnson, Jack Kerouac, and Jack Spicer. McGonigle remains fixated with the self-imposed German exile of the Irish novelist Francis Stuart and the voluntary exile of the Russian writer Vladimir Nabokov. Stylistically, McGonigle exhibits the influence of both the Austrian writer Thomas Bernhard and the bleaker broodings of Samuel Beckett.

For several years in the 1980s, McGonigle edited *Adrift,* an Irish-American magazine that published a wide variety of Irish-American prose and poetry of merit; the magazine was launched at the now-defunct Facsimile Book Shop in midtown Manhattan, where books from Ireland were found in abundance between 1978 and 1988. Clearly belonging to the postmodern European tradition, McGonigle lives his life as an exile in America with a public hardly familiar with the nouveau roman tradition, nor able to comprehend how an American, much less an Irish-American, could possibly consider himself alienated in the United States. But there is no commercial market for writing that eschews complex plot, romance, or easy rewards for readers impatient with parody, sarcasm, satire, surreal organization, and panoptic irony. McGonigle's genial book reviews on non-American novelists frequently appear in such newspapers as *New York Newsday, The Los Angeles Times,* and *The Washington Post.*

Kevin T. McEneaney

See also: BECKETT, Samuel

References

Fanning, Charles. *The Irish Voice in America: 250 Years of Irish American Fiction.* Lexington: University Press of Kentucky, 2000.

Wall, Eamonn. *From the Sin-é Café to the Black Hills: Notes on the New Irish.* Madison: University of Wisconsin Press, 1999.

McGRAW, JOHN JOSEPH (1873–1934)

John McGraw was born in Truxton, New York, on April 7, 1873, to John McGraw, an Irish immigrant railroad laborer, and Ellen (Comerfort). After losing his mother and four siblings to a diphtheria epidemic, McGraw devoted himself to athletics; by

Portrait of professional baseball player and manager John Joseph McGraw. (Library of Congress)

age 16 he was playing baseball professionally for Olean of the New York-Pennsylvania League. In August 1891, after a stint with several minor league teams, McGraw joined the Baltimore Orioles, then a member of the American Association. In 1892, the American Association disbanded and the Orioles entered a reorganized National League. McGraw became the league's foremost third baseman and one of its top hitters as the Orioles won three consecutive championships (1894–1896). His playing style has been described as everything from hard-nosed to dirty: typically, he would obstruct base runners, intimidate umpires, and otherwise distract opponents. Standing only 5 feet 6 inches tall and weighing but 120 pounds, McGraw made up in determination and tenacity what he lacked in size. In 1897 McGraw batted .391, still the highest single-season batting average for a third baseman; he ended his career with a lifetime batting average of .334 and a remarkable .465 on-base percentage. He averaged more than 40 stolen bases throughout his career and twice led his league in both bases on balls and runs scored (1898 and 1899). In 1899 McGraw became the Orioles manager and began to develop his reputation for genius. When the National League reorganized the following year, dropping Baltimore and three other franchises, McGraw joined the St. Louis Cardinals. He returned as player-manager of the new American League Baltimore franchise in 1901, but frequent clashes with owner Ban Johnson ended the reunion. In 1902 McGraw signed a four-year contract to manage the New York Giants for an annual salary of $11,000, the highest in baseball history to that point.

McGraw served as player-manager of the Giants from 1902 to 1906, winning his first pennant in 1904. Dubbed "Little Napoleon" by New York sportswriters, and working in the spotlight of America's media capital, McGraw became one of the sport's most dominating personalities. International fame followed off-season tours of Europe, the Caribbean, and Latin America. From 1904 to 1924 the Giants won 10 pennants and three world championships as McGraw—a master tactician, bullier of umpires without equal, and martinet with his players—solidified his reputation as baseball's best manager. An innovative tactician credited with implementing the hit and run, squeeze play, and other strategic moves, McGraw is seen by many as being responsible for baseball's growing popularity and success before the appearance of Babe Ruth and other home run champions.

Despite having more future Hall of Famers on his roster than any other manager, McGraw never won another pennant after 1924. In 1932, McGraw—in failing health and unable to rally his team into contention—yielded the managerial reins to Bill Terry, ending a 30-year tenure with the Giants. Despite his retirement, McGraw was named the manager of the National League squad in the following year's inaugural all-star game.

McGraw currently ranks second all-time in games managed with 4,845 and in wins with 2,840 wins. Though known for his combative style, McGraw gave away much of his baseball income (which reached $70,000 per annum) to needy former ballplayers and others who were down and out. Having lost as much as $100,000 on real estate speculation, McGraw died broke in New Rochelle, New York, on February 25, 1933. Twice married (in 1897 to Minne Doyle, who passed away two years later, and in 1902 to Blanch Sindall), McGraw had no children.

Tim Lynch

See also: BASEBALL; BASEBALL MANAGERS, IRISH-AMERICAN

References

Alexander, Charles. *John McGraw.* Lincoln: University of Nebraska Press, 1999.

McGraw, John. *My Thirty Years in Baseball.* Lincoln: University of Nebraska Press, 1995.

McGuckian, Medbh (1950–)

A widely recognized Northern Irish Catholic poet, translator, editor, and teacher, Medbh McGuckian is best known for her poems, which evoke an enigmatic personal mythology as they challenge linguistic conventions through ambiguous syntax and pronoun usage. McGuckian derives much of her symbolism from nature and from the home, both of which she frequently evokes through images of plants, flowers, weather, motherhood, domestic spaces, and colors. Unlike the work of many Northern Irish poets, McGuckian's does not overtly engage with the political atmosphere. Instead, she opts for a covert, indirect exploration of the role of language, territory, gender, and art in the Northern Irish arena. Though she does not profess to be a feminist, her fluid, sensual poetry is often associated with French feminist Hélène Cixous' concept of women's language and writing called *écriture féminine.* McGuckian's poetic style alternately fascinates, frustrates, and challenges readers and critics. McGuckian has produced more than a dozen collections of poems since 1980, including *The Flower Master* (1982), *On Ballycastle Beach* (1988), *Marconi's Cottage* (1991), *Captain Lavender* (1994), *Shelmalier* (1998), *Drawing Ballerinas* (2001), *The Face of the Earth* (2002), and *The Book of the Angel* (2004). She has also edited *Fortnight* and an anthology, *The Big Striped Golfing Umbrella: Poems by Young People from Northern Ireland* (1985), translated Nuala Ní Dhomhnaill's *The Water Horse* from Irish into English in collaboration with Eiléan Ní Chuilleanáin, and authored a study of Seamus Heaney's poetry entitled *Horsepower Pass By!* (1999).

McGuckian is the third of six children born in Belfast, Northern Ireland, to Hugh Albert McCaughan, a schoolteacher, and Margaret (Fergus) McCaughan. She attended Holy Family Primary School in Newington and the Dominican Convent in Fortwilliam Park from 1961 to 1968. McGuckian earned a Sullivan Scholarship to Queen's University Belfast, where she earned her BA in 1972. She continued her studies there, earning an MA in Anglo-Irish literature and a DipEd in 1974. At Queens, McGuckian studied under Seamus Heaney, who was already a significant Irish poet by that time. She attended classes with poets Paul Muldoon and Frank Ormsby, although McGuckian declined the invitation to join their poetry group, which Heaney moderated. McGuckian taught English at Dominican Convent and at St. Patrick's College, Knock, Belfast. She soon returned to Queens, serving as the first female writer-in-residence from 1986 to 1988. In 1991, McGuckian was a visiting fellow at the University of California, Berkeley. She taught creative writing to suspected or accused paramilitaries held in the Maze prison in 1994. She was a writer fellow at Trinity College Dublin in 1999–2000 and maintains her involvement with the creative writing department at Queens.

In 1979, McGuckian won the National Poetry Competition with her poem, "The Flitting," which she submitted under a male pseudonym. She won an Eric Gregory Award in 1980, the year her poetry appeared in two pamphlets, *Portrait of Joanna* and *Single Ladies: Sixteen Poems.* Her first book of poems, *The Flower Master,* earned her a Rooney prize (1982), the Irish Arts Council Award (1982), and the Alice Hunt Bartlett Award (1983). The collection probes generativity and postnatal experience, and arrived shortly after McGuckian gave birth to her first child. By the time *Venus and the Rain* appeared in 1984, her poetic reputation was firmly established. In this collection, McGuckian writes of borders, boundaries, and obliquely gendered relationships where Venus and the Moon symbolize femininity while Mars, the Sun, and the rain represent masculinity.

Geographical locality and history echo in *On Ballycastle Beach* (1988). As both McGuckian and her father were born in Ballycastle, this locale is linked to her anticipation of and reaction to her father's approaching death. Likewise, McGuckian is interested in generational relation and transmission in *Marconi's Cottage* (1991), which involves themes of birth sparked by the arrival of McGuckian's first daughter Emer Mary Charlotte Rose. The collection takes its title from the Ballycastle beach house where Nobel Prize winner Guglielmo Marconi transmitted from Rathlin Island to the mainland with his wireless telegraph. McGuckian won the Cheltenham Prize for *On Ballycastle Beach* in 1989 and was shortlisted for the Irish Times Irish Literature Prize for Poetry for *Marconi's Cottage* in 1992, the same year she was awarded the Helen Waddell Award. *Captain Lavender* (1994) grieves the 1992 death of her father and for a society she proves increasingly willing to confront more openly. Her work in the latter 1990s and early 2000s had consolidated her stellar reputation.

Kelly J. S. McGovern

See also: HEANEY, Seamus; MULDOON, Paul

References

Hogan, Robert, ed. *Dictionary of Irish Literature.* Westport, CT: Greenwood, 1996.

O'Connor, Mary. "Medbh McGuckian." In *Modern Irish Writers: A Bio-Critical Sourcebook,* edited by Alexander G. Gonzalez, 182–187. Westport, CT: Greenwood, 1997.

Olendorf, Donna, ed. *Contemporary Authors.* Vol. 143. Detroit: Gale, 1994.

Riggs, Thomas, ed. *Contemporary Poets.* 7th ed. Detroit: St. James, 2001.

McGuckin, Barton (1852–1913)

Barton McGuckin spent a year in America in 1887 singing in opera and concerts. In his early career, he started as a chorister in the Armagh Cathedral, where he received vocal training and studied the organ, violin, and piano. In 1871 he became the principal tenor soloist at Saint Patrick's Cathedral, Dublin. Here he also studied with Joseph Robinson, a prominent local musician and vocalist. McGuckin made a successful appearance at the Crystal Palace concerts in 1875. McGuckin went to Milan toward the end of 1875, where he pursued his vocal studies further for the next year, returning to England to perform in the Crystal Palace concerts in October 1876. In November 1876 he again appeared in Dublin, this time at the Ancient Concert Rooms in Great Brunswick Street. His operatic debut was made as Thaddeus in Balfe's *The Bohemian Girl* at Birmingham in September 1880 with the Carl Rosa Opera Company. Invitations quickly followed to sing at various leading musical festivals in Bristol, Hereford, Leeds, Norwich, and elsewhere in England. During this period he also sang in oratorios. His first operatic role in Dublin was as William Meister in *Mignon* in 1881. He successfully premiered Balfe's opera *Morro, the Painter of Antwerp* at Her Majesty's Theatre in January 1882. He continued to sing with the Carl Rosa Opera Company in London and the provinces, taking on the leading tenor roles in, *Faust, Carmen, Mignon Lohengrin,* and *Manon.*

During the years 1883–1887, while at the Theatre Royal, Drury Lane, in London, McGuckin created a number of new operas by English composers, such as A. G. Thomas, A. C. Mackenzie, and F. Corder. In 1887, McGuckin visited New York with the National Opera Company. He sang various operatic roles from the standard repertoire at the Academy of Music on 14th Street. He then went on tour to Boston and other places in New England, performing in opera and concerts before returning to New York. In 1888 he returned to London to rejoin the Carl Rosa Opera Company. He continued to sing principal parts with the company until 1896. It was during this period that he reached his peak when he sang the title role in the first English-language version of Verdi's *Otello* at Manchester in 1892. In later life McGuckin became associated with the Royal Irish Academy of Music in Dublin, where he endeavored to set up a competition in his name. This association was brief when he disagreed with the constraints placed on his involvement. McGuckin did live long enough to be able to make some recordings of Irish songs at the dawn of the recording industry in 1905. In recent years one of these recordings, a ballad by Irish composer Thomas Moore, *Avenging the Bright,* was reissued on the Symposium label in London.

Basil Walsh

See also: MOORE, Thomas; MUSIC, COUNTRY AND IRISH

References

Brown, J. D., and S. S. Stratton. *British Musical Biography.* Birmingham: S. S. Stratton, 1897.

Grove, George, ed. *Dictionary of Music and Musicians.* Vol. 4. Philadelphia: Theodore Presser, 1889.

Pine, Richard, and Charles Action, *To Talent Alone.* Dublin: Gill & Macmillan, 1998.

White, Eric Walter. *A Register of First Performances of English Opera.* London: The Society for Theatre Research, 1983.

McGwire, Mark D. (1963–)

Mark David McGwire—"Big Mac"—was born in Pomana, California, on October 1, 1963. Although McGwire is not usually regarded as Irish American, he is of Irish descent and had a large fan base in Ireland. McGwire was a first baseman who starred initially at the college level, with the University of Southern California (he had been drafted by the Montreal Expos but declined in favor of USC for financial reasons), and at the Olympic level, winning a silver medal with the USA amateur team in Los Angeles in 1984. He left USC after three years, signing with the Oakland Athletics. He played his first Major League game for them in August 1986. The following year, 1987, he was named Rookie of the Year after hitting a rookie record 49 home runs for the Oakland Athletics. The previous record of 38 had been jointly held by Frank Robinson and Wally Berger. He won his only World Series with Oakland in 1989, when they swept the San Francisco Giants. During this time with Oakland McGwire would form a colorful and successful relationship with Jose Canseco—one that would later prove controversial.

With McGwire about to become a free agent at the end of the 1997 season, he was traded midseason to the St. Louis Cardinals, where he completed a second successive season with 50 or more home runs—a deed only accomplished previously by Babe Ruth.

In 1998 McGwire and Sammy Sosa of the Chicago Cubs began their attempt to beat Roger Maris's 1961 home run record of 61 in a single season. McGwire equaled the record on September 7 and broke it September 8. Extra drama was added to the night by the fact that Sammy Sosa was playing right field, Maris's family was in the stands, and McGwire's young son, Matthew, was the Cardinal's batboy. The game was delayed 11 minutes for the celebration that followed. Sosa would hit his 60th home run on September 12.

McGwire finished the season with 70 home runs, having hit two in the last game. Sosa finished with 66. Both men shared *Sports Illustrated* magazine's "Sportsman of the Year" award. The following year McGwire hit 65 runs, and Sosa hit 63; both men became the only people in baseball history to hit 60 home runs in successive seasons. That same season McGwire became only the 17th player to hit more than 500 home runs in his career.

McGwire's record was eventually beaten in 2001 by Barry Bonds, who hit 73 home runs in a season. McGwire retired from baseball in 2001, finishing with 583 lifetime home runs. Despite his records McGwire will also always be controversially linked with the use of steroids. He admitted using androstenedione, a bodybuilding drug banned in most sports but allowed in baseball. He later stopped taking the supplement, saying he did not want to encourage young people to take it. However, the publication of Canseco's 2005 autobiography, *Juiced,* brought such a public outcry that President George W. Bush mentioned steroids and their abuse in baseball as part of his State of the Union address. Congress responded by asking McGwire and others to testify. McGwire under oath refused to deny or confirm that he had used performance-enhancing drugs during his career and instead asked that Congress concentrate on the future rather than the past. The controversy continues to blight his record. McGwire married Stephanie Slemer in 2002, and the couple has a son, Max. McGwire has another son, Matthew, from his first marriage.

Brid Nicholson

References

Hall, Jonathan. *Mark McGwire: A Biography.* New Jersey: Simon Spotlight Entertainment, 2001.

Miklasz, Bernie. *Celebrating 70: Mark McGwire's Historic Season.* New York: McGraw-Hill, 1998.

McMANUS, GEORGE (1884–1954)

Corned beef and cabbage, Dinty Moore's stew, a gimlet-eyed wife, and a husband entering his house carrying his shoes or leaving it amid a hail of dishes—these were everyday occurrences in George McManus's long-running comic strip, *Bringing Up Father,* featuring the adventures of Jiggs and Maggie. McManus was born on January 23, 1884, into an immigrant Irish family living in St. Louis, Missouri. His father was a theater manager, and McManus had many opportunities to absorb the elements of stage comedy and vaudeville humor that he would later work into this comic strip. He started cartooning at the age of 16, and in 1904 he went to New York City, where he eventually landed a position at Joseph Pulitzer's *The World.* One of his early strips, *Nibsy the Newsboy in Funny Fairyland,* shared some of the fantastic, dreamlike qualities of Winsor McCay's *Little Nemo in Slumberland.*

In 1912, McManus moved over to *The World*'s rival, the *Journal American,* run by William Randolph Hearst. A year later he started the strip that made his name, *Bringing Up Father,* syndicated by King Features. Part of the strip's success was based on McManus's ability to turn into humor three themes that dominated early twentieth-century American popular culture: the tensions between husband and wife, between the generations, and between the classes. Interestingly, all of these themes had particular meaning within the Irish-American community.

The inspiration for *Bringing Up Father* was an 1893 lace-curtain comedy, *The Rising Generation,* by William Gills, which McManus had seen during his days in St. Louis. McManus had already experimented with satire on marriage and the family in an earlier strip, *The Newlyweds,* which he had brought with him from *The World.* In *Bringing Up Father,* McManus set his comedy within an Irish-American family. His character Jiggs was a hod carrier who, having come into money, wanted to retain the comfortable habits and friends of his working-class background. On the other hand, Maggie, his wife, and Nora, the daughter, eagerly sought to emulate the life of the upper class. The interplay between father and daughter reflected the comedy of Will M. Cresey's popular Mag Haggerty vaudeville sketches. However, the focus of the strip was on Jiggs's and Maggie's version of the battle of the sexes as fought out over lace-curtain aspirations. In Irish-American popular culture, wives were frequently depicted as the engines of social ambitions, while their working-class husbands shrank from the embarrassments of living beyond their means. This theme first emerged in Edward Harrigan's Mulligan

Guard musicals in the 1870s and 1880s, and became a staple in Tin Pan Alley comic Irish songs, vaudeville sketches, and some of Finley Peter Dunne's Mr. Dooley pieces.

The success of *Bringing Up Father* extended beyond the funny papers. In the 1920s *Father*, a play based on the strip, toured America, with McManus occasionally playing the leading role. After first appearing in silent animated cartoons, Jiggs and Maggie were featured in at least eight films. McManus, playing himself, appeared in several of those produced in the 1940s. A more unlikely by-product of the comic strip derived from Jiggs's legendary addiction to the beef stew served in Dinty Moore's saloon. The establishment and the stew were allegedly inspired by one of McManus's favorite eateries, run by a friend, James Moore. Moore tacked the name "Dinty" onto his establishment. Eventually, "Dinty Moore" appeared as a brand of canned goods.

As a comic strip artist, McManus combined stereotypes and caricatures with a high level of fashionable decorative draftsmanship. Jiggs, the father, was drawn with a long-upper lip and a pug nose, inherited from anti-Irish nineteenth-century political cartoons and from the vaudeville stage. However, McManus's scenes of upper-class life were filled with art deco–style architecture and decorations. At the same time, the zaniness that characterized the early comic strips was evident in the pictures on the walls, in which figures broke out of the frame and seemed to be leading a life of their own.

McManus retired from the strip in the 1940s. By that time, some of the early comic strips had become habitual fare for many newspaper readers. Jiggs and Maggie continued their marital combat for another 60 years, an unlikely remnant of the once ubiquitous Irish-American humor. *Bring Up Father* was last published on May 28, 2000, in its 87th year, a world record among comic strips.

William H. A. Williams

See also: DUNNE, Finley Peter; HARRIGAN, Edward, and HART, Tony

References

McManus, George. *Bringing Up Father,* edited by Herb Galewitze. New York: Scribner's, 1973.

McManus, George. *Jiggs Is Back.* California: Celtic Book Company, 1986.

Williams, William H. A. "Green Again: Irish-American Lace-Curtain Satire." *New Hibernia Review* 6, no.2 (Summer 2002): 9–24.

McNutt, Alexander (1725–1811)

The details of Alexander McNutt's birth, including the identity of his parents and earliest years, are unclear. Born in Londonderry, Northern Ireland, he first came to North America as a young man, around 1753, at which point his life becomes better documented. His first place of American settlement was Staunton, Virginia. There, as a militia officer under Major Andrew Lewis, he fought against the Shawnee of the Ohio River Valley. By 1758 McNutt had moved north, settling in Londonderry, New Hampshire. The next year his attention had turned further north yet, when he became involved in schemes for colonizing Nova Scotia, for which he is best remembered today.

The earliest settlers that McNutt attracted to Nova Scotia came from New Hampshire. But in his effort to populate Acadia with Protestants, and to turn a profit doing so, he soon turned his gaze across the Atlantic to Ireland. In the spring of 1761 McNutt actively sought immigrants from Londonderry and its hinterland. News of his settlement scheme spread further afield by word of mouth and in print, in newspapers such as the *Belfast News-Letter*. Some 300 colonists acted on his offer to relocate to Nova Scotia, where the head of each migrating family would receive 200 acres as well as 50 acres for each member of the family. While McNutt acted on his scheme with support from Lt. Gov. Jonathan Belcher (with whom McNutt had a good relationship), and the Board of Trade in London, the Privy Council turned him down. Fearing the consequences of a declining Protestant population in Ireland, the Privy Council looked no more favorably on McNutt's grander scheme hatched in 1762. Without support from the Privy Council, McNutt could not succeed in his plans. However, in 1765, he was compensated with 13,500 acres for the losses he reportedly incurred in 1761.

After the French and Indian War ended, McNutt aimed to take advantage of the consequences of the Proclamation of 1763 by attracting potential settlers to Nova Scotia from other (Pennsylvania in particular) colonies in British North America. In late 1765 he secured several land grants, but for several reasons little colonization followed. McNutt himself lived in Nova Scotia for a time in the late 1760s and early 1770s. During the War for American Independence (1776–1783) he was suspected by both the British government and the American rebels of being sympathetic toward the other side. McNutt lived on McNutt Island during the late 1780s, but he moved to Virginia in 1794, and that is where he spent his final years.

Mark G. Spencer

References

Blakeley, Phyllis R. "Alexander McNutt." In *Dictionary of Canadian Biography*, edited by Ramsay Cook. Toronto: University of Toronto, 2005.

Dickson, R. J. *Ulster Emigration to Colonial America, 1718–1775*. London: Routledge and Kegan Paul, 1966.

Eaton, A. W. H. "Alexander McNutt, the Colonizer." *Americana* 8 (1913): 1065–1106.

Wright, Esther Clark, *The Petitcodiac: A Study of the New Brunswick River and of the People Who Settled Along it*. Sackville, New Brunswick: The Tribute Press, 1945.

McSWINEY, PAUL (1856–1890)

Nothing is known about Paul McSwiney's early life and education before the first performance of his opera *Amergen* in the Cork Opera House on February 23, 1881. A significant event in local music history, the opera to his own libretto was praised for its drama and melodic content, but less so for its musical craftsmanship. Soon after the successful week of performances, McSwiney went to London and then in 1883 to New York, where he became the musical director of the New York branch of the Society for the Preservation of the Irish Language. The first work he produced in that capacity was *An Bárd 'gus an Fó,* subtitled *A Gaelic Idyll,* a dramatic cantata for soloists, choir, and orchestra, first performed at Steinway Hall on November 28, 1884. However, it was not until 1885, when the work was produced in an English version as *The Bard and the Knight,* that it could attract a larger audience. Other works to which he contributed both music and words were *Alexander, a Musical Drama* and *John McHale* (unfinished). He further produced a number of plays, such as *Brian, The*

Fairies Doll, and a novel called *Nirvana.* McSwiney's failure with *An Bárd 'gus an Fó* is significant as it shows the diminishing importance of the Irish language among the immigrant Irish.

Axel Klein

References

Klein, Axel. "Stage-Irish, or the National in Irish Opera, 1780–1925." *Opera Quarterly* 21 (2005): 1–41.

O'Donoghue, David J. *The Poets of Ireland.* Dublin: [for the author], 1912.

MEAGHER, THOMAS FRANCIS (1823–1867)

A Young Ireland revolutionary, orator, politician, and American Civil War hero, Thomas Meagher was born in Waterford in 1823, the son of a distinguished citizen. His father, a member of the Repeal Association, served twice as mayor and as the parliamentary representative from that district. Meagher attended the Jesuit school at Clongowes, Co. Kildare, where he fashioned his future as an orator. He then attended Stonyhurst, a Catholic college in Lancastershire where his interest in Irish history was stimulated by the anti-Irish atmosphere. Joining his father in the Repeal Association back in Waterford, he served a short term as secretary and then left for Dublin, where he intended to study for the bar. His involvement in the Repeal Association fostered his friendships with Young Irelanders Gavan Duffy and Thomas Davis, among others. His talents as an orator brought him quick notice, despite his English accent, disciplined through elocution at the English boarding school. There he had also developed suspicions of the Whig government, whose leaders were courted by Daniel O'Connell.

Thomas Francis Meagher, hero of the American Civil War and Irish revolutionary. (Library of Congress)

On July 28, 1846, Meagher delivered his famous "Sword Speech" at Dublin's Conciliation Hall, wherein he argued against the O'Connell peace resolution before the Repeal Association. Although Meagher agreed that peaceful means of achieving repeal were most preferred, the British parliament had repeatedly thwarted efforts to give Ireland its own representative government. Arguing that independence could be won only through a show of strength, Meagher cited violent rebellions that had led to independence. His allusions included Judith's assassination of the Assyrian invader and a rebellion by Belgian priests. John O'Connell, son of the Liberator, interrupted Meagher, and after a dispute, the Young Irelanders walked out of the meeting, resulting in the rift between Young Ireland and Old Ireland over repeal strategy. The Sword Speech became legendary and made Meagher an international celebrity.

In February 1847, Meagher lost an election in his home district, Waterford, where the seat went to a Tory, the repeal ticket having been split between Old and Young Ireland. In February 1848, widespread revolutions in continental Europe excited Young Irelanders' imaginations, and Meagher with other leaders formed a delegation to enlist French support for a planned Irish revolt. The new French President Alfonse de Lamartine, a poet-politician, refused. The new French government had no intention of engaging England in a war over Ireland. Meagher, however, did return with a gift crafted by an admirer, the Irish tricolor flag, fashioned after the French flag.

In March, a demonstration against British rule resulted in Meagher's arrest along with William Smith-O'Brien and John Mitchel. The resulting trials for sedition resulted in not guilty verdicts for Meagher and Smith-O'Brien, but Mitchel's jury was packed in favor of the prosecution, and he was convicted. That July, Meagher organized a demonstration fashioned after O'Connell's "monster meetings." It was held on Slievenamon, a mountain in Co. Tipperary, where a reported 50,000 attended. The British response was to suspend habeas corpus and to arrest Meagher and others for treason. His trial resulted in conviction for high treason, which demanded hanging followed by drawing and quartering, but the government, uneasy that Meagher and others might be hailed as martyrs and thus further inflame hostilities, had the sentence commuted. Meagher was transported to Van Dieman Land, Australia, on July 29, 1849.

Meagher's confidence and jovial nature enhanced his popularity. He won friends in the colony and joined other Young Ireland felons. He was awarded a ticket of leave, which allowed him to live freely in that land on his honor that he would not try to escape. Escape, however, he did, returning his ticket to the police in Ross district—a matter of honor. The Irish chief constable, however, refused to arrest Meagher, and English settlers threatened to shoot any constable who dared to make the arrest.

While in Tasmania, Meagher married Catherine Bennet, whom he called Bennie. They had a son, Henry Emmett Fitzgerald, born while the father was making his escape to the United States. Bennie sailed to Ireland, where she was cared for by the Meagher family in Waterford. The elder Thomas Meagher escorted her to New York to join her husband, but after four months, Meagher undertook a speaking tour and insisted that she return to Ireland. Bennie bore a second son, Thomas Francis Meagher III, but she died of typhus shortly after giving birth in 1854.

Meagher arrived in New York in May 1852. He gave lectures for the following two years on the subjects of Australia, Irish history, literature, and politics. He also assisted John Mitchel in establishing an Irish-American newspaper, the *Citizen.* In 1856, he married Elizabeth Townsend, and he established his own newspaper, the *Irish News.* He soon lost interest in journalism, and the paper closed in 1860. In 1857, Meagher left the *Irish News* in the hands of Richard J. and Gerald R. Lalor while he joined an exploratory expedition to Central America, from which he published two articles: "Holidays in Costa Rica" and "The New Route Through Chirigus." When the U.S. Civil War broke out,

Meagher organized a company of Irish volunteers, serving under Colonel Michael Corcoran's 69th New York Regiment. Meagher saw action in Virginia, at the first Battle of Bull Run (Manassas, July 21, 1861) where his horse was struck by cannon shot and fell from beneath him. He organized the Irish Brigade that same year and became a colonel. On February 3, 1862, in command of the 69th Regiment, he was appointed brigadier-general. He fought at the second Battle of Bull Run in August and at Antietam in September, where he again lost his horse to gunfire. He received high praise for his fierceness in battle from his opponent General Robert E. Lee. At the Battle of Fredericksburg, in December, Meagher incurred a gunshot wound to the leg and saw many of his men fall in battle.

In 1863, Meagher ran into conflict with the Union Army command when he insisted that he be allowed to recruit for his regiment. Refused, he tendered his resignation in protest but was again refused. He served in several other campaigns before resigning on May 15, 1865.

After the war, President Andrew Johnson appointed Meagher to serve as temporary governor of the Montana territory, a post in which he served from 1865 to July 1, 1867. During his career in the American West, Meagher wrote "Rides through Montana," reprinted in *The River We Carry With Us: Two Centuries of Writing from the Clark Fork Basin.*

Meagher's term in office ended with his fall into the Missouri River from a steamboat near Fort Benton. His death was reported in the American press as caused by drunkenness, but in Waterford, a popular story contends that he was attacked by Know-Nothings, an anti-immigrant society aimed at preventing immigrants from serving in political office. Meagher published two books: *Recollections of Ireland and the Irish* and *The Last Days of the 69th in Virginia,* a Civil War history.

Katherine Parr

See also: MITCHEL, John

References

Davis, Richard. *The Young Ireland Movement.* Dublin: Gill and Macmillan, 1987.

Meagher, Thomas F. "Rides through Montana." In *The River We Carry With Us: Two Centuries of Writing from the Clark Fork Basin.* Clark City, MT: Clark City Press, 2002.

O'Sullivan, T. F. "Thomas Francis Meagher." *The Young Irelanders.* Tralee: Kerryman, 1944: 191–207.

MELLON, ANDREW WILLIAM (1855–1937)

The fourth son of Thomas Mellon and Sarah Jane Negley, Andrew Mellon was born March 24, 1855, in Pittsburgh, Pennsylvania. In 1868 he enrolled in the Western University of Pennsylvania, the forerunner of the University of Pittsburgh, but left in 1872, three months before graduation, to open a lumber and construction company. The dislocations of the Panic of 1873 led Mellon to believe bankers and businessmen best served the United States by imparting order to the economy, and in 1874 he entered T. Mellon and Sons, the bank his father had founded. In January 1882 Mellon's father was so impressed with his son's abilities that he gave him the bank. During the next four decades Mellon would use the bank to finance the growth of industry. In January 1890 he invested in the operations of chemist Charles M. Hall, which would grow into the Aluminum Company of America. In the 1890s he

President Warren Harding (left) receives treasury savings certificates from Andrew Mellon (right). Mellon was a successful banker and treasury secretary to Presidents Warren Harding, Calvin Coolidge, and Herbert Hoover. (Library of Congress)

invested in oil wells in western Pennsylvania and in 1891 founded with local investors what would become the Gulf Oil Corporation. In 1902, in his capacity as bank president, Mellon reorganized T. Mellon and Sons as the Mellon National Bank.

Bank associate and industrialist Henry Clay Frick had in 1898 introduced Mellon to Nora Mary McMullen, the daughter of a wealthy brewer, and the two married in 1900. Mrs. Mellon gave birth to Ailsa in 1901 and Paul in 1907. Although the couple vacationed every year but one in England, Andrew Mellon otherwise immersed himself in work. Nora Mellon resented his absence, disliked Pittsburgh, and in 1909 separated from her husband. The two divorced in 1910, deepening Mellon's absorption in work.

By then Mellon had turned toward politics. He disapproved of government intervention in the economy in the belief that only bankers and businessmen were adept at managing the economy. He supported a high tariff to protect industry despite the harm tariffs did to agriculture. Mellon opposed a minimum wage as a burden to business and favored low corporate and individual taxes. These views led him to finance the campaigns of local Republicans and in 1916 of Republican presidential candidate Charles Evans Hughes. Warren G. Harding's election as president in 1920 brought Mellon to the fore. Friend and former Secretary of State Philander C. Knox recommended Mellon to Harding, who in 1921 named him secretary of the treasury. Accustomed to austerity in his own life Mellon demanded the same of government. Not content merely to balance the budget, Mellon aimed for a surplus to pay down the country's $24 billion debt. To achieve this goal Mellon proposed to reduce federal expenditures faster than taxes. In the name of economy Mellon opposed the payment of a bonus to World War I veterans, writing the text of Harding's 1922 veto. For the same reason he opposed aid to farmers, writing the 1926 and 1928 vetoes of the McNary-Haugen Bill. His central aim as treasury secretary was to reduce taxes on the wealthy in the belief that business, free from the burden of taxes, would generate more money and thus more revenue for government and more jobs. The benefits of low taxes on the wealthy would therefore trickle down to the poor. The emergency of Word War I at an end, in 1921 Mellon sought to repeal the Excess Profits Act, which taxed corporate profits above 8 percent. Congress obliged and heeded Mellon's counsel in reducing the tax rate on incomes above $1 million from 66 to 50 percent. Mellon sought a second round of cuts in 1923 and a third in 1926. As a consequence, an individual who paid $663,000 in income taxes on $1 million in 1921 paid less than $200,000 in 1929. Mellon offset these reductions with increases in taxes on stamps, cars, and bank checks and an increase in postage. Critics charged that these actions benefited the wealthy at the expense of the poor. Defenders lauded him the greatest treasury secretary since Alexander Hamilton. Treasury secretary to presidents Harding, Calvin Coolidge, and Herbert Hoover, Mellon has had the longest tenure in that role to date. In 1932 Hoover named Mellon ambassador to Great Britain. In 1933 Pennsylvania Congressman Louis T. McFadden charged Mellon with underpaying his taxes by more than $2 million in 1931. After Mellon's death the Board of Tax Appeals set the amount at $485,809 rather than $2 million. In 1937 Mellon bequeathed his art collection, $15 million for the construction of a building, and $5 million for an endowment to establish and maintain the National Gallery of Art. Mellon died of pneumonia on August 26, 1937.

Christopher Cumo

See also: MELLON, Thomas

References

Hersh, Burton. *The Mellon Family: A Fortune in History.* New York: William Morrow and Company, 1978.

Koskoff, David E. *The Mellons: The Chronicle of America's Richest Family.* New York: Thomas Y. Crowell Company, 1978.

Murray, Lawrence Leon. "Andrew W. Mellon, Secretary of the Treasury, 1921–1932: A Study in Policy." PhD thesis. Michigan State University, Lansing, 1970.

MELLON, THOMAS (1813–1908)

The son of Andrew Mellon and Rebecca Wauchob, Thomas Mellon was born February 3, 1813, in Co. Tyrone, Ireland. In October 1818 the family left Ireland for Baltimore, Maryland, and then Westmoreland County, Pennsylvania. Benjamin Franklin's *Autobiography,* which Mellon read as a teen, fired his ambition to be more than a farmer. In 1834 he enrolled at Jefferson College in Canonsburg, Pennsylvania, transferring that October to the Western University of Pennsylvania, the forerunner of the University of Pittsburgh.

In September 1837 Mellon graduated from the university and that fall was its Latin professor. In 1838 he studied law with Charles Shaler, former judge of the Court of Common Pleas of Allegheny County, Pennsylvania. In December 1838 Mellon passed the bar examination and opened an office in Pittsburgh.

In 1843 he married Sarah Jane Negley, the daughter of a wealthy landowner. She gave birth to Thomas Alexander Mellon in 1844, to James Ross Mellon in 1846, to Sarah Emma Mellon in 1847, to Annie Rebecca Mellon in 1851, to Samuel Selwyn Mellon in 1853, to Andrew William Mellon in 1855, to Richard Beatty Mellon in 1858, and to George Negley Mellon in 1860. To stimulate their work ethic, Thomas Mellon paid his children for their chores. Discontented with public schools because students were unruly and with private schools because parents interfered in the curriculum, Mellon built a schoolhouse and hired a tutor for his children.

Now a father Mellon sought to increase his income. Chiding himself for charging too little for his services, in the 1840s Mellon loaned money at 10 to 15 percent interest. After fire swept Pittsburgh in 1845 he bought land at discount. In 1846 alone he built 18 apartments. In 1849 he bought a 60-acre coal mine. In 1859 he became partner in J. B. Corey and Company, opening mines in Braddock and Sandy Creek, Pennsylvania. That year he won election as the Republican candidate for judge of the Court of Common Pleas in Allegheny County. In his decade on the bench he came to distrust juries, believing the common man incapable of reaching the correct verdict. As he had as a lawyer, Mellon grew dissatisfied with the pay and yearned to make his mark in business. In 1869 he did not run for reelection but instead opened a bank, T. Mellon and Sons. Business was brisk until the Panic of 1873 reduced the bank's holdings that October to $12,000. Unlike many other banks, however, T. Mellon and Sons did not close its doors. In 1877 Mellon financed completion of the Ligonier Valley Railroad, linking Ligonier and Latrobe, Pennsylvania. To ensure a compliant labor force, Mellon paid $1 a day, 10¢ above the prevailing wage. Between 1881 and 1887 he sat on the Pittsburgh City Council. In the name of economy he opposed an increase in property taxes for public schools and the construction of a public library.

In 1882 Mellon retired from the bank, giving it to his son Andrew. In 1890 Mellon transferred his assets to Andrew to hold in trust for the family. That year Mellon moved to Kansas City, Missouri, to consult a medium in hopes of communicating with his deceased children. In 1895 he returned to Pittsburgh and died on his 95th birthday, February 3, 1908.

Christopher Cumo

See also: MELLON, Andrew William

References

Hersh, Burton. *The Mellon Family: A Fortune in History.* New York: William Morrow and Co., 1978.

Koskoff, David E. *The Mellons: The Chronicle of America's Richest Family.* New York: Thomas Y. Crowell Co., 1978.

Mellon, Thomas. *Thomas Mellon and His Times.* Pittsburgh: University of Pittsburgh Press, 1994.

MICHIGAN

In the early 1700s, Irish immigrants arrived on the peninsulas that now make up the state of Michigan, initiating three centuries of Irish-Michigan relations. The Irish were one of the first groups to settle Michigan, soon after the French, and long before the Germans and Dutch who later became the dominant ethnic groups. Michigan's European population was small until large-scale immigration began in the 1820s, totaling just 4,000 when the Michigan Territory was created in 1805. After statehood in 1837, the number of Irish immigrants steadily increased, reaching a peak during the middle of the century, coinciding with the Potato Famine. Until the late 1850s, the Irish were the largest ethnic group in Michigan, making up about a third of the population. Irish immigrants widely practiced "chain migration," a process by which an individual immigrant established a new life and then helped family and friends to follow. Immigrants usually settled in established Irish communities centered on the church and workplace. Because of the expense and harshness of the journey from Ireland to Michigan, returning to Ireland was often impossible. Thus, until the latter half of the twentieth century, relationships between Irish immigrants and their family and friends in Ireland were conducted almost solely by means of written correspondence.

Catholic Church records indicate that by 1879 more than 3,000 Irish families were in the Detroit area, with a further 12,000 families throughout the state. The 1870 Mortality Schedule includes many Irish surnames, such as O'Reilly, Sullivan, Ryan, McLaughlin, Caffrey, Coleman, O'Brien, Murphy, and Quinn. More than 2,500 Irish surnames are currently represented in Michigan. Irish settlers ensured that Michigan has many Irish place-names, naming four of Michigan's counties Clare, Wexford, Roscommon, and Antrim; establishing the towns of Bangor, Dublin, Buckley, Dundee, Sullivan, and Tyrone; and naming an area of Lenawee County the Irish Hills. Irish immigrants were instrumental in building and governing Michigan. The Irish worked as miners, laborers, farmers, sailors, engineers, carpenters, lawyers, and stonemasons. Irish workers opened up the state to settlement by constructing railroads and digging canals, while those who settled in urban areas often worked for fire and police departments. The Irish were predominantly drawn to the Democratic Party and dominated Detroit politics until the end of the nineteenth century. During the twentieth century, Frank Murphy, Frank Fitzgerald, Frank Kelley, and Patrick McNamara were influential politicians. Frank Murphy, a Democrat, was elected mayor of Detroit in 1931 and governor in 1936. Frank Fitzgerald, a Republican, was governor from 1935 to 1937, and defeated Murphy to serve again in 1939. Harry Kelly was governor from 1943 to 1947, and Jerry Cavanagh was mayor of Detroit from 1962 to 1969. Henry Ford, arguably Michigan's most famous and powerful citizen, was descended from Irish immigrants from Co. Cork.

The Irish have maintained a strong presence within Michigan society. The Corktown area, settled in 1834 by Cork immigrants, is Detroit's oldest surviving neighborhood. Detroit's annual Saint Patrick's Day Parade is the state's oldest continuing ethnic parade. A number of Irish festivals are held annually, such as the Clare Michigan Irish Festival and the Michigan Irish Music Festival in Muskegon. Michigan contains dozens of Irish organizations, such as the Ancient Order of Hibernians, which aims to help newly arrived immigrants, both socially and politically, and to preserve Irish arts, dance, music, and sports. The Muskegon Irish American Society promotes Irish culture through education, activities, and gatherings and by providing lessons in Irish language, dance, and music. Recent guest speakers include Myles O'Reilly, senior vice president of the Irish Development Agency, the Irish government's office in charge of recruiting business to Ireland.

Although the Irish-American community in Michigan is large—1,067,474 people identified themselves as Irish in the 2000 census (almost 11 percent of the state's population)—the number of Irish-born Michigan residents has decreased since the 1940s, numbering just 2,303 in 1990. Historically, the Michigan-Ireland relationship has been one-sided: the Irish immigrated to Michigan and contributed significantly to the state's industrial, economic, and social development, but Michigan's contributions to Ireland have been relatively few, including motor vehicle exports and music from Motown to Madonna and Eminem. However, during recent decades, increasing numbers of Michigan's citizens have engaged more directly with Ireland and its culture, from attending Irish festivals, U2 concerts, and productions of *Riverdance,* to reading Irish literature, or actually traveling to Ireland for vacations. Many Michigan universities, such as the University of Michigan and Michigan State University have study abroad arrangements with Irish universities, such as University College Dublin and University College Cork, allowing Michigan students to spend a semester living in Ireland, studying the culture, and forging relationships with their Irish peers.

Nathanael O'Reilly

See also: ANCIENT ORDER OF HIBERNIANS; CATHOLIC CHURCH, the; FORD, Henry; GREAT FAMINE, The; IRISH DANCING IN AMERICA

References

Bak, Richard. *Detroit Across Three Centuries.* Chelsea, MI: Sleeping Bear Press, 2001.

Coffey, Michael, ed. *The Irish in America.* New York: Hyperion, 1997.

Glazier, Jack, and Arthur W. Helweg. *Ethnicity in Michigan: Issues and People.* East Lansing: Michigan State University Press, 2001.

McGee, John Whalen. *The Passing of the Gael: Our Irish Ancestors, Their History & Exodus.* Grand Rapids, MI: Wolverine, 1975.

Rubenstein, Bruce A., and Lawrence E Ziewacz. *Michigan: A History of the Great Lakes State.* 3rd ed. Wheeling, IL: Harlan Davidson, 2002.

Vinyard, Jo Ellen. *The Irish on the Urban Frontier: Nineteenth-Century Detroit, 1850–1880.* New York: Arno Press, 1976.

MILWAUKEE IRISH FEST (FOUNDED 1981)

Milwaukee, Wisconsin, once famous for its beer, has always been perceived as a predominantly German city. In the early 1980s, however, the city's Irish residents decided to assert their presence in the community. As a result, the Milwaukee Irish Fest was founded in 1981 under the direction of Ed Ward. Since 2000, attendance figures have run from around 127,000 to more than 132,000. Apart from its size, three things make Irish Fest unique: the wide diversity of Irish music presented, the emphasis on Irish and Irish-American culture, and the evolution of auxiliary events and organizations that complement the festival and extend its impact throughout the year and beyond Milwaukee. Musically, the festival presentations range from Celtic rock bands and Riverdance-style dancing on large stages to *seán nós* singers and traditional solo performers from Ireland and North America in more intimate settings. The elongated shape of Milwaukee's festival park, which curls along the western shore line at the end of Lake Michigan, provides sufficient space and separation to minimize the type of sound bleeding that often plagues traditional singers and instrumentalists.

The same availability of space allows the festival to present a variety of opportunities for visitors to become acquainted with different aspects of Irish culture. Traditional crafts are demonstrated in some areas and currachs are raced in others. Every year there are special exhibitions built around themes, such as the Irish Famine or the history of Irish radio. Experts are brought from Ireland to curate the exhibits and to talk about the displays. A community-based Irish repertory company presents Irish and Irish-American plays at the theater on the festival grounds. During the week preceding the festival, Irish Fest Summer School, held at the University of Wisconsin-Milwaukee, provides a multigenerational program of lectures on Irish history and culture and workshops in the Gaelic language and Irish music, dance, and crafts.

Finally, the dynamics of Irish Fest have led to the creation of several entities that have extended the organization's efforts beyond the annual festival. The Irish Fest Foundation, established in 1993, channels some of the festival's revenue to organizations and activities that further Irish culture in the United States and Ireland. In 1998, the Irish Fest Center opened its doors, offering a year-round venue for lectures, concerts, and workshops. The center's School of Music began in 2002, providing instruction in Irish instrumental music and singing. The center also houses the John J. Ward, Jr., Irish Music Archives, named after the father of the festival's founder. The archives have more than 50,000 artifacts, most of them relating to Irish and Irish-American music and entertainment. The collection includes songbooks, sheet music, and sound recordings ranging from cylinders to CDs and covering Irish traditional and popular music. In a little more than two decades, the Milwaukee Irish Fest has evolved into an organization that is unique in the history of Irish-American culture.

William H. A. Williams

MISSOURI

The region of Missouri formed part of an ancient Native American culture located around Cahokia, the largest pre-Columbian settlement north of Mexico. In 1764, St. Louis was chosen as the site of a trading post by Pierre Laclède Liguest, who had been given a land grant by the French king Louis XV. The area became part of the United States in 1803 after the Louisiana Purchase, doubling the size of America. St. Louis subsequently became famous for being the springboard for the Meriwether Lewis and William Clark expedition, tasked with exploring the vast, newly acquired lands.

Missouri grew as emigrants moved westward from the coast and New England, but it retained an early French character. Much of the growing activity was based around the Mississippi River and the growing number of steamboats. The emerging sectionalism between the free North and slave South flared up around the issue of Missouri's statehood, and the dispute was addressed with the Missouri Compromise of 1820, wherein Missouri was admitted as a slave state while Maine was simultaneously admitted as a free state to preserve the balance of power.

The state population continued to grow, particularly rapidly from 1835 to 1860. Many Scots-Irish arrived in this period, both from Ireland and the upper South, all groups settling in cities and farmland along the Mississippi and Missouri rivers, some of the latter group being slave owners. Both Mark Twain, whose childhood home was in Hannibal, and Ulysses S. Grant, who had a Missouri farm, were descended from the Scots-Irish.

As numbers grew, Irish farming communities were both consolidated and established, one of the earliest being Saint Patrick's in Clark County, established in 1833. Part of southern Missouri was known as the Irish Wilderness; this included an 1859 settlement of 40 Irish families that did not survive the Civil War.

The majority of Irish immigrants settled in the urban centers of Kansas City and St. Louis (43 percent of the St. Louis population was Irish or German in 1850 and on the eve of Civil War St. Louis had the largest non–American-born city population in the country). Many new arrivals in Kansas City were aided by Bernard Donnelly, an immigrant and Catholic priest who established a quarry and a brickyard, providing jobs for hundreds of Irish immigrants paving early roads and in construction work.

A small group, known as the Irish Crowd, constituted part of the upper-class society in St. Louis before the Civil War and included John O'Fallon, Robert Campbell, Joseph Charles, who edited the city's first newspaper, and John Mullanphy. Mullanphy was born near Enniskillen (in 1758), immigrated to America in 1778, and settled in St. Louis in 1804. Various business interests yielded enough money for him to become a prominent philanthropist; he established convents, churches, and a hospital and donated a tract of land to ease the overcrowded Irish settlement. One of his 15 children became mayor of the city in 1847 and left a sizable amount of money to provide relief for poor emigrants moving west.

The urban experience for the vast majority, however, was characterized by living in a city struggling to accommodate so many people. Many Irish immigrants were unskilled or semiskilled, were subject to high levels of nativist resentment in the 1840s and 1850s, and in many cases competed for lower-level jobs with the city's free black population or with slaves who were contracted out by their owners. Consequently, many Irish workers were pro-slavery largely out of fear of a large pool of free labor undercutting their wages. Many lived in riverfront districts or the Irish shantytowns that quickly spread on the city's edge and became known as the Kerry Patch. This area was considered a dangerous community that essentially became a slum after the Civil War. Many of those who had fled conditions in Ireland would be affected by a severe cholera epidemic that swept St. Louis in 1849, killing an estimated 10 percent of the population.

The overall population increase was mirrored by the growth in churches that helped provide cohesiveness and identity for the communities. In mid-century many Irish laborers worked within the city political machines that gripped Kansas City and St. Louis into the first half of the twentieth centuries, both of which were controlled for differing periods by Irishmen—Ed Butler in St. Louis and the notorious Tom Pendergast in Kansas City in the 1920s–1930s. Despite deep-rooted civic corruption involving gambling and prostitution, Pendergast held substantial influence within the Democratic Party nationally and would help elect Missourian Harry S. Truman to the Senate in 1934.

During the American Civil War Missouri Irish fought for both sides—many perceived similarities between the Confederate cause and the Irish independence movement. For example, Joseph Kelly, an Irish immigrant and grocer in St. Louis, organised an Irish militia in 1857 and would lead them as part of the Confederate 5th Missouri during the war, known as Kelly's Boys.

In a postwar Missourian landscape, taking advantage of industrial opportunity, Irish in the area began to move into trades and professions. In a geographically central location, with rail and water transportation, industries flourished and St. Louis became the nation's fourth largest city by the 1890s. The city hosted the 1904 World's Fair (and Olympics), which included an exhibition showcasing Ireland, replete with singers, fiddlers, harpists, pipers, bands, dancers, and a visit from the poet W. B. Yeats, who traveled from Ireland for the event.

St. Louis is famed for its large steel arch in downtown, completed in 1965 to commemorate the city's historical importance as the "Gateway to the West," especially in regard to being used as a springboard during the gold rush. St. Louis has seen a steady suburbanization of residents, losing half its population between 1950 and 1990, and has been overtaken in size by Kansas City. The state's population as a whole continues to grow, and of its population of 5,595,211, 23.5 percent claim German ancestry (the largest ethnic ancestry group) and 12.7 percent claim Irish descent (the second largest).

Sam Hitchmough

References

Doyle, David Noel, and Owen Dudley Edwards, eds. *America and Ireland, 1776–1976: The American Identity and the Irish Connection,* Westport, CT: Greenwood Press, 1980.

Kenny, Kevin. *The American Irish.* New York: Longman, 2000.

Miller, Kerby A. *Emigrants and Exiles: Ireland and the Irish Exodus to North America.* 1985. Reprint, Oxford: Oxford University Press, 1988.

Spencer, Thomas M. *The Other Missouri History.* Columbia: University of Missouri Press, 2005.

MITCHEL, JOHN (1815–1875)

The Young Ireland revolutionary, journalist, and author John Mitchel was regarded as a hero-martyr for Irish nationalism in mid-nineteenth-century Ireland. Born November 3, 1815, in Camish, Co. Derry, the son of a Unitarian minister and member of the United Irishmen, Mitchel entered Trinity College in 1840, where he received his BA degree. He then studied law and became a solicitor, practicing in Newry, where he married Jenny Verner. He moved to Bainbridge and continued to practice law. Here he met the founders of Young Ireland, a politically active group of Trinity students who supported Daniel O'Connell. Mitchel was already a member of O'Connell's Repeal Association, and his friendships with Thomas Davis and Charles Gavan Duffy resulted in his editorial career for the pro-repeal newspaper the *Nation.* At Davis's request, Mitchel wrote the *Life of Aodh O'Neal* for a literary series,

Portrait of Irish nationalist activist and political journalist John Mitchel. (Library of Congress)

the *Library of Ireland.* When Davis died suddenly of scarletina in 1845, Mitchel joined Duffy as coeditor. During the Famine, Mitchel wrote anti-British editorials that demanded radical opposition to colonial rule. His militant political leanings eventually caused him to break from Young Ireland's leadership, because he was angered at their reluctance to endorse violent insurrection. Further, he believed the Famine was deliberately orchestrated to diminish the dependent Irish population and thereby increase colonial coffers. Mitchel argued that Ireland had no choice but to engage in armed resistance against landlords and exports of Irish commodities. In February 1848, Mitchel broke with Duffy and established his own newspaper, the *United Irishman,* wherein he continued to assail English officials and their representatives in Ireland.

In early 1848, Mitchel and Young Ireland leaders William Smith-O'Brien and Thomas F. Meagher were arrested for treason-felony. Smith-O'Brien's and Meagher's trials resulted in acquittal, because substantive evidence of treason was lacking, but the prosecution successfully packed Mitchel's jury, and he was found guilty. The trial generated anti-British sentiment in Dublin, and Mitchel's planned rescue would have been followed by an uprising. Young Ireland leaders, however, feared that a preemptive insurrection would fail and determined instead to delay the uprising until the fall harvest. To the dismay of many, and to Mitchel, he was led from the prison on May 27, placed in a police van, and carried to the Dublin docks where he boarded a prison ship. He would find himself in Bermuda before being shipped a second time to Van Diemen Island in Australia. Over the course of his imprisonment, he kept a detailed journal beginning with the date of his deportation. His *Jail Journal* became an important statement of Irish nationalism.

Mitchel enjoyed celebrity status and at various ports he was hailed by the public as a hero. On arrival in Australia, in ill health from recurring asthma, he was able to obtain a ticket of leave, a permit to live freely under his promise that he would not try to escape. His wife, Jenny Verner, and five children joined him, and they moved to a farm in Bothwell where he served his sentence as a sheep rancher. He maintained friendships with other Young Irelanders who had also been deported, many after the 1848 Rising: Smith-O'Brien and Meagher, Kevin O'Doherty, John Martin, Terrence B. McManus, and Patrick O'Donoghue. In 1853, however, the journalist P. J. Smyth arrived with a plan to aid in Mitchel's escape. The ticket of leave required that should he renege on his promise, he must turn himself into authorities, a question of honor with which Mitchel complied. He and Smyth entered the constabulary in Bothwell where Mitchel declared his intention. The police were slow to absorb the implication of his declaration, and Mitchel, with Smyth, escaped by horseback. Mitchel found shelter among Irish patriots, including Irish priests who disguised him as a cleric. Meanwhile, Smyth arranged for Mitchel and his family to sail first to Tahiti and then to San Francisco. On August 2, 1853, six weeks after turning in his ticket, having served five years of his 14-year sentence, Mitchel sailed from Australia. His wife sold the farm and household belongings and joined him in Tahiti. There the family boarded a U.S. ship bound for San Francisco on September 13.

The Mitchel family arrived in New York on November 29, 1853, where they settled in Brooklyn. John Mitchel declined an invitation to practice law and returned instead to journalism, serving as publisher and editor of the *Citizen,* assisted by Thomas Meagher. Mitchel continued his editorial style established years earlier in the *Nation* and in the *United Irishman.* He fiercely defended Irish Catholics against Know-Nothings (National Council of the U.S. of North America), a political organization engaged in defamatory practices against immigrants. Mitchel also embroiled himself in a controversy with the Roman Catholic Church when he criticized church doctrine regarding the infallibility of the pope. New York's Archbishop Hughes successfully debated Mitchel in the New York press. Mitchel later expressed regret over the dispute.

In yet another controversy, Mitchel supported southern slavery. The Reverend Henry Ward Beecher argued that Mitchel's stance was inconsistent with his position on Irish independence, yet Mitchel argued that slaveholding was not a crime and that Negroes enjoyed the protection of their southern owners, unlike tenants in Ireland. In 1854, Mitchel received an invitation to address the University of Virginia in Charlottesville. His popularity in the North had diminished, and his reception in the South brought about his decision to move to Tennessee. In Tuckaleechee, he again turned to farming, supplementing his income with lectures. He then moved to Knoxville, and in October 1857 established the *Southern Citizen,* an antiabolitionist newspaper that he later moved to Washington, D.C., where he published a series of articles on Young Ireland. At that time, Mitchel was approached by the Fenians, but he refused to use his newspaper as a means of Fenian fund-raising because, as he later explained, he distrusted the secretive nature of the organization.

In 1859, Mitchel pulled up roots again and moved to Paris, where he reported for the *Charleston Standard,* the *Irish-American,* and the *Irishman,* a Dublin publication. He returned to New York in 1862 during the War Between the States. Mitchel's southern sympathies took him to Richmond, Virginia, where he served in the Confederate ambulance corps and where his three sons joined Confederate forces. Both James and William died in service; John served on the staff of General John B. Gordon. While serving in the ambulance corps, Mitchel edited the Richmond *Examiner.*

After the war, Mitchel returned with his remaining family to New York and became editor of the *Daily News.* He had lost three children, yet his misfortunes continued. His defense of the South, and especially of Jefferson Davis, caused General Ulysses S. Grant to order his arrest. Again faced with a treasonable offense, Mitchel served five months at Fort Monroe. His health failed him, and through the efforts of the Fenians, he was released in October 1865. Mitchel joined the Fenian organization and served as treasurer, returning to Paris with the hope that another planned insurrection in Ireland would succeed where Young Ireland had failed. In Paris, Mitchel realized that the Fenians had misrepresented their capacity to organize and fund another Irish revolt.

Upon his return to New York, Mitchel began the *Irish Citizen,* assisted by his son John. He continued to lecture, wrote articles on Irish history, and published his collection of articles on Ireland, *The Last Conquest of Ireland (Perhaps).* He also contributed to *Appleton's Cyclopaedia.* With his health continuing to fail, Mitchel determined to visit his homeland, which he had left 26 years before. In July 1874, he landed with his daughter and a physician-friend at Queenstown (Cobh). Once again on Irish soil, he was concerned that he might be arrested. Mitchel, however, moved freely across the island and returned to Dublin, where he met old friends and his family. Before returning to the United States, he agreed to allow his name to be place in nomination for a parliamentary seat, although he stated that he would never sit in the House of Commons. In February 1875, he was elected to represent Tipperary. The vote was challenged by the Tory parliament, a new election was called, yet Mitchel was confirmed by a 2,368 majority vote in a second election held March 11.

Mitchel traveled to Tipperary with his son John on the initial news that he had been elected and was in Tipperary for the second vote. Exhausted, he spoke to crowds in Tipperary and Clonmel, but he grew too weak to continue. A speech scheduled at the Theatre Royal in Cork on February 26, was given by his friend John Dillon who read from notes. In those notes, Mitchel stated that the significant aspect of his election was its defiance of Parliament: a convicted Irish felon had been elected to a parliamentary seat.

After a period of rest, Mitchel determine to revisit his home in Newry. It was there he received news of the second election results. On March 20, 1875, John Mitchel passed away. He is buried in the Newry Unitarian cemetery.

Katherine Parr

See also: MEAGHER, Thomas Francis

References

Davis, Richard. *The Young Ireland Movement.* Dublin: Gill and Macmillan, 1987.

Kearns, G. "'Educate That Holy Hatred': Place, Trauma and Identity in the Irish Nationalism of John Mitchel." *Political Geography* 20, no. 7 (2001): 885.

McGovern, Bryan. "John Mitchel: Ecumenical Nationalist in the Old South." *New Hibernia Review* 5, no. 2 (2001): 99–110.

O'Sullivan, T. F. "John Mitchel." In *The Young Irelanders.* Tralee: Kerryman, 1944: 191–207.

MITCHELL, GEORGE J. (1933–)

Senator George J. Mitchell was born on August 20, 1933, in Waterville, Maine. His father, George Mitchell, Sr., was a laborer of Irish ancestry and his mother, Mary Saad, a textile worker of Lebanese ancestry. After graduating from Bowdoin College in 1954, Mitchell served for two years as an officer in the U.S. Army Counter Intelligence Corps in Berlin. He earned a law degree from Georgetown University in 1960 and then worked as a trial lawyer in the Justice Department in Washington, D.C., for two years. From 1962 to 1965, Mitchell served as executive assistant to Senator Edmund S. Muskie, whom Mitchell would later replace in the Senate. In 1965 Mitchell returned to Maine and engaged in the private practice of law. He ran unsuccessfully for governor of Maine in 1974 but was appointed U.S. attorney for Maine in 1977 and U.S. district judge for Maine two years later.

Mitchell was initially appointed to the U.S. Senate in 1980 to complete the term of Senator Muskie, who had resigned to become secretary of state. Mitchell was elected to his first full term in the Senate in 1982 and went on to a distinguished career that included positions on the Finance, Veterans Affairs, and Environment and Public Works committees. Among other notable work in the Senate, Mitchell played an instrumental role in the passage of the Americans with Disabilities Act, the ratification of the North American Free Trade Agreement, and the creation of the World Trade Organization. He also served as Senate majority leader from 1989 until he left the Senate in 1995.

After retiring from the Senate, Mitchell returned to the private practice of law but remained active in international politics. In 1995 President Bill Clinton appointed Mitchell special adviser to the president and secretary of state for economic initiatives in Ireland. The former senate majority leader then chaired the peace negotiations in Northern Ireland that culminated in the historic Good Friday accord of 1998, an agreement reached by the governments of Ireland and the United Kingdom and the political parties of Northern Ireland. In a May 1998 referendum the voters of Ireland overwhelmingly endorsed the agreement. Mitchell recounts his experience in the Northern Ireland peace negotiations in his 1999 book, *Making Peace.* President Clinton awarded Mitchell the Presidential Medal of Freedom on March 17, 1999, in recognition of the former senator's role in the Northern Ireland peace process.

Senator Mitchell's experience as a negotiator in international conflicts was not limited to Northern Ireland. He served as chairman of the International Crisis Group, an independent, nonprofit conflict resolution organization founded in 1995. In 2000, President Clinton, Israeli Prime Minister Ehud Barak, and Palestinian Liberation Organization Chairman Yasser Arafat asked Mitchell to chair an International Fact Finding Committee on violence in the Middle East. The Bush administration, the European Union, and many other governments endorsed the committee's recommendation, widely known as the Mitchell Report.

Kathleen Ruppert

References

George J. Mitchell Department of Special Collections. "Biography." http://library.bowdoin.edu/arch/mitchell/research/bio.htm (accessed August 13, 2007).

"Mitchell, George John, (1933)." Biographical Directory of the United States Congress. http://bioguide.congress.gov/scripts/biodisplay.pl?index=M000811 (accessed August 13, 2007).

MITCHELL, JOHN (1870–1919)

John Mitchell, president of the United Mine Workers of America (UMWA), was one of the most prominent and successful

American labor leaders of the early twentieth century. Born on February 4, 1870, in Braidwood, Illinois, the son of Martha Halley and Robert Mitchell, a Protestant native of Dublin, Mitchell became an orphan at age six and began mining work six years later. He had little formal education and left home at 16 to work in Colorado, New Mexico, and Wyoming coal mines before returning to Illinois. He married Katherine O'Rourke, a Catholic, in 1892 and their marriage produced six children.

Mitchell successfully organized miners in southern Illinois for the UMWA and by 1897 had a national reputation in the union. When UMWA President Michael Ratchford resigned in 1898, Mitchell took over leadership of the organization and served for 10 years. As a labor leader Mitchell favored collective bargaining agreements, which he believed would end labor violence and class warfare. Unlike radical labor leaders and socialists, Mitchell rejected the inevitability of class conflict. He presented a public image of a politically and socially conservative labor leader dedicated to caution. He did, however, create a highly centralized union organization to guarantee the union's commitment to negotiated agreements.

Mitchell achieved success in regional collective bargaining with the Interstate Joint Agreement in 1898, which covered the bituminous coal region between western Pennsylvania and Illinois known as the Central Competitive Field. Mine operators agreed to increase pay for the miners and to institute an eight-hour workday. This success spurred a great increase in union membership and convinced Mitchell of the value of trade agreements.

Mitchell's fame as a labor leader came during the Anthracite Strike of 1902 in the anthracite coal regions of eastern Pennsylvania. Here Mitchell demonstrated his abilities and political sophistication. Mitchell's union became a model of industrial unionism, enlisting the membership of all occupations in the mining industry, unlike the narrowly enrolled craft unionism prevalent in its parent organization, the American Federation of Labor. It also strove to overcome ethnic, religious, and linguistic divisions among the miners, recruiting heavily among recently arrived immigrant miners from Italy and Eastern Europe. Mitchell also courted journalists, who responded with favorable stories, as well as local religious leaders such as Bishop Michael Hoban of Scranton and Father John J. Curran of Wilkes-Barre.

Mitchell handled the strike of some 150,000 miners for more than five months to near tactical perfection. Not only did he maintain effective control over the striking miners and prevent violence, but he also masterfully won over American public opinion through the press. Rejecting any calls for revolutionary social change, Mitchell set the standard for future labor leaders as a reasonable, respectable, and peaceful figure who placed labor's demands in the context of the public interest. President Theodore Roosevelt ultimately encouraged government arbitration to settle the strike that had paralyzed the anthracite industry. The Anthracite Coal Strike Commission of 1903 granted a 10 percent wage increase, a nine-hour workday, and the creation of a board to arbitrate labor-management disputes. For the first time the government had intervened in an American labor dispute to settle a strike peacefully rather than simply to break the strike. Mitchell had achieved the only major American labor victory over a monopolized industry before the 1930s.

During his presidency coal miners gained higher pay, shorter working hours, and safer working conditions, and the UMWA went from 30,000 members to 300,000 members, becoming the largest labor union in the United States.

Mitchell had become a national figure with the Anthracite Strike and the leading spokesman for organized labor, but after 1902 his natural conservatism and commitment to mutual agreements made him increasingly cautious in protecting the institutional gains of the United Mine Workers. He never again threatened massive labor action. The strains of office eventually caught up with Mitchell, who battled problems with alcohol, insomnia, and chronic illnesses. Mitchell sought spiritual relief in 1907 by converting to Catholicism. He retired from his UMWA presidency in 1908 to become head of the Trade Agreement Department of the National Civic Federation, a coalition of capitalist, labor, and public officials, a post he held until 1911. Mitchell later became the chairman of the New York Industrial Commission, which he headed until he died of pneumonia in 1919 at age 49.

Joseph P. Finnan

See also: MOLLY MAGUIRES

References

Gowaskie, Joseph M. "John Mitchell and the Anthracite Coal Strike of 1902: A Century Later." In *'The Great Strike': Perspectives on the 1902 Athracite Coal Strike*. Easton, PA: Canal History and Technology Press, 2002.

Laslett, John H. M., ed. *The United Mine Workers of America: A Model of Industrial Solidarity?* University Park: The Pennsylvania State University Press, 1996.

Phelan, Craig. *Divided Loyalties: The Public and Private Life of Labor Leader John Mitchell*. Albany: State University of New York Press, 1994.

Taft, Philip. *Organized Labor in American History*. New York: Harper & Row, 1964.

MITCHELL PRINCIPLES, THE

The principles of democracy and nonviolence, or the "Mitchell Principles," were issued in January 1996 as part of the ongoing peace process in Northern Ireland. Named for former U.S. Senator George Mitchell, chairman of the peace negotiations in Northern Ireland from 1996 to 1998, the Mitchell Principles helped pave the way for the Good Friday Agreement reached by the governments of Ireland and the United Kingdom and the political parties of Northern Ireland in 1998.

Following a 1994 ceasefire by the Irish Republican Army (IRA) and the main loyalist paramilitary organizations in Northern Ireland, Taoiseach Albert Reynolds, Social Democratic and Labour Party leader John Hume, and Sinn Féin leader Gerry Adams met in Dublin and all declared their commitment to solving the Northern Ireland question peacefully and democratically. An impasse was reached, however, when the two main Unionist parties in Northern Ireland (the Ulster Unionist Party and the Democratic Unionist Party) refused to enter negotiations with Sinn Féin until the latter had demonstrated its commitment to democracy through the decommissioning of IRA arms. Sinn Féin considered such a demand unacceptable, and the opening of all-party negotiations was therefore put on hold.

The governments of the United Kingdom and the Republic of Ireland invited former U.S. Senator George Mitchell, who had served for a year as special adviser on economic initiatives in Northern Ireland, to chair the peace negotiations. Mitchell was given the task of exploring how paramilitary arms might be decommissioned and all-party negotiations advanced. In a January 1996 report, Mitchell concluded that decommissioning in advance of talks was unrealistic. He recommended instead a twin-track approach in which all parties to the negotiations would affirm their total and absolute commitment to democracy and nonviolence. The decommissioning of arms could then move forward once talks had begun.

In addition to discussing the decommissioning process and suggesting a number of confidence-building gestures, Mitchell's report outlined six principles that each party must accept before reaching the negotiating table. The acceptance of the so-called Mitchell Principles would indicate a commitment to democracy and nonviolence and so, it was hoped, take the gun out of Irish politics once and for all. As a test of their bona fides in the peace process, all parties were asked to affirm their total commitment to the following six principles: (1) democratic and exclusively peaceful means of resolving political disputes; (2) the complete disarmament of paramilitary organizations; (3) the use of an independent commission to verify that disarmament was satisfactorily completed; (4) the renunciation of the use of force (or the threat of force) to influence the course of negotiations; (5) an agreement to abide by the terms of any agreement reached in all-party negotiations; and (6) an end to "punishment" killings and beatings.

Even after the release of Mitchell's report, the peace process in Northern Ireland continued to be beset by controversy, delays, and occasional bouts of violence. The British government under Prime Minister John Major agreed to the Mitchell Principles but insisted that elections be held for a negotiating convention before talks could begin. Interpreting Major's request as a delaying tactic, republicans were outraged. On February 9, 1996, just two and a half weeks after the Mitchell Commission published its report, an IRA bomb killed two people and injured more than 100 in the Docklands area of London. Sinn Féin's leader Gerry Adams voiced his willingness to adhere to the Mitchell principles on May 20, but other parties insisted in the wake of the Docklands bombing that nothing short of an IRA cease-fire would suffice. When talks opened on June 10, 1996, Sinn Féin, the political arm of the IRA, was therefore excluded. Progress was slow during the first year of talks, and little significant advance occurred for some time. When a new Labour government under Tony Blair was elected in May 1997, however, renewed attention was given to the Northern Ireland peace process and a schedule was set for substantive talks over the course of the next year. The IRA restored its cease-fire in July and Sinn Féin was admitted to the talks six weeks later. After considerably more wrangling, an agreement was finally reached at approximately 5 p.m. on Good Friday, April 10, 1998. The Mitchell Principles had laid the foundation for the negotiations that eventually culminated in this historic Good Friday Agreement.

Kathleen Ruppert

References

Cox, Michael, et al., eds. *A Farewell to Arms? From "Long War" to Long Peace in Northern Ireland.* Manchester, UK: Manchester University Press, 2000.

Mulholland, Marc. *The Longest War: Northern Ireland's Troubled History.* Oxford: Oxford University Press, 2002.

MOLLY MAGUIRES

The term Molly Maguires was applied in Ireland to those who used violence against landlords and their agents. No evidence has ever been found to connect the Molly Maguires of the anthracite coal region of eastern Pennsylvania with those in Ireland, however, other than common use of the name. Both the Molly Maguires in Ireland and Pennsylvania shared a common belief that the use of violence was justified because economic and political power was overwhelmingly against them. Members of the Molly Maguires who were convicted were also members of the Ancient Order of Hibernians and the Workingmen's Benevolent Association (WBA), even though these groups and the majority of their members opposed violence.

Between 1862 and 1875 16 murders in the anthracite coal region of Pennsylvania were attributed to the Molly Maguires. Targets included mine owners, foremen, a judge, a police officer, and others. Ethnic rivalry and competition for jobs with Welsh miners contributed to the violence. The patterns of assassinations can be broken down into two distinct periods. The first lasted from 1862 to 1868 and was a reaction to the Civil War era draft and the difficulty in organizing a union during the national crisis. The immigrant Irish miners resisted the draft, and during the war, mine operators fought unionization, charging that it was unpatriotic. These unpopular positions permanently damaged the standing of the Irish miners in the eyes of the public. In the following decade the public was receptive to exaggerated stories of Irish terrorism and secret societies on the coalfields.

In 1869 the WBA got the operators to agree to a contract favored by the miners, including a sliding pay scale. When the price of coal fell, the operators wanted to lower wages. In addition, Franklin B. Gowen of the Reading Railroad was consolidating ownership of the mines, and the smaller operators thought they had to cut costs to remain competitive. Having heard rumors that the Irish miners had a terrorist organization called the Molly Maguires, Gowen hired the Pinkerton Detective Agency to infiltrate the alleged secret society. Pinkerton assigned the task to James McParlan, an Ulster Catholic, who believed the Molly Maguires were an organization imported from Ireland.

After stockpiling coal throughout 1874, the operators presented the miners with a new contract, complete with a significant pay cut. In January 1875 the WBA called a strike. Over the next six months, in what was called "the long strike," the WBA failed to obtain any concessions from the operators. In June the operators invited the miners who so desired to return to work with the pay cut. Many accepted the offer. Such a devastating loss virtually destroyed the WBA. It also caused a group of men to consider that violence was the only tool available to achieve social justice for the workers. On the inside, McParlan, as he reported later on the stand, witnessed the planning of assassinations and beatings. In the summer of 1875 the pattern of assassinations resumed, initiating the second period of violence, drawing national attention and feeding anti-Irish sentiment. In addition to the nativists and businessmen, the Catholic Church and organized labor unions condemned the Molly Maguires.

The trials began in January 1876 and lasted until August 1878. McParlan abandoned his undercover operations and immediately gave his testimony to the prosecutors. In all, fifty Molly Maguires were indicted, based almost exclusively on McParlan's word. The prosecutors were mostly corporation lawyers and Franklin

Gowen was their leading witness. The prosecutors used the trials to convict all labor organizing as antidemocratic, un-American and potentially murderous. When the verdicts were finally tallied, 20 were hanged and another 20 imprisoned. Ten had received amnesty for providing evidence against the others.

Gregory J. Dehler

References

Bimba, Anthony. *The Molly Maguires.* New York: International Publishers, 1932.

Broehl, Wayne G., Jr. *The Molly Maguires.* Cambridge, MA: Harvard University Press, 1964.

Gudelunas, William A., and William G. Shade. *Before the Molly Maguires: The Emergence of the Ethno-Religious Factor in the Politics of the Lower Anthracite Region, 1844–1872.* New York: Arno Books, 1976.

Kenny, Kevin. *Making Sense of the Molly Maguires.* New York: Oxford University Press, 1998.

MOLONEY, MICK (1944–)

For more than 30 years Mick Moloney has been at the center of the revival of interest in traditional Irish music in the United States. A gifted musician, steeped in the tradition, a scholar with years of experience in fieldwork, and a tireless organizer of recording sessions and concerts, Moloney has been uniquely situated to bring Irish music to America and America to Irish music.

Like many young urban Irish of his generation, young Moloney's initial interest in folk music was sparked by the British "skiffle" movement of the 1950s and then by the phenomenal international success of the Clancy Brothers and Tommy Makem. Drawn to the tenor banjo, Moloney sought out the rich musical tradition on the other side of the Shannon in Co. Clare. By the early 1960s, when he enrolled in University College Dublin, he was an active musician. While completing his bachelor's (politics) and master's (economics) degrees, he played in a variety of folk groups and organized several folk clubs. He eventually joined the Johnsons, bringing his flatmate, guitarist Paul Brady, into the group. The Johnsons were an international success, but five years of touring was enough for Moloney. After a stint in education in Norway and social work in London, he took up a suggestion by Dr. Kenneth Goldstein and enrolled in the doctoral program in Goldstein's department of folklore at the University of Pennsylvania.

With Irish traditional music in the United States as his thesis subject, Moloney found himself traveling around the country recording the tunes and memories of a generation of aging immigrant musicians. In spite of the obscurity that had overtaken it after World War II, the music had been kept alive by the likes of Mike Flanagan and Ed Reavy. Drawing on his background as a professional musician, Moloney was soon producing recordings of Irish-American musicians of the rising, as well as the passing, generation. By 2000, Moloney had produced almost 50 recordings.

In 1976, Moloney was asked to organize the Irish section of the Smithsonian Institution's Festival of American Folklife, bringing Irish and Irish-American musicians of all ages together on the Mall in Washington, D.C. It was partly for this event that Moloney put together the Greenfields of America, a group of traditional musicians and dancers who have brought Irish music to almost every corner of the country. Over the years, Moloney has continued to perform and record with the Greenfields, Eugene O'Donnell,

Robbie O'Connell, Jimmy Keane, and Séamus Egan. He has accompanied numerous other musicians on their recordings.

Keenly aware of the relationship between music and society in America, Moloney has worked hard to bring Irish music and dance into contact with other ethnic cultures. He has directed and coordinated American multicultural dance festivals that have been sent to West Africa and South and Central America by the United States Information Agency.

Moloney's talents as a musician and a scholar, combined with his extraordinary range of contacts among Irish-American musicians, have involved him in various projects for National Public Radio and the Public Broadcasting System. Among these are the PBS documentaries *Out of Ireland* (1998) and *The Irish in America: Long Journey Home* (1999). He was also a consultant for the BBC/RTÉ series *Bringing It All Back Home* (1991).

The academic side of Moloney's career has involved him in teaching ethnomusicology, folklore, and Irish studies courses at the University of Pennsylvania, Georgetown University, Villanova University, and New York University. He is the author of numerous articles and a combination book and CD, *Far From the Shamrock Shore: The Story of Irish American History through Song* (2002).

William H. A. Williams

See also: CLANCY BROTHERS, the

References

"A Conversation with Mick Moloney: Part I." *The Folk Life* 1, no. 9 (July 1977).

"A Conversation with Mick Moloney: Part II." *The Folk Life* 1, no. 10 (August, 1977).

Winick, Steve. "From Limerick to Solid Man: The Musical Life of Mick Moloney." *Dirty Linen* 48 (October/November 1993).

MONTAGUE, JOHN (1929–)

John Montague was born in Brooklyn, New York, in 1929. His father, James Montague, an Ulster Catholic from Co. Tyrone, had moved to America in 1925. He was joined in 1928 by his wife and their two elder sons. Unable to find steady work during the Depression, the children were sent back to Ireland in 1933. John went to live with his aunts in Garvaghey, Co. Tyrone. He was educated in St. Patrick's College, Armagh, the junior Diocesan Seminary. One of his teachers was Sean O' Boyle, one of the leading experts on Ulster folk song and Irish poetry. He encouraged Montague's exploration of Irish poetry. In 1946, Montague won a Co. Tyrone scholarship to attend University College Dublin. Inspired by the example of other student poets (including Thomas Kinsella) he began to publish his first poems in *The Dublin Magazine, Envoy,* and *The Bell,* edited by Peadar O'Donnell. In 1952, Montague left for Yale on a Fulbright Fellowship. He worked at the Iowa Writers Workshop in 1954–1955. After a further year of graduate study in Berkeley, he returned to Dublin, where he married and began to work in the Irish Tourist Office.

Montague continued to write poetry and published his first collection, *Poisoned Lands,* in 1961. He lived for a number of years in Paris, where he befriended Samuel Beckett. His first book of stories, *Death of a Chieftain,* was published in 1964. Further collections of poetry, *A Chosen Light* (1967) and *Tides* (1970), followed. During the 1960s, Montague continued to work on a long autobiographical poem about Northern Ireland, *The Rough Field,* which was finally published in 1972. *The Rough Field* was slowly recognized as a major achievement. *Hymn to the New Omagh*

Road (1968) and *The Bread God* (1972) also reflect his interest in Northern Ireland's affairs. In 1976, Montague was presented with the Award of the Irish American Cultural Institute, the first Marten Toonder Award in 1977, and the Alice Hunt Bartlett Award for *The Great Cloak* in 1978. A Guggenheim fellowship in 1979–1980 enabled Montague to complete his *Selected Poems* (1982) and his second long poem, *The Dead Kingdom* (1984), which were published in Ireland, Britain, the United States, and Canada. In 1987, New York's governor, Mario Cuomo, presented Montague with a citation for his literary achievements and contributions to the people of New York. Montague taught for two decades at University College Cork, influencing a generation of Irish poets in the Republic—among them Tom McCarthy, Greg Delanty, and Nuala Ní Dhomhnaill. Author of 10 major collections of poems dating from *Poisoned Lands* (1961) to *Smashing the Piano* (2001), Montague was the first holder of the Ireland Chair of Poetry at Queen's University Belfast.

Aoileann Ní Eigeartaigh

References

Brady, Anne M., and Brian Cleeve. *A Biographical Dictionary of Irish Writers.* Dublin: The Lilliput Press Ltd., 1985.
Gonzales, Alexander G., ed. *Modern Irish Writers: A Bio-Critical Sourcebook.* Westport, CT: Greenwood Press, 1997.

MONTREAL

The flag of the city of Montreal is a Christian cross on a white background with a flower in each quadrant representing the four founding communities of the city. In the lower right-hand quadrant is the shamrock. The significance of this homage to the Irish community rests on their presence and their contribution for over a century, in making Montreal a modern economic center for the northeastern part of North America.

Before the first wave of Irish immigration of the 1840s, there was a small Irish community within Montreal and parts of the surrounding areas. Imbued with the ideas of republicanism and progressive politics, many in this burgeoning community supported the 1837–1838 Patriot Rebellion in Lower Canada. This rebellion, lead by French Canadian elites such as Louis Joseph Papineau, rejected British colonialism, wanted to establish a republican form of government, and wanted to implement progressive ideas such as separation of church and state, rights for women, and equality for aboriginals. Irishmen such as Daniel Tracy and Edmund Bailey O'Callaghan joined the cause of the rebellion. Both members of the *fils de la liberté;* Tracy was the founder in 1828 of the Irish newspaper *The Vindicator,* which espoused republican ideals and supported the "92 resolutions," the political manifesto for the Patriot Rebellion. O'Callaghan, who later became the editor of *The Vindicator,* was also an instigator with Louis Joseph Papineau of the rebellion. Both supported and were also members of the Patriot Party and worked to forge unity between the Irish and French Canadians against the British colonialists.

The wave of Irish immigrants that came to Montreal settled in the southwestern part of the city. The vast majority settled in areas around the Lachine Canal. Because the Lachine Canal, built in 1825, was the link between the Saint Lawrence River and the Great Lakes, this area quickly became in the mid-nineteenth century the center of Canada's and in particular Montreal's industrial revolution. The Irish immigrants therefore settled where the jobs were. They quickly became part of Montreal's working class.

Because of the Irish influx into the city, Saint Patrick's Church (now named a Basilica) was built in 1847 to fulfill the religious needs of Irish Catholicism. But Saint Patrick's was a little far removed (placed in the center core of the city) from the concentration of the working-class Irish. Working in the industries around the Lachine Canal (railways, the port of Montreal, textiles, steel foundries), the Irish concentrated in St. Ann's ward (near the port) and later in Point St. Charles (along the Lachine Canal). Saint Ann's, or, as it came to be named, Giffintown, quickly became the largest area of Irish settlement and a beacon of Irish working class culture for the city of Montreal. By 1845 there were approximately 500,000 Irish in Canada; 30,000 of these lived in Griffintown, making it the largest English-speaking community in Quebec. Thomas D'Arcy McGee would become the member of Parliament for the area. Because of these numbers a new Irish Catholic Church, Saint Ann's, was built in 1854. The Irish workers of Griffintown would build the Victoria Bridge (the first railway bridge across the Saint Lawrence River that would link Montreal's industrial sector to the New England States), and would erect at the entrance of the bridge, seen until this day, a monument (the Black Rock) to all Irish immigrants who had died coming to Canada. Griffintown was transformed beyond all recognition by municipal planning initiatives in 1970, depriving the city's working class Irish community of its traditional environs.

As industrialization proceeded west and east along the Saint Lawrence, Irish workers started to inhabit new areas of Montreal. The Lachine Canal was still a focal point for the Irish community, which increasingly moved towards the Point St. Charles neighborhood. In 1895, a new Irish Catholic Church, Saint Gabriel's, was built, and it is still the center of cultural activity for the Irish community of Montreal. Here, as in Griffintown, the Irish working class would provide the labor for the railway yards, the port, and the rising steel industry in southwest Montreal.

Industrial expansion by the turn of the twentieth century turned eastward, along the Saint Lawrence to areas around Maisonneuve and Rosemont. Again, as in the past, Irish workers would go to where the jobs were. In 1911, Canadian Vickers, a subsidiary of British Vickers of Northern Ireland, constructed a shipbuilding plant in East End Montreal. This plant built ships for the British navy and had the largest dry dock in the world. Here again job opportunities for Irish workers led to their migration to the eastern part of the city. The management of Canadian Vickers was British and Scots-Irish, while the workers were French Canadian and Irish. At the height of its activity between 1930 and 1960, Vickers employed up to 10,000 people, working in three shifts. By 1920, because of their growing numbers, a new Irish Catholic parish was created. Saint Aloysius was built in 1927, and, until its demolition in 1980, it was the focal point of the Irish cultural community in the eastern part of the city.

A little north of Maisonneuve was an area called Rosemont. Here the Canadian Pacific Railroad (CPR), Canada's oldest and largest railway, established its main Canadian plant, named the Angus Shops after one of the Canadian Pacific Railroad's presidents. The Angus Shops built and repaired railway cars for the entire Canadian Pacific Railroad network; during World War II. It also produced a large number of tanks for the Allies. As before, Irish workers followed the employment opportunities. To work for the CPR guaranteed a family's future. The same pattern prevailed with the construction of Saint Brendan's church (still in operation today), built to fulfill the religious needs of the Irish workers who now worked and lived in Rosemont.

The peculiarity that marked these early Irish working-class parishes was that for more than 100 years the parish priests came from Ireland. This policy was instituted by the Irish branch of the Catholic Church to promote and protect Irish Catholicism and culture in a sea of French Canadian culture and French Catholicism. Each parish had its corresponding elementary school (grades one through seven) where the curriculum was taught by the Presentation Brothers brought over from Ireland. With the Irish churches and schools, the preservation of Irish culture and religious practices was rooted in Canadian society and permitted to grow.

Many other ethnic and cultural groups (Italians, Poles, Ukrainian Catholics, French Canadians who wished to learn English) who practiced Catholicism and lived in these neighborhoods profited from this Irish presence by attending the only English-language schools in these working-class areas. They learned about Irish culture and history, and in many ways their schools were forerunners of a multicultural Canadian society. The last brother of the Presentation order in Canada left in the mid-1990s. Certain Irish Catholic high schools, such as Cardinal Newman High School and Thomas D'Arcy McGee High School, were more regional and catered to a wide English-speaking Catholic clientele. Many of these schools, as with the parishes, no longer exist, because of the Irish community's displacement to the suburbs or Toronto.

There were other Irish Catholic parishes, which were built over the years, always following the movement of the Irish community into different sections of Montreal and into suburbs. Some examples would be Saint Mark's and Saint Anthony's in the Mile End district, Saint Mary's in the lower city, and Transfiguration of Our Lord in the West Island.

As of 2005 the core of the Irish community of Montreal is now dispersed throughout the city and surrounding suburbs, but the energy of the community persists in the form of numerous organizations such as the United Irish Societies of Montreal (who organize the annual Saint Patrick's Day parade), Cine Gael (Irish film society), Canadian Association for Irish Studies, and the Concordia University Centre for Canadian Irish Studies to name but a few. An excellent example of this continued vivacity and contribution of the Irish community to cosmopolitan Montreal is the Saint Patrick's Day parade, started in 1824, which has become the longest uninterrupted Irish festivity in North America.

Donald Cuccioletta

See also: McGEE, Thomas D'Arcy

References

Bradbury, Bettina. *Working Families, Age, Gender and Daily Survival in Industrializing Montreal.* Toronto: McClelland and Stewart, 1993.

Burns, Patrica. *The Shamrock and the Shield: An Oral History of the Irish in Montreal.* Montreal: Véchicule Press, 1998.
Trigger, Rosalyn. "The Role of the Parish, Fostering Irish Catholic Identity in the 19th Century." Master's thesis, McGill University, Montreal, Canada, 1997.

MOORE, BRIAN (1921–1999)

Brian Moore's first novel, *The Lonely Passion of Judith Hearne* (1956), established this Irish expatriate and conservative stylist as a significant voice in the modern novel tradition. A Belfast-born author of almost 30 novels, Moore has been labeled Irish, British, Canadian, and American during the course of his career, as a consequence of his self-imposed exile from Ulster to North America. During his lifetime, he was admired in the writing community, especially by Graham Greene, and was thrice shortlisted for the Booker Prize for *The Doctor's Wife* (1976), *The Colour of Blood* (1987), and *Lies of Silence* (1990). His second novel, *The Luck of Ginger Coffey,* won the prestigious Canadian Governor General's Award in 1960. Several of his other works—including *Catholics* (1972), *The Temptation of Eileen Hughes* (1981), and *Cold Heaven* (1983)—have also appeared in film. The protagonist's motto delivered in *I Am Mary Dunne* (1968), "*memento ergo sum*" ("I remember, therefore I am"), epitomizes Moore's ultimate concern: the influence of the cultural and religious past on existence in the present and future.

Exile and emigration emerge as consistent themes in Moore's writing, along with explorations of memory, loss of faith, ordinary lives, loneliness, and spiritual paralysis. Catholicism also haunts his novels, although Moore opposed being labeled a Catholic writer on the grounds that he falls short of the ideal. Many of Moore's earlier characters and situations are drawn from his own experience. *The Emperor of Ice-Cream* (1965), with its protagonist who fails his Leaving Certificate, takes a job with the Air Raid Precautions Unit, and serves as a paramedic coffining bodies during the Blitz of Belfast, is Moore at his most clearly autobiographical. Later character renderings, such as the missionary priest in *Black Robe* (1985) or the nineteenth-century French woman who travels to Algeria in *The Magician's Wife* (1997) display Moore's increasingly broad interest in the aftereffects of colonialism and religion.

Moore was born August 25, 1921 in Belfast, Northern Ireland, the fourth of nine children that were conceived by James Bernard Moore, a doctor and converted Catholic, and Eileen McFadden Moore, a former nurse. Like his father, Moore studied at St. Malachy's College Belfast. Unlike his father, he was unable to pass mathematics and, consequently, failed the school Leaving Certificate, to his father's displeasure. It was his mother who regarded him as a favorite son. Their warm relationship helped balance the repressive atmosphere of his father's rigid Catholicism. Moore lost his own Catholic faith while still a young man, and regarded the Catholic Belfast society of his youth as stifling; only after emigrating could Moore begin his authorial career. Moore became a Canadian citizen and later moved to the United States. He never returned to Ireland. After serving as a paramedic during World War II and a postwar stint with the United Nations, Moore decided to immigrate to Montreal, Canada, in 1948, and soon found a position at the *Montreal Gazette.* He married Jacqueline (Scully) Siros, a talented staff writer at the *Montreal Standard* in 1951. The couple would have one son, Michael Brian, in 1953 and would divorce in 1967. Moore's later marriage to Jean Denney, another Canadian, would last the rest of his life.

Moore left his position as a reporter in 1952 to become a full-time writer of books, and he authored several pulp novels under pseudonyms such as Michael Bryan and Bernard Mara before *Judith Hearne,* Moore's first literary novel, appeared in 1955. It was issued in the United States under the longer title the following year. *The Feast of Lupercal* (1957) soon followed. The family moved to New York City in 1959, where he wrote *The Luck of Ginger Coffey,* for which he won the Governor-General's Award in 1960. He would also earn the same award, Canada's highest literary honor, for *The Great Victorian Collection* (1975). In 1964, Moore converted *The Luck of Ginger Coffey* into screenplay form, prompting an admiring Alfred Hitchcock to ask Moore to write another screenplay. The film *Torn Curtain* (1966) was a disappointment for Moore, though the project did induce his permanent move to Malibu, California, which he found a beneficial climate for his writing. He accepted a position teaching in the English department at the University of California-Los Angeles and continued to produce novels every two or three years until his death.

Kelly J. S. McGovern

References

Blades, John. "Brian Moore: Travels of a Literary Infidel." *Publishers Weekly* 245, no. 1 (January 5, 1998): 44–45.

Gonzales, Alexander G. *Modern Irish Writers: A Bio-Critical Sourcebook.* Westport, CT: Greenwood, 1997.

Moritz, Charles, ed. *Current Biography Yearbook.* New York: H. W. Wilson, 1986.

O'Donoghue, Jo. *Brian Moore: A Critical Study.* Dublin: Gill and Macmillan, 1990.

MOORE, CHRISTY (1945–)

Born in Newbridge, Co. Kildare, Christy Moore was steeped in music and politics from an early age. Moore graduated from the folk circuits of Ireland and England during the 1960s and became a solo performer of iconic status, with a string of successful albums and a discography that spans more than 500 songs and 30 albums. He has been recording and performing his music for more than 40 years and has collaborated with other legendry figures along the way, such as Shane McGowan, Sinead O'Connor, Elvis Costello, and Bono among others. Moore has been a central figure in two of the most influential Irish bands of the past 30 years, namely Planxty and Moving Hearts, along with his key musical collaborator Donal Lunny.

His repertoire is both wide ranging and eclectic, and it can move seamlessly from bawdy entertainment to biting political and social protest songs aimed at events in Ireland and on the international stage. The breadth of Moore's repertoire reflects the personal and political development of the man himself and the span of time across which he has been writing and performing. During the course of his career, Moore has been a regular visitor to North America and has a large following among Irish diaspora communities in large cities such as Boston and New York.

In musical terms, Moore was initially influenced by the Clancy Brothers (he would later follow in their footsteps to play Carnegie Hall in New York) but was also infused with the more radical tradition of singers such as Ewan MacColl, Bob Dylan, and Woody Guthrie. In 1988, Atlantic Records capitalized on U.S. interest after the sold-out Carnegie Hall gig by releasing a special *Compilation USA* album.

Moore has created a substantial body of work in the recording studio; his albums include *Prosperous, The Spirit of Freedom, H-Block, Ride On, Ordinary Man, This Is The Day,* and the recently released *Burning Times* in 2005. Many of these albums have revitalized songs that had nearly been lost by the Irish folk tradition, and some of his own early albums have become collectors, items in their own right. Perhaps more importantly, Moore has functioned as an aural archive of his political and social times, writing and singing about the H-Block protests and republican hunger strikes in Northern Ireland in the 1980s with "90 Miles From Dublin"; attacking the abuses of the Catholic Church in *Strange Ways;* and critiquing U.S. foreign policy with such songs as "El Salvador," "America, We Love You," and more humorously "Hey Ronnie Reagan." Moore's music has also reflected concerns about unemployment in "Ordinary Man"; the nuclear arms race in "Hiroshima, Nagasaki Russian Roulette"; and international human rights abuses in "Biko Drum." In recent years, Moore has campaigned against the U.S.-led War in Iraq and President George W. Bush's visit to Ireland. In June 2004 he headlined a group of Irish acts at a concert in Dublin organized by the Irish Anti-War Movement entitled When Bush Comes to Shove. In the past, Moore has had to cancel concerts in Northern Ireland because of bomb threats from loyalist paramilitary groups. More recently, he was controversially detained for more than two hours in October 2004 by British police under the Prevention of Terrorism Act at Holyhead while on his way to a concert in Liverpool.

While often pigeonholed as an Irish folksinger, Moore has transcended this categorization and has emerged as a political, social, and cultural commentator with an international relevance. Apart from his studio recording, Moore will also be remembered by those who have seen him in concert, for a number of electric live performances charged with humor, political anger, and emotional connections with an audience for whom the pain of migration is infused into the national consciousness. These concerts are built on a powerful roller coaster of affection and connection between Moore and his audience, along with periodic admonishments by the singer for overenthusiastic audience participation. His music has inspired and consoled the Irish diaspora, as well as his audience within Ireland, and is built upon a deep spirituality, humanitarianism, intelligence, wit, and poetic talent.

Feargal Cochrane

See also: CLANCY BROTHERS, the

References

Connolly, Frank, ed. *The Christy Moore Songbook.* Tralee: Brandon Books, 1984.

Moore, Christy. *One Voice: My Life in Song.* London: Hodder & Stoughton, 2000.

MOORE, MARIANNE (1887–1972)

Marianne Moore was one of the most innovative and idiosyncratic of modern American poets, an original and influential editor and reviewer, and a prolific correspondent. Her writing spans a crucial period in twentieth-century literature, forming a bridge between the inventiveness of early modernist peers (H.D., Ezra Pound, and T. S. Eliot) and the lyrical voices of her successors (including Sylvia Plath, whom she met in 1958, and Elizabeth Bishop). Moore has been described as a "Kleptomaniac of the mind" (Costello, 5),

Portrait of poet Marianne Moore who, during the course of her career, won the Pulitzer Prize, the National Book Award, and the Bollingen Prize. (Library of Congress)

and it is evident that her interests were varied, ranging from the Brooklyn Dodgers to zoology. T. S. Eliot suggests that Moore's art is the product of "many soils" (Costello, 12), and although she is typically regarded as an American writer, she expresses a persistent affinity with the Ireland of her distant inheritance. Moore did not actually visit Ireland until 1964 and, after she had done so, enthused about its ability to live up to her expectations (Willis, 665).

Moore was born in 1887 in Kirkwood, Missouri, and she and her older brother were raised by their mother and their grandfather, a Presbyterian pastor. In a letter to Ezra Pound, Moore elaborates on these origins, suggesting that she is of Irish, and possibly Scottish, but certainly Celtic ancestry (Tomlinson, 16). Moore studied at Bryn Mawr from 1905 until 1909 and then taught at an Indian School in Pennsylvania before moving to New York in 1918. By this time, she had become acquainted with avant-garde poets, and her work had begun to appear in literary magazines. In 1921 her first volume, *Poems,* was published, without Moore's knowledge, by acquaintances H.D. and Winifred Bryher. This was followed by numerous other collections, including *Observations* (1924), *Selected Poems* (1935), *The Pangolin and Other Verse* (1936), *What Are Years* (1941), *Like a Bulwark* (1956), and *Complete Poems* (1967). Moore also wrote a play, *The Absentee* (1962), based on Maria Edgeworth's novel of the same title.

Moore became a familiar and iconoclastic figure on the New York poetry scene. She edited the magazine *The Dial* during the 1920s, and it was in this capacity that she published some of W. B. Yeats's work, including autobiographical essays and one poem, "Among School Children." Yeats is a poet to whom Moore repeatedly turns. His complaint from *Ideas of Good and Evil* about William Blake's imaginative reach informs Moore's thoughts about truth, language, and the imagination in 'Poetry'—one of her best-known works. Moore values sincerity and commitment in poetry, and it is a similar attentive directness that she recognizes and approves in Yeats's work. Moore is critical, though, about Yeats's complex and often-shifting views about women (Willis, 314).

The association of Ireland with femininity, of national with gender identity, reemerges in Moore's "Sojourn in the Whale" (1917)—a poem that takes Ireland and Irishness as explicit themes. The poem originates in and reflects on Moore's early struggle to gain admission to the New York poetry establishment. It draws on the mythology, rhetoric, and imagery of the Ireland with which Moore claimed kinship to fully figure experiences of exclusion, circumscription, and frustration. Ireland, here, is personified as female and is addressed directly in a heartfelt appeal for solidarity in resistance to oppressive forces. This is particularly resonant, given both Moore's history as a supporter of the suffragettes, and the genesis of the poem in the period after the Easter Rising of 1916.

"Spenser's Ireland" (1941), too, takes Ireland as its subject (and Edmund Spenser's *A View of the Present State of Ireland* [1596] as its stimulus). It is frank, even defiant, in its acknowledgment that this is an Ireland that the speaker knows only in her imagination. It is an idealized place that is available to her only through folklore and literature. The poem is complex in its sympathies, both delighting in and skeptical about the Irish habits and customs that it describes. Like "Sojourn in the Whale," it strives to envisage individual and collective freedom but is frustrated by an inability to broach the multiple forms of enslavement that pertain in the culture.

"Spenser's Ireland" closes on an ambiguous note that yokes the uncertainty and dissatisfaction of the speaker's position with her Irish identity. Fiona Green cites the opening line of an early draft of the poem, which sees the speaker falling out of love with Ireland (181), and suggests that the text as a whole reflects a growing ambivalence on Moore's part about Irish neutrality during the World War II period. Arguably, the final line of the published version reflects Marianne Moore's own troubling situation of being simultaneously committed to, and dissatisfied with, her identity as an Irish-American writer.

Jo Gill

See also: YEATS, William Butler

References

Costello, Bonnie. *Marianne Moore: Imaginary Possessions.* Cambridge, MA: Harvard University Press, 1981.

Green, Fiona. "'Your trouble is their trouble': Marianne Moore, Maria Engeworth and Ireland." *Symbiosis* 1, no. 2 (October 1997): 173–185.

Moore, Marianne. *Complete Poems.* London: Faber and Faber, 1984.

Tomlinson, Charles, ed. *Marianne Moore: A Collection of Critical Essays.* Englewood Cliffs, NJ: Prentice-Hall, 1969.

Willis, Patricia C., ed. *The Complete Prose of Marianne Moore.* London: Faber and Faber, 1987.

MOORE, THOMAS (1779–1852)

Thomas Moore was one of the most popular poets writing in English in the nineteenth century. He helped to establish

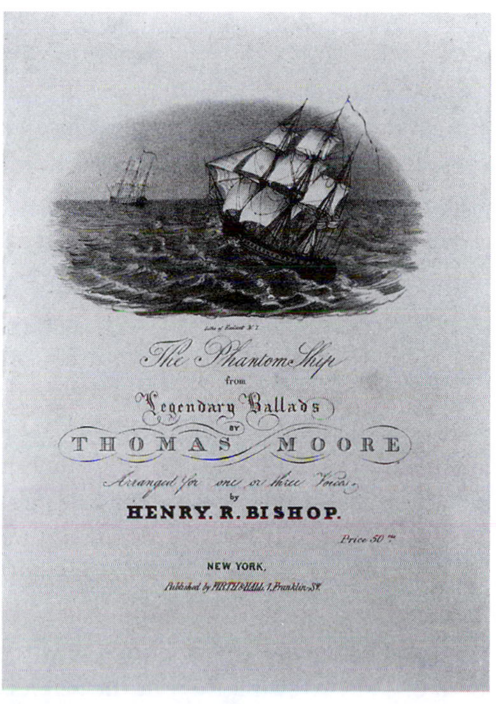

Title page from a collection of ballads by Thomas Moore. (Library of Congress)

the themes of nineteenth-century romantic poetry and song. He was the bard of nostalgia, the half-pleasurable, half-sad emotional recollection of bygone days and departed friends, as seen through "the light of other days" (from "Oft in the Stilly Night"). However, he was best known for his *Irish Melodies* (issued from 1808 to 1834), which were acclaimed on both sides of the Atlantic. These poems, which Moore set to his adaptations of traditional Irish airs, helped to establish the romantic, sentimental image of Ireland in Victorian parlor ballads. Few American households boasting an organ or a piano would have been without their copy of Moore's *Melodies.*

Although a Roman Catholic, Moore attended Protestant Trinity College in his native Dublin. While a student there he befriended Robert Emmet and Lord Edward Fitzgerald, who became leaders of the United Irishmen. Moore did not join the radical group or take part in its risings in 1798 and 1803, but he mourned the deaths of his friends, evoking their memories in the *Melodies.* However, because he feared being labeled as a republican, Moore never mentioned the names of the rebels he memorialized in such songs as "Oh! Breath Not His Name" or "When He Who Adores Thee." When he did celebrate Irish heroism and national sacrifice, he was careful to set his poems in the long dead, half-mythologized past. His odes to freedom did not rage against the English power of his own day. As a consequence, Moore has been criticized for having popularized images of Ireland as glorious in defeat and pitiable in subordination, as represented by the self-sacrificing warrior bard of "The Minstrel Boy" or the helpless maiden of "Erin! The Tear and Smile in Thine Eyes." Yet this last song also invoked a hope for Irish unity, symbolized by a "rainbow—One Arch of peace." Moore had married a Protestant (his "heretic girl" of "Come, Send Round the Wine"), and in several songs he called for an end to Ireland's sectarian discord. He was, nevertheless, a strong supporter of Catholic Emancipation.

The political subtleties of Moore's popular songs were probably lost on their many admirers in the United States, Irish and non-Irish alike. Yet even those Yankees who were unmoved by Moore's stirring celebrations of Irish patriotism embraced the sentimental romanticism of his love songs, which held their place in the popular repertory well into the twentieth century. Today, however, when placed alongside modern poetry, even Moore's best efforts may seem effusive and conventional. The close readings of academic critics find little to engage them, while postcolonial theorists fret about how accommodating Moore's brand of Irish nationalism was to British imperialism.

Whatever his shortcomings as a poet, Moore's true genius lay in his ability as a songwriter. Drawing on the traditional Irish airs published by Edward Bunting and others, Moore was highly skilled in adapting them to his poems, uniting melody and lyrics into smooth flowing lines. Part of this ability was due to the fact that he performed his own material and so brought a singer's sense to the construction of his songs. The musicality of his melodies even survived the often fussy piano arrangements of the composers his publishers hired to provide settings for the songs. Even though they were far removed from their folk sources, Moore's songs were one of the principal conduits for Irish traditional music into Anglo-American popular music. His influence can easily be seen in the melodies of Stephen Foster.

William H. A. Williams

References

Flannery, James W. *Dear Harp of My Country: The Irish Melodies of Thomas Moore.* Nashville, TN: J. S. Sanders, 1997.

Tessuier, Thérèse. *The Bard of Erin: A Study of Thomas Moore's Irish Melodies, 1808–1834,* translated by George P. Mutch. Salzburg: Institut für Anglistik und Amerikanistik, Universität Salzburg, 1981.

White, Harry. *The Keeper's Recital: Music and Cultural History in Irish Music, 1770–1970.* Critical Conditions. Field Day Essays. Cork: Cork University Press, 1998.

Williams, William H. A. *'Twas Only An Irishman's Dream: The Image of the Irish and Ireland in American Popular Song Lyrics, 1800–1920.* Urbana: University of Illinois Press, 1996.

MORRISON, BRUCE (1944–)

Born in New York City, Bruce Morrison was brought up in Northport, New York, on Long Island. He attended the Massachusetts Institute of Technology and graduated with a degree in chemistry before going on to receive a master's degree in organic chemistry at the University of Illinois at Urbana-Champaign. He later attended Yale Law School. He worked for New Haven Legal Services before running for the United States Congress in 1982. From 1983 until 1991 he represented the Third District of Connecticut (New Haven) in the House of Representatives, having narrowly defeated his opponent in both the primary and the congressional elections. During his time in the House of Representatives he served on the Judiciary Committee and the Banking Committee. He also served on the Committee for Veterans Affairs and the Select Committee on Children, Youth and Families. He visited Cuba, Paraguay, and Chile to promote human rights and democracy. He left Congress to run as the Democratic candidate for governor of Connecticut but finished third behind the Independent candidate, Lowell Weicker, and the Republican, John Rowland. In 1995 President Clinton appointed Morrison as the chairman of the Federal Housing Finance Board, in charge of the 12 Federal Home Loan Banks. He oversaw the passing of the Federal Home Loan Bank Modernization Act of 1999, and he remained in this position until 2000. In 2001 he founded Morrison Public Affairs Group, a lobby group of which he is currently the chairman.

Links with Ireland have been visible at different stages of his career. As a member of the House of Representatives he was chairman of the Immigration Subcommittee. In 1990, along with prominent Irish-American Senator Edward Kennedy, he sponsored the Immigration Act. This act granted 48,000 visas to Irish emigrants who wished to live and work in America. Many of the Irish people who availed themselves of these visas later ended up becoming American citizens. At a time when the Irish economy was in recession and large numbers of Irish illegal immigrants were in America, his role in this legislation was important, and it made his name well known in Ireland. This led to the visas in question being commonly referred to as "Morrison visas." However, some in America claimed that as opposed to those immigrants from other countries, there was special treatment for the Irish as a result of the Irish-American lobby. Because of this alleged favoritism, they maintained that Ireland, a country with a relatively small population, had received a disproportionately high allotment of visas. In spite of these claims, many in Ireland regarded the visa program as a success. In 1994 the Irish national television station RTÉ broadcast a program called *The Morrison Tapes,* which followed three groups of Irish emigrants to America who had availed themselves of the Morrison visas. Ten years later, they revisited the same people—a family, two young men, and a single mother—to track the changes in their lives over the intervening period.

Later Morrison also played an important role in the Irish peace process, and he was a key adviser to President Bill Clinton in the negotiations that took place both before and after the Irish Republican Army cease-fires. He was the cochairman of Irish-Americans for Clinton-Gore in the two presidential elections. From 1991 to 1995 he was a partner in the law firm Morrison & Swaine, where he specialized in immigration. From 1992 to 1997 he also served on the U.S. Commission for Immigration Reform. With the growth of the Irish "Celtic Tiger" economy in the 1990s, the drop in Irish people immigrating to America was accompanied by a rise in the number of people from other countries coming to live and work in Ireland. In 2003, at a conference of the Immigrant Council of Ireland, Morrison urged the Irish government to bring in a new immigration system in Ireland. He envisaged that the country would need more immigrants to maintain its current rate of economic growth and that there would have to be large-scale reform of Ireland's immigration system. He called for a coherent immigration policy that would allow people to settle in Ireland with the possibility of their eventually becoming Irish citizens. In 2004 he criticized the citizenship referendum that was being held in Ireland, calling it "dangerous," "unnecessary," and "premature."

David Doyle

Reference

"Bruce Morrison." Stennis Center for Public Service website. www.stennis.gov/Congressional%20Bios/brucemorrison.htm (accessed August 13, 2007).

MORRISON, VAN (1945–)

Singer, composer, and musician Van Morrison has proven that an Irish artist can assimilate and reinvent in an original way the essence of American music from the 1950s and 1960s, especially the African-American tradition and rhythm and blues. He has recorded more than 20 albums over four decades, remaining Ireland's most durable popular singer and a respected songwriter worldwide.

At age 18, Van Morrison began his recording career with a pop group named Them (from 1963), having a debut success with a single titled "Don't Start Crying Now" (1964), followed by a cover of a blues classic, "Baby Please Don't Go" (1964), first recorded by U.S. blues legend Big Joe Williams. The group combined covers of American music and original compositions.

As a composer for Them, Morrison released his first classic, the hit song "Gloria," in 1965, which would later become a major anthem for U.S. singer Patti Smith in 1978. When the group Them disbanded in 1966, after a successful American tour, Van Morrison immigrated to the United States, where he stayed and recorded as a solo artist from 1967 until 1973.

Under his own name (from 1967), Van Morrison has had a long, successful career as a solo performer and songwriter, with classic albums such as his debut for Warner Records (and second album as a solo artist), *Astral Weeks* (1968), and his third as a solo artist, titled *Moondance* (1970), which featured songs like "Caravan," "Into the Mystic," and the title song, in a fine synthesis of jazz, pop, and rock. In 1973 Morrison confirmed his attachment to African-American music, covering many bluesy standards on a live album titled *It's Too Late to Stop Now* (1973), which was recorded in Los Angeles and London. Among the blues and soul songs covered by Van Morrison on his 1973 tour were Sam Cooke's "Bring It On Home," Ray Charles's "I Believe To My Soul," Willie Dixon's "I Just Want to Make Love to You," and two older tracks composed by Sonny Boy Williamson: "Help Me" and "Take Your Hand Out Of My Pocket."

Back in Ireland from 1973 to 1976, Van Morrison recorded a new album almost every two years, although some of those went unnoticed. On film, Morrison briefly appeared in Martin Scorsese's documentary *The Last Waltz* (1978), about the farewell concert of Canadian group the Band, with whom he performed one of his most famous songs, "Caravan." Van Morrison also appeared onstage as a guest star with U.S. legend Bob Dylan at a London concert in 1984, doing a duet of Dylan's "It's All Over Now Baby Blue."

Exploring his own roots from the mid-1980s, Van Morrison traveled Ireland and recorded 10 Irish folk songs with the Irish folk ensemble the Chieftains in 1988 (on a CD titled *Irish Heartbeat*), featuring Gaelic lyrics like "Carrickfergus," "Ta Mo Chleamhnas Deanta (My Match It Is Made)," and the title song. That celebrated collaboration exposed Van Morrison to a new, younger audience.

Van Morrison's interest in African-American music, which his own father collected, led him to record with his long-time idol, bluesman John Lee Hooker, who did two duets with him for Morrison's CD *Too Long In Exile* (1993). In 2000, Van Morrison recorded a whole duet album titled *You Win Again* with Linda Gail Lewis, the younger sister of rock-and-roll singer Jerry Lee Lewis; the album included standards like Hank Williams's country song "Jambalaya," and John Lee Hooker's "Boogie Chillen."

After more than 40 years of song writing, Van Morrison remains a distinctive, powerful singer and sometimes a spiritual lyricist, who can create moody atmospheres and intense performances (see his underrated LP *Poetic Champions Compose,* from 1987). He also recorded two live albums in Belfast: *Live at the Grand Opera House, Belfast* (1985) and *The Skiffle Sessions: Live in Belfast 1998* (2000), on which he included traditional folk songs like "Goodnight Irene," composed in 1935 by African-American songster Huddie Leadbelly.

Yves Laberge

See also: CHIEFTAINS, The

Reference

Hinton, Brian, *Celtic Road: The Art of Van Morrison.* London: Sanctuary Publishing Limited, 2003.

MOTT, LUCRETIA COFFIN (1793–1880)

Lucretia Coffin Mott was a Quaker minister and reformer whose transatlantic experience contributed to the expression of her reform impulses; likewise, her presence at the first World Anti-Slavery Convention, held in London in 1840, encouraged and challenged both local reformers, for example Richard Davis Webb and, to a lesser extent, the Irish politician Daniel O'Connell. These contacts, made and fostered within the Quaker and reform circles, formed part of a transatlantic network of like-minded reformers who refined and circulated their ideals and traded reform news in their letters and pamphlets. These primary documents give insights into the advances and conflicts that accompanied involvement in reform groups.

Mott attended the 1840 World Anti-Slavery Convention as an American delegate but was refused admission to the proceedings. Frederick Tolles explains that the religious and political beliefs that inspired Mott demanded that she take sides in both Quaker and abolitionist circles. In both cases, her choice was less favored amongst English Quakers. Lucretia Mott and her husband were Hicksite Quakers, who "emphasized the inward more than the historic Christ" (Tolles 1952, 4), whereas the English Quakers favored the more orthodox approach to their religious experience. Lucretia supported the abolitionist leader, William Lloyd Garrison, and his call for immediate emancipation of the black slaves through peaceful means, rather than the gradualist approach of the more militant American Anti-Slavery Society. Consequently, the English mistrusted Mott and refused to admit her to the proceedings. While sitting outside the door, Mott met Elizabeth Cady Stanton, and most commentators suggest that this meeting inspired the beginning of the first Women's Rights Convention, held at Seneca Falls in 1848.

While at the first World Anti-Slavery Convention, Mott met the Irish leader Daniel O'Connell, who was not a delegate but attended the conference. Mott asked O'Connell to respond to the fact that she had been snubbed. This challenged O'Connell to reconsider his initial misgivings about the place of female delegates at this conference.

After the conference, Mott visited Ireland and met with several Quaker and abolitionist reformers she had previously met in London. One of these was the Quaker printer from Dublin, Richard Davis Webb. Lucretia and Webb became firm friends; indeed, Webb was so impressed by Mott, he described her as the "Lioness of the Convention" (Harrison 1993, 24). They discussed matters of a philanthropic and reform nature. Despite such pleasant company, Mott was very conscious of Irish poverty and noted it in her diary. She was also interested in the education of women, and this topic also appears in her diary. These are just some of the many reform issues that inspired her to speak for the freedom of those marginalized by race or gender, education of boys and girls, and temperance; her 49 public addresses dwell on these themes. However, she is most commonly associated with the twin causes of the abolition of slavery and women's rights.

Ann Coughlan

See also: ABOLITIONISM AND SLAVERY; WEBB, Richard Davis

References

Harrison, Richard S. *Richard Davis Webb: Dublin Quaker Printer (1805–1872).* Cork: Red Barn Publishing, 1993.

Tolles, Frederick. *Slavery and the Woman Question: Lucretia Mott's Diary of Her Visit to Great Britain to Attend the World's Anti-Slavery Convention of 1840.* London: Friends Historical Society, 1952.

MOYNIHAN, DANIEL PATRICK (1927–2003)

Born in Tulsa, Oklahoma, Daniel Patrick Moynihan grew up in New York City. He was educated at Benjamin Franklin High School in Harlem, from which he graduated first in his class. His father deserted the family when Daniel was young, leaving his mother to raise the children by herself. After a series of odd jobs, which included working as a longshoreman and shining shoes, he briefly attended the City College of New York before joining the Navy in 1944. After the war he attended Tufts University and received a bachelor's degree in 1948. He received a master's degree in 1949 and a doctorate in 1961 from the Fletcher School of Law and Diplomacy. He also studied at the London School of Economics as a Fulbright Fellow in 1950–1951. He worked as assistant and secretary to Governor W. Averell Harriman of New York, and he was a member of the New York State Tenure Commission before writing papers for the presidential campaign of John F. Kennedy. When Kennedy was elected president, Moynihan was appointed special assistant to Secretary of Labor Arthur Goldberg. Later, he became assistant secretary of labor and helped draft legislation that would become President Johnson's Equal Opportunities Act. Following an unsuccessful bid for the Democratic nomination for president of the New York City Council, he was named director of the Joint Center for Urban

Former United States Democratic senator for New York Daniel Patrick Moynihan is sworn in as U.S. ambassador to the United Nations by Justice Byron White (left). United States President Gerald Ford (right) stands nearby at the White House on June 30, 1975. (Getty Images)

Affairs at Massachusetts Institute of Technology and Harvard in 1966. He subsequently became a professor of government at the Kennedy School of Government at Harvard, a position he left to join the Nixon administration as adviser to the president for urban affairs. He resigned this position in 1971 and returned to Harvard, where he was a professor of sociology until 1973, when he was appointed ambassador to India, a position he remained in for two years. Before returning briefly to Harvard, he was named as permanent representative to the United Nations in 1975. He resigned his post and returned to Harvard before being elected the U.S. senator for the state of New York in November 1976. He was reelected as senator on three occasions: in 1982, 1988, and 1994. In 2000 he declared that he would not seek reelection to the Senate. In the same year, President Clinton awarded him the Presidential Medal of Freedom, the nation's highest civilian honor. Moynihan was professor at Syracuse University's Maxwell School, and for the final year of his life he was senior scholar at the Woodrow Wilson International Center for Scholars. He died of complications from a ruptured appendix on March 26, 2003, and he is buried at Arlington National Cemetery. In addition to his career in public service, Moynihan was a noted author. His 19 books include *Beyond the Melting Point* (1963), a study of American ethnicity that he coauthored with Nathan Glazer, and *The Negro Family: The Case for National Action,* which became popularly known as the Moynihan Report. Other publications included *The Politics of a Guaranteed Income* (1963), *Family and Nation* (1986), *Came the Revolution* (1988), *On the Law of Nations* (1990), and *Secrecy: The American Experience* (1998).

Moynihan, along with New York Governor Hugh Carey, Speaker of the House Tip O'Neill, and Senator Edward Kennedy, was known as one of the "Four Horsemen," an informal group of senior Irish-American politicians who promoted Irish interests in Washington. He was also known as a supporter of the moderate nationalist Social Democratic and Labour Party and its leader John Hume, and he became a vocal opponent of violent Irish republicanism. He joined forces with other Irish American politicians to appeal to Irish Americans to stop sending money to the Provisional Irish Republican Army. However, in 1994, with the emergence of the Irish peace process, along with Senator Kennedy, he appealed to President Clinton to grant the Sinn Féin leader Gerry Adams a visa to enter America. On his death tributes were paid to him by the Taoiseach Bertie Ahern, who said he was "a great intellectual and a great friend to Ireland." Enda Kenny, the leader of Fine Gael, the main oppostion party in Ireland, said "his tireless commitment to finding a peaceful solution to the conflict in Northern Ireland was instrumental in encouraging the U.S. government to become involved in supporting the peace process."

David Doyle

References

Deedy, John. "Daniel Patrick Moynihan." In *The Encyclopedia of the Irish in America,* edited by Michael Glazier. Notre Dame, IN: University of Notre Dame, 1999.

Hodgson, Godfrey. *The Gentleman from New York: Daniel Patrick Moynihan—A Biography.* New York: Houghton Mifflin, 2000.

Katzmann, Robert A., ed. *Daniel Patrick Moynihan: The Intellectual in Public Life.* Washington, DC: The Woodrow Wilson Center Press, 1998.

MULDOON, PAUL (1951–)

Born in Eglish, Co. Tyrone, Paul Muldoon grew up on a farm near the Moy, Co. Armagh. He was educated at St. Patrick's College Armagh and Queen's University Belfast. At Queen's he established relationships with members of the Belfast Group, including Seamus Heaney, Derek Mahon, and Michael Longley. From 1973 to 1986 he worked for BBC Northern Ireland in Belfast. The collections published during this time—*Mules* (1977), *Why Brownlee Left* (1980) and *Quoof* (1983)—reflect turbulence in Muldoon's personal life and escalating political violence in Northern Ireland. After short periods spent living in Co. Kerry and in England, Muldoon settled permanently in the United States with his second wife, Jean Hanff Korelitz. Between 1987 and 1990, he lectured at Columbia University, the University of California, and the University of Massachusetts and since 1990 has worked at Princeton University. In 1999, he was appointed Oxford Professor of Poetry. Since his immigration to the United States, Muldoon has published several collections of poetry, including the important books *Madoc (*1990) and *The Annals of Chile* (1994). He has also written for the opera (his three libretti are all concerned with American themes), stage, and television. His collected *Poems 1968–1998* was published in 2001.

America, North and South, has always assumed a large place in Muldoon's poetry. "Lunch with Pancho Villa," in *Mules,* represents an early excursion into a fantasy South America that Muldoon revisited and expanded upon two decades later. "Immram," an experiment in combining Irish and American idiom, appears in *Why Brownlee Left.* In *Quoof* the sonnet sequence "The More a Man Has the More a Man Wants," follows the fortunes of a terrorist mercenary, Gallogly, and his vengeful nemesis and alter ego, an "Oglala Sioux" named Mangas Jones. A note to the poem claims it is "loosely based on the Trickster cycle of the Winnebago Indians." "7, Middagh Street," in *Meeting the British* (1987), concerns transatlantic exchange of a different kind. This densely allusive poem is a sequence of interlinked dramatic monologues spoken by the inhabitants of the house on Thanksgiving Day 1940; these inhabitants included W. H. Auden, Benjamin Britten, Salvador Dali, and Louis MacNeice. These literary concerns combine with the picaresque narrative of earlier poems in *Madoc.* The 233-poem sequence, "Madoc—A Mystery," which occupies almost all of this volume, mixes various genres (literary and philosophical history, science fiction, the western adventure story) to imagine what might have happened had Coleridge and Robert Southey (Muldoon's poem is a '"re-make" of Southey's 1806 epic) succeeded in their scheme to establish a utopian pantisocracy on the banks of the Susquehanna. These oblique, linguistically playful poems, each "surtitled" by the name of a philosopher in brackets, confront issues of gender, race, conquest, and colonization, by implication in their Irish as well as American contexts. Muldoon's poetry of the mid-1990s is characterized by a growing interest in South American–Irish cultural exchange. Throughout *The Annals of Chile,* Muldoon's childhood home is associated with South American landscapes; while the poems' formal and thematic preoccupation with repetition is influenced by Jorge Luis Borges, particularly his essay "A New Refutation of Time."

Muldoon's three latest collections, *Hay* (1998), *Moy Sand and Gravel* (2001), and *Horse Latitudes* (2006), continue to draw parallels between the Ireland of his childhood and youth and his adopted home in the United States. Muldoon's commitment to a historical understanding of the Irish diaspora, his dismantling of prevailing notions of the importance of place in Irish poetry, his combination of American experimental idiom with a more traditionalist post-Romantic Irish poetic confirm his important place in any survey of Irish-American cultural exchange.

See also: HEANEY, Seamus

Kit Fryatt

References

Kendall, Tim. *Paul Muldoon.* Bridgend: Seren, 1996.

Wills, Clair. *Improprieties: Politics and Sexuality in Northern Irish Poetry.* Oxford: Oxford University Press, 1993.

Wills, Clair. *Reading Paul Muldoon.* Newcastle upon Tyne, UK: Bloodaxe, 1998.

MULHALL, MICHAEL GEORGE (1836–1900)

Michael G. Mulhall, a writer, journalist, and statistician born in Dublin in 1836, was the son of Thomas Mulhall (1803–1856) and Catherine Flood (1807–1849). Mulhall studied for the priesthood at the Irish College in Rome. He abandoned the idea of religious life, and then went to Buenos Aires in 1860, where his brother Edward Thomas Mulhall (1832–1899) had already been settled since the mid-1850s. In May 1861, Michael and Edward Mulhall founded the *Standard,* which became the first daily newspaper in English published in South America (though the weekly *British Packet* had been published since 1810). The *Standard* was founded, as it declared in the first issue, "not as the emblem of a party or the watchword of rivalry, but as the bond of fellowship between the various members of our Anglo-Celtic race [. . .]. We have all come from the British Isles and English, Irish, Scotch, and American acknowledge one mother tongue. Monopoly is unjust and bigotry hateful. To crush one and prevent the other is our object." Although in fact Irish, the Mulhall brothers usually referred to themselves as English, championing the interests of the British community; these views were reflected in the paper, and the brothers were often criticized for this stance. The *Standard* ceased publication in 1959, but its archives remain one of the most important sources for the history of English-speaking communities in Argentina.

In 1863 Mulhall published *The Handbook of the River Plate,* allegedly the first book in English printed in South America; it was followed by five subsequent editions in 1869, 1875, 1876, 1885, and 1892, reaching a total of 11,500 copies sold. In 1876 an edition in Spanish was ordered by President Sarmiento. The 1892 edition of the *Handbook* offers 686 pages full of plenty of minute information about Argentina—its natural features, population, industries, railways, finance and commerce—and a detailed description of provinces, departments, and cities. Abundant information about Uruguay and Paraguay is also included. The inclusion of elaborate information about the journey from Europe to Argentina and routes in the latter country suggests that the main readers were potential English-speaking emigrants. A separate edition for Brazil (*Handbook of Brazil*) was published by the brothers Mulhall in 1877. Other books published by Michael G. Mulhall were *The*

English in South America (1878), *Progress of the World in Arts, Agriculture, Commerce, Manufactures, Instruction Railways, and Public Wealth Since the Beginning of the Nineteenth Century* (1880), *Balance Sheet of the World for Ten Years, 1870–1880* (1881), *History of Prices Since the Year 1850* (1885), and his famous *Mulhall's Dictionary of Statistics* (1883). In fact a compilation of statistics rather than a dictionary, the *Dictionary of Statistics* is valuable for its contents of the nineteenth century and unique for this period, including statistics arranged alphabetically by specific subject—accidents, age, crime, debt, drunkenness, eggs, fires, insane, and so on—for the United States, Europe, and other countries. It was published in seven editions up to 1911.

In 1878 Pope Leo XIII decorated Mulhall in recognition of his literary work. He traveled extensively in Europe collecting material for a committee of the English parliament reporting on a proposed department of agriculture for Ireland in 1896. Mulhall died in Dublin on December 12, 1900. His wife Marion MacMurrogh Murphy was also a writer and the first president of the St. Joseph Ladies Society in Buenos Aires.

Edmundo Murray

See also: PRESS, THE IRISH IN LATIN AMERICA

References

Coghlan, Eduardo A. *Los Irlandeses en la Argentina: Su Actuación y Descendencia.* Buenos Aires: Author's Edition, 1987.

Marshall, Oliver. *The English-Language Press in Latin America.* London: Institute of Latin American Studies, University of London, 1996.

Meehan, Thomas F. "Michael George Mulhall." In *The Catholic Encyclopedia,* vol. X.

Murray, Thomas. *The Story of the Irish in Argentina.* New York: P. J. Kenedy & Sons, 1919.

MULRONEY, BRIAN (1939–)

Although Brian Mulroney was Canada's prime minister for almost a decade, for many people the most defining moment of his political career was perhaps not legislation signed or a speech given, but a duet. In March, 1985, Mulroney met with Ronald Reagan in Quebec City in what became known as the Shamrock Summit—so-called because of the two leaders' shared Irish heritage and the meeting's coincidence with Saint Patrick's Day. Irishness was played up by all involved, most delegates wearing green somewhere on their person. At the conclusion of the summit, Mulroney, Reagan, and their wives, in a televised broadcast, appeared on stage to sing "When Irish Eyes Are Smiling." Mulroney's defenders would claim that the event was a success, marking a rapprochement between the United States and Canada after years of stressed relations under Pierre Trudeau's governance. Detractors, and most public opinion, considered the event to be symbolic of Mulroney's willingness to play lapdog to Reagan's neoconservative program, which was actualized in the negotiations that took place behind closed doors and would lead to the North American accord. The Irish heritage and friendship of the two was reinforced at Reagan's funeral in 2004, where Mulroney was an official pallbearer and gave a eulogy quoting from the poetry of W. B. Yeats and Seamus Heaney.

Brian Mulroney was born in Baie Comeau, a paper-mill town on the northeastern shore of Quebec's Saint Lawrence River coast, on March 20, 1939. He is the eldest son and the third of six children born to Benedict Mulroney, an electrician employed at the paper mill, and his wife Irene (O'Shea). His parents met in the parish of

Sainte-Catherine-de-Portneuf, a small town to the west of Quebec City that was home to both Irish and French Canadian Catholics. It was in this parish that the Mulroney family originally settled upon their arrival in the 1840s, after emigrating from Ireland during the Famine.

Despite his working-class origins, Mulroney was sent to St. Thomas, a well-respected Catholic boarding school in Chatham, New Brunswick. He graduated with a bachelor's degree from St. Francis Xavier University in Antigonish, Nova Scotia, and a law degree from Laval University in Quebec. Upon graduation from Laval, he was employed by a prestigious Montreal law firm where he practiced labor law, settling several high-profile labor disputes for management teams who would remain grateful and loyal to him in his future life as a politician. From 1977 until 1983 he was the head of Iron Ore Company of Canada.

In 1976, Mulroney made a failed attempt to lead the federal Progressive Conservative Party, losing out to Joe Clark because of what many viewed as a campaign that was too flashy and arrogant. When Clark resigned as the party's leader in 1983, a more mature and better organized Mulroney took over the leadership reigns of the party. Buoyed by general public discontent after more than a decade and a half of Pierre Trudeau's Liberal rule, Mulroney was elected in September 1984; it was the largest landslide victory in Canadian federal political history. He led his party and the country as prime minister from 1984 until his resignation in 1993.

Mulroney and his politics are often viewed in the context of the rule of Margaret Thatcher and Ronald Reagan. He led his government as a right-wing reformer, cutting social programs while dismantling impediments to international trade and Canadian business. His most memorable legislation includes the Goods and Services Tax and the North American accord, the latter of which would set the groundwork for the North American Free Trade Agreement. Although his government was rocked by successive scandals involving various members of Parliament, he himself was never found culpable despite his initial implication in what became known as the Airbus Scandal. Though Mulroney has officially retired from public life to practice law, he is still a major influence on the policies and direction of the Conservative Party and its leaders.

Brad Kent

See also: REAGAN, Ronald Wilson

References

McDonald, Marci. *Yankee Doodle Dandy: Brian Mulroney and the American Agenda.* Toronto: Stoddart, 1995.

Murphy, Rae, Robert Chodos, and Nick Auf der Maur. *Brian Mulroney: The Boy from Baie-Comeau.* Toronto: James Lorimer & Company, 1984.

Savoie, Donald. *Thatcher, Reagan, Mulroney: In Search of a New Bureaucracy.* Pittsburgh, PA: University of Pittsburgh Press, 1994.

MULVANY, JOHN (CA. 1839–1906)

Born in Moynalty, Co. Meath, John Mulvany immigrated to the United States at about 12 years of age. After studying at the National Academy of Design in New York, from 1861 he worked in Chicago as a freelance artist for Irish newspapers. He was with the Union Army during the Civil War, returning pictorial records to newspapers in New York. At the end of the war, he went to Europe to study—to Düsseldorf and Munich, Germany, and Antwerp, Belgium—exposures that are stylistically evident in his work. In turn, he decisively influenced Frank Duveneck, William Merrit Chase, and Frederick Remington.

On his return to the United States, Mulvany moved to Chicago, then Cincinnati, and from there to the Iowa-Nebraska border, where he began his western paintings, such as *The Preliminary Trial of a Horse Thief,* which was shown to great acclaim at the National Academy of Design in 1876; *Trappers of the Yellowstone* (1877); and *Lynch Law, A Comrade's Appeal.* Mulvany then moved to Kansas City, where he spent two years on the prototypical rendition of *Custer's Last Rally* (1881), commemorating the defeat of General Custer by Native Americans in June 1876 at the Little Big Horn. The original painting is thought to be nonextant, but an artist's copy has recently emerged. This dramatic painting depicts Custer at the center of a vivid and crowded canvas, holding a revolver in one hand and a saber in the other. Extraordinarily, the painting had a 17-year tour. At its first stop in Boston, it was commended for its realism, its fidelity to detail, and its knowledge of contemporary American warfare. In New York, Walt Whitman eulogized its "native," "autochtonic" qualities at length in the *New York Tribune.* In Louisville, Kentucky, the *Courier-Journal* pronounced Mulvany "a genius," and the painting's popular appeal was such that, in Chicago, the painting was lithographed for mass distribution.

Mulvany was also an accomplished portrait painter, painting portraits of, among others, Brigham Young, Robert Emmet, Mayor Dunne, and Sitting Bull. Nationalist views were inculcated in Mulvany during his early schooling in Ireland, furthered through his association with exiled Fenians, such as John Devoy, and his own association with Clan na Gael. His Irish political pictures, such as the *Battle of Aughrim* and *The Anarchists,* exemplify his exploration of momentous political events in Irish history. The Irish American Club in Chicago probably commissioned *The Battle of Aughrim* in 1883, leading to Mulvany's return to Ireland between 1883 and 1885. In pursuit of authenticity, he applied to the Tower of London for permission to research the arms and uniforms of the time. While waiting for his permit, he was advised by a friend to get out of London fast. Days later, on January 25, 1885, a series of bombs exploded in the Tower, courtesy of Clan na Gael. According to Mulvany, had he not fled, he would have spent the rest of his life in jail.

Because of his political connections, Mulvany's work underwent a significant deterioration in status. And in his later years, he was variously described as "an eccentric," "a down-and-out," and "a drunkard." Nonetheless, he continued to paint, producing, notably, *The Anarchists,* the political painting that would appear to have been his undoing. Dr P. H. Cronin's role in the Clan na Gael crisis came to an end with Cronin's murder in Chicago in 1889—a murder justified on the accusation of treason. In fact, Cronin was beaten to death with an ice hatchet to prevent his exposure of Alexander Sullivan. *The Anarchists* depicts six men cutting cards to select the murderer. This painting may have rendered the protagonists identifiable, so that, rather than committing suicide, as reported, Mulvany may have been "assisted" to his death in 1906.

Mulvany is now almost totally forgotten, notwithstanding a major international reputation in his own lifetime. Other than an invaluable, unpublished monograph by Mulvany's great-grand niece, Anne Weber, very little has been written about this important Irish-American artist. That so many paintings nodal to Irish and Irish-American history should remain unlocated is a tragedy.

Niamh O'Sullivan

References

Taft, Robert. *Artists and Illustrators of the Old West 1850–1900.* New York, Charles Scribner, 1953.

Tuite, Thomas P. "John Mulvany, Great Irish Painter." *Gaelic American* (New York), March 6, April 3, and April 10, 1909.

Weber-Scobie, Anne. *The Life and Work of Irish-American Artist John Mulvany (1939–1906).* Unpublished MS, 1993.

Portrait of Charles Francis Murphy, New York City politician. (Library of Congress)

MURPHY, CHARLES FRANCIS (1858–1924)

Charles Francis Murphy, one of the greatest Democratic political bosses of the early twentieth century, led Tammany Hall in New York City. He was born in a tenement on Manhattan's Lower East Side on June 20, 1858, the second of nine children of Irish Roman Catholic immigrants Dennis (or John M.) and Mary Prendergrass (or Prendergast) Murphy. He attended public school until the age of 14, when family need forced him to find work. Murphy picked up money in wire factories and as a part-time handyman in a saloon. He left the factories to become a caulker along the East River waterfront, meeting many of the young Irish men who would later form the core of his political support. In 1875, Murphy became the driver of a public horsecar; his route covered most of lower Manhattan, making him a familiar sight to many commuters. In 1878, Murphy purchased the first of his four saloons. The saloon, which did not serve women, was a gathering place for local dockworkers and laborers. The second floor of the building housed the Sylvan Social Club for young men ages 15 to 20, whose baseball team Murphy had organized in 1875. With the saloon, club, and baseball team as his anchors, Murphy began to emerge as a political figure. In 1892, he became the Democratic leader of the 18th Assembly District and a member of the executive committee of Tammany Hall.

Politics brought Murphy social mobility and respectability. In 1897, Murphy was appointed commissioner of docks, the only paid position he ever held in government. He was proud of the position and retained the title "Commissioner" as his preferred form of address for the rest of his life. During his tenure in office, Murphy set up a system of dock leasing that greatly benefited Tammany Hall. Murphy, a taciturn and puritanical man, engaged only in so-called honest graft. He steadfastly refused to accept money connected to illegal activity such as prostitution or gambling but thought nothing of using inside information to profit and routinely demanded fees from contractors seeking to do business with the city. Murphy stayed in power by being accessible. He made it a practice to station himself beneath a gas lamp in front of a Democratic club for several hours each night. Anyone could approach him for assistance, and he won many votes by providing social services to families in need. On election day, he made sure that Democratic voters made it to the polls by sending messengers to anyone who had not cast a ballot by midafternoon.

A model district leader, Murphy brought more votes for Tammany than any of his peers. On September 19, 1902, when the corrupt leader of Tammany was pushed out of office, the dependable and comparatively honest Murphy succeeded him. He remained leader of Tammany for the remainder of his days. Other than golf, he had few interests outside of politics. Earlier that year, in June 1902, Murphy married widow Margaret J. Graham and adopted her daughter. The Murphys had no other children.

None of Murphy's predecessors enjoyed his power on the municipal, state, or national level. He was responsible for the election of three New York City mayors and three New York State governors, including Al Smith. He helped advance the career of Robert Wagner, the U.S. senator from New York during the New Deal and a great advocate for organized labor. Unlike many political bosses, Murphy supported progressive legislation and efficiency in government. Widely commended for his mild rule, he nevertheless bore chief responsibility for the impeachment of corrupt Governor William Sulzer, whom he had helped to elect in 1912. At the time of his death Murphy planned to nominate Smith for president at the 1924 Democratic National Convention.

Murphy died suddenly in New York City on April 25, 1924, from an ailment that the attending physician labeled as indigestion. He left an estate of more than $2 million, although his Tammany post was formally unsalaried and he never held elective office. A crowd estimated by newspapers at more than 50,000 attended Murphy's funeral at Saint Patrick's Cathedral.

Caryn E. Neumann

See also: NEW YORK CITY; TAMMANY HALL

References

Connable, Alfred, and Edward Silberfarb. *Tigers of Tammany: Nine Men Who Ran New York.* New York: Holt, Rinehart and Winston, 1967.

Weiss, Nancy Joan. *Charles Francis Murphy, 1858–1924: Respectability and Responsibility in Tammany Politics.* Northampton, MA: Smith College, 1968.

MURPHY, HERMANN DUDLEY (1867–1945)

Hermann Dudley Murphy was a second-generation Irish American who, at the turn of the twentieth century, was an influential artist and frame maker. A painter of portraits, landscapes, and still lifes, Murphy was a participant in the Boston School of Painting, a teacher at the Harvard School of Architecture, and a founding member of the Guild of Boston Artists. As a designer, carver, and gilder, working out of his shop, named Carrig-Rohane in tribute to his Celtic ancestry, he was a seminal figure in the history of framing and was chiefly responsible for Boston being the center of innovative frame design.

Murphy was born in Marlborough, Massachusetts, on August 25, 1867. His father was a native of Cork and a shoe manufacturer in Stoneham, Massachusetts; his mother was descended from Royal Governor Joseph Dudley of New Hampshire. Hermann was educated at Boston's Chauncy Hall School and the Boston Museum School. After a few years as an illustrator for newspapers and periodicals and a brief stint as artist and surveyor for a Nicaragua canal survey expedition, Murphy traveled to Paris in 1891. There he studied painting at the Academie Julian, garnering awards in drawing and composition. In 1895 he married fellow art student Caroline Bowles, and the couple settled in Winchester, Massachusetts, where, in 1903, he built a house and studio. Nearly 6 feet 6 inches tall with abundant red hair and a beard, Murphy was a lifelong sportsman, winning American Canoe Association championships in sliding deck-seat canoeing in 1902, 1909, 1910, and 1931. He belonged to the Union Boat Club of Boston and the Winchester Boat Club.

In contrast to his size and athleticism, Murphy was considered an aesthete, and his art was noteworthy for its delicacy, subtlety, and refinement. Initially, he painted portraits and landscapes, but as his career in landscape painting flourished, he ceased to paint portraits except for family and friends. Much of his work focused on New England, as he recreated scenes from around Winchester and Marblehead, on Cape Cod, in Ogunquit, Maine, and at Mt. Monadnock. Later, he traveled and captured the landscapes of Italy, Holland, England, Puerto Rico, and Mexico. From the 1920s until his death in 1945, he primarily painted still lifes and florals, for which he received critical and popular acclaim.

Murphy took his public artistic responsibilities seriously. From 1902 to 1937 he taught life drawing at the Harvard School of Architecture and taught at the Worcester (Massachusetts) Art Museum School. From 1916 to 1943 he was a member of the Massachusetts Arts Commission, and between 1928 and 1935 he led the art committee of the Boston Art Club. He was also a member of the National Academy of Design, the Copley Society, the Guild of Boston Artists, and the New York and Boston Watercolor Societies.

Artistically, Murphy was most influenced by the work of James McNeill Whistler, and like Whistler, he was concerned with the totality of any artwork, including its framing. After learning to carve and gild to frame his own works appropriately, Murphy set up a frame shop at his home in Winchester. Two years later, he moved the shop to Boston where he designed and constructed frames for many leading artists of the period, including Childe Hassam and William Merrit Chase. Believing the frame itself was a work of art, Murphy signed his frames and, in 1907, participated in an exhibition devoted to frames as an art form held at Boston's Copley Hall. Frames from Murphy's studio were considered some of the most beautiful frames ever made. In 1917 he turned his

Carrig-Rohane shares over to his studio artisans and sold the company to Vose Galleries of Boston.

Throughout his career he exhibited widely and won many awards. One-man exhibitions of his work were held in such museums as the Wadsworth Athanaeum, the Pennsylvania Academy of Fine Arts, and the St. Louis Museum of Art. His awards included a bronze medal at the Pan-American Exposition of 1901 and a silver medal at the Panama-Pacific International Exposition of 1915.

Following a lengthy estrangement, in 1915 Caroline and Hermann Murphy were divorced, and a year later Murphy married Nellie Littlehale Umbstaetter, a recent widow whom he had courted decades earlier. He and Nellie built a house and studio in Lexington, Massachusetts, where he died in 1945. Murphy's paintings can be found in many public collections, including the Museum of Fine Arts, Boston, the Cleveland Museum of Art, the Art Institute of Chicago, and the Portland Art Museum.

Patricia Fanning

See also: BOSTON; MASSACHUSETTS

References

Coles, William A. "Hermann Dudley Murphy: An Introduction." *Hermann Dudley Murphy (1867–1945): "Realism Married to Idealism Most Exquisitely."* New York: Graham Gallery, 1982.

Cooke, Edward S., Jr. "The Aesthetics of Craftsmanship and the Prestige of the Past: Boston Furniture-Making and Wood-Carving." In *Inspiring Reform: Boston's Arts and Crafts Movement.* Wellesley, MA: David Museum and Cultural Center, 1997: 42–56.

Smeaton, Suzanne. "American Picture Frames of the Arts and Crafts Period, 1870–1920." *Antiques* 136, no. 6 (November 1989): 1124–1137.

MURPHY, JOHN JAMES (1822–1909)

John James Murphy was born in 1822 in Haysland, Kilrane parish, Co. Wexford, to Nicholas Murphy and Catherine Sinnott. At age 22, he emigrated to South America together with his cousins John and Lawrence Murphy and neighbors John O'Connor, Nicholas Kavanagh, Thomas Saunders, James Pender, Patrick Howlin, and others. They were part of an emigration scheme arranged from Buenos Aires by Wexford-born merchant James Pettit. On April 13, 1844, they left home in Wexford and sailed directly to Liverpool, where they waited to depart in the brig *William Peile.* The ship left Liverpool on April 21, 1844, with 115 Irish passengers onboard, called at Cape Verde islands on May 13, and finally sailed into the mouth of the River Plate on June 25. A century later these emigrants and their journey—the first organized emigration from Ireland to Argentina—inspired Walter MacCormack's epic ballad "The Kilrane Boys," which was included by Joseph Ranson in his *Songs of the Wexford Coast* (Wexford: John English & Co., 1975).

Once in Argentina, Murphy took advantage of his British citizenship and his Irish origin, which connected him to the British merchants and the Irish Catholic priests in Buenos Aires. Like many of his fellow countrymen he stayed a short time in the city and then he went to the *campo* or countryside. He and a friend worked near Chascomús with an Argentine family and left when they realized that they would never get paid for their work of digging ditches. The next years he spent in Chacabuco working as a shepherd in the profitable sheep business.

In 1855, 11 years after his arrival, Murphy owned 1,750 hectares in Salto that he had purchased from John McKiernan, with whom he had been working in halves. He named his ranch La Flor del Uncalito. In 1864 he acquired La Caldera of 4,050 hectares in neighboring department Rojas. Murphy was the first landowner in Buenos Aires to enclose his property with wire. In 1859 he had a bad year because of want of water. Murphy saved his sheep by constantly throwing buckets of water over the parched land, and the sheep were able to eat the roots of grass or weeds they found, surviving on this and water. As his daughter recalled, Murphy "did this day and night and the sheep would rush towards him as soon as they saw him coming."

Murphy made every possible effort to convince family members, neighbors, and friends in Wexford to immigrate to Argentina. According to his letters it was "the best country under the sun." In 1866, all the shepherds, hands, and laborers working in his ranches in Salto and Rojas were from Wexford except for one from Westmeath. Murphy sent so many passengers to Argentina through Lamport & Holt shipping company that his brother Martin Murphy, who remained in Wexford and acted as his representative in Ireland, received an agent commission for every ticket purchased. With the immigrants working for him, Murphy often paid their tickets in advance, and they committed to stay in their ranches for at least 14 months working to repay their passage. Murphy was also an ardent advocate of sheep farming in Argentina, and sometimes the *Wexford People* published his letters promoting the business and emigration to Argentina.

In 1878 Murphy traveled with his family back to Ireland and rented his lands in Argentina. Being the elder brother, he had the idea of returning definitively to Ireland to take care of the family farm, and possibly be appointed as Argentine consul in Dublin. But two of his children died in Ireland, and the family returned to Argentina in January 1882. Under the favorable conditions created after the war against the Indians, on March 15, 1883, Murphy bought 18,600 hectares in Venado Tuerto (southern Santa Fe) from Eduardo Casey. With the help of his family and others, he immediately settled the new ranch, San Juan, and began wire fencing, building outposts, and planting trees. He paid off the last of his debts the year before his death. By the end of the century the prosperous wool business was declining and was replaced by cattle, and later by grain. Murphy started to let his land to Italian settlers, who dedicated it mostly to corn and wheat.

Murphy died on July 13, 1909, in Buenos Aires, leaving a large family and an important estate to his heirs. A railway station in Santa Fe province was named after him, and most of the land was rented out to tenants. Some of these tenant farmers were evicted by the agents of his daughter Elisa Murphy Gahan, who was living in England, therefore confirming the remarks of Timothy Horan, Irish diplomatic envoy to Argentina in 1958: "It is one of history's little ironies that our emigrants to Argentina [helped] to assist in building up a system and a class the creation of which in Ireland had led to their own emigration."

Edmundo Murray

See also: ARGENTINA; CASEY, Eduardo

References

Coghlan, Eduardo A. *Los Irlandeses en la Argentina: Su Actuación y Descendencia.* Buenos Aires: Author's Edition, 1987.

Landaburu, Roberto. *Irlandeses: Eduardo Casey, Vida y Obra.* Venado Teureto: Fondo Editor Mutual Venado Teureto, 1995.
Murray, Edmundo. "From Kilrane to the Irish Pampas: The Story of John James Murphy." in *The Southern Cross* 127, no. 5860 (2002): 5.
Ortigüela, Raúl. *Murphy, en Tierras Benditas.* Venado: Tuerto, 1991.

MURRAY, LUIS ALBERTO (1923–2002)

Journalist, writer, historian, and poet born in Buenos Aires, Luis Alberto Murray was the son of Miguel Juan Murray and Teresa Munnier, and the great-grandson of John Murray (1826–1907) of Derraghanbeg, Newtowncashel parish (Co. Longford). A historian of the revisionist school, supporter of the Peronist movement founded by President Juan D. Perón, and supporter of the Roman Catholic tradition, Murray joined *Crítica* newspaper in 1948 and contributed to *Democracia, Vea y Lea, El Pueblo, Confirmado, Mayoría,* and *Clarín* in their political sections. He worked for the latter newspaper for more than 20 years. Murray began writing poetry in 1943 and published, among other works: *Desintegrada voz, Tránsito, Una mujer y un hombre, América clavada en mi costado,* and *De pie, entre los relámpagos.* He also translated Argentine poetry and tango lyrics into English. Together with Argentine intellectuals Fermín Chávez, José María Castiñeira de Dios, José María Rosa, and Osvaldo Guglielmino, Murray structured an ideological base for the Peronist movement. He was also a member of the Rosas Institute of Buenos Aires, and, in the line of historical revisionism, he defended the rule of Rosas as positive contribution for Argentina against the powers of British and other colonialist European nations.

In Argentine historiography Murray represents the nationalist-revisionist trend of the 1940s, with his essays *Pro y Contra de Alberdi, Pro y Contra de Sarmiento, Caseros y Pozo de Vargas: Dos Derrotas Argentinas,* and *Vida, Obra y Doctrina de Roberto Noble.* Opposite to the perspectives of liberal historians, who wished to replace the native cultures with European (especially British) enlightenment, Murray envisioned a new reading of postindependence texts, in which he searched the elements of the proposed Argentine nation, including the Spanish language, Catholicism, and Hispano-Creole cultural tradition. His religious traditionalism within the Roman Catholic doctrine was parallel to that proposed in times of the "Santa Federación" of Buenos Aires governor Juan Manuel de Rosas, focusing on the ideological relations between religion and state instead of dogmatic matters. Although a vast majority of the Irish-Argentine elite (to which Murray's family belonged) followed the Argentine landed class in its noticeable anti-Peronist attitudes, Murray found in the nationalist aspect of Peronism similar values of conservatism and defense of the Catholic culture. Murray died on August 1, 2002.

Edmundo Murray

See also: PRESS, the Irish in Latin America

References

Coghlan, Eduardo A. *Los Irlandeses en la Argentina: Su Actuación y Descendencia.* Buenos Aires: Author's Edition, 1987.
www.academiaperiodismo.org.ar/ (accessed January 20, 2004).

MURRAY, THOMAS (1871–)

Thomas Murray was a historian and author of the first and only history of the Irish in Argentina published in English to date. It is generally thought that Murray was born in 1871 in Kilbeggan, Co. Westmeath, the son of Patrick Murray and Anne Molloy. In 1897 he emigrated with his family to the United States, and in the early 1900s he went to Buenos Aires. He probably remained in the city and worked with records and files related to the Irish in Argentina. The main circle of Murray's friends included some of the most notorious Irish nationalists of the time: Francis O'Grady, P. F. Byrne, McCorry, Michael (Mícheal Ban) Murphy, and the *Southern Cross*'s editor Gerald Foley. In 1913, he left Argentina for New York, where he published *The Story of the Irish in Argentina* (1919) and some of his poems. Murray returned to Buenos Aires in 1924 to promote his book, which was received unsympathetically by the Irish-Argentine media and the community in general. According to the first reviews in the *Southern Cross,* the author "has devoted a great deal of time and concentration to his work, and his sources of information are copious." But some weeks later the same paper remarked that "there are some assertions, when the author advances his own personal opinions, with which we are not in agreement."

Murray's 512-page book describes the history of the Irish community from the perspective of an outside observer intimately familiar with Irish Argentina's people and places, in the language characteristic of early twentieth century Irish Catholic nationalism. Criticism of the *Standard*'s Dublin-born publisher Michael G. Mulhall as a *shoneen* (or West Briton) illustrates how contemporary political divisions in Ireland were reflected in Argentina's Irish community. The book includes an account of the first Irish visitors to the River Plate, the initial Irish settlers in Buenos Aires during colonial times, Irish in the British campaigns of 1806 and 1807, military men in the wars of independence like William Brown, Peter Campbell, and John T. O'Brien, Irish sheep farmers, the account of William McCann's trips through Buenos Aires province, Father Anthony Fahy and his relations, useful lists of contributors to Irish charities within Argentina and Ireland, as well as individual chronicles for each Irish community in the provinces, Irish chaplains and religious orders, schoolmasters, the press, and Irish societies. Among the sources Murray consulted were the *Standard,* the *Southern Cross, Fianna* review, the *British Packet, La Gaceta Mercantil, La Nación, Revista del Plata,* and many works of Argentine political and social writers like Mariano Moreno, Domingo F. Sarmiento, Bartolomé Mitre, Adolfo Alsina, and Vicente F. Lopez. Murray's work remains the only published history (in English) of the Irish emigration to Argentina.

Edmundo Murray

See also: ARGENTINA; FAHY, Anthony; MULHALL, Michael George

MUSIC, COUNTRY AND IRISH

Country and Irish music is a popular music genre that first appeared in Ireland in the 1960s and is still popular in Ireland today. The term "country and Irish music" is an allusion to American country and western music, a hybrid popular music genre that grew out of traditional folk music idioms played by settlers living in the rural southeastern United States in the 1800s. By the early twentieth century, American country music began to be featured on commercial recordings, and throughout the twentieth and twenty-first centuries it was tremendously successful on a global scale. American country music was popular in Ireland from the early twentieth century, and by the 1960s Irish artists began performing and recording country music in Ireland and the United States, Britain, and Europe. Country and Irish music differs very little in sound, instrumentation, or lyrical content from its American counterpart; instead, the phrase exists primarily as a marketing term to differentiate between country music created by Irish-born artists and country music imported to Ireland from the United States or other regions of the world.

Ireland has had a connection to American country music from its earliest inception, which can be largely attributed to the fact that the roots of early American country music share much in common with Irish traditional music and folk song. In the seventeenth and eighteenth centuries, thousands of Scots-Irish, Scots, and English immigrated to the United States, many of whom settled in rural areas of the United States, including the Appalachian Mountain region. British, Scots, and Irish settlers continued performing musical traditions from their homelands, such as folksinging and instrumental dance tunes. In time, however, musicians came into contact with other styles and genres of music, and in Appalachia this ultimately resulted in the blending of British and Irish folk ballads and fiddle tunes, blues music of southern African Americans, southern religious hymns, and American popular music. The resultant melding of these seemingly disparate music traditions led in the 1800s to the birth of two music forerunners to country music: "hillbilly" music and old-time music—a type of music ensemble most commonly featuring a vocalist, fiddle, banjo, and guitar.

In the early 1920s commercial recordings of old-time music first began to appear. The development of the recording industry in the 1920s as well as the establishment of radio stations throughout America in the early twentieth century helped transform country music from a regional vernacular music into a commercially successful popular music genre. As the country music recording industry grew, more and more recordings found their way to areas outside the United States, including Ireland. From the early 1900s Irish immigrants to the United States—whose ranks had by that time swelled to millions—sent American records home to their families, and country music was no exception. In addition, the establishment of a nationally funded radio network in Ireland by the early 1960s also furthered mass consumption of various American popular music styles, including country music.

The first Irish country music artists emerged in Ireland in the 1960s, a time in which popular music genres, such as rock and roll, skiffle, ceilidh, showband, and folk were growing in popularity throughout Ireland because of newly formed radio and television media outlets as well as live music performances. Many early country artists got their start in other musical genres that were popular in Ireland at the time before finding a place in the burgeoning country music scene.

Céilí music—a modern take on Irish traditional dance music that includes sound amplification, tighter orchestrations and fuller musical instrumentation—developed in the dance halls of New York, Britain, and Ireland in the 1920s and grew in popularity through the 1960s. Irish and country artist Philomena Begley, the "Queen of Irish Country" got her musical start as lead singer of the Old Cross Céilí Band in the 1960s, which later changed its name to Country Flavour to better suit its country music sound. In 1971 the band made the Irish Top 10 with "Here Today, Gone Tomorrow" and "Never Again." Begley later formed her own band, the Ramblin' Men, and she released several songs that topped the Irish charts, including "Ramblin' Man," "Blanket on the Ground," "Wait a Little Longer," "Once Around the Dance Floor," and "Whiskey Drinkin' You." Country singer Susan McCann entered the music business as a teenager singing with the John Murphy Country Céilí Band. She embarked on a highly successful solo career as a country singer several years later and subsequently earned a place on the Irish charts with such hits as "Big Tom is Still King" and "String of Diamonds."

Showband music emerged in Ireland in the 1950s and featured lively, choreographed numbers in many musical idioms, including rock and roll, country, skiffle, and Dixieland, as well as slower love songs and ballads. Most of these performances took place in ballrooms and dance halls that were built throughout Ireland at that time to accommodate the booming interest in this popular music entertainment form. Showband groups such as the Capitol Showband and the Dixies often included country music in their acts.

Artists such as Big Tom McBride, Larry Cunningham, and Brian Coll got their start in country music by fronting showbands. Big Tom first attracted attention by performing with the Mainliners on the Irish televised *Showband Show* and subsequently became one of the leading country acts of the 1970s. Big Tom also had a succession of hit singles in Ireland as a solo artist, including "Log Cabin for Sale," and "Back to Castleblayney." He also fronted the Travellers in the 1970s and rejoined the Mainliners in the late 1980s. Larry Cunningham entered the showband scene with the Mighty Avons, who released the hugely popular single "Lovely Leitrim." He is also identified with many country singles, including "Pretty Little Girl from Omagh" and "Among the Wicklow Hills." Cunningham left the Mighty Avons in the late 1960s to front the Country Blue Boys, a group that toured successfully for decades. Brian Coll began his musical career as lead vocalist with the Polka Dots and later performed with the highly successful showband group the Plattermen, before forming his own band, the Buckaroos, in 1968. Coll and the Plattermen had a number of hit singles, including "Give an Irish Girl to Me," "These are My Mountains," and "When My Blue Moon Turns to Gold."

Although the showband phenomenon lost its momentum in the early 1970s, showband artists who had specialized in country and western music continued to successfully tour and perform throughout Ireland after its demise. In addition, new artists emerged on the country and Irish music scene, including such superstars as Ray Lynam—the undisputed "King of Irish Country"—and Daniel O'Donnell. Lynam fronted the Hillbillies for many years and had hit singles on the Irish chart with "Sweet Rosie Jones" and '"Gypsy, Jo and Me." Daniel O'Donnell got his start as guitar player for his sister Margo's country group before embarking on a solo career in the early 1980s with the single "Donegal Shore." He released his first album, *Two Sides of Daniel O'Donnell,* in 1985 and released numerous albums throughout the

1980s and 1990s. O'Donnell has toured widely, produced several television shows in Ireland, and garnered numerous awards and accolades in Ireland, Britain, and the United States.

Irish-language country and Irish music (referred to in Irish Gaelic as *Gaelcheoil Tiré*) emerged in the 1980s in the Conamara *Gaeltacht* and enjoyed popular success for years to follow. Singers such as John Beag Ó Flatharta, Peader Ó Flatharta, Martin Joe Ó Flatharta, Beairtle Ó Domhnaill, Pádraig Mac Donncha, Dara Bán Mac Donncha, Tomás Mac An Iomaire, Tomás Mac Eoin, and Annamaria Nic Dhonncha released *Gaelcheoil Tiré* recordings through the publishing company *Chló Iar-Chonnachta,* performed on Irish-language radio station Raidió na Gaeltachta, and appeared in local pubs and halls throughout Conamara.

Numerous country and Irish artists enjoyed success in the 1980s, 1990s, and beyond, including Declan Nerney, Áine Cromie, Mick Flavin, Kathy Durkan, Anne Breen, Louise Morrissey, John Hogan, Michael O'Brien, Mary Duff, Paddy O'Brien, Mike Denver, Patrick Feeney, Barry Doyle, Helen McCabe, Michael English, and Kieran McGilligan. Although country and Irish music is not as popular as it was in its heyday, it still attracts a loyal following to the present day.

Erin Stapleton-Corcoran

See also: APPALACHIA

References

Carthy, Brian. *The A-Z of Country and Irish Stars.* Dublin: Gill and MacMillan, 1991.

O'Connor, Nuala. *Bringing it all Back Home: The Influence of Irish Music at Home and Overseas.* 2nd ed. Dublin: Merlin Publishing, 2001.

Power, Vincent. *Send 'em Home Sweatin': The Showbands' Story.* Dublin: Kildanore Press, 1990.

MUSIC IN AMERICA, IRISH

American music history owes much to its many immigrant populations, for the musical traditions they brought to their new homeland have made an undeniable impact on the American musical landscape. The musical relationship between the United States and Ireland is long, beginning with the first Irish settlers to the United States in the late seventeenth century. However, the greatest period of musical exchange between America and Ireland began in the mid-1800s and continued through the early 1900s, when millions of Irish immigrated to the United States. Many of these immigrants were amateur musicians and dancers, and they continued to play traditional music and to dance in their new homeland. Irish-American music and dance performance continue today, particularly in metropolitan centers. However, the American performance context had an undeniable impact upon Irish music, for it accelerated musical exchange among musicians from various regions of Ireland and created a demand for new styles of musical performance to mirror the ever-changing position of the Irish in American society. In the nineteenth and twentieth centuries the advent of new theatrical traditions and commercial sound recordings as well as the dissemination of music on radio and television further transformed Irish music in both the United States and Ireland, and Irish musicians in America have produced music in Irish traditional, folk, popular, and rock idioms. Today there remain strong cultural ties between Ireland and America, as evidenced by the active Irish festival circuit in the United States and the ongoing popularity of Irish traditional, rock, folk, and pop music in the United States today.

Irish Traditional Music in Ireland

Traditionally, the Irish possess various styles and repertoires of vocal performance, all of which have found their way—although with varying degrees of success and visibility—into the Irish-American performance tradition. Irish traditional song, like Irish traditional instrumental music, is transmitted and performed orally and comprises regional repertoires and variations. Because of the bilingualism of the island the Irish song repertoire consists of songs in both the Irish and English languages. The oldest type of Irish traditional singing—called *sean nós* (meaning "old style") is unaccompanied, unmetered, and highly ornamented. This style of singing is generally associated with rural regions of Ireland, is more frequently performed in the Irish language (although strong arguments may be made for the existence of English language *sean nós*), and was traditionally performed in small community gatherings. Most Irish-language songs are lyrical in nature, for they express personal stories in poetic language and imagery rather than in an explicit narrative form. Themes of love are the most common, although songs that praise specific locales or recount history and lore are also prevalent. English-language songs contain features from both the Irish-language song tradition and ballads imported from Britain. Themes found in English-language songs are as numerous as the experiences that may befall a person in the course of daily life; but broad categories of English-language song include lullabies, love songs, work songs, political songs, and religious songs.

Irish instrumental music traditionally referred to a number of dance styles including jigs, reels, hornpipes, polkas, mazurkas, flings, barn dances and waltzes, as well as other instrumental pieces such as slow airs, marches, and planxties. The melodic line of Irish instrumental music was usually played on the fiddle, uilleann pipes, harp, wooden flute, tin whistle, accordion, or concertina, while the bodhrán and bones played Irish traditional dance music, which was originally intended for accompaniment to set, step, *céilí,* or *sean-nós* dance, but music was also performed solely for listening and entertainment at informal community contexts, such as sessions or *céilídh.* Traditionally, Irish songs and instrumental music were orally transmitted from one musician to another, and because of the personal nature of the music they featured stylistic features and repertoires that were tied to specific regions of Ireland.

The Arrival of Irish Musicians in America

The first Irish musicians to arrive in the United States were among the nearly half million Irish who immigrated to the United States in the seventeenth and eighteenth centuries, most of whom were of Scots-Irish descent. The Scots-Irish were predominantly Protestants from Ulster, and they settled in both rural and urban areas scattered throughout the United States. They made their most pronounced and recognizable musical contribution in the southeastern states of West Virginia, Virginia, North Carolina, South Carolina, Tennessee, and Kentucky. Scots-Irish settlers continued performing musical traditions from their homelands, such as folksinging and instrumental dance tunes, but over time their musical traditions melded with other styles and genres of music performed in the region, such as British ballads and fiddle tunes, African-American vernacular music, southern religious hymns, and American popular music. This musical amalgam became the foundation for Appalachian folk, old time, and hillbilly music, ultimately leading in the twentieth century to the creation of country and bluegrass music.

Between 1845 and 1920 over a million Irish emigrants arrived in the United States, mainly in the aftermath of the Great Irish Famine. Irish immigrants of this period were predominantly Catholics from rural, impoverished, and remote regions of Ireland. These areas of Ireland were known for their strong familial and community bonds as well as their wealth of folk traditions, including Irish traditional song, music, and dance. Many of the Irish emigrants of this period settled in urban areas such as New York, Boston, Chicago, Philadelphia, and San Francisco. Those who had been musicians and dancers in Ireland often continued to play traditional music and to dance in America. However, Irish musicians—many of whom were for the first time residing in close proximity to people from villages and counties outside their own—sang, played music, and danced together, which ultimately contributed to the exchange and assimilation of musical styles and repertories once associated with specific localities in Ireland.

Irish traditional musicians continued to gather and perform together throughout the twentieth century, particularly in cities such as New York, Boston, Chicago, Philadelphia, and San Francisco. In America Irish musicians would play at private house parties, pubs, taverns, at Irish music clubs, and for céilídh and *feisanna* (music and dance festivals that often included competitive events). In addition, new performance contexts had a definite impact on Irish traditional music. During the first half of the twentieth century, particularly in the 1930s, dance halls sprang up in all major American cities, and many of these featured Irish traditional musicians. Dance hall bands were often asked to play a variety of music styles, and because of the size of the halls and the number of participants they began playing music that featured a more forceful rhythm and louder dynamics. In the first half of the twentieth century Irish dance bands—such as the Four Provinces Orchestra (Philadelphia), Dan Sullivan's Shamrock Band (Boston), the Harp and Shamrock Orchestra (Chicago), and the Flanagan Brothers (New York) performed in dance halls throughout the United States (e.g., Celtic Hall in New York City or Erin's Isle in Chicago). These céilí bands forged a hybrid Irish-American musical idiom in which traditional instruments were combined with the piccolo, saxophone, piano, and drum set, the musical parts were arranged in a manner similar to mainstream big bands, and they played current hits of the days in addition to Irish music.

The Irish in American Musical Theater

The emergence of popular theater in the early 1800s had a massive impact on various styles and genres of music in America at that time, including Irish music. A career in the burgeoning entertainment industry offered new employment opportunities to those—including the Irish—whose options had generally been limited to work in manual labor or civil service. As a result, numerous Irish who showed talent in music, singing, or dancing entered the theater business, thereby playing a pivotal role in the development of American popular theater forms of minstrelsy, variety shows, and vaudeville. In addition, the image of the Irish in America was deeply influenced by this newly emergent performance medium, for images of the Irish—both negative and humorous—were plentiful on stage from its early years.

The minstrel show emerged in the 1830s and quickly became the most popular form of public entertainment in the United States. Early minstrel shows featured working-class white men who blackened their faces and performed music and dance, most commonly in parody of plantation slave culture. The Irish had a prominent role in minstrelsy from the beginning, as most minstrel companies featured Irish tenors and Irish dancers, many of the music and dances in the productions were based on or featured elements of Scottish and Irish dance tunes (e.g., "Jimmy Crack Corn" or "Blue Tail Fly" was based on an Irish hornpipe), and elements of Irish step dance were used to create soft shoe, the style of dancing often featured on stage. Daniel Decatur Emmett (1815–1904), a composer and performer of Irish ancestry, is credited, along with a performance group known as the Virginia Minstrels, with creating the first full-length minstrel show, entitled *The Essence of Old Virginny* (1833), and he wrote "Dixie," perhaps the most successful song ever performed on the minstrel stage.

Minstrelsy was very successful through the 1870s, but by the 1880s it declined in popularity because its racist overtones grew increasingly objectionable to audiences, particularly after the Civil War. Irish and Irish-American minstrel performers of note include George Primrose, Billy West, Edwin Kelly of Leon and Kelly's Minstrels, R. M. Hooley, J. W. Raynor, Daniel Webster O'Brien, Matt Peel, Barney Fagen, Frank McNish, and Sam Decere. In addition, many Irish performers got their start in minstrelsy before moving on to a career in vaudeville, solo singing, or drama, including Dan Bryant, John Murphy of Murphy and Mack's Minstrels, John Collins, Patrick Sarsfield Gilmore, and Chauncey Olcott.

The variety show emerged in America by the 1840s. Variety shows were offered at variety saloons, and they shared common features with minstrelsy, in particular its use of loosely connected skits. However, variety shows differed from minstrelsy in that they featured a wider range of subject matters. Catering strictly to male audiences, variety saloons offered performances that were often unrefined in production and crude in tone. The stereotype of the stage Irishman—inebriated, overly sentimental, dense, illogical, and pugilistic—was born in variety saloons, and songs and stage numbers that reinforced the stereotype of the "Paddy" were plentiful. Irish entertainers played an important role in this theatrical genre, acting as singers, dancers, musicians, and sketch comedians.

American variety saloons remained popular through the 1870s, when they were supplanted by vaudeville, a theatrical genre that evolved from the "oleo," a short variety segment once showcased between numbers in minstrel performances. Theater owner and variety show performer Tony Pastor (1837–1908) saw the opportunity to draw larger audiences by creating a cleaner, more refined theatrical genre that catered to both genders. In 1865 Pastor opened Tony Pastor's Opera House in New York City, and his theater productions quickly became wildly popular with middle-class audiences. A typical vaudeville show consisted of eight to 20 different acts, ranging from silent pantomime animal tricks, and contortionists to musical number, songs, comedy acts, and monologues.

Other vaudeville theater houses opened as a result of Pastor's success, a vaudeville circuit was created, and vaudeville grew to become the most popular form of entertainment from the 1860s through the mid-1920s. Most vaudeville productions featured a jovial, lighthearted atmosphere, which appealed to audiences seeking a release from the stress and tedium of daily life. Comedy teams, such as the Irish "double act," and the Irish "four act" became a common feature on vaudeville stages, represented by duos such as McNulty and Murray, Clooney and Ryan, Needham and Kelly, and Kelly and Ryan, as well as quartets such as the Four Shamrocks, the Four Emeralds, the Four Mortons, and the Four Cohans. Many performers of Irish descent got their start in vaudeville, including performer and songwriter William J. Scanlan (1856–1908), actress and comedian Gracie Allen (1895–1964), Maggie Cline (1857–1934), and playwright and production team Edward (Ned) Harrigan (1844–1911) and Tony Hart (born Anthony Cannon, 1855–1891), as well as performer George M. Cohan (1878–1942).

Ned Harrigan, a New York native of mixed English and Irish ancestry, performed banjo and acted in both minstrel shows and variety shows as a youth. Harrigan met Tony Hart in 1871, who was then a 16-year-old minstrel and variety show performer of Irish descent. Harrigan and Hart began their career together performing short humorous sketches that satirized various issues facing ethnic and immigrant groups in post–Civil War New York, such as political corruption, race relations and ethnic conflict, and issues of class and social standing. These skits soon evolved into multi-scene, stand-alone theatrical performances. The duo created more than three dozen original productions, but their most famous works featured the Mulligan Guards, a quasi-military unit that mocked military organizations sponsored by New York politicians in the 1870s. Focusing specifically on the politically ambitious saloon owner Dan Mulligan, these productions included comedic repartee, battles between various militia units, and musical numbers. Several songs from the Mulligan Guard franchise—in particular "St. Patrick's Day" and "The Mulligan Guard"—were incredibly popular, with the latter finding its way to India, where British troops used it as a marching tune. After the phenomenal success of *The Mulligan Guard* (1873), Harrigan and Hart further explored the life of Dan Mulligan, his family, and friends in subsequent productions. They became household names among theatergoers of the late nineteenth century, and their musical productions are widely credited for setting the stage for the American musical comedy that emerged on Broadway in the 1920s.

George M. Cohan was America's first show business superstar, known coast to coast as a successful actor, singer, dancer, playwright, composer, librettist, director, and producer. Raised in a second-generation Irish-American theatrical family, Cohan began performing with the family vaudeville troupe the Four Cohans as a child. After successfully producing his first musical play, Cohan moved away from vaudeville and embarked on a career in the newly emerging theatrical form known as the musical, which differed from vaudeville in that each song or musical number was connected by a theme or story line. Cohan produced numerous plays and musicals during his lifetime, many of which contained Irish-themed numbers such as "Harrigan," "Nellie Kelly, I Love You," and "Molly Malone." However, Cohan is probably better known for his songs "Yankee Doodle Dandy," "Give My Regards to Broadway," "You're a Grand Old Flag," and "Over There," all of which focused on American and patriotic themes. Countless Irish and Irish-American performers followed in Cohan's path, making their name in musical theater—both on Broadway and on screen—including James Cagney (1899–1986), Gene Kelly (1912–1996), Judy Garland (1922–1969), and Debbie Reynolds (1932–).

The Popularization of Irish Music in America

Various technological advances, such as music publishing and sound recordings, affected Irish music performance from the late 1700s onward. Within the American context music publishing permanently affected Irish musical performance and practice as well as the Irish traditional music and song repertoire in both the United States and Ireland, for the publication of music created an enduring, unchanging, written musical record within a musical practice that had previously been solely oral and ephemeral. By the early 1800s, the music publishing business was firmly established in the United States, due in part to the rising interest in music that could be played at home on the piano. Irish songs were popular with music publishers and their audiences from the very beginning of the music publishing enterprise, and many of these published pieces found their way back to Ireland, influencing the musical scene there as well.

Throughout the late eighteenth and nineteenth centuries, thousands of American songbooks were published that featured Irish or Irish-themed songs. Indicative of the experiences of the Irish in America, Irish songs published in America during the eighteenth and nineteenth centuries included subjects such as emigration, the voyage to America from Ireland, the Irish involvement in the Revolutionary and Civil wars, the Irish involvement within politics and trade organizations, livelihood and employment of the Irish, familial and community life, stereotypical portrayals of the Irish in America, as well as nostalgic, romanticized odes to the "Auld Sod."

The most famous Irish songwriter of the early 1800s was Thomas Moore (1779–1852), whose music was characterized by resetting ancient Irish harp tunes to sentimental, oftentimes nationalistic lyrics. Moore's music grew in currency as popular music entertainment in England, Ireland, and the United States soon after the publication of his *Irish Melodies* in 1808. Moore was the most popular songwriter in America throughout the 1820s and 1830s, and he was the leading contributor to American song collections published between 1825 and 1850. Moore's *Irish Melodies* set the standard for countless songwriters; his music directly influenced the works of other Irish-born composers, including Samuel Lover (1797–1868), Peter Moran, William Balfe (1808–1870), and James Gaspard Maeder (1809–1876), as well as the American composer Stephen Foster (1826–1864). Foster, who was of Scots-Irish ancestry, produced music that appeared in songbooks and on the minstrel stage. Foster is most well-known for his songs "Oh! Susanna," "Old Folks At Home," "My Old Kentucky Home," and "Jeanie with the Light Brown Hair."

Irish instrumental music was also featured in collections of Irish music from the 1800s onward. Music collector Francis O'Neill (1848–1936) made a tremendous impact on Irish traditional music through his printed compilations of Irish dance music. O'Neill immigrated to America as a young man, joined the Chicago police force in the 1870s, and became chief of police by 1901. When O'Neill arrived in Chicago, he found a thriving musical community in which he was an active participant. Beginning in the 1880s, he began collecting music from Irish traditional musicians living in Chicago as well as other previously printed sources. He produced *O'Neill's Music of Ireland* in 1803, which was the largest collection of Irish music ever published at that time. He followed this seminal work with several other tune collections, including *The Dance Music of Ireland: 1001 Gems* (1907) as well as two treatises on Irish music.

By the early 1900s a sizable portion of the American population was foreign born. With the invention of the sound recording and the gramophone in the late 1800s, industrialists within the newly emerging recording industry seized on the opportunity to make a profit by producing ethnic recordings targeted for the immigrant population. Because of the sizable Irish-born population in America at that time, Irish and quasi-Irish recordings appeared on record from the very beginning of the industry. During this so-called "golden age of Irish music" of the early twentieth century, a vast body of Irish music was recorded by major recording labels. These recordings—first on wax cylinders and later on phonograph recordings—included instrumental music, vocal recordings, and Irish-themed musical numbers from theatrical productions. Irish music recordings were hugely successful with Irish Americans, non-Irish Americans, and the Irish in Ireland.

Several Irish instrumentalists made names for themselves in the burgeoning Irish music recording industry in America, including such pivotal figures as uilleann piper Patsy Touhey (1865–1923), flutist John McKenna (1880–1947), and fiddlers James Morrison (1893–1947) and Michael Coleman (1891–1946). These artists as well as numerous others produced Irish instrumental recordings of such note in the early 1900s that they continue to guide Irish musicians in Ireland and America.

Many styles of song were well received during the early years of the American recording industry, such as traditional ballads, stage skits, comic songs, vaudeville routines, and nostalgic compositions of Tin Pan Alley. However, the most popular type of Irish song recorded was that of the Irish tenor, a style of singing that was most typified by sentimental, melodramatic songs executed in an operatic singing style. Two formidable Irish tenors of this period were Chauncey Olcott (1860–1932; born Chancellor John Olcott) and John McCormack (1884–1945). Olcott was born in New York State to an Irish-born mother and grew up in an "Irish shanty" along the banks of the Erie River. Olcott made his debut on the minstrel stage in Chicago at age 19, after which he toured throughout the United States and Britain. Olcott was very successful in the minstrel shows, but he soon garnered special attention for his remarkable tenor voice and was encouraged to sing Irish ballads and to take leading roles in plays, operas, and operettas. Olcott acted in several Broadway plays, including *Barry of Ballymore, Isle O' Dreams, The Heart of Paddy Whack,* and *Machusla.* Olcott collaborated with George Graff and Ernest Ball on the composition of many famous Irish ballads, including "Mother Machree," "When Irish Eyes Are Smiling," "Goodbye My Emerald Land," "The Wearing of the Green," and "Sure They Call It Ireland," but he was wholly responsible for the lyrics to "When Irish Eyes Are Smiling," and he composed both the melody and lyrics for "My Wild Irish Rose."

John McCormack (1884–1945) was an Irish-born choir and operatic singer who enjoyed tremendous success as a live performer and recording artist. After studying the bel canto style of operatic singing in Italy in the early 1900s McCormack made his opera debut (1906) and began presenting ballad concerts shortly thereafter. He spent time touring in America after World War I, and his concerts featured German lieder; works by Handel, Mozart, and various Italian composers; and Irish folk and popular songs. McCormack's recordings of Irish songs such as "The Minstrel Boy," "The Harp that Once through Tara's Hall," "Dear Harp of My Country," "The Last Rose of Summer," "The Rose of Tralee," and "Believe Me If All Those Endearing Young Charms" made him a household name in Ireland and America, and his recordings sold several million copies.

Although Irish traditional music has never disappeared from the American landscape, from the early 1900s on Irish music that was produced in America revealed increasingly closer ties to mainstream American popular culture. This may be partly explained by the rapidly expanding entertainment industry of that time, which offered many mediums of performance and dissemination, such as theater, film, radio, and television. In addition, the Irish themselves became more assimilated into American society over time and, as a result, their Irish ethnic identity—while still incredibly important—evolved from being an everyday reality to one that could be adopted or omitted at will. Now perceiving themselves as "Irish Americans" rather than as the ethnic Irish residing in America, Irish-American audiences craved productions by Irish-American performers that not only entertained, but that also reflected their newly emergent Irish-American identity while simultaneously keeping pace with developments in the American popular music scene.

Throughout the twentieth century, Irish-American musicians made a name for themselves in American classical music as well as in every genre of American popular music. Elements of Irish traditional, folk, and theatrical music have found their way into the work of several American composers of classical music, such as Victor Herbert (1859–1924), Edward Collins (1886–1951), Henry Cowell (1897–1965), and Samuel Barber (1910–1981). Within the jazz scene, several musicians of Irish ethnicity enjoyed highly successful careers, including Jimmy Dorsey (1904–1957) and Tommy Dorsey (1905–1956) of the Dorsey Brothers, Gerry Mulligan (1927–1996), and Roland Bernard "Bunny" Berigan (1908–1942). Countless singers of the 1930s, 1940s, 1950s, and 1960s sang sentimental, Irish-themed songs on the radio, in movies, and on television programs, and Irish-American singers Bing Crosby (1904–1978), Dennis Day (1918–1988), and Ruthie Morrissey in particular showcased their Irish identity through song.

During the early 1960s, Irish folk song found a new audience base in the United States and Ireland, spurred by the commercial success of the Clancy Brothers and Tommy Makem. Influenced by the American folk revival of the late 1950s and 1960s, Makem and the Clancys updated Irish songs—particularly traditional Irish ballads—by adding guitar or banjo accompaniment, which resulted in the introduction of rhythm and harmonic accompaniment to the Irish singing tradition. The so-called "Irish Beatles" made their debut on the *Ed Sullivan Show* and performed at the White House during the John F. Kennedy administration. Numerous Irish "ballad bands" emerged in Ireland and the United States after the phenomenal success of the Clancy Brothers and Tommy Makem.

Throughout the late twentieth and early twenty-first centuries, various elements of Irish traditional music—from the lyrical style and melodic line of Irish traditional ballads and dance tunes to less tangible elements such as imagery and poetry that evoke Irish identity and sentiment—have become enmeshed in rock, pop, country, folk, jazz, new age, and punk music. Examples include groups and solo artists such as U2, Hothouse Flowers, Horslips, Thin Lizzy, Clannad, Afro Celt Sound System, Van Morrison, Sinéad O'Connor, Thin Lizzy, the Corrs, the Cranberries, the Pogues, Black 47, Flogging Molly, and the Dropkick Murphys. Although the music performed by these and countless groups often bears little resemblance to Irish traditional music, it has offered additional genres of music through which Americans of Irish ethnicity as well as non-Irish Americans may explore Irish culture or express their own Irish cultural identity. In addition, the reception and enjoyment of Irish popular music has at times served as the entry point through which individuals become involved with more traditional Irish cultural expressions such as Irish dance and music.

The Revival of Irish Traditional Music in America

By the late 1960s, Irish immigration to America had lessened to a great degree, and this reality, combined with the continuing assimilation of the Irish in America and the popularization of Irish music, all had negative implications for Irish traditional music performance. Irish traditional music in America was in serious decline as a public musical form, instead being performed and enjoyed primarily by small groups of musicians in private settings. However, during the 1970s, government organizations such as the Smithsonian Institute and the National Endowment for the Arts began providing funds to promote Irish traditional musicians in America. These endeavors were significant, for they funded concerts by Irish traditional musicians; allowed notable, yet underrepresented Irish traditional musicians, such as Joe Shannon, John McGreevy, Eleanor Neary, James Keane, Frank Thornton, Terry Teahan, Sean McGlynn, Gus Collins, Gene Kelly, Eddie Cahill, and Maureen McGlynn, to be recorded for the first time on commercial recordings like *Traditional Irish Music in America: Chicago* (1978) and *Traditional Irish Music in America: The East Coast* (1970s); and supplied funds to support Irish organizations.

During the late 1970s, 1980s, and 1990s, Irish traditional music study and performance reemerged and evolved in the United States because of the revival of Irish traditional culture under way at that time and a new wave of Irish immigration to America, as well as the universal movement to explore one's ethnic roots that emerged in America in the 1970s. Many young American-born Irish and recent immigrants to America participated in Irish traditional music, with key figures such as Laurence Nugent, John Williams, Eileen Ivers, Martin Hayes, Joannie Madden, John Whelan, Jerry Sullivan, Seamus Egan, and Liz Carroll achieving particular success, either by winning musical competitions in America and Ireland, teaching and lecturing throughout the United States, or touring with traditional groups such as Solas, Cherish the Ladies, Trian, and many others. Folklorist, scholar, and musician Mick Moloney has contributed immensely to the ongoing revival of Irish traditional music through his research on Irish-American music, his frequent concert and lecture appearances pertaining to Irish music in America, and the 1977 founding of *The Green Fields of America,* a multiyear concert tour that has funded concerts of immigrant Irish and native-born players of Irish music.

Today, Irish traditional music is highly visible in American society and people interested in attending Irish traditional music performances or taking up Irish traditional music or dance have a myriad of opportunities and means by which to do so. These include the multitude of Irish festivals and concerts sponsored by organizations throughout the country, countless music sessions held at Irish pubs throughout the United States, the growing number of Irish cultural centers and academic departments on university campuses, a booming Irish music recording industry, the appearance of Irish traditional music in commercial films (e.g., *The Brothers McMullen* and *Michael Collins*) and dance spectacles (e.g., *Riverdance* and *Lord of the Dance*), and the frequent performance of Irish traditional music on public radio and television. Links between Irish musicians in America and Ireland are stronger than ever before because of affordable and air travel, a vigorous, international Irish concert circuit, and advances in information technology, all of which encourage Irish musicians on both sides of the Atlantic to collaborate and exchange music more frequently, often in new and innovative ways. Today, Irish music in America successfully bridges popular and traditional realms of performance and draws audiences and participants regardless of their ethnic background.

Erin Stapleton-Corcoran

See also: BALFE, Michael W.; BALL, Ernest R.; BOSTON; CAGNEY, James; CLANCY BROTHERS, the; COHAN, George M.; COLEMAN, Michael; FOSTER, Stephen Collins; HARRIGAN, Edward, and HART, Tony; HERBERT, Victor August; KELLY, Gene; McCORMACK, John; MOLONEY, Mick; MOORE, Thomas; MORRISON, Van; NEW YORK CITY; OLCOTT, Chauncey; SAN FRANCISCO; SCANLAN, William J.; SCOTS-IRISH CULTURE; U2

References

Carolan, Nick. *A Harvest Saved: Francis O'Neill and Irish Music in Chicago.* Cork: Ossian, 1997.

Grimes, Robert R. *How Shall We Sing in a Foreign Land: Music of Irish Catholic Immigrants in the Antebellum United States.* South Bend, IN: Notre Dame University Press, 1996.

McCullough, Lawrence. "Irish Music in Chicago: An Ethnomusicological Study." PhD dissertation, University of Pittsburgh, Pittsburgh, Pennsylvania, 1978.

Miller, Rebecca. "Irish Music." In *The Garland Encyclopedia of World Music: The United States and Canada,* edited by Ellen Koskoff, 842–846. New York: Garland, 2001.

Moloney, Mick. *Far From the Shamrock Shore: The Story of Irish Immigration through Song.* New York: Crown, 2002.

Moloney, Mick. "Irish Ethnic Recordings and the Irish American Imagination." In *Ethnic Recordings in America: A Neglected Heritage.* Washington, DC: American Folklife Center, Library of Congress, 1982.

Moloney, Mick. "Irish Music in America: Continuity and Change." PhD Dissertation, University of Pennsylvania, Philadelphia, 1992.

O' Connor, Nuala. *Bringing it all Back Home: The Influence of Irish Music at Home and Overseas,* Dublin: Merlin Publishing, 2001.

Williams, William H. A. *'Twas Only an Irishman's Dream: The Image of Ireland and the Irish in American Popular Song Lyrics, 1800–1920.* Urbana: University of Illinois Press, 1996.

MYLES, EILEEN (1949–)

Eileen Myles was born in Cambridge, Massachusetts, to Terrence Myles, a postman with Irish ancestry, and Genevieve Preston Myles Hannibal, a secretary of Polish descent. She was educated in Catholic schools and went on to take her bachelor's degree from the University of Massachusetts (Boston) in 1971. She attended graduate school at Queens College in New York before embarking on a career as a full-time writer. She gave her first reading of her poetry in the famous New York music club CBGB's on the Lower East Side of Manhattan. She became involved in the Poetry Project of Saint Mark's Church, serving as artistic director there from 1984 to 1986. During her time there she cowrote two plays. The first, *Joan of Arc, a Spiritual Entertainment,* was written with Barbara McKay and Elinor Naven in 1979, and *Patriarchy, a Play* was written the following year. *The Irony of the Leash* (1978), which was her first published collection of poetry, was followed by *A Fresh Young Voice from the Plains* (1982). She edited *Ladies Museum: An Anthology of New Downtown Women Poets* (1977) with Susie Timmons and Rochelle Kraut. She also edited a poetry magazine, *dodgems,* from 1977 to 1979, as well as a book with Liz Kotz entitled *The New Fuck You: Adventures in Lesbian Reading,* which won a Lambda Book Award in 1995. Her own work has been included in anthologies such as John Ashberry's *The Best American Poetry, 1988* and *Postmodern American Poetry* (1994). As well as writing on culture and literature for the *Village Voice* and *The Nation,* she has written art criticism for *Art in America.* Her poetry has been included in periodicals such as *The New England Review, The Kenyon Review, The American Poetry Review, The Partisan Review,* and many other publications. She has taught at New York University, the New School for Social Research, the California Institute of the Arts, and the Memphis College of Art, among other institutions. She ran for the office of U.S. president in the 1992 election. She is currently the professor of writing at the University of California, San Diego.

Myles is one of the few lesbian poets in America today who is consistently able to attract a general readership as well as the interest of critics. She has worked in a wide array of media ranging from drama and autobiography to the public performance of her poetry, which makes it difficult to confine her work to any single category. In a poetry review written for *The Nation* Myles says, "poetry's so tiny it's universal: A famous painter might be invited by *The New York Times* to give us a tour of the Met, to show us what he knows, but for poets there's no such building, or even the book-store. It's simply the world." Since she came out as a lesbian in 1977, her work has often been solely identified as that of a lesbian poet. However, it was only with her collection of poems entitled *Sappho's Boat* (1982) that her lesbian identity was first explicitly expressed in her work. In her essay "The Lesbian Poet," which is the clearest articulation of the way in which her sexuality is related to her poetry, she states that "more men ought to start unwriting themselves." Most of the poems contained in her next collection, *Bread and Water* (1985), were written during an extended stay in Mexico. Her next work was an autobiographical memoir, *Chelsea Girls* (1994), in which she recounts her own upbringing in Boston and the effect of living with her alcoholic father. She also recalled her own struggles with alcoholism and drug use. In 1990 she took to the stage to perform *Leaving New York,* a fusion of different literary genres and her poetry and stories. Later, she saw her decision to run for the presidency in 1992 as an extension of her poetic and artistic interests.

David Doyle